LAW AND GENDER IN MODERN IRELAND

Law and Gender in Modern Ireland: Critique and Reform is the first generalist text to tackle the intersection of law and gender in this jurisdiction for over two decades. As such, it could hardly have come at a more opportune moment. The topic of law and gender, perhaps more so than at any other time in Irish history, has assumed a dominant place in political and academic debate. Among scholars and policymakers alike, the regulation of gendered bodies, and the legal status of sexual and gendered identities, is now a highly visible fault line in public discourse.

Debates over reproductive justice (exemplified by the recent referendum to remove the '8th Amendment'), increased rights for lesbian, gay, bisexual and transgender persons (including the public-sanctioned introduction of same-sex marriage) and the historic mistreatment of women and young girls have re-shaped Irish public and political life, and encouraged Irish society to re-examine long-unchallenged gender norms. While many traditional flashpoints remain such as abortion and prostitution/sex work, there are also new questions, including surrogacy and the gendered experience of asylum frameworks, which have emerged. As policy-makers seek to enact reforms, they face a population with increasingly polarised perceptions of gender and a legal structure ill-equipped for modern realities.

This edited volume directly addresses modern Irish debates on law and gender. Providing an overview of the existing rules and standards, as well as exploring possible options for reform, the collection stands as an important statement on the law in this jurisdiction, and as an invaluable resource for pursuing gendered social change. While the edited collection applies a doctrinal methodology to explain current statutes, case law and administrative practices, the contributors also invoke critical gender, queer and race perspectives to identify and problematise existing (and potential) challenges. This edited collection is essential reading for all who are interested in law, gender and processes of social change in modern Ireland.

Law and Gender in Modern Ireland

Critique and Reform

Edited by
Lynsey Black
and
Peter Dunne

•HART•
OXFORD • LONDON • NEW YORK • NEW DELHI • SYDNEY

HART PUBLISHING

Bloomsbury Publishing Plc

Kemp House, Chawley Park, Cumnor Hill, Oxford, OX2 9PH, UK

HART PUBLISHING, the Hart/Stag logo, BLOOMSBURY and the Diana logo are trademarks of Bloomsbury Publishing Plc

First published in Great Britain 2019

A catalogue record for this book is available from the British Library.

Library of Congress Cataloging-in-Publication data

Names: Black, Lynsey, editor. | Dunne, Peter, editor.

Title: Law and gender in modern Ireland : critique and reform / edited by Lynsey Black, Peter Dunne.

Description: Oxford [UK] ; Portland, Oregon : Hart Publishing, 2019. | Includes bibliographical references and index.

Identifiers: LCCN 2018049641 (print) | LCCN 2018050021 (ebook) | ISBN 9781509917235 (EPub) | ISBN 9781509917211 (hardback)

Subjects: LCSH: Sex and law—Ireland. | Gender identity—Law and legislation—Ireland. | Sex discrimination—Law and legislation—Ireland. | Law reform—Ireland. | BISAC: LAW / Constitutional. | LAW / Civil Rights.

Classification: LCC KDK1771.S49 (ebook) | LCC KDK1771.S49 L39 2019 (print) | DDC 342.41708/78—dc23

LC record available at https://lccn.loc.gov/2018049641

ISBN: HB: 978-1-50991-721-1
ePDF: 978-1-50991-722-8
ePub: 978-1-50991-723-5

Typeset by Compuscript Ltd, Shannon

ACKNOWLEDGEMENTS

There are a number of institutions and individuals to whom we owe a significant debt in bringing this project to fruition.

In particular, we are grateful to the School of Law, Trinity College Dublin (TCD). Both editors met and conceived of this collection while completing our doctoral studies at TCD. From the beginning, the School of Law has shown consistent support and encouragement, without which we would not have been able to realise this project.

In July 2017, the School of Law provided both financial and logistical assistance for a *Law and Gender in Modern Ireland* workshop. This allowed both the editors and the contributors to share ideas and flesh out the shape of individual chapters. The workshop was an invaluable part of the process and we are very grateful, particularly to the former Head of School, Professor Oran Doyle, and Catherine Finnegan and Beth Whitney, who were instrumental in making the day happen.

During our PhD studies, we were generously supervised by Professor Ivana Bacik (Lynsey Black) and Professor Mark Bell (Peter Dunne). Not only have Ivana and Mark been a consistent support, they also provided essential advice and feedback as we navigated the process of developing this collection, and were always willing to offer assistance and guidance.

Lynsey Black was an Irish Research Council Government of Ireland Postdoctoral Fellow throughout the period the book was in preparation. Lynsey was based in the Sutherland School of Law, University College Dublin, and she would like to thank both the Irish Research Council, and the Sutherland School of Law which provided a collegiate and stimulating space to work on this project. She would also like to thank Professor Ian O'Donnell, who was a supportive mentor throughout.

Peter Dunne began this project as an Ussher Doctoral Fellow at TCD. He is extremely grateful for the financial support provided by TCD throughout the period of his fellowship. Since August 2017, he has been a lecturer-in-law at the University of Bristol. Peter is grateful for Bristol's ongoing institutional support, and for colleagues who constantly challenge the boundaries of law and gender in modern society.

This project would not have been possible without the professional, thoughtful and supportive advice of Hart Publishing, and its wonderful editorial staff. Since the early stages of the collection, we have been grateful for the openness and expertise of all those with whom we have had the pleasure to work, particularly Rosamund Jubber, Bill Asquith, and Kate Whetter. Hart's willingness to explore innovative questions of law and gender, and their encouragement to consider our subject matter from new and varying perspectives has significantly enhanced the quality of the collection.

We are particularly grateful to our family and friends – particularly our partners, parents and siblings – who have supported us throughout the process, offered invaluable advice and tolerated us during stressful moments! And, finally, but most crucially, we must thank the contributors. Without their efforts the book would not exist. It has been a pleasure working with the authors, and a privilege getting to know them.

CONTENTS

TABLE OF CASES

Ireland

England and Wales

European Union

Council of Europe

TABLE OF STATUTES

Ireland

United Kingdom

European Union

LIST OF CONTRIBUTORS

Ivana Bacik is the Reid Professor of Criminal Law, Criminology and Penology at the School of Law, Trinity College Dublin, and a Senator for Dublin University. She has a law degree from Trinity College Dublin and an LLM from the London School of Economics. She is a barrister and teaches courses in Criminal Law, Criminology, and Feminist Criminology at Trinity. She has published widely in the areas of criminal law, criminology, gender and law, and human rights law. Her publications include Bacik and Rogan (eds), *Legal Cases that Changed Ireland* (Clarus Press, 2016).

Alan DP Brady BL is a practising barrister. He is a graduate of Trinity College Dublin, the London School of Economics and the King's Inns. He has worked as a legal researcher at the Law Reform Commission and has taught at the London School of Economics, University College London and Trinity College Dublin. Alan has published in the areas of gender and the Irish Constitution, human rights, and corporate homicide.

Patricia Brazil is the Averil Deverell Lecturer in Law at Trinity College Dublin where she lectures in refugee and immigration law, family law and child law. She has also practised as a barrister since 2004, specialising in the areas of asylum and immigration, family and child law. She regularly delivers conference papers at both domestic and international conferences pertaining to refugee, immigration and child law and has extensive publications in these areas.

Fiona Buckley is a Lecturer in the Department of Government and Politics, University College Cork (UCC) specialising in gender politics. Fiona is a graduate of Queen's University Belfast (QUB), being conferred with a PhD in Political Science in 2016. Fiona's research is largely focused on gender politics, in particular gender and cabinet government and gender quotas, but she also publishes on Irish politics, electoral administration and voting behaviour.

Lucy-Ann Buckley is a Senior Lecturer in Law at NUI Galway, where she is also a Vice Dean. She holds a law degree and masters in law from University College Cork, a second masters in law from the University of Oxford, and a PhD from Trinity College Dublin. She has also qualified as a solicitor. She specialises in equality law, labour law and family property, and has published widely on issues such as prenuptial agreements, financial provision on divorce, sexual harassment and employment equality. She is also active in international policy development, contributing to the draft *Joint Statement towards Inclusive Social Protection Systems Supporting the Full and Effective Participation of Persons with Disabilities* prepared by the International Labour Organisation in 2015–2016. She is currently an expert advisor to the States of Guernsey in relation to the development of multi-ground equality legislation.

Louise Crowley is a Senior Lecturer in Family Law in the Law School at University College Cork. Louise is a graduate of University College Cork (BCL 1996, LLM 1997, PGDTL 2010), and Cardiff University (PhD 2010). She is the author of Family Law (Roundhall), the leading Irish family law text and has published widely in national and international journals on regulatory approaches to marital breakdown, asset distribution and marital agreements, and on issues relating to the legal responses for those affected by domestic and intimate partner violence. Her research has been informed by engagement with both victims and perpetrators of domestic abuse, based on collaborations with Tusla and victim support services and participants of the perpetrator programmes provided by MOVE (Ireland). Since 2016 Louise has piloted the bystander Intervention programme at University College Cork, which seeks to encourage a greater understanding and awareness of the normalisation of sexual misconduct and to empower students to challenge these perceived behavioural norms, whilst recognising their role as contributors to a safer campus and society. Louise is the Director of the Children's Rights and Family Law LLM at UCC, which incorporates two clinical modules, allowing faculty and students to conduct research and develop initiatives to enhance the user experience in the Irish family law system. Louise is also a member of the Governing Body of UCC.

Mary Donnelly is Professor in the Law School at University College Cork. She is a University College Dublin (BCL 1986), University College Cork (MA 1993), Trinity College Dublin (MLitt 1995) and University of Wales, Cardiff (PhD 2007) graduate. Her books include *Healthcare Decision-Making and the Law: Autonomy, Capacity and the Limits of Liberalism* (Cambridge: Cambridge University Press, 2010) and *The Law of Credit and Security* (Round Hall, 2011; 2nd ed 2015). She has collaborated on projects funded by the European Commission, the Irish Research Council for the Humanities and Social Sciences, the National Children's Office and the Irish Hospice Foundation and has acted as consultant for public agencies and legal firms. She was a member of the Expert Group to review the Mental Health Act 2001 (2013–2015). She is a member of the Health Service Executive National Consent Advisory Group/Assisted Decision Making Steering Group and the Legislation Committee of the Mental Health Commission and is Chair of the Expert Technical Group to develop Codes of Practice for the Assisted Decision-Making (Capacity) Act 2015.

Máiréad Enright is a Senior Lecturer in Birmingham Law School. Her research is in feminist legal studies, and law and religion, particularly how patriarchal legal and religious structures can be resisted and changed. Her research in this respect looks beyond traditional methods of law reform to consider illegality, protest, private litigation, and experimental legal drafting. She is Co-Director of the *Northern/Irish Feminist Judgments Project* and consults with and advises groups campaigning around the reproductive rights and historical gender-based violence in Ireland. Máiréad has published widely within the areas of reproductive rights, and feminist legal theory, and recently edited *Northern/Irish Feminist Judgments: Judges' Troubles and the Gendered Politics of Identity* (Hart, 2017).

James Gallen is a Lecturer in the School of Law and Government at Dublin City University. His PhD thesis examined the relationship between transitional justice, peace-building and economic development in international law. His research interests include human rights, international law and legal and transitional justice. His present research agenda and recent publications concern transitional justice and jus post bellum, and a transitional justice approach to historical abuse in consolidated democracies, especially child sex abuse in the Roman Catholic Church. In 2017 he was appointed as an Expert Advisor on Transitional Justice by the Department of Children and Youth Affairs to advise on a transitional justice approach to the issue of Mother and Baby Homes.

Yvonne Galligan is a professor of comparative politics and Director of Equality, Diversity and Inclusion in the Technological University Dublin. She has written extensively on women and politics in Ireland and Europe. Her research focuses on two areas: political representation and the relationship between gender and democracy. She has published in major international journals such as International Political Science Review, Gender and Society, Policy and Politics, and others. Her book publications include *Sharing Power: Women, Parliament, Democracy* and *Gender Politics and Democracy in Post-socialist Europe.* Yvonne is frequently invited to bring her expertise to bear on governmental and political party initiatives supporting women. She has participated in events organised by the Council of Europe, Northern Ireland Assembly, Dáil Eireann, Ministry of Justice, Equality and Law Reform (RoI), the Women and Equality Unit (UK), and OFMDFM (NI).

Susan Leahy is a Lecturer in the School of Limerick, University of Limerick. Her PhD research was funded by the Irish Research Council for the Humanities and Social Sciences. Her thesis was entitled The Rules and Realities of Consent in Irish Sexual Offences Law: Perspectives on Reform and examined the rules relating to consent in Irish sexual offences legislation. She has published her research on sexual offences in both national and international journals, including the Common Law World Review, the International Journal of Evidence and Proof, the Journal of Criminal Law and the Irish Journal of Family Law. She recently co-authored (with Dr Margaret Fitzgerald-O'Reilly) a book entitled *Sexual Offending in Ireland: Laws, Procedures and Punishment*, published by Clarus Press. Susan's primary research interests lie in the area of criminal justice and family law.

Deirdre McGowan is Head of Law, Dublin Institute of Technology. She holds a BCL (Hons) from University College Dublin and a Doctor of Philosophy from Maynooth University. Deirdre is a qualified solicitor and has worked with a number of firms, including M J O'Connor & Company and Mary Cowhey & Company. Deirdre served as an adjudicator with the Residential Tenancies Board from 2014 to 2018. Previously, she was Director of the North Kildare Citizens Information Service Limited. Deirdre's research interests lie in the fields of Michel Foucault and post-structuralist legal theory; feminist legal theory; social policy and social law (personal taxation, social welfare, family law, housing law and policy etc); and law and social government.

Andrea Mulligan BL is an Assistant Professor in the School of Law, Trinity College Dublin, where she lectures in Medical Law and Ethics, Law and Bioethics, and Insolvency Law. Andrea's research specialisation is in the legal regulation of human reproductive technologies ranging from established technologies such as IVF, surrogacy and donor-assisted conception to emerging and future technologies such as gene editing and human enhancement. She is interested in both the public law and private law aspects of this research field. Andrea also has research interests across the broader fields of Medical Law and Bioethics, and is co-author of *Medical Law in Ireland* (Bloomsbury Professional, 2017). Her current research projects include researching the right to identity in donor assisted human reproduction and surrogacy, and tortious liability for mistakes in the course of reproductive treatment.

Andrea graduated from the LLB programme at the School of Law, Trinity College Dublin, before going on to study on the LLM programme at Harvard Law School, where she specialised in reproductive technologies and constitutional law. She was awarded her doctorate by TCD in 2014, and was called to the Bar of Ireland in 2012.

Tanya Ní Mhuirthile joined the School of Law and Government, Dublin City University, in September 2015. Her research interrogates the interaction between the body and law and draws on human rights law, medical law, law and gender theory and feminist jurisprudence. Tanya is a legal consultant to both Transgender Equality Network Ireland and IntersexUK. She has advised Government ministers, public representatives and civil and public servants on the drafting of legislation and the development of public policy in particular in relation to the *Criminal Justice (Female Genital Mutilation) Act, 2012* and *Gender Recognition Bill 2013, Legal Recognition of Gender Bill 2013* and the *Gender Recognition Act 2015.* Tanya has also advised NGOs, including Amnesty International, Irish Council of Civil Liberties, Transgender Equality Network Ireland, IntersexUK, International Lesbian, Gay, Bisexual, Trans and Intersex-Europe (ILGA-Europe), and Transgender Europe on their policy initiatives relevant to her research expertise, both in Ireland and abroad. In November 2017, Tanya was appointed to the Gender Recognition Act Review Group by Minister Regina Doherty.

Monica O'Connor is a Researcher with the 'Sexual Exploitation Research Project' at the School of Social Policy, Social Work and Social Justice, University College Dublin and is a Research fellow with the WiSE Research Centre at Glasgow Caledonian University. Monica was previously an Irish Research Council Government of Ireland Doctoral scholar at St. Patrick's College, where she researched issues of choice, consent, agency and harm in the lives of prostituted and trafficked women in Ireland. Monica received her doctorate in 2014. Monica has worked as an independent researcher conducting EU research in comparative research projects on human trafficking, led by the Immigrant Council of Ireland across six Member States of the EU. Monica has been an independent consultant in the statutory and voluntary sector, advising on the development of services to women subjected to violence and working as Manager of Policy, Training and Research in Women's Aid.

Mary O'Toole SC was called to the Bar of Ireland in 1980. She took silk in 2000. She is also an accredited mediator. She practices in the area of constitutional, family and mental health law. Mary has been involved in numerous landmark cases in Irish law, including *Attorney General v X* (establishing the constitutional parameters of the right to seek an abortion in Ireland under Art. 40.3). Throughout her career, she has participated in many campaigns for legal reform, most recently as Chair of the Lawyers for Yes coalition during the 2015 marriage equality referendum. In 2015, Mary was jointly honoured as the "Woman of the Year" by the Irish Women Lawyers Associations. She has recently been appointed by the Government to carry out a review of the Magdalene Laundry Redress Scheme.

Fergus Ryan is a Senior Lecturer in the Department of Law, Maynooth University. He holds an LLB and PhD from Trinity College Dublin. His research interests are in the areas of family law, constitutional law, gender, sexual orientation, and human rights. He has previously lectured at the Dublin Institute of Technology, where he served as Head of the Department of Law. Fergus has published in the areas of immigration, refugee and citizenship law, contract law, constitutional law, family law, LGBT rights and civil partnerships.

Fergus has advised the Equality Authority, the Irish Human Rights Commission and the Law Reform Advisory Committee of Northern Ireland on issues of family law and human rights. He has assisted in drafting legislation and legislative amendments for several members of Seanad Éireann, including the Adoption (Identity and Information) Bill 2014. Fergus is a former President of the Irish Association of Law Teachers. He is the Irish representative on ECSOL (the European Commission on Sexual Orientation Law).

Brian Tobin is a Lecturer in the School of Law, NUI Galway. Brian holds an LLB and a PhD from Trinity College Dublin. His doctoral thesis examined the socio-legal assimilation of same-sex family structures in Ireland. His primary research interests are in the areas of family and child law, with a focus on the recognition of contemporary family forms and the position of children born via assisted human reproduction. Brian has published in leading peer-reviewed journals such as the *Irish Jurist*, the *International Journal of Law, Policy and Law* and the *Journal of Social Welfare and Family Law*. In April 2014, Brian was invited to provide expert legal opinion on the General Scheme of the Children and Family Relationship Bill to the Oireachtas Joint Committee on Justice, Defence and Equality.

Nusha Yonkova is the Anti-trafficking Manager at the Immigrant Council of Ireland, an independent human rights organisation and a licensed Law Centre. Presently, she is conducting employment-based doctoral research overseen by University College Dublin, School of Social Policy, Social Work and Social Justice, exploring gender-sensitive approaches to assistance and protection of victims of human trafficking. This work is sponsored by the Irish Research Council. Nusha has been working exclusively in the area of human trafficking for the last 9 years and has authored a range of policy documents and reports as well as coordinated research activities undertaken by national and transnational teams. She holds a MSc in Engineering and a MA in Intercultural Studies from Dublin City University in Ireland. In 2008, she became the first migrant woman elected to the Executive Board of the National Women's Council of Ireland. In 2013 and 2014, Nusha served as the elected Chair of the European Network of Migrant Women, a pan-European network.

INTRODUCTION

LYNSEY BLACK AND PETER DUNNE

I. Overview

Law and Gender in Modern Ireland: Critique and Reform is the first generalist text to tackle the intersection of law and gender in Ireland for over two decades. As such, it could hardly have come at a more opportune moment. The topic of law and gender, perhaps more so than at any other time in Irish history, has assumed a dominant place in political and academic debate. Among scholars and policy-makers alike, the regulation of gendered bodies, and the legal status of sexual and gendered identities, is now a highly visible (and continuously divisive) fault line in public discourse. Indeed, beyond these spheres, discussion of how our laws should conceptualise issues of gender and sex has assumed a critical function throughout all sections of Irish society.

The growing importance of the intersection of law and gender in recent years has manifested across many discrete areas. Debates over reproductive justice, increased rights for lesbian, gay, bisexual, transgender and intersex (LGBTI) persons, and the historic mistreatment of women and girls have dominated public discourse, encouraging Irish society to re-examine long unchallenged gender norms. While many traditional flashpoints such as abortion and prostitution/sex work remain, new issues have emerged, such as surrogacy, and the gendered experience of the asylum process.

Many of the chapters in this collection address issues that were less visible, or entirely invisible, as recently as the 1990s. Subjects such as transgender rights had little public or political traction until recently. Over the past three decades, significant changes have occurred in Irish attitudes towards sexuality, alongside the inevitable expansion in gender models that this allows. The decriminalisation of sodomy in 1993 was just over 20 years removed from the 2015 referendum to affirm same-sex marriage rights. Meanwhile, although many married couples in Ireland experienced separation, until 1996 none of these couples could obtain a divorce. The shifts in relationships, and in the official sanctioning of different forms of relationship, which have taken place have occasioned reforms in areas such as leave entitlements for parents, the provisions of custody arrangements for separating parents, and framing a new legislative structure for surrogacy.

The position of women in these years has undergone something of a cultural shift. In 1996, Ireland's last Magdalene Laundry closed its doors, without fanfare or public comment. This edited collection reflects on the twists and turns of public and official conceptions of institutions such as these and their new status as symptoms of a shameful past. The recognition of such institutionalisation as a form of gendered harm, has joined other developments in recent decades to signal a (slightly) greater willingness to name harms which have been experienced – often at disproportionate rates by women. The criminalisation of marital rape in 1990, for example, offered some recognition of bodily autonomy. The reforms to our law on sexual offences continue this process but fall short in many ways.

In May 2018, the bodily autonomy rights of women in Ireland experienced a highly symbolic moment: the repeal of the 8th Amendment to the Constitution. The 8th Amendment recognised the equal right to life of women and of the 'unborn child', resulting in the criminalisation of abortion save where there existed a threat to the life of the woman. Since its passage into law (with overwhelming public support) in 1983, it has stood, perhaps more than any other legal instrument, as the representation of past and present State control over female bodies, of a denial of women's agency and consent, and as a reminder of the explicit ways in which, since the foundation of the State, Irish law has hidden, censored and punished female sexuality. While repealing the 8th Amendment will have great practical implications for the many thousands of Irish women who, for decades, have faced the necessity to travel to the United Kingdom and Europe to access basic reproductive healthcare, it also stands as a symbolic affirmation of the changing status of women in Irish society.

Perhaps it is no coincidence that, in the past three decades, women's visibility in Ireland's public sphere has increased and women's voices have been heard more clearly. Women have entered the workforce in ever-greater numbers and begun (very slowly) to enter the realm of politics and, alongside, critical questions have been raised regarding fundamental notions of gender.

Ireland's new position in a globalised world has also brought new challenges related to gender and sexuality. Although traditionally a country of net outward migration, in recent years, the position of persons seeking asylum in Ireland has taken on significant salience and urgency, provoking necessary legislative responses, which must be cognisant of the role of gender and sexuality. In sum, the list of subjects which have attained greater salience in recent years is staggering, and it is no coincidence that most revolve around questions of gender and sexuality. The chapters of this volume ably demonstrate the seismic shifts in this area which have occurred over recent decades in Ireland.

The book is not, however, an unqualified celebration of gendered laws and gendered experiences of legal regulation. While, as compared with the position of women and LGBTI persons three decades ago, there is much to praise in contemporary laws and policies, the various chapters in this volume illustrate an acute awareness of the ways in which gendered inequality and stereotyped norms remain key features of contemporary Irish law. In some respects, what the contributions to this volume reveal is a twenty-first century Ireland where, although the prevailing legal structures suggest a departure from historic inequity, the lived-experience of law, for many persons, remains anchored to gender-related vulnerability, precariousness and risk. This book acknowledges and highlights this experience – drawing attention, across the Irish legal and political landscape, to the ways in which women and LGBTI populations continue to be economically, socially and culturally marginalised. The editors and contributors are committed to offering an honest and critical assessment of the relationship between law and gender in the modern Irish State.

In 1993, Alpha Connelly's edited collection, *Gender and the Law in Ireland*,[1] was published. Although the current text is not an updated edition of that work, it is, in many

[1] Alpha Connelly (ed), *Gender and the Law in Ireland* (Cork, Oak Tree Press, 1993).

ways, its spiritual successor. While numerous recent works have considered specific cases, individual topics and feminist methodologies,[2] the present work, as a broad, generalist text, offers an introduction to law and gender in Ireland, incorporating recent reforms, current debates, and possible future developments. Through the contributions to follow, this book provides a holistic 'state of the nation' for gender and Irish law.

Crucially, the book is not, and cannot be, a comprehensive treatment of all facets of gender and the law in Ireland. No such book could be written, nor indeed should it be, as there can be no definitive 'truth' on the myriad issues suggested by such a title. However, the text does provide a considered analysis of many areas of central concern. To that end, 17 substantive legal or socio-legal topics have been identified, and each chapter provides an accessible overview of the law in this area. In particular, contributors have attempted to answer three general questions:

(1) What is the existing law?
(2) What are the critiques of the existing law?
(3) What are the suggestions for reform?

It is hoped that these lines of enquiry will frame the chapters for the reader. Individual contributors look at international best practice, international comparators and employ existing research and commentary from non-governmental organisations, academics, and policy-makers to overview the good, the bad and the potential for reform.

In terms of approach, the contributions incorporate a descriptive methodology to explain current statutes, case law and administrative practices. There is no single theoretical perspective running through the chapters, but the individual authors have drawn on critical feminist, queer and race perspectives where relevant, and where theoretical frameworks can illuminate key insights on a topic. In this vein, the chapters also reveal the tensions within theoretical approaches. This is evident, for example, in Ivana Bacik's contribution, highlighting that even choices of terminology – such as either 'prostitution', 'sex work' or 'sexwork' – can be a telling reflection of ideology.

II. Structure

The book is organised into three parts: 'Gender and the Criminal Law', 'Family and Relationships', and 'Law in a Changing Society'.

A. Gender and the Criminal Law

Susan Leahy (Chapter 1) examines the law on sexual offences, looking at the recent Criminal Law (Sexual Offences) Act 2017, and focusing specifically on the issue of consent.

[2] See eg Jennifer Redmond, Sonja Tiernan, Sandra McAvoy and Mary McAuliffe (eds), *Sexual Politics in Modern Ireland* (Newbridge, Irish Academic Press, 2015); Máiréad Enright, Julie McCandless and Aoife O'Donoghue (eds), *Northern/Irish Feminist Judgments: Judges' Troubles and the Gendered Politics of Identity* (Oxford, Hart, 2017); Ivana Bacik and Mary Rogan (eds), *Legal Cases that Changed Ireland* (Dublin, Clarus Press, 2016).

Leahy explores the legal framework of sexual offences within the context of socio-cultural expectations of gendered behaviour and gendered violence, and the influence of rape myths. The chapter looks closely at the definition of consent, introduced for the first time in Irish law through the 2017 legislation. Leahy welcomes this development, and the introduction of ideas of mutuality and communicative sexuality into Irish law. However, she highlights the ongoing issues, focusing in particular on the problem of the 'honest belief' defence in Irish law, and looking at some of the persistent critiques of Ireland's law on sexual offences.

In her contribution on prostitution/sex work, Ivana Bacik (Chapter 2) adopts a comprehensive policy and political analysis to investigate the motivating factors behind the Criminal Law (Sexual Offences) Act 2017. This legislation introduced the new offence of the purchase of sex, and effectively decriminalised the selling of sex. Bacik outlines the political currents which led to this substantial law reform, which saw the 'Nordic' model adopted in Ireland. Notably, Bacik's chapter outlines the contentious nature of the debate on prostitution/sex work, between those who view prostitution as a gendered form of exploitation and harm, and those who adopt a harm reduction and agency-focused approach.

The global phenomenon of trafficking forms the subject of Monica O'Connor and Nusha Yonkova's contribution (Chapter 3), which takes as its focus the issue of trafficking for sexual exploitation. Examining the EU and Irish legislative framework, the chapter enumerates the various measures in place to tackle trafficking and offers a critique of the effectiveness of these measures, in particular, Ireland's Criminal Law (Human Trafficking) Act 2008 and the relevant EU Directives. Notably, the authors contend that until anti-trafficking provisions reflect the complex interplays between gender, migration, trafficking for sexual exploitation, and prostitution, they will be of little practical use to victims of trafficking.

Máiréad Enright (Chapter 4) explores the contentious issue of abortion. As a subject which, in many ways, has framed the Irish political landscape for several generations, Enright considers the constitutionalisation of abortion through the 8th Amendment. Her chapter addresses and reveals the pernicious ways in which the domestic law – constitutional, legislative and judicial – curtailed women's agency, denied basic physical autonomy and fell hardest upon individuals who lay at the intersection of multiple vulnerabilities. Enright discusses historic strategies for reform, landmark moments in the campaign towards reproductive justice and, ultimately, the transformative 'Together for Yes' movement, which resulted in the successful repeal of the 8th Amendment in May 2018. Looking to the future, Enright outlines proposed legislative intervention, and asks what this will mean for bodily autonomy rights in modern Ireland.

B. Family and Relationships

Fergus Ryan (Chapter 5) discusses movements towards greater rights in Irish law for gay, lesbian and bisexual (LGB) persons. From a recent position of criminality (for gay men), Ryan charts legal developments in the areas of, inter alia, hate speech legislation, employment equality and, ultimately, partnership recognition. Ryan addresses the legal and social context in which such reforms came about, and he reflects upon the impact of rapid (legal) change, culminating in the popular affirmation of same-sex marriage rights in

2015. Ryan does not offer a utopian vision of LGB equality in modern Ireland. Recognising the significant law-based and cultural barriers which remain, Ryan provides a balanced analysis of the transformations which LGB individuals have experienced over the past quarter century.

Brian Tobin (Chapter 6) considers the gendered dimensions of Ireland's parental laws, placing a particular focus on the status of 'guardians'. Noting how automatic guardianship rights operate only in favour of married couples and unmarried women, Tobin suggests that current laws reinforce the privileged position of marital unions and discriminate against unmarried men. His chapter advocates a more balanced, modern vision of parenthood in Ireland, where men's legal role in their children's lives does not depend upon formal relationship or legal gender.

Andrea Mulligan (Chapter 7) explores the intersections of law, surrogacy and gender. She approaches the topic through a clearly defined lens: the way in which surrogacy law in Ireland impacts on women. Mulligan has four women in contemplation in her chapter: the surrogate; the egg donor; the commissioning mother with a genetic link to the child; and the commissioning mother without a link to the child. She begins by setting out the existing legal framework (or lack thereof), and proceeds to critique the law from the perspective of the women involved, with a particular focus on the protective purpose of the law. Mulligan's central thesis is that the absence of specific legal regulation of surrogacy has unwittingly resulted in a de facto legal regime for the regulation of surrogacy which is male-centred, and which fails to protect the interests of the female parties to a surrogacy transaction.

Louise Crowley (Chapter 8) looks at how issues of gender interweave with social, legal and political responses to domestic violence. She recalls how Irish law's attempts to protect victims of domestic violence have been frustrated by a combination of historical reluctance to intervene and a begrudgingly piecemeal approach to remedies. The pre-1976 absence of State action, the non-criminalisation of marital rape until 1990, the vague evidentiary thresholds in the governing statutes, and the longstanding restriction of the availability of remedies to married applicants have perpetuated and sustained the weaker position for domestic violence victims (most typically women suffering at the hands of men). However, Crowley also outlines recent international developments, including the Istanbul Convention, which better prioritise the needs of victims. She concludes with the hope that the Domestic Violence Act 2018 (explained in detail) can (and will) enhance the rights of domestic violence victims in this jurisdiction.

Deirdre McGowan (Chapter 9) addresses the law governing property rights on the breakdown of marital unions. She begins with an outline of property ownership during marriage, contextualising the relevant rules by reference to social practice and behaviours. As the chapter progresses, McGowan introduces the current framework for property allocation when marital unions end, placing particular focus on court applications for judicial separation and divorce. McGowan explains the pertinent legislative principles and how they are applied by the Irish courts, drawing specific attention to the impact of gender roles in marriage. Finally, as the chapter concludes, McGowan identifies key difficulties with the existing marital property framework. She reflects upon both the potential for, but also the limitations of, marriage law reform as a way to promote gender equality.

Mary Donnelly (Chapter 10) views the gendered narratives of the financial crisis through the lens of 'sexually transmitted debt'. Looking first at the treatment of this issue outside of Ireland, Donnelly contrasts two dominant trends, the gender-neutral approach espoused by the House of Lords in *Royal Bank of Scotland plc v Etridge (No 2)* and the gender-specific approach adopted by the High Court of Australia in *Garcia v National Australia Bank*. She then turns to the relevant jurisprudence in Ireland, selecting cases for closer analysis both in terms of the gender narratives which emerge from them, and the judicial approaches employed. Through her research, Donnelly makes visible the gendered nature of this aspect of the Irish financial crisis. She concludes by locating her discussion within the broader context of feminist critiques of private law and advocates a structural analysis of private law in Ireland, grounded in the identification of the impact of factors, such as gender, which are otherwise hidden in plain sight.

Tanya Ní Mhuirthile (Chapter 11) considers the development of transgender and intersex rights in Ireland. Describing the historical moves towards legal recognition of preferred gender, Ní Mhuirthile recalls the highly publicised litigation pursued – over a period of nearly two decades – by Dr Lydia Foy, who sought a new birth certificate with her correct, female, gender marker. Ní Mhuirthile explores various efforts by successive Irish governments to resist Dr Foy's demands, and the resulting, ultimately successful, litigation, in which Dr Foy engaged. In 2015, the Oireacthas passed the Gender Recognition Act, which now permits individuals to obtain formal State acknowledgment of their affirmed identity. While praising the positive (even transformative) nature of the 2015 Act, which incorporates and prioritises the principle of self-determination, Ní Mhuirthile also observes how such legislation continues to fail and erase key demographics, including transgender children, non-binary individuals and those who experience intersex variance.

C. Law in a Changing Society

Alan DP Brady (Chapter 12) looks at the relationship between gender and the Constitution, with a particular emphasis upon care and the status of women who work in the home. Brady reflects on the symbolism of Article 41.2 of the Constitution and discusses the historical and contemporary arguments for reform. Throughout the chapter, Brady critically engages with High Court and Supreme Court jurisprudence, suggesting that Ireland's senior judges have (to a large extent) endorsed existing substantive inequalities in the name of preserving freedom between unequally situated parties (often opposite-sex spouses). Finally, in the latter part of his chapter, Brady argues that judicial resistance to positive obligations and socio-economic rights is both a perpetuating factor for gender inequality (regardless of the wording of Article 41.2) and also a reason to be sceptical about the potential for a gender-neutral recognition of care in the Constitution to achieve any meaningful change.

Lucy-Ann Buckley (Chapter 13) explores the concept of 'doing gender' in the context of Irish employment law, drawing upon the Employment Equality Acts 1998–2015, and the relevant EU law provisions. Ireland has historically had very low levels of female participation in the workforce. Buckley examines the development of women's role in paid employment and investigates the binary gender regime which relegated women to the domestic sphere. The chapter explores the law's failure to adequately respond to complaints of discrimination experienced by transgender persons, and its inability to consider the effects of intersectionality in discrimination. Buckley then turns to look at protective leave entitlements – specifically maternity, adoptive and parental leave – and argues that these are structured in such a way as to reinforce the existing gender binary, further pushing women away from full workforce participation.

Patricia Brazil (Chapter 14) considers the role and status of gender within Ireland's asylum decision-making processes. Noting that gender/sex is not specifically mentioned within the Convention Relating to the Status of Refugees 1951, Brazil nevertheless observes how – within international 'best practice' – gender has been identified as a potential source of unlawful persecution, placing women within the framework of a 'particular social group'. Brazil's chapter explores Irish judicial (and administrative) responses to gender as a ground for asylum and illustrates how the existing case law has failed to properly vindicate the rights of female-identified asylum applicants.

James Gallen (Chapter 15) explores redress mechanisms for historical mistreatment in Ireland, examining in particular the Magdalene Laundries, symphysiotomy (a surgical procedure carried out during childbirth) and Mother and Baby Homes. Gallen's discussion situates these institutions/practices within a broader nation-building project, which aimed to produce a narrow morality and role for women in early-twentieth-century Ireland. Through his contribution, Gallen illustrates how, although past rights violations and harm are increasingly being addressed, there remains a gendered dimension in the sequencing of investigation and redress. Gallen evaluates these latter processes as they apply to Magdalene Laundries, symphysiotomy and Mother and Baby Homes. He identifies a piecemeal approach – which seeks to minimise legal recognition of wrongdoing – across all three institutions and practices, and he concludes that challenges remain to effectively confront the gendered nature of the harm and the failures to date of redress strategies.

Throughout the contributions in the collection, the necessity of political representation to achieve progressive aims is clear. Fiona Buckley and Yvonne Galligan (Chapter 16) explore women's political representation in Ireland and look at the trajectory of women's participation in politics from independence in 1922 up to the most recent general election. In particular, Buckley and Galligan analyse the Electoral (Amendment) (Political Funding) Act 2012, which holds that political parties will forfeit 50 per cent of funding unless at least 30 per cent of their candidates are women. The chapter examines the intangible but very real structural barriers to women's participation in politics in Ireland and examines the moment of change presented through the 2008 financial crisis. Buckley and Galligan note that the political will to act stemmed from dissatisfaction with Ireland's informal and localised political nature. However, while they welcome the 2012 legislation, they affirm a need to monitor its effectiveness in light of case studies from elsewhere in Europe.

Finally, Mary O'Toole (Chapter 17) looks at the lived-experiences of female practitioners within the Irish legal system. Drawing from data across the legal profession, but with a particular emphasis on the Bar, O'Toole identifies key access barriers – such as informal 'old boys' networking, financial precariousness and childcare responsibilities – which obstruct female advancement within the law. While, as is evident throughout the collection, many of these factors also impede women's opportunities in other spheres of society, they are particularly exclusionary in the individualised and idiosyncratic context of the legal profession. O'Toole considers the structural changes that would be required to better accommodate female participation (including baseline acknowledgment among male practitioners that gender inequality exists) and evaluates the measures which the professional bodies are already applying.

III. Themes

Throughout this volume, there are a number of themes which recur with some frequency. These themes are considered and analysed in depth in the concluding chapter, providing a holistic assessment and reflection upon the relationship between law and gender as revealed in the 17 substantive contributions. However, as a final introductory note, and in order to create a frame through which readers can approach the chapters, these themes are identified and (briefly) overviewed in this section.

One bright thread evident throughout the text is the role of activism and cultural shifts in achieving legal changes in recent years. The tireless advocacy of many individuals and groups over two decades has caused fundamental shifts in how Irish society views itself. This flurry of hopeful advocacy and campaigning stands in marked contrast to the historic function of gender as a tool in nation-building. Many of the revolutions occurring in contemporary Ireland are happening against and in opposition to independence-era aspirations. The founders of the new Irish State envisioned a nation made stable through the strong bonds of family – based on marriage – with a conservative and communitarian society which favoured conformity over individualism. The very tangible repercussions of this ideology pervade discussion of the intersections of law and gender in Ireland and have circumscribed the roles available for women and other marginalised groups in Irish society for decades.

Pertinent to the national and conservative hopes for a newly independent Ireland, was the minimising of women's agency and bodily autonomy, and the downgrading of women's consent – in women's confinement in religious institutions, sexual contact or medical procedures, or indeed in the inability of women to make decisions about their own health. Attempting to 'unpick' this pernicious legacy, one of the persistent questions has been the extent to which law should embrace either gender-neutrality or gender-specificity. It seems that Ireland has the worst of both worlds. At the constitutional level, Ireland enshrines the role of women in the home, as domestic and maternal. Meanwhile, elsewhere, there is refusal to recognise the lived experience of certain harms as uniquely gendered.

In remaking Ireland's relationship with gender, the influence of international law stands out. Many of the most progressive legal reforms have come about because of Ireland's obligations as a member of various supranational bodies. This stands true for the recognition of transgender individuals and the decriminalisation of sodomy. This sphere also suggests some future reforms, for example in the legal recognition of cross-border surrogacy. The influence of international opinion, for example in the UN criticism of Ireland's treatment of the victim-survivors of Magdalene Laundries, cannot be underestimated. The criticism in this specific instance caused embarrassment on the international stage and was a factor which helped persuade law-makers to consider how they wished Ireland to be viewed.

Related to the nature of globalised law-making, the exploration of intersectional concerns also comprises a central aspect of the chapters herein, evident for example in the discussions of trafficking or refugee law. Elsewhere, other contributions consider the differential impacts of various policies, such as the contention that unpaid parental leave will, inevitably, be availed of by the lower earning parent – who is most likely to be a woman, as women continue to earn less than men – thereby perpetuating gendered and classed caring imbalances. Some of the contributions particularly highlight the seeming unwillingness by legislators to conceptualise the multiplicative effects of factors such as gender, class and race. Both O'Connor and Yonkova, and Brazil, are critical of the unidimensional nature of State understandings of hardship.

The exposure of this failure to assess lived-experience as a holistic and complex phenomenon, rather than a checklist of attributes, perhaps leads well to the final overarching strand which one can draw from the contributions to this book: the idea that the law is limited in what it can achieve. No collection on gender and the law can avoid this conclusion. While legal reform has been welcome, it is not a simple stand-in for societal values and norms. Legal protections can speak to, but cannot resolve, the structural barriers to equality which persist in Irish society.

PART I

Gender and the Criminal Law

1

Sexual Offences Law in Ireland

Countering Gendered Stereotypes in Adjudications of Consent in Rape Trials

SUSAN LEAHY

I. Introduction

Set as it is against a backdrop of society's understandings of appropriate and inappropriate sexual behaviour, there are few areas of the law more impacted by gender roles and stereotypes than the law on sexual offences. Ideals and societal expectations of appropriate socio-sexual behaviour for men and women, boys and girls, permeate every aspect of the law in this area. Indeed, entire volumes have been dedicated to discussions of these issues.[1] Given the inevitable space limitations of one chapter, it is not possible to fully rehearse the myriad ways in which gender considerations have influenced the development and implementation of the substantive and procedural law on sexual offences. The substantive rules relating to adjudications of consent in rape trials is the chosen focus here, as they represent a paradigm example of the impact of gendered stereotypes on the operation of sexual offences law. Further, an examination of this area of the law is timely, as the Criminal Law (Sexual Offences) Act 2017 has for the first time introduced a statutory definition of consent in Ireland. Although welcome, this reform effort remains unfinished as the rules relating to the defendant's mens rea regarding consent, namely, the honest belief in consent defence, have yet to be reformed. This chapter is an opportunity to reflect on recent achievements whilst highlighting that much remains to be done if the influence of gendered stereotypes on the difficulties of proving an absence of consent in rape trials is to be tackled effectively.

The chapter begins with a consideration of how societal factors affect the operation of rape law and, specifically, impact upon adjudications of consent in rape trials. The substantive rules on consent and honest belief will then be discussed and critiqued and suggestions

[1] See generally S Brownmiller, *Against Our Will: Men, Women and Rape* (New York, Fawcett Books, 1987); S Estrich, *Real Rape: How the Legal System Victimizes Women Who Say No* (Cambridge MA, Harvard University Press, 1987); S Lees, *Ruling Passions: Sexual Violence, Reputation and the Law* (Buckingham, Open University Press, 1997); S Lees, *Carnal Knowledge: Rape on Trial*, 2nd edn (London, The Women's Press, 2002); J McGregor, *Is it Rape? On Acquaintance Rape and Taking Women's Consent Seriously* (Farnham, Ashgate 2005); J Temkin, *Rape and the Legal Process*, 2nd edn (Oxford, Oxford University Press 2002).

for further reform will be offered. The chapter concludes with a reflection on the need for change outside the formal legislative process if real progress is to be made in this area.

II. Rape Myths and Realities: The Attitude Problem in Rape Trials

The impact which prejudicial and erroneous attitudes about rape and rape victims exert on the operation of the law was first highlighted by radical feminists in the latter decades of the twentieth century. Commentators like Estrich suggested that the problem with rape law was 'not the wording of statutes per se but rather our understanding of them … how a judge interprets and directs a jury, the "common sense" understandings of rape against which a juror will assess a rape allegation'.[2] Unfortunately, these 'common sense' understandings are often imbued with misperceptions about rape and rape victims. These misperceptions may be classified as 'rape myths', that is, 'descriptive or prescriptive beliefs about rape (ie about its causes, context, consequences, perpetrators, victims and their interaction) that serve to deny, downplay or justify sexual violence that men commit against women'.[3] Although the theory that societal attitudes (which may be erroneous and/or prejudicial) influence sexual offence trials was originally posited by feminists, it is now a generally accepted fact. For example, in the first edition of his seminal text on Irish sexual offences law, O'Malley acknowledges that 'The study of sexual offences is in many ways a study of social values'.[4] Similarly, McCullagh suggests that jurors' 'common sense' understandings of consent 'may reflect and embody the range of sexual stereotypes of rape that exist in Irish society'.[5]

The most oft-cited rape myth is the 'real rape' stereotype. Estrich defines 'real rape' as 'a sudden surprise attack by an unknown, often armed, sexual deviant' which 'occurs in an isolated, but public, location and the victim sustains serious physical injury, either as a result of the violence of the perpetrator or as a consequence of her efforts to resist the attack'.[6] The effect of this myth is that attacks which do not adhere to the 'violent stranger in a dark alley' stereotype are less likely to be seen as rape. This is problematic because, contrary to the myth, the majority of rapes involve offenders who are known to their victims, occur in private locations and typically involve little, if any, physical violence and serious injury such as wounds or broken bones. The erroneous nature of the 'real rape' stereotype is neatly illustrated by the findings in *Rape and Justice in Ireland* (hereafter '*RAJII*'), the most comprehensive and detailed Irish research on rape.[7] There were three strands to this research, focusing on the primary attrition points for rape cases: (1) the victim's decision to

[2] Estrich, *Real Rape* (n 1) 4.

[3] G Bohner et al, 'Rape Myth Acceptance: Cognitive, Affective and Behavioural Effects of Beliefs that Blame the Victim and Exonerate the Perpetrator' in M Horvath and J Brown (eds), *Rape: Challenging Contemporary Thinking* (Cullompton, Willan Publishing, 2009) 19.

[4] T O'Malley, *Sexual Offences: Law, Policy and Punishment* (Dublin, Round Hall Sweet and Maxwell, 1996) 1.

[5] C McCullagh, *Crime in Ireland: A Sociological Introduction* (Cork, Cork University Press, 1996) 107.

[6] Estrich, *Real Rape* (n 1) 4.

[7] C Hanly et al, *Rape and Justice in Ireland, A National Study of Survivor, Prosecutor and Court Responses to Rape* (Dublin, The Liffey Press, 2009).

report to the Gardaí;[8] (2) the Director of Public Prosecution's (DPP) decision to prosecute;[9] and (3) the trial.[10] The reality of rape identified across the three strands of this research is squarely at odds with stereotypical expectations of 'real rape'.

First, the majority of victims were raped by someone they knew. Of the victims interviewed in strand one of the research, 34 per cent had been raped by a stranger, with 25 per cent and 14 per cent reporting acquaintances and friends, respectively, as their attackers.[11] In the DPP files surveyed, 58.2 per cent of defendants were classified as 'friend' or 'acquaintance' with only 10.9 per cent identified as strangers.[12] Within the Central Criminal Court files analysed, nearly three-quarters of the complainants identified their attacker as someone with whom they had some form of prior relationship.[13] Second, private as opposed to public locations were the most likely locations for rape. In the Central Criminal Court files, approximately three-quarters of the incidents in which the setting was specified occurred in a private place or vehicle.[14] The complainant's home was the most common location for attacks in both the interviews with victims[15] and the DPP files.[16] Finally, while the *RAJII* findings revealed that the majority of rapes involved some degree of force, the physical injuries sustained by victims tended to be relatively minor. For example, in the victim interviews, 71 per cent reported that the defendant used physical force against them,[17] but 44 per cent of those reporting the use of force stated that the physical injury they incurred was relatively minor (eg bruises, cuts or scratches).[18] Similarly, in the Central Criminal Court files, 70 per cent of complainants for whom medical reports were compiled reported physical injuries[19] but only a minority of these were recorded as serious (ie broken bones,[20] strangulation marks[21] or knife wounds[22]).[23] Thus, the typical rape in Ireland is quite unlike the 'real rape' stereotype.

The other key, possibly even more pernicious, rape myth relates to expectations about victims themselves. Within rape trials, victim behaviour is scrutinised to determine whether the complainant is a 'real victim'. As Larcombe notes:

> Law's 'ideal victim' is no longer sexually chaste but she is consistent, rational and self-disciplined; she rarely has a history of mental illness or sexual abuse, and she does not drink alcohol to excess or otherwise engage in 'risky' behaviour.[24]

[8] ibid 111. This involved a national survey of 100 rape victims.

[9] ibid 120. A quantitative analysis was undertaken of materials received from the Office of the DPP on 597 reported rapes received by the DPP from the beginning of 2001 to the end of 2004.

[10] ibid 339. The researchers undertook a review of 173 rape case files which were received by the Central Criminal Court between 2000 and 2005 and analysed 35 trial transcripts.

[11] ibid 133.

[12] ibid 220.

[13] ibid 268–69.

[14] ibid 269.

[15] ibid 132, 32%.

[16] ibid 220, 30.1%.

[17] ibid 135.

[18] ibid 136.

[19] ibid 274.

[20] 3.7%.

[21] 2.78%.

[22] 2.78%.

[23] ibid 274.

[24] W Larcombe, 'Falling Rape Conviction Rates: (Some) Feminist Aims and Measures for Rape Law' (2011) 19 *Feminist Legal Studies* 27, 37.

Of course, in reality, rape victims will rarely conform to this idealised archetype. Most notably, alcohol is a regular feature in rape cases and was a common factor across all three strands of *RAJII*. For example, in strand one, over two-thirds of the victims interviewed reported that they had been drinking at the time of the incident, the majority having consumed three or more drinks.[25] The DPP files showed that 80 per cent of the complainants had consumed alcohol around the time of the incident, with 45.4 per cent described as severely intoxicated.[26] Similarly, in the Central Criminal Court files, nearly two-thirds of complainants had engaged in what is officially medically classified as 'binge-drinking'[27] prior to the incident.[28] Fifteen per cent reported consuming illegal drugs (predominantly cannabis or marijuana).[29] The expectation of consistency and rationality is also misguided. Given the trauma of rape and the fact that victims are very likely to blame themselves for their victimisation, expecting consistent accounts to be given throughout the investigation and trial is a fallacy. Nonetheless, expectations of ideal victim behaviour allow for victims to be portrayed as unreliable or unworthy of the victim label.

Despite the erroneous nature of rape myths, they are still prevalent in Irish society,[30] as demonstrated in the results of a recent Eurobarometer Report which surveyed perceptions of EU citizens about gender-based violence.[31] Twenty-four per cent of those surveyed agreed that women are more likely to be raped by a stranger than someone they know.[32] Twenty-three per cent agreed that women often make up or exaggerate claims of abuse or rape.[33] Further, although the numbers are considerably lower, there are still stereotypical expectations of 'real' victims. Eleven per cent of respondents believed that if someone is drunk or on drugs, that may make having sexual intercourse with them without consent justified. Further, 9 per cent of participants believed that voluntarily going home with someone or wearing revealing, provocative or sexy clothing could justify non-consensual sexual activity.[34] Although these figures demonstrate that rape myth acceptance (RMA) does not prevail amongst the majority of the population, attachment to ideals of 'real rape' and 'real victims' persist amongst a not insignificant proportion of society. Indeed, the existence of RMA may be higher than the statistics suggest. Ellison and Munro argue that 'participants who respond to questionnaires may be well-versed in the socially "appropriate" attitudes to be voiced at this abstract level, and so may present a more progressive profile to the researcher than they in fact endorse'.[35] If this is the case, then attitudes which are not articulated by the majority in surveys may surface in real-life assessments of rape allegations.

[25] Hanly et al, *Rape and Justice in Ireland* (n 7) 138.

[26] ibid 224.

[27] That is, the consumption of seven or more units of alcohol on a single occasion: Health Service Executive, *Less Alcohol is More Money, Energy and Control* (Dublin, Department of Health, 2008) 3.

[28] Hanly et al, *Rape and Justice in Ireland* (n 7) 272.

[29] ibid 273.

[30] For further discussion of the impact of Irish attitudes to rape on the operation of the law, see eg S Leahy, 'Bad Laws or Bad Attitudes? Assessing the Impact of Societal Attitudes upon the Conviction Rate for Rape in Ireland' (2014) 14(1) *Irish Journal of Applied Social Studies*, Article 3, see https://arrow.dit.ie/ijass/vol14/iss1/3.

[31] European Commission, *Special Eurobarometer 449 Report: Gender-Based Violence* (European Commission, 2016). The study involved surveying EU citizens in the 28 Member States of the EU; 1,002 Irish adults were surveyed. The results discussed here focus on the findings from the Irish participants only.

[32] ibid 57.

[33] ibid 58.

[34] ibid 64.

[35] L Ellison and V Munro, 'A Stanger in the Bushes, or an Elephant in the Room? Critical Reflections upon Received Rape Myth Wisdom in the Context of a Mock Juror Study' (2010) 13 *New Criminal Law Review* 781, 799.

If these attitudes persist in society, they are likely to influence juror deliberations in rape trials. As Temkin and Krahé highlight, jurors do not leave their long-held attitudes behind in the cloakroom when they enter a courtroom.[36] Research with juries is prohibited in Ireland and as yet mock jury research has not taken place in this area in this jurisdiction, but English research demonstrates the impact which RMA can have upon mock juror deliberations in rape trial simulations. Research conducted by Temkin and Krahé showed that jurors were more convinced that a defendant should be held liable and placed less blame on the complainant in stranger rapes than in rapes by acquaintances, and in particular, rapes by ex-partners.[37] Further, in mock jury research conducted by Ellison and Munro participants

> exhibited a strong and, in many cases, unshakeable expectation that a genuine victim of rape would engage in vigorous physical resistance against her attacker, and that, as a result, there would be corroborative evidence of injury on the body of either.[38]

Traces of 'real victim' stereotyping are evident in Finch and Munro's research which showed that women who consume alcohol in the presence of a male drinker will be perceived as being more sexually available than a non-drinking counterpart. Even in situations where the complainant's intoxication was not wholly voluntary (ie where her drink was spiked with additional alcohol) the complainant was frequently viewed as partially responsible.[39] Although it is not safe to draw definitive conclusions from mock jury research from another jurisdiction, the Eurobarometer statistics on UK attitudes to rape are not dissimilar to the Irish statistics, with low levels of RMA amongst the majority of respondents.[40] Thus, the mock jury research demonstrates that despite relatively progressive attitudes being displayed in attitude surveys, stereotypical attitudes may still influence juror deliberations.

Perhaps more troubling than the results of mock jury studies is recent research which suggests that even if jurors do not come to trial subscribing to prejudicial beliefs about rape, applying them spontaneously in their deliberations, 'other forces in trial proceedings work to reintroduce rape myths'.[41] Duncan and Henderson suggest that

> shared understandings within the courtroom are not necessarily the same as the assumptions and knowledge individual jurors hold outside the courtroom space, but are generated within it, for the duration of the trial, within the context of that specific case. Individualising a case has the effect of removing it from the broader context of sexual violence statistics and any awareness of gendered power relations jurors might carry with them as *contemporary* common knowledge.

[36] J Temkin and B Krahé, *Sexual Assault and the Justice Gap: A Question of Attitude?* (Oxford, Hart Publishing 2008) 69.

[37] ibid 48.

[38] L Ellison and V Munro, 'Better the Devil You Know? "Real Rape" Stereotypes and the Relevance of a Previous Relationship in (Mock) Juror Deliberations' (2013) 17 *International Journal of Evidence and Proof* 299, 315.

[39] E Finch and V Munro, 'The Demon Drink and the Demonized Woman: Socio-Sexual Stereotypes and Responsibility Attribution in Rape Trials Involving Intoxicants' (2007) 16 *Social and Legal Studies* 591, 599.

[40] For example: 27% of UK respondents agreed that women are more likely to be raped by a stranger than someone they know; 30% agreed that women often make up or exaggerate claims of abuse or rape; 12% believed that being drunk or on drugs may make having sexual intercourse without consent justified; 5% believed that voluntarily going home with someone could justify non-consensual sexual activity; and 6% believed that wearing revealing, provocative or sexy clothing could justify non-consensual sexual activity: European Commission, *Special Eurobarometer 449 Report* (n 31) 57–64.

[41] K Duncanson and E Henderson, 'Narrative, Theatre and the Disruptive Potential of Jury Directions in Rape Trials' (2014) 22 *Feminist Legal Studies* 155, 160.

> Thus removed, it becomes possible to view the specific case in question as an exception, one to which traditional narratives might apply even if jury members have pre-existing objections to such narratives.[42]

Thus, defence counsel tactics can encourage jurors to reason according to erroneous and prejudicial rape stereotypes. This is evident in trial observations. For instance, a pre-occupation with victim resistance and physical struggle was observed in Smith and Skinner's observations of rape trials in England, 'with any failure [to resist or struggle] being portrayed as abnormal and therefore suspicious'.[43] The researchers found that 'Rape myths were … routinely discussed and used to oversimplify the incidents being discussed'.[44] Zydervelt et al uncovered similar results in a New Zealand study of defence cross-examinations of complainants in rape trials.[45] They found that:

> The most common method of challenging the plausibility of the complainant's allegation was citing the complainant's behaviour immediately before the offence (eg willingly accompanying the defendant to a secluded place) or immediately afterwards (eg returning to the party with the defendant).[46]

Hence, whether jurors hold erroneous beliefs about rape before entering the courtroom, or whether defence tactics make stereotypical notions about rape seem to represent reality, rape stereotypes are an inescapable element of rape trials.

Of course, it would be disingenuous to suggest that the interplay between societal factors and the operation of the law in rape trials is confined to the influence of rape myths. The fact patterns of the typical rape case, as illustrated in the data from *RAJII* above, demonstrate that rapes occur in private spaces, with no witnesses, little corroborating evidence and often involve alcohol, meaning that memory recall can be impacted. In the stark 'swearing contest' nature of rape trials where jurors must be sure beyond reasonable doubt of guilt, it is inevitable that jurors will have difficulty in reaching their verdicts. As Hanly et al note:

> [I]n an ideal world, it would be possible always to distinguish between the innocent and the guilty. But this world is far from ideal. We have chosen to insist upon credible and reliable evidence as a foundation for conviction, and the existence of proper attrition is a necessary consequence of that choice.[47]

While it may be an 'unpalatable truth',[48] it is important to accept that, even without the influence of rape myths, there will be some allegations of rape which cannot be proved to the satisfaction of our criminal standard of proof.

However, whilst the social realities which impact upon adjudications of consent in rape trials involve more than rape myths, societal attitudes about rape must be considered in

[42] ibid 169.

[43] O Smith and T Skinner, 'How Rape Myths Are Used and Challenged in Rape and Sexual Assault Trials' (2017) 26 *Social and Legal Studies* 449.

[44] ibid 461.

[45] They studied transcripts from cases heard in New Zealand between 1996 and 2011: S Zydervelt et al, 'Lawyers' Strategies for Cross-examining Rape Complainants: Have We Moved beyond the 1950s?' (2016) 57 *British Journal of Criminology* 551, 555.

[46] ibid 561.

[47] Hanly et al, *Rape and Justice in Ireland* (n 7) 367.

[48] ibid 370.

reform efforts if legal change is to yield positive results. Reformers must concentrate on 'improving the "legal" story of rape', that is,

> bring[ing] the legal definition of rape and sexual assault into line with women's experiences so that legal definitions and presumptions do not reinforce false stereotypes or 'myths' about rape and effectively 'disqualify' the rape complaints of the majority of women.[49]

The remainder of this chapter considers whether recent Irish reform achieves this objective.

III. Defining Consent: The Criminal Law (Sexual Offences) Act 2017

In Irish law, a man commits rape if:

(a) he has sexual intercourse with a woman who at the time of the intercourse does not consent to it, and
(b) at that time he knows that she does not consent to the intercourse or he is reckless as to whether she does or does not consent to it.[50]

Consent is integral to this definition, representing 'the hinge on which a sexually penetrative act is rendered legal or criminal'.[51] Despite its centrality, the concept was not positively legislatively defined in Irish law until the enactment of the Criminal Law (Sexual Offences) Act 2017. Instead, the presence or absence of consent was determined with reference to common law rules. In *The People (DPP) v C*,[52] Murray J described consent as

> voluntary agreement or acquiescence to sexual intercourse by a person of the age of consent with the requisite mental capacity. Knowledge or understanding of facts material to the act being consented to is necessary for the consent to be voluntary or constitute acquiescence.[53]

At common law, an apparent consent to sexual activity may be vitiated by force, fear of adverse consequences,[54] fraud as to the nature of the act,[55] or the identity of one's partner[56] or incapacity[57] (eg through sleep,[58] unconsciousness or intoxication[59]). The only positive statutory guidance which was offered on this issue prior to the 2017 reforms was section 9 of the Criminal Law (Rape) (Amendment) Act 1990 which provided that

> in relation to an offence that consists of or includes the doing of an act to a person without the consent of that person any failure or omission on the part of that person to offer resistance to the act does not of itself constitute consent to the act.

[49] Larcombe, 'Falling Rape Conviction Rates' (n 24) 34.
[50] Criminal Law (Rape) Act 1981, s 2(1).
[51] Duncanson and Henderson, 'Narrative' (n 41) 162.
[52] *People (DPP) v C* [2001] 3 IR 345.
[53] ibid 360.
[54] *R v Olugboja* [1982] QB 320.
[55] *R v Flattery* (1877) 2 QBD 410; *R v Williams* (1923) 1 KB 340.
[56] *People (DPP) v C* [2001] 3 IR 345.
[57] Capacity to consent requires that an individual be over the legal age of consent (17 years) and have the requisite mental capacity to consent. Where individuals lack capacity to consent due to age or limited decision-making capacity, sexual activity with them is prohibited.
[58] *R v Mayers* (1872) 12 Cox CC 311; *R v Larter & Castleton* [1995] Criminal Law Review 75.
[59] *R v Lang* (1976) 62 Cr App R 50.

This provision sought to offset the expectation which jurors might have that victims should resist the efforts of their attacker. Although this was a welcome declaratory provision, in practice, a failure to offer resistance was still something that was likely to be taken into account by a jury as evidence from which consent could be inferred.[60]

There were a number of problems with the reliance on common law to define consent which prevailed until the introduction of the 2017 Act. The guidance provided on consent was both vague and stagnant. For example, although fear of adverse consequences was capable of vitiating an apparent consent to sexual activity, it was very unclear what forms of sexual coercion might be included within this. Would, for example, a threat of job loss or of harm to a third party suffice? Without specific guidance, it is unlikely that jurors would view these sorts of threats as sufficient to find a defendant guilty of rape. Similarly, the lack of direction on intoxication meant that jurors were not receiving guidance on how to appropriately and dispassionately assess whether consent was present where the complainant was intoxicated at the time of the impugned encounter. Admittedly, the common law was sufficiently elastic to allow for progressive interpretations and development of the understanding of consent but without legislative prompting, this was unlikely to occur. As Temkin suggests, the net effect of a failure to spell out or provide criteria by which lack of consent can be judged is that 'much oppressive behaviour is likely to go unpunished'.[61] The law was certainly not robust enough to overcome the effects of societal attitudes about rape.

In light of the challenges posed by relying on the common law rules on consent, it is unsurprising that Irish legal commentators and victim support groups repeatedly called for the introduction of a legislative definition which was ultimately enacted in section 48 of the 2017 Act.[62] The latter substitutes the following for section 9 of the Criminal Law (Rape) (Amendment) Act 1990:

(1) A person consents to a sexual act if he or she freely and voluntarily agrees to engage in that act.[63]

(2) A person does not consent to a sexual act if –

- (a) he or she permits the act to take place or submits to it because of the application of force to him or her or to some other person, or because of the threat of the application of force to him or her or to some other person, or because of a well-founded fear that force may be applied to him or her or to some other person,
- (b) he or she is asleep or unconscious,
- (c) he or she is incapable of consenting because of the effect of alcohol or some other drug,
- (d) he or she is suffering from a physical disability which prevents him or her from communicating whether he or she agrees to the act,[64]

[60] C Hanly, *An Introduction to Irish Criminal Law*, 3rd edn (Dublin, Gill and MacMillan, 2015) 323.

[61] Temkin, *Rape and the Legal Process* (n 1) 93.

[62] See eg Law Reform Commission, *Report on Rape and Allied Offences* (Dublin, Law Reform Commission 1988) para 16; Rape Crisis Network of Ireland, *Agenda for Justice I: Towards Ending Injustice for Survivors of Sexual Violence* (Dublin, Rape Crisis Network of Ireland, 2005) 4; *Consent on Sexual Contact: RCNI Discussion Document* (Dublin, Rape Crisis Network of Ireland, 2008) 2; *RCNI Agenda for Justice Discussion Document* (Dublin, Rape Crisis Network of Ireland, 2009) 12; S Leahy, 'Reform of Irish Rape Law: The Need for a Legislative Definition of Consent' (2014) 43 *Common Law World Review* 231.

[63] This is defined as: (a) an act consisting of sexual intercourse or buggery; (b) an act described in s 3(1) or s 4(1) of the 1990 Act (ie aggravated sexual assault or rape under s 4), or; (c) an act which if done without consent would constitute a sexual assault: s 9(6) (as amended).

[64] Examples of individuals who might be affected by this provision are those suffering from cerebral palsy or the effects of the stroke and thus may not be able to express themselves fully.

(e) he or she is mistaken as to the nature and purpose of the act,
(f) he or she is mistaken as to the identity of any other person involved in the act,
(g) he or she is being unlawfully detained at the time at which the act takes place,
(h) the only expression or indication of consent or agreement to the act comes from somebody other than the person himself or herself.

This two-tiered definition of consent provides a positive statement of what consent means (thus marking a break with the negative approach to definition found in the common law), followed by a non-exhaustive list of situations where consent will be deemed to be absent.[65] The focus on 'free agreement' in the first tier can be seen to introduce the idea of communicative sexuality into Irish law, that is, a requirement of mutuality in sexual encounters which is evidenced by effective communication. The positive definition which sets out the requirements for a valid consent should shift the focus in sexual offence trials to seeking to identify that these elements (freedom, capacity and choice) are present as opposed to looking for signs of non-consent (eg force, fraud, incapacity). Of course, as outlined below, the definition in itself is not sufficient to achieve this goal and must be supported by additional initiatives if it is to meaningfully impact on adjudications of consent in rape trials.

The list of situations where consent is deemed to be absent largely replicates the common law but there is some expansion of the understanding of the factors which are contra-indicative of genuine sexual choice. For example, the new definition provides greater guidance on force and threats, clarifying that submission to sexual activity due to the application of force towards a third party or the threat thereof does not constitute a legally valid consent. It also seems that the force or threat thereof does not have to come from the defendant. Further, the second tier confirms that fraud includes fraud as to the purpose of the act and not just its nature. Thus, the 2017 reforms cover frauds like that in *R v Tabassum*,[66] where individuals consent to what would otherwise be a non-consensual sexual touching because they have been led to believe it is a necessary medical procedure. This clarification is welcome and increases protection from sexual abuse and exploitation. Since the express inclusion of fraud as to purpose within sexual fraud in England and Wales, there have been a number of convictions on this ground. For example, in *R v Piper*[67] it was held that the complainant had not consented where she had agreed to be measured for a bikini by the defendant for the purpose of determining her suitability for a modelling job when in fact this was done for the sexual gratification of the defendant.[68] Such convictions would have been unlikely under the common law rules.

Another noteworthy inclusion in the second tier is verification that consent expressed by a third party other than the complainant is not a valid consent. This aligns with the ideal of communicative sexuality and offers greater protection from sexual abuse for vulnerable individuals, such as trafficked persons or sex workers, who may be offered for sexual services without their consent. Further, section 9(5) reproduces the message of the original section 9, providing that 'Any failure or omission on the part of a person to offer resistance to an act does not of itself constitute consent to that act'. Additionally, section 9(4) clarifies

[65] Section 9(3) provides that '[t]his section does not limit the circumstances in which it may be established that a person did not consent to a sexual act'.
[66] *R v Tabassum* [2000] 2 Cr App R 328.
[67] *R v Piper* [2007] EWCA Crim 2131.
[68] See also *R v Jheeta* [2007] EWCA 1699; *R v Matt* [2015] EWCA Crim 162.

that 'Consent to a sexual act may be withdrawn at any time before the act begins, or in the case of a continuing act, while the act is taking place'.[69]

Although the list of situations where consent will now be deemed to be absent is very welcome and to some extent develops the understanding of consent which prevails at common law, the legislature could have gone further and sought to more directly tackle the rape myths discussed above. Most notable in this regard is the stance taken on threats, the understanding of which is confined to threats of force. Despite some limited expansion (eg the inclusion of threats of force towards a third party), the legislature did not stray far from the traditional, indeed stereotypical, understandings of force which are found within the common law. It is a pity that the list did not acknowledge that there are a number of threats other than those of force which can obviate sexual choice (eg threats to abduct or detain a third party;[70] expose a secret that would be highly damaging to the complainant's interests;[71] or to withdraw financial support where the complainant is wholly dependent on the defendant for survival[72]). Elsewhere, this author has suggested that the list of situations where consent will be deemed to be absent should include the situation where 'the complainant submits to sexual activity as a result of threats of serious harm or serious detriment of any type to the complainant or a third party'.[73] Of course, as the second tier is non-exhaustive,[74] the definition of consent in the first tier can be used by judges to extend the legal understanding of threats which are contra-indicative of consent to include those listed above. Nonetheless, given the conservative judicial development of understandings of consent to date in this jurisdiction and the persistence of the 'real rape' stereotype which continues to create an expectation that rape involves forcible compulsion, positive legislative action emphasising that unjustifiable sexual coercion involves more than physical force and threats thereof would have been beneficial. It is unfortunate that the legislature did not opt to provide greater guidance here. It is also regrettable that, when defining consent, the legislature did not also re-evaluate the honest belief in consent defence, reform of which is discussed in the next section. As will be argued below, both issues are so closely related, to reform one without at least re-assessing the other, seems incongruous.

IV. Unfinished Business: The Honest Belief Defence

The honest belief defence operates to exculpate a defendant who, at the time of the impugned sexual encounter, honestly believed that the complainant was consenting. This defence can be defined objectively (ie a belief will exculpate where it is based on reasonable grounds) or subjectively (ie a belief in consent exculpates once honestly held – no matter how unreasonable it is to hold such a belief). A subjective construction of the honest belief defence is provided for in section 2(2) of the 1981 Act:

> It is hereby declared that if at a trial for a rape offence the jury has to consider whether a man believed that a woman was consenting to sexual intercourse, the presence or absence of reasonable

[69] This places the common law rule in *Kaitmaki v R* [1985] 1 AC 147.
[70] Temkin, *Rape and the Legal Process* (n 1) 101.
[71] ibid.
[72] Leahy, 'Reform of Irish Rape Law' (n 62) 254.
[73] ibid 261.
[74] Section 9(3) of the Criminal Law (Rape) (Amendment) Act (as amended).

> grounds for such a belief is a matter to which the jury is to have regard, in conjunction with any other relevant matters, in considering whether he so believed.[75]

The history of the application of this provision has not been straightforward. A series of cases in the 1990s considered when and how judges should instruct juries about honest belief.[76] Ultimately, the Supreme Court, in *People (DPP) v McDonagh*,[77] confirmed that section 2(2) should only be explained to a jury when an issue of mistaken belief arises, that is, in 'cases in which, the jury having found that the complainant had not in fact agreed to intercourse, an issue is raised that the accused had mistakenly believed that she had consented'.[78] That section 2(2) should only be explained to the jury in exceptional cases was recently re-iterated by the Supreme Court in *DPP v O'R*,[79] Charleton J emphasising that

> in the vast majority of cases no specific issue as to any belief aspect of the mental element in rape arises. … The circumstances are very rare indeed where a genuine issue could arise that even though the woman did not consent, the man nonetheless believed that she was consenting.[80]

The learned judge also highlighted that where the defendant's assertion was that the complainant consented, then a claim of honest belief in consent is not available. In such cases it is unnecessary 'to embark on the issue of mistaken belief as it simply does not arise. Nor can anyone credibly plead alternative facts: that there was a consensual sexual encounter but if there was not then that the accused nonetheless believed that the woman consented'.[81]

Although a defendant's belief need not be objectively reasonable to exculpate, Charleton J notes that irrational unfounded assertions of honest belief need not be accepted by jurors:

> [N]o jury is under any obligation to believe an obviously false story. A jury is entitled to accept or reject any prosecution or defence evidence. In these cases, every jury is entrusted, using shrewdness and commonsense, to judge what the accused claims as to his mistaken belief against their view of what an ordinary or reasonable man would have realised in the circumstances. This defence requires genuine belief.[82]

The *O'R* judgment stresses that the honest belief defence should only be raised where there is a solid evidential basis for it. Moreover, the judgment makes clear that the defendant cannot claim that there was consent and also seek to rely on the defence of honest belief. Justice Charleton places significant faith in jurors' ability to spot a spurious claim of honest belief, thereby suggesting that the defence is not open to abuse and that the subjective construction of the defence is not creating injustice. However, given the role of rape myths in the trial process and the inherent complexities of rape cases, jurors may not be as impervious to contrived claims of honest belief as the judgment suggests. Thus, the defence may have greater practical impact than is described here. Further, the

[75] This defence originated in the now infamous English judgment in *R v Morgan* [1975] AC 182.
[76] *People (DPP) v Gaffey*, Unreported, Court of Criminal Appeal, 10 May 1991; *People (DPP) v F*, Unreported, Court of Criminal Appeal, 27 May 1993; *People (DPP) v Creighton* [1994] 1 ILRM 551; *DPP v Rock*, Unreported, Court of Criminal Appeal, 29 July 1993.
[77] *DPP v McDonagh* [1996] 1 IR 565.
[78] ibid 573.
[79] *DPP v O'R* [2016] IESC 64.
[80] ibid para 40.
[81] ibid para 41.
[82] ibid.

connotations of the subjective formulation of the defence are squarely at odds with the message of communicative sexuality which the new definition of consent promotes. Allowing a subjective construction of the defence to prevail arguably sends a message that a unilateral interpretation of a sexual partner's willingness to engage in sexual activity is permissible, thereby undermining the message of mutuality and communication in sexual encounters which is offered by the definition of consent. As Pickard observes, an unreasonable belief in consent is no more than 'an easily avoided and self-serving mistake produced by the actor's indifference to the separate existence of another'.[83] Consequently, reform of this defence is vital for both practical and principled reasons. Given the strong inter-linkage between honest belief and the definition of consent, to reform one and not at least review the other is incongruous and it is hoped that the Government's commitment to consider reform of this defence[84] will result in swift efforts to align this defence with the statutory definition of consent. This author has previously proposed the following reformulation of the honest belief defence:

> A defendant will not be guilty of rape where he held a reasonable belief that the complainant was consenting. Whether a belief was reasonable is to be determined according to all the circumstances, including any steps which the defendant took to ascertain whether the complainant was consenting.[85]

This recommendation is based upon the construction of honest belief in the English Sexual Offences Act 2003.[86] Significantly, although the English law is understood as introducing an objective approach to honest belief, an element of subjectivity is retained in order to offset any potential interference with defendants' rights.[87] Guidance accompanying the English legislation provides that the reference to 'all the circumstances' includes a defendant's attributes such as disability or extreme youth, but not any particular fetishes which he may possess.[88] Thus, in deciding whether a defendant's belief in consent was reasonable, any characteristic of the defendant which might affect his ability to perceive or understand whether the complainant was consenting should be taken into account.[89] Of course, careful line-drawing is required here to make sure that an accused's characteristics are only taken into account where genuinely relevant. Methods of ensuring this are discussed below.

[83] T Pickard, 'Culpable Mistakes and Rape: Relating Mens Rea to the Crime' (1980) 30 *University of Toronto Law Journal* 75, 83. Pickard's views are cited and echoed by J Temkin, *Rape and the Legal Process* (n 1) 126–27.

[84] S Bardon, 'State to Review Use of Honest Belief of Consent as Rape Defence' *The Irish Times* (24 January 2017); Department of Justice and Equality, *National Strategy for Women and Girls 2017–2020* (Dublin, Department of Justice & Equality, Stationery Office, 2017) objective 5.10.

[85] S Leahy, 'When Honest is not Good Enough: The Need for Reform of the Honest Belief Defence in Irish Rape Law' (2013) 23 *Irish Criminal Law Journal* 2.

[86] Honest belief is no longer formulated as a defence to rape in English law. Rather, it is a constituent element of the mens rea. However, the English rules in this area are still instructive.

[87] Concerns have traditionally been expressed that the move to an entirely objective construction of the defence runs the risk of unfairly convicting individuals who are incapable of acting reasonably. The most famous exposition of this concern is offered by Glanville Williams who opined that 'to convict the stupid man would be to convict him for what lawyers call inadvertent negligence – honest conduct which may be the best that this man can do but that does not come up to the standard of the so-called reasonable man', Glanville Williams, in a letter to *The Times* (London, 8 May 1975), quoted in Estrich, *Real Rape* (n 1) 97.

[88] Crown Prosecution Service, Guidelines on the Sexual Offences Act 2003, 7.

[89] R Card, *Sexual Offences: The New Law* (Bristol, Jordan Publishing, 2004) 39. Examples of such characteristics might include learning disabilities, mental illness, impairment of sight or hearing, level of maturity or level of sexual experience.

The benefits of the proposed approach to re-formulating the honest belief defence is that it introduces an objective construction of the defence without raising concerns about potential unfairness for defendants who, for legitimate reasons, are not able to reach the standard of objective reasonableness when interpreting a sexual partner's consent. Importantly, requiring the jury to consider 'all the circumstances, including any steps … taken to ascertain whether the complainant was consenting' prompts jurors to consider the context of the impugned encounter when determining whether a claimed honest belief in consent was reasonable. To do this, the jury would have to look at the actions of both parties, what the relationship between them was prior to the alleged incident, the circumstances in which they had placed themselves, and the level of responsibility exercised by both parties.[90] The express reference to steps taken to ascertain consent is also significant, aligning with the ideal of communicative sexuality in the definition of consent, re-iterating that consent to sexual activity should be communicated and that it is incumbent upon individuals to make sure that their partners are freely consenting to sexual activity.

Admittedly, given the vagueness of the phrase 'all the circumstances', care is needed so that the reformulation of the defence achieves real changes and that a resort to traditional and/or stereotypical attitudes does not undermine the effectiveness of the new provision. Commenting on the English law in this area, Temkin and Ashworth voice concern that the broad reference to 'all the circumstances' is an invitation for the jury to scrutinise the complainant's behaviour, and thus necessarily employ 'real victim' imagery, in order to determine whether there was anything about the complainant which could have induced a reasonable belief in consent.[91] If the interpretation of honest belief developed so as to permit complainant behaviour to be scrutinised in this way, reformulation would contain 'no real challenge to society's norms and stereotypes about either the relationship between men and women or other sexual situations, and leaves open the possibility that those stereotypes will determine assessments of reasonableness'.[92]

Indeed, mock jury research conducted by Finch and Munro on the English definition of honest belief suggests that, without guidance, the looseness of the phrase 'all the circumstances' is likely to be interpreted by jurors in a broad manner which will greatly reduce the significance of the more objective approach to mens rea. The researchers found that reference to wider circumstantial factors generates an opportunity for the introduction into the jury room of a range of (ill-founded) views about 'appropriate' socio-sexual interaction, either on the basis that they are shared by jurors who are assessing the signals sent out by the complainant's conduct, or on the basis that jurors, while not sharing these views themselves, nonetheless consider that they may have been harboured by the defendant and so may be relevant to the question of reasonableness.[93] This research illustrates a number of examples where the reference to 'all the circumstances' allowed questionable stereotypes to creep into determinations of whether a defendant's belief in consent was reasonable.

[90] Home Office, Protecting the Public: Strengthening Protection against Sex Offenders and Reforming the Law on Sexual Offences (London, Home Office, 2002) 17.

[91] J Temkin and A Ashworth, 'The Sexual Offences Act 2003: Rape, Sexual Assault and the Problems of Consent' (2004) *Criminal Law Review* 328, 342.

[92] ibid.

[93] E Finch and V Munro, 'Breaking Boundaries? Sexual Consent in the Jury Room' (2006) 26 *Legal Studies* 303, 317.

For example, the jurors took into account 'the whole situation, the party, the drinking and so on' or 'the fact that she is at a party, she does look and appear to be drunk, she hasn't told him no'.[94]

It is clear then that additional measures are required to ensure that a reformulated honest belief defence is not undermined by a resort to stereotypical thinking about appropriate socio-sexual behaviour, or by defendants being able to rely on inappropriate grounds to assert an honest belief in consent. A possible intervention would be to replicate the approach to defining consent and include a 'second tier' in the reformulation of the honest belief defence, creating a list of claims which are not sufficient to raise the defence (eg the fact that the defendant previously had sex with the complainant or that she did not physically resist).[95] This approach would limit the potential for defendants to raise spurious, unfounded assertions of honest belief which rely on stereotypes. It is also possible that the legislature could go even further and shift the burden of proving an honest belief in consent to the defendant. Shifting a burden of proof to defendants in criminal trials is not uncontroversial and may raise concerns about protection of the defendant's constitutional right to the presumption of innocence. However, the Irish legislature has already adopted this approach for the mistake of age defence in statutory rape law where a defendant's mistake must not only be reasonable but must be proven by the defendant on the balance of probabilities.[96] Thus, it is feasible that the honest belief in consent defence could be reformed so that a defendant raising the defence would have to bear the legal burden of proving it on the balance of probabilities. An alternative, more moderate, approach would be to shift a persuasive burden of proof to the defendant, that is, a burden of establishing a reasonable doubt in the mind of the jury.[97]

A comprehensive review of the merits and appropriate method of shifting the burden of proving honest belief to the defendant is beyond the scope of discussion here but it may be a viable option for ensuring that only genuine and robust claims are put before a jury. Overall, the foregoing discussion illustrates that there are a number of viable options which can be considered for ensuring that the positive benefits of moving to an objective formulation of the honest belief defence will not be undermined by recourse to stereotypical beliefs about appropriate socio-sexual behaviour. Undoubtedly, there is much to consider here but reform of the substantive rules on consent will be incomplete until the issue of honest belief in consent is effectively reformed.

[94] ibid 318.

[95] The benefits of clear direction on what is reasonable or unreasonable, potentially by enactment of a list of examples has been posited by S Cowan, 'Freedom and Capacity to Make a Choice: A Feminist Analysis of Consent in the Criminal Law of Rape' in V Munro and C Stychin (eds), *Sexuality and the Law: Feminist Engagements* (Abingdon, Routledge-Cavendish, 2007) 66. A similar recommendation has been made by Flynn and Ring, who argue for a list of considerations which the jury should have regard to when considering a claim of honest belief, see E Flynn and S Ring, 'Judgment: *DPP v C*' in M Enright et al (eds), *Northern/Irish Feminist Legal Judgments* (Oxford, Hart Publishing, 2017) 554.

[96] See ss 2(3)–(5) and 3(3)–(5) of the Criminal Law (Sexual Offences) Act 2006, as inserted by ss 16 and 17 of the Criminal Law (Sexual Offences) Act 2017, respectively.

[97] This approach to shifting the burden of proof to defendants was discussed and approved in *People (DPP) v Egan* [2010] 3 IR 561 in relation to a consideration of the pre-2017 definition of the mistake of age defence in Irish statutory rape law. It was held that a defendant could discharge a persuasive burden of proof 'by reference to some evidence in the case, whether by cross-examination or otherwise, but not necessarily by giving evidence himself', ibid 572.

V. Beyond Legislative Reform: Extra-Legal Initiatives to Tackle Rape Stereotypes in the Courtroom and Beyond

The introduction of a statutory definition of consent has the potential to act as a catalyst for change in adjudications of consent in rape trials, especially once the honest belief defence is also appropriately reformed. Progress will not, however, be achieved by legislative change alone. Additional extra-legislative initiatives are vital if rape law reform and its significance are to be effectively conveyed to jurors and to minimise the potential for progressive interpretation of the definition to be undermined by continued adherence to rape stereotypes within the courtroom. One method of helping judges to achieve this is the use of model jury directions which could be provided to judges via bench book guidance. An example of the use of such directions can be found in the English *Crown Court Compendium*[98] which includes guidance for judges when directing juries in rape trials both on the issue of consent and honest belief and on the avoidance of reliance on stereotypes in deliberations. Such directions can be given at the start of the trial or when summing up for the jury and it is recommended that any proposed direction be discussed with counsel in advance.[99]

The *Compendium* contains a number of model directions, which judges can use to direct jurors to be wary of drawing unwarranted assumptions from issues such as: delayed complaint; inconsistent accounts; lack of emotion/distress when giving evidence; or the clothing worn by the complainant at the time of the attack. An example of guidance which the *Compendium* provides for trial judges when directing jurors on consent is the direction on the fact that fear other than fear of force is also inconsistent with consent, thus targeting any potential for jurors to be influenced by stereotypical expectations of force and physical injury:

> V gave evidence that although D did not threaten her or use any force on her, she did not consent to [specify act] because she was so frightened by what D was doing that she froze and was unable to speak or to move. It is important to draw a distinction between consent and submission. A person consents to something if, being capable of making a choice and being free to do so, s/he agrees to it. Consent in some situations may be given enthusiastically, whereas in others it is given with reluctance, but nevertheless, it is still consent. Where however a person is so overcome by fear that she lacks any capacity either to give consent or to resist, that person does not consent but is submitting to what takes place.[100]

Instructions like this seek to offset the potential ill-effects of unwarranted assumptions about rape and appropriate socio-sexual behaviour, whilst remaining sufficiently nuanced so as not to create unfair prejudice for the defendant. Providing such directions would be discretionary and they are sufficiently flexible to be tailored to suit individual cases. Consequently, their use would not interfere with judicial autonomy in directing jurors but would assist judges in neutrally advising jurors about the realities of rape. Although there is no equivalent of the *Compendium* in Ireland, perhaps this is an initiative which could be undertaken once a statutory Judicial Council is established and greater commitment and

[98] D Maddison et al, *The Crown Court Compendium Part I: Jury and Trial Management and Summing Up* (Judicial Council, 2017).

[99] ibid 20–22.

[100] ibid 20–18.

resources are directed towards judicial training and guidance.[101] Indeed, training for judges and barristers who practice in the area of sexual offences is vital if reform is to be implemented progressively and the continuing effects of stereotypes are to be eliminated from the trial process.

Of course, it is also vital that stereotypical attitudes outside the courtroom are tackled. Changing stereotypical societal attitudes about sexual violence is crucial both to ensure that negative attitudes do not find their way into courtrooms in the first place and to foster healthier attitudes about appropriate socio-sexual behaviour, thereby curbing the prevalence of sexual violence. The new statutory definition of consent (and hopefully, reform of honest belief) provides the impetus for opening a national conversation about attitudes to appropriate socio-sexual behaviour. Although efforts have already been made with regard to education of young people in Ireland,[102] what is required is a government-sponsored, national awareness and education campaign which is targeted at all age demographics. Any such campaign must be carefully researched and designed and be offered in a targeted and sustained manner to maximise its effectiveness in all echelons of society. Although training and education initiatives along these lines are costly to devise and deliver, they are indispensable if the ill-effects of rape myths are to be tackled successfully both within the criminal justice process and in society more generally.

VI. Conclusion

This chapter has illustrated the complex effects which gendered stereotypes exert on adjudications of consent in rape trials. The introduction of a statutory definition of consent is a very welcome and long-awaited reform but it is just the beginning of the process of change in this area. Further law reform in the form of reformulation of the honest belief in consent defence is urgently required if the message of the new communicative model of consent is not to be undermined. Additionally, although outside the scope of this chapter, reform of the rules of evidence which control the information which jurors have access to when adjudicating on consent also requires consideration, most notably the rules regulating the admission of sexual experience evidence. However, what the discussion here has also demonstrated is that law reform by itself cannot hope to counter the negative effect of gendered stereotypes on rape trials. Certainly, law can seek to 'push forward' and change societal attitudes by sending a message about appropriate socio-sexual behaviour.[103] It must, however, be accompanied by more deep-seated social change if it is to be effective. Thus, any

[101] The Judicial Council Bill 2017 is currently progressing through the legislative process. Once enacted, a Judicial Studies Committee will be established to provide training for judges: s 17. At present, the Judicial Studies Committee is under-resourced and thus judicial training and support is limited: see www.aji.ie/supports/judicial-education.

[102] Consent workshops have been developed by researchers in National University of Ireland, Galway, see P MacNeela et al, *Development, Implementation, and Evaluation of the SMART Consent Workshop on Sexual Consent for Third Level Students* (2017), available online at www.nuigalway.ie/smartconsent. Dublin Rape Crisis Centre also runs an 'Ask Consent' campaign, see www.drcc.ie/get-informed/campaigns/ask-consent-campaign. A government-supported education campaign for secondary school students has also been announced, see K Doyle, 'Secondary School Students to get Classes on Sexual Consent' *Irish Independent* (30 December 2017).

[103] Estrich, *Real Rape* (n 1) 101.

reform effort must entail a broadly-based strategy, encompassing not just legal reforms but also extra-legal initiatives, which seek to tackle negative societal attitudes both within the courtroom and in wider society.[104] In this respect, extra-legal measures suggested here, such as model jury directions and public awareness and education campaigns, are an indispensable part of the reform effort. There is no quick fix for the challenges encountered here. Law reform must be seen as a first step in a much lengthier, and, inevitably, expensive and time-consuming project. This will involve educative and awareness-raising endeavours, as well as 'perpetual vigilance' in the form of monitoring and evaluation to establish whether legal and non-legal initiatives are achieving their intended consequences.[105] Thus, while the recent reforms of Irish sexual offences law have sown the seeds of change, much work remains to be done before the impact of gendered stereotypes is eliminated from both the courtroom and Irish society.

[104] Temkin, *Rape and the Legal Process* (n 1) 355.

[105] V Nourse, 'The "Normal" Successes and Failures of Feminism and the Criminal Law' (2000) 75 *Chicago-Kent Law Review* 951, 978.

2

Prostitution Law

IVANA BACIK

I. Introduction

Irish prostitution law has 'developed historically in a clearly gendered way'.[1] Until the introduction of statutory reform in 2017,[2] a prohibitionist model of legal regulation was in place, focused upon the public display of selling sex, rather than the sale of sex itself, with offences framed in gender-neutral language under the Criminal Law (Sexual Offences) Act 1993. However, even after 1993, the criminal law continued to be applied in a gendered way, targeting only the visible manifestations of prostitution, not the private exploitation of the (mostly) women selling sex. Only the offer of sex for sale in public was criminalised, through offences based on 'loitering' and 'soliciting' for the purposes of prostitution; but it was not an offence for a person to buy sex, either in public or in private. The focus was on concealing the sale of sex, not explicitly outlawing it: a double standard; a 'distinctly ambivalent' legal structure;[3] or a 'prostitution tolerance regime'.[4] Prostitution was legally framed as a 'public nuisance', not private exploitation.

In a significant change of approach in 2017, law reform was introduced in Ireland to criminalise the purchase of sex, based on the 'Nordic model' law first adopted by Sweden in 1999.[5] Similar laws have also been passed in Norway, Iceland, Canada, Northern Ireland and France.[6] This model is associated with a perspective that sees prostitution as inherently exploitative and causing harm to the (predominantly) women engaged in it; a societal gender inequality.[7] The Swedish law thus sought 'to tackle prostitution through a statement

[1] I Bacik, *Kicking and Screaming: Dragging Ireland into the Twenty-First Century* (Dublin, O'Brien Press, 2004) 149.

[2] Criminal Law (Sexual Offences) Act 2017. The author is a member of Seanad Éireann and was involved as a Senator in the passage of the legislation. Seanad Éireann is the upper house of the Oireachtas, the Irish parliament.

[3] T O'Malley, *Sexual Offences*, 2nd edn (Dublin, Round Hall, 2013) 202.

[4] M O'Connor, 'Consent, Agency and Harm: A Phenomenological Inquiry into the Experience of Women in Prostitution and Women Trafficked for Sexual Exploitation in Ireland' (Dublin City University, Unpublished PhD Thesis, 2014) 78.

[5] Violence Against Women Act (*Kvinnofrid*). See eg G Ekberg, 'The Swedish Law that Prohibits the Purchase of Sexual Services: Best Practices for Prevention of Prostitution and Trafficking in Human Beings' (2004) 10 *Violence Against Women* 1187.

[6] The Irish law reform is contained in pt 4 of the Criminal Law (Sexual Offences) Act 2017.

[7] See eg the Swedish government's explicit definition of prostitution as gender-based violence (the 'Regeringskansliet' strategy on 'gender mainstreaming', implemented in 2012), cited in M Skilbrei and C Holmstrom,

about prostitution as a phenomenon and practice of gender inequality that is incompatible with a gender equal society.'[8] A growing momentum in support of this approach may be identified among policy-makers in different countries. By contrast, academic discourse on prostitution has become increasingly dominated by feminist scholars who challenge the view of prostitution as exploitation, arguing instead that women exercise agency by engaging in 'sexwork'. This perspective supports legal structures in which prostitution is decriminalised or legalised, as in jurisdictions such as the Netherlands or New Zealand. The divide between the 'exploitation' and 'sexwork' feminists has become entrenched in recent years. A review of the Irish prostitution laws and the 2017 reform will be provided here in the context of these contemporary feminist debates.

II. Historical Development of Irish Prostitution Law

Irish prostitution law has a long and complex history – from the Contagious Diseases Acts and Vagrancy legislation of the nineteenth century, to the focus on the so-called 'common prostitute' in early twentieth century legislation. Difficulties around providing proof of 'indecent exposure' in order to secure convictions in the 1980s led to a change in the law; legislation enacted in 1993 formed the basis for regulating prostitution until 2017. But despite these changing legal regimes, some themes have remained constant throughout. Above all, the criminal law was, until 2017, not designed to suppress prostitution itself, just to curb its public display.

An examination of early statutes dealing with prostitution, such as the Vagrancy Act 1824, demonstrates that legislative concern centred not on the existence of prostitutes, but on the visible manifestation of their activities.[9] An analysis of early case law shows that judges, too, were most concerned with keeping prostitution out of public sight. Gendered judicial interpretations became part of the common law on prostitution; Maria Luddy writes that the prostitute was constructed in Ireland as 'an infectious creature, a carrier of disease and immorality which was transferable to the respectable men and women of society'.[10] In the 1860s, this gendered construction was expressed through the notorious Contagious Diseases Acts 1864–69, which introduced registration and compulsory medical examination for prostitutes, ostensibly in order to protect soldiers from venereal disease. After a long reform campaign by groups appalled at the brutal treatment of women under these laws,

Prostitution Policy in the Nordic Region: Ambiguous Sympathies (Farnham, Ashgate, 2013) 138. Skilbrei and Holmstrom cite a comment made to a journalist at the time of the law reform by then Minister for Equality Mona Sahlin, 'If you are a feminist, you cannot relate to prostitution in any other way than to see it as male domination', 138. See also Y Svanstrom, 'Criminalising the John – a Swedish Gender Model?' in J Outshoorn (ed), *The Politics of Prostitution: Women's Movements, Democratic States and the Globalisation of Sex Commerce* (Cambridge, Cambridge University Press, 2004).

[8] J Erikson, 'The Various 'Problems' of Prostitution – a Dynamic Frame Analysis of Swedish Prostitution Policy' in M Coy (ed), *Prostitution, Harm and Gender Inequality: Theory, Research and Policy* (Farnham, Ashgate, 2012) 159.

[9] S 3 of the 1824 Act provided that 'every common prostitute wandering in the public streets or public highways, and behaving in a riotous or indecent manner, shall be deemed an idle and disorderly person within the true intent and meaning of this Act'.

[10] M Luddy, *Prostitution and Irish Society 1800–1940* (Cambridge, Cambridge University Press, 2007) 7.

the Acts were finally repealed in the 1880s.[11] The Criminal Law (Amendment) Act 1885 was then passed, giving the police extensive powers against procurers and brothel keepers. The implementation of the new legislation caused a reduction in the number of brothels, but had the effect of forcing prostitutes back onto the streets.[12]

The withdrawal of the British garrison in Dublin following independence in 1922 led to the decline of prostitution in the previously notorious area of 'Monto' in Dublin.[13] New legislation was introduced in 1935, through the Criminal Law (Amendment) Act of that year. While it also contained provisions on other issues, this was the first post-independence Irish law to deal with prostitution. Margaret Ward places it within the context of a series of laws repressive of women's sexuality, illustrating the strengthening influence of the Catholic Church in the new State.[14]

The 1935 provisions on prostitution were drafted in similar terms to those of the nineteenth century statutes, containing a comprehensive prohibition on 'public indecency', and making it an offence for a 'common prostitute' to loiter in a public place and to solicit passers-by for the purposes of prostitution. Beyond some minimal policing, however, no relevant developments in policy took place for over 20 years.[15] By the 1960s, brothels were well-established in parts of Dublin city, as prostitution began to shift from an on-street to an off-street activity.[16] In 1964, a major initiative in policing commenced, using the newly established Ban Gardaí (women police) to 'entrap' men.[17] Apparently the policy was discontinued 'with indecent haste', due to publicly expressed concerns about the safety of the women police, as well as the supposed desire to protect clients' families.[18]

However, the practice of charging women as 'common prostitutes' under the 1935 Act continued until the landmark 1980 Supreme Court decision in *King v AG*.[19] King had been convicted under the Vagrancy Act 1824, for the offence of 'loitering' as a 'suspected person or reputed thief'. Evidence of his previous bad character was therefore used to convict him,

[11] For an account of the reform campaign, see eg T Sanders, M O'Neill and J Pitcher, *Prostitution: Sex Work, Policy and Politics* (London, Sage, 2009) 114, referring to the 'pivotal' role of reformer Josephine Butler.

[12] See eg J Walkowitz, *Prostitution and Victorian Society: Women, Class and the State* (Cambridge, Cambridge University Press, 1980); J Walkowitz, 'The Politics of Prostitution' (1980) 6 *Signs: Journal of Women in Culture and Society* 123.

[13] North inner-city Dublin, north-east of the Custom House; for more detail see eg Luddy, *Prostitution and Irish Society* (n 10), 33–36.

[14] M Ward, *Hanna Sheehy Skeffington, Suffragette and Sinn Féiner* (Dublin, UCD Press, 2017) 309.

[15] By contrast, in England, the Report of the Committee on Homosexual Offences and Prostitution (the Wolfenden Report) (London, HMSO, 1957) was published in 1957, its recommendations subsequently forming the basis for the passage there of the Sexual Offences Act 1959.

[16] E Ward, 'From Prohibitionism to a Globalised Sex Trade' (2010) 25 *Irish Political Studies* 47.

[17] I Gannon and J Gannon, *Prostitution: The Oldest Male Crime?* (Dublin, Jig Publications, 1980) 10.

[18] ibid 12.

[19] *King v AG* [1981] IR 233. In the subsequent case of *Dillon v DPP* [2008] 1 IR 383, a similar provision, s 3 of the Vagrancy (Ireland) Act 1847, which prohibited 'wandering abroad and begging', was also found unconstitutional, although an offence of begging was then legislated for through the Criminal Justice (Public Order) Act 2011. In *Douglas v DPP* [2013] 2 ILRM 324, the offences of causing scandal or injuring community morals were found unconstitutional; and in *McInerney v DPP* [2014] IEHC 181, Hogan J found the offence of 'offending modesty' similarly to be unconstitutional. In the more recent case of *Douglas v DPP* [2017] IEHC 248, McDermott J in the High Court again found a similar offence unconstitutional, namely that of 'outraging public decency contrary to common law' due to the difficulty with precise definition of its constituent elements, but confirmed the existence of the common law offence of 'committing an indecent act in public', an offence now effectively substituted by s 45 of the Criminal Law (Sexual Offences) Act 2017, which provides for an offence of 'exposure, offensive conduct of sexual nature'.

but the Supreme Court overturned his conviction, holding the offence unconstitutional as it was 'so arbitrary, so vague, so difficult to rebut'.[20]

After *King*, for a time, women engaged in prostitution were prosecuted either for the common law offence of breach of the peace or for aiding and abetting indecent exposure.[21] Both these approaches proved ineffective in securing convictions, and the number of prosecutions for prostitution-related activities generally declined. Between 1984 and 1992, only 10 prosecutions for prostitution were recorded; in three separate years there were no prosecutions.[22]

In 1985, prostitution policy was considered by the Law Reform Commission (LRC), which recommended the introduction of a 'specific offence of loitering or soliciting by prostitutes in streets and public places'.[23] Rejecting the option of decriminalisation, the LRC commented that:

> Freedom of operation for prostitutes on the street would be highly offensive to the great majority of people … The public nuisance that would ensue would be unacceptable and would outweigh other considerations.[24]

This report represented the first attempt by a State body to tackle the issue of prostitution in a considered fashion, but unfortunately it accepted the 'public nuisance' rationale of the nineteenth-century legislation, albeit recommending that the terms 'loitering' and 'soliciting' should be rendered gender neutral, so that both clients and prostitutes could be prosecuted.

No further action was taken for a number of years. Then, in January 1993, the Second Commission on the Status of Women reported on a range of policy issues, including prostitution.[25] The report again described prostitution as a 'potential public nuisance', and expressed concern that in certain areas 'any woman may be approached on the erroneous assumption that she may be a prostitute … [giving] rise to considerable distress and fear on the part of women so approached'.[26] However, the report did offer some recognition for the harms caused to women by prostitution, recommending supports to assist in leaving prostitution, and it also endorsed the LRC recommendation that 'the person soliciting and the client [would be made] open to the same sanctions'.[27]

III. The Criminal Law (Sexual Offences) Act 1993

Just a few months following this report, reform finally came with the passage of the Criminal Law (Sexual Offences) Act 1993. This Act was most noteworthy for bringing about

[20] *King v AG* [1981] IR 233, 257.

[21] Under the Summary Jurisdiction (Ireland) Act 1871.

[22] Those years were 1988, 1989 and 1991; see Commissioner of the Garda Síochána, 'Report on Crime' 1988–89, and 1991. In 1979, Rosita Sweetman quoted a Garda spokesperson as saying 'Brothels as such are not known to us. There have been no prosecutions in recent years': R Sweetman, *On Our Backs: Sexual Attitudes in a Changing Ireland* (London, Pan Books, 1979) 183–84.

[23] Law Reform Commission, *Law Reform Commission Report on Vagrancy* (Dublin, Government Publications, 1985) (LRC 11-1985) 102.

[24] ibid 102.

[25] *Report of the Second Commission on the Status of Women* (Dublin, Stationery Office, 1993).

[26] ibid 51.

[27] ibid 51.

the decriminalisation of male homosexual activity;[28] but it also introduced new offences related to prostitution. It was given a short two-day debate in the Oireachtas (the Irish parliament). Unsurprisingly, most debating time was devoted to the provisions decriminalising homosexuality, but some legislators expressed regret that so little time could be given to the significant changes in prostitution law.

In its favour, the 1993 Act represented a limited attempt to modernise the law on prostitution – but it retained much of what was objectionable about the old law. It ended the use of the term 'common prostitute,' and created an expanded gender-neutral definition of 'soliciting' for the 'purpose of prostitution' in line with the LRC recommendation, thus extending the criminal law to cover men as well as women engaged in prostitution; and to cover clients and touts, not just prostitutes. Greatly increased penalties were also introduced for all prostitution-related offences.

Despite the expanded definitions, the new offences were based upon the traditional legal premise in criminalising those soliciting in a public place; or those loitering in a public place in order to solicit, who fail to move on after being directed to do so by police.[29] The 1993 Act, like the earlier legislation, was clearly based upon the traditional view of prostitution as public nuisance.[30]

Thus, little changed following the passage of the 1993 Act. Although its enactment had been intended to make prostitution offences easier to prosecute,[31] subsequent crime statistics do not bear this out. A 2008 Trinity College Dublin (TCD) report on prostitution highlighted the low numbers of prosecutions taken annually under the Act.[32] More recently, only 120 incidents of prostitution-related offences were recorded by Gardaí in 2013; and a startlingly low total of 36 incidents in 2016.[33] Unfortunately, no breakdown by gender is provided, but later research provides a clear indication that those engaged in prostitution are predominantly women. In particular, in 2009 the first comprehensive study on sexual exploitation of trafficked and migrant women in Ireland (the Kelleher report) was published.[34] The report estimated that about 1,000 women were engaged in indoor prostitution in Ireland on any one day.[35] More recent figures based on audits of escort sites

[28] Following the ECHR decision that Ireland's criminalisation of homosexuality was in breach of the European Convention on Human Rights in *Norris v Ireland* (1991) 13 EHRR 186.

[29] Offences created under ss 7 and 8 of the 1993 Act.

[30] For an analysis of the effect this legal approach has upon gendered constructions in the media, see L Ryan, *Reading the Prostitute: Appearance, Place and Time in British and Irish Press Stories of Prostitution* (Farnham, Ashgate, 1997).

[31] ME Ring, 'Casting a Wider but More Complex Net against Prostitution' The Irish Times (Dublin, 19 December 1996). These difficulties were of course based on the problem of proving that a person was a 'common prostitute', once the decision in *King v AG* [1981] IR 233 established that evidence tending to show prior convictions was inadmissible.

[32] Trinity College Dublin Centre for Gender and Women's Studies, 'Interdisciplinary Report on Prostitution in Ireland' (Report for the Irish Human Rights Commission, Dublin, TCD, 2008) 57. The report noted that in 2003, proceedings were commenced in respect of only 214 'loitering and soliciting' offences; and just 95 such offences in 2005.

[33] In 2014, 129 such incidents were recorded but in 2015, the total figure recorded dropped dramatically to only 56 incidents, and a further drop was recorded in 2016, with a total of only 36 incidents (only five for prostitution generally, 29 for brothel keeping and two for organisation of prostitution). Data provided by the Minister for Justice, Seanad Debate, 23 November 2017, Vol 254, No 8. The figures provided were described as 'provisional and … subject to further revision'.

[34] Kelleher Associates, M O'Connor and J Pillinger, *Globalisation, Sex Trafficking and Prostitution: The Experiences of Migrant Women in Ireland* (Dublin, Immigrant Council of Ireland, 2009).

[35] ibid 21.

showed advertisements for 1,052 women and 1,124 women for 2011 and 2012 respectively.[36] Research into levels of prostitution for a television documentary broadcast in February 2012 found that, over 'a period of 12 months, more than 8800 profiles were advertised on the escort web sites monitored by the research team, the daily average being 693'.[37]

By the late 1990s, just as increased focus had turned to the issue of trafficking internationally, so in Ireland, criminal justice policy had begun increasingly to focus on transnational aspects of prostitution. The first research attempting to estimate the extent of trafficking into Ireland was conducted by Ward and Wylie, published in 2007, which found a minimum of 76 cases and an additional possible 75 cases of trafficking for sexual exploitation over a seven-year period.[38] The 2009 Kelleher report provided a more detailed overview of the extent of trafficking in Ireland, concluding that the overwhelming majority (97 per cent) of escorts advertising online were stated to be from outside Ireland.[39]

In 2008, legislation was finally passed criminalising the trafficking of persons for sexual exploitation, defining 'sexual exploitation' to include prostitution.[40] Since then, prosecuting rates have remained low.[41] As with the prostitution-related offences discussed above, low levels of trafficking offences being prosecuted do not reflect the true extent of trafficking for the purposes of sexual exploitation. Indeed, increasing awareness about exploitation of the migrant women engaged in prostitution in Ireland became a significant factor in the 2017 law reform process; the traditional 'public nuisance' focus came increasingly under criticism for failing to address the harms caused to women exploited through prostitution.

IV. The 2017 Reform

Monica O'Connor (who, along with Nusha Yonkova, also contributed Chapter 3 to this volume) suggests that the first emergence of a radical feminist discourse on prostitution in Ireland, focusing on the experiences of women, came with the publication in 2004 of a report by the Irish Observatory on Violence Against Women, stating that prostitution was a 'fundamental violation of women's human rights' and recommending adoption of the

[36] ibid 13.

[37] ibid 13.

[38] E Ward and G Wylie, 'The Nature and Extent of Trafficking of Women into Ireland for the Purposes of Sexual Exploitation 2000–2006: A Report from Findings' (2007) 39 *SSRS Research Papers and Reports* (SSRC, NUI Galway).

[39] Kelleher Associates et al, *Globalisation, Sex Trafficking and Prostitution* (n 34).

[40] The Criminal Law (Trafficking) Act 2008 was necessary to comply with EU Council Framework Decision of 19 July 2002 on Combating Trafficking in Human Beings and to give effect to the UN Protocol to Prevent, Suppress and Punish Trafficking in Persons; and the Council of Europe Convention on Action Against Trafficking in Human Beings. Other aspects of the definition of 'exploitation' were amended by s 1 of the Criminal Law (Human Trafficking) (Amendment) Act 2013, but the definition of 'sexual exploitation' remained unchanged. Since 2008, increased focus has been placed on the need for greater support services for those trafficked; an EU-funded Dignity Project was developed in Ireland to improve services for victims of trafficking. See also L Sweeney and S FitzGerald, 'A Case for a Health Promotion Framework: The Psychosocial Experiences of Female, Migrant Sex Workers in Ireland' (2017) 13 *International Journal of Migration, Health and Social Care* 419.

[41] Only five convictions for trafficking-related offences were secured in 2010; seven prosecutions were commenced in 2011, and two further convictions obtained that year: Joint Oireachtas Committee on Justice, Defence and Equality, 'Report on Hearings and Submissions on the Review of Legislation on Prostitution' (Dublin, Stationery Office, 2013) 36. See also annual statistics compiled by the Department of Justice Anti-Trafficking Unit, www.blueblindfold.gov.ie.

Nordic model.[42] Then, in 2008, the TCD report similarly concluded that Irish prostitution law was flawed, and that the Swedish legislation was preferable as it 'most fully encapsulates human rights protections as provided for in United Nations (UN) human rights treaties'.[43] Shortly after that, the Kelleher report also recommended the Nordic model, and the Immigrant Council of Ireland (ICI) became more prominently engaged in highlighting the exploitation of migrant women engaged in prostitution.[44] Arising out of these initiatives, the ICI initiated the formation of a new organisation, 'Turn Off the Red Light' (TORL). This became a campaigning coalition of non-governmental organisations (NGOs), trade unions, political organisations and other groups advocating as a policy goal the reduction or elimination of prostitution through criminalising the purchase of sex. However, an alternative 'sexwork' perspective on prostitution was emerging in Ireland at the same time, heralded by the formation in 2006 of the Sex Workers Alliance Ireland (SWAI), which argued for a harm reduction model and opposed the criminalisation of the purchase of sex.[45]

Despite these developments, the political momentum behind the Nordic model was accelerated by a change of government following the February 2011 general election. The coalition that came to power was made up of the larger Fine Gael party and their smaller partner, the Labour Party. Labour had previously adopted a policy in favour of the Nordic model, and although no reference to prostitution law was made in the 2011 Programme for Government, the issue was soon brought up within parliamentary debates in motions supporting the Nordic model tabled in the Seanad (Senate) by Senator Katherine Zappone.[46]

These motions were defeated, but during the debates the Government promised to undertake a review of the law. In June 2012, a discussion document published by the Department of Justice acknowledged 'compelling reasons to review the criminal law on prostitution'.[47] The report raised a series of questions as to how to frame future prostitution law. In response, at the request of then Minister for Justice Alan Shatter TD, the Joint Oireachtas Justice Committee initiated a public consultation on prostitution law reform.[48] The Committee received over 800 written submissions, of which approximately 80 per cent

[42] National Observatory on Violence Against Women, 'First Country Report from the Republic of Ireland' (May 2004) 10 (this is an independent monitoring mechanism made up of NGOs, academics and others). Cited in O'Connor, 'Consent, Agency and Harm' (n 4) 94.

[43] Trinity College Dublin Centre for Gender and Women's Studies, 'Interdisciplinary Report on Prostitution in Ireland' (Report for the Irish Human Rights Commission, Dublin, TCD, 2008) 15.

[44] Kelleher Associates et al, *Globalisation, Sex Trafficking and Prostitution* (n 34). See also O'Connor, 'Consent, Agency and Harm' (n 4) 96. The EU-funded Dignity project was led by the Immigrant Council of Ireland (ICI), and it facilitated a visit to Sweden by governmental and non-governmental Irish organisations to share 'knowledge and experience of the Swedish approach', resulting in the 2011 publication by the Department of Justice and Equality of a report on the possible adoption in Ireland of a Swedish-type approach to prostitution law: Department of Justice and Equality, 'Report of Visit of Dignity Project Partners to Stockholm 14–16 September 2010' (Dublin, Government Publications, 2011).

[45] O'Connor, 'Consent, Agency and Harm' (n 4) 98. A similar approach was also advocated in a 2009 research publication by the National Advisory Committee on Drugs, which examined risks taken by drug-using sex workers: G Cox and T Whitaker, 'Drug Use, Sex Work and the Risk Environment in Dublin' (Dublin, Government Publications, 2009).

[46] Newly-appointed Independent Senator Katherine Zappone tabled motions on human trafficking and prostitution on 12 October 2011 and again on 18 April 2012 in the Seanad, calling on the government to criminalise the purchase of sex.

[47] Department of Justice and Equality, 'Discussion Document on Future Direction of Prostitution Legislation' (Dublin, Government Publications, 2012) 4–5.

[48] This author was a member of the Committee and of the delegation which visited Sweden in November 2012.

supported the Nordic model. A series of public hearings were held, and a Committee delegation visited Sweden to meet those involved in implementation of the law there.

The Committee process culminated in publication of a June 2013 report which noted that the 'vast majority of women in prostitution in Ireland today … [are] believed to be of non-Irish nationality'.[49] The Committee heard extensive evidence on the harms associated with prostitution, and on the reduction of demand for prostitution in Sweden since 1999, concluding

> such a reduction in demand will lessen the incidence of harms associated with prostitution and – particularly in view of the predominance of migrant women in prostitution in Ireland – the economic basis for human trafficking into this State for the purpose of sexual exploitation … the approach adopted in Sweden has had a strongly positive normative effect on social attitudes to sexuality and gender equality in that country.[50]

Thus, the report recommended the adoption of an offence 'penalising the purchase of sexual services of another person by means of prostitution'.[51] Other significant recommendations included

> properly resourced policies relating to health, education, training, housing and immigration status of men and women who work in prostitution so as to minimise harms risked or suffered by them and to support the exit from prostitution of those who wish to do so.[52]

Further correspondence ensued between Minister Shatter and the Committee following the report, but no policy developments took place while he remained Minister.[53] Following his resignation (for unrelated reasons) in May 2014 and the ministerial appointment of Frances Fitzgerald TD, a marked change in policy approach became discernible, with indications that the report's recommendations would be accepted.[54] Thus, when the heads of the Criminal Law (Sexual Offences) Bill were published in November 2014, new provisions criminalising the purchase of sexual services were included.[55] The Bill itself was eventually published in September 2015, nearly a year later. Apart from the prostitution-related provisions, it also included a wide range of substantive and procedural reforms relating to the prosecution of sexual offences generally, in particular new offences addressing sexual abuse and exploitation of children. Because of its extensive scope, the Bill was strongly welcomed,

[49] Joint Oireachtas Committee on Justice, Defence and Equality, 'Review of Legislation on Prostitution' (2013) 1–2.

[50] ibid 69–70. Prior to the publication of the report, a private members' bill seeking to criminalise the purchase of sexual services had been introduced into the Dáil by Thomas Pringle TD; the Criminal Law (Sexual Offences) (Amendment) Bill 2013, debated on Second Stage on 3 May 2013 and defeated by majority vote on 7 May 2013.

[51] Joint Oireachtas Committee on Justice, Defence and Equality, 'Review of Legislation on Prostitution' (2013) 73.

[52] ibid 74.

[53] See A Shatter, *Letter to David Stanton TD*, 25 September 2013; D Stanton, *Letter of Response to Minister Shatter*, 6 November 2013; and, A Shatter, *Letter to David Stanton TD*, 1 December 2013. The Minister said in his final letter that he had sought advices from the Attorney General and the Minister for Health, www.oireachtas.ie/parliament/media/committees/justice/archivejustice/Addendum-to-Prostitution-Report.pdf.

[54] Minister Fitzgerald is described by Ward as having been 'a long-standing TORL supporter', see E Ward, 'The Irish Parliament and Prostitution Law Reform: A Neo-Abolitionist Shoe-In?' in E Ward and G Wylie (eds), *Feminism, Prostitution and the State: The Politics of Neo-Abolitionism* (London, Routledge, 2017) 87.

[55] Department of Justice and Equality, Press Release, 'Minister Fitzgerald Publishes Heads of New Criminal Law (Sexual Offences) Bill 2014', 27 November 2014, www.justice.ie/en/JELR/Pages/PR14000349.

both by the TORL campaign and by rape crisis centres and victims' rights groups; but the provisions on prostitution were criticised by the SWAI.[56]

Prior to the introduction of the Bill, the process of change in Irish law had been overtaken by more rapid developments in Northern Ireland, with the enactment in January 2015 of a Nordic model law there.[57] The law started life in the Stormont Assembly as a private members' bill introduced by Democratic Unionist Party (DUP) Peer Maurice Morrow and passed through the Assembly with support from Sinn Féin, but it was opposed by some academics, and by groups representing women in prostitution.[58] Opposition to the Nordic model was similarly expressed by the Irish branch of Amnesty International, which in August 2015 voted to support decriminalisation of prostitution.[59] This position placed Amnesty in direct confrontation with the TORL campaign, which by then had over 70 Irish NGOs as affiliates. It meant however that by the date of the Bill's publication in September 2015, a concerted opposition to the introduction of the Nordic model had emerged in Ireland.[60]

During the Oireachtas debates introducing the Bill in October 2015, Minister Fitzgerald referred to this development in describing criminalisation of the purchase of sexual services as 'a matter which has already been the subject of considerable debate both inside and outside the Houses and beyond the State', further stating that in accepting the Justice Committee recommendation for reform, she had concluded that 'there is undoubtedly evidence of a wider exploitation of persons involved in prostitution outside of those trafficked such as those who are coerced or otherwise forced through circumstances to engage in the activity' and that she had become 'convinced that targeting the exploitation associated with prostitution requires targeting those who demand these services'.[61]

Other legislators expressed support in similar terms for the new prostitution-related provisions, referring for example to the emergence of an 'all-island consensus on targeting the exploitative nature of prostitution' and to the view that 'prostitution is intrinsically a violation of human rights', with one Opposition Senator stating:

> The massive explosion in the number of foreign prostitutes operating in Ireland compared to a decade ago raises a question about the extent of the trafficking of women into and within Ireland

[56] See eg 'Sex Workers Hit Out at New Bill Criminalising Prostitution Clients' (*The Journal*, 23 September 2015) www.thejournal.ie/child-grooming-bill-2-2347763-Sep2015/.

[57] The Human Trafficking and Exploitation (Criminal Justice and Support for Victims) Act (Northern Ireland) 2015. S 15 of this Act created the new offence of 'paying for sexual services of a person', inserting a new Art 64A into the Sexual Offences (Northern Ireland) Order 2008. Art 64A (7) requires that a review be conducted of the operation of the new offence over a three-year period following its coming into effect.

[58] See eg 'Law to Ban Paying for Sex in North Passes Final Stage in Stormont' *The Irish Times* (Dublin, 9 December 2014) www.irishtimes.com/news/social-affairs/law-to-ban-paying-for-sex-in-north-passes-final-stage-in-stormont-1.2031693. See also S Huschke et al, 'Research into Prostitution in Northern Ireland' (Department of Justice, October 2014), which concluded that criminalisation of clients could endanger those engaged in prostitution and that 'Only 2% of the sex workers who responded to our survey supported the criminalisation of clients', 11. See also S Huschke, 'Victims Without a Choice? A Critical View on the Debate about Sex Work in Northern Ireland' (2016) 14 *Sexualities Research and Social Policy* 192; S Huschke and S Schubotz, 'Commercial Sex, Clients, and Christian Morals: Paying for Sex in Ireland' (2016) 19 *Sexualities* 869; S Huschke and E Ward, 'Stopping the Traffic? The Problem of Evidence and Legislating for the "Swedish Model" in Northern Ireland' (2017) 8 *Anti-Trafficking Review* 16.

[59] Vote taken at an Amnesty International conference in Dublin on 11 August 2015; see K Holland, 'Amnesty Votes to Decriminalise Sex Work and Prostitution' *The Irish Times* (Dublin, 11 August 2015) https://www.irishtimes.com/news/social-affairs/amnesty-votes-to-decriminalise-sex-work-and-prostitution-1.2313863.

[60] See eg S FitzGerald and K McGarry, 'Problematizing Prostitution in Law and Policy in the Republic of Ireland' (2016) 25 *Social and Legal Studies* 289.

[61] Seanad Debate, 6 October 2015, Vol 242, No 6.

for sexual exploitation. … The issue at stake in the Bill is the exploitation of these women and the need to develop a fresh approach to the problem.[62]

However, the progress of the Bill, which had begun in the Seanad in October 2015 and eventually passed there in January 2016 after lengthy and contentious debate, was interrupted by a change of government following the February 2016 general election.[63] Even following the re-appointment of Frances Fitzgerald TD as Minister for Justice, some months' delay ensued before the Bill resumed in the Dáil in October and November 2016.

Several TDs then expressed opposition to or concern about the prostitution provisions at Second Stage, and at later stages put down amendments seeking, for example, to decriminalise brothels. The assertion that the Nordic model had reduced demand elsewhere was contested, one TD arguing for example that 'demand has not been reduced but rather … displaced and put somewhere … much more dangerous … for sex workers'.[64] In the Seanad, similarly, where the Bill returned in February 2017 having concluded in the Dáil, Senator Michael McDowell was highly critical of the Bill's premise, positing that

> there are people who passionately believe that the solution to the problem is stopping the demand for prostitution and hitting the purchaser rather than the supplier of sex for money. I know there are people who passionately believe that but they are wrong. The oldest profession will not be suppressed by this.[65]

Writing prior to the conclusion of the bill's progress through the Oireachtas, Eilís Ward had been strongly critical of the Justice Committee process, describing it as a 'neo-abolitionist shoe-in', and arguing that

> by the time the Committee's work began, the political debate was, in fact, all but over. ToRL's representation of the problem of prostitution (and its solution), had already been internalised by the political elite such that the Committee process closed down consideration of the range of policy options set out by the government … and served to institutionalise neo-abolitionist discourse already hegemonic in Irish society.[66]

However, a careful reading of the Oireachtas debates on the Bill over the many months between its introduction and eventual passage shows instead that robust opposition to the prostitution-related provisions was expressed by many legislators, and that these provisions were amended significantly during the legislative process. The Bill was finally passed in February 2017 as the Criminal Law (Sexual Offences) Act 2017.[67] The Nordic model

[62] Senator Catherine Noone; Senator Katherine Zappone; and Senator Denis O'Donovan, Seanad Debate, 6 October 2015, Vol 242, No 6.

[63] By the end of January 2016, the Bill had begun in the Dáil having concluded its passage through the Seanad, despite strong opposition to the Nordic model approach expressed by Senator David Norris, in particular; see eg Senator Norris at Second Stage criticising the Swedish law, and urging the Minister 'to take on the welfare of the people engaged in this business, not the ideological pretensions of what amounts to an ideologically driven lobbying group'. Senator Mary White similarly expressed opposition, stating: 'Evidence is growing in Sweden of the adverse effects of the ban on sex worker's lives.' Seanad Debate, 6 October, Vol 242, No 6.

[64] Clare Daly TD, Select Committee on Justice and Equality Debate, 7 December 2016.

[65] Seanad Debate, Report Stage, 14 February 2017.

[66] Ward, 'The Irish Parliament and Prostitution Law Reform', 86–87, citing E Ward and G Wylie, 'Reflexivities of Discomfort: Researching the Sex Trade and Sex Trafficking in Ireland' (2014) 21 *European Journal of Women's Studies* 251.

[67] A vote was called on the Bill at final stages in the Dáil on 7 February 2017; it was passed by 94 votes to 6, with 3 abstentions; those who voted against included the two Green Party TDs and a number of Independent TDs

is effectively applied through section 25, which creates a new offence of 'payment etc for sexual activity with prostitute'.[68] Significantly, while the purchase of sex is thus now criminalised, following amendment during debates, the offence of soliciting or importuning no longer applies to a person who offers sex for sale – thus effectively decriminalising the sellers of sex.

A number of other crucial amendments were also made during the Oireachtas process. In particular, an amendment providing for a review of the new law within three years was introduced at Report stage in the Dáil, and may be seen as representing a concession to those members (TDs) who had expressed concern that criminalising clients might endanger those engaged in prostitution.[69]

V. Context for the 2017 Law Reform

Any gendered analysis of the 2017 law reform in Ireland must examine the context of contemporary feminist debates. As mentioned earlier, a divide between 'exploitation' and 'sexwork' perspectives developed following the emergence of second-wave feminism, when feminist theorists began to question biologically determinist explanations for female offending and to challenge the assertions of earlier criminologists that prostitution is the 'typical female crime'.[70]

Clear differences of view soon began to emerge over prostitution. By 1992,[71] leading feminist legal scholar Mary Joe Frug noted that 'although the feminists I've read all agree that prostitution should be decriminalized, they disagree about *how* decriminalization should occur'.[72]

(Dáil Debate, 7 February 2017). The Bill was then returned to the Seanad, and finally passed there without a vote on 14 February 2017 (Dáil Debate, 7 February 2017, Vol 937, No 3). The prostitution-related provisions in pt 4, along with most of the Act's other provisions were commenced on 27 March 2017 by way of SI 112/2017, Criminal Law (Sexual Offences) Act 2017 (Commencement) Order 2017.

[68] The offence is contained in a new s 7A of the 1993 Act. S 27 provides that the Minister for Justice must prepare a report on the operation of s 7A for the Oireachtas within three years of its commencement: ie by 27 March 2020.

[69] This was a government amendment (introduced at Dáil Debate, Report Stage, 2 February 2017, Vol 937, No 2). In introducing it, Minister Fitzgerald commented: '... the report shall include information as to the number of arrests and convictions in respect of the new offence under s 7A as created by this Bill. This is the provision that targets the demand for sexual services and I have limited the review to this particular provision, as it is this that has given rise to some concern regarding the impact on the safety and well-being of sex workers.' Many Opposition TDs however sought a shorter review period of two years; some sought a more extensive review of all prostitution-related offences, not just of s 7A. This report must provide information on the number of arrests over the three-year period in respect of the new offences, as well as an assessment of the impact of the offences on those who provide sexual services for payment. Speaking about the review provision in the Seanad on 27 March 2018, Justice Minister Charlie Flanagan TD commented: 'The exact nature of the report mandated under the new Act has not yet been decided. Information provided by the women's health service of the HSE and by organisations such as Ruhama and An Garda Síochána will form part of the report ... Officials from my Department have been engaged in discussions with these and other organisations as part of a civil society-led working group to support the implementation of the Act.' (Speech made in response to a Commencement matter raised by the author, Seanad Debate, 27 March 2018, Vol 257, No 1.)

[70] See generally I Bacik, 'Women and the Criminal Justice System' in P O'Mahony (ed), *Criminal Justice in Ireland* (Dublin, IPA, 2002) 137.

[71] Frug, MJ, 'A Postmodern Feminist Legal Manifesto (an unfinished draft)' (1992) 105 *Harvard Law Review* 1045, 1052.

[72] ibid 1058.

Over the decades since, the disagreement has been described as 'the most divisive distinction in feminist thinking'.[73] Broadly speaking, the 'exploitation' approach may be associated with radical feminist theory, and the 'sexwork' approach with liberal or postmodern feminist theory. An immense range of academic literature on prostitution from both perspectives has been generated over recent decades; Jo Phoenix writes that '[t]he literature on prostitution is now so voluminous that there are textbooks provided to help students navigate their way through the empirical studies'.[74]

In one of the best-known early radical feminist arguments, Catharine MacKinnon described prostitution as a form of sexual violence against women: 'rape, battery, sexual harassment, … prostitution, and pornography … form a distinctive pattern: the power of men over women in society'.[75] Other theorists like Kathleen Barry[76] and Sheila Jeffreys[77] have also considered prostitution as 'the institutionalization of women's dependence on men … therefore exploitative and inherently violent and oppressive'.[78] Thus, radical feminist scholarship 'perceives prostitution as gender-based violence, a practice that de-humanizes and objectifies women'.[79]

Maddy Coy has argued that prostitution constitutes a gender regime.[80] It involves a gendered division of labour, since it 'disproportionately involves men buying access to women's bodies'; it enables men to exercise power over women's bodies; it involves emotional labour, 'minimization of self'; and it reproduces heteronormativity.[81] Coy concludes that 'prostitution as a gender regime reproduces gender as a hierarchy … and thus undermines movements towards gender equality'.[82]

This perspective has had increased influence in recent years upon policy-makers in moving from the traditional 'public nuisance' view of prostitution to an alternative perspective which emphasises the harm it causes to women, particularly in the context of trafficking, and its impact upon gender relations in society. Sutherland thus concludes: 'Radical feminists … have had a substantial impact on the development and adoption of anti-trafficking legislation and instruments in various countries and at the international level.'[83]

[73] S Kingston, *Prostitution in the Community: Attitudes, Action and Resistance* (London, Routledge, 2014) 10.

[74] J Phoenix, 'Prostitution and Sex Work' in A Liebling, S Maruna, and L McAra (eds), *Oxford Handbook of Criminology*, 6th edn (Oxford, Oxford University Press, 2017) 685–703, 700. See also R Matthews and M O'Neill (eds), *Prostitution* (Farnham, Ashgate, 2003).

[75] C MacKinnon, *Feminism Unmodified: Discourses on Life and Law* (Cambridge MA, Harvard University Press, 1987) 5.

[76] K Barry, *Female Sexual Slavery* (New York, NYU Press, 1984).

[77] S Jeffreys, *The Idea of Prostitution* (Melbourne, Spinifex Press, 1997). See also C Pateman, 'What's Wrong with Prostitution?' (1999) 27 *Women's Studies Quarterly* 53.

[78] Kingston, *Prostitution in the Community* (n 73) 10.

[79] M Segrave et al, *Sex Trafficking: International Context and Responses* (Cullompton, Willan, 2009) 3.

[80] M Coy (ed), *Prostitution, Harm and Gender Inequality: Theory, Research and Policy* (Farnham, Ashgate, 2012) 4, referring to the 'gender regime' model developed by R Connell, *Gender*, 2nd edn (Cambridge, Polity Press, 2009). Walby writes that gender regimes are 'systems of gender relations', referring to the same underlying concept as 'patriarchy'; see S Walby, *The Future of Feminism* (Cambridge, Polity Press, 2011) 7, 104.

[81] ibid 5.

[82] ibid 5. This approach is taken in an Irish context by Monica O'Connor, who used the theoretical framework of a continuum of sexual exploitation in her research exploring the experiences of seven women in prostitution, O'Connor, 'Consent, Agency and Harm' (n 4) 2.

[83] K Sutherland, 'Work, Sex and Sex-Work: Competing Feminist Discourses on the International Sex Trade' (2004) 42 *Osgoode Hall Law Journal* 139, 140.

By contrast, within academic writing, the alternative 'sexwork' perspective has become dominant with a marginalisation of the radical feminist perspective.[84] Coy suggests this may be due to what Sylvia Walby has identified as 'a 'neoliberal' turn in the academy – 'a shift in intellectual enquiry about systems of power to that of agency … [which] functions in practice towards deflecting analytic interest away from the powerful and from systems of power'.[85] Indeed, Walby suggests that the celebration of individual agency and of 'raunch culture' within contemporary third-wave feminist writing effectively masks the way in which commercialised sexuality represents a new form of control over women, an exploitative neoliberal gender regime.[86]

While in contemporary debates, a 'sexwork' position may be offered from a liberal or postmodern perspective, many of its advocates take an explicitly standpointist position, arguing that they represent the voices of those engaged in prostitution.[87] 'Sexwork' proponents also emphasise the centrality of women's agency. In arguing that women may make an informed 'rational choice' to work in prostitution, Sanders et al suggest:

> The backlash against radical feminist ideas centres on the notion that by constructing women involved in prostitution as only 'victims', the objects of male oppression and passive in their own lives, the 'agency' of women is denied. This argument about 'agency' essentially refers to women's free will and their ability to make decisions about their circumstances and how they use their bodies.[88]

The argument that women's moral agency should be respected has a powerful resonance for many feminists, with obvious parallels for debates on reproductive rights and bodily autonomy. There is a real concern that the 'exploitation' model can lead to a paternalistic approach which denies women autonomy. Scoular and O'Neill, for example, argue that the radical approach has created a rhetoric around victimhood of women who sell sex; whereas in reality, 'women who sell sex do not always experience themselves as victims'.[89]

Those who advocate a 'sexwork' approach also tend to be highly critical of what they describe as the 'abolitionism' of the radical feminist perspective, favouring instead a harm reduction policy of decriminalisation and improved conditions for those in prostitution.[90] 'Abolitionism' is presented by many as an alliance between radical feminists and religious conservatives. Ronald Weitzer, for example, refers to the emergence of 'a powerful moral crusade' which has 'advocated a strict abolitionist orientation towards all forms of commercialized sex … increasingly conflated with sex trafficking'.[91] He suggests that 'right-wing

[84] See eg J Bindel, *The Pimping of Prostitution: Abolishing the Sex Work Myth* (London, Palgrave Macmillan, 2017) ch 9.

[85] Coy, *Prostitution, Harm and Gender Inequality* (2012) 3, citing Walby, *The Future of Feminism* (n 80) 23.

[86] Walby, ibid, 19–20.

[87] J Nagle, *Whores and Other Feminists* (New York, Routledge, 1997). See also M Chateauvert, *Sex Workers Unite: A History of the Movement from Stonewall to Slutwalk* (Mass, Beacon, 2013).

[88] Sanders et al, *Prostitution: Sex Work, Policy and Politics* (n 11), 9.

[89] J Scoular and M O'Neill, 'Legal Incursions into Supply/Demand: Criminalising and Responsibilising the Buyers and Sellers of Sex in the UK' in V Munro and M Della Giusta (eds), *Demanding Sex: Critical Reflections on the Regulation of Prostitution* (Farnham, Ashgate, 2008) 25.

[90] A position taken for example at international level by UNAIDS, *The Report of the UNAIDS Advisory Group on HIV and Sex Work* (Geneva, UNAIDS, 2011).

[91] R Weitzer, 'The Movement to Criminalize Sex Work in the United States' (2010) 37 *Law and Society* 61, 61.

political and religious forces' are 'the dominant forces in the anti-trafficking, abolitionist crusade' in the US.[92]

It is difficult to square this hypothesis with the political reality that applied in the Swedish context, referred to above. The Swedish law introduced in 1999 was explicitly based on a theoretical approach which sees prostitution as a feature of gender inequality in society.[93] In her analysis of the process through which the Swedish law reform was carried out, Yvonne Svanstrom says that a unique feature of the process was the early emergence of a consensus among feminist activists and political actors as to the appropriate theoretical and legal model on which prostitution law reform should be based: 'there was more or less unanimous support among the feminists in the established political parties for seeing prostitution as patriarchal oppression of women'.[94]

In his discussion of the philosophical underpinnings for prostitution law reform, Peter de Marneffe argues that the exploitation/sexwork debate represents a clash between civil libertarian and progressive principles. He says that progressives believe government is justified in limiting individual liberty to reduce harm, even where it is not necessary to protect anyone's rights from being violated; thus, prostitution laws may be justified to protect individuals from self-inflicted harm; there are many examples of such laws being justified in other contexts, such as bans on smoking in public places, or laws to restrict shop opening hours to protect workers' rights. He says thus that, from a progressive perspective, the 'most active opponents of prostitution and its legalisation today … are left-leaning feminists who see prostitution as a form of violence against women; they are not sexual traditionalists or religious conservatives'.[95] Julie Bindel similarly places the Nordic model within a progressive political context, pointing out that the abolitionist movement was from its origins

> indivisible from the feminist anti-male violence movement, with little or no interference from the religious right, or conservative moralists. Just as the wider feminist movement sought to end male violence rather than contain or make it more palatable, the abolitionist movement sought the end of the sex trade.[96]

VI. Conclusion

In the context of ongoing feminist debates, how is the 2017 reform best seen? Markedly different views have been offered, with many highly critical academic commentaries. Some, like Weitzer, have suggested such reforms are motivated by conservative or religious

[92] ibid 83–84.

[93] See the Swedish government's explicit definition of prostitution as gender-based violence (Regeringskansliet 2012), cited in Skilbrei and Holmstrom, *Prostitution Policy in the Nordic Region* (n 7) 138. See further n 7 above. See also Svanstrom, 'Criminalising the John?' (n 7).

[94] Svanstrom, 'Criminalising the John' (n 7) 225.

[95] P De Marneffe, *Liberalism and Prostitution* (Oxford, Oxford University Press, 2010) 155. De Marneffe also reviews the empirical evidence that prostitution causes harm (including harm of stigmatisation, even where it is legalised) to most of those engaged in it; and argues that 'paternalistic' anti-prostitution laws may be philosophically justified on the grounds that prostitution causes harm to those engaged in it; even if it is freely chosen and even if harm is not caused to all of those so engaged. He gives other examples of justified paternalistic laws; for example, the Irish smoking ban, or laws to restrict shop opening hours to protect workers' rights.

[96] Bindel, *The Pimping of Prostitution* (n 84), 8–9. See also K Banyard, *Pimp State: Sex, Money and the Future of Equality* (London, Faber, 2016).

ideology; Ward and Wylie argue that 'neo-abolitionism' arises from a convergence between radical feminism and State interests, based upon an 'unlikely collaboration of feminism and fundamentalism'.[97] Graham Ellison asserts that

> for some religious fundamentalists in Northern Ireland the debate about prostitution is really a debate about moral turpitude, uncontrolled sexuality and idealized femininity that in turn link to a broader sense of anxiety around the nature of social change and societal liberalism.[98]

Others critique the reform as failing to recognise women's agency or to protect those engaged in prostitution. FitzGerald and McGarry argue that Irish 'neo-abolitionist discourse' has operated 'through gendered and racialized assumptions about sex workers and migrant women' and has mis-framed and misrepresented 'sex-working women'.[99] David Ryan argues that decriminalisation would instead represent 'the most viable chance of practically addressing the needs of sex workers and developing the systems in which their safety can be better protected'.[100] Ward asserts that the 2017 law represents a 'move to deny consent to all sex workers as a group, as a principle of law'.[101]

This assertion is challenged however by Monica O'Connor, who criticises the 'liberal emphasis on the concepts of personal choice and agency [which] … reflects a narrow neo-liberal focus on individualism … [and] fails to fully consider the impacts of socio-economic, cultural and affective inequalities on a person's range of choices'.[102] She uses a continuum concept to describe how 'choice, agency and coercion co-exist' for women within prostitution, so that 'consent' is effectively compromised, as for women experiencing domestic violence.[103] Further, she argues that criminalising the purchase of sex removes 'consent as the defining factor for determining criminal acts of sexual exploitation', enabling 'a more integrated policy and legislative framework which recognises and addresses the harm to both prostituted and trafficked women'.[104]

This analysis, proffered by one of the leading advocates for the 2017 reform, provides support for the contention that it is best seen as part of an international feminist movement for change based on recognition of harm caused to women through prostitution, rather than as the product of particular conservative or religious ideologies.[105] Support for

[97] Ward and Wylie, *Feminism, Prostitution and the State* (n 53) 3, citing E Bernstein, 'Carceral Politics as Gender Justice? The "Traffic in Women" and Neo-Liberal Circuits of Crime, Sex and Rights' (2012) 41 *Theory and Society* 233. They refer to Northern Ireland as a particular example of the influence of 'conservative and fundamentalist religious forces' upon the adoption there of prostitution law reform modelled on the Swedish approach. See also G Wylie, *The International Politics of Human Trafficking* (London, Palgrave, 2016).

[98] G Ellison, 'Criminalizing the Payment for Sex in Northern Ireland: Sketching the Contours of a Moral Panic' (2017) 57 *British Journal of Criminology* 194, 210–11. To support this assertion of a split in the US feminist movement, Ellison refers to R Weitzer, *Legalising Prostitution: From Illicit Vice to Lawful Business* (New York University Press, 2011) and Bernstein, 'Carceral Politics as Gender Justice?' (n 97).

[99] FitzGerald and McGarry, 'Problematizing Prostitution' (n 60). See also K McGarry and S FitzGerald, 'The Politics of Injustice: Sex-Working Women, Feminism and Criminalizing Sex Purchase in Ireland' (2017) *Criminology & Criminal Justice*, DOI: 10.1177/1748895817743285.

[100] D Ryan, 'The Proposed Reform of Prostitution Law in Ireland – Moral Discourse and the Perpetual Exclusion of Sex Workers' (2017) 27 *Irish Criminal Law Journal* 12.

[101] E Ward, 'The Irish Parliament and Prostitution Law Reform', 99.

[102] O'Connor 'Consent, Agency and Harm' (2014) 206.

[103] ibid 195–96.

[104] ibid 201. See also M O'Connor, 'Choice, Agency, Consent and Coercion: Complex Issues in the Lives of Prostituted and Trafficked Women' (2017) 62 *Women's Studies International Forum* 8.

[105] Banyard portrays the Irish reform as a recent example of the way in which the growing feminist movement internationally to criminalise buyers of sex is having an impact on legal change, see *Pimp State* (n 96), 230.

this contention may lie in the political reality that key champions of the reform, notably Senator Zappone and Minister Fitzgerald, had previously taken anti-clerical stances on women's rights and LGBT campaigns.[106] While the relevance of positions taken by individual political actors on different policy issues may be questioned by advocates of the 'sexwork' approach who see the Nordic model as inherently conservative in denying women's moral agency,[107] nonetheless, as de Marneffe argues, a significant impetus for Nordic model laws derives from a progressive 'left-leaning feminist' movement, which he contrasts with a more 'libertarian' perspective that opposes laws which limit individual liberty to reduce harm.

It is argued that de Marneffe's distinction is apposite in an Irish context – just as it applied in the original Swedish context with the introduction of the Nordic model there in 1999. The contention that 'paternalistic' anti-prostitution laws may be justified from a progressive feminist perspective is borne out in Ireland by much of the language used in the Oireachtas Committee report recommending the reform, and in subsequent parliamentary debates, with the Minister and other legislators expressly referring to the Bill's purpose in seeking to tackle exploitation of women. It is also borne out by the fact that the NGOs signed up to the TORL campaign had long experience on human rights and feminist issues, with noteworthy support from the trade union movement.[108]

Support for the 2017 reform as an example of progressive feminist law-making is also evident from academic sources. For example, Rebecca Beegan and Joe Moran conclude that the 2017 law 'targets demand, challenges society's attitudes to men's violence against women and sends a clear message that the body cannot be sold, bought or violated'.[109] In addition, there are some early indications that it may have real impact on demand: writing in July 2017, journalist Conor Gallagher noted that:

> There is anecdotal evidence to suggest the new law change is having a small effect on the industry. There has been a drop in women advertising on the main sites and men looking to buy sex are becoming more cautious.[110]

These indications remain anecdotal, as no figures on prosecutions under the 2017 Act are yet available. One year on from the commencement of the relevant provisions, the Minister for Justice however confirmed that the 'Garda national protective services bureau is monitoring the impact of the offences and is developing initiatives to ensure adequate and proper enforcement'.[111] While the impact of the new legislation thus remains to be seen, feminist

[106] Both were prominent in the 2015 marriage equality referendum campaign, unsuccessfully opposed by the Catholic Church, which resulted in legal recognition of the right of same-sex couples to marry; Katherine Zappone had previously asserted this right in a legal case taken against the State, in which this author acted as legal counsel: *Zappone & Gilligan v Revenue Commissioners* [2006] IEHC 404. Both, along with this author and indeed several of those TDs who opposed the reform, were also highly active in the 2018 Eighth Amendment referendum campaign for legal abortion in Ireland, again a campaign opposed by the Catholic Church.

[107] See for example M Sibley, 'Owning Risk: Sex Worker Subjectivities and the Reimagining of Vulnerability and Victimhood' (2018) 58 Brit. J. Criminol. 1462.

[108] The Irish Congress of Trade Unions (ICTU) and many individual unions all signed up to support the Nordic model prior to its introduction, 'Congress Supports Launch of "Turn Off the Red Light: End Prostitution in Ireland" Campaign' (2 February 2011) www.ictu.ie/equality/2011/02/02/congress-supports-launch-of-turn-off-the-red-light/.

[109] R Beegan and J Moran, 'Prostitution and Sex Work: Situating Ireland's New Law on Prostitution in the Radical and Liberal Feminist Paradigms (2017) 17 *Irish Journal of Applied Social Studies* 59, 72.

[110] C Gallagher, 'It's Clearly a Brothel, Yet Nothing Can be Done' *The Irish Times* (Dublin, 29 July 2017).

[111] Minister for Justice Charles Flanagan TD (Speech made in response to a Commencement matter raised by the author, Seanad Debate, 27 March 2018, Vol 257, No 1).

debates on prostitution policy are now so polarised that every assertion made about the impact of the 2017 law is likely to be contested. For now, it appears that while the 'sexwork' perspective remains dominant in academic discourse, the view of prostitution as an inherently exploitative gender regime has exerted greater influence on Irish civil society and policy-makers. The 2017 reform, like the 1999 Swedish legislation, represents recognition of prostitution as a practice of gender inequality incompatible with a gender equal society.

While those opposed may argue that the reform will be ineffective in abolishing prostitution, legislators are entitled to adopt measures that, by tackling demand, are likely at least to have a reductive effect. And it is unarguable that the new law has ended the traditional double standard, marking a significant shift in perspectives on prostitution, from 'public nuisance' to 'private exploitation', in Irish legal and political discourse.

3

Gender, Prostitution and Trafficking for Sexual Exploitation

MONICA O'CONNOR AND NUSHA YONKOVA

I. Introduction

This chapter provides a critique of the legislative framework pertaining to trafficking for sexual exploitation in Ireland and in the European Union (EU) from a gender perspective. Concern regarding trafficking into and within the EU has led to the introduction of specific laws and policies in Member States including Ireland, with the introduction of the Criminal Law (Human Trafficking) Act 2008 criminalising the trafficking of humans for the purpose of sexual or labour exploitation or the removal of organs. This chapter focuses on two core elements: the criminalisation of the buyer of sex where the person selling sex is known to be a victim of trafficking and the response of the State to women who have been trafficked for sexual exploitation.[1] Drawing on research and evidence in Ireland and Europe, it demonstrates that: the legal provisions seeking to stop the demand for buying victims of trafficking do not act as a deterrent to buyers; the law is inoperable and ineffective; the current approach fails to recognise the intersection of gender, migration and trafficking for sexual exploitation and prostitution; and the absence of a gender-specific approach regarding the needs of victims of sexual exploitation has resulted in inappropriate and harmful responses. The Irish legislative and policy framework is examined within the context of the European Directive provision relating to the purchase of sex from victims of trafficking and similar legislative frameworks in other Member States.[2] The authors suggest that the evidence increasingly indicates that attempts to address trafficking without addressing the wider demand for women and girls within the commercial sex trade of destination countries will inevitably fail.

II. Trafficking for Sexual Exploitation: The Global and European Context

There are several different forms of trafficking in human beings identified to date, and newer forms are continuously emerging. However, the trafficking of women and girls

[1] See also Ivana Bacik's contribution in this volume (Chapter 2).

[2] Directive 2011/36/EU of the European Parliament and of the Council of 5 April 2011 on preventing and combating trafficking in human beings and protecting its victims, and replacing Council Framework Decision 2002/629/JHA [2011] OJ L101/1.

for the purposes of sexual exploitation is the most widespread form of this crime in Europe.[3] The international definition of human trafficking, which was first introduced by the United Nations in 2000, has been adopted and expanded by the EU to include the following:

> The recruitment, transportation, transfer, harbouring or reception of persons, including the exchange or transfer of control over those persons, by means of the threat or use of force or other forms of coercion, of abduction, of fraud, of deception, of the abuse of power or of a position of vulnerability or of the giving or receiving of payments or benefits to achieve the consent of a person having control over another person, for the purpose of exploitation.[4]

While agreed definitions are helpful in guiding laws and policy, trafficking of women and girls for the purpose of sexual exploitation is a multifaceted phenomenon, which needs to be understood in the context of globalisation, poverty, war and conflict, migration, gender inequality and violence against women. The migratory flow of people from impoverished regions and countries seeking to migrate into richer, post-industrialised areas of the world is estimated to be over 244 million.[5] At the same time, restrictive migration policies and limited legal avenues for migration create a context in which a range of people seek to profit by 'facilitating' movement and migration, including smugglers and traffickers, placing people in precarious situations where they are 'embarking on ever more hazardous crossings'.[6] Trafficking, smuggling and illegal migration intersect and overlap in origin countries, and what may begin as voluntary migration 'can result in trafficking and/or exploitation at a later stage'.[7] Once people embark on a route of irregular migration, the potential for exploitation is high, and thus it is perhaps best to conceptualise these processes as existing on a 'continuum of predatory and exploitative practices'.[8]

Figures indicate that trafficking is a highly gendered phenomenon. The US State Department estimates that between 600,000 and 800,000 men, women and children are trafficked across international borders each year.[9] Of these, 80 per cent are women and girls, and up to 50 per cent are minors, the majority of whom are trafficked into commercial sexual exploitation. Data from the United Nations Office on Drugs and Crime (UNODC) indicates that 96 per cent of the identified victims of trafficking in human beings for sexual exploitation are female.[10] Trafficking into and within the EU reflects a similar gendered profile, with 75 per cent of victims being female. Data from Eurostat indicate that 'a distinct gender split

[3] Eurostat, 'Statistical working papers: Trafficking in human beings, 2015 edition' (Luxemburg, Publication Office of the European Union, 2015).

[4] Art 2, Directive 2011/36/EU (n 2).

[5] United Nations, 'International Migration Report 2015' (Department of Economic and Social Affairs, ST/ESA//SER.A/375, 2016).

[6] United Nations Population Fund (UNFPA), *State of the World Population: A Passage to Hope, Women and International Migration* (UNFPA, 2006) 10.

[7] B Anderson and B Rogaly, 'Forced Labour and Migration to the UK' (London, study prepared by Compas in collaboration with the Trades Union Congress, 2005) 19.

[8] M Melrose, 'Mercenary Territory: A UK Perspective on Human Trafficking' in KA McCabe and S Manian (eds), *Sex Trafficking: A Global Perspective* (Plymouth, Lexington Books, 2010) 59–71, 60.

[9] Office to Monitor and Combat Trafficking in Persons, 'Trafficking in Persons Report' (Washington, US Department of State, 14 June 2004).

[10] United Nations Office on Drugs and Crime (UNODC), *The Globalization of Crime: A Transnational Organized Crime Threat Assessment* (Vienna, UNODC, 2010).

can be seen within the different types of exploitation'[11] with trafficking for the purpose of sexual exploitation being the most prevalent form of trafficking in the EU (69 per cent, of whom 95 per cent are women).

The routes of many migrant women into prostitution and international trafficking continue to follow the common migration pattern of movement from less developed and poorer regions to richer ones, leading from the Global South to the Global North. However, in the European context, the majority of victims of trafficking for the purpose of sexual exploitation are now female EU nationals moving from the poorer regions in Central and Eastern European states to the wealthier Western EU Member States.[12] It is also worth noting that estimates of victims of trafficking are based on those identified and registered as such in nation states. The ratio between estimates of those who are identified as victims of trafficking and those who remain unidentified varies according to expert opinion, with estimates ranging from 1 in 4, to 1 in 10, to 1 in 20.[13]

The current migration crisis created by war and conflict has exacerbated the risks for vulnerable people of being trafficked, with the forced displacement of large masses of people and the increasing number of people who are desperately seeking to migrate. Women and girls are highly at risk in these precarious situations.[14] It is within this global context that 'fertile fields of exploitation' are created, where vulnerable girls and women are easily targeted by illegal operators who rapidly identify the potential for huge profit in 'facilitating' illegal migration and trafficking.[15] This ensures a supply of people to meet the demand for cheap, migrant labour, which in turn furnishes opportunities for exploitation in certain sectors of destination countries.[16] The demand for cheap labour continues to grow, particularly in 'markets of exploitation' in richer countries; most irregular migrants and trafficked people will find themselves within this 'shadow economy'.[17] Within such locations, as many commentators have observed, the normal protections of the State and the legal systems are largely absent.[18] Female migrants are mainly located within the personal services or 'tertiary sector', including care work, catering, domestic labour, contract cleaning, and the 'sexual entertainment' and prostitution sectors.[19] Migrant women now make up an average

[11] Eurostat, 'Statistical working papers: Trafficking in human beings, 2015 edition' (Luxemburg, Publication Office of the European Union, 2015) 11.

[12] Europol, 'Situation Report: Trafficking in Human Beings' (The Hague, February 2016, No 765175).

[13] A Di Nicola et al, *Prostitution and Human Trafficking: Focus on Clients* (New York, Springer-Verlag, 2005); B Kutnik, P Belser and G Danailova-Trainor, *Methodologies for Global and National Estimation of Human Trafficking Victims: Current and Future Approaches* (Geneva, International Labour Organisation (ILO), Working Paper, January 2007); UNODC, *The Globalization of Crime* (n 10).

[14] RKQ Akee et al, 'Ethnic Fragmentation, Conflict, Displaced Persons and Human Trafficking: An Empirical Analysis' (Discussion Paper No 5142, Institute for the Study of Labor, August 2010), www.papers.ssrn.com/abstract=1667766.

[15] L Kelly, *Fertile Fields: Trafficking in Persons in Central Asia* (Vienna, International Organization for Migration, IOM, April 2005) 5.

[16] L Kelly, *Journeys of Jeopardy: A Review of Research on Trafficking in Women and Children in Europe* (Vienna, International Organisation for Migration, IOM Migration Research Series No 11, November 2002).

[17] S Sassen, 'Global Cities and Survival Circuits' in B Ehrenreich and A Russell Hochschild (eds), *Global Women: Nannies, Maids and Sex Workers in the New Economy* (London, Granta Books, 2003) 264.

[18] A Aronowitz, G Theuermann and E Tyurykanova, *Analysing the Business Model of Trafficking in Human Beings to Better Prevent the Crime* (Vienna, OSCE, 2010); G Van Liemt, 'Human Trafficking in Europe: An Economic Perspective' (Geneva, International Labour Organisation (ILO), Working Paper, Declaration/WP/31/2004, June 2004).

[19] P Monzini, *Sex Traffic: Prostitution, Crime and Exploitation* (London, Zed Books, 2005) 70.

of 84 per cent of women in prostitution across the EU.[20] The UNODC estimates that as many as one million women in Europe are involved in prostitution and one in seven of the women involved in this industry are trafficking victims, amounting to 140,000 women in total.[21]

The commercial sex trade in the destination countries is regarded as a particularly lucrative activity due to: the demand for a constant new supply of girls and women; the level of criminality, illegal activity, coercion and violence; the high profit margins for pimps and brothel owners in the organisation of the sale of commercial sex; and the potential for multiple occasions of use and exploitation of victims.[22] Furthermore, research consistently reveals that the female prostitution market includes adult women as well as underage girls, who are inserted into the same cycle of exploitation and intended for the same kind of customer, where they are regarded as 'interchangeable goods'.[23] It is estimated that in any prostitution regime, between 10 and 24 per cent of women will fit the international definition of being trafficked,[24] and that the profits from trafficked women alone in Europe could be as high as €2.5 billion.[25] The commercial sex trade in Ireland reflects similar patterns. Research reveals a highly organised sex trade in which international traffickers and Irish pimps and prostitution agencies collaborate in the commercial sexual exploitation of Irish, migrant and trafficked women. Of the estimated 800–1,000 women exploited in the Irish commercial sex trade at any given time, between 87 and 97 per cent are migrant women, with 51 nationalities identified, at least 10 per cent being trafficked women and girls.[26]

III. International Response

Concern regarding trafficking has been reflected in numerous international instruments including: the United Nations 'Protocol to Prevent, Suppress and Punish Trafficking in Persons, Especially Women and Children', from 2000 (the Trafficking Protocol);[27] the 2005 Council of Europe Convention on Action against Trafficking in Human Beings (the Trafficking Convention); and two EU Directives, respectively Directive 2011/36/EU on preventing and combating trafficking in human beings and protecting its victims (the Anti-Trafficking Directive), and Directive 2012/29/EU establishing minimum standards on the rights, support and protection of victims of crime (the Victims' Rights Directive).[28] This has

[20] UNODC, *The Globalization of Crime* (n 10).

[21] ibid.

[22] J D'Cunha, 'Legalizing Prostitution: In Search of an Alternative from a Gender and Rights Perspective' (Seminar on the Effects of Legalization of Prostitution Activities: A Critical Analysis, Stockholm, 5–6 November 2002); Monzini, *Sex Traffic* (n 19); P Kelleher et al, *Globalisation, Sex Trafficking and Prostitution: The Experiences of Migrant Women in Ireland* (Dublin, Immigrant Council of Ireland/Women's Health Project/HSE/Ruhama, 2009).

[23] Monzini, *Sex Traffic* (n 19) 3.

[24] Kutnik, Belser and Danailova-Trainor, *Methodologies* (n 13); C Seo-Young, A Dreher and E Neumayer, 'Does Legalized Prostitution Increase Human Trafficking?' (2012) 41 *World Development* 67.

[25] UNODC, *The Globalization of Crime* (n 10).

[26] Kelleher et al, *Globalisation, Sex Trafficking and Prostitution* (n 22).

[27] The Treaty was adopted as an Optional Protocol to the UN Convention on Transnational Organised Crime.

[28] Directive 2012/29/EU of the European Parliament and of the Council of 25 October 2012 establishing minimum standards on the rights, support and protection of victims of crime, and replacing Council Framework Decision 2001/220/JHA [2012] OJ L315/57.

resulted in the introduction of comprehensive legislative and policy frameworks in nation states including Ireland and the provision of major resources by international bodies to address trafficking.[29] Targeting the demand that leads to human trafficking has been part of virtually every modern legal instrument, including Article 9(5) of the Trafficking Protocol and Article 6 of the Trafficking Convention, which call for legislative and other measures to discourage the demand 'that fosters all forms of exploitation of persons, especially women and children'. However, the continuing rise in the number of trafficked people into and within the EU has led to a sharpened focus on the need to address demand. A recent report of the European Commission examining the progress under the EU strategy towards the eradication of trafficking in human beings, states:

> Trafficking in human beings is a crime driven by demand and profit. The profits, in both the legal and illegal economies, result in a complex interplay between supply and demand that must be addressed if the crime is to be eradicated.[30]

In relation to trafficking for sexual exploitation, this 'complex interplay' involves the supply of vulnerable girls and women to the commercial sex trade by traffickers and pimps to meet the demand of the local prostitution organisers and buyers of sex. A major study on gender and trafficking carried out for the European Commission in 2016 states:

> Demand reduction concerns changing the wider environment into which people may be trafficked so as to reduce incentives for trafficking. In the case of trafficking for purposes of sexual exploitation, this wider environment is critically shaped by the institution of prostitution.[31]

However, opposing approaches to prostitution continue to underpin policy and directives of the EU. Countries such as the Netherlands and Germany draw a strict demarcation between trafficking for sexual exploitation and legal 'sex work', and resist the Swedish/Nordic approach which involves an integrated strategy to address prostitution and trafficking, criminalising the purchase of sex from any person and de-criminalising those exploited in prostitution.[32] Consequently, Article 18 of the 2012 Anti-Trafficking Directive requires Member States to reduce demand: 'Member States shall take appropriate measures, such as education and training, to discourage and reduce the demand that fosters all forms of exploitation related to trafficking in human beings.' However, it goes on in Part 4 to require Member States to introduce a limited legislative provision to discourage demand:

> Member States shall consider taking measures to establish as a criminal offence the use of services which are the objects of exploitation as referred to in Article 2, with the knowledge that the person is a victim of an offence referred to in Article 2.

Thus, Member States are only required to introduce a highly restrictive criminal offence for the use of the services of a victim of exploitation and trafficking, with the proviso that

[29] For a full description of the Irish legislative and policy framework, see generally M O'Connor, *Upholding Rights: Early Legal Intervention for Victims of Trafficking*, Comparative Report ELY Project (Dublin, Immigrant Council of Ireland, 2015).

[30] European Commission, 'Report on the Progress Made in the Fight Against Trafficking in Human Beings as Required under Article 20 of Directive 2011/36/EU on Preventing and Combating Trafficking in Human Beings and Protecting its Victims' (Brussels, COM (2016) 267 final).

[31] S Walby et al, *The Study on the Gender Dimension of Trafficking in Human Beings: Final Report* (Luxemburg, European Commission, Migration and Home Affairs, 2016) 23.

[32] This approach has now also been introduced in Iceland, Norway, France, Northern Ireland and Ireland.

the person must have knowledge that this involves a person who is a victim of a trafficking offence. Translated into the realm of trafficking for sexual exploitation, this infers that the buyer of sexual services must be aware that the person being engaged for sex is a victim of human trafficking.

IV. An Ill-Informed Legal Approach

This legal approach discouraging sex trafficking demand, with the condition that the customer is aware of the vulnerability of the sellers of sex, does not appear to be informed by any of the extensive studies of the phenomenon of the purchase of sex conducted in various EU Member States to date. Rather, this legal approach as proposed is a minimalistic measure that attempts to satisfy the widely diverging strategies on prostitution that exist between countries. There is an increasing body of research exploring the demand side of prostitution, focusing on the interests of buyers, who are primarily men, to purchase access to sex from sellers, who are primarily women. The impetus for such studies has also been generated by the desire to explore human trafficking for sexual exploitation that occurs in the same environment – the market for the sale of sex. These studies have by now established the characteristics of the average buyer of sex and their attitudes to the persons involved in selling it, as well as to paid sex in general. A study was conducted in 2014 across five EU Member States (Bulgaria, Cyprus, Finland, Ireland and Lithuania) which included interviews or completed surveys with 763 purchasers of sex, 71 face-to-face interviews and 692 online survey responses.[33] The average buyer of sex is male, well-educated, with middle to high income, and in a relationship at the time of the sex purchase. In the main, the male buyers viewed the females involved in the transactions as consenting adults and were unlikely to conceptualise the women from whom they purchased sex as potential victims of human trafficking, even though almost one third of male respondents who reported purchasing sex also reported encountering some form of exploitation including sellers who were legally under the age of consensual sex.

The interviewed men displayed a complex view of the act of purchasing sex and those involved in the sale of sex. On the one hand, they overwhelmingly believed that the sale of sex is a transaction between two consenting adults, and, on the other hand they would not want to see any close friend or family member become involved in this practice. Most buyers viewed sellers of sex as being different from other women. The study shows that, when practised over a long time, purchasing sex largely becomes a planned activity for the buyers, compared to first-time experiences. A large proportion of respondents avoided answering the question of whether they had reported suspicions of trafficking to the authorities or responded that they had not considered reporting suspicions to the police. When asked what would make them refrain from buying, the primary deterrents indicated were public exposure and/or legal sanctions.

A qualitative study conducted in Cyprus by the Mediterranean Institute of Gender Studies, casts further light on the attitude of buyers to the women they purchase.[34]

[33] N Yonkova and E Keegan, 'Tackling Demand for Sexual Services of Trafficked Women and Girls: Study' (Dublin, Immigrant Council of Ireland, Stop Traffick! EU Project, 2014).

[34] J Christodolou, 'National Report from Cyprus' (Mediterranean Institute of Gender Studies, forthcoming).

Most interviewees were aware that women in prostitution may be victims of trafficking and had witnessed coercion and methods of control, but they still wanted the 'services' they had paid for and did not ask whether the woman was forced into prostitution or not:

> Sex buyers adopt a position of conscious non-responsibility ... they are not concerned about the personal histories or circumstances of women ... what brings many men into the market of commercial sex, is the unrealistic and socially ingrained, sense of entitlement to have their 'sexual needs' met under any circumstances, and to obtain what they consider rightfully theirs.[35]

The study further suggested that one of the major factors affecting demand for sexual services in Cyprus is the tendency to stereotype and objectify women, and particularly Eastern European women, as sex symbols:

> Racial and ethnic stereotypes play a prominent role in the sex industry and this inherent sexism and racism led to the stereotype that Eastern European women – poor, white, blond, tall and thin – are sexually available, willing to please, and with no sexual inhibitions.

This intersection of sexism and racism is also reflected in a study of buyers in Finland, with men who mostly bought in Baltic countries, in particular Tallinn in Estonia.[36] The study revealed that part of the attraction of prostitution is a desire to have sex in the context of a traditional gender order and male dominance, accompanied by 'ethno-sexualisation of "other" women' which 'may be used to justify the objectification and exploitation of women of a different nationality'.[37] Given the hugely disproportionate number of migrant women in prostitution, these are critical issues which demand further research.

In Ireland, an analysis of over 1,000 postings on the website Punter.net Ireland, where buyers post reviews of the women, reveals a consumerist attitude to women with key ratings for: good value for money; the physical attributes of the women; the degree of sexual gratification/satisfaction, with explicit details of sexual acts demanded; the expectation that the women should enjoy the sex, with severe criticism of women who did not appear engaged; and an expectation of 'the girlfriend experience'.[38] Interviews with trafficked women also indicate that being distressed or unwilling to participate in sexual acts did not elicit sympathy or concern in relation to possible coercion or trafficking among buyers, but rather elicited criticism and dissatisfaction on their part.[39] These findings reflect international studies which consistently find a commodifying attitude among buyers, who display a strong sense of entitlement as consumers to have their sexual demands met once payment has been made.[40]

[35] ibid 25.

[36] AM Marttila, 'Desiring the "Other": Prostitution Clients on a Transnational Red-Light District in the Border Area of Finland, Estonia and Russia' (2008) 12 *Gender Technology and Development* 31.

[37] ibid 42.

[38] Kelleher et al, *Globalisation, Sex Trafficking and Prostitution* (n 22).

[39] M O'Connor, 'Choice, Agency, Consent and Coercion: Complex Issues in the Lives of Prostituted and Trafficked Women' (2017) 62 *Women's International Studies Forum* 8.

[40] M Coy, M Horvath and L Kelly, *'It's Just like Going to the Supermarket': Men Buying Sex in East London*, Report for Safe Exit (London, London Metropolitan University, 2007); J MacLeod et al, *Challenging Men's Demand for Prostitution in Scotland: A Research Report Based on Interviews with 110 Men Who Bought Women in Prostitution* (Glasgow, Women's Support Project, April 2008); M Monto, 'Prostitutes' Customers: Motives and Misconceptions' in R Weitzer (ed), *Sex for Sale: Prostitution, Pornography and the Sex Industry*, 2nd edn (New York, Routledge,

These studies reveal that the purchase of sex is a highly gendered activity that is carried out exclusively by men. The primary concern of buyers is to have their sexual demands met; it would appear unlikely that they will exhibit discernment or be concerned about the circumstances or conditions women are currently under or whether they have been trafficked. The sense of entitlement among the habitual users of prostitution consistently emerges, indicating they cannot be easily deterred in practice. Measures that rely on the conscious observations of buyers and their willingness to enquire about the vulnerability of the seller when purchasing sex are clearly based upon unrealistic assumptions.

V. An Inoperable Law

In Ireland, section 5 of the Criminal Law (Human Trafficking) Act 2008 introduced an offence which made it illegal to 'solicit or importune' a trafficked person for the purpose of prostitution. The Act criminalises a person found guilty of paying for sexual services with a victim of trafficking, with liability for a fine of up to €5,000 and a prison sentence of up to five years. However, *lack of knowledge* of the trafficking circumstances of the victim can be used as a defence by the buyer, which makes a conviction highly problematic. It was suggested at the time of adoption of the law, that section 5 gave the Gardaí significant additional powers in relation to prosecuting buyers who have sex with trafficked persons in any location, including indoors, but to date there has not been a single conviction under this provision. Recent examination of the implementation of this approach in Finland, Cyprus and Lithuania, illustrates that similar conditional laws, whereby the knowledge of the buyer determines his culpability in the trafficking crime, have also failed to result in prosecutions or to have any meaningful impact on demand.[41]

For nearly a decade, Finland operated a partial sex-purchase ban, which outlawed the purchasing of sex only when the seller was a victim of procuring and human trafficking and the offender was aware of the circumstances and the attempt was intentional. In 2015, further changes to the law were made where the purchase of sex from victims of the sexual trade through negligence was criminalised, making it a criminal offence to engage in sexual intercourse or comparable sexual act for payment when there was a reason to suspect that the person referred to is a victim of pandering or human trafficking. This means the buyers of sex can no longer avoid legal responsibility by gaining as little information as possible from the person selling sex and the conditions surrounding them. The new provision is meant to be easier to apply. There have been some charges taken against men who have sexually abused a victim of trafficking or procuring, but they have resulted in minimal fines, despite the fact that the maximum sentence is imprisonment for six months. The Finnish

2010) 233–55; M Tyler and N Jovanovski, 'The Limits of Ethical Consumption in the Sex Industry: An Analysis of Online Brothel Reviews' (2018) 66 *Women's Studies International Forum* 9; J O'Connell Davidson, *Prostitution, Power and Freedom* (Cambridge, University of Michigan, 1998).

[41] O'Connor, 'Comparative Report from the "Disrupt Demand" Project' (Part of the 'Study Examining Campaign Strategies in Member States to Introduce Legislative Measures to Discourage Demand for Sex Trafficking', funded by the Internal Security Fund of the European Union, under the call HOME/2015/ISFP/AG/THBX (forthcoming 2018).

expert cited in the report concluded that the partial sex-purchase ban is unlikely to have had any effect in relation to the reduction of the demand for prostitution, since there are few prosecutions, which result in minimal sanctions.

Similarly, in Cyprus a legal provision penalising persons who use services provided by victims of trafficking has been introduced but only if the person is considered to have been reasonably able to assume that the service was provided by a victim of trafficking. If found guilty, the person is subject to imprisonment for to up to three years, or to a fine not exceeding €15,000, or both. To date there have been no convictions under this provision. There is some pressure from human rights and feminist organisations to remove the wording 'reasonable assumption' and this proposal is currently under discussion at the Parliamentary Committee of Human Rights and Equal Opportunities for Men and Women.[42]

In Lithuania, a law on trafficking penalties for users of forced labour and services has been introduced. The law makes clear that it is only applicable where the use of force can be demonstrated; no buyers of sex have been prosecuted under this law to date. The issue of the liability of a client for buying sexual services is further addressed in the Administrative Violations Code, which was originally intended as a measure to reduce the demand for prostitution services in Lithuania. The offence criminalises both persons who earn from prostitution and persons who use paid prostitution services; however, it exempts persons involved in prostitution on several grounds: being dependent or under physical or psychological violence or deception, by any means, or being a minor or/and a victim of human trafficking when the status is recognised in the criminal proceedings. According to this provision, a fine from 300 to 1000 LTL may be imposed on the prostitute and the client. In reality, the Lithuanian expert asserted that the evidence consistently indicates that women in prostitution are the primary focus of law enforcement. Buyers, on the other hand, are rarely prosecuted, and in these rare cases the penalty is a minimal fine as it is a minor administrative offence.[43]

It must be observed that even though all of the countries referred to in this section are nominally compliant with the minimal standards for the discouragement of demand that fosters trafficking for sexual exploitation as the legal treaties require, no discernible effects have been achieved in these jurisdictions from the introduction of these specific laws.

VI. Failure to Recognise the Intersection of Gender, Migration, Prostitution and Trafficking for Sexual Exploitation

As noted at the outset of this chapter, the issue of human trafficking is positioned at the elaborate intersection of gender, migration and prostitution, and the experiences of victims of this crime are similarly complex. Unfortunately, it appears that anti-trafficking responses are failing the victims precisely because the complex nature of their circumstances and experiences remains unrecognised by the authorities of the EU Member States. Despite the increasing recognition that trafficking for sexual exploitation such as prostitution is a

[42] ibid.
[43] ibid.

highly gendered phenomenon, contemporary EU anti-trafficking responses are consciously removed from any considerations regarding the inherently exploitative nature of prostitution, as the latter is seen as a point of unnecessary contention. Measures seeking to address trafficking for sexual exploitation must recognise that victims 'can be hidden within mixed populations of independent, exploited and coerced prostitutes and in mixed migration flows'.[44]

Even though EU-wide statistics indicate that the number of EU citizen victims is on the rise, the significant increase of third country national victims associated with forceful and conflict-predicated migration cannot be ignored. In the last three years alone, Italy has witnessed an almost 600 per cent increase in the number of potential sex trafficking victims arriving by sea. This upward trend continued during the first six months of 2017, with most victims arriving from Nigeria being girls aged 15–17.[45] Consequently, responding to victims of human trafficking within this largely foreign population requires an acknowledgement that their entitlements to services may be highly problematic. This is true for victims of trafficking who are third country nationals as well as for EU citizen victims, who need to prove their habitual residence to gain access to services.[46]

There is an increasing body of evidence on the traumatic impact of sexual exploitation and the 'severe, brutal and long-term, gender-specific physical, gynaecological and mental health harms, risks to life and traumas from trafficking for purposes of sexual exploitation'.[47] In a study of 207 girls and women who had been trafficked, almost all (95 per cent), had been subjected to severe and ongoing physical and sexual violence; over half (57 per cent) reported physical injuries; 89 per cent reported threats of violence to themselves and their families including threats to kill; and 70 per cent reported that they had no freedom of movement.[48] But it is also important to note that gender-specific harm is not confined to women who have been trafficked. Numerous studies indicate that being exploited in prostitution brings severe consequences for women's physical, sexual, reproductive and mental health and that the rates and frequency of extreme violence experienced, including homicide, are exponentially higher for women in prostitution than the general population of women and girls.[49]

[44] Walby et al, *The Study on the Gender Dimension of Trafficking* (n 31).

[45] International Organisation on Migration IOM, 'UN Migration Agency Issues Report on Arrivals of Sexually Exploited Migrants, Chiefly from Nigeria' (IOM, 21 July 2017), www.iom.int/news/un-migration-agency-issues-report-arrivals-sexually-exploited-migrants-chiefly-nigeria.

[46] Habitual residence is a condition that an EU citizen residing in a Member State, different from their country of citizenship, must satisfy in order to qualify for various State supports and welfare payments. The condition is linked to length and continuity of residence, satisfying the EU right to reside and the general nature of the residence.

[47] Walby et al, *The Study on the Gender Dimension of Trafficking* (n 31) 8.

[48] C Zimmerman et al, *Stolen Smiles: Report on the Physical and Psychological Health Consequences of Women and Adolescents Trafficked in Europe* (London, London School of Hygiene and Tropical Medicine, 2006) 56.

[49] M Coy, 'Invaded Spaces and Feeling Dirty: Women's Narratives of Violation in Prostitution and Sexual Violence' in M Horvath and J Brown (eds), *Rape: Challenging Contemporary Thinking* (Portland, Oregon, Willan, 2009) 184–207; M Farley et al, 'Prostitution and Trafficking in Nine Countries: An Update on Violence and Post-Traumatic Stress Disorder' in M Farley (ed) *Prostitution, Trafficking and Traumatic Stress* (New York, Haworth Press, 2003); C Høigård and L Finstad, *Backstreets: Prostitution, Money and Love* (University Park, Pennsylvania State University Press/Polity Press, 1992); Kelleher, et al, *Globalisation, Sex Trafficking and Prostitution* (n 22); JJ Potterat et al, 'Mortality in a Long Term Open Cohort of Prostitute Women' (2004) 159 *American Journal of Epidemiology* 778; J Raphael and DL Shapiro, 'Sisters Speak Out: The Lives and Needs of Prostituted Women in Chicago' (Chicago, Center for Impact Research, August 2002); J Raymond et al, 'A Comparative Study of Women

Despite this evidence, the lack of synchronicity in planning human trafficking measures, migration regimes and strategies on violence against women, creates a disjointed national effort leaving those in need of support with limited provisions that are largely tokenistic in nature and benefit small numbers of individuals formally identified as 'victims'. Sadly, even the identified victims surviving trafficking for sexual exploitation are not adequately supported within the present policy and legal framework due to the largely gender-blind provisions failing to take into account the type of trauma and harm experienced by women in the sex trade. Arguably, most detrimental of all for the protection of sexually exploited women is the intentional disconnect between the system for identification and support of victims of trafficking and the strategy on prostitution, which does not envisage a corresponding support structure or access to an existing one.

The recently commissioned legal analysis of the Anti-Trafficking Directive from a perspective of women trafficked for sexual exploitation (including forced marriages) concludes that the law, as complemented by the Victims' Rights Directive, could provide a viable system for support, assistance and protection of women and girls trafficked for sexual exploitation, provided certain conditions are fulfilled.[50]

In the first place, there is a need to give sufficient weight and attribute concrete meaning to the gender-specific aspects of implementation. Second, efficient implementation of the anti-trafficking measures for support, assistance and protection requires the acceptance and utilisation of the legal standards established in the wider area of violence against women as well as the maintenance of synchronicity with such standards at all times. For example, the analysis establishes that theoretical eligibility for protection, assistance and compensation does not automatically deliver results for such victims due to their diminished capacity to participate in and benefit from the welfare and justice system as a result of trauma and economic disadvantage, which is common for women who are survivors of violence against them. Third, and uniquely for victims of trafficking, is the need for gender-specific identification and recognition of such victims in the context of an extremely complex legal definition of trafficking in human beings, which is a multifaceted crime, with several elements that must be evidenced. The highly traumatic and gender-specific nature of the exploitation in these crimes calls for special competence and gender sensitivity by those responsible for victim identification.

The European Parliament's Committee on Women's Rights and Gender Equality (FEMM) commissioned a review of the implementation of the Anti-Trafficking Directive from a gender perspective, which concluded that Ireland lacked a comprehensive legal and policy framework that could guarantee the rights of female victims.[51] The measures put in place are gender-neutral, which ignores the prevalent victim profile – an adult or

Trafficked in the Migration Process: Patterns, Profiles and Health Consequences of Sexual Exploitation in Five Countries (Indonesia, the Philippines, Thailand, Venezuela and the United States' (Coalition Against Trafficking in Women, funded by the Ford Foundation, 2002); EG Krug et al (eds), *World Report on Violence and Health* (Geneva, World Health Organization (WHO), 2002).

[50] N Yonkova, S Gillan, E Keegan, M O'Connor, D Charlton and A Zobnina, *An analysis of the Anti-trafficking Directive from the perspective of a victim of a gender-based violence* (Vilnius: European Institute for Gender Equality, forthcoming).

[51] D Charlton and N Yonkova, 'The Implementation in Ireland of Directive 2011/36/EU from a Gender Perspective' in A Scherrer and H Werner (eds), *Trafficking in Human Beings from a Gender Perspective: Directive 2011/36/EU: European Parliament Assessment Report* (Brussels, European Parliamentary Research Service, 2016).

female minor, trafficked for the purposes of sexual exploitation. The Irish statistics mirror the EU statistics in that they show that the most widely reported form of exploitation is trafficking for sexual exploitation, and that women and girls constitute the majority of victims.[52] Nonetheless, the national legislative and policy framework does not demontrate a response to this evidence. The gender dimension of human trafficking in Ireland is not acknowledged in the National Action Plan,[53] and references to gender-sensitive assistance to victims, in line with Article 1 and Recital 3 of the Anti-Trafficking Directive, are missing. The identification process fails victims of trafficking who originate in another EU Member State or who seek international protection, which primarily affects female victims of sex trafficking.[54] In the context of the recent migration crisis and the commitments taken by the State to welcome significant numbers of refugees, it is timely to review the blanket exclusion of trafficked victims in the asylum process from the possibility to be identified and supported.[55]

Especially problematic in Ireland is the provision of accommodation to victims, in what are known as Direct Provision centres for asylum seekers. Direct Provision has been severely criticised from a human rights perspective, in terms of: long delays in processing applications (up to eight years); inadequate welfare payments of only €21.60 per week; poor conditions; the lack of access to education and limited permission to work, resulting in people having no skills to enter the labour market if they are finally given status; and a failure to provide any form of adequate compensation schemes.[56] Presently, the blanket prohibition to work has been lifted on a conditional basis to allow asylum seekers to apply for a work permit if they manage to secure a job offer of a salary exceeding €30,000 per annum. If they are successful, they have to pay a work permit fee of €1,000 for a year. These are unrealistic targets for the vast majority of victims of trafficking for sexual exploitation, many of whom have never acquired a formal education or held an occupation prior to the trafficking experience. These arrangements have been found by international monitoring bodies and NGOs providing services to be particularly detrimental to female victims of trafficking.[57] Women are placed in mixed accommodation where they are vulnerable to further sexual exploitation and re-trafficking; there are no specialist services provided on sexual assault and rape.

Other examples of failure to recognise the sexual violation that women trafficked for sexual exploitation experience is evident in their secondary victimisation by repetition of

[52] *National Statistical Reports for Trafficking in Human Beings in Ireland*, 2008–2015 www.blueblindfold.gov.ie.

[53] Department of Justice and Equality (DJE), *Second National Action Plan to Prevent and Combat Trafficking in Human Beings* (Dublin, DJE 2016).

[54] Immigrant Council of Ireland (ICI), *Submission to the Anti Human Trafficking Unit of the Department of Justice and Equality: Second National Action Plan* (Dublin, ICI, July 2015) 5.

[55] For further analysis of gender and asylum law, see Patricia Brazil's contribution in this volume (Chapter 14).

[56] E Keegan, N Yonkova and A Valderrama, 'Identification and Response to the Needs of Trafficked Asylum Seekers: Summary Report National Focus Ireland' (TRACKS Project, Dublin, Immigrant Council of Ireland, 2017).

[57] Free Legal Advice Centres (FLAC), *One Size Doesn't Fit All: A Legal Analysis of the Direct Provision and Dispersal System in Ireland, 10 Years On* (Dublin, FLAC, November 2009) www.flac.ie/download/pdf/one_size_doesnt_fit_all_full_report_final.pdf; AkiDwa, '"Am Only Saying It Now": Experiences of Women Seeking Asylum in Ireland' (AkiDwa, Dublin, March 2010); Immigrant Council of Ireland (ICI), 'Asylum Seeking Victims of Trafficking: Legal and Practical Challenges' (Dublin, ICI/Sponsored by the UN Global Initiative to Fight Human Trafficking, November 2011) www.immigrantcouncil.ie/files/publications/84faa-18.11.2011un_gift_report.pdf; Charlton and Yonkova, 'The Implementation in Ireland of Directive 2011/36/EU' (n 51).

traumatic accounts and the lack of compensation avenues that could realistically benefit such victims, outside of the employment-based schemes. The existing compensation avenues in Ireland put victims of trafficking for sexual exploitation at a disadvantage because, in the vast majority of cases, they do not have verifiable expenses or employment losses to present to access the Criminal Justice Compensation Tribunal or any of the work-related bodies.[58] Given the potential that compensation carries to offer a viable future for women with scarce educational and professional skills, it is fair to conclude that the present response fails such victims.

VII. The Wider Implications

Introducing a criminal offence which *only* applies to the buying of a person for sex who has been trafficked into the sex trade is, as we have seen, ineffective as a deterrent and inoperable from a policing perspective. However, it is important to recognise that laws on sexual crime not only act as a deterrent or as a punitive sanction; they also have a declarative and normative function in indicating the legitimisation, or not, by the State of specific sexual acts. For example, the abolition of the spousal rape exemption in Ireland in the Criminal Law (Rape) (Amendment) Act 1990 ensured that a husband could be prosecuted for raping his wife; but it was also a declaration by the Irish State that it was no longer acceptable or legal to assume that marriage conferred the right to sexual access to women and thus that such a right to sex could be enforced with impunity.[59] In a similar way, there are wider implications of limiting the punitive, declarative and normative power of the law to the sexual victimisation only of those identified as trafficked. Crucially, it suggests that the concern of the State is confined to the protection of a minority of women within the sex trade – those who are deemed to be trafficked – and, by implication, that it is acceptable and legal to buy 'other' women who have 'chosen' to be in prostitution. By creating a rigid demarcation between trafficked and prostituted women, this legal approach disregards the circumscribed conditions which drive women and girls into prostitution, as well as the endemic violence and sexual exploitation to which they are subjected to once they are entrapped within the commercial sex trade. This demarcation creates problematic 'hierarchies of seriousness' as described by Kelly and Radford in relation to sexual violence which, as they argue, then become 'embodied in legal and other discourses'.[60]

Furthermore, legitimising by omission the buying of non-trafficked women creates a flawed presumption of consent on the part of such women as it ignores the compromised nature of consent within the prostitution contract; submission or acquiescence to unwanted sexual acts because of economic need does not constitute meaningful consent.[61]

[58] Charlton and Yonkova, 'The Implementation in Ireland of Directive 2011/36/EU' (n 51); O'Connor, *Upholding Rights* (n 29).

[59] T O'Malley, *Sexual Offences: Law, Policy and Punishment* (Dublin, Round Hall, 1996).

[60] L Kelly and J Radford, 'Sexual Violence against Women and Girls: An Approach to an International Overview' in RE Dobash and RP Dobash (eds), *Rethinking Violence Against Women* (Thousand Oaks, Sage Press, 1998) 53–76, 57.

[61] R Moran, *Paid For: My Journey through Prostitution* (Dublin, Gill and Macmillan, 2013); O'Connor, 'Choice, Agency, Consent and Coercion' (n 39).

From the perspective of buyers, who as we know are indiscriminate in identifying trafficking or coercion in any context, this law re-enforces their view that as long as women appear to consent, their demand for buying sexual gratification is perfectly legitimate. Regardless of the coercive circumstances in which that consent is gained, the buyer is exonerated from responsibility or criminal sanction. From a wider societal perspective, this approach narrows the public perception of harm to those who are trafficked, while women who are perceived to have 'chosen' to be in the trade are regarded as individually responsible for the subsequent violations to which they are subjected. For women exploited in the commercial sex trade, this law sends a message that the harm they experience in prostitution is of little concern to the State and that their right to bodily integrity is of lesser value than the same right of women recognised as trafficked, regardless of the similar, or in some cases greater, degree of violation that they have experienced.

The brief analysis of the current anti-trafficking measures in this chapter exposes only the surface of the deeper conceptual misunderstanding and misinterpretation of the societal obligations on the one hand, and the gender-specific needs of trafficked victims on the other. The situation of the vast majority of women in the sex trade, who are excluded even from the very limited considerations for support and recovery from commercial sexual abuse, is further more precarious. Such women would ultimately benefit from a possible future incorporation of gender-specific orientation into the anti-trafficking measures, should political leadership to this effect emerge.

VIII. Conclusion

This chapter has aimed to highlight the inevitable failure of the current EU legal approach which seeks to address demand by the criminalisation of the buying of sex only from victims of trafficking. Specific targeted measures by EU and Member States in relation to trafficking in human beings are necessary. However, measures which do not recognise the intersection of trafficking for sexual exploitation, migration and prostitution, in terms of targeting and recruitment by traffickers, the indiscriminate attitude of the buyers of sex, and the specific trauma of gender-based harms, are ineffective. If the EU is serious about addressing demand, it must recognise that the Swedish/Nordic approach has demonstrated irrefutably that it is effective, not only as an anti-trafficking measure, but also as an approach which reduces the numbers of girls and women exploited in prostitution. Walby et al calculate that the Netherlands now has nine times the rate of prostitution in Sweden, and that Germany appears to have a rate of prostitution of between 30 and 40 times that of Sweden.[62] The authors conclude that the evidence is clear that the enforcement of the sex-buyer law creates a context which is less conducive to human trafficking.

Following the Nordic approach, through a provision in the Criminal Law (Sexual Offences) Act 2017, Ireland has now made it a criminal offence for any person to purchase or attempt to purchase sexual activity from another person; the Act also ensures that those exploited in prostitution are de-criminalised. While buying a person who is known

[62] Walby et al, *The Study on the Gender Dimension of Trafficking* (n 31).

to be trafficked remains a more serious offence, the prior rigid demarcation between the buying of trafficked and prostituted persons no longer pertains. However, states such as Ireland, which have introduced similar laws, need to recognise the extensive infrastructure and implementation framework which the Swedish government has established, and the resources allocated to providing comprehensive services and exit routes for women.[63] The continued commitment to education and public awareness programmes ensures the law acts as an effective deterrent to the demand that fosters human trafficking but also fulfils the wider objectives of the law in relation to gender equality.

[63] GS Ekberg, 'Swedish Laws, Policies and Interventions on Prostitution and Trafficking in Human Beings: A Comprehensive Overview' (Stockholm, 22 November 2017) www.researchgate.net/publication/321254711_SWEDISH_.

4

Abortion Law in Ireland: Reflecting on Reform

MÁIRÉAD ENRIGHT

I. Introduction

On 25 May 2018, the Irish people, in a referendum, voted to remove Article 40.3.3 of the Constitution, and replace it with the 36th Amendment, affirming the Oireachtas' power to pass legislation on abortion. At the time of writing, the government has published its proposed abortion legislation, the General Scheme of the Health (Regulation of Termination of Pregnancy) Bill 2018[1] (HRTPA). Space here does not allow for a complete re-telling of the history of the constitutional near-prohibition of abortion, of recent efforts to repeal that legislation, or indeed for a comprehensive analysis of the many facets of the proposed new Irish abortion law. Instead, this chapter will offer a critical thematic overview of recent reforms in the law, before sketching some aspects of the feminist campaign for that reform and evaluating some legal outcomes.

II. A New Constitutional Landscape

If passed, the HRTPA would radically alter Irish abortion law. Currently, abortion is only legal in Ireland where the test in the *X* case is satisfied:[2] that is, where the woman's life is at 'real and substantial' risk, and that risk can only be avoided by terminating the pregnancy.[3] If the HRTPA is passed, abortion will be legal without any requirement to disclose reasons within the first 12 weeks of pregnancy. After 12 weeks, it will be available on three restricted grounds: risk to life; risk of serious harm to health; and fatal foetal abnormality. The government assumes that repeal of the 8th Amendment and its replacement with the 36th Amendment will make constitutional space for this legislation. Under the 8th Amendment, which is the core of Article 40.3.3, the government must ensure that pregnancy is maintained to birth, wherever 'practicable', in order to safeguard the right to life of

[1] Available at www.health.gov.ie/blog/publications/updated-general-scheme-of-the-health-regulation-of-termination-of-pregnancy-bill-2018/.

[2] *Attorney General v X* [1992] 1 IR 1.

[3] The Amendment will read: 'Provision may be made by law for the regulation of termination of pregnancy.'

the 'unborn', which is 'equal' to that of the pregnant woman. Shortly before the May 2018 referendum, in a deportation case called *M v Minister for Justice*,[4] the Supreme Court brought years of constitutional debate to an end when it held that the only constitutional right of the foetus is the 'right to life of the unborn' under the 8th Amendment. The implication is that are no rights of the foetus elsewhere in the Constitution that could survive removal of the Amendment from the Constitution, and no unenumerated right to life which preceded the Amendment and would prevail despite repeal.[5] With the Amendment removed from the Constitution, any obstacles to liberalisation of abortion law derived directly from a foetal right to life should also be removed. The text of the 36th Amendment then confirms that the Oireachtas is entitled to pass law regulating the termination of pregnancy.[6]

Of course, the Oireachtas has no firm precedent to guide it here, and so it seems to be legislating on the basis of a series of new constitutional assumptions:

(i) The foetus may no longer be understood as an independent rights-bearer or, if it is, its rights or interests cannot ground an absolutist abortion law of the kind developed under Article 40.3.3.
(ii) The pregnant woman, although she has no absolute right to access abortion, enjoys a range of constitutional rights worthy of respect. Abortion might, then, be considered from a relational perspective which bears in mind, at least, that measures taken to protect prenatal life may have profound consequences for pregnant women.
(iii) The State may have an interest in protecting prenatal life in the interests of the common good, as acknowledged obiter in *M*.[7] However, this must be pursued in proportion[8] to its duties to vindicate the personal rights of the pregnant woman.
(iv) The State's interest in protecting prenatal life grows stronger as the pregnancy progresses, and will only be trumped in late pregnancy in exceptional circumstances.

These assumptions are very much in keeping with the abortion decisions of constitutional courts elsewhere. If this is an accurate sketch of the effects of the referendum on 25 May, however, then the constitutional law of pregnancy in Ireland has changed dramatically. The constitutional abortion law developed since 1983, and especially since the *X* case in 1992, has five key features:[9] First, the foetus and the woman carry equal constitutional weight as lives-in-being, irrespective of the circumstances of the pregnancy,[10] or of how advanced it is.[11] Second, the foetus is an independent rights-bearer, often represented by its own

[4] *M v Minister for Justice* [2018] IESC 14.

[5] F de Londras and M Enright, *Repealing the 8th* (Bristol, Policy Press, 2018) 28.

[6] ibid 54–55.

[7] '[T]he State is entitled to take account of the respect which is due to human life as a factor which may be taken into account as an aspect of the common good in legislating.' *M v Minister for Justice* [2018] IESC 14 [10.63].

[8] This is not an especially strong protection for women's rights, since the Oireachtas enjoys significant discretion in balancing individual rights and the common good. See further www.aboutthe8th.com/2018/04/09/if-the-referendum-passes-might-a-future-constitutional-challenge-require-the-government-to-lift-the-time-limits-for-abortion-access/.

[9] See more fully in de Londras and Enright, *Repealing the 8th* (n 5) 1–5.

[10] In *X* itself, for example, the girl's rape was a secondary concern – if she could have survived the pregnancy she would have been expected to bear it.

[11] See further R Fletcher, 'Post-Colonial Fragments: Representations of Abortion in Irish Law and Politics' (2001) 28 *Journal of Law and Society* 568; F De Londras, 'Constitutionalizing Fetal Rights: A Salutary Tale from Ireland' (2015) 22 *Michigan Journal of Gender and the Law*, available at www.papers.ssrn.com/abstract=2600907.

counsel, effectively separable from the pregnant woman's body, and thus her constitutional adversary.[12] It has a right to be born alive where practicable, even if it may only live for a short time.[13] Third, the abortion-seeking woman's right to life is effectively compromised by the foetus' entitlement to be born alive. The competing rights are not modified by any relational interpretation. She may not legally terminate the pregnancy merely because her life is at risk or her quality of life is diminished by the pregnancy. A risk which is predicted to arise in future, but which has not yet materialised, cannot be taken into account.[14] She must wait until her life is at 'real and substantial' risk. This was made vividly apparent by the death of Savita Halappanavar in 2012. She contracted sepsis – the result of an inevitable miscarriage at 17 weeks' pregnancy that took seven days to unfold. She was refused an abortion despite repeated requests. The case illustrated the difficulties doctors face in determining whether a woman has reached the threshold of 'real and substantial' risk to life.[15] Few women can pass that test; in 2017, just 15 legal terminations were carried out in Ireland.[16] Fourth, the abortion-seeking woman enters a zone of exception,[17] in which she has no constitutional rights except this compromised right to life. Very little case law describing Irish women's constitutional rights in pregnancy is available, and none, of course, in the context of abortion. Because the pregnant woman enjoys no other constitutional rights, she may be treated cruelly. Her health may be permanently damaged in order to preserve the pregnancy, as long as she survives it. Doctors owe a duty to do everything practicable to preserve foetal life, whatever the consequences for the woman.[18] For example, in 2014, a suicidal asylum-seeker, Ms Y, pregnant through rape, was denied an abortion under the Protection of Life During Pregnancy Act 2013 (PLDPA). Her pregnancy was prolonged using forcible methods, with the approval of the High Court, until a viable foetus could be delivered. This decision had long-term consequences for her health.[19] As with any pregnant woman in Ireland, she was not entitled to refuse any medical treatment which would place her foetus' life at significant risk.[20] The case of *PP v HSE* illustrated what can happen

[12] S Ahmed, *Differences That Matter: Feminist Theory and Postmodernism* (Cambridge, Cambridge University Press, 1998) 39.

[13] de Londras and Enright, *Repealing the 8th* (n 5) 7.

[14] See eg the case of Clare Malone, K Holland, 'Heart Patient Unable to get an Abortion as Life not at Immediate Risk' *The Irish Times* (Dublin, 27 April 2018), and the case of Michelle Harte, Irish Council for Civil Liberties, 'Case in Focus: Michelle Harte', available at www.iccl.ie/her-rights/health/michelle-harte/.

[15] Health Services Executive, 'Final Report: Investigation of Incident 50278 from Time of Patient's Self Referral to Hospital on the 21st of October 2012 to the Patient's Death on the 28th of October, 2012' (Health Services Executive, 2013) 69; Health Information and Quality Authority, 'Investigation into the Safety, Quality and Standards of Services Provided by the Health Service Executive to Patients, Including Pregnant Women, at Risk of Clinical Deterioration, Including Those Provided in University Hospital Galway, and as Reflected in the Care and Treatment Provided to Savita Halappanavar' (Health Information and Quality Authority, 2013) 212.

[16] Annual Report of Notifications in Accordance with the 'Protection of Life During Pregnancy Act 2013' 2017; in 2016, there were 25 such terminations.

[17] See further de Londras and Enright, *Repealing the 8th* (n 5) 34 et seq.

[18] See eg Protection of Life During Pregnancy Act 2013, ss 7 and 8.

[19] See R Fletcher, 'Contesting the Cruel Treatment of Abortion-Seeking Women' (2014) 22 *Reproductive Health Matters* 10. Ms Y subsequently settled her actions against the State. She had sought an abortion much earlier in pregnancy when viability would not have been an issue, but because of the negligence of various actors, her access to abortion was delayed, M Tighe, 'HSE Willing to Compensate Refugee Rape Victim Ms Y over Denied Abortion' *Sunday Times* (Dublin, 10 June 2018).

[20] *HSE v B* [2016] IEHC 605. See further discussion of the effects of the Amendment on childbirth and labour in de Londras and Enright, *Repealing the 8th* (n 5) 9–12.

when the woman is reduced to a bare body.[21] P had suffered brain-stem death, but her body was kept under experimental somatic care in an effort to bring her early pregnancy to fruition. In her case, the efforts to bring the pregnancy to its conclusion were found to be 'futile' as her body was too degraded by infection to endure for many more weeks. If the pregnancy had been more advanced, or Ms P's body had been in better condition, there would have been no constitutional obstacle to continuing to experiment with somatic care, irrespective of her own wishes or those of her family. Finally, the abortion-seeking woman may avoid the implications of the test in *X* by travelling to another jurisdiction, often along the established abortion trail to England, and the State may not stop her. But the State is entitled to deprive her of certain supports necessary to make that journey, in full knowledge that delaying access to abortion means later more expensive terminations, and even the possibility of refusal of care on arrival.[22] Irish constitutional law, at one time, did not recognise the right to travel or to information – the courts held that women's clinics and student union officers acting in solidarity with abortion-seeking women could be punished in an effort to protect the life of the 'unborn'.[23] Today, again because women are stripped of most constitutional rights, the law does not recognise that the obligation to travel to access healthcare, at a time of psychological distress, is a violation of human rights, even though this is recognised by international human rights law.[24] Of course, some women, who are unable or unwilling to attempt travel, will use illegal abortion pills instead.[25] Although the pills are not inherently dangerous, this practice is criminalised, so that it is heavily stigmatised, and women may be discouraged from seeking abortion care when needed for fear of prosecution. These expulsions and punishments are hardest on women who are already at the margins of Irish society; as Ms Y's case demonstrates,[26] for example, asylum seekers and women in poor health will struggle to navigate and use the few narrow routes available to circumvent the Amendment.

This is a summary, rather than a comprehensive overview of Ireland's constitutional abortion law. Its simplicity may obscure the uncertainty which characterised the law for decades during which the State refused to legislate on abortion, and apparently considered it acceptable to require women to go to the High Court if they wanted to confirm their right to access an abortion. Some of the points of constitutional law above are working interpretations espoused by government which have never been tested in the courts. The aim of advancing this summary, however, is to outline the resolutely foetocentric nature of the Irish abortion law in principle and in practice. By this is meant, simply, that Irish abortion law has emphasised the protection of prenatal life in ways which efface women's personhood

[21] *PP v HSE* [2014] IEHC 622.

[22] M Clarke, 'The Women We Can't Help', *Abortion Rights Campaign* (6 November 2016), available at www.abortionrightscampaign.ie/2016/11/06/guest-post-the-women-we-cant-help-by-mara-clarke-founder-and-director-of-abortion-support-network/.

[23] Attorney General (SPUC) v Open Door Counselling & Well Woman Centre Ltd [1988] IR 593; SPUC v Grogan [1989] IR 753.

[24] See eg *Mellet v Ireland*, Human Rights Committee, Communication 2324/2013 (2016); *Whelan v Ireland*, Human Rights Committee, Communication 2425/2014 (2017).

[25] S Sheldon, 'Empowerment and Privacy? Home Use of Abortion Pills in the Republic of Ireland' (2018) 4 *Signs* 823.

[26] See discussion of this case in K Side, 'A Geopolitics of Migrant Women, Mobility and Abortion Access in the Republic of Ireland' (2016) 23(12) *Gender, Place & Culture* 1788.

in pregnancy. Few women are known to have died because of the law, but women are required to bear a great deal in order that an unborn child will survive. The test in *X* refers to 'real and substantial' risk to life; this is an acknowledgment that every pregnancy can be dangerous to some degree, but that most women will be expected to endure this risk. The foetus deserves this sacrifice because it is always innocent, unblemished and vulnerable; in Berlant's evocative language it is 'the unprotected person, the citizen without a country or future … unjustly imprisoned in its mother's hostile gulag'.[27] Echoes of such language are apparent in *PP v HSE*:

> The unfortunate unborn has suffered the dreadful fate of being present in the womb of a mother who has died, and in which the environment is neither safe nor stable, and which is failing at an alarming rate … It has nothing but distress and death in prospect.[28]

If the foetus is the innocent, desperately in need of State protection,[29] then, by turn, there will be something anomalous or deviant about the woman who asserts an entitlement to end a pregnancy under law.[30] Arguably, a desire to punish deviant women is apparent in the zeal with which the law has been enforced. Foetal life is protected, not only by the criminalisation of abortion, but by subjecting women to extraordinary risk assessment processes when they attempt to claim entitlement to a life-saving abortion. Since 2013, under the PLDPA, a woman requesting an abortion is required to go through a risk assessment procedure without parallel anywhere else in Irish medical law. If her life is at risk from physical illness, she must see two doctors, and two more if her application is refused and she appeals. If she is suicidal, she must see three doctors, and three more if she appeals.[31] The PLDPA's distinction between physical illness and suicidality, in particular, speaks to a mistrust of women who will not endure severe mental illness – even if that involves detention or unwanted treatment in pregnancy – for their child.[32] Few women are granted terminations under the PLDPA on suicide grounds, and there are cases where women who have made attempts on their life have been refused.[33] In *HSE v BS*,[34] a young woman was detained for psychiatric treatment when she requested an abortion on grounds of risk of suicide, even though there were no independent grounds for her detention under the Mental Health Act. It can comfortably be said, that Irish law is based, to use Geunther's language, on a 'maternal ethics of embodiment for the Other' which requires self-sacrifice, valorising 'the persecution, trauma and displacement of the maternal self'.[35] Any women refusing this duty, however vulnerable they may be, are either displaced through travel or criminalised.

[27] L Berlant, *The Queen of America Goes to Washington City: Essays on Sex and Citizenship* (Durham, Duke University Press, 1997) 97.

[28] *PP v HSE* [2014] IEHC 622.

[29] A Cavarero, *In Spite of Plato: A Feminist Rewriting of Ancient Philosophy* (Abingdon, Taylor & Francis, 1995) 76.

[30] R Braidotti, *Nomadic Subjects: Embodiment and Sexual Difference in Contemporary Feminist Theory* (New York, Columbia University Press, 2011) 213; L Zerilli, 'A Process without a Subject: Simone de Beauvoir and Julia Kristeva on Maternity' (1992) 18 *Signs* 111.

[31] Protection of Life During Pregnancy Act 2013, s 9.

[32] See further C Murray, 'Suicide, Dignity and the Irish Discourse on Abortion' (2016) 25(6) *Social & Legal Studies* 667.

[33] See E Coyne, 'Suicidal Woman Was Refused an Abortion' *The Times* (London, 29 June 2018); E Coyne, 'Abortions Were Denied to Suicidal Women' *The Times* (London, 20 January 2017).

[34] *HSE v BS* [2017] IEDC 8.

[35] L Guenther, *Gift of the Other, The: Levinas and the Politics of Reproduction* (Albany, SUNY Press, 2012) 143.

Set the new constitutional assumptions, which arguably animated drafting of the HRTPA (discussed above), and the constitutional principles which have governed access to abortion in Ireland for 35 years, side-by-side, and the difference is stark. It is not clear that Irish law will immediately shed its foetocentrism. However, the demise of Article 40.3.3 may mean, at last, that there is some space for moving away from its sacrificial vision of maternity. That said, under the 36th Amendment, abortion, though regulated in new ways, remains an exceptional constitutional issue, worthy of specific naming in the text. Before looking at the HRTPA in more detail, it may be useful to explore the political foundations of any shift in constitutional position, from Article 40.3.3 to the 36th Amendment.

III. Political Change towards Constitutional Reform

The formal institutional journey to the referendum on Article 40.3.3 is well-known in Ireland. A 2010 European Court of Human Rights decision, arising from strategic litigation in *A, B and C v Ireland*,[36] highlighted that Ireland's abortion law was unworkable even in those few cases where women might have a claim to a constitutional, life-saving abortion in Ireland. Because the law was unclear, doctors were unwilling to apply or interpret it in practice; generating so-called 'chilling effects' within the law. In an unusually deferential judgment,[37] the Court held that women in Ireland had procedural rights to access constitutionally permissible abortion, but the State was not required to liberalise its abortion law. Feminists responded with the 'Action on X' campaign, a demand for the government to finally pass legislation to give effect to the *X* case.[38] In late 2012, as the Oireachtas was about to deliberate on legislative responses to that judgment, Praveen Halappanavar's story of the death of his wife Savita broke, and provoked mass vigils in her honour.[39] The government nevertheless followed through with plans to legislate for the prevailing constitutional position – the PLDPA was debated in 2013, and passed into law in 2014, over 21 years after *X* was decided. However, it was already clear that broader change was needed. Doctors contributing to the Oireachtas debates on the legislation emphasised that, issues of legal clarity aside, the 'real and substantial risk to life' test was incompatible with safe medical practice. Earlier that year, the pressure group Termination for Medical Reasons Ireland (TFMRI) began to campaign to draw attention to the position of parents who had received a diagnosis of a fatal foetal anomaly.[40] The story of Ms Y's case, reported in 2014, again had the effect of undermining the PLDPA, by demonstrating the cruelty it had licensed.[41] Human rights treaty bodies and tribunals repeatedly condemned the Irish law, and encouraged

[36] *A, B and C v Ireland* [2010] ECHR 2032.

[37] See further C Ryan, 'The Margin of Appreciation in A, B and C v Ireland: A Disproportionate Response to the Violation of Women's Reproductive Freedom' (2014) *UCL Journal of Law and Jurisprudence* 1.

[38] H O'Connell, 'Action on X Group Plans Rally to Mark 21st Anniversary of Case' *Journal.ie* (1 March 2013).

[39] 'Rallies Held Around Ireland in Memory of Savita Halappanavar' *RTÉ* (18 November 2012).

[40] K Sheridan, 'I Believe in a Loving God and that I won't be Damned for what I Did' *The Irish Times* (Dublin, 17 April 2012).

[41] C Bohan, 'Hundreds of Protestors Turn Out in Dublin Over Ireland's Abortion Laws' *Journal.ie* (20 August 2014).

constitutional reform.[42] Radical politicians in the Oireachtas repeatedly pushed for legislation to repeal the Amendment. Eventually the Fine Gael government agreed to establish a Citizens' Assembly: a group of 99 citizens who met in the Spring of 2017, considered public submissions and advocates' arguments, and produced surprisingly liberal recommendations for legislative reform.[43] These included the recommendation that abortion should be available on request until 12 weeks' pregnancy. These were scrutinised by a Joint Oireachtas Committee, which heard a series of expert submissions, modified the Assembly's recommendations, and made the proposals which eventually became the 36th Amendment and the HRTPA.[44] This formal institutional story of legal change contains typical ingredients: (i) external international pressure and mobilisation of human rights arguments; (ii) internal protest and mobilisation; (iii) political engagement by a new generation of high status experts, such as senior doctors, and contestation of that expertise; (iv) citizen consultation, to a limited extent; (v) an incremental process of reform, beginning with limited legislation before attempting subsequent liberalisation; and (vi) women's increased formal participation in the political process, especially as TDs and Senators.

The political movement towards removal of Article 40.3.3, which gathered under the slogan 'Repeal the 8th' and which was crucial to the mobilisation of a 'Yes' vote in May 2018, cannot be wholly contained within this simple story of institutional reform. Feminists have campaigned in opposition to the Amendment since it was first proposed. In 1983, it was difficult for Irish activists to make a case for abortion access as a basic human right. The first Women's Right to Choose group had only formed in 1980; it had few members, and the wider women's movement was not unified on the abortion issue. Influential bodies such as the Council on the Status of Women[45] were unable to reach a shared position among their members. As a result, the Anti-Amendment Campaign (AAC) formed to resist the insertion of the Amendment into the Constitution did not campaign directly for abortion access, but rather made a strategic decision to mount a neutral campaign against the legal form of the Amendment itself.[46] The AAC argued that the Amendment would do nothing to prevent unwanted pregnancy, while denying access to abortion in cases of rape and serious risk to health. It also emphasised the Amendment's inherent uncertainty and the likelihood that it would generate difficult unforeseen consequences.[47] The victorious Pro Life Amendment Campaign (PLAC) and their successors, since they were appealing to majority morality, seemed to have the more persuasive argument: they could frame reproductive rights as an alien irritant to a Catholic Irish constitution,[48] and a threat to the vulnerable

[42] International Human Rights Observations on Abortion in Ireland.

[43] See www.citizensassembly.ie/en/The-Eighth-Amendment-of-the-Constitution/.

[44] Joint Committee on the Eighth Amendment of the Constitution, see webarchive.oireachtas.ie/parliament/oireachtasbusiness/committees_list/eighthamendmentoftheconstitution/.

[45] The forerunner of the National Women's Council of Ireland.

[46] C Hug, *The Politics of Sexual Morality in Ireland* (London, Palgrave, 1998) 148.

[47] Anti-Abortion Campaign, see www.irishelectionliterature.com/2018/05/07/1982-leaflet-from-the-anti-amendment-campaign/#more-37675.

[48] See further L Smyth, *Abortion and Nation: The Politics of Reproduction in Contemporary Ireland* (London, Ashgate, 2005); R Fletcher, 'Post-Colonial Fragments' (n 11); R Fletcher, 'Pro-Life Absolutes, Feminist Challenges: The Fundamentalist Narrative of Irish Abortion Law 1986–1992' (1998) 36 *Osgoode Hall Law Journal* 1; B Collins and P Hanafin, 'Mothers, Maidens and the Myth of Origins in the Irish Constitution' (2001) 12 *Law and Critique* 53; L Smyth, 'Narratives of Irishness and the Problem of Abortion: The X Case 1992' (1998) 60 *Feminist Review* 61.

infant who was such a potent symbol of the nation's future.[49] They captured an apparently unassailable Catholic nationalism. Women, because of their reproductive role, have always been the bearers of national identity and social order;[50] the uterus, in Preciado's evocative words is 'not a private organ, but a biopolitical space of exception … a laboratory of the nation state on whose management depends the purity of the national ethnos'.[51] This was not a new problem. There had been a tendency in Irish law, going back to the foundation of the State and the criminalisation of contraception,[52] to use law to enforce women's presumptive obligation to bear children and mother them for the nation.[53] This gelled, of course, with conservative Catholic ideology,[54] which frames mothering as a protective but self-sacrificing role, involving obligations to bear pain for the foetus.[55] Although this joining of maternity and national obligation was not overt government policy, the substantial social capital of its proponents – clerics and leading professionals – lent it a legitimacy which was considered at least equal to the views of those who resisted the Amendment. This persisted even as public support for their broader position weakened. For many years, the State's stock argument when criticised by international human rights experts was that the Amendment was a unique pillar of Irish legal culture: a 'nuanced and proportionate response to the views of the Irish electorate on the highly politicised and divisive question of the extent to which the right to life of the foetus should be balanced against the rights of the woman'.[56]

However, as a new generation of feminist activists came of age in the 2000s, the politics of reproductive rights in Ireland had fundamentally altered, and it was possible to articulate new visions of the relationship between abortion and the nation. Feminist pro-choice activism gained a greater legitimacy as the power of the Catholic hierarchy and Catholic social teaching waned in the late 1990s, in the wake of a series of scandals around sexual and institutional abuse of women and children. Irish law was secularising rapidly, as indicated, for example, by new laws on divorce and same-sex marriage. Feminism was a counter-culture in Ireland, but an important one. Nevertheless, a great deal of pro-choice energy was concentrated not on advocating for more liberal laws, but on supporting women who needed to travel, defending the suicide exception to the *X* judgment, and persuading government to legislate to clarify the law in the *X* case. The events of 2012 and 2013

[49] L Edelman, *No Future: Queer Theory and the Death Drive* (Durham, Duke University Press, 2004) 14.

[50] A Ong and M Peletz, *Bewitching Women, Pious Men: Gender and Body Politics in Southeast Asia* (Oakland, University of California Press, 1995) 6.

[51] B Preciado, 'Uterus Strike', see www.hiredknaves.wordpress.com/2014/02/18/uterus-strike/. To similar effect see A McCulloch, 'The Rise of the Fetal Citizen' (2012) 26 *Women's Studies Journal* 17 and Berlant's work on the 'intimate public sphere', L Berlant, 'The Intimate Public Sphere' in JA Radway and others (eds), *American Studies: An Anthology* (NJ, John Wiley & Sons, 2009) 111.

[52] S McAvoy, 'Regulation of Sexuality in the Irish Free State' in G Jones and E Malcolm (eds), *Medicine, Disease and the State in Ireland, 1650–1940* (Cork, Cork University Press, 1999) 254.

[53] See further M Enright, 'Involuntary Patriotism: Judgment, Women and National Identity on the Island of Ireland' in M Enright et al (eds), *Northern/Irish Feminist Judgments* (Oxford, Hart Publishing, 2017) 27, 37–38.

[54] These are not only Catholic ideas. On the non-religious origins of cultures of fetality see eg: D Haraway, *Modest–Witness@Second–Millennium.FemaleMan–Meets–OncoMouse: Feminism and Technoscience* (London, Psychology Press, 1997) 202–04.

[55] See J Kristeva, 'Stabat Mater' in S Suleiman (ed), *The Female Body in Western Culture: Contemporary Perspectives* (Cambridge, Harvard University Press, 1986) on the inevitable tempering of maternal joy with pain.

[56] See eg www.justice.ie/en/JELR/Pages/SP14000193.

allowed a shift in focus, which energised pro-choice campaigners to campaign for repeal of Article 40.3.3. By 2018, so many different entities supported the campaign for repeal that it is difficult to speak of it as a unitary movement. However, key participants included the Abortion Rights Campaign (founded 2012) and the Coalition to Repeal the 8th (founded 2013), which was an umbrella group for a range of smaller pro-choice campaigning groups, often coalescing around shared identities as doctors, lawyers, artists, parents, grandparents, migrants and so on.[57] These two organisations came together with the National Women's Council of Ireland to form the official platform for a 'Yes' vote in the May 2018 referendum, called 'Together for Yes'.[58]

This six-year Repeal movement was 'about' law; however, although some lawyers were involved in various ways, it was not dominated by technical formalistic arguments about constitutional principle. It articulated a new political account of abortion-seeking women's collective relationship to law, which dissented from the narrow position of flawed or damaged mother, ascribed to women in nationalist anti-abortion discourse. The Repeal movement's work had many strands, but here just three will be discussed. First, the movement repeatedly questioned the abortion law's legitimacy at its foundations. They made manifest the public demand for change. This work often took the form of shows of public strength and anger such as the annual March for Choice, and the Strike 4 Repeal,[59] which protested delays in calling a referendum on abortion. In more everyday ways, the use of apparel, such as the Repeal Project's well-known black sweaters,[60] demonstrated mass support for abortion law reform in the streets. Second, they developed a range of languages for critiquing the law. One, of course, drew in vernacular terms on constructions of Irish abortion law as a breach of human rights. Another had an historical focus, particularly in the context of celebrations of the centenary of the 1916 Rising. At this time, awareness of Ireland's history of denial of reproductive rights to women was growing. Through the work of survivors and their advocates, scandals such as the practices of the Magdalene Laundries and the Mother and Baby Homes, and the use of symphysiotomy were seeping into the public consciousness, and some were the subjects of public inquiries and (limited) redress (see Chapter 15). Campaigners began to trace the connections between older methods of disciplining women's erotic embodiment[61] in Ireland and contemporary abortion law. The prohibition on abortion, particularly its discussion in artistic works,[62] became widely understood as one in a long succession of state techniques of biopower, by which good self-sacrificial maternal lives were celebrated while others were repeatedly foreclosed, radically erased or disregarded.[63] Drawing attention to women's history had many effects, but one

[57] See www.repealeight.ie.

[58] See www.togetherforyes.ie.

[59] See strike4repeal.org.

[60] See https://www.her.ie/repeal/repeal-project-founder-anna-cosgrave-repeal-project-is-my-micro-contribution-to-a-movement-spanning-decades-308025.

[61] A Jaggar and S Bordo, *Gender/body/knowledge: Feminist Reconstructions of Being and Knowing* (New Brunswick, Rutgers University Press, 1989) 54.

[62] See further N NicGhabhann 'City Walls, Bathroom Stalls and Tweeting the Taoiseach: The Aesthetics of Protest and the Campaign for Abortion Rights in the Republic of Ireland', Continuum, DOI: 10.1080/10304312.2018.1468413.

[63] See J Halberstam, *In a Queer Time and Place: Transgender Bodies, Subcultural Lives* (New York, NYU Press, 2005) 3.

was to frame the modern state as complicit with the oppressions worked by its predecessors and, accordingly, as obliged to change the law. This set of arguments was so effective that it became part of mainstream political discourse. For example, the Minister for Health invoked it in opening the Oireachtas' debate on proposed legislation in January 2018,[64] tracing the connection between the legislation and the nation's attempts to understand a history of punishment of unmarried mothers.

Second, the movement publicised women's methods of circumventing the law, including illegal methods, such as the use and distribution of the abortion pill. This included direct action events, by groups such as ROSA, at which activists consumed or circulated the pill,[65] and smaller interventions in public space, such as displays of stickers and posters, or use of social media which both informed women about the availability of the pill, and showed that women were using it and indeed, supporting each other to use it. During the referendum campaign, there was a tendency to frame pill use as unsafe, and the experience as one of lonely abandonment.[66] This framing helped support the argument for regulating pill use within the healthcare service, which may mean that these challenges failed to disrupt the assumption that someone other than women themselves should be in charge of their reproductive lives. The illegality of these actions, of course, inhibited detailed storytelling about pill distribution across the country, and so the emphasis in media reports tended to be on individual procurement of the pill by ordering from websites run by foreign telemedicine organisations. However, in drawing attention to pill use, activists demonstrated that the prevailing abortion law was effectively unenforceable and that, as with travel, feminists could work together to ensure access to healthcare not provided by the State.

Third, and perhaps most strikingly, the movement used personal narrative to generate plural public understandings of the abortion-seeking woman. Although women had been leaving Ireland to terminate pregnancies for generations, it was not usual to speak publicly about that experience in public forums. This was an indicator of the relentless stigmatisation of abortion and unwanted pregnancy.[67] Abortion was an open secret. Human rights organisations did a great deal to communicate the reality of denial of abortion care, and of abortion travel, but the stories used to illustrate these issues were generally anonymous. In recent years, campaigners have refused that secrecy, de-privatising abortion, by telling personal abortion stories, not only in the media, but in the arts; for example, in the photographs of the X-ile project,[68] in social media projects such as 'In Her Shoes'[69] and in theatre work such as Grace Dyas' *Not At Home*.[70] These stories were important because they allowed women, rather than foetuses, to be centred as agents in the Irish story of abortion access, and to

[64] Speech by Mr Simon Harris TD, Minister for Health (17 January 2018) available at www.merrionstreet.ie/en/News-Room/Speeches/Speech_by_Mr_Simon_Harris_TD_Minister_for_Health.html.

[65] Abortion Pill Train, www.womenonweb.org/en/page/9127/abortion-pill-train.

[66] See eg 'Women in Ireland should not take Abortion Pills, says Harris' *The Irish Times* (Dublin, 12 April 2018).

[67] See further R Fletcher, 'Silences: Irish Women and Abortion' (1995) *Feminist Review* 44; A Smyth, 'Telling the Truth About Women's Lives' (2015) 10 *Estudios Irlandeses* 115; C Sanger, 'Talking About Abortion' (2016) 25(6) *Social and Legal Studies* 651, DOI 10.1177/0964663916668250.

[68] See http://www.x-ileproject.com/.

[69] See https://www.facebook.com/InHerIrishShoes/.

[70] See theatreclub.ie/not.

reframe that agency. Writing about 'subaltern pain', Lauren Berlant warns about appeals to law that depend on individuals' disclosure of stories of personal suffering.[71] There is a risk that women's stories will only be heard insofar as they can be made safe and assimilable to national norms, and there is a suffering entailed in disclosure of private pain to an often hostile audience.[72] Women's abortion story-telling was radical because campaigners insisted on telling stories which normalised and de-stigmatised everyday abortions. The movement for a referendum was precipitated by the stories of Savita Halappanavar and TFMRI – stories of fatal foetal abnormality and life-saving termination, and so there was a real danger that, in the movement for reform, women's trauma would become 'the index of the meaning and value of … [their] citizenship'.[73] However, women's demands were ultimately more expansive; they were not contained by stories of death and grief. Rather, women told unashamed stories of ordinary abortions; explaining that they terminated their pregnancies, not for exceptional reasons, or because they were tragic victims of circumstance, but because they simply could not be pregnant. Many women, particularly activists in Parents for Choice, and TFMRI were able to trouble the assumption that abortion was a rejection of motherhood and present it instead as a common episode in many women's lives as mothers. This work of narrative production continued right up until the last days of the referendum campaign.

It could be said that the Repeal movement articulated a new nationalism around abortion. This is always a partial, and risky, if effective, strategy. In particular, activists have pointed out that a coherent claim about an abortion law which affected women 'like' undecided Irish voters – 'our friends and neighbours, our sisters, cousins, mothers. aunts wives'[74] – is always necessarily exclusionary of different or less palatable voices. For example, the stories of migrant women, like Ms Y and Savita Halappanavar, were emblematic of the campaign.[75] Much of the Irish law on reproductive rights was worked out on the backs of minority women. The legal cases which applied the 8th Amendment in the years leading up to Repeal were not about abortion, but about reproductive justice. They concerned whether the future rights of unborn children could be invoked to prevent their migrant parents' deportation.[76] However, migrants' stories were often centred within the final referendum campaign or in government discourse. As new abortion law is developed, implemented or even reformed, an intersectional approach to reproductive justice, which acknowledges the specific needs of women in minority communities in Ireland, will be essential to genuine progress.

[71] L Berlant, 'The Subject of True Feeling: Pain, Privacy and Politics' in J Dean (ed), *Cultural Studies and Political Theory* (Ithaca, Cornell University Press, 2000) 55, 59.

[72] L Kavanagh, Speech at NWCI AGM, available at www.thedailyslog.com/in-the-future-i-would-like-us-to-be-able-to-make-change-without-the-constant-bearing-of-our-souls-and-our-wounds/.

[73] Berlant, 'The Subject of True Feeling: Pain, Privacy and Politics' (n 71) 52.

[74] Speech by Mr Simon Harris TD, Minister for Health (17 January 2018) available at www.merrionstreet.ie/en/News-Room/Speeches/Speech_by_Mr_Simon_Harris_TD_Minister_for_Health.html.

[75] 'Savita's Law: The Race Politics of Repeal' *The New Pretender* (28 June 2018) available at www.new-pretender.com/2018/06/28/ireland-savitas-law-the-racial-politics-of-repeal/.

[76] *Ugbelese v MJELR* [2009] IEHC 598; *E v MJELR* [2008] IEHC 68 (cited with approval by MacEochaidh J in *FO v Minister for Justice* [2013] IEHC 236 and again in *Dos Santos v Minister for Justice* [2013] IEHC 237); *Baby O v MJELR* [2002] IR169.

IV. A New Legislative Landscape

Has there been a revolution in Irish abortion law to match the revolution in public discourses of abortion worked by the Repeal movement? Law is always indeterminate, and the constitutional law of pregnancy in Ireland, discussed above, now seems fresh, open-ended and ripe for woman-centred interpretation. However, the HRTPA suggests a conservative approach to these constitutional possibilities. Although it would bring Irish abortion law into compliance with international human rights obligations for the first time, there remains a tendency to frame abortion in terms of public morality rather than of private medical decision-making. It is largely exceptions-based legislation. Access to abortion will be heavily restricted after 12 weeks. A woman will only be able to access an abortion: (i) if the foetus is diagnosed with a fatal foetal anomaly; a condition which means that it is highly likely to die in the womb, or during birth or within 28 days of birth;[77] (ii) if her life is at risk;[78] or (iii) if her health is at risk of serious harm.[79] These exceptions will not cover the situation of some women who are unable to access a termination before 12 weeks or do not realise that they need one. There is no provision for waiver of the statutory time limit, even if the woman misses it by only a few days. In exceptions-based legislation, only certain categories of 'deserving' abortion, or 'hard cases' are addressed. So, for example, the legislation omits to provide for women who may need a later abortion for socio-economic reasons. It also omits terminations for very severe but non-fatal foetal anomalies, in part because of a marked refusal to engage with the 'No' campaign's linking of abortion to the eradication of children with disabilities.[80] Undoubtedly, some women will continue to use abortion pills, and some will continue to travel.

Certainly, the HRTPA, if passed, will improve Irish abortion law. The structure of the legislation suggests that some important lessons have been learned from the PLDPA. Unlike the PLDPA, the draft legislation draws no distinction between risks arising from physical and mental illness. It has also abandoned the distinction between risk to health and risk to life, and the qualifying language of 'real and substantial' risk, which made the original *X* case test so difficult to apply in practice. The text of the draft legislation has also shed some of the rhetoric of the Amendment; whereas the PLDPA referred to the 'unborn', the draft legislation speaks of the foetus. And whereas the PLDPA only regulated procedures 'as a result of which, or in the course of which' unborn life was ended,[81] the draft legislation would regulate procedures intended to end the life of the foetus. We have not yet, apparently, reached the stage where our abortion legislation can refer directly to abortion by name. Crucially, the legislation will allow a woman to access legal abortion in Ireland up to 12 weeks pregnancy, if she needs one. If she terminates her own pregnancy after that period has elapsed, she will no longer be criminalised, though a person who assists her may be.[82] Before 12 weeks, GPs will be able to provide abortion services, but will have no role in 'gate-keeping' access by

[77] Head 6.
[78] Heads 4 and 5.
[79] Heads 4 and 5.
[80] H McDonald, 'Irish Abortion Vote: "propagandistic" use of Children with Down's Syndrome Condemned' *Guardian* (London, 22 May 2018).
[81] PLDPA, s 9.
[82] Head 14.

evaluating the woman's reason for terminating the pregnancy. Their function will be to date the pregnancy, and certify and arrange the termination.[83] After certification, the woman will have to wait three days before she can access a termination.[84] The '12 weeks' provision was controversial within the Joint Oireachtas Committee, and some TDs only publicly supported it as provision for rape victims;[85] acknowledging that it was inappropriate and re-traumatising to ask women who have been raped to go through special procedures to test the veracity of their claim. The '12 weeks' provision was often represented in terms of 'unrestricted' access to abortion, but in fact it is restricted in three ways: by (i) by time limit; (ii) by medical oversight; and (iii) by a mandatory waiting period. The waiting period is not medically required – it is there, presumably, to ensure that women take the decision to terminate pregnancy seriously. The legislation makes no guarantee of provision of abortion care,[86] and this means that real work will have to be done to ensure that women, particularly those from minority populations, have meaningful access to services.

The HRTPA does not create a purely 'private' model of abortion, since it does not accept that the decision is the woman's alone. It is deeply reliant on medical oversight – and particularly obstetric oversight[87] – for its legitimacy. During the referendum campaign, medical oversight was opposed to the alternative of presumptively 'dangerous' pill distribution networks. Doctors rather than women (or, for example, midwives) are positioned as gatekeepers of access to morally difficult late abortion. This should not be accepted uncritically. 'Good' abortion legislation on its own will not guarantee abortion access; that legislation must be implemented within pro-choice cultures,[88] not least cultures of everyday interpretation of the HRTPA. Medicine is not always practiced neutrally or dispassionately, and recourse to 'evidence' and 'best practice' does not in itself purge medicine of all infirmities.[89] One site of potential difficulty for interpretation of the HRPTA is the 'risk of serious harm to health' ground. This ground was heavily critiqued by the 'No' campaign during the referendum as a 'vague mental health ground', which would lead to 'abortion on demand up to six months'.[90] It will be important, not only to women who fall ill during pregnancy, but to a range of vulnerable populations, including women with pre-existing physical and psychosocial disabilities. Except in emergencies, where a woman's health is at immediate risk requiring immediate termination of the pregnancy, the relevant risk will be certified by two doctors.[91] There are three issues here: health, appropriateness and viability. First, 'health' is

[83] Head 7.

[84] Head 7(2).

[85] B Kelleher, 'Why I was persuaded abortion up to 12 weeks should be allowed' *The Irish Times* (Dublin, 21 March 2018).

[86] In contrast to provisions in Spain, for example.

[87] Oversight is a different question from direct interference, which will also be an important dimension of reform. This may mean controlling interferences with that access; for example, by regulating 'rogue' abortion counsellors and clinics, and criminalising protests outside locations where abortion care is provided. While the Minister for Health has spoken about 'exclusion zones' to this end, these are not mentioned in the HRPTA. See S Murray, 'Harris Planning Exclusion Zones' *Irish Independent* (Dublin, 31 May 2018).

[88] See L Oja, 'Why is a "Good Abortion Law" Not Enough? The Case of Estonia' (2017) 19(1) *Health and Human Rights* 161.

[89] J Law and A Mol, *Complexities: Social Studies of Knowledge Practices* (Durham, Duke University Press, 2002) 11; M Berg and A Mol, *Differences in Medicine: Unraveling Practices, Techniques, and Bodies* (Durham, Duke University Press, 1998) 3.

[90] See eg loveboth.ie/category/vote-no-blog.

[91] Heads 4–6.

not defined in the legislation. It is important that it is not read too rigidly; for example, by confining its application to cases where a risk to life is foreseeable, or grave and permanent injury is predicted. Ideally, any deterioration in a woman's health should be evaluated in the context of her whole life, because the significance of a condition will vary from one woman to the next. The World Health Organisation's definition of 'health', which is not confined to diagnosis of an illness, but also takes account of the patient's social context, could be used to ensure more expansive access to abortion on health grounds where needed in later pregnancy.[92] Women themselves, of course, should also be consulted in abortion decision-making, though the HRPTA does not require doctors to do so. Second, the HRPTA provides that, even if doctors agree that a woman's health is at risk of serious harm, the abortion may be refused if it is not 'appropriate'.[93] This language could either be read flexibly, or to justify refusal of an otherwise legitimate termination. Finally, in cases where the woman's life or health is at risk,[94] the expectation is that a viable foetus will be delivered alive – since termination of a viable pregnancy will be criminalised – and so pregnancies will rarely be terminated in Ireland after 23 weeks.[95]

It is clear that the interaction of health, appropriateness and viability will be crucial to the operation of this ground. Guidance and training for doctors should direct human-rights compliant balancing of these factors. Guidance and training should directly address factors which might legitimate unduly conservative interpretation of the HRPTA to refuse terminations and substitute coercive treatment. It is important to remember that, even within the current law, at least some of women's suffering is attributable, not only to the law itself, but to unduly rigid interpretation of the law, whether motivated by caution or conservatism. *PP v HSE*[96] is one example; there was nothing in the jurisprudence on the 8th Amendment to suggest that somatic care was justified in this instance, and indeed the High Court confirmed that it was not. Ms Y's case was another; nothing in the jurisprudence on the Amendment suggested that she should be subjected to inhuman and degrading treatment to prolong her pregnancy to viability. Arguably, the interpretation of the Amendment in Savita Halappanavar's case was similarly flawed, as her doctors could reasonably have disregarded her foetus' heartbeat once it became clear that miscarriage was inevitable. This issue has received little public discussion.

It is crucial that the role of everyday legislative interpretation is understood and addressed as the new abortion law is implemented.[97] Criminalisation is important here: under the HRPTA, doctors who provide abortions outside the law will remain liable to imprisonment. If there is uncertainty about how the ground should be applied, renewed 'chilling effects' may emerge, blocking women's access to healthcare and producing ancillary abuses of human rights. Indirect conscientious objection, whereby a doctor who disagrees

[92] Health is defined as 'a state of complete physical, mental and social well-being and not merely the absence of disease or infirmity'. Preamble to the Constitution of the World Health Organization as adopted by the International Health Conference, New York, 19–22 June 1946.

[93] Head 4(1)(c).

[94] Head 4(1)(b).

[95] Head 19.

[96] *PP v HSE* [2014] IEHC 622.

[97] See, to this end, the work of La Mesa in Colombia, AC González Vélez, 'Legal Knowledge as a Tool for Social Change: La Mesa por la Vida y la Salud de las Mujeres as an Expert on Colombian Abortion Law' (2017) 19(1) *Health and Human Rights* 109–18.

with abortion in a particular case does not declare his objection, preferring to participate in order to obstruct access to legal healthcare, may also be an issue. A regime for open advance declaration of conscientious objection, and enforcement of the statutory obligation to refer the patient to a colleague willing to perform the procedure, will be necessary to avoid this difficulty.[98] In order to manage and respond to wrongful denial of access, it is important that abortions refused as well as abortions granted are monitored and reported, so that any patterns of obstruction or refusal can be addressed. It would be advisable to provide for regular independent review of the operation of legislation so that any necessary amendments can be proposed efficiently, at natural intervals, without the need for renewed political campaigning. Currently, it is only proposed to monitor abortions granted,[99] as if to suggest that the performance of abortions, rather than the broader provision of accessible services, is the target of regulation. Finally, where a woman is refused an abortion and appeals that decision,[100] consideration should also be given to including lawyers, as well as doctors, on decision-making review panels, to discourage needlessly restrictive interpretation. The point, in engaging with questions of interpretation of the new abortion law, is to ensure that there is always space for the voice of the woman being cared for – that is, that the moralisation of abortion has not been removed from the Constitution only to be reproduced at the level of day-to-day care.

V. Conclusion

The 8th Amendment made each Irish abortion a matter of national value. When abortion becomes a matter for the nation, each abortion is a threatening act of disobedience and disloyalty; in Penelope Deutscher's words, each abortion-seeking pregnant woman becomes a 'murderous competing sovereign whose self-interest would thwart the intervening motivations of the state'.[101] Irish abortion law under the Amendment could be read, in this sense, as a punishment for women who, in their efforts to maintain their self-sovereignty,[102] or to preserve their bodily integrity,[103] were simultaneously understood as undermining the Irish State. It is hard to say, at this point, whether the referendum has undone Irish abortion law's relation to punitive nationalism. Certainly, there is an acceptance, reflected in the structure of the proposed legislation as well as in the language of 'compassion' and 'care' centred in the Together for Yes campaign,[104] that 'good' Irish women will need abortions in exceptional cases. 'Yes' campaigners in the referendum successfully articulated an alternate Irish nationalism. However, the legislation stops short of meeting the demand for 'free, safe,

[98] See further de Londras and Enright, *Repealing the 8th* (n 5) 81.

[99] Head 17. Some refusals will come to government attention if they are the subject of reviews under Head 13.

[100] Head 13.

[101] P Deutscher, 'The Inversion of Exceptionality: Foucault, Agamben, and "Reproductive Rights"' (2008) 107 *South Atlantic Quarterly* 55, 66.

[102] Cavarero, *In Spite of Plato* (n 29) 78.

[103] D Cornell, 'Dismembered Selves' in W Brown and J Halley (eds), *Left Legalism/Left Critique* (Durham, Duke University Press, 2002) 350.

[104] S Bardon, 'Repeal Campaigners to Focus on Compassion, Care and Change' *The Irish Times* (Dublin, 22 March 2018).

legal' abortion;[105] that is, a demand for access to abortion as normalised healthcare which is not subject to any distinctive legal regime. So, a question remains about how a campaign for reproductive justice has been translated, first, into a campaign for law reform, and then into legal structures. There is a danger that Ireland's exceptions-based abortion law 'minorises' women; identifying categories of women who can safely be granted abortions within Ireland, while excluding other significant populations from provision. The relationship between abortion-seeking women and the law may be one of limited benevolent protection, rather than of deference to women's self-actualisation; to what the Italian philosopher Adriana Cavarero calls the 'sovereign subjectivity of maternal power'.[106] Despite the reform, women will not have control over their own pregnancies. They will have more options for accessing safe, early and confidential abortion[107] than they do under the current law. However, these options only run along certain limited, medically supervised and tightly-constrained modalities.[108] It may be some time before abortion in Ireland is legally unremarkable, and genuinely a matter for individual women making healthcare decisions in privacy and security.

[105] See www.abortionrightscampaign.ie/2018/07/10/universalaccesstoabortionwelcomed/.
[106] Cavarero, *In Spite of Plato* (n 29) 79. See also www.abortionrightscampaign.ie/tag/free-safe-legal/.
[107] This formula is Sally Sheldon's, see Sheldon, 'Empowerment and Privacy?' (n 25).
[108] Cavarero, *In Spite of Plato* (n 29) 76.

PART II

Family and Relationships

5

Mapping a Transformed Landscape: Sexual Orientation and the Law in Ireland

FERGUS RYAN

I. Introduction

A seemingly minor amendment to legislation can sometimes speak volumes. Buried deep in the detailed Schedules to the Civil Partnership and Certain Rights and Obligations of Cohabitants Act 2010[1] is a provision that amends the Presidential Establishment Act 1938.[2] The amendment allows for the payment of a pension to the surviving civil partner of the President of Ireland.[3] Given that only couples of the same sex could enter into civil partnership,[4] the legislation clearly envisaged what must have been unthinkable a mere 20 years earlier: that a future President (holding the highest office in the land) might have a same-sex partner.

Few phenomena better illustrate the extent to which Ireland has changed in the past 50 years than the evolution of the law as it relates to sexual orientation. Up until 1993, consenting adult males still faced the prospect of criminalisation for homosexual sexual acts, regardless of the age, context or consent of the parties.[5] A relatively short 22 years later, in 2015, Ireland became the first sovereign state in the world to introduce marriage for same-sex couples by constitutional referendum.[6] The contrast could not be more striking. In the space of 25 years, social attitudes and, with them, laws have incrementally evolved in a manner that once might have been thought unimaginable. The underlying reasons for this transformation in perspectives are complex, but the net effect is that a country once

[1] On which see F Ryan, *Civil Partnership and Certain Rights and Obligations of Cohabitants Act 2010* (Dublin, Round Hall, 2011).

[2] Civil Partnership and Certain Rights and Obligations of Cohabitants Act 2010 (hereinafter '2010 Act'), s 99(2) and Items 6, 7 and 8, Pt 2 of the Schedule, amending s 4 of the Presidential Establishment Act 1938 as substituted by s 3 of the Presidential Establishment (Amendment) Act 1991.

[3] Although largely a ceremonial role, Art 12(1) of the Constitution of Ireland describes the President of Ireland as taking 'precedence over all other persons in the State'.

[4] See the 2010 Act, ss 3, 7(3) and 107(e).

[5] The Offences Against the Person Act 1861 ss 61 and 62, and the Criminal Law (Amendment) Act 1885, s 11.

[6] 34th Amendment to the Constitution (Art 41.3); Marriage Act 2015. On which, see below and F Ryan, 'Ireland's Marriage Referendum: A Constitutional Perspective', *DPCE Online (Diritto Pubblico Comparato Ed Europeo) 2015-2.*

profoundly uncomfortable with the concept of homosexuality has actively embraced its lesbian, gay, bisexual and transgender (LGBT) population in a resounding popular affirmation of LGBT equality. The culmination of this transformation, one might say, was the 2017 appointment as Taoiseach[7] of Leo Varadkar, an openly gay man, an event made all the more remarkable given how (relatively) uncontroversial a factor his sexual orientation proved to be in his appointment.

This chapter chronologically traces the legislative and other legal steps that mark this transformation, with particular emphasis on laws concerning relationship recognition. While underlining the tremendous legal progress and social change that has occurred, the conclusion emphasises that formal legal equality does not necessarily mean that the LGBT population is now invulnerable, or that the historic prejudices and attitudes have entirely been swept away.

II. Criminal Laws and the Path to Decriminalisation

Sexual orientation describes the condition of being emotionally, romantically and sexually attracted to other persons, whether of the same sex, opposite sex, or regardless of sex or gender.[8] It is distinct from the concepts of gender identity and gender expression, which concern how a person perceives and expresses their own gender (and which are addressed in Chapter 11). What causes these variations in sexual orientation is unclear. What is clear, however, is that diversity in sexual orientation is experienced in every society and culture.

Nonetheless, to a greater or lesser degree, the prevalent social 'heteronormative'[9] expectation in most societies is that people who are male will generally be attracted to those who are female and vice versa. Historically, many societies and cultures have regarded (and many still regard) homosexuality and bisexuality (and in particular homosexual sexual acts) as aberrant. As a result, these sexual orientations have widely been the subject of social, religious and legal disapproval and attempted suppression. Many major world religions still disapprove of homosexual acts, some quite strongly. This social and religious disapproval regularly manifests itself in practices such as bullying, harassment, verbal abuse, denigration and discrimination directed at people who are gay and bisexual. Even within Europe, laws, policies and social attitudes vary widely, with negative attitudes hardening as one moves towards the east and southeast of the continent.[10]

[7] Prime Minister and Head of Government. See Art 28 of the Constitution of Ireland 1937.

[8] M Foucault, in *The History of Sexuality* (New York, Vintage Books, 1976), suggests that the concept of sexual orientation as an identity is a relatively modern phenomenon, emerging in Europe during the industrial revolution. Historically, he argues, people were not classified by orientation per se and the concepts of homosexuality and bisexuality as identities are relatively recently conceived.

[9] 'Heteronormativity' describes the social phenomenon that positions heterosexuality as the norm, to the exclusion of homosexual and bisexual orientations. Heteronormative assumptions promote heterosexuality as the natural (and therefore 'default') sexual orientation.

[10] See eg A Bodnar and A Śledzińska-Simon, 'Between Recognition and Homophobia: Same-Sex Couples in Eastern Europe' in D Gallo, L Paladini, and P Pustorino (eds), *Same-Sex Couples before National, Supranational and International Jurisdictions* (Berlin, Springer-Verlag, 2014) 211–47. See also Eurobarometer 437 (Special) 2015.

A. Criminalisation

Historically, opposition to homosexuality has typically resulted in laws banning and penalising consensual same-sex sexual activity. In 2018, male homosexual acts (even where consensual) remain unlawful in 72 states, with lesbian sexual acts banned in 45 states.[11] In a small number of jurisdictions, homosexual sexual acts may even potentially result in the death penalty at the hands of the state.[12] Even where these laws are not directly enforced in all cases, they can result in extortion and blackmail, and may provide moral justification for oppression of and discrimination against sexual minorities.

While a majority of world states (particularly those in Europe and the Americas) no longer criminalise homosexual sexual acts,[13] Ireland was a relative latecomer to the trend towards decriminalisation. Prior to 1993, male homosexual sexual acts had long been the subject of both legal and social sanction in Ireland. The act of anal intercourse was, for centuries, treated as a common law offence,[14] and described in the Offences against the Person Act 1861 as the 'abominable crime of buggery'. At one point it attracted the death penalty,[15] though the 1861 Act imposed a maximum penalty of penal servitude for life.[16] The act of buggery applied to anal intercourse by a man with a man or woman, as well as intercourse with an animal.[17] Consent under the 1861 Act was no defence (indeed, if he or she consented, the recipient or 'patient' party could potentially be prosecuted alongside the active party (the 'agent')).[18]

While the buggery offence applied to both heterosexual and homosexual anal intercourse, section 11 of the Criminal Law (Amendment) Act 1885 created a homosexual-specific offence of gross indecency between men. What constituted gross indecency is not defined in the Act, but the measure seemed targeted primarily at oral sex and mutual masturbation (though strictly speaking, the offence did not require the parties even to make physical

[11] See A Carroll and L Ramón Mendos, *State Sponsored Homophobia*, 12th edn (ILGA (the International Lesbian, Gay, Bisexual, Trans and Intersex Association), 2017) 8.

[12] Carroll and Mendos, ibid, remark that, as of 2017, four sovereign states and two regions of other states prescribed the death penalty as a penalty for same-sex acts: 'non-State actors apply it across two more States'. They note that five more states, in theory, allow the death penalty to be applied though, they note, 'there appears to be no data to suggest the death penalty has been implemented in those States for consensual same-sex sexual acts between adults and in private'.

[13] For instance, sodomy was decriminalised in France in 1791, with an equal age of consent for heterosexual and homosexual offences being introduced in 1982.

[14] For instance, T O'Malley, *Sexual Offences*, 2nd edn (Dublin, Round Hall, 2013) refers to the Fleta and Britton treatises from around 1290. The former describes the punishment for 'sodomy' as burial alive, while the latter prescribes burning.

[15] See 10 Chas I, Cap 20, 'An act for the punishment of the vice of buggery' 1634. For instance, Bishop John Atherton suffered death by hanging in 1640 for buggery with his steward, J Childe. See also Offences Against the Person Act 1829, s 18.

[16] Strictly speaking, buggery was a common law offence, the penalty for which was imposed by the 1861 Act. See *DPP v Devins* [2012] IESC 7 where the Supreme Court confirmed this was a common law offence. See also PA Ó Síocháin, *The Criminal Law of Ireland*, 7th edn (Foilseacháin Dlí, 1981); P Charleton, *Offences against the Person* (Dublin, Round Hall Press, 1992); SE Quinn, *Criminal Law in Ireland*, 3rd edn (Irish Law Publishing 1998).

[17] As McWilliam J observed in *Norris v Attorney General* [1984] IR 36 at 41: 'Leaving the reference to animals aside, the offence of buggery consists of the insertion of the penis into the anus and may be committed between two men or between a man and a woman but cannot be committed between two women.'

[18] *R v Jellyman* (1838) 8 C & P 604. O'Malley notes that 'At common law, both parties, irrespective of gender, were equally liable, assuming that both were consenting'. O'Malley, *Sexual Offences* (n 14) 5–15.

contact).[19] It applied even where the parties both consented[20] (indeed, some case law suggests that the parties must act 'in concert').[21] The fact that the parties may both have been adults and the acts committed in private provided no defence.

A curious aspect of the pre-1993 legislative landscape is there was comparatively little regulation of lesbian sexual activity.[22] It remained largely beyond the remit of the criminal law save in the case of indecent assault upon a female, in respect of which the age of consent was 15.[23] In *Norris v Attorney General* O'Higgins CJ (for the majority) reasoned:

> The legislature would be perfectly entitled to have regard to the difference between the sexes and to treat sexual conduct or gross indecency between males as requiring prohibition because of the social problem which it creates, while at the same time looking at sexual conduct between females as being not only different but as posing no such social problem.[24]

The relative absence of criminal legislation did not, however, mean that lesbian women were necessarily privileged. Female sexuality – though not subject to the same extent to the restrictions of the criminal law – was nonetheless policed carefully by social and cultural norms that informally penalised deviation from feminine norms. One might also argue that the absence of legislation reflected the social invisibility of lesbianism as a phenomenon, and highlighted a distinct tendency not to regard lesbian sexuality seriously. Indeed, an ironic side-effect of the ban on male homosexual sexual acts was that it arguably drew attention to and made visible the phenomenon of male homosexuality and bisexuality, at the possible expense of female sexual minorities.

B. Challenges to Criminalisation

Although Ireland inherited the UK's 1861 and 1885 Acts, these laws were carried over without much question into the legal framework of the Irish Free State on independence and remained in force without alteration until 1993.[25] The State did not always enforce these laws with vigour, though there were certainly prosecutions under the Acts throughout the early history of the State and bouts of prosecutorial zeal blighted the lives of many homosexual men.[26] These laws arguably had a chilling effect on the gay population, even those

[19] *R v Hunt and Badsey* [1950] 2 All ER 291 and *R v Preece and Howells* [1977] QB 50.

[20] In *Norris v Attorney General* [1984] IR 36, 51, O'Higgins CJ notes 'the section applies irrespective of the ages of the male persons involved and irrespective of whether the act is committed in public or private, or with or without consent'.

[21] *R v Hornby and Peaple* [1946] 2 All ER 487 and *R v Preece and Howells* [1977] QB 50.

[22] At various points in history, however, the criminal law has sought to target lesbian activity: see L Crompton, 'The Myth of Lesbian Impunity: Capital Laws from 1270 to 1791' (1981) 6 *Journal of Homosexuality* 11–25.

[23] Indecent assault (now called sexual assault) usually requires, as an essential element, that one party has not consented, unless the victim is under 15, in which case the victim's consent is not available as a defence. Criminal Law (Amendment) Act 1935, s 14. Since the Criminal Law (Sexual Offences) Act 2006, various specified sexual acts (including some lesbian sexual acts) engaged in with a person under 17 are unlawful.

[24] *Norris v Attorney General* [1984] IR 36, 59.

[25] The provisions of Art 73 of the Constitution of the Irish Free State 1922 and of Art 50 of the Constitution of Ireland 1937 carried over pre-independence laws into the law of the new states, to the extent that they were in force in Ireland at the time of the foundation of the relevant states and were not inconsistent with the constitutions thereof.

[26] See N McCafferty, 'In the Eyes of the Law: Two Consenting Adults Learn that it's an Offence Over Here' *The Irish Times* (Dublin, 12 September 1975) 13; C Hug, *The Politics of Sexual Morality in Ireland* (London, Palgrave

who were not directly prosecuted. The ban served indirectly as a justificatory backdrop for a variety of anti-gay practices including police harassment of gay men, media censorship and inaction in the face of the HIV/AIDS crisis of the 1980s.[27]

A legal challenge to these laws resulted in a 1984 Supreme Court verdict upholding their constitutionality. In *Norris v Attorney General*,[28] the Supreme Court, by a 3-2 majority, held that the laws in question did not infringe the plaintiff's constitutional rights to privacy, equality, free expression or free association. Speaking for the majority, O'Higgins CJ invoked the Constitution's strong religious references[29] in support of his argument that it could not recognise a right to engage in activity long considered by most Christian churches to be morally wrongful.[30] The Chief Justice held that the State was entitled to consider homosexual acts as inimical to family life, marriage and public health, and therefore it lay within the power of the State to restrict their practice.[31] In particular, the majority judgment implicitly stressed what it saw as the 'contagious' nature of homosexuality, O'Higgins CJ reasoning that, left unchecked, the exclusively homosexual 'may lead a mildly homosexually orientated person into a way of life from which he may never recover'.[32] Exclusive homosexuality he added 'can result in great distress and unhappiness for the individual and can lead to depression, despair and suicide'.[33]

A minority of the Supreme Court, however, recognised that while some restrictions on sexual conduct would be valid, the then existing laws encroached on the right to privacy. Justice Henchy noted how these laws 'blight[] and thwart[] in a variety of ways the life of a person who is by nature incapable of giving expression to his sexuality except by homosexual acts, and who wishes to be entitled to do so consensually in private'.[34] He concluded that the relevant laws were unconstitutional because 'by their overreach and lack of precision and of due discrimination, they trench on an area of personal intimacy and seclusion which requires to be treated as inviolate for the expression of those primal urges, functions and aspirations which are integral to the human condition of certain kinds of homosexuals'.[35] Justice Henchy noted that the 'essence of the unconstitutionality' lay not in banning homosexual conduct per se but in applying without qualification these laws 'to consenting adult males who are exclusively and obligatorily homosexual'.[36] This left the

Macmillan, 1999); P Ryan, 'The Pursuit of Gay and Lesbian Sexual Citizenship Rights, 1980–2011' in M Leane and E Kiely (eds), *Sexualities and Irish Society; A Reader* (Dublin, Orpen Press, 2014) ch 4, 108; The Government claimed in the European Court of Human Rights in *Norris v Ireland* [1988] 13 EHRR 186, at 19–20, that between 1974 and 1988 prosecutions were only mounted under these provisions in cases of non-consensual or public sex, or sex involving minors, though the State denied having a policy not to prosecute consensual adult sexual activity.

[27] K Rose, *Diverse Communities: The Evolution of Lesbian and Gay Politics in Ireland* (Cork, Cork University Press, 1994) 19–20, 22; F Ryan, '"Queering" the Criminal Law: Some Thoughts on the Aftermath of Homosexual Decriminalization' (1997) 7(1) *Irish Criminal Law Journal* 38–47; F Ryan, "We'll Have What They're Having': Sexual Minorities and the Law in the Republic of Ireland' in M Leane and E Kiely (eds), *Sexualities and Irish Society: A Reader* (Dublin, Orpen Press, 2014) 59–60.

[28] *Norris v Attorney General* [1984] IR 36.

[29] See the Preamble to the Constitution of Ireland, as well as Art 44.1 thereof.

[30] [1984] IR 36, 64.

[31] ibid 63–65.

[32] ibid 64. Earlier, at 63, he notes: 'The homosexually orientated can be importuned into a homosexual lifestyle which can become habitual.'

[33] ibid 63.

[34] ibid 72.

[35] ibid 79.

[36] ibid 78.

latter with the 'stark and (for them) inhumane choice' between abstinence and the risk of criminalisation or exposure to 'intolerance, harassment, blackmail and other forms of cruelty at the hands of those who would batten on the revulsion that such acts elicit in most heterosexuals'.[37] Justice McCarthy agreed, noting that

> a very great burden lies upon those who would question personal rights in order to justify State interference of a most grievous kind (the policeman in the bedroom) in a claim to the right to perform sexual acts or to give expression to sexual desires or needs in private between consenting adults, male or female.[38]

C. Decriminalisation

Despite the majority ruling, Henchy J's observation that these laws 'One way or the other … seem doomed to extinction'[39] proved prescient. In *Dudgeon v United Kingdom*,[40] the European Court of Human Rights (ECtHR) found the same laws (as applied in Northern Ireland) to be in breach of the right to respect for private life under Article 8 of the European Convention on Human Rights. The ECtHR reasoned that the prohibition on consensual adult sex 'by reason of its breadth and absolute character, is, quite apart from the severity of the possible penalties provided for, disproportionate to the aims sought to be achieved'.[41] A similar outcome prevailed in the ECtHR in respect of the Irish ban on male homosexual acts in *Norris v Ireland*,[42] though the latter 1988 ruling did not lead to immediate change. It was not until 1993 (the Criminal Law (Sexual Offences) Act 1993) that the Oireachtas amended the law to remove the offences of buggery as it applied to humans and gross indecency between men, replacing these offences with crimes applying specifically to the same conduct with persons under 17 years.[43] This meant that while non-consensual homosexual and heterosexual activity continue to be criminalised,[44] consensual acts between males aged 17 years or over are (generally) no longer an offence.[45] Broadly speaking, the same age of consent now applies to a variety of sexual acts, with no distinction between same-sex and opposite-sex activities (save for an exemption applying specifically to underage girls where there is a risk of pregnancy).[46]

[37] ibid.

[38] ibid 102.

[39] ibid 78.

[40] *Dudgeon v United Kingdom* (1981) 4 EHRR 149.

[41] ibid 61.

[42] *Norris v Ireland* (1991) 13 EHRR 186.

[43] The relevant laws have since been superseded by the Criminal Law (Sexual Offences) Act 2006 (as amended).

[44] For instance, non-consensual anal and oral intercourse constitute rape under s 4 of the Criminal Law (Rape) (Amendment) Act 1990. Sexual assault or aggravated sexual assault are offences under ss 2 and 3 of that Act.

[45] Consensual sexual acts causing serious harm being a possible exception.

[46] The Criminal Law (Sexual Offences) Act 2006 criminalises persons (both men and women) who engage in a variety of sexual acts with persons under the age of 17 (with more serious penalties where the victim is under 15). These sexual acts include sexual intercourse, anal or oral penetration by the penis, vaginal penetration by an object, and acts that would constitute aggravated sexual assault if committed without consent on an adult. An exemption applies in respect of girls under 17 who engage in sexual intercourse with a boy under 17; the girl is not guilty of an offence under the Act (see s 5). The Criminal Law (Sexual Offences) Act 2017 creates an exemption in respect of voluntary, non-exploitative underage sex between parties where the alleged victim is 15 or over and the defendant

III. Equality and Non-discrimination

Decriminalisation in Ireland came very late by comparison with other European jurisdictions. Nonetheless, and by contrast, Ireland was a relatively early adopter of anti-discrimination legislation. Historically, people who were gay and lesbian faced a very real threat to their livelihoods through the possibility of being dismissed from employment or otherwise being discriminated against on grounds of sexual orientation or, perhaps more commonly, for being open about their sexuality.[47] Senator David Norris noted, in 1993, that he was aware of a number of cases where people had lost their jobs due to their sexual orientation.[48] Their employers, he said, were careful not to document sexual orientation as the reason for dismissal, and the employees proved unwilling to complain of such treatment for fear of further exposure and out of a sense of shame.

It is perhaps debatable whether dismissal on this ground was in fact lawful in Ireland before 1993,[49] though there was certainly no explicit protection based on sexual orientation up to that date.[50] In England and Wales, case law suggested that, in the absence of express protection, dismissals on this basis would be lawful.[51] The criminalisation of male homosexual acts in Ireland prior to 1993 may have given an employer wishing to dismiss a gay employee some indirect justification in doing so.[52] A 1989 survey by Gay Health Action revealed a substantial fear among LGBT people of discrimination, with 11 per cent reporting actual workplace discrimination on grounds of sexual orientation.[53] While ostensibly low, the figure arguably reflects the fact that many employees may have escaped discrimination by concealing their sexuality. In the 1989 survey, less than one-third of respondents

is younger or less than two years older than the alleged victim. The age of consent in respect of sexual assault is 15 (Criminal Law (Amendment) Act 1935, s 14). The law on sexual assault applies equally to both sexes, regardless of sexual orientation.

[47] Bob Cant offers a number of accounts of workers in the UK being dismissed from employment effectively for being gay and lesbian and, critically, for being open about it at work. In the UK, for instance, Louise Boychuk lost her job in 1975 for wearing a badge with the words 'Lesbians Ignite' at work. See B Cant, 'Coming Out in the Trade Union Movement' (*Notches*, 17 October 2017), www.notchesblog.com.

[48] Seanad Éireann debate on the Unfair Dismissals (Amendment) Bill 1993, Second Stage (resumed), 31 March 1993, Vol 135 No 11, *Seanad Debates*, 1194.

[49] The Unfair Dismissals Act 1977, s 6(1), deems a dismissal unfair 'unless, having regard to all the circumstances, there were substantial grounds justifying the dismissal'. Whether homosexuality per se was a 'substantial ground' justifying dismissal prior to 1993 is debatable.

[50] In *Equality Now for Lesbians and Gay Men* (Dublin, ICCL, 1990) 38, the authors state that the Unfair Dismissals Act 1977 did 'not outlaw discrimination on the basis of sexual orientation'. They nonetheless point to an Employment Appeals Tribunal decision from 1978 finding that sexual orientation was not a substantial ground for dismissal, though they acknowledge 'we are not confident that this decision will be treated as a precedent' (ibid). They highlight the decision in *Flynn v Power* [1985] ILRM 336, where an unmarried female teacher was dismissed from employment for having a relationship with a married man, as a result of which she become pregnant outside marriage. The High Court found that her dismissal from a teaching post in a Catholic school, on religious ethos grounds, was not unlawful. The decision had, in the ICCL's words 'disquieting implications for lesbian and gay men' (ibid).

[51] In *Saunders v Scottish National Camps Association* (1980) IRLR 174, (1981) IRLR 277, the Employment Appeals Tribunal upheld the dismissal of a maintenance worker at a children's camp on grounds that he was gay. The EAT acknowledged that there was no evidence of any danger to children.

[52] Compare: *Wiseman v Salford City Council* [1981] IRLR 202.

[53] Cited by Senator David Norris, Seanad Éireann debate on the Unfair Dismissals (Amendment) Bill 1993, Second Stage (resumed), 31 March 1993, Vol 135 No 11, *Seanad Debates*, 1194–95. Senator Norris observed that Gay Switchboard Dublin had also reported high levels of fear of workplace discrimination.

reported being 'out' at work, with 58 per cent reporting a fear of discrimination if they were to be open about their sexuality at work.[54] A common coping mechanism, therefore, was to remain discreet or closeted at work.

Although Irish public opinion was not, historically, sympathetic to LGBT liberation claims, Irish political and social history arguably created a certain sensitivity to claims of discrimination. This is not to say, of course, that Irish people are less prone to discriminate on various grounds, but rather that an awareness of historical religious and ethnic discrimination has perhaps attuned Irish policy-makers more readily to the merits of anti-discrimination measures.[55] Indeed, Senator Norris himself noted in a 1993 debate:

> Despite the fact that I have on occasion rebuked the Government for their laxity on rights of sexual orientation, a humane and compassionate policy on the subject has been pursued by a Fianna Fáil Government over a number of years.[56]

From the late 1980s onwards, there was concrete evidence in Ireland of openness to change and a willingness to address unequal treatment. Spurred by trade union activism, in 1988, a Department of Finance Circular declared 'discrimination on the basis of sexual orientation or medical condition … will not be tolerated in the civil service'.[57] The Prohibition of Incitement to Hatred Act 1989 and Video Recordings Act of the same year both addressed public incitement to hatred on grounds (inter alia) of sexual orientation. It is notable that the State adopted these measures even before the decriminalisation of homosexual acts, signalling an early thawing of attitudes.

A. Anti-discrimination Laws

The 1990s also saw a range of equality laws put in place that formally prohibited discrimination on grounds of sexual orientation in a number of contexts. The Unfair Dismissals (Amendment) Act 1993 explicitly deemed dismissal to be automatically unfair on the ground of sexual orientation where it results wholly or mainly from the sexual orientation of that person.[58] The Health Insurance Act 1994 prevents premiums payable under health insurance contracts from being varied by reference (inter alia) to sexual orientation.[59] Since 1999, the law also prohibits sexual orientation discrimination in the context of employment (including access to, the terms and conditions of, promotion within and dismissals

[54] See also GLEN/Nexus, *Poverty: Lesbians and Gay Men, The Economic and Social Effects of Discrimination* (Combat Poverty Agency, 1995). A majority of respondents in that study were not 'out' at work; 39% reported self-selecting out of applying for certain jobs for fear of discrimination or harassment; 7% reported being sacked for being gay; while a further 14% left employment due to their sexual orientation.

[55] See K Rose, *Diverse Communities: The Evolution of Lesbian and Gay Politics in Ireland*, (Cork, Cork University Press, 1994) 3, who remarks that memories of the colonial history of religious and ethnic discrimination in Ireland fostered an innate aversion to inequality.

[56] Seanad Éireann debate on the Unfair Dismissals (Amendment) Bill 1993, Second Stage (resumed), 31 March 1993, Vol 135 No 11, *Seanad Debates*, 1193–94.

[57] Department of Finance Circular 12/88, Civil Service Policy on AIDS, http://circulars.gov.ie/pdf/circular/finance/1988/12.pdf.

[58] Unfair Dismissals Act 1977, s 6(2)(e) as amended by Unfair Dismissals (Amendment) Act 1993, s 5(a).

[59] As amended by the Health Insurance (Amendment) Act 2012, which prevents different treatment based on 'health risk status' which is defined as including sexual orientation.

from employment) under the Employment Equality Act 1998. European Union (EU) law also bans such discrimination in the workplace,[60] though the 1998 Act preceded EU action on this point. The Equal Status Act 2000 placed similar restrictions on sexual orientation discrimination in the context of the supply of goods, services, accommodation and education. Discrimination for these purposes includes harassment on grounds, inter alia, of sexual orientation and civil status.[61] Notably, under the Employment Equality Act and Equal Status Act a person may claim discrimination by imputation (where others believe a person to be of a particular sexual orientation, even where they are not) and by association (where a person suffers discrimination because of an association with another person who has a particular sexual orientation). Thus, for instance, an employer or service provider cannot treat a mother differently because her son is gay.

Cumulatively, these provisions have important symbolic and practical implications. Symbolically, these equality measures signify in a very powerful way a collective social disapproval of sexual orientation discrimination. It is not legitimate, they signal, to treat a person differently because that person is gay, lesbian, bisexual or indeed heterosexual. Although they apply in specific contexts, the broader message is that the former social disapproval of homosexuality is no longer to be tolerated.

Practically speaking, the Acts provide important protections to LGBT people, and remedies where discrimination occurs. The existence of these protections, particularly in the context of employment, also means that gay, lesbian and bisexual people who might formerly have feared career repercussions of coming out have a visible legal safety net. This is not to say that legal protections completely ease the process of coming out, or eliminate prejudice. Nonetheless, the former possibility of being removed from or treated differently in employment (or at least the law's uncertainty on this point) arguably played a big part in prompting LGBT people in the past to remain closeted and discreet about sexuality, particularly in the workplace.

These prohibitions also offer important protections to *heterosexuals*. A heterosexual person may justifiably take legal action where his or her sexual orientation is the basis for unfavourable treatment (subject to some limited exceptions). These laws to some extent therefore lean against the ghettoisation of LGBT communities, a process where minorities withdraw into themselves and do business only with LGBT and LGBT-friendly businesses.

B. Asylum

The Refugee Act 1996 (since replaced by the International Protection Act 2015) provided a powerful symbolic marker of the extent to which official attitudes to sexual orientation had changed in a relatively short time. The Act expressly extended the option of refugee status to a person where there is a well-founded fear of being persecuted for reasons (inter alia) of 'membership of a group of persons whose defining characteristic is their belonging to

[60] Council Directive 2000/78/EC of 27 November 2000 establishing a general framework for equal treatment in employment and occupation.

[61] 'Civil status' includes the condition of being married, separated, divorced, widowed or single, as well as being a civil partner or former civil partner. It does not expressly include being a cohabitant or former cohabitant.

the female or the male sex or having a particular sexual orientation'. Although the International Protection Act 2015 has replaced the 1996 Act, the same principles apply in the later Act.[62] In practice, securing asylum on this ground can prove challenging, due to requirements of establishing credibility and the difficulty in proving one's sexual orientation and providing evidence of likely persecution.[63] Nonetheless, the express reference to the possibility of asylum on this ground speaks volumes. A country that had only just decriminalised consensual homosexual acts three years previously was now expressly offering refuge to those who otherwise faced persecution because of their sexual orientation. Notably, the Court of Justice of the European Union has ruled against credibility assessments based on stereotypical characteristics, as well as invasively intimate techniques of establishing sexual orientation.[64] It has also concluded that a state cannot compel asylum applicants to conceal or be discreet about their sexuality in order to avoid persecution, a point affirmed by the High Court in Ireland.[65] If a person wishes to live openly as LGB, the state cannot deny that person asylum on the basis that he or she could avoid persecution in a particular state by hiding his or her sexual orientation.[66]

C. Religion and Sexual Orientation

It is interesting to speculate on the impetus for these changes. Political factors played a part. The presence of the Labour Party and Democratic Left in coalition governments in the mid-1990s arguably made a significant impact in prompting reform; both parties' socially liberal credentials made them a ready ally for LGBT causes. The election of Mary Robinson as President in 1990 also signalled a sea change in social attitudes; the election was notable not simply because of President Robinson's gender, but also her well-established credentials as a campaigner and legal advocate for socially liberal causes (including decriminalisation).[67]

The push for equality also closely tracked a demise in widespread public allegiance to the Roman Catholic Church. Although it remained a powerful social and political force throughout the 1970s and 1980s, challenges to its domination were already afoot during that era. The 1990s witnessed a number of sexual scandals involving clergy, including accusations of clerical sexual abuse of minors, coupled with claims that the Church sought to cover up or conceal such incidents. While the Church had formally warned of what it saw

[62] See International Protection Act 2015, ss 2 and 8.

[63] P Brazil, 'Applications for Asylum by Lesbian, Gay, Bisexual, Transgender and Intersex (LGBTI) Persons' (2011) 6(1) *The Researcher* 8–14. See eg *MCA v Refugee Appeals Tribunal* [2014] IEHC 504.

[64] Such as a psychologist's expert report on a person's sexual orientation; see Case C-473/16 *F v Bevándorlási és Állampolgársági Hivatal* 25 January 2018. See also Cases C-148-150/13 *A, B and C v Staatssecretaris van Veiligheid en Justitie* EU:C:2014:2406, [2015] 2 CMLR 5.

[65] Cases C-199/12, C-200/12, C-201/12 *X, Y and Z v Minister voor Immigratie en Asiel* EU:C:2013:720, [2014] 2 CMLR 16. See also *HJ (Iran) and HT (Cameroon) v Secretary of State for the Home Department* [2010] UKSC 31. This line of reasoning has also been followed in Ireland: see *MA v Minister for Justice, Equality and Law Reform* [2011] 3 IR 41; *SQ v Minister for Justice* [2013] IEHC 94; and *EPA v Refugee Appeals Tribunal* [2013] IEHC 85.

[66] See also the UNHCR Guidance Note on Refugee Claims Relating to Sexual Orientation and Gender Identity (UNHCR, 2008) 12: '25. A person cannot be expected or required by the State to change or conceal his or her identity in order to avoid persecution.'

[67] On which, see E O'Reilly, *Candidate: The Truth Behind the Presidential Campaign* (Cork, Attic Press, 1991).

as the risks of decriminalisation,[68] its moral authority throughout the 1990s waned significantly by comparison with earlier decades. The 1970s and 1980s witnessed the beginning of a struggle against Church influence in socio-sexual laws, and a gradual secularisation across Irish society. In the face of Church opposition, the Health (Family Planning) (Amendment) Acts 1985, 1992 and 1993 substantially liberalised the law on contraception in Ireland, in particular by gradually removing restrictions on access to condoms.

While religious adherence has waned in intensity in the intervening period, it is still relevant in this specific legal context. A recurring theme in legal discourse around sexual orientation is the extent to which the law should allow sincere religious viewpoints to justify derogations from the ban on sexual orientation discrimination. If, for instance, the owner of a hotel genuinely believes, for sincere religious reasons, that homosexual sexual acts are wrong, can she lawfully refuse to accommodate a gay couple? Can a religious-run school require gay employees to refrain from discussing their sexuality in front of students?

In the context of employment, the issue most notably arises in section 37(1) of the Employment Equality Act 1998.[69] This clause, as initiated, provides that a religious, educational or medical institution run by a body established for religious purposes or which seeks to promote certain religious values will not be treated as discriminating under Parts II or IV of the Act where

> (a) it gives more favourable treatment, on the religion ground, to an employee or a prospective employee over that person where it is reasonable to do so in order to maintain the religious ethos of the institution, or (b) it takes action which is reasonably necessary to prevent an employee or a prospective employee from undermining the religious ethos of the institution.

What this means is that a religious-run educational or medical institution, such as a faith-based school or hospital, may sidestep equality law in certain circumstances (though those circumstances have been greatly limited by subsequent legislation). First, where it is reasonable to do so in order to maintain its religious ethos, a school or hospital can favour a person on the ground of religion, effectively allowing a person's religious beliefs to be used as a reason for employing or not employing a person. Given that 'religion' under the Act includes 'religious outlook', one might potentially argue that a school could, for instance, favour a person with more orthodox religious views on homosexuality over a more liberal person of faith. The second clause is of particular relevance to LGBT staff, allowing a denominational school or hospital to take action to prevent its religious ethos from being undermined. Notably in this context such action must be 'reasonably necessary'.

Given the number of schools and hospitals in the State run in accordance with religious values, this clause had potentially significant implications for LGBT staff. Section 37, prior to recent reforms restricting its impact, arguably had a 'chilling effect' on teachers in particular.[70] It is arguable that the main impact of the section was to discourage LGBT teachers from discussing their sexual orientation or gender identity with students and

[68] Statement of the Irish Episcopal Conference, 'Law on Homosexuality', 22 June 1993. See also Cardinal CB Daly, *Law and Morals* (Dublin, Four Courts Press, 1993).

[69] See also Art 4 of Council Directive 2000/78/EC of 27 November 2000 establishing a general framework for equal treatment in employment and occupation. See M Coen, 'Religious Ethos and Employment Equality: A Comparative Irish Perspective' (2008) 28(3) *Legal Studies* 452.

[70] On LGBT school teachers' experiences, see S Gowran, 'See No Evil, Speak No Evil, Hear No Evil: The Experiences of Lesbian and Gay Teachers in Irish Schools' in J Deegan, D Devine, and A Lodge (eds),

colleagues, for fear of being accused of undermining the school's ethos. As such, in practice, the law arguably did not necessarily exclude people who were LGBT from faith-based schools and hospitals (though that possibility cannot be discounted) so much as police their behaviour and expression in the workplace, enforcing a 'virtual closet' in religious-run contexts.

Although section 37 still applies, the Equality (Miscellaneous Provisions) Act 2015 has greatly dented its impact. The 2015 Act amends section 37 to restrict the right to invoke religious ethos to justify discrimination in schools and hospitals that are maintained, wholly or partly, by public funding (which includes most faith-based schools).[71] The amendment is complex, but effectively it allows an institution to act against an employee so as to safeguard its ethos only in very exceptional cases where a number of rigorous conditions are met.[72] Most notably, it appears to prevent a State-funded faith-based school or hospital from discriminating against a person on the ground of sexual orientation per se.

When it comes to the provision of goods and services, the Equal Status Act 2000 allows 'differences in the treatment of person on the religion ground in relation to goods or services provided for a religious purpose' and permits school admission policies that prefer students of particular religions over others. (This right, however, has been qualified significantly by the Education (Admission to Schools) Act 2018.) 'Religion' for this purpose includes religious outlook and may therefore, possibly, be used to justify discrimination against those with more liberal religious views. The Marriage Act 2015, in section 7, exempts religious denominations and registered solemnisers of marriages who are nominated by religious bodies from any requirement to celebrate marriages of same-sex couples.

Nonetheless, outside the context of the provision of religious goods and services, the law generally does not permit religion to trump the ban on sexual orientation discrimination. Whether this infringes the right of free practice of religion is debatable. Challenges to bans on sexual orientation discrimination based on freedom of religion have generally proved unsuccessful in the UK[73] and in the ECtHR[74] and attempts to include religious exemptions in civil partnership legislation failed. While religious freedom is an important value, exemptions that allow businesses to use faith as a reason for discrimination risk significantly undermining equality laws, providing a ready excuse for most instances of sexual orientation discrimination. One would hardly tolerate using faith to justify racial discrimination, so why should sexual orientation be any different? People of faith remain free to live their own lives in accordance with their faith, believing and professing what they believe. Equality laws in this context prevent them only from penalising others for not practising the same beliefs, thus safeguarding freedom *from* religion for LGBT employees and consumers.

Primary voices: Equality, Diversity and Childhood in Irish Primary Schools (Dublin, Institute of Public Administration, 2004) 37–55; A Neary, 'Lesbian and Gay Teachers' Experiences of "Coming Out" in Irish Schools' (2012) 34(4) *British Journal of Sociology of Education* 563–602.

[71] See the Equality (Miscellaneous Provisions) Act 2015, s 11.

[72] For instance, for an action against an employee to be lawful it must be objectively justified by the institution's aim of preventing the undermining of its religious ethos, and the means of achieving that aim must be appropriate and necessary. The action must also be proportionate, rationally and strictly related to its ethos, and must be a response to conduct rather than a response (inter alia) to a person's sexual orientation. See the Equality (Miscellaneous Provisions) Act 2015, s 11.

[73] *Ladele v London Borough of Islington* [2009] EWCA Civ 1357; *Bull and Preddy v Hall and another* [2013] UKSC 73; *Lee v McArthur and Asher's Bakery* [2016] NICA 29. Though see *Lee v Asher's Bakery* [2018] UKSC 49.

[74] *Eweida v United Kingdom* [2013] ECHR 37.

IV. Relationship Recognition: Civil Partnership

The equality reforms of the 1990s were deficient in one important respect. While they protected individuals from discrimination on the basis of sexual orientation, they did little to provide legal recognition for same-sex couples. A same-sex couple who experienced discrimination in the context of employment or the provision of goods or services on the basis of their sexual orientation could both potentially argue discrimination on that ground.[75] Yet beyond that, same-sex couples had little substantive recognition in law prior to 2010. In 2000, the sole model for recognition of intimate relationships in Ireland was marriage, from which same-sex couples were excluded.[76] Cohabitation outside marriage attracted only isolated legal rights and obligations.[77] Even in the limited contexts in which cohabitants were legally recognised, such recognition appeared often to be worded in such a way as to exclude same-sex cohabitants.[78]

In 1989, Denmark became the first country in the world to allow 'registered partnerships' for same-sex couples.[79] This marriage-like union allowed same-sex couples to formalise their unions, and gain some legal recognition and protection. The idea gradually gathered pace, with similar legislation being passed in Norway in 1993, Sweden in 1995 and Iceland in 1996.[80] The Nordic states were initially outliers, but by the early 2000s various models of relationship recognition for same-sex couples had been adopted throughout parts of Europe and North America.

[75] Though, as Bruce Carolan points out in 'Judicial Impediments to Legislating Equality for Same-Sex Couples in the European Union' (2005) 40(3) *University of Tulsa Law Review* 527, 542–44, the Employment Equality Act 1998 did not provide comprehensive protection to same-sex couples. In particular, as enacted, the Act allowed unmarried couples (which, prior to 2015, included all same-sex couples) to be denied spousal employment benefits (s 34). The civil status provisions, additionally, apply (among others) to married and single persons (and now civil partners), but do not expressly make reference to cohabitants.

[76] Civil Registration Act 2004, s 2(2)(e).

[77] See generally J Mee and K Ronayne, *The Partnership Rights of Same-Sex Couples* (Equality Authority, 2000); Equality Authority, *Implementing Equality for Lesbians, Gays and Bisexuals*, (Equality Authority 2001); National Economic and Social Forum, *Equality Policies for Lesbian, Gay and Bisexual People: Implementation Issues* (Forum Report No 27, April 2003); Irish Council for Civil Liberties, *Equality for All Families* (Dublin, ICCL, 2006); J Walsh and F Ryan, *The Rights of De Facto Couples* (Irish Human Rights Commission, 2006); Law Reform Commission, *The Rights and Duties of Cohabitants*, LRC-82-2006 (Dublin, Law Reform Commission, 2006).

[78] See, for instance, as initially passed, the Domestic Violence Act 1996, s 3, the Civil Liability (Amendment) Act 1996, and the Residential Tenancies Act 2004, s 39. All three pieces of legislation extended certain rights to cohabitants but used gendered language that appeared to suggest that the couple must have been of opposite sex. See also s 3(10) and (11) of the Social Welfare Consolidation Act 2005, as enacted, which defined a spouse as including 'a man and woman who are not married to each other but are cohabiting as husband and wife'. (Since 2010, these measures have been amended to include same-sex cohabiting couples.) For instance, as initially passed, s 3(1)(b) of the Domestic Violence Act 1996 spoke of an applicant who was 'not the spouse of the respondent but has lived with the respondent as husband or wife'. Though the point is debatable, the formula appeared to presuppose that the parties had to be of opposite sex. See *Harrogate Borough Council v Simpson* (1984) 17 HLR 205 and *Fitzpatrick v Sterling Housing Association* [2001] 1 AC 27. See, however, *Ghaidan v Godin-Mendoza* [2004] UKHL 30 where the House of Lords interpreted 'living with the original tenant as his or her wife or husband' in light of the European Convention on Human Rights as including cohabiting same-sex couples.

[79] Lov nr 372/ af 01.06.1989 om registreret partnerskab, (D/341- H- ML Act no 372 of June 1, 1989 on registered partnership) (Denmark).

[80] See generally H Friðriksdóttir, 'The Nordic Model: Same-Sex Families in Love and Law' in D Gallo, L Paladini, and P Pustorino (eds), *Same-Sex Couples before National, Supranational and International Jurisdictions* (Berlin, Springer-Verlag, 2014).

In 2004, the UK introduced civil partnerships for same-sex couples, allowing same-sex couples to formalise their relationships and gain recognition and protection under the law.[81] In almost all respects, the rights and obligations flowing from civil partnership mirrored those applying to married couples. Indeed, the differences between marriage and civil partnership in the UK are minimal. Notably, the UK legislation applies to Northern Ireland, allowing same-sex couples to enter into a formally recognised union similar in almost all respects to marriage. This led some to argue that, under the terms of the Good Friday agreement, equivalent human rights measures were required south of the border.

The present author has noted elsewhere a possible 'neighbour effect' in this context, a phenomenon where innovations in the field of sexual orientation in law in one state can sometimes spill over into neighbouring states.[82] The close cultural, social and legal links between Ireland and the UK led some to question why civil partnerships should not also be available in the Republic.

The Irish Government, however, initially proved reluctant to grant relationship recognition to same-sex couples. In the rare instances where legislation recognised unmarried couples, the legislative wording often appeared to indicate a requirement or expectation that the parties be of opposite sex. Certain provisions of the Domestic Violence Act 1996, Civil Liability (Amendment) Act 1996 and Residential Tenancies Act 2004 that applied to cohabitants were, as originally drafted, worded using gendered language that appeared to require the parties to be, respectively, male and female.[83] Prior to 2010, social welfare legislation recognised only opposite-sex cohabitants.[84] Notably, the Social Welfare (Miscellaneous Provisions) Act 2004 went so far as to expressly deny recognition of same-sex couples in the context of access to administrative schemes. The legislation arose from controversy over the refusal to grant a free travel pass to the same-sex partner of a pensioner, on the basis that the pass was only available to opposite-sex partners. The Equality Authority claimed that this constituted sexual orientation discrimination under the Equal Status Act 2000, resulting in an initial reversal of the refusal. By extending a restrictive definition of spouse to various administrative schemes, however, the 2004 Act copper-fastened the exclusion of same-sex couples from recognition under the social welfare code, effectively ensuring that only married couples and opposite-sex couples would be recognised.[85]

Nonetheless, the introduction of civil partnership in the UK in 2004 and in other jurisdictions arguably added to the impetus for the adoption of a similar scheme in Ireland, though progress towards legislative recognition of same-sex couples initially proved slow. The Parental Leave (Amendment) Act 2006 extended parental leave to persons in loco parentis (including, potentially, the cohabiting same-sex partners of parents) and allowed persons in a 'relationship of domestic dependency' to claim force majeure leave

[81] Civil Partnership Act 2004 (UK).

[82] F Ryan, 'Book Review: D Gallo, L Paladini and P Pustorino (eds), *Same-Sex Couples before National, Supranational and International Jurisdictions* (Berlin, Springer-Verlag, 2014)' in (2016) 14 *International Journal of Constitutional Law (ICON)* 310, 315.

[83] See above (n 78).

[84] See s 3(10) and (11) of the Social Welfare Consolidation Act 2005.

[85] The Equal Status Act 2000 does not apply where discrimination is required by another enactment. The Minister in question argued that the restrictive measure was a temporary measure pending a comprehensive review of the social welfare system.

in respect of a partner's illness. An influential *Options Paper* on Domestic Partnership (the 'Colley' Report)[86] as well as an Irish Human Rights Commission Report on the *Rights of De Facto Couples*[87] strengthened the impetus for a substantial form of civil partnership for same-sex couples.[88] Two private members' bills on civil unions added to the momentum for reform.[89]

Notably, arguably at the insistence of the Green Party, the Programme for Government 2007–2012 made a formal commitment to the establishment of civil partnership[90] though it was vague on exactly what form that would take. The Government published a General Scheme of a Civil Partnership Bill in 2008, followed by a full bill in 2009. The bill included not just provision for civil partnership but also a scheme for the limited protection of cohabiting couples, both same-sex and opposite-sex.[91] The provisions were detailed and relatively comprehensive, though the bill fell short on the issue of couples raising children. The bill passed through the Dáil without a dissenting vote, and was opposed by only four senators. Signed by the President in July 2010, the Civil Partnership and Certain Rights and Obligations of Cohabitants Act 2010 ('2010 Act') came into force in January 2011 with the first full-notice civil partnerships celebrated in April 2011.

A. Perspectives on Civil Partnership

Conservative opposition to the 2010 Act proved relatively muted and ultimately ineffective. The Roman Catholic Church formally opposed the measures.[92] In public discourse, however, the Act's civil partnership provisions seemed to attract only relatively isolated opposition from conservatives, though its proposals on cohabitation law proved somewhat controversial among farming groups.[93]

Ironically, civil partnership probably proved to be most controversial among LGBT activists in Ireland. While some saw civil partnership as representing significant progress, others decried it as a form of second-class citizenship.[94] The former saw civil partnership, while not ideal, as offering significant legal protection and recognition for same-sex couples. Indeed, with the notable exception of provisions relating to children, almost all of the legal protections offered to spouses applies also to civil partners. The 2010 Act grants (inter alia)

[86] *Options Paper presented by the Working Group on Domestic Partnership* (Department of Justice, 2006).

[87] J Walsh and F Ryan, *The Rights of De Facto Couples* (IHRC, 2006).

[88] See also the remarks of the Minister for Justice at the launch of the aforementioned IHRC report. C Coulter, '"Equal" Status for Cohabiting Couples Ruled Out' *The Irish Times* (Dublin, 13 May 2006).

[89] Senator David Norris' Civil Partnership Bill 2004 and Labour's Civil Unions Bill 2006.

[90] Programme for Government 2007–2012 (2007) 87: 'This Government is committed to full equality for all in our society. Taking account of the options paper prepared by the Colley Group and the pending Supreme Court case, we will legislate for Civil Partnerships at the earliest possible date in the lifetime of the Government.'

[91] See Pt 15 of the 2010 Act.

[92] See 'Archbishop Warns Against Marital Rights for Cohabitation' *The Irish Times* (Dublin, 4 November 2008).

[93] S Collins, 'Partnership Bill to include Five-year Cohabitation Period for Property Rights' *The Irish Times* (Dublin, 19 May 2010) notes the concerns expressed by the Irish Creamery Milk Suppliers' Association and Irish Farmers' Association regarding the cohabitation provisions of the 2010 Act.

[94] On reactions within the LGBT community, see Ú Mullally, *In the Name of Love: The Movement for Marriage Equality in Ireland* (Dublin, The History Press Ireland, 2014).

shared home protection,[95] rights of maintenance[96] and inheritance,[97] remedies for domestic violence,[98] pension entitlements,[99] and remedies following dissolution[100] that largely match the entitlements, obligations and remedies extended to married couples. Equality laws were amended to prevent discrimination against current and former civil partners.[101] Subsequent legislative changes meant that civil partners are treated the same as spouses for the purposes of tax,[102] social welfare[103] and citizenship.[104] Moreover, civil partners are, as a matter of policy, treated the same as spouses for the purpose of immigration. The process for entering into civil partnership also largely mirrored the formalities for marriage, the most notable difference being that there was no provision for religious ministers to formalise civil partnerships.[105]

On the other hand, however close civil partnership is to marriage, it is not marriage. Notably, civil partnership does not attract the protection of Article 41 of the Constitution, which, according to Supreme Court jurisprudence, continues to apply only to families based on marriage.[106] The Supreme Court decision in *JMcD v PL and BM*[107] starkly illustrated this point, in holding that an unmarried lesbian couple and their child were not a family for the purpose of the Constitution. Civil partners, while legally recognised, are also not 'family' for the purpose of Article 41, a point underlined by the reference in Part 4 of the 2010 Act to the home of civil partners as their 'shared home' rather than the term 'family home', which was normally applied to the matrimonial home. Indeed, while there are some exceptions, the 2010 Act generally tends to avoid using the term 'family' to describe civil partners.

B. Children

The most notable weakness in the Act, as initially passed, related to couples raising children.[108] The proposition that adult same-sex relationships deserved legal recognition ultimately proved to be relatively uncontroversial. Indeed, in many respects the extent of recognition in the Act was remarkable, given how closely civil partnership mirrors the legal model for marriage. It appeared, however, that the issue of children presented something

[95] Pt 4 of the 2010 Act.
[96] Pts 5–7 of the 2010 Act.
[97] Pt 8 of the 2010 Act.
[98] Pt 9 of the 2010 Act.
[99] Ss 99–100 of the 2010 Act.
[100] Pt 12 of the 2010 Act.
[101] Ss 102–03 of the 2010 Act.
[102] Finance (No 3) Act 2011 and Finance Act 2012.
[103] Social Welfare and Pensions Act 2010.
[104] Civil Law (Miscellaneous Provisions) Act 2011, s 33.
[105] Pt 3 of the 2010 Act and Pt 7A of the Civil Registration Act 2004.
[106] See, in particular, *State (Nicolaou) v An Bord Uchtála* [1966] IR 567; *G v An Bord Uchtála* [1980] IR 32; *O'B v S* [1984] IR 316; *WO'R v EH* [1996] 2 IR 248; *JMcD v PL and BM* [2010] 2 IR 199; and *CO'S & TB v Judge Doyle & Ors* [2013] IESC 60. See also *Mokrane v Minister for Justice*, Equality and Law Reform, unreported, High Court, Roderick Murphy J, 28 June 2002, and *GT v KAO* [2008] 3 IR 567, 600.
[107] *JMcD v PL and BM* [2010] 2 IR 199.
[108] See, generally, F Ryan, *Civil Partnership and Certain Rights and Obligations of Cohabitants Act 2010* (Dublin, Round Hall, 2011) 24–29; P Dunne, 'Civil Partnership in an Ireland of Equal Marriage Rights' (2015) 53(1) *Irish Jurist* 77–99; F Ryan, 'The Rise and Fall of Civil Partnership' (2016) 19(3) *Irish Journal of Family Law* 50–62.

of a red line for the Government. Although many individual TDs and Senators pressed for recognition of civil partners raising children, the Government proved reluctant to cross that line. The reluctance may have reflected an instinctual lack of ease around facilitating the raising of children by same-sex couples, particularly male couples.

While the Act as initiated was not entirely silent in relation to the children of individual civil partners,[109] as originally passed it studiously avoided recognising or facilitating any legal relationship between a child and the child's parent's civil partner (outside the context of conflict of interests)[110] or requiring the latter to provide financially for the former. The Act as originally passed exhibits a distinct nervousness around legislating for LGBT-headed families with children. This was reflected most starkly in the provisions for dissolution of civil partnership, which (as originally passed) allowed dissolution without regard to the need for proper provision for children being raised by the couple.[111] The Act as first enacted also made no provision for maintenance of children by the parent's civil partner or remedies for the benefit of children following civil partnership dissolution. Given the emphasis in family law on the welfare and best interests of children,[112] these omissions seemed out of kilter with general legal policy.

Most of these gaps have since been removed by the Children and Family Relationships Act 2015 ('2015 Act'). The 2015 Act allows a civil partner (A) to be sued for maintenance in respect of a child of his or her civil partner (B), where A 'being aware that he or she is not the parent of the child, has treated the child as a member of the family'.[113] The 2010 Act has also been amended so that a dissolution cannot be granted unless (inter alia) 'provision that the court considers proper having regard to the circumstances exists or will be made for the civil partners and any dependent child of the civil partners'.[114] The various remedies available to former civil partners following dissolution are now also available for the benefit of dependent children of the civil partners.[115] Various other amendments allow orders to be made in respect of the child of the civil partners. Additionally, the spouses, civil partners and cohabitants of parents may apply for guardianship and custody in respect of a child of the parent after two years of co-parenting, subject to certain conditions.[116] The 2015 Act as passed contains measures that allow the spouses (including, since the Marriage Act 2015, same-sex spouses), civil partners and cohabitants of mothers who give birth following a donor-assisted conception (where eggs, sperm or embryos are donated) to be treated as legal parents of the child along with the mother.[117] These provisions, however, are (as of

[109] While the Act as enacted made no direct provision for children, it required the interests of children to be taken into account in some contexts. See s 45(3)(b)(ii) and s 129(2)(l) of the 2010 Act, which require the courts, when considering whether to grant maintenance and remedies following dissolution, to take account of any financial and other obligations a civil partner has towards his or her children. See also ss 73 and 86 of the 2010 Act, on succession.

[110] S 97, and Sch, Pt 1, on conflicts of interests, recognise that a conflict of interest may arise between a person and his or her civil partner's child.

[111] 2010 Act, s 110 (as initially enacted).

[112] See UN Convention on the Rights of the Child, Art 3; Constitution of Ireland 1937 (as amended), Art 42A; Guardianship of Infants Act 1964, s 3; Adoption Act 2010, s 19; Child Care Act 1991, s 24.

[113] See s 135 and 140 of the 2015 Act, amending ss 2 and 45 of the 2010 Act.

[114] See s 150 of the 2015 Act, amending s 110 of the 2010 Act.

[115] See eg ss 153–58 of the 2015 Act.

[116] See s 6C of the Guardianship of Infants Act 1964 as inserted by s 49 of the 2015 Act.

[117] Pt 2 of the 2015 Act.

July 2018) not yet in force (although there are signs that the current Government intends to act on this matter). The Adoption (Amendment) Act 2017 extends the right to apply to adopt a child as a couple (jointly) to civil partners and cohabitants (the right to apply as a couple had previously applied only to spouses, though this has included same-sex spouses since 2015).[118] Under that same Act, spouses, civil partners and cohabitants of a parent (A) may now adopt their stepchildren without requiring A to join in the adoption in order to preserve A's parental rights.[119]

C. The Verdict on Civil Partnership

Civil partnership represented a very significant advance on the law as it had previously stood. For the first time, same-sex couples had access to a substantial legal status that afforded (at least for the adult partners in an LGBT-headed family) significant rights and protections. With hindsight, after the marriage referendum, it is easy to forget how momentous an initiative civil partnership was. A state that had traditionally eschewed all but the most limited recognition for non-marital partners had created, from scratch, a union for same-sex couples with substantial rights, obligations and protections, modelled closely on rules that formerly had been strictly reserved to marital couples. This legal recognition was all the more remarkable given the marriage-centric focus of the Constitution. It was clear also that whether or not this was constitutionally possible, the political will did not exist among mainstream politicians in 2010 to facilitate full access to marriage. There was nonetheless a broad political consensus that the exclusion of same-sex couples from marriage required some alternative, and a reasonably substantial one at that.

It is difficult to avoid the conclusion, however, that civil partnership represented a form of second-class citizenship for same-sex couples. The implicit message was that, although entitled to substantial recognition, same-sex partners were fundamentally not worthy of and not suited to marriage. Given that marriage is widely regarded (not unproblematically) as a gold standard for romantic relationships, exclusion from marriage powerfully signalled the subordinate status of same-sex couples. No wonder, then, that some LGBT activists viewed civil partnership with less than warm enthusiasm.[120]

Purely from an administrative point of view, the introduction of civil partnership seemed profoundly inefficient. Between 2011 and 2016, 2,078 civil partnerships took place in Ireland, a small fraction of the over 127,944 marriages celebrated during the same period.[121] Given the relatively small numbers involved, administratively speaking, it would have been much simpler and more cost-efficient to allow same-sex couples access to marriage rather than creating an entirely new mechanism for relationship formation. The fact that a separate regime was designed specifically for a minority underlined the perception that the State regarded same-sex couples as unworthy of marriage.

[118] S 33 of the Adoption Act 2010 as amended by the Adoption (Amendment) Act 2017.
[119] S 58A of the Adoption Act 2010 as inserted by s 26 of the Adoption (Amendment) Act 2017.
[120] See Ú Mullally, *In the Name of Love: The Movement for Marriage Equality in Ireland* (Dublin, The History Press Ireland, 2014).
[121] See 'Marriages and Civil Partnerships' CSO Statistical Releases for 2011–2016, www.cso.ie.

In some respects, civil partnership was problematic precisely because it so closely mirrored marriage. It was modelled on and benchmarked against marriage to such extent that it could not be said to be a particularly unique or radically different institution.[122] Arguably, the understandable emphasis among activists was to make it as close to marriage as possible (so that civil partners would be fully protected, and also so that the case for denying marriage to same-sex couples would be weakened). Indeed, analyses of the deficiencies of civil partnership (including some of those conducted by the present author) usually focused on benchmarking civil partnership against marriage, the aim being to see how closely civil partnership matched marriage and where it diverged.[123] The assumption underpinning these analyses was that deviation from marriage was bad; similarity was good.

In retrospect, there was comparatively little examination of the merits of civil partnership for same-sex couples independently of its similarity to marriage. Indeed, the focus on the extent to which it matched marriage arguably detracted from an on-the-merits assessment of civil partnership. As Olivia Rundle has observed, applying heterosexual norms to same-sex couples does not necessarily result in appropriate outcomes for the latter. Same-sex couples have very particular experiences and perspectives that may demand a somewhat different approach.[124]

In particular, civil partnership matched marriage in ways that one might not have considered entirely beneficial or useful. Like divorce legislation, civil partnership legislation generally offers no formal clean financial break option on dissolution; remedies available following dissolution are, in the main, available at the time of dissolution or at any time thereafter.[125] This opens up the possibility of life-long dependency on a former civil partner when it is arguable that, in at least some cases, a clean break with the possibility of short-term rehabilitative maintenance should be made available. In short, the civil partnership regime largely replicated what was available for spouses, without any deep assessment as to whether the marital regime was suitable or appropriate to begin with. (Admittedly, however, an improved regime for civil partners might have fallen foul of the Constitution, given that measures that treat unmarried couples more favourably than similarly positioned married couples may breach the requirements of Article 41's constitutional protections for marriage and the family).[126]

[122] Compare C Stychin, 'Couplings: Civil Partnership in the United Kingdom' (2005) 8 *NY City L Rev* 543, who speaks of civil partnership as an 'awkward category that both is and is not marriage'.

[123] See eg P Fagan, *Missing Pieces* (Marriage Equality, 2012). See also F Ryan, '"Benchmarking" Civil Partnership: Comparing Civil Partnership with Marriage and Considering the Legal Position of Children' in *ICCL Seminar Series*, Vol 1, 'The General Scheme of the Civil Partnership Bill: Legal Consequences and Human Rights Implications' (Dublin, ICCL, 2009).

[124] O Rundle, 'Following the Legislative Leaders: Judicial Recognition of Same Sex Couples in Australia and New Zealand' in D Gallo, L Paladini, and P Pustorino (eds), *Same-Sex Couples before National, Supranational and International Jurisdictions* (Berlin, Springer-Verlag, 2014).

[125] While some ancillary remedies are not available to a former spouse or civil partner who has remarried or entered into a new civil partnership after divorce or dissolution, the option of seeking ancillary remedies following divorce and dissolution is generally open-ended. See, Pt 12 of the 2010 Act, particularly ss 117–128. See also D Byrne, 'Foreword' (vii) and G Shannon, 'Preface', (xi) in G Shannon (ed), *The Divorce Act in Practice* (Dublin, Round Hall, 1999); *JD v DD* [1997] 3 IR 64. The superior courts have indicated, however, a preference for finality and certainty where possible, particularly in 'big money' divorce cases (see *DT v CT* [2003] 1 ILRM 321, *WA v MA* [2005] 1 IR 1, *YG v NG* [2011] IESC 40) though the overriding requirement is that proper provision be made for children and former spouses.

[126] *Murphy v Attorney General* [1982] IR 241.

D. Superior in Some Respects?

Where there are differences between civil partnership and marriage, the default assumption seemed to be that such differences were a negative. In fact, far from signalling the deficiencies of civil partnership, at least some of these differences marked civil partnership out as an improvement on marriage. For instance, civil partnership dissolution is available within a more reasonable timeframe than divorce. A married couple must be living apart for four of the previous five years, with no prospect of reconciliation, before they may even apply for a divorce (the court must be satisfied, additionally, that proper provision has been or will be made for both spouses and any children).[127] A civil partnership, by contrast, can be dissolved after two years living apart (though the same proper provision condition also applies here).[128] Arguably, this much less prolonged living apart requirement is preferable to that which applies to marriage. Civil partners can start afresh and formalise new relationships much earlier than separated spouses. The two-year living apart requirement reduces the need for interim solutions such as judicial separation,[129] which is not available to civil partners. While the absence of judicial separation for civil partners represents a departure from the legal regime applicable to marriage, it is arguable that it is not necessary in a context where civil partners can dissolve their relationship after two years (and enter into separation agreements in the interim). Indeed, the Government has proposed a constitutional referendum to reduce the living apart requirement for divorce to two years.[130] In short, civil partnership dissolution now provides the policy template for reform of marital dissolution rules.

It is arguable also that civil partnership is more modern in several respects than marriage, and avoids some of the ideological baggage associated with the latter. Civil partnership, for instance, boasts a codified provision on annulment that greatly improves on the piecemeal and in some cases rather antiquated laws on nullity of marriage.[131] For those who favour a wholly secular and egalitarian union, civil partnership comes with no religious or patriarchal baggage. This point was emphasised by the litigants in the UK case of *Steinfeld and Keidan v Secretary of State for Education*,[132] a heterosexual couple who wished, for reasons of principle, to enter into a civil partnership rather than a marriage. Indeed, even with the availability of marriage for same-sex couples in the England and Wales, a minority of same-sex couples still opt for civil partnerships, and some heterosexual couples in that

[127] These requirements are embedded into the Constitution in Art 41.3.2. See also Family Law (Divorce) Act 1996, s 5.

[128] 2010 Act, s 110.

[129] See the Judicial Separation and Family Law Reform Act 1989.

[130] See S Bardon, 'Government Agrees on Seven Referendums in 2018 and 2019' *The Irish Times* (Dublin, 26 September 2017).

[131] 2010 Act, s 107.

[132] *Steinfeld and Keidan v Secretary of State for Education* [2017] EWCA Civ 81. In England and Wales, civil partnership is available to same-sex couples but not opposite-sex couples. Marriage, by contrast, is available to both. See Arden LJ, at 5: '[Steinfeld and Keidan] wish to formalise their relationship, but they have deep-rooted and genuine ideological objections to marriage based upon what they consider to be its historically patriarchal nature. They consider that the status of civil partnership would reflect their values and give due recognition to the equal nature of their relationship.' The majority of the Court of Appeal found that the State was entitled to have some time to evaluate the options before deciding whether to extend civil partnership to opposite-sex couples or entirely abolish it. In June 2018, however, the UK Supreme Court found that the distinction between same-sex and opposite-sex couples contravened the ECHR.

jurisdiction have campaigned for civil partnership to be open to them too. In June 2018, the UK Supreme Court held that maintaining the option of civil unions for same-sex couples (who can also marry), but excluding opposite-sex couples, is inconsistent with the European Convention on Human Rights.[133] The UK Government has since announced proposals to extend civil partnership in England and Wales to opposite-sex couples.

E. The Decline of Civil Partnership

Despite these potential advantages, civil partnership in the Republic of Ireland is no longer available to new entrants. With the introduction of marriage for same-sex couples in the Marriage Act 2015, the Oireachtas closed off the option of new civil partnerships for same-sex couples, subject to temporary transitional provisions.[134] The reasoning for this step appears to be that allowing couples who can marry to choose between civil partnership and marriage might potentially undermine the special constitutional status of marriage.[135] While existing civil partnerships are unaffected by this move, the Act allows two people in an existing civil partnership to marry each other, thus terminating the civil partnership. The closing off of civil partnership to new entrants heralds the decline of an interesting chapter in the history of family diversity in Ireland, though admittedly, there appears to have been relatively little concern in the LGBT community at the phasing out of this legal status.

V. The Path to Equal Marriage

If the Government's intention in introducing civil partnership was to short-circuit moves for marriage, it was not to have its way. The impetus for equal marriage gathered pace.

In 2001, the Netherlands became the first state in the world to extend marriage to same-sex couples.[136] Belgium followed suit in 2003, with Canada enacting similar legislation in 2005[137] and Spain and South Africa[138] in 2006. While reform in European states generally

[133] [2018] UKSC 32.

[134] Ss 8–10 of the Marriage Act 2015. Couples who had already given notice of their intention to enter into civil partnership and who had received civil partnership registration forms before the Act came into force were still allowed to enter into a civil partnership after the Act was commenced. Transitional provisions were also made for couples whose civil partnerships were delayed by unsubstantiated objections. Subject to these exceptions, no new civil partnerships are permitted after November 2015.

[135] Art 41.3.1 of the Constitution of Ireland 1937. See the comments of the Minister for Justice and Equality in *Dáil Debates* Vol 890, 23 September 2015 and *Select Committee on Justice, Defence and Equality* Vol 2, No 47, 30 September 2015. See also *MhicMhathúna v Ireland* [1989] IR 504, [1995] 1 IR 484; J Mee, 'Cohabitation, Civil Partnership and the Constitution' in O Doyle and W Binchy (eds), *Committed Relationships and the Law* (Dublin, Four Courts Press, 2007) 201–06; O Doyle, *Constitutional Law: Texts, Cases and Materials* (Dublin, Clarus Press, 2008), 226–30. P Dunne, in 'Civil Partnership in an Ireland of Equal Marriage Rights' (2015) 53(1) *Irish Jurist* 77–99 provides a very compelling counterpoint to the line of thinking.

[136] De Wet Openstelling Huwelijk (An Act on the Opening Up of Marriage) of December 21, 2000, Official Journal of the Kingdom of the Netherlands, Stb 2001, 9 (Netherlands).

[137] Civil Marriage Act 2005.

[138] *Minister of Home Affairs and Another v Fourie and Another* [2005] ZACC 19; Civil Union Act, 2006 (Act No 17 of 2006).

followed a legislative route, litigation provided the main (though not the exclusive) impetus for reform in North America. The courts in various Canadian provinces and territories provided the initial impetus for the adoption of marriage in Canada, by striking down laws banning same-sex marriage.[139] Litigation also featured prominently in the struggle for marriage equality in the United States[140] culminating in the 2015 Supreme Court decision in *Obergefell v Hodges*[141] opening up marriage to same-sex couples across the United States. Various South American states have also legislated for the marriage of same-sex couples, as have New Zealand and Australia.

In Ireland, at common law, two persons of the same sex could not contract a valid marriage.[142] The Civil Registration Act 2004 expressly stipulated that it was an impediment to marriage if the intending parties were of the same sex. This did little more, however, than codify the already existing and well-settled common law understanding of marriage as an exclusively opposite-sex union. Prior to 2015, Irish law also refused to recognise foreign marriages between people of the same sex, a stance challenged by the litigants in *Zappone and Gilligan v Revenue Commissioners*.[143] In that case, a lesbian couple, Dr Katherine Zappone and Dr Ann-Louise Gilligan, sought to have their Canadian marriage recognised in Ireland for tax purposes. The Revenue Commissioners maintained that the marriage was not a marriage in Irish law, a perspective with which the High Court agreed. Ms Justice Dunne concluded that marriage at common law, under legislation and under the Constitution (as it stood at that time) was a heterosexual union, and that there was no constitutional right to marry a person of the same sex or to require recognition of such a marriage celebrated abroad. There was, she added, little evidence of a consensus in favour of change in this context from which one might argue for an 'updating' of the interpretation of the Constitution.[144]

A. The Momentum for Equal Marriage

Although unsuccessful, the *Zappone and Gilligan* case arguably generated a momentum for the equal marriage movement in Ireland (indeed, a direct consequence of the case was the establishment of the campaigning group, Marriage Equality). Dr Zappone and Dr Gilligan ably personified the campaign for equal marriage and proved formidable and charismatic

[139] At provincial/territorial level see, for instance, *Halpern v Canada* 95 CRR (2d) 1 (Ontario Superior Court, 12 July 2002); *Hendricks v Quebec* [2002] RJQ 2506 (Quebec Superior Court, 6 September 2002); *Barbeau v British Columbia* 2003 BCCA 251 (Court of Appeal for British Columbia, 1 May 2003); *Dunbar & Edge v Yukon and Canada*, 2004 YKSC 54; at federal level: *Reference Re Same-Sex Marriage* [2004] 3 SCR 698, 2004 SCC 79.

[140] At state level see, for instance, *Baehr v Lewin* 852 P 2d 44 (Haw, 1993); *Goodridge v Dept. of Public Health*, 798 NE 2d 941 (Mass 2003); *In re Marriage Cases* (2008) 43 Cal.4th 757; *Strauss v Horton* 46 Cal.4th 364, 93 Cal.Rptr.3d 591, 207 P.3d 48; *Varnum v Brien* 763 NW 2d 862 (Iowa, 2009). At federal level see *Baker v Nelson* 291 Minn. 310 (Minn. 1971), 409 U.S. 810 (1972); *Perry v Schwarzenegger; Perry v Brown* (4 August 2010); *Windsor v New York* 570 US (2013); *Hollingsworth v Perry* 570 US (2013); *Obergefell v Hodges* 576 US___ (26 June 2015).

[141] *Obergefell v Hodges* 576 US___ (26 June 2015).

[142] *Talbot (orse. Poyntz) v Talbot* 111 Sol Jo 213 (1967, HC (England and Wales)); *Corbett v Corbett* [1971] Probate 83 (England and Wales).

[143] *Zappone and Gilligan v Revenue Commissioners* [2006] IEHC 404, [2008] 2 IR 417.

[144] Indeed, aspects of her decision suggest that an updating interpretation may not have been possible in the context of Art 41.

role models in this context. Although one might have thought that the adoption of civil partnership blunted the case for marriage, it arguably strengthened the case for further reform. If same-sex couples could acquire a status that had so many of the hallmarks of marriage, the case for exclusion from marriage became profoundly weaker.

During and after the 2011 elections, political reticence around equal marriage dissipated as various political parties came out in favour of marriage. Most notably, the Labour Party, in its 2011 election manifesto, committed the party 'to holding a referendum to provide for constitutional recognition of same-sex marriage' as well as various improvements to the law relating to civil partnership.[145] Sinn Féin[146] and the Green Party[147] also committed to equal marriage. Although Fianna Fáil and Fine Gael initially proved more reticent on the issue, the formation of the Fine Gael-Labour Government in 2011 saw a commitment to examining the issue of marriage equality in a Constitutional Convention.[148] Made up of a chairperson, 33 political representatives and a representative sample of 66 lay people, the Convention deliberated on the issue in April 2013, with 79 out of 99 members ultimately recommending constitutional change to allow civil marriage for same sex couples.[149] What was, perhaps, more remarkable was that 81 members agreed with the proposition that 'In the event of changed arrangements in relation to marriage, the State shall enact laws incorporating necessary changed arrangements in regard to the parentage, guardianship and upbringing of children'.[150] Given the reticence to address the position of civil partners raising children in the 2010 Act, this outcome was telling. It suggests that the former reluctance to contemplate children being raised by same-sex couples was dissipating.

B. Was a Referendum Required?

The Convention result arguably boosted momentum for a referendum on the topic. Whether a referendum was strictly necessary remained a cause of some academic disagreement. Changes to the Constitution of Ireland require approval by popular vote in a referendum.[151] While the Oireachtas is empowered to make law, it cannot act in breach of the Constitution.[152] The question thus arose: did the Constitution (prior to 2015) permit ordinary legislation extending marriage to same-sex couples? Several academic commentators cogently maintained that a referendum was not in fact necessary, and that the Oireachtas could extend marriage to same-sex couples by ordinary legislation.[153]

[145] *One Ireland: Jobs, Reform, Fairness* (Labour Party, 2011) 78.

[146] *There is a Better Way* (Sinn Féin, 2011) 35.

[147] *Renewing Ireland* (Green Party, 2011) 19.

[148] *Programme for Government 2011–2016* (Department of An Taoiseach, 2011) 17: 'We will establish a Constitutional Convention to consider comprehensive constitutional reform, with a brief to consider, as a whole or in sub-groups, and report within 12 months on the following: … Provision for same-sex marriage.'

[149] *Third Report of the Convention on the Constitution* (Constitutional Convention, 2013) 6.

[150] ibid.

[151] See Arts 46 and 47 of the Constitution of Ireland. Only Dáil Éireann may initiate a constitutional amendment bill, which the Oireachtas must approve, but the people of Ireland, through the referendum, have the final say on any amendment.

[152] See Arts 15.2 and 15.4 of the Constitution of Ireland.

[153] See eg B Tobin, 'Law, Politics and the Child-Centric Approach to Marriage in Ireland' (2012) 47 *Irish Jurist* 210; C O'Mahony, 'Constitution is Not an Obstacle to Legalising Gay Marriage', *The Irish Times* (Dublin, 26 July 2012); E Daly, 'Same-sex Marriage Doesn't Need a Referendum' (Human Rights in Ireland Blog, 15 July 2012).

Notably, the Constitution (prior to 2015) was silent on the topic. Article 41, as initiated, did not refer to the sex or gender of the parties to marriage. On matters of social policy, particularly controversial or socially sensitive matters, the general approach of the courts in constitutional challenges is to defer to the Oireachtas, giving it relatively wide latitude to legislate for what it considers to be in the common good.[154] Indeed, in *Zappone and Gilligan*, Ms Justice Dunne appears to suggest that the issue of legal recognition for same-sex couples was fundamentally a matter for the legislature,[155] implying that the courts would be likely to give the Oireachtas wide latitude in this context (though it is possible, from the context, that she was thinking specifically of civil partnership). She relied on the legislative passage of the Civil Registration Act 2004 (expressly ruling out same-sex marriage) as support for her conclusion that there was no consensus in favour of marriage for same-sex couples at the time of her ruling. This suggests a reliance on the legislative will, and therefore, possibly, a judicial deference towards parliamentary freedom in this context.

On the other hand, it is very difficult to argue that marriage in 1937 meant anything other than a heterosexual union. References in Article 41 and 42 to the role of women and mothers and to parents and children seemed broadly to support that view. As Dunne J noted in *Zappone and Gilligan*:

> [O]ne has to bear in mind all of the provisions of Articles 41 and 42 in considering the definition of marriage. Read together, I find it very difficult to see how the definition of marriage could, having regard to the ordinary and natural meaning of the words used, relate to a same sex couple.[156]

Similarly, in the Supreme Court in *JMcD v PL* in 2009 Denham J had remarked (albeit obiter) that 'arising from the terms of the Constitution, "family" means a family based on marriage, the marriage of a man and a woman'.[157] (Of course, with the passage of the 34th Amendment in 2015, 'family' in this context now also includes married same-sex couples.) The Attorney General's office and successive governments maintained that the Constitution would not permit legislation without a referendum. Legislative change would be risky and prone to challenge, they maintained.

Whatever the legal position, it was clear that the political view was that a referendum was necessary. It is arguable, however, that holding a referendum on the human rights of a minority is highly problematic. As Encarnación argues 'there is something inherently unseemly about putting the civil rights of any group, especially a historically oppressed one, to a popular vote'.[158] Research by Dane, Short and Healy demonstrates how the referendum debate – notwithstanding its outcome – generated considerable stress and anxiety among the LGBT population, particularly younger people.[159] While the ultimate result arguably gives considerable democratic legitimacy to equal marriage, the debate was not without negative consequences for LGBT people.

[154] See eg, *D (a minor) v Ireland* [2012] 1 IR 697; *OR and others v An tArd Chláraitheoir* [2014] 3 IR 533. See also the comments of Murray CJ in *Roche v Roche* [2010] 2 IR 321.

[155] [2008] 2 IR 417, particularly 506 and 513.

[156] ibid 506.

[157] *JMcD v PL* [2009] IESC 81, [2010] 2 IR 199, 270.

[158] O Encarnación, 'Ireland's Referendum, However Inspiring, is not a Step Forward for Gay Rights', *The Irish Times* (Dublin, 26 May 2015).

[159] S Dane, L Short, and G Healy, *Swimming with Sharks: The Negative Social and Psychological Impacts of Ireland's Marriage Equality Referendum 'NO' Campaign* (University of Queensland/Victoria University, 2016); P Karp, 'Same-sex Marriage: Irish Campaign had Negative Effect on Most LGBTI People' *The Guardian (Australia)*

C. The 2015 Referendum

The 34th Amendment to the Constitution was put to the people in a referendum held on 22 May 2015. It proposed the insertion into the Constitution of a new Article 41.4 stating that 'Marriage may be contracted in accordance with law by two persons without distinction as to their sex'.[160] The referendum saw an extraordinary, unprecedented mobilisation in favour of equal marriage. The newly formed Yes Equality (YE) campaign (made up of the Gay and Lesbian Equality Network, the Irish Council of Civil Liberties and Marriage Equality) proved remarkably successful in marshalling the LGBT community and allies (many of whom had never previously been involved in an election or political campaign) to canvass and campaign.[161] Social media played a prominent role in mobilisation, though the YE campaigners also excelled in the more traditional art of door-to-door canvassing. The narrative largely eschewed abstract human rights arguments in favour of personal narratives not only of individual LGBT people but also of family and friends thereof.

The emphasis in the No campaign was largely on the impact of same-sex couples raising children. Indeed, the anti-amendment campaign largely avoided narratives addressing the merits of homosexuality and same-sex relationships per se, instead focusing on maintaining that a father and mother together were best placed to raise a child.[162] The discourse emphasised the complementarity of male and female parenting, based on an essentialist viewpoint that fathers and mothers respectively contributed in different but complementary ways to the raising of children. This was manifested in a prominent poster campaign declaring that 'children deserve a mother and a father'. The campaign also maintained that marriage equality would prevent the courts and State from favouring what anti-amendment campaigners saw as the preferable model of child-rearing. One particularly curious line of argument suggested that the marriage amendment would, if passed, lead to a constitutional right to surrogacy, a contention that was ably debunked by several commentators.[163]

The 'No' side argument was in certain respects rather sophisticated, though perhaps only superficially so. One might argue that the State is entitled to privilege heterosexual unions because these are the only unions from which new life can be formed. A State depends for its future sustenance on new generations being born. A conjugal heterosexual union is the only form of union that can – without outside assistance – perform this task. The difficulty with this argument is that marriages are recognised as valid in law even where heterosexual couples cannot bear children – due to infertility or age – or mutually decide not to do so.[164] The argument, furthermore, ignores the fact that children are also born because of the

(Sydney, 8 October 2016); F de Londras, 'A Referendum on Marriage: Social Costs and Political Choices' (Human Rights in Ireland Blog, 11 November 2013).

[160] For an analysis of the wording, see C O'Mahony, 'Same-sex Marriage Referendum: A Legal Review', *The Irish Times* (Dublin, 22 January 2015).

[161] See G Healy, B Sheehan, and N Whelan, *Ireland Says Yes: The Inside Story of How the Vote for Marriage Equality Was Won* (Newbridge, Irish Academic Press, 2015).

[162] See eg the 'Mothers and Fathers Matter' campaign.

[163] See eg C O'Mahony, 'The Constitution, the Right to Procreate and the Marriage Referendum' (Constitution Project Blog, 21 April 2015) www.constitutionproject.ie/?p=503.

[164] In *D-e v A-g*, 1 Rob Eccl 296, Dr Lushington observed that: 'mere incapability of conception is not a sufficient ground on which to found a decree of nullity'. See also *L v L (orse. D)* (1922) 38 TLR 697, Lord Stair's *Institutions* (1832) I tit 4, para 6, *Baxter v Baxter* [1947] 2 All ER 886, and *MM (orse. G) v PM* [1986] ILRM 515.

conscious acts of lesbian and gay couples, through assisted human reproduction and surrogacy. One might also argue that there are various social benefits (such as mutual support and care) that flow from intimate unions and that the State should encourage such unions, even where children are not born of those unions.

Broadly, with some exceptions on the fringes, the No campaign avoided religious narratives and moral critiques of homosexuality. Indeed, the official No campaign sought to steer clear of what might have been perceived as an anti-homosexual narrative, even appearing (tacitly) to favour civil partnership. Although the referendum carried comfortably, it is worth bearing in mind that the 'No' side sowed enough doubt to gain a 38 per cent vote, a sizeable proportion of the voting population. The emphasis on children may have had an impact, though it is equally arguable that the 'children deserve a mother and a father' strategy may have backfired in some quarters, particularly among lone parent families.

The referendum ultimately took place on 22 May 2015. On a turnout of 60 per cent, the vote was 62 per cent in favour of the 34th Amendment, with all but one of the 43 constituencies voting in favour.[165] Urban areas returned a particularly high 'Yes' vote, but the 'Yes' vote also prevailed in more rural constituencies. Working class constituencies seemed to vote heavily in favour of the 'Yes' side. Undoubtedly, the vote also mobilised young voters in an unprecedented way, though Elkink, Farrell, Reidy and Suiter suggest that the vote would have carried even in the absence of an upsurge in the normal pattern of youth voting.[166] They suggest 'a generational shift is clearly visible in the survey data over time. Conservative Ireland is slowly dying'.[167]

There is no doubt that the vote stands as an impressive signal of social acceptance for LGB people and families. In a sense, however, the referendum takes on a wider significance. It is likely that the poll also offered an opportunity to make an implicit break with the conservative Ireland of the past. The vote, in particular, allowed electors to distance themselves from the socio-sexual scandals of earlier years, to signal that the Ireland of the Magdalene Laundries, Mother and Baby homes, of contraceptive bans, and censorship had long been abandoned. Symbolically, the vote is as clear a signal as any of the demise of the Roman Catholic Church's former social and political influence, particularly in the sphere of sexual mores.

D. Subsequent Legislation

In the wake of the referendum, two members of the public sought permission to lodge referendum petitions challenging the result on the basis of alleged flaws in the process.[168]

[165] For an analysis of the voting patterns in the referendum, see J Suiter 'Lessons from the Yes and No Campaigns' *The Irish Times* (Dublin, 27 May 2015); J Elkink et al, 'Understanding the 2015 Marriage Referendum in Ireland: Constitutional Convention, Campaign, and Conservative Ireland', UCD Geary Working Paper 2015/21, 9 November 2015.

[166] J Elkink et al, 'Young People Voted in Droves for Marriage Equality in Ireland: Equality Would have Won Without Them' *Washington Post* (Washington, 30 June 2015) http://www.washingtonpost.com/blogs/monkeycage/wp/2015/06/30/young-people-voted-in-droves-for-marriage-equality-in-ireland-equalitywould-have-won-without-them/.

[167] ibid.

[168] *Lyons v Ireland* [2015] IESCDET 38.

The litigation was ultimately unsuccessful, though it delayed the passage of marriage legislation by several months.

Given the very momentous and ground-breaking nature of the changes effected by it, the Marriage Act 2015 proved to be a remarkably short Act. It formally removed the former impediment to marriage based on identity of sex, thus clearing the way for the marriage of same-sex couples.[169] The Act also extended the prohibited degrees of relationship (banning marriage between close relatives) to relatives of the same-sex.[170] It made provision for the recognition of foreign marriages between couples of the same sex.[171] As previously noted, the 2015 Act closed off civil partnerships to new entrants[172] and exempted religious denominations from having to celebrate marriages between persons of the same sex.[173] This means that while churches and faiths may choose to marry couples of the same sex, they cannot be compelled to do so, either under the 2015 Act or any other enactment (including the Equal Status Act 2000). It also provides for the recognition of foreign marriages between same-sex couples.

The marriage referendum seemed to embolden the government in other ways. The year, 2015, also saw the passage of the ground-breaking Gender Recognition Act 2015, allowing legal recognition of a person's preferred gender (discussed in Chapter 11). The Gender Recognition Bill 2014, as originally initiated, had proposed that gender recognition would be open only to people who were not married or in a civil partnership (a 'single status requirement') and only if a doctor certified that the applicant was transitioning or had transitioned to that person's preferred gender.[174] The Government initially seemed stubbornly intent on insisting on the latter requirement, thus making legal gender recognition subject to medical approval and control. In the wake of the marriage referendum, however, the Government quite suddenly relented, removing the requirement of medical certification, and adopting a 'self-declaratory' model. As noted elsewhere in this collection, adult applicants may now apply for gender recognition simply by making an autonomous personal declaration, with no requirement for any evidence of transition, social, physical or otherwise. Additionally, the Act's 'single status requirement' was never brought into force and was ultimately repealed by the Marriage Act 2015.[175] Arguably, the strong 'Yes' vote signalled to politicians either that they could afford to be generous or that an overly cautious approach to LGBT rights would no longer be tolerated.

VI. Unfinished Business?

A distinct risk arises that one might confuse legal progress with social acceptance. Formal equality does not automatically translate into equality of outcomes and experiences. The Eurobarometer survey shows that people in Ireland are among the most accepting in Europe

[169] Marriage Act 2015, s 4.
[170] ibid s 5.
[171] ibid s 12.
[172] ibid pt 4.
[173] ibid s 7.
[174] Gender Recognition Bill 2014 as initiated by Seanad Éireann, s 8(2)(b), s 9(1)(f)(i) and (g).
[175] Gender Recognition Act 2015, s 9(2)(b) and s 10(1)(f)(i) were both repealed by Marriage Act 2015, s 24.

of people who are LGBT.[176] Nonetheless, despite considerable social and legal strides, people who are LGBT remain vulnerable in certain respects, particularly those who are younger as well as those who are transgender and intersex. In particular, mental health outcomes for younger LGB and transgender populations are decidedly less positive than for their straight and cisgender counterparts.[177] Challenges also remain in relation to sexual health among men who have sex with men. An absence of comprehensive hate crime legislation also compromises Ireland's position as a leader in LGBT rights.[178] Notwithstanding highly progressive gender recognition legislation, Ireland provides no means of gender recognition for a vulnerable population of transgender people who are under 16 years old, and cleaves to a gender binary that denies full recognition to people who are of non-binary gender. Even with the extension of marriage to same-sex couples, some of the underlying rules applicable to marriage remain distinctly heteronormative.[179]

In the legal context, some gaps remain in relation to parenting by same-sex couples. Civil partners and long-term cohabitants, as well as same-sex spouses, may now apply to adopt their stepchildren[180] and may apply jointly to adopt children.[181] Additionally, same-sex partners and spouses of parents (inter alia) may acquire guardianship and custody rights.[182] Nonetheless, the position of lesbian couples who parent children through assisted human reproduction (AHR) remains (in July 2018) legally precarious. Parts 2 and 3 of the Children and Family Relationships Act 2015 will, once implemented, address the situation of a woman who gives birth to a child conceived using donor eggs, or sperm, or who gives birth following the implantation of a donated embryo. In such cases, and subject to various conditions, the parents of the child will be the mother and her spouse (husband or wife), civil partner or cohabitant. Subject to the consent of all parties, the donor will not be treated as a parent of the child. These provisions are particularly relevant to lesbian couples who have children through AHR. Nonetheless, over three years after their enactment, these provisions are (as of July 2018) not yet in force. (The Government has indicated its intention to bring these provisions into operation in late 2018.) Despite proposals for reform,[183] laws concerning parentage following surrogacy are also not yet in place (as is discussed in Chapter 7).

It is arguable also that the legal changes made in recent years predominantly favour middle class LGBT populations, and may be less favourable to more marginalised LGBT people[184] (despite the myth of the 'pink pound', research shows that LGBT populations,

[176] Eurobarometer 437 (Special) 2015.

[177] A Higgins et al, *The LGBT Ireland Report* (GLEN/Belongto, 2016).

[178] A Haynes, J Schweppe, and S Taylor, *Critical Perspectives on Hate Crime: Contributions from the Island of Ireland* (London, Palgrave Macmillan, 2017).

[179] For instance, adultery as a ground for judicial separation and the concept of consummation in nullity law (inability to consummate ordinarily renders a marriage voidable) both apply only acts of heterosexual sexual intercourse. See F Ryan, '"Playing Away from Home on an Uneven Pitch?" Spouses, Civil Partners and Adultery in Irish and UK Law' (2014) 17(2) *Irish Journal of Family Law* 41–51. See also *UF v JC* [1991] 2 IR 330.

[180] Adoption Act 2010, s 58A, as inserted by the Adoption (Amendment) Act 2017.

[181] Adoption Act 2010, s 33, as amended by the Adoption (Amendment) Act 2017.

[182] Guardianship of Infants Act 1964, s 6C and s 11E, as inserted by the Children and Family Relationships Act 2015.

[183] *Report of the Commission on Assisted Human Reproduction* (Department of Health and Children, 2005); General Scheme of the Assisted Human Reproduction Act 2017.

[184] See R Colker, 'Marriage' (1991) 3(2) *Yale Journal of Law and Feminism* 321.

on average, can be particularly vulnerable to poverty[185]). For instance, the tax and pension advantages of marriage and civil partnership may be of little consequence to couples on low incomes and single LGBT people. Changes to social welfare law[186] provided some benefits for same-sex couples, but in some cases, legal recognition *reduces* the payments available to a couple.[187]

Additionally, while civil partners and same-sex married couples, in principle, enjoy equal rights in relation to pensions (and must be treated the same as opposite-sex spouses), some pension schemes deny pension-holders recognition of their civil partners and spouses where the legal relationship is formalised after retirement or after reaching a particular age.[188] This is despite the fact that the State did not recognise same-sex unions prior to some older pension-holders' retirement dates, thus preventing them, prior to retirement or reaching a specific age, from meeting pension scheme requirements relating to spouses/civil partners. In *Parris v TCD*[189] the Court of Justice of the European Union ruled that denying spousal pension benefits to same-sex partners because they did not marry or enter into a civil partnership before reaching a particular age or before retiring (even where the law did not allow them to do so prior to reaching that age or retiring) did not constitute sexual orientation or age discrimination under EU law.[190] The Court also dismissed the claim of compound discrimination based on both factors combined.

The extension of marriage to same-sex couples, in addition, does little to address the need to provide greater recognition for a diversity of family types outside of marriage. Indeed, it is arguable that the discourse of equal marriage potentially has further privileged and exalted marriage as the ideal model of relationship, to the exclusion of alternative family types. One might argue, of course, that the underlying emphasis in the marriage referendum debate was on equality and diversity. A High Court judge has recently suggested that the marriage amendment and other social and legal developments[191] potentially provide the basis for a more expansive constitutional understanding of the inherent constitutional rights of members of non-marital families.[192] Nonetheless,

[185] See eg MVL Badgett, LE Durso and A Schneebaum, *New Patterns of Poverty in the Lesbian, Gay, and Bisexual Community* (Williams Institute, 2013) and TNT Brown, AP Romero and GJ Gates, *Food Insecurity and SNAP Participation in the LGBT Community* (Williams Institute, 2016).

[186] The Social Welfare and Pensions Act 2010 formally recognises same-sex cohabiting couples and civil partners as couples for social welfare purposes. Previously, social welfare law recognised only spouses and opposite-sex cohabiting couples.

[187] Because spouses, civil partners and cohabiting couples are means tested on their joint income as a precondition to certain social welfare payments, legal recognition of their relationship may result in lower social welfare payments. The One Parent Family Payment is not available to cohabiting parents. While social welfare recipients may claim for an adult dependent, where both parties receive certain social welfare payments, the total payment to the couple may be capped.

[188] While the Government has promised to address this issue, a proposal to rectify this, in certain circumstances, in the General Scheme of the Social Welfare and Pensions Bill 2017 (Head 14) has not been enacted and was not replicated in the Social Welfare, Pensions and Civil Registration Bill 2017, at least as initiated. The Government has indicated, however, that it intends to introduce amendments at committee stage of the 2017 bill to address the issue. See also the Pensions (Equal Pension Treatment in Occupational Benefit Scheme) (Amendment) Bill 2016.

[189] *Parris v TCD* C-443/15 [2017] 2 CMLR 17.

[190] Specifically, Council Directive 2000/78/EC of 27 November 2000 establishing a general framework for equal treatment in employment and occupation.

[191] Such as the 31st Amendment to the Constitution (new Art 42A) confirming the natural rights of *all* children.

[192] *IRM v Minister for Justice and Equality* [2016] IEHC 478 (Humphreys J) 99. On appeal, the Supreme Court declined to comment definitively on this point, as it was not relevant to the outcome ([2018] IESC 14).

to date, Supreme Court jurisprudence consistently confines the family for the purpose of Article 41 of the Constitution to the family based on marriage alone.[193] While the 2010 Act improved legal protection for vulnerable long-term cohabitants, couples who wish to access various substantial rights and protections have little option but to marry. The push for marriage, one might argue, has displaced a radical queer social and political vision (encompassing the aspiration to dignity, freedom and equality for all and solidarity with marginalised and oppressed peoples) in favour of more conservative, assimilationist goals.[194] Aoife Neary, for example, argues that 'mobilizing a politics of change and a concept of "equality" that is based on normalization and sameness simultaneously forefronts and reproduces a certain model of "acceptable" sexual-citizen subject while reassigning "others" with peripheral status'.[195] '[A] model of progressive change based on normalization and sameness' she concludes, 'has implicit heteronormative constraints and consequences'.[196] Indeed, one might argue that institutions such as civil partnership and marriage serve to police and constrain LGBT populations.[197] The focus on marriage has also served to mask the relatively privileged legal and social position of romantic unions as compared with non-conjugal household units. Why should the law treat a married couple any more favourably in law and in policy than other family members who provide caring functions within a household?[198]

Nonetheless, one cannot deny the extraordinary sea change in the law and social policy as it applies to LGBT populations. Over the space of 30 years, Ireland has transformed from what Chris Robson termed 'on paper at least, the worst legal regime in Western Europe for lesbians and gay men'[199] to a state that not only allows gay couples to marry but entrenches the right to do so in its Constitution. It would be a mistake, however, to imagine that these changes were the product of inevitable or irresistible progress. They reflect the brave incremental efforts of a great many dogged and determined advocates and campaigners. Nor should we assume that the task of achieving full legal protection for and social acceptance of people who are LGBT is complete.

[193] See above (n 106).

[194] See eg R Conrad (ed), *Against Equality: Queer Critiques of Gay Marriage* (Against Equality Press, 2010) and I Kamikaze, 'I Used To Be an Activist, But I'm Alright Now' in Í O'Carroll and E Collins (eds), *Lesbian and Gay Visions of Ireland; Towards the Twenty-first Century* (London, New York, Cassell, 1995) 110–21.

[195] A Neary, 'Civil Partnership and Marriage: LGBT-Q Political Pragmatism and the Normalization Imperative' (2016) 19(7) *Sexualities* 757–79, 769.

[196] ibid 774.

[197] See C Stychin, '"A Stranger to its Laws": Sovereign Bodies, Global Sexualities and Transnational Citizens' (2000) 27(4) *Journal of Law and Society* 601–25.

[198] See C Stychin, 'Couplings: Civil Partnership in the United Kingdom' (2005) 8 *NY City L Rev* 543.

[199] C Robson, 'Anatomy of a Campaign' in Í O'Carroll and E Collins (eds), *Lesbian and Gay Visions of Ireland; Towards the Twenty-first Century* (London, New York, Cassell, 1995) 47–59.

6

Law and Parental Rights

BRIAN TOBIN

I. Introduction

This chapter examines whether gender discrimination exists in relation to the acquisition of the fundamental parental rights of guardianship, custody and access in Ireland. While an unmarried mother is automatically a guardian of her child once it is born, the Guardianship of Infants Act 1964, as amended by the Status of Children Act 1987 ('1987 Act'), only allows an unmarried father to apply to the court to be appointed a guardian of his child. This chapter will analyse the initial judicial unease with guardianship applications by unmarried fathers in the early years, post-1987, and the sea change that has occurred in judicial attitudes to such applications in recent times. The chapter will also demonstrate that further statutory innovations in the area of guardianship over the past 20 years have had the effect of giving rise to a legislative approach that in practice favours guardianship rights only for those unmarried fathers who have some form of a relationship with the child's mother. Rather than introducing automatic guardianship on the birth of the child and finally equalising the position of the unmarried father with that of the unmarried mother, the prevailing legislative approach to guardianship is largely aligned with the early, conservative judicial approach that fully endorsed differentiating between unmarried fathers depending on the strength of the relationship with the child's mother. This chapter will demonstrate that the prevailing legislative approach is out of sync with the modern, flexible, child-centric judicial approach that sees beyond gender and relationship status in the context of guardianship applications. Finally, this chapter will examine whether there is any clear gender bias by judges when deciding custody and access cases in the courts.

II. Guardianship under Irish Law – *Prima Facie* Gender Discrimination

The concept of guardianship relates to the rights and duties of a person as regards making decisions about a child's overall welfare. A person who is a guardian of a child has the right and duty to decide how the child will be raised. A guardian makes decisions about the most significant aspects of a child's upbringing, such as where the child will live and be educated, health requirements, religion and so forth. In Ireland, natural parents have different legal rights in relation to their children depending on whether they are married or unmarried. Where children are born to married parents or, indeed, where their parents subsequently marry, Irish law confers equal and joint rights of guardianship on both the mother and the father. This statutory equality between married parents in the context of guardianship is provided for under the Guardianship of Infants Act 1964 ('1964 Act').[1] It complies with the express constitutional protection of the marital family under Article 41.3.1.

Where a child is born to unmarried parents, however, only the natural mother enjoys an automatic right of guardianship.[2] The unmarried father is expressly excluded from enjoying automatic rights by virtue of the 1964 Act.[3] By contrast, the unmarried mother's right to automatic guardianship of her child is recognised, and it is a personal right under Article 40.3 of the Constitution.[4] The unmarried father does not enjoy an automatic statutory or constitutional right of guardianship in respect of his biological child at the time of the child's birth, and this remains the case despite legislative amendments to the law in this area over the last 30 years. Thus, the natural, unmarried father of a child is prima facie discriminated against under Irish law on the grounds of his gender and relationship status.

III. Judicial Unease with Early Legislative Innovation

The Status of Children Act 1987 amended the Guardianship of Infants Act 1964 and granted an unmarried father the right to apply to the court to be appointed a guardian of his child.[5] This was the first statutory reform to benefit unmarried fathers in the context of guardianship. However, it was for the court to decide whether an unmarried father making such an application should be appointed as a guardian. In the early case law following the introduction of this statutory entitlement, the Irish superior courts treated the unmarried father with a high degree of circumspection.[6] In *JK v VW*, Finlay CJ in the Supreme Court made it clear that the unmarried father does not, as a result of the 1987 Act, enjoy an automatic legal right to be appointed a guardian; he merely has the right to *apply* to be so appointed.[7] Chief Justice Finlay also stated that 'although there may be rights of interest or concern arising from the blood link between the father and the child, no constitutional right to

[1] Guardianship of Infants Act 1964, s 6(1), provides that 'the father and mother of an infant shall be guardians of the infant jointly'.

[2] The definition of guardianship adopted by Finlay Geoghegan J in *RC v IS* [2003] 4 IR 431 is that it 'describes the group of rights and responsibilities automatically vested in the parents of a child born within marriage and in the mother of a child born outside marriage in relation to the upbringing of a child'. This useful definition was adopted by Finlay Geoghegan J from A Shatter, *Family Law*, 4th edn (Dublin, Bloomsbury Professional, 1997) 531.

[3] The definition of 'father' in s 2 of the 1964 Act does not include the natural father of a child born outside of wedlock. Therefore, such a father cannot fall within the ambit of s 6(1).

[4] *State (Nicolaou) v An Bord Uchtála* [1966] IR 567. Under the Constitution, it is a personal right under Art 40.3 rather than a familial right under Art 41 because, in *State (Nicolaou) v An Bord Uchtála* [1966] IR 567, 644, Walsh J in the Supreme Court stressed that 'the mother of an illegitimate child does not come within the ambit of Articles 41 and 42 of the Constitution'.

[5] S 12 of the Status of Children Act 1987 inserted s 6A into the Guardianship of Infants Act 1964.

[6] See *JK v VW* [1990] 2 IR 437; *WO'R v EH* [1996] 2 IR 248.

[7] *JK v VW* [1990] 2 IR 437, 446 (Finlay CJ).

guardianship in the father of the child exists'.[8] The Chief Justice made it abundantly clear that the outcome of an unmarried father's guardianship application could vary significantly depending on the extent of his relationship with the child's mother:

> The range of variation would, I am satisfied, extend from the situation of a child conceived as a result of casual intercourse, where the rights might well be so minimal as practically to be non-existent, to the situation of a child born as a result of a stable and established relationship and nurtured at the commencement of his life by his father and his mother in a situation bearing nearly all of the characteristics of a constitutionally protected family, when the rights would be very extensive indeed.[9]

Thus, the early judicial approach to guardianship applications was to equate the probability of success regarding such applications as being dependant on the strength of the relationship between the child's unmarried parents. In his judgment, Finlay CJ seems to regard only those unmarried fathers in a relationship akin to a marriage with the child's mother as deserving of success in the courts. It would appear that an unmarried father's application for guardianship could easily have been dismissed by the court where the child was conceived through casual sexual intercourse. This is striking when one considers that less than two decades later, the Supreme Court had radically altered its position and was open to the possibility of appointing as a guardian a man who had never even had sexual intercourse with the child's mother and who was envisaged as merely a sperm donor.[10] As we shall see, under the judicial approach, the strength of a man's relationship with the child's mother is no longer a significant obstacle to a potentially successful guardianship application.[11]

IV. An Alignment of Judicial Attitudes and Legislative Policy Concerning Guardianship?

Although the reform introduced by the 1987 Act enabled an unmarried father to apply to the court to be appointed a guardian of his child, this meant that all unmarried fathers had to endure the time and expense of a court application, even those unmarried fathers who were in the courts' preferred, stable, 'marriage-like' relationship with the child's mother. Therefore, section 4 of the Children Act 1997 ('1997 Act') inserted a new section 2(4) into the 1964 Act. In so doing, it introduced a straightforward procedure to allow an unmarried father to become a guardian. This reform obviated the need for an application to the court by enabling the mother and father, by agreement, to make a statutory declaration conferring the status of guardian on the father. Although Crowley observes that this declaration is 'the easiest way for the unmarried natural father to become a guardian of his child',[12] the obvious drawback is that the child's mother has to consent to the making of the declaration appointing the father as guardian. Therefore, the unmarried father must have an amicable relationship with the child's mother.

[8] ibid 447 (Finlay CJ).
[9] ibid.
[10] *McD v L* [2009] IESC 81.
[11] *MR v SB* [2013] IEHC 647; *McD v L* [2009] IESC 81.
[12] L Crowley, *Family Law*, 2nd edn (Dublin, Thomson Round Hall, 2013) 91.

Similarly, the most recent reform in this area also makes the unmarried father's guardianship rights dependent on a 12-month cohabiting relationship with the child's mother. Section 43 of the Children and Family Relationships Act 2015 ('2015 Act') amended section 2 of the 1964 Act to provide for automatic guardianship in the case of an unmarried father who has cohabited with the child's mother for a period of 12 months, including cohabitation of *at least* three months after the birth of the child.[13] Thus, the unmarried father's right to guardianship under the 2015 Act depends on his having enjoyed a somewhat lengthy and durable cohabitating relationship with the child's mother. Shannon asserts that this guardianship reform introduced via the 2015 Act means that '[f]or the first time in Irish law, a non-marital father will *automatically* be the guardian of his child'.[14] However, it is not really an 'automatic' guardianship right when guardianship is only acquired *at least* three months after the birth of the child, rather than immediately upon birth.

The original guardianship proposal contained in the General Scheme of the Children and Family Relationships Bill 2014 was more favourable to unmarried fathers cohabiting with the mother. Part 7 of the original General Scheme provided that an unmarried father, who was cohabiting with the child's mother for at least 12 consecutive months *before* the child's birth, which cohabitation ended (if applicable) not less than 10 months before the child's birth, would, akin to the mother, acquire automatic guardianship rights on the birth of the child.[15] This proposal would still only have benefitted unmarried fathers cohabiting with the mother. However, at least that particular cohort would have acquired automatic guardianship rights upon the birth of the child if it had been enacted, thus somewhat reducing gender discrimination between unmarried parents regarding the acquisition of guardianship rights.

Thus, since 1997, statutory reforms to make it easier for an unmarried father to become a guardian of his child by obviating the need for a court application have stopped short of equating his position with that of the unmarried mother by granting him automatic guardianship rights upon the birth of the child. Further, his right to become a guardian under the reforms introduced by the 1997 and 2015 Acts is very much dependent on the quality of his relationship with the child's mother. In this respect, it is interesting to note that the 1997 and 2015 reforms bring the legislature's approach to guardianship very much in line with the judicial approach as enunciated by Finlay CJ in *JK v VW* in 1990.[16] The legislative reforms introduced in 1997 and 2015 only benefit unmarried fathers insofar as they are on good terms with, or are cohabiting with, the child's mother, and therefore these reforms, while beneficial to some, still leave a large number of unmarried fathers who must have recourse to the courts in order to acquire guardianship rights in relation to their child.

By continuing to discriminate against fathers on grounds of gender and relationship status, the statutory approach to guardianship rights for natural, unmarried fathers is out of sync with other progressive statutory developments concerning guardianship. The Children

[13] S 43 was commenced on 18 January 2016 by virtue of the Children and Family Relationships Act 2015 (Commencement of Certain Provisions) Order 2016. This section also provides that an unmarried father who satisfies this 12-month cohabitation period is also automatically recognised as the 'father' of his child.

[14] G Shannon, *Children and Family Relationships Law in Ireland: Practice and Procedure* (Dublin, Clarus Press, 2016) 58.

[15] See pt 7 of the General Scheme of the Children and Family Relationships Bill 2014.

[16] *JK v VW* [1990] 2 IR 437.

and Family Relationships Act 2015 extended the right to apply to the courts to be appointed a guardian to non-biological social parents.[17] A spouse, civil partner or cohabitant[18] of the child's natural parent can now apply to be appointed a guardian once they have shared with the natural parent responsibility for the child's day-to-day care for a period of more than two years. Parts 2 and 3 of the 2015 Act purport to regulate parentage of a child born via donor assisted human reproduction (DAHR).[19] In this context, the unmarried father is treated even less favourably than the non-biological, intended parent of a child born through DAHR. Where a woman conceives a child through DAHR and her husband or same-sex civil partner is not a biological parent of the child but has consented to parentage under the 2015 Act, then that person will be a second, automatic guardian of the child once it is born.

The guardianship reforms for non-biological intended parents that were introduced under the 2015 Act serve to accentuate the unfairness of the natural, unmarried father's position. These reforms sanction automatic guardianship rights for non-biological intended parents because of their relationship status with the child's mother (marriage or civil partnership). In contrast, the 2015 Act prima facie discriminates against the natural, unmarried father by denying him automatic guardianship on the birth of his child because, by not being part of a State-sanctioned registered relationship,[20] he lacks a relationship status in relation to the mother.[21]

V. Guardianship in the Courts Today: Beyond Gender, Biology and Relationship Status

It is disappointing that the Children and Family Relationships Act 2015 did not go further and eliminate the subsisting, prima facie statutory discrimination by finally equating the position of the unmarried father with that of the unmarried mother as regards guardianship, especially when one considers the recent liberalisation of the judiciary's attitude towards guardianship applications that have come before the courts pursuant to section 6A

[17] Children and Family Relationships Act 2015, s 49 (inserting s 6C into the Guardianship of Infants Act 1964).

[18] A cohabitant must have been cohabiting for over three years with the child's biological parent in order to be eligible.

[19] However, pts 2 and 3 of the 2015 Act are not yet in force. See B Tobin, 'We still don't have crucial parental rights for same-sex couples' (*The Journal*, 29 May 2017) www.thejournal.ie/readme/opinion-we-still-dont-have-crucial-parental-rights-for-same-sex-married-couples-3410543-May2017/. However, in July 2018, the Children and Family Relationships (Amendment) Bill 2018 was passed by the Houses of the Oireachtas in order to facilitate commencement of Parts 2 and 3 of the 2015 Act in the Autumn/Winter of 2018.

[20] Civil partnership was only available to same-sex couples. However, as Fergus Ryan notes in Chapter 5 of this volume, the introduction of marriage equality spelled the end for civil partnership. S 8 of the Marriage Act 2015 repealed s 2(2A) of the Civil Registration Act 2004, which was inserted by s 7(2) of the Civil Partnership and Certain Rights and Obligations of Cohabitants Act 2010. This means that it is no longer possible to enter into a civil partnership in Ireland post-marriage equality (subject to transitional provisions). The repeal of s 2(2A) does not affect any subsisting civil partnership; such unions will continue to be governed by the 2010 Act. An unmarried father would have been unable to enter into a civil partnership with the child's mother in any event.

[21] Under the 2015 Act the unmarried father's position as regards automatic guardianship is identical to that of a cohabiting, non-biological intended parent in a DAHR scenario. A cohabitant of the mother of the child in a DAHR scenario who has consented to parentage will be a guardian of the child where that person and the mother have cohabited for 12 consecutive months, including at least three months after the birth of the child. See Children and Family Relationships Act 2015, s 49 (inserting s 6B into the Guardianship of Infants Act 1964).

of the 1964 Act.[22] Currently, not only are the vast majority of unmarried fathers successful in their guardianship applications before the courts,[23] but recent case law demonstrates that the courts are even open to appointing as guardians men who were expected to be mere sperm donors or, in certain exceptional cases, men who have acted *in loco parentis* for a significant period of time but who in fact have no biological connection to the child.

The case of *McD v L* involved a known sperm donor[24] who entered into an agreement with a female same-sex couple to provide sperm that would enable them to have a child together.[25] It was agreed between the parties in the sperm donation contract that the female same-sex couple would be the child's 'parents' and the known sperm donor would act in a more limited role, akin to that of a 'favourite Uncle'.[26] Subsequently, the known donor supplied sperm, and this was used by one member of the female same-sex couple to conceive a child. Following the birth of the child the parties had a falling out and the known sperm donor, as the natural father, sought guardianship of and access to the child by virtue of the provisions of the Guardianship of Infants Act 1964.[27] There had been limited contact between the sperm donor and the child following the birth and so a limited bond had been established. Previous judgments of the superior courts had indicated that such a limited bond between a natural father and his child was likely to be anathema to a ruling in his favour in a guardianship application before the courts.[28] Indeed, in the High Court, Hedigan J denied the known sperm donor both guardianship and access rights but, on appeal, the Supreme Court granted him access to the child and even embraced the possibility of his being appointed a guardian of the child in changed circumstances in the future.

The Supreme Court regarded the situation of a known sperm donor as akin to that of a natural father because throughout the judgment the appellant was referred to as 'the father', and Denham J made it quite clear that 'The father, who was a sperm donor, has rights as a natural father, as provided for in s.6A of the Guardianship of Infants Act 1964, as amended, to apply to be appointed guardian of the child'.[29] Consequently, as Fennelly J acknowledged, 'it is not suggested, in the present case, that the father is *any less* the biological father of the child by reason of being a sperm donor' (emphasis added).[30] Justice Denham also recognised the appellant as 'the biological father' and concluded that 'there is benefit to a child, in general, to have the society of its father'.[31] Justice Fennelly accorded significant weight to

[22] See Guardianship of Infants Act 1964, s 6A (inserted by Status of Children Act 1987, s 12).

[23] In 2014, 2121 guardianship applications by unmarried fathers were granted, with a mere 46 being refused; 526 applications were withdrawn/struck out. See Courts Service Annual Report 2014 www.courts.ie/Courts.ie/library3.nsf/(WebFiles)/76D5C7C737385EFF80257E91002F3D7A/$FILE/Courts%20Service%20Annual%20Report%202014.pdf.

[24] A known sperm donor is a man known to the child's natural mother and its non-biological intended parent. He may be a friend, neighbour, colleague, acquaintance, etc. A non-anonymous sperm donor is a man who is not known to the child's natural mother and its non-biological intended parent. However, identifying information about this man will be recorded by a DAHR facility when he donates sperm and such information may be accessed by the child upon reaching adulthood.

[25] *McD v L* [2008] IEHC 96 (High Court); [2009] IESC 81, [2010] 1 ILRM 461 (Supreme Court).

[26] The superior courts held that the sperm donation contract was unenforceable. Thus, it would appear that in Ireland a known donor cannot be contractually excluded from pursuing parental rights in relation to the child.

[27] See Guardianship of Infants Act 1964, s 6A (inserted by Status of Children Act 1987, s 12), and s 11.

[28] See generally *JK v VW* [1990] 2 IR 437; *WO'R v EH* [1996] 2 IR 248.

[29] *McD v L* [2010] 1 ILRM 461, 493.

[30] ibid 523.

[31] ibid 494.

the biological link and regarded the appellant as a 'parent' of the child. For Denham J, since the same-sex couple was not a family under the Constitution, their relationship could not 'be weighed in the balance against the father'.[32] She, and the other members of the Supreme Court, refused the appeal on the issue of guardianship but they allowed it in relation to access.

By acknowledging that the known sperm donor's statutory rights are akin to those of other natural, unmarried fathers, the Supreme Court's decision emphasises that the genetic link alone is sufficient for a natural father to seek both guardianship of, and access to, his child. In the more recent High Court case of *MR and Another v An tArd Chláraitheoir*, Abbott J acknowledged that it was clear from *McD v L* that 'the concept of blood relationships or links are paramount in deciding parenthood'.[33] The judge went on to state that 'the male input into the make-up of the child makes him a parent just because he gave the genetic material'.[34] Nonetheless, Leonard-Kane was rather critical of *McD v L* from an LGBT rights perspective: 'Whilst the decision is undoubtedly a significant development in the context of non-marital fathers' rights, it has completely undermined the stability and autonomy of lesbian families conceived using donor sperm.'[35] However, Ryan was not so critical of *McD v L* because:

> While the Supreme Court went out of its way to deny the couple's formal claim to be a family, the reality of the decision is that by denying the father guardianship, and thus excluding the father from a decision-making role in respect of the child, the Supreme Court implicitly endorsed the couple's central role in the child's upbringing.[36]

While it is notable that the appeal was dismissed insofar as it related to guardianship, this author does not entirely share Ryan's optimism as regards the Supreme Court's tacit endorsement of same-sex family units. Elsewhere in the judgment, it becomes apparent that the couple's fundamental role in the child's upbringing could quite easily be diluted by the courts in the not-too-distant future. The members of the Supreme Court made it clear that the known sperm donor 'father' in this case stands every chance of being granted guardianship at a later date should the evolution of his relationship with the child warrant it.[37] Justice Denham felt that 'there should be no order of guardianship made in relation to the father *at this time*. As in all family law matters, issues may be re-addressed in changed circumstances' (emphasis added).[38] Justice Fennelly also held that 'it is, of course, possible that a time will come when [a guardianship] application might be renewed in the High Court in

[32] ibid 494.

[33] *MR and Another v An tArd Chláraitheoir* [2013] IEHC 91 [102]. Indeed, this High Court decision reinforced the significance of genetic parentage in Irish law.

[34] ibid [42].

[35] M Leonard-Kane, 'Lesbian Co-Parenting and Assisted Reproduction: In an Age of Increasing Alternative Family Forms, Can Ireland Continue to Ignore the Need for Legislative Boundaries to be Placed on "Fertile" Ground?' (2010) 13 *Trinity College Law Review* 5, 23.

[36] F Ryan, 'Are Two Irish Mammies (even) Better than One? Heteronormativity, Homosexuality and the 1937 Constitution' in E Carolan (ed), *The Constitution of Ireland: Perspectives and Prospects* (Dublin, Bloomsbury Professional, 2012) 425, 440.

[37] Hence it is respectfully submitted that Mulligan was not necessarily correct to state in relation to *McD v L* that 'For the Supreme Court, the applicant in this case … was eligible to apply for access, but not for guardianship'. See A Mulligan, 'Constitutional Parenthood in the Age of Assisted Reproduction' (2014) 49 (1) *Irish Jurist* 90, 101.

[38] *McD v L* [2009] IESC 81, [2010] 1 ILRM 461 (Supreme Court) 494.

different circumstances'.[39] Hence, the Supreme Court judges seem to envisage that, if the access arrangements put in place result in the child establishing a strong attachment to its father over time, then an application for guardianship might be approved by the High Court one day.[40] The judicial approach to unmarried fathers and guardianship in *McD v L* stands in stark contrast to the legislative approach under the Children and Family Relationships Act 2015. Whereas the 2015 Act remains concerned with the strength of a cohabiting relationship between a child's unmarried parents for quite some time before and after birth, the Supreme Court in *McD v L* was open to the possibility of one day appointing (as a guardian) a man who had in fact never cohabited with the child's mother and had merely donated his sperm for use by the child's mother and her same-sex partner in a 'home-insemination' scenario.

An equally flexible approach to guardianship was taken in the more recent case of *MR v SB*,[41] where Abbott J appointed as a guardian of two children a man who had no biological connection to them, but had acted 'very strongly in a position of loco parentis',[42] in circumstances where the children's mother had abandoned them and their non-guardian fathers did not have an active role in their upbringing. The children's mother was seeking their return and the applicant, who had previously been in a relationship with the children's mother and who had been left raising them, wished to be appointed as their guardian.[43] Justice Abbott observed that section 16 of the Guardianship of Infants Act 1964 provided that, where a parent has abandoned or deserted a child or allowed a child to be brought up by another person at that person's expense, the court can decline to return the child to that parent. The judge was of the view that, in such cases, the party who has successfully resisted the return of the child is, in effect, the parent of such a child and it would be a dereliction of the duty of the courts not to treat him as such to the detriment of the interests of the child.[44] A corollary of this finding was that the court could appoint the man in this case as a guardian, even though he had no biological link to the children. However, Abbott J did acknowledge the 'exceptional circumstances' of that case.[45]

Therefore, unlike the recent legislative approach, the judicial approach to guardianship is no longer tied to a man's relationship status with the child's mother or, in certain exceptional

[39] ibid 533.

[40] In *A v B&C* [2012] EWCA Civ 285, 48, a case in England and Wales involving a known sperm donor seeking access to a child being raised by lesbian parents, Black LJ recognised that 'the role of the father in the child's life will depend on what is in the child's best interests at each stage of the child's childhood and adolescence. As with any other child, the father/child relationship may turn out to be close and fulfilling for both sides, it may be no more than nominal, or it may be something in between.'

[41] *MR v SB* [2013] IEHC 647. For an analysis of this case, see generally 'Family Law' in R Byrne and W Binchy (eds), *Annual Review of Irish Law 2013* (Dublin, Thomson Round Hall, 2014) 324–25.

[42] ibid [2] (Abbott J). In *Hollywood v Cork Harbour Commissioners* [1992] 1 IR 457, 465, O'Hanlon J described *in loco parentis* as 'any situation where one person assumes the moral responsibility, not binding in law, to provide for the material needs of another'.

[43] This case was decided prior to the enactment of s 49 of the Children and Family Relationships Act 2015 (inserting s 6C into the Guardianship of Infants Act 1964), which enables a person other than a child's parent to apply to the court to be appointed as a guardian where they have provided for the child's day-to-day care for a continuous period of more than 12 months and the child has no parent or guardian who is willing or able to exercise the rights and responsibilities of guardianship.

[44] ibid [19] (Abbott J).

[45] ibid [24] (Abbott J).

cases, to his biological connection to the child. Consequently, the approach to guardianship in the Irish courts feels far less discriminatory on the grounds of gender and relationship status than the prevailing legislative approach.

VI. Reform of the Law on Guardianship

In 1982, in its *Report on Illegitimacy*, the Law Reform Commission (LRC) first recommended that both parents of a child should be joint guardians under Irish law, whether a child is born within or outside of marriage.[46] A similar recommendation was made by the LRC in its more recent *Report on the Legal Aspects of Family Relationships* in 2010.[47] The LRC felt that equality between parents was important and recommended that legislation be enacted by the Oireachtas (the Irish parliament) to vest automatic joint guardianship in both the mother and the father of any child. The LRC noted that unmarried fathers were the only group excluded from automatic recognition 'of the relationship between a parent and a child, which brings with it significant responsibilities and the correlative rights'.[48] Thus, the LRC concluded that 'all parents should be treated equally in respect of their relationship with their children regardless of gender or marital status'.[49] The LRC considered that this approach was generally in the best interests of the child.

Despite these recommendations, the Children and Family Relationships Act 2015 did not embrace this gender-neutral approach to automatic joint guardianship rights for unmarried parents on the birth of the child. As discussed, the 2015 Act only grants guardianship rights a minimum of three months after the birth of the child, and only then to those unmarried fathers who have cohabited with the child's mother for a period of 12 months, including at least three months after the birth. Thus, 36 years after the LRC's initial recommendations, automatic joint guardianship rights for both unmarried parents on the birth of a child are still not a statutory reality in Ireland. Viewed from a gender equality perspective, the provisions of the 2015 Act are disappointing given the LRC's recommendations and the fact that, when it was published in early 2014, the General Scheme of the Children and Family Relationships Bill provided for a form of automatic joint guardianship rights for *both* unmarried parents on the birth of the child, without the need for any post-birth temporal cohabitation requirement between mother and father.

As the situation stands, the unmarried father remains the subject of prima facie discrimination on the grounds of gender and relationship status when it comes to obtaining automatic guardianship rights under Irish law. However, Irish law is not unique in this regard. In England and Wales, the unmarried father only has the right to apply to the court for a parental responsibility order in relation to his child.[50] He is not automatically vested

[46] Law Reform Commission, *Report on Illegitimacy* (LRC 4 – 1982) 177.

[47] Law Reform Commission, *Report on the Legal Aspects of Family Relationships* (LRC 101 – 2010) 18.

[48] ibid.

[49] ibid 16–17.

[50] Children Act 1989, s 4(1). Parental responsibility is the equivalent of guardianship in England and Wales. Shannon observes that 'effectively there is no practical difference between this concept and the concept of guardianship'. See generally G Shannon, *Child Law*, 2nd edn (Dublin, Thomson Round Hall, 2010) 726.

with parental responsibility on the birth of the child, although he can acquire it shortly thereafter if the mother consents to registering him as the father on the child's birth certificate.[51] The unmarried father can also acquire parental responsibility via a 'parental responsibility agreement' with the child's mother.[52] This is virtually identical to what is provided for in this jurisdiction under section 2(4) of the Guardianship of Infants Act 1964, as amended by section 4 of the Children Act 1997. Interestingly, the means by which an unmarried father can acquire guardianship rights under legislation in England and Wales without going to court all depend on the quality of his relationship with the child's mother. This is identical to the approach taken under legislative reforms enacted in this jurisdiction.

During Dáil (parliamentary) debates on the Children and Family Relationships Bill, the then Minister for Justice and Equality, Frances Fitzgerald TD, stressed that the guardianship reforms contained in the Bill 'reflect existing constitutional protection for marital fathers and are the consequence of legal advice'.[53] The Minister appeared to be suggesting that, in relation to guardianship, the legal position of married and unmarried fathers could not be equalised by legislation because this would be contrary to the constitutional protection of the married family in Article 41. However, the Minister's argument does not take account of the Children's Amendment, Article 42A, which, from a child-centric perspective, would surely serve to counter any argument based on Article 41 and favour equating the position of married and unmarried fathers á la guardianship? Whenever the Oireachtas has a moral discomfort about legislating in a controversial area it hides behind the smokescreens of 'legal advice' and the need to respect the 'constitutional position'. In 2008, when civil partnership legislation was proposed, the then Minister for Justice, Dermot Ahern TD, claimed that the Government was legislating for civil partnership instead of same-sex marriage because the advice of the Attorney General was that 'anything that would provide, or try to replicate "marriage" in this legislation would not stand constitutional scrutiny'.[54] In fact, same-sex marriage legislation would most likely have been constitutionally compliant.[55] Similarly, in light of Article 42A, legislation extending automatic guardianship rights to unmarried fathers would most likely be in harmony with the Constitution. In 2015, the Oireachtas was clearly as uncomfortable with extending guardianship rights to unmarried fathers as it was with extending marriage rights to same-sex couples in 2008. It seems that Irish politicians will rush to justify their conservative stance on an issue by claiming that they are acting on legal advice from the Attorney General's office and trying to respect the constitutional position. Nonetheless, in 2015, Minister Fitzgerald did commit to a review of the legislation in two years.[56] However, in September 2017, the current Minister for Justice and Equality, Charles Flanagan TD, stated in the Dáil that he has 'no plans at present

[51] See Adoption and Children Act 2002, s 111 (amending s 4(1) of the Children Act 1989). In Ireland, placing the unmarried father's name on the child's birth certificate does not grant him guardianship rights; it simply means that the presumption of paternity applies to him. See Status of Children Act 1987, s 46.

[52] Children Act 1989, s 4(1).

[53] *Dáil Debates*, 12 March 2015, Vol 871, No 3.

[54] M Hennessy and C O'Brien, 'Bill to Grant Legal Protection to Same-Sex Couples' *The Irish Times* (Dublin, 25 June 2008) 3.

[55] See B Tobin, 'Marriage Equality in Ireland: The Politico-Legal Context' (2016) 30(2) *International Journal of Law, Policy and the Family* 115.

[56] *Dáil Debates*, 12 March 2015, Vol 871, No 3.

for further amendment of the Guardianship of Infants Act 1964 to provide for automatic guardianship for unmarried fathers'.[57]

Apart from the alleged constitutional concerns, one reason why the law might tie an unmarried father's 'automatic' guardianship rights following the birth of the child to the quality of his relationship with the child's mother might be to prevent those unmarried fathers in domestic violence situations who are no longer living with the mother from acquiring automatic guardianship rights. However, in Ireland, this does not appear to have been a reason for the denial of automatic guardianship rights to unmarried fathers when the Children and Family Relationships Bill was being debated by the Oireachtas in 2015. Speaking on domestic violence and automatic guardianship rights, Minister Fitzgerald stated that 'we should not make a decision as to the rights of a non-marital father on the basis of the poor behaviour of *some*' (emphasis added).[58] While it is understandable that policy-makers may not want automatic guardianship rights to be obtained and used by violent men as a means of threatening and harassing their ex-partners, Minister Fitzgerald is correct in stating that this should not dictate the policy adopted on automatic guardianship rights for *all* unmarried fathers. As stated in the Consultation Paper issued by the Lord Chancellor's Department in the UK in 1998: 'It is clearly impossible to assume that most unmarried fathers are irresponsible or uninterested in their children, and do not deserve a legal role as parents.'[59]

VII. Gender, Custody and Access

Custody refers to a person's right to the day-to-day physical care and control of a child. Custody rights are automatically vested in married parents because, as Henchy J observed in *G v An Bord Uchtála*:

> Custody will normally be necessary for the effectuation of the parents' constitutional right and duty to provide, according to their means, for the religious and moral, intellectual, physical and social education of their children.[60]

Although an unmarried mother enjoys an automatic right to the custody of her child,[61] the unmarried father can apply for custody under the Guardianship of Infants Act 1964.[62] Indeed, even if the unmarried father is not a guardian of the child, he nonetheless has a statutory right as a 'parent' to apply for custody. In a recent empirical study of the treatment of fathers in the Irish family courts, Egan concluded that in custody cases, joint custody is now the option preferred by judges in the system.[63] The option of joint custody was placed

[57] *Dáil Debates*, 20 September 2017, Vol 959, No 1.
[58] *Dáil Debates*, 12 March 2015, Vol 871, No 3.
[59] Lord Chancellor's Department, *Consultation Paper on Procedures for the Determination of Paternity and the Law on Parental Responsibility for Unmarried Fathers* (1998) 26. See also J Wallbank, 'Clause 106 of the Adoption and Children Bill: Legislation for the 'Good' Father?' (2002) 22 *Legal Studies* 276.
[60] *G v An Bord Uchtála* [1980] IR 32, 85 (Henchy J).
[61] *State (Nicolaou) v An Bord Uchtála* [1966] IR 567, 644 (Walsh J).
[62] Guardianship of Infants Act 1964, s 11.
[63] A Egan, 'Are Fathers Discriminated against in Irish Family Law? An Empirical Study' (2011) 14(2) *Irish Journal of Family Law* 38.

on a statutory footing when the Children Act 1997 amended the 1964 Act.[64] The courts are willing to order joint custody in cases involving both married and unmarried parents, even where there is significant acrimony between them.[65]

Crowley observes that, in practice, despite an order for joint custody, the children tend to reside with one parent while exercising access rights with the other parent.[66] She emphasises that joint custody 'does not afford each party rights to equal time with the child, but rather ensures that each parent *has rights* and corresponding obligations to the child' (emphasis added).[67] Coulter observes that, in practice, there is a 'distinct preference among judges' for the child's 'primary residence' to be with the mother, with access to the father.[68] However, this should not lead one to conclude that judges are biased against fathers in custody disputes; rather, as Coulter observes, it is because, even today, mothers are 'more likely to be available to the children after school'.[69] Coulter highlights the fact that although in contemporary times the majority of women with children are in the workforce, they are often 'in part-time work or lower-paid work'[70] than men; thus they are simply more readily available to their children on a daily basis.[71] Rather than being based on any gender bias, it appears that the judicial preference for 'primary care and control' of the child to go to the mother in joint custody cases is actually driven by what is in the best interests of the child. When a judge orders that 'primary care and control' of a child should go to the mother, Coulter observes that this is rarely opposed by the father.[72] This is most likely because the father appreciates that this is in the best interests of the child in cases where the mother can, because of her circumstances, be more available to cater for the child's needs on a daily basis. Nonetheless, in those cases where a father seeks a more equal time-sharing arrangement by having the children stay with him half the time, and he argues cogently for this, Coulter states that it is 'most often' granted by the judge.[73] Egan found that judges are open to awarding sole custody to a father where the mother has alcohol or drug addiction problems.[74]

Gender discrimination does not seem to factor into judicial decisions surrounding custody. The welfare of the child seems to be the determinative factor in custody disputes. Fathers are not really treated any less favourably than mothers because, as Egan points out: 'While joint custody is now the preferred option by the courts following relationship breakdown, mothers still have day-to-day care and control of the children, *but in reality*, that is more attributable to practicalities than to the courts system'.[75]

Similarly, gender discrimination does not appear to arise in practice where the court is tasked with awarding access rights to a parent. A parent can apply for access under the

[64] S 9 of the Children Act 1997 amended s 11 of the Guardianship of Infants Act 1964.
[65] *DFO'S v CA*, Unreported, High Court, April 20, 1998.
[66] Crowley, *Family Law* (n 12) 178.
[67] ibid 179.
[68] C Coulter, *Family Law in Practice: A Study of Cases in the Circuit Court* (Dublin, Clarus Press, 2009) 103.
[69] ibid.
[70] ibid.
[71] On this basis, one might argue that – as women's likelihood to receive greater custody rights reflects their position as primary caregivers, a position which is facilitated/imposed as a consequence of Irish labour laws which encourage women into child caregiving roles – the preference which women typically receive in custody hearings is a reflection of their disadvantaged position within the labour market.
[72] ibid.
[73] ibid.
[74] Egan, 'Are Fathers Discriminated against in Irish Family Law?' (n 63) 41.
[75] ibid 47.

1964 Act.[76] Crowley observes that 'it is extremely unusual for a court to refuse a parent access'.[77] During the course of her empirical research, Egan found that 'for the most part, those parents who applied for access were granted some form of contact with their children'.[78] Indeed, in *McD v L*, the Supreme Court awarded access rights to a known sperm donor who had formed but a limited bond with the child.[79] The courts' willingness to award access rights to a parent is probably because access is seen as a right of the child both under domestic law,[80] and under Article 8 of the European Convention on Human Rights.[81] Indeed, the importance to a child of access rights for persons other than parents is recognised by statute. Blood or adoptive relatives or other persons who have been involved in the child's upbringing can apply to the courts for access. The Guardianship of Infants Act 1964, as amended, enables relatives or 'a person with whom the child resides or has formerly resided' to apply to the courts seeking access to the child.[82]

VIII. Guardianship, Custody and Access and Article 42A

Notwithstanding the success of the Children's Referendum in November 2012, where 58 per cent of the electorate voted in favour of the 31st Amendment to the Constitution, Article 42A was only inserted into the Constitution in 2015, following an unsuccessful legal challenge to the outcome of the referendum.[83] Article 42A provides express constitutional recognition and protection for children's rights. Article 42A.4.1 not only places the 'best interests' test on a constitutional footing, but it requires that 'provision shall be made by law that in the resolution of all proceedings concerning the … guardianship or custody of, or access to, any child, the best interests of the child shall be the paramount consideration'.[84] It is clear from the judiciary's approach to guardianship, custody and access even prior to the enactment of Article 42A, the welfare of the child can trump gender, the relationship between a child's parents, and even an applicant's lack of biological connection to the child when the courts are deciding whether to make an order.

IX. Conclusion

Shared parenting in the form of joint custody arrangements between mothers and fathers is now the preferred option in the Irish courts. Although, in practice, this means that most

[76] Guardianship of Infants Act 1964, s 11.
[77] Crowley, *Family Law* (n 12) 180.
[78] Egan, 'Are Fathers Discriminated against in Irish Family Law?' (n 63) 47.
[79] *McD v L* [2009] IESC 81. However, the case was remitted to the High Court to decide on the access arrangements, and Hedigan J granted access subject to strict conditions. See *McD v L* [2010] IEHC 120.
[80] *MD v GD*, Unreported, High Court, 30 July 1992.
[81] *Eriksson v Sweden* [1989] 12 EHRR 200.
[82] S 11 of the Guardianship of Infants Act 1964, as amended by s 9 of the Children Act 1997 and s 55 of the Children and Family Relationships Act 2015.
[83] *Jordan v Minister for Children and Youth Affairs* [2014] IEHC 327.
[84] S 45 of the Children and Family Relationships Act 2015 gives statutory effect to Art 42A.4.1 by amending s 3 of the Guardianship of Infants Act 1964. This section of the 2015 Act was commenced on 18 January 2016 by virtue of the Children and Family Relationships Act 2015 (Commencement of Certain Provisions) Order 2016.

children will still have their primary residence with their mother, it is clear that this is not due to any gender bias by judges when making an order, but because it is usually in the best interests of the child in circumstances where the mother can be more readily available to take care of the child's needs. Further, gender bias does not appear to factor into judicial decisions concerning access rights.[85]

Nonetheless, despite calls for reform dating back to 1982, the unmarried father remains the subject of prima facie discrimination on the grounds of his gender and relationship status in the context of statutory guardianship rights. This reticent approach by the legislature is disappointing when one considers that initial judicial unease has recently given way to a more flexible, inclusive and child-centric approach. The prevailing judicial attitude to guardianship applications looks beyond gender, the unmarried father's relationship with the child's mother and, in certain exceptional cases, even biological connections to a child. While the lack of automatic guardianship rights for unmarried fathers is frustrating, Ireland is not alone in failing to provide for this.[86] Given that the current Minister for Justice and Equality has made it clear that he is unwilling to revisit the question of whether to provide automatic guardianship rights for unmarried fathers in the near future, it would appear that equal guardianship rights for unmarried fathers are not yet on the horizon.

[85] *McD v L* [2009] IESC 81.
[86] In England and Wales, see the Children Act 1989, s 4(1), as amended.

7

Surrogacy Law in Ireland: The Troubling Consequences of Legislative Inertia

ANDREA MULLIGAN

I. Introduction

Surrogacy is intimately bound up with gender. It challenges us to interrogate our understanding of parenthood and what it means to enter into parenthood ethically.[1] At the time of writing, surrogacy law in Ireland is in transition. As matters stand, 'surrogacy law in Ireland' means the absence of law.[2] There remains no legal regulation of surrogacy in this jurisdiction, aside from European directives governing the quality and safety of human tissues and cells.[3] Irish surrogacy law, insofar as we can say it exists, means the way that commissioning couples use the provisions of Irish family law to allow them to regularise their relationships with surrogate-born children. In October 2017, the Department of Health released the long-awaited General Scheme of the Assisted Reproduction Bill 2017 (the 'General Scheme').[4] The General Scheme sets out relatively detailed proposals for a comprehensive scheme of regulation for surrogacy and for other aspects of assisted human reproduction. This chapter considers the law as it stands, and the proposals for reform.

[1] Surrogate motherhood, or 'surrogacy' describes a situation where a woman gestates a pregnancy on behalf of another person or couple (the intended parents), on the understanding that she will hand the child over to them on its birth. There are two forms of surrogate motherhood: traditional surrogacy and gestational surrogacy. In a traditional surrogacy arrangement, the surrogate uses her own eggs and is genetically related to the child. Conception usually takes place using artificial insemination. In gestational surrogacy, an egg donor is used and the surrogate has no genetic relationship to the resulting child. For a full discussion of these definitions, see PR Brinsden, 'Surrogacy's Past, Present and Future' in E Scott Sills (ed), *Handbook of Gestational Surrogacy* (Cambridge, Cambridge University Press, 2016). On the ethics of surrogacy see generally L Van Zyl and A van Niekerk, 'Interpretations, Perspectives and Intentions in Surrogate Motherhood' (2000) 26 *Journal of Medical Ethics* 404; P Abrams, 'The Bad Mother: Stigma, Abortion and Surrogacy' (2015) 43(2) *Journal of Law, Medicine and Ethics* 179.

[2] For a discussion of Irish law on assisted reproduction generally, including surrogacy, see S Mills and A Mulligan, *Medical Law in Ireland*, 3rd edn (Oxford, Bloomsbury Professional, 2017) ch 14.

[3] Directive 2004/23/EC on setting standards of quality and safety for the donation, procurement, testing, processing, preservation, storage and distribution of human tissues and cells [2004] OJ L102/48, Directive 2006/17/EC implementing Directive 2004/23/EC of the European Parliament and of the Council as regards certain technical requirements for the donation, procurement and testing of human tissues and cells [2006] OJ L38/40 and Directive 2006/86/EC implementing Directive 2004/23/EC of the European Parliament and of the Council as regards traceability requirements, notification of serious adverse reactions and events and certain technical requirements for the coding, processing, preservation, storage and distribution of human tissues and cells [2006] OJ L294/32.

[4] The General Scheme can be accessed at: www.health.gov.ie/blog/publications/general-scheme-of-the-assisted-human-reproduction-bill-2017/.

There are a great many ways in which surrogacy intersects with gender.[5] A full analysis of all the many gender-related perspectives on surrogacy is beyond the scope of this chapter, and it will, therefore, focus on one particular viewpoint: the way in which surrogacy law in Ireland impacts on women. There are four women in contemplation, some, but not all, of whom will be involved in every surrogacy arrangement. These are: the surrogate, the egg donor, the commissioning mother with a genetic link to the child, and the commissioning mother without a genetic link to the child. Each of these women has her own particular vulnerabilities, arising from the nature of the surrogacy transaction and potentially arising from the woman's own circumstances.

Before analysing and critiquing Irish law, it is important to recognise that legal regulation in the surrogacy context has a number of discrete functions. First, law regulates the legal status of persons involved in surrogacy transactions and governs the legal relationship between those persons. This comprises the laws regulating the persons who are entitled to apply to be recognised as a parent, and to apply to be appointed as a guardian of the surrogate-born child. Second, legal regulation governs the surrogacy transaction itself, and regulates the legal relationship between the surrogate and the commissioning parents, as well as the transaction concerning the obtaining and use of the sperm, embryo or eggs, including donated embryos and gametes where donation is involved. The core function of the law in respect of the surrogate and the egg donor is to ensure that, if these processes are legally permissible, they proceed on the basis of properly informed and fully voluntary consent. Law's function in regulating these transactions comprises the legal status of the agreements themselves, and the question of whether they take effect as enforceable legal contracts, or whether they have a separate status in law. In respect of all parties to a surrogacy arrangement, it can be said that the law serves a protective purpose.

This chapter will begin by setting out the law in Ireland, and then proceed to evaluate that law from the perspective of the women involved, and in particular by reference to the protective purpose of the law. The central thesis is that the absence of specific legal regulation of surrogacy has unwittingly resulted in a de facto legal regime for the regulation of surrogacy which is male-centred, and which fails to protect the interests of the female parties to a surrogacy transaction. This critique of the law will argue that commissioning mothers, surrogates and egg donors are rendered invisible at Irish law. The paradigm case is one in which a heterosexual couple engages a surrogate to carry a pregnancy, using an embryo formed from the commissioning father's sperm and either the commissioning mother's egg, or the egg of a donor.[6]

The chapter will then proceed to consider the proposals for a new scheme of regulation for assisted reproduction. The chapter will conclude with an examination of the case law of the European Court of Human Rights in the field of surrogacy and provide some analysis on how Ireland's Convention obligations must be respected within any new legal regime.

[5] One other important intersection concerns same-sex male couples, who have a special interest in surrogacy, for obvious reasons. This has long provoked debate about the capacity of men to take on traditional female mothering roles. See eg H Kim 'Family Building by Same-Sex Male Couples via Gestational Surrogacy' (2017) 35(5) *Seminars in Reproductive Medicine* 408; M Saez, 'Same-Sex Marriage, Same-Sex Cohabitation, and Same-Sex Families around the World: Why Same is So Different' (2011) 19(5) *European Review of Private Law* 631.

[6] It is, of course, acknowledged that surrogacy occurs in other contexts and in other family arrangements.

II. Legal Regulation of Surrogacy in Ireland

A. Surrogacy in Ireland

Before examining the law, it makes sense to consider the reality of surrogacy practice in Ireland. Occupying, as it does, an unregulated space, there are no comprehensive statistics available on surrogacy in Ireland. Information that is available is gained from legal and medical practitioners in the field.[7] It would appear that there is little or no practice of surrogacy within Ireland.[8] This is not to say that Irish people are not engaged in surrogacy arrangements. When Irish people seek surrogacy services, they look overseas. Countries such as the US and Ukraine are attractive destinations. As certain jurisdictions gradually crack down on the practice of international surrogacy – India, Nepal and Thailand, for example – Irish business necessarily moves elsewhere. Currently therefore, when we talk about surrogacy in Ireland, we primarily mean surrogacy arrangements entered into by Irish people overseas and which those Irish people seek to have recognised in Ireland. It is assumed that the vast majority, or even all, of these agreements are made on a commercial basis where the surrogate is paid for her services.[9] This reality must be recognised as a key facet of the regulatory challenge in making law for surrogacy in Ireland.

B. The Law on Surrogacy

Irish law makes no specific provision for the practice of surrogacy, or for the regulation of the familial relationships that arise from surrogacy. While parental relationships arising from donor-assisted human reproduction are governed by the Children and Family Relationships Act 2015 ('2015 Act'), parental relationships arising from surrogacy are not governed by that Act. Interestingly, surrogacy was included in early drafts of the 2015 Act but excluded during the course of the legislative process.[10] Surrogacy falls, therefore, to be governed by the general provisions of Irish family law. In Irish law, the mother of a child is the birth mother, regardless of whether that woman is the child's genetic mother or not, and regardless of whether she is a surrogate. There is currently no way in which that can be changed at Irish law: the birth mother remains the mother forever. The legal position was briefly changed by the High Court decision in *MR v An t-Árd Chláraitheoir*,[11] but the holding was reversed by the Supreme Court and the status quo restored. This case remains the leading case on surrogacy in Irish law, and it is considered in detail below. If the birth mother is married, her husband will benefit from the presumption of paternity, unless this is displaced by the genetic father.

[7] Including the author's experience of the practice of the Irish courts.

[8] Note, however, that the surrogacy arrangement in *MR v An t-Árd Chláraitheoir* [2013] IEHC 91, [2014] IESC 60 did take place in Ireland.

[9] This view is necessarily anecdotal.

[10] See General Scheme of a Children and Family Relationships Bill 2014: www.justice.ie/en/JELR/General%20Scheme%20of%20a%20Children%20and%20Family%20Relationships%20Bill.pdf/Files/General%20Scheme%20of%20a%20Children%20and%20Family%20Relationships%20Bill.pdf.

[11] *MR v An t-Árd Chláraitheoir* [2013] IEHC 91, [2014] IESC 60.

Genetic fathers are very differently situated. At Irish law, the genetic father of a surrogate-born child is treated in the same way as any genetic father who is not cohabiting with the birth mother of the child (discussed in other contributions to this collection, see for example Chapter 6). He is entitled to apply for a declaration of parentage under section 35 of the Status of Children Act 1987. The commissioning father will need to provide DNA evidence from a reliable source in support of his application for a declaration of parentage. On foot of that parental status, the genetic father can apply to be appointed a guardian of the child pursuant to the Guardianship of Infants Act 1964. Such applications are generally made in one set of proceedings in the Circuit Court, as only the Circuit Court has jurisdiction in Status of Children matters. The State must be served with such proceedings pursuant to section 35(5) of the Status of Children Act 1987. If the genetic father is successful in his Status of Children application, the Court will proceed to consider his application to be appointed guardian of the child. In deciding whether the appointment of the genetic father as guardian is appropriate, the Court must regard the welfare of the child as the paramount consideration.[12] The welfare principle also has constitutional status in Ireland, pursuant to Article 42A.4 of the Constitution, which provides:

> 1 Provision shall be made by law that in the resolution of all proceedings
>
> i. brought by the state, as guardian of the common good, for the purpose of preventing the safety and welfare of any child from being prejudicially affected, or
>
> ii. concerning the adoption, guardianship or custody of, or access to, any child,
>
> the best interests of the child shall be the paramount consideration.

Commissioning fathers with no genetic connection to the child have no entitlement to apply for parental status. Where a child is born through surrogacy and neither parent is a genetic father, there is no way in which either commissioning parent may be recognised as a parent at Irish law.

While the Children and Family Relationships Act 2015 does not regulate surrogacy it may allow for guardianship orders to be made in respect of the commissioning parents of surrogate-born children. Section 6C of the Guardianship of Infants Act 1964, as inserted by section 49 of the Children and Family Relationships Act 2015, provides that a District or Circuit Court may appoint a person as guardian of a child where that person is married to, civil partner of, or has cohabited for more than three years with the child's parent, and has shared parental responsibility with that parent for more than two years. Where a genetic father has been recognised as the parent of a surrogate-born child, and been appointed as guardian on that basis, this section allows a court to make a guardianship order in favour of his spouse, civil partner or cohabitee after a period of two years.

There is no doubt that this section was not drafted with the intention of applying to commissioning parents of surrogate-born children, but it may include them in its scope, albeit unintentionally. The practical effect of this section is that the second parent of a surrogate-born child, whether male or female, may apply to be appointed guardian of that child after the necessary period of parental responsibility has elapsed.[13] Anecdotal evidence

[12] Guardianship of Infants Act 1964, s 3.

[13] After Pt 2 and 3 of the 2015 Act are commenced, the retrospective provisions for the establishment of parental status may provide a more attractive option to second commissioning parents. See Children and Family Relationships Act 2015, ss 20–22.

exists to suggest that such orders have been made in surrogacy cases, indicating that certain judges have been convinced that the 2015 Act conferred such jurisdiction on the District and Circuit Courts, whether or not the legislature intended that effect. The intricacies of this particular issue are beyond the scope of this chapter, but given the complexity of the matter it may be appropriate for the District Court to state a case to the High Court to seek clarification of this jurisdiction.

Unlike surrogacy, the legal relationships arising from egg donation are regulated in Irish law, although the relevant provisions have not yet been commenced. Part 2 of the 2015 Act governs parentage in cases of donor-assisted human reproduction. It establishes a regime whereby the parental relationships arising from such procedures are defined by reference to the intention of the parties as long as proper consent was provided. However, the 2015 Act does not govern maternal status in the surrogacy context, because it retains the rule that the mother is the birth mother, even if a donor egg was used. Furthermore, it governs donor-assisted human reproduction procedures, described in the Act as a DAHR Procedure. This is defined as:

> [A] donor-assisted human reproduction procedure, being any procedure performed in the State with the objective of it resulting in the implantation of an embryo in the womb of the woman on whose request the procedure is performed, where—
>
> (a) one of the gametes from which the embryo has been or will be formed has been provided by a donor,
>
> (b) each gamete from which the embryo has been or will be formed has been provided by a donor, or
>
> (c) the embryo has been provided by a donor.[14]

The reference to the 'woman on whose request the procedure is performed' suggests that this only includes women who are themselves the commissioning parents, and excludes surrogates. Furthermore, it excludes procedures performed outside the State, so where the surrogacy arrangement takes place abroad and includes egg donation this would in any event fall outside the scope of the Act.

Aside from the law of guardianship, there is a theoretical possibility that the Irish law on adoption would allow for the adoption of a surrogate-born child by the commissioning parents.[15] However, there are no known examples of this procedure being executed. Furthermore, the Supreme Court commented in *MR* that it did not regard that there was clear evidence that it was possible for the commissioning parents to adopt.[16]

A soft law aspect of the legal regime that should be noted is the Department of Justice guidelines on the procedures for the repatriation of surrogate-born children, entitled 'Citizenship, Parentage, Guardianship and Travel Document Issues in Relation to Children Born as a Result of Surrogacy Arrangements Entered Into Outside the State'. Issued in response to the growing phenomenon of Irish couples travelling abroad to enter into commercial surrogacy arrangements, this document explains, in layman's terms, the law governing the citizenship of children born through international surrogacy arrangements. As the legal mother of the child is the surrogate, Irish citizenship, and on foot of that an

[14] Children and Family Relationships Act 2015, s 4.
[15] Adoption Act 2010.
[16] *MR v An t-Árd Chláraitheoir* [2014] IESC 60, O'Donnell J [16].

Irish passport, may only be claimed through the genetic father. The Department of Justice facilitates parents in bringing newborn babies into the jurisdiction on the basis of an Emergency Travel Certificate. These are issued on a discretionary basis, but as a general rule, the Department must be satisfied:

1 that the child is or may be an Irish citizen, and
2 that the application for the ETC is being made by a parent or guardian of the child, and
3 that—

   (i) the consent of all of the child's guardians to the issuing of an ETC has been obtained, or
   (ii) such consents have been dispensed with by an Irish court, or
   (iii) there are exceptional circumstances involving an immediate and serious risk of harm to the child's life, health or safety requiring the child to undertake travel for which a travel document is required and that for the purpose of securing the welfare of the child a travel document should be issued to the child,

and

4 that the issuing of an ETC is in the best interests of the child[17]

The Irish authorities take the view that it is not generally in the best interests of the child to be present in a jurisdiction without any adult to whom they have a recognised legal relationship. Therefore, before an ETC is granted, parents must undertake to notify their local health centre of the arrival of the child within two working days of arrival, and the genetic father must undertake to make an application to court to establish his parental status within 10 working days of arrival.

The Irish law of surrogacy is in no sense a bespoke, considered, legal regime. Rather, it is the result of a legal vacuum and the apparent reluctance on the part of the legislature to address the issue of surrogacy. The situation is the result of a combination of legislative inertia and unintended consequences, a situation which ultimately fails to secure the interests of any party, except arguably those of the genetic father.

C. Commissioning Mothers

In Irish law, the commissioning mother is perhaps the woman who fares worst. In the case of heterosexual couples, it is important to note that it is often the commissioning mother's fertility difficulties that lead a couple to engage a surrogate in the first place. Before getting to the birth of the surrogate-born child, the commissioning mother will usually have experienced the long, hard journey of infertility and all the pain that that entails. The commissioning mothers can be presumed to play an equal part in the parental project that leads to the child being born. She can further be presumed to play a key caring role in the child's life, and indeed is far more likely than the commissioning father to be the primary carer (see Chapters 6 and 13). Section 6C of the Guardianship of Infants Act is the only prospect that Irish law offers for the recognition of the commissioning mother's legal status

[17] *Citizenship, Parentage, Guardianship and Travel Document Issues in Relation to Children Born as a Result of Surrogacy Arrangements Entered Into Outside the State* (Department of Justice, 2012) 4–5 https://www.dfa.ie/media/dfa/alldfawebsitemedia/childrens-issues-surrogacy-guidance-document.pdf.

and, as discussed, the jurisdiction of the courts to make such an order is potentially uncertain. In any event, this procedure is of no avail until the commissioning mother has been caring for the child for a period of two years.

i. The Invisibility and Inequality of Genetic Motherhood

The first perspective to be considered is that of the genetic mother of the surrogate-born child. She enjoys no status at Irish law whatsoever. She may, it seems, apply to be appointed a guardian on foot of her husband or partner's parenthood pursuant to the 2015 Act, but that application is not in any way premised on, or supported by, her position as a genetic mother, except to the extent that the court would be entitled to take into account the genetic relationship as part of its general best interests inquiry.[18] The problematic nature of the genetic mother's legal position is highlighted by the contrast between her position and that of the commissioning father who enjoys a genetic connection. He is a parent in precisely the same sense as the genetic commissioning mother: they both share 50 per cent of their DNA with the child, and yet he is granted precisely the same status as any non-cohabiting father. By contrast, the genetic mother enjoys no recognition whatsoever. She is deemed not to be a mother because another person has carried out an essential function of mothering: gestation. Fatherhood does not have a gestational component, and so a genetic father in the surrogacy context is not disadvantaged. The position of the genetic mother is therefore one of inequality as well as invisibility.

The iniquitous position of the genetic, commissioning, mother gave rise to the leading case on surrogacy in Ireland, *MR v An t-Árd Chláraitheoir*.[19] This case concerned a commissioning mother who engaged her sister to act as a surrogate. The commissioning mother and her husband were able to provide their own gametes for the formation of embryos. The surrogate carried the pregnancy and gave birth to twin boys. Under Irish law the commissioning father was appointed guardian on foot of his paternal status. There was, however, no provision for the commissioning mother to have her parental status recognised. The surrogate – the genetic aunt – remained the legal mother of the twins. The genetic parents requested that An t-Árd Chláraitheoir (the Chief Registrar) register the commissioning mother as the legal mother of the child, on the basis of her genetic connection. That request was refused and the commissioning parents issued proceedings against the Chief Registrar, arguing that the genetic mother was entitled to be registered as the mother.

At first instance, the commissioning parents were successful.[20] Justice Abbott ordered that the genetic mother be registered as the legal mother of the children.[21] Justice Abbott showed no discomfort with the magnitude or import of the matter he was asked to adjudicate: he fully embraced the challenge of deciding whether the true meaning of 'mother' in Irish law was the genetic or the gestational mother. Justice Abbott's analysis of the constitutional case law led him to conclude that the sine qua non of motherhood was the blood link

[18] Pursuant to the general requirement that the best interests of the child be the paramount concern in matters of guardianship, see Guardianship of Infants Act 1964, s 3.

[19] *MR v An t-Árd Chláraitheoir* [2014] IESC 60, [2013] IEHC 91.

[20] *MR v An t-Árd Chláraitheoir* [2013] IEHC 91.

[21] For a full discussion of this case, see A Mulligan, 'Constitutional Parenthood in the Age of Assisted Reproduction' (2014) 48(1) *Irish Jurist* 90.

between parent and child, and that this blood link meant DNA.[22] While acknowledging the role of epigenetics and emerging scholarship in that area, he concluded that it was DNA that was truly definitive of motherhood. Though this led Abbott J to an attractive conclusion on the facts of the case, his judgment risked overreaching and was described as 'broad ranging' by the Supreme Court.[23] The logical extension of his analysis was that the parenthood in all cases was truly defined by DNA. This would mean that, in the case of an egg or sperm donor, the true parent was the donor, not the commissioning parent. The decision of the State to appeal Abbott J's decision seems to have been motivated by such concerns: there were concerns that such a holding could constrain the discretion of the legislature to legislate for surrogacy in due course.[24]

The Supreme Court overturned Abbott J's holding, setting aside his order. This order was subsequently overturned by the Supreme Court. The Supreme Court primarily approached the question as a narrow one of statutory interpretation, stating that the core issue in the appeal was whether the genetic mother was entitled to have her maternity registered on the birth certificates pursuant to the Civil Registration Act 2004. Importantly, there was no challenge to the constitutionality of the Civil Registration Act 2004, so it was not open to the Court to decide whether the Act was unconstitutional by reason of failing to recognise the genetic mother's status. In coming to its conclusion, the Supreme Court made a number of important comments which are relevant to the broader issues concerning the legal regulation of surrogacy.

The Court's core holding was on the narrow issue of the interpretation of the Civil Registration Act 2004. A majority of the Court concluded that applying ordinary principles of statutory interpretation, the word 'mother' under that Act referred to the birth mother. Looking to the legislative context of the Act, and to its purpose, the Court concluded that it was clear that, under the Act, the person to be registered as the mother was the person giving birth. Advances in assisted human reproduction had not changed that. Justice O'Donnell observed: 'Science may have undermined or at least qualified the assumptions upon which the Act was based, but that does not alter the interpretation of the Act.'[25]

The majority was also keenly aware of its institutional role in trying to accommodate advances in assisted reproduction. It was keenly aware of the inadequacy of the law as it stood, but believed that the courts could not fill what was a highly problematic legislative vacuum. Chief Justice Denham referred to a 'lacuna' in the law which the court could not address. Justice O'Donnell observed that it was 'surely wrong' that Irish society had not had the opportunity to address these issues via legislation.[26] Justice Hardiman stated that the regulation of surrogacy – and indeed the specific issue of the definition of mother – required policy choices that should only be made by the legislature. He commented, in memorable terms, that the failure of the law to respond to developments in assisted reproduction was 'as if Road Traffic Law had failed to reflect the advent of the motor car'.[27]

[22] *MR v An t-Árd Chláraitheoir* [2013] IEHC 91 [102-03].

[23] *MR v An t-Árd Chláraitheoir* [2014] IESC 60, Denham CJ [14].

[24] See press release by Department of Social Protection, 'Statement in relation to High Court judgment in the case of *MR, DR, OR and CR v An tÁrd Chlaraitheoir* [Registrar General], Ireland & the Attorney General' (6 June 2013). It states, in part: '[The High Court decision] may also have the effect of tying the hands of the Oireachtas in how it may legislate, in the future, for the complex areas of surrogacy and assisted human reproduction.'

[25] *MR v An t-Árd Chláraitheoir* [2014] IESC 60, O'Donnell J [32].

[26] ibid [6].

[27] ibid Hardiman J [4].

Most members of the majority steered clear of constitutional issues or, as in the case of Denham CJ, took the view that the Constitution was effectively silent on the issue of maternal status in surrogacy. It is important to note, however, that this was not the view of O'Donnell J, who found that there was no constitutional objection to a system of birth registration which registered the birth mother as the mother *initially*. However, in his view, 'serious constitutional issues must necessarily arise if that position is maintained for all time and for all purposes'.[28] This illustrates an interesting division in the Court. Justice O'Donnell clearly left open the possibility that the current regime was vulnerable to constitutional challenge on the basis that it made no provision whatsoever for the reassigning of maternal status.

The lengthy and novel dissent of Clarke J (as he then was) is worthy of individual consideration. While focusing essentially on the same question as the majority, he framed it in broader terms, observing that 'these proceedings are about the current legal definition of motherhood and the current legal identity of the person or persons who might properly be regarded as a mother'.[29] The case could only be resolved, he said, by looking to the meaning of the term 'mother' in general law, and then considering whether the 2004 Act displaced that meaning.[30] For him, the first question in interpreting the 2004 Act was what the pre-existing common law position was, as regards the definition of mother. Justice Clarke found that there was no basis to say that the common law of Ireland defined mother as the birth mother. Like Denham CJ, he found that the Latin maxim *mater semper certus est*[31] had no place in the common law of Ireland. However, Clarke J concluded that the true common law position was that both the birth mother and the genetic mother were the mother of a child, given that, when that common law evolved, there was no possibility of those being different people. In his view, neither the 2004 Act, nor the Status of Children Act 1987, altered that common law position.

Turning to the requirements of the Constitution, Clarke J found that there was nothing to suggest that the constitutional definition of mother was different to the common law definition.[32] He acknowledged that it was counterintuitive to recognise two persons as the mother, but argued that it was equally counterintuitive to refuse to acknowledge either the birth or genetic mother as a mother. This led Clarke J to conclude that the Oireachtas was entitled to adopt a policy choice as to which person was recognised as mother for particular purposes. Those policy choices were not, however, to lie beyond the reach of the Court's review. Justice Clarke commented, echoing the views of O'Donnell J in this regard:

> They are also issues which, in my view, necessarily would loom large if either the genetic mother or the birth mother were, by definition, in all circumstances, and without any possibility of legal intervention, to be excluded by definition from being a mother for constitutional purposes.[33]

Such issues did not arise on the facts of the case at hand.[34]

[28] ibid O'Donnell J [38].
[29] ibid Clarke J [1.1].
[30] ibid [9.8].
[31] ibid [7.1].
[32] ibid [8.7].
[33] ibid [8.9].
[34] See also comments, ibid Clarke J [9.6].

Clarke J ultimately concluded that under the law both the genetic mother and the birth mother have some of the characteristics of mothers as used in Irish law. This, he reasoned, was the situation prior to the 2004 Act, and the Act had not stripped them of that status. As such, both the birth mother and the genetic mother were entitled to be registered as the mother of the child. Acknowledging that this was a messy result, he commented that it was 'the least bad solution'[35] and said that, if his view had commanded a majority, he would have directed the Chief Registrar to take steps necessary to ensure registration of both women.

Though *MR* did not ultimately improve the position of the genetic mother, it serves as a valuable precedent – and in essence, the only precedent – in the area of Irish surrogacy law. The decision is to be commended to the extent that it corrected the potential overreach of the High Court. Justice Abbot's analysis had potentially troublesome consequences, entailing what appeared to be a general holding that parenthood was to be defined by genetics alone. The Supreme Court's approach was entirely different to that of the High Court. Far from overreaching, it refused to 'reach' at all, with a majority of the Court emphasising that the regulation of surrogacy was a task for the legislature, and an arena in which the courts were not competent to interfere. Importantly, however, there was a discernible difference of opinion amongst the members of the Court as to whether there are constitutional rights that are engaged by laws governing the establishment of parental status in the context of surrogacy arrangements. Denham CJ suggested that there were not, that the Constitution was effectively silent on surrogacy. Clarke J and O'Donnell J disagreed: while not in agreement on the appropriate orders to be made in the case, they did agree that a continued failure on the part of the State to recognise parental status would give rise to constitutional concerns.

It is submitted that, on this issue, the view of Clarke J and O'Donnell J is the better one. The Irish Constitution is a constitution that is distinctively concerned with rights concerning families,[36] marriage,[37] parents and children.[38] Irish statute law in all of these arenas operates with a constitutional underpinning, and is constrained by the constitutional rights in play. It is implausible to suggest that a constitution which is so uniquely involved in the regulation of family life would be silent on the matter of parental status in surrogacy arrangements. The only interpretative approach which would support such a conclusion is an originalist or strict historical approach, approaches which have not been especially favoured by the Irish courts. This is not to say that the Oireachtas would not be entitled to a reasonably wide degree of deference in the balancing of constitutional rights in the surrogacy context: it undoubtedly would enjoy such deference as regards its approach to a difficult matter of social policy.[39] The courts according due deference to the legislative balancing of rights is, however, quite a different situation to constitutional silence.

[35] ibid [10.4].

[36] See also Art 41, *CO'S v Judge Doyle* [2014] 1 IR 556, *J.McD. v PL* [2010] 2 IR 199, *Nicolau v An Bord Uchtala* [1966] 1 IR 567.

[37] See also Art 41.3, *Murray v Ireland,* [1985] IR 532, *Ennis v Butterly* [1996] 1 IR 426, *HAH v SSA & Ors* [2017] 1 I.R. 372.

[38] See also Art 42A, *G v An Bord Uchtala* [1980] IR 32, *North Western Health Board v HW* [2001] 3 IR 622, *N v HSE* [2006] 4 IR 374, *JH, An Infant* [1985] IR 375.

[39] On deference to legislative balancing of rights, see eg *Tuohy v Courtney* [1994] 3 IR 1.

ii. The Invisibility of Intention

The commissioning mother without a genetic connection is similarly invisible. Unlike the genetic commissioning mother, this commissioning mother does not have an equality-based complaint. The commissioning father with no genetic link is invisible also. The invisibility of commissioning mothers highlights the fact that, as well as ignoring the genetic element of motherhood, Irish law sets no store by the place of intention in parenthood. To ignore the intentional element of parenthood is to fail to appreciate the fundamental changes that the development of surrogacy – and assisted reproduction more broadly – has meant for the institution of parenthood.[40]

Surrogacy arrangements require a richer understanding of parenthood. Parenthood in surrogacy involves not just a genetic component and a gestational component, but also an intentional component.[41] A person may have intentional and causative responsibility for the birth of a child, and yet have no genetic or gestational relationship to that child. We might illustrate the significance of the intentional element of parenthood by looking at the example of a person born through surrogacy, where there is no genetic link to either parent. This person has genetic parents, a gestational parent (the surrogate), and intended parents; the intended parents being the people who caused this child to be born. It might also be the case that this person has just one intended parent, to whom he or she may or may not be related. We might describe this person as having genetic parents – the egg and sperm donors – and a gestational parent – the surrogate. It would seem absurd to not describe as parents those people who commissioned the surrogacy arrangement.[42]

Horsey has argued that the intentional element of parenthood is not just significant in surrogacy but that it alone should be the pre-birth determinant in assigning parental status for children born through surrogacy and assisted reproduction.[43] She highlights a range of arguments for why intention is the most compelling form of parental claim in the assisted reproduction context.[44] The most compelling of these is the fact that the intended parents are the ones whose initiative and motivation caused the child to come into existence.[45] Applying the standard legal concept of causation, one can say that, but for the actions of the intended parents, this child would never have existed.[46] In Irish law, the central causative

[40] The author has made a similar argument in the context of ECHR identity rights in respect of surrogacy. See A Mulligan, 'Identity Rights and Sensitive Ethical Questions: The European Convention on Human Rights and the Regulation of Surrogacy Arrangements' (2018) 26(3) *Medical Law Review* 449–75.

[41] See also Chapter 13 in this volume for a discussion of the need for an evolving understanding of parenting in relation to protective leave entitlements.

[42] Note that the proposed surrogacy legislation does not provide for parental orders in the absence of a genetic link.

[43] K Horsey, 'Challenging Presumptions: Legal Parenthood and Surrogacy Arrangements' [2010] 22(4) *Child and Family Law Quarterly* 449.

[44] On intentional parenthood, see also RF Storrow, 'Parenthood by Pure Intention: Assisted Reproduction and the Functional Approach to Parentage' (2002) 53 *Hastings Law Journal* 640; G Douglas, 'The Intention to be a Parent and the Making of Mothers' (1994) 57(4) *Modern Law Review* 636.

[45] Horsey acknowledges that intention is only an appropriate determinant in assisted reproduction where, for the child to exists, there must be a definite intention. This is in contrast to natural reproduction, which of course can be wholly unintentional, and indeed wholly undesired.

[46] Horsey notes the reasoning in the decision of the Supreme court of California in the case of *Johnson v Calvert* [1993] 851 P 2d 774.

role of intention is entirely ignored. One would not have to go quite so far as Horsey – and say that intention is the preeminent element of parenthood – to believe that the invisibility of intention in Irish law in problematic.

Of course, commissioning mothers with a genetic link to the child are also intended parents, and their role as intentional parent is as invisible as their role as genetic parent. *MR* strongly suggests that there are constitutional concerns in respect of commissioning genetic mothers. This begs the question as to whether a commissioning mother with no genetic link to the child might also be able to assert constitutional rights and maintain a constitutional argument. Justice Clarke and O'Donnell J both spoke in terms of the constitutional position of the genetic mother, so their comments do not directly support the assertion of constitutional rights on the part of the commissioning mother. However, the position of a commissioning mother without a genetic link did not arise on the facts, so the absence of any mention does not necessarily mean that she is invisible under the Constitution. It is significant to note that some members of the Supreme Court observed that one problem with the High Court analysis was its emphasis on genetic parenthood to the exclusion of other considerations, asking how the analysis of Abbott J would operate in cases of egg and sperm donation.[47] This suggests an acceptance on the part of the Court that the role of the genetic parent varies by reference to the circumstances. It should be noted, however, that in the case of *JMcD v PL*[48] the Supreme Court set very little store by the agreement concluded between a lesbian couple and a friend of theirs who agreed to act as sperm donor in assessing the constitutional rights at play. It focused almost exclusively on the sperm donor's genetic fatherhood, and his intentions towards the child subsequent to its birth.[49] Together, these decisions provide scant precedent for the establishment of constitutional rights for commissioning mothers with no genetic connection. Such rights would have to be argued and established in the constitutional context by reference to general arguments supporting the recognition of the intentional element of parenthood.

D. Surrogates and Egg Donors

The surrogate mother suffers from a different kind of invisibility at Irish law. In one sense, it could be said that she enjoys extensive legal protection: she, as the birth mother, will remain the child's mother forever, as a matter of Irish law, enjoying at the statutory and constitutional level the right to guardianship. She is not, therefore, invisible to the law in the context of the surrogacy arrangement. But what is invisible is her status as a surrogate, and this is the source of her difficulties. A woman who decides to act as a surrogate does not want to have the status of mother. In all but a tiny minority of cases,[50] the surrogate sees herself as a surrogate, not as a mother, and wants the law to reflect that. As well as rights, motherhood confers on her responsibilities. Under Irish law, a surrogate retains the obligation of

[47] *MR v An t-Árd Chláraitheoir* [2014] IESC 60, McMenamin J [56].

[48] *JMcD v PL* [2010] 2 IR 199.

[49] The applicant, the sperm donor, had at the outset agreed to have the role of a 'favourite uncle' in the child's life but subsequent to the child's birth sought to be recognised as a parent.

[50] This situation is extremely rare. Internationally, the leading example is *In re Baby M* 109 N.J. 396 (NJ Feb 3, 1988).

maintenance of the child. However unlikely it may be that a child would ever enforce that right,[51] the theoretical possibility remains. Unless the Circuit Court dispenses with the need for the mother's consent,[52] her consent will be required on an ongoing basis for the child to obtain an Irish passport. Ironically, by according the surrogate the high status of 'mother', Irish law acts precisely against the interests of the vast majority of surrogates.

In practice, the Irish courts confer certain procedural protections on the surrogate mother. In the vast majority of cases, the surrogate is resident outside Ireland. To obtain orders in respect of paternity and guardianship for the genetic father, it is usually necessary to name the surrogate mother in the proceedings, as well as her husband if she is married, and to serve all documentation on them. Ordinarily, the father will need to provide the court with an affidavit sworn by the surrogate[53] in which she indicates her consent to the orders being sought. In such proceedings, the court is usually provided with a copy of the surrogacy agreement.

Questions must be asked about the real value of such procedural protections. Courts are, of course, operating in an unregulated space, and doing all in their power to protect the parties involved. In reality, however, those procedural guarantees may have little impact. Some foreign surrogates are empowered and well protected, and have the benefit of independent legal advice. American surrogacy arrangements, in particular, usually involve well paid, experienced surrogates operating in jurisdictions which protect their interests. These women may benefit from the procedural protections imposed by the Irish courts which supplement the security of their position in their home jurisdiction. Surrogates from less developed countries may be quite differently situated. Such women rarely have independent legal advice, and in many cases will be depending on translations of the surrogacy contract and of the other documents.

In virtually all such arrangements, the surrogate provides her services on a commercial basis, and motivated by that commercial purpose. Commercial surrogacy contracts are often criticised as raising a risk of exploitation of the surrogate, and this is the primary argument in favour of legal prohibitions on commercial surrogacy.[54] Unfortunately, the procedural safeguards imposed by the Irish courts, and the substantive position at Irish law, do little to provide real protection for a commercial surrogate at risk of exploitation. In reality, if the commercial surrogacy arrangement is exploitative, the surrogate has already been exploited by the time the matter reaches the Irish courts. By the time a surrogate has had a child and has sent it home with its Irish commissioning parents, it is far too late to address any risk of exploitation. Neither the procedural protections imposed by the Irish courts nor the fact

[51] Consider unusual cases where donor-conceived children have attempted to enforce rights of maintenance against donors, eg Miles Brignall, 'Gay Sperm Donor Told to Pay Child Maintenance For "His" Two Children' *The Guardian* (London, 26 October 2012) www.theguardian.com/money/2012/oct/26/gay-sperm-donor-pay-child-support-maintenance.

[52] The Circuit Court is often willing to dispense with consent.

[53] An affidavit sworn by the surrogate's husband, if she is married, is also required.

[54] R Storrow, 'New Thinking on Commercial Surrogacy' (2013) 88(4) *Indiana Law Journal* 1281; K Drabiak et al, 'Ethics, Law, and Commercial Surrogacy: A Call for Uniformity' (2007) 35(2) *Journal of Law, Medicine and Ethics* 300–09; A Van Niekerk and L Van Zyl 'Commercial Surrogacy and the Commodification of Children: An Ethical Perspective' (1995) 14(2) *Medicine and Law* 163–70; I Jargilo 'Regulating the Trade of Commercial Surrogacy in India' (2016) 15(2) *Journal of International Business and Law* 337; X Tang, 'Setting Norms: Protections for Surrogates in International Commercial Surrogacy' (2016) 25(1) *Minnesota Journal of International Law* 193–216.

that the surrogate remains the mother at Irish law – a status which she almost certainly does not want – provide her with any real protection from exploitation.

Finally, it should be noted that an argument could be made that surrogacy contracts have an informal status at Irish law. All the indications are that such contracts would not be enforceable in Ireland,[55] and yet they form a routine part of surrogacy proceedings in the Circuit Court. As regards egg donors, the 2015 Act establishes procedures regulating donor-assisted human reproduction. These are aimed at ensuring that donors are provided with comprehensive information, and that they give fully free and informed consent. It would appear, however, that the 2015 Act does not apply to donor-assisted reproduction in the context of a surrogacy arrangement, and furthermore it does not apply where the procedure takes place outside the State. As such, there is no protection whatsoever at Irish law for the egg donor in a surrogacy arrangement.

III. Reform: The Proposed Surrogacy Legislation

Against such a background, proposals for a bespoke surrogacy regime are long overdue and most welcome. This section will set out in outline what those proposals are, and offer some commentary on them and the organising principles which appear to underpin the legislative approach.

Part 6 of the General Scheme addresses the regulation of surrogacy. The regime it proposes to establish is one under which commercial surrogacy is prohibited but altruistic surrogacy is permitted, as long as certain legal and factual criteria are fulfilled.[56] Only gestational rather than traditional surrogacy is to be permitted. The surrogacy agreement is to be approved in advance by the Regulatory Authority, which will be established under the new legislation.[57] The surrogate must fit within certain criteria. She must be between 25 and 47 years of age, must have previously given birth to a child, and she must be assessed by a medical practitioner and by a counsellor, and approved as an appropriate person to act as a surrogate.[58] It will be possible for both couples and single people to enter into a surrogacy arrangement as long as they can demonstrate their medical inability to conceive and/or gestate a pregnancy, and as long as one intended parent is under 47. All surrogacy arrangements must involve at least one gamete provided by an intending parent.[59] The surrogate will be the mother of the child on birth,[60] and the intending parents can apply for a parental order, which will appoint them as the parents of the child. Parental orders will only be granted where the surrogacy arrangement is a permissible surrogacy arrangement under the law.[61]

[55] In *JMcD v PL* [2010] 2 IR 199, there was agreement on the Supreme Court that an agreement was only enforceable subject to the best interests of the child. In *Roche v Roche* [2010] 2 IR 321, the court was sceptical as to the role of contracts in resolving the disposition of frozen embryos. See in particular comments of Geoghegan J at [2010] 2 IR 321, 389.

[56] General Scheme, Head 36.

[57] ibid.

[58] ibid Head 38.

[59] ibid Head 39.

[60] If married, the surrogate's husband will be the child's father.

[61] General Scheme, Heads 47, 48 and 49.

In these general requirements, a number of significant policy choices can be discerned. First, surrogacy that involves no genetic link to the resulting child is not permissible. The rationale that underpins this would appear to be that surrogacy, to be ethically permissible, must bear some resemblance to natural human reproduction. The situation it seems intended to prevent is one in which it is possible for a couple to commission all aspects necessary to conceive and gestate a child. Even in the absence of payment, perhaps such a situation is regarded as unduly consumerist. Another significant policy choice is that the General Scheme suggests that surrogacy arrangements will be open to single men as well as single women.[62] Given the requirement for a genetic link, that single man would have to be capable of providing sperm for use with a donated egg.[63]

Perhaps the central feature of the scheme is that only altruistic surrogacy will be permissible. A notable feature of the scheme is that it permits the payment of reasonable expenses to surrogates, but defines reasonable expenses extremely restrictively. Reasonable expenses are defined as costs associated with:

(a) becoming or trying to become pregnant;
(b) the pregnancy or a birth;
(c) entering into and giving effect to a surrogacy agreement.[64]

Surrogates may be paid in respect of lost earnings arising from the pregnancy, but this is limited to:

(i) a period of not more than two months during which the birth happened or was expected to happen;

(ii) any other period during the pregnancy when the surrogate was unable to work on medical grounds related to pregnancy or birth.[65]

This tight definition would appear to be intended to ensure that the prohibition on commercial surrogacy is not thwarted by the payment of large sums of money in respect of reasonable expenses, often characterised as loss of earnings during the period of the pregnancy in which the surrogate is in effect working as a surrogate for the commissioning couple. An interesting comparison can be drawn with surrogacy law in the United Kingdom where commercial surrogacy is illegal, but sums are on occasion paid to surrogates and retrospectively approved by the courts.[66] Such payments would appear to be prohibited under the proposed Irish legislation.

Another aspect of the General Scheme which appears to be targeted at commercial surrogacy is Head 42, which provides that it will be illegal to advertise the availability of surrogacy services of a particular person, or to advertise that one is seeking a surrogate. It seems that it would still be permissible for a fertility clinic to advertise that it provided

[62] The explanatory note to Head 39 states that 'If the surrogacy agreement involves a single intending parent then s/he must meet all of the criteria as an individual', suggesting that both single men and women can be intending parents.

[63] It is interesting to note that the proposed regime contrasts with that in effect in the UK where single people are not eligible for parental orders. See Human Fertilisation and Embryology Act 2008, s 54(1).

[64] General Scheme, Head 41.

[65] ibid.

[66] Human Fertilisation and Embryology Act 2008, s 54(8). See discussion in *Surrogacy in the UK: Myth Busting and Reform* (Surrogacy UK, 2015).

medical surrogacy services in respect of altruistic arrangements already in place, but it could not advertise assistance in finding a surrogate. These provisions would seem to be designed to avoid the growth of a surrogacy marketplace in which surrogates and intended parents could make contact and potentially enter into illegal commercial arrangements. If that is the purpose, however, the section may potentially overreach its intent. Altruistic surrogacy is permitted under the General Scheme, but if one cannot publicly advertise in respect of altruistic surrogacy arrangements, then presumably the only arrangements which will occur are those where the intended parents and the surrogate already know each other. It is not immediately clear why this should be the case. It is possible that a woman may altruistically wish to carry a pregnancy for strangers, and therefore needs a way to make contact with them. To the extent that Head 42 prevents such arrangements being made, it would seem to go too far.

It is worth considering what effect this strict approach to the prohibition of commercial surrogacy is likely to have on the development of surrogacy practice in Ireland. The regime demands a very high degree of altruism from a surrogate. Not only can she not be paid reasonable expenses for the duration of the pregnancy, she may only be paid for a two-month period at the time of the birth, and if she is medically unfit to work. Given that Head 42 will make it very difficult to identify strangers willing to act as a surrogate, the only surrogacy arrangements that will be facilitated are those between friends or family members. This will likely leave many intended parents unable to find a surrogate, raising the prospect that they will attempt to enter into an arrangement in breach of the regulations, or go abroad to circumvent the law.

Perhaps the most distinctive aspect of the General Scheme is that it makes extensive provision for the recording of information about the surrogacy arrangement and for ensuring that the resulting child will have access to information concerning the surrogate.[67] The legislation will establish a National Surrogacy Register.[68] This register will contain details on the surrogate, the donor (where a donor is involved), the intended parents and the child. Importantly, the National Surrogacy Register will be coordinated with the national register of births, with the effect that where a surrogate-born person who is over 18 years of age applies for a copy of their birth certificate, they will be informed that 'further information relating to him or her is available from the National Surrogacy Register'.[69] The purpose of this provision is clearly to ensure that a surrogate-born person can access contact details of their surrogate. If the person does not already know he or she is surrogate-born, they may find this out in the course of accessing a copy birth certificate. This provision mirrors analogous provisions under the 2015 Act which govern access to donor-related information by donor-conceived persons. Under that Act, a National Donor Conceived Person Register[70] is created, which provides analogous functions to those provided by the National Surrogacy Register. As in the case of surrogacy, the National Donor Conceived Person Register interacts with the register of births with the effect that a donor-conceived person over the age of 18 who applies for a birth certificate will be informed that information concerning them is held by the National Donor Conceived Person Register.

[67] General Scheme, Heads 44, 50 and 51.
[68] ibid Head 50.
[69] ibid Head 51.
[70] Children and Family Relationships Act 2015, s 33.

These measures are designed to vindicate the right of the person to identity, by ensuring that they can access identifying material concerning their genetic or gestational parents. Anonymous gamete donation has long been a subject of controversy in assisted reproduction, and in that context there has been extensive discussion of the right to access identifying details of sperm and egg donors.[71] The right of the child to access identifying information on their surrogate has been much less discussed. The Irish legislative approach puts information on both genetic and gestational parents on the same footing, taking a normative position that each is equally important to the resulting child.

The General Scheme would appear to make no provision for the making of parental orders in respect of surrogacy arrangements concluded prior to the enactment of the legislation. This is in contrast to the 2015 Act which does establish a limited regime for the retrospective recognition of parental status.[72] This may be something of a weakness in the proposed regime, as it would make no allowances for the recognition of parental status even where the surrogacy arrangement in question was an altruistic one. Admittedly, it may well be the case that there have been few if any such arrangements in Ireland, but in principle it would seem to be unfair not to make any provision for arrangements which would have fallen within the regime, if enacted earlier. The applicants in *MR*, for example, seem to fit the criteria. Surely they, alongside the handful of other people in the same position, should be entitled to retrospective recognition.

The Act is also silent on the status of children and parents who enter into surrogacy arrangements, which fall outside the category of permissible arrangements. This silence is not unusual – legal regimes across the world struggle with the question of how to cope with these situations.[73] There is a fundamental tension arising from the fact that the commissioning parents have circumvented the law, but the child is a wholly innocent party. In the great majority of cases, the best interests of the child are served by remaining in the care of the commissioning parents, given that it is highly unlikely that there is anyone else who wants to be recognised as the child's parent. Justice Clarke adverted to this problem in *MR*, commenting:

> Whatever form of regulation is considered appropriate to prevent abuse, exploitation or other practises which may be considered to be undesirable, there is always the risk that a child will come into existence in circumstances which are a breach of those regulations. Such a situation will not be the child's fault. The law will have to deal with that child as that child is. Any legislation needs not only to deal with the proper regulation of practise and methodology in this area but also the proper recognition of the status of children who result from advances in modern science. In the context of new advances in science the law will have to deal with the problem of what to do in

[71] See eg N Cahn, 'Necessary Subjects: The Need for a Mandatory National Donor Gamete Databank' (2009) 12 *DePaul Journal of Health Care Law* 203. For the opposite view, compare: IG Cohen, 'Rethinking Sperm-Donor Anonymity: Of Changed Selves, Nonidentity, and One-night Stands' (2012) *Georgetown Law Journal* 431. See generally, see DR Beeson, PK Jennings and W Kramer, 'Offspring Searching for their Sperm Donors: How Family Type Shapes the Process' (2011) *Human Reproduction* 26(9) 2415–24.

[72] Children and Family Relationships Act 2015, ss 20–22.

[73] Fenton-Glynn has explored the difficulties the English courts have experienced in relation to children born through international, commercial surrogacy arrangements which are illegal as a matter of English law. See C Fenton-Glynn, 'The Regulation and Recognition of Surrogacy under English Law: An Overview of the Case Law' (2015) 27 *Child and Family Law Quarterly* 83; C Fenton-Glynn, 'Outsourcing Ethical Dilemmas: Regulating International Surrogacy Arrangements' (2016) 24(1) *Medical Law Review* 59.

> circumstances where, in breach of whatever regulation may be put in place, a new human being has come into the world.[74]

The General Scheme, whether deliberately or inadvertently, fails to tackle this issue.

A further issue for the General Scheme is the fact that it is expressly directed at surrogacy arrangements which take place in Ireland. Permissible surrogacy arrangements include only domestic surrogacy arrangements,[75] and surrogates must be habitually resident in Ireland. It seems therefore that the legislation will not regulate surrogacy arrangements entered into abroad by Irish people, and more importantly will not regulate the legal status of those parents and children when they return to Ireland. Given that such foreign surrogacy arrangements currently constitute the vast majority of 'Irish' surrogacy arrangements, this would seem to be a significant lacuna. This omission may also fail to vindicate the rights of the child under the European Convention on Human Rights, as discussed in the next section.

IV. Cross-border Surrogacy and the European Convention on Human Rights

The final dimension of Irish surrogacy law which must be addressed is the extent of the State's obligations under the European Convention on Human Rights (ECHR).[76] In recent years, the European Court of Human Rights (ECtHR) has decided a number of cases concerning cross-border surrogacy, and states' obligations in respect of the rights of persons concerned when they return to their country of origin.[77] While it is clear that states are entitled to maintain domestic prohibitions on surrogacy, they may have obligations in respect of children born abroad.

The leading case on this is *Mennesson v France*,[78] which concerned a French couple who entered into a surrogacy agreement in California with a Californian surrogate, which led to the birth of twins. The commissioning father was the genetic father, but the commissioning mother had no genetic link. Surrogacy was illegal as a matter of French law.[79] The French authorities refused to record the legal relationship between the parents and children in the French register of births, marriages and deaths, on the basis that it was contrary to the principles of French law 'to give effect, in terms of the legal parent-child relationship, to a surrogacy agreement'.[80] While the legal relationship between the parents and the children

[74] *MR v An t-Árd Chláraitheoir* [2014] IESC 60, [2.21].

[75] Defined as 'a surrogacy agreement undertaken by a surrogate and an intending parent who are habitually resident and where the embryo transfer is carried out in this State', Head 35, General Scheme.

[76] For a more in-depth discussion of this case law, see A Mulligan, 'Identity Rights and Sensitive Ethical Questions (n 40).

[77] *Mennesson v France* App no 65192/11 (ECtHR, 26 June 2014), *Labassee v France* App no 65941/11 (ECtHR, 26 June 2014), *Paradiso and Campanelli v Italy* Appl no 25358/12 (ECtHR, 27 January 2015, Second Chamber) (ECtHR, 24 January 2017, Grand Chamber).

[78] *Mennesson v France* App no 65192/11 (ECtHR, 26 June 2014).

[79] French Civil Code, Civil Code, Art 16-7. This prohibition addressed altruistic as well as commercial surrogacy agreements.

[80] *Mennesson v France* App no 65192/11 (ECtHR, 26 June 2014) 27, quoting the decision of the Court of Cassation of 6 April 2011.

was not recognised as a matter of French law, the parents enjoyed full legal responsibility for the children, granted on the basis of the US civil status documents. The parents challenged this refusal to recognise the legal parent-child relationship, arguing that it violated the right to private and family life of both the parents and the children, as protected by Article 8 of the Convention.

The applicants were ultimately successful in this challenge, and the Court identified a breach of the children's right to respect for private life arising from the refusal of the French authorities to recognise the children as the children of their biological father, and as French citizens by reason of that relationship. This conclusion was premised on the existence of that genetic link, with the Court commenting:

> It cannot be said to be in the interests of the child to deprive him or her of a legal relationship of this nature where the biological reality of that relationship has been established and the child and parent concerned demand full recognition thereof.[81]

As is clear from this quote, the welfare of the children was central to the Court's conclusions.

It is not clear precisely what effect *Mennesson* will have on the obligations of Member States in the surrogacy arena more broadly, but what does seem to be clear is that Member States have some obligation to recognise the legal relationship between a child born through cross-border surrogacy and its biological father, even where surrogacy is itself illegal as a matter of domestic law. The ECtHR has been significantly less sympathetic to surrogacy-related claims where there is no biological relationship.[82] It is also important to note that the surrogacy arrangement in *Mennesson* appears to have been a commercial one, but this had no bearing on the Court's analysis. It seems, therefore, that the obligation to recognise the parental relationship arises even where the child is born through a surrogacy arrangement which is illegal as a matter of domestic law. This may arguably apply to surrogacy arrangements carried out within the home state which are in breach of domestic law, as well as those entered into abroad.

As discussed, the General Scheme makes no provision for children born outside of the proposed regime, whether at home or abroad. The ECHR case law on surrogacy raises the prospect that a failure to make provision for these children may constitute a breach of the Convention, at least where there is a genetic link with the commissioning father. Irish law will, in due course, have to ensure that the State fulfils its obligations in this regard.

V. Conclusion

This is an exciting moment for Irish surrogacy law. It seems that the major policy decisions have been made by the relevant government departments, and it is now for the legislature to scrutinise and fine tune those proposals. After many years of neglect, it seems that Irish law may finally be getting to grips with the legal and ethical challenge of surrogacy. It is to be hoped, in particular, that the new regime will render visible and protected those women who previously were invisible and exploited.

[81] ibid 100.

[82] *Paradiso and Campanelli v Italy* Appl no 25358/12 (ECtHR, 27 January 2015, Second Chamber).

8

Domestic Violence Law

LOUISE CROWLEY

I. Introduction

Domestic and relationship violence is a significant social evil, and as regards the statistical evidence relating to its incidence, has always predominantly presented as abuse against women. The capacity of the law to protect victims of domestic violence in Ireland has been frustrated by the combination of historical reluctance to intervene followed by a begrudgingly piecemeal approach to the availability of remedies for victims. The inadequacy of the responses and the associated prioritising of rights of privacy and property over the immediate needs of victims of abuse serves to vividly demonstrate the longstanding failure of the Irish State to effectively and comprehensively protect victims of domestic abuse. The Irish State has, in this context, repeatedly failed women through its inability to intervene robustly. The pre-1976 absence of State capacity to intervene, the non-criminalisation of marital rape until 1990, the vague evidentiary thresholds in the governing statute, and the longstanding restriction of the availability of remedies to married applicants, have merely perpetuated and sustained the weaker position of victims of domestic violence, most typically women suffering at the hands of men. However recent international developments, including the EU Victims of Crime Directive and the Council of Europe Convention on Preventing and Combating Violence Against Women and Domestic Abuse (the 'Istanbul Convention'), have better prioritised the needs of the victim, while also expressly highlighting the gendered nature of this abuse. It is hoped that Ireland's victims of domestic abuse will be better served by the Irish legal system upon the given the recent enactment of the Victims of Crime Act 2017 and the Domestic Violence Act 2018, as mandated by these international obligations.

II. The Prevalence and Gendered Nature of Domestic and Relationship Violence

The prevalence of domestic abuse is impossible to gauge accurately, given both its under-reporting and the systemic reluctance to prosecute offenders. The unwillingness by victims to report incidents of abuse and to pursue the matter through the criminal justice system, as well as the historic under-recording and miscategorisation of incidents by the State, has resulted in a failure to capture the true nature and extent of the abuse being inflicted. Government-commissioned reports to assess the prevalence nationally in Ireland have been sporadic, but when published demonstrate the predominantly gendered nature of domestic violence incidents. The seminal 2005 report entitled *Domestic Abuse of Women and Men in Ireland*,[1] produced by Watson and Parsons for the Economic and Social Research Institute (ESRI) and the National Crime Council, reported that one in seven women in Ireland, compared with one in 17 men, experience severe abusive behaviour of a physical, sexual or emotional nature, from a partner at some stage in their lives.[2] While the data reveal that, at the time of reporting, approximately 88,000 men and 213,000 women in Ireland had been severely abused,[3] it was also reported that the abuse suffered by women was likely to be more severe – it was seven times more likely to be sexual in nature, and women were more likely than men to suffer serious injuries.[4]

This distinct gendered imbalance is also reflected in international research; a study conducted in 2001 reported that '90% of the more systematic, persistent and injurious violence that is instrumental in the maintenance of power, is perpetrated by men'.[5] Separately, a cross-jurisdictional study of police reports and crime surveys involving the UK, the US and Canada reported that between 90–97 per cent of perpetrators of relationship violence are men.[6] More broadly, Heise et al have reported that at least one in three women, which they estimate equates to up to one billion women, have been beaten, coerced into sex, or otherwise abused in their lifetimes.[7]

National statistics and related data are published more frequently by a number of Irish domestic violence support services, including Women's Aid,[8] the Dublin Rape Crisis Centre[9] and Safe Ireland.[10] The stark prevalence of domestic violence against women is evident in all reports issued by these organisations; for example, Women's Aid has repeatedly reported that one in five women in Ireland who have been in a relationship have been abused by a current or former partner.[11] In 2016, Women's Aid received 16,946 disclosures of domestic violence against women, made during 19,115 contacts with Women's Aid Direct Services.[12] These included a range of incidents: 11,078 incidents of emotional

[1] D Watson and S Parsons, *Domestic Abuse of Women and Men in Ireland Report of the National Study of Domestic Abuse* (National Crime Council/ESRI, 2005) www.esri.ie/pubs/BKMNEXT56.pdf.

[2] ibid 24.

[3] ibid.

[4] Women's injuries tended to be more serious – women are nearly twice as likely as men to require medical treatment for their injuries and 10 times more likely to require a stay in hospital. Women are also over twice as likely as men to have experienced severe physical abuse, seven times more likely to have experienced sexual abuse, and almost three times more likely to have experienced severe emotional abuse.

[5] MS Kimmel, *Make Victims of Domestic Violence: A Substantive and Methodology Research Review* (2001 report to the Equality Committee of the Department of Education and Science); subsequently published as MS Kimmel, '"Gender Symmetry" in Domestic Violence: A Substantive and Methodological Research Review' (2002) 8(11) (November) *Violence Against Women*, Special Issue: Women's Use of Violence in Intimate Relationships, Part 1.

[6] RE Dobash and RP Dobash, *Women, Violence and Social Change* (London, Routledge, 1992).

[7] L Heise, M Ellsberg and M Gottemoeller, *Ending Violence Against Women* (Series L No 11) (Johns Hopkins University School of Public Health, Population Information Program, 1999).

[8] 'National and International Statistics' (*Women's Aid*) www.womensaid.ie/about/policy/natintstats.html.

[9] 'Policy and Publications' (*Dublin Rape Crisis Centre*) www.drcc.ie/get-informed/policy-publications/.

[10] 'Knowledge Centre' (*Safe Ireland*) www.safeireland.ie/knowledge-centre/.

[11] M O'Connor and Kelleher Associates, *Making the Links* (Women's Aid, 1995).

[12] Women's Aid, *Impact Report 2016* (Women's Aid, 2016) www.womensaid.ie/download/pdf/womens_aid_impact_report_2016.pdf.

abuse; 3,502 incidents of physical abuse; and 1,671 incidents of financial abuse were disclosed. Additionally, in that year, Women's Aid received 695 reports of sexual abuse, including 316 rapes. In 2015, 76 per cent of the 11,789 helpline contacts received by the Dublin Rape Crisis Centre were from female victims.[13] Although not differentiated by gender in its 2016 report, engagement with the Dublin Rape Crisis Centre increased to 12,388. As regards accommodation support, a one-day survey conducted by Safe Ireland in 2014 reported that 475 women and 301 children were accommodated and/or received support from a domestic violence service.[14]

The prevalence of domestic violence amongst women across the European Union was also recently captured by an EU-wide survey based on interviews conducted with 42,000 women across the 28 Member States. The Report compiled by the European Union Agency for Fundamental Rights entitled *Violence Against Women – An EU-wide Survey*,[15] published in March 2014, confirmed that gender-based violence disproportionately affects women, noting that while both genders can commit acts of relationship violence, violence against women is predominantly perpetrated by men, most especially in respect of sexual violence and sexual harassment. The survey asked women about their experiences (current and historical) of physical, sexual and psychological violence, including incidents of intimate partner violence. It also included questions on acts of stalking, sexual harassment, and the impact of new technologies in their experiences of abuse. What was uncovered, across the 28 Member States, was that:

> One in 10 women has experienced some form of sexual violence since the age of 15, and one in 20 has been raped. Just over one in five women has experienced physical and/or sexual violence from either a current or previous partner, and just over one in 10 women indicates that they have experienced some form of sexual violence by an adult before they were 15 years old. Yet, as an illustration, only 14 per cent of women reported their most serious incident of intimate partner violence to the police, and 13 per cent reported their most serious incident of non-partner violence to the police.[16]

Both the prevalence of the violence, and the systematic underreporting to the authorities, caused the Agency to regard gender-based violence as an ongoing, extensive human rights abuse that must be addressed.[17] In addition to the startling levels of abuse disclosed by the participants in the survey, it was equally evident that the majority of victims of such abuse do not report the incidents to the authorities in their Member State. Research conducted by the

[13] Dublin Rape Crisis Centre, *Annual Report 2017* (Dublin Rape Crisis Centre, 2017) www.drcc.ie/wp-content/uploads/2017/07/Annual-Report-2016.pdf.

[14] 'New Domestic Violence Statistics Show 14 Requests for Accommodation could not be met every day' (*Safe Ireland*, 16 February 2016) www.safeireland.ie/2016/new-domestic-violence-statistics-show-14-requests-for-accommodation-could-not-be-met-every-day/.

[15] European Union Agency for Fundamental Rights, *Violence Against Women: An EU-wide Survey – Main Results Report* (Publication Office of the European Union, 2015).

[16] European Union Agency for Fundamental Rights, *Violence Against Women: An EU-wide Survey. Results at a Glance* (Publication Office of the European Union, 2014).

[17] ibid 7. The Report acknowledged that 'It is only since the 1990s that violence against women has emerged as a fundamental rights concern that warrants legal and political recognition at the highest level, and as an area where State Parties, as those with a duty to protect, have an obligation to safeguard victims'. In a Red C poll carried out for SAFE Ireland in December 2015, nearly 90% of people said that domestic violence is an issue all of society should be concerned with. Over 80% of respondents, rising to 87% amongst female respondents, were of the view that the issue of domestic violence should be prioritised by Government.

National Office for the Prevention of Domestic, Sexual and Gender-based Violence reflects the extent of under-reporting in the Irish context, emphasising the proactive responsibility on the State through appropriate support services, to connect with those women who have not accessed a frontline domestic violence service in Ireland.[18]

III. Historical Reluctance of the Irish State to Intervene in Family Life

The identification of the family unit in Article 41 of the Constitution as being 'antecedent and superior to all positive law', served to establish the inviolability of the family by mandating the State's obligation to respect the family in its constitution and authority.[19] This stance traditionally served to prevent the State from intervening in the privacy of the family unit despite alleged adverse effects on individual members.[20] However, the rights of the family are not absolute,[21] and ultimately the obligation on the State to intervene in cases of domestic abuse gave rise to the enactment of section 22 of the Family Law (Maintenance of Spouses and Children) Act 1976 ('1976 Act'). However, in balancing the rights of the different parties, the State accorded significant weight to the rights of the respondent, both as a member of a family unit deserving of significant deference by the State, and also as traditionally the property owner, whose rights have continuously restricted the capacity of the law to robustly protect the victim of such abuse. As a result, when first given a statutory footing, the capacity for intervention was relatively minimal; section 22 introduced the barring order which empowered the court to remove a violent spouse from the home where there were reasonable grounds for believing that the safety or welfare of the applicant spouse or any dependent child of the family required it, representing the first statutory basis for a civil application to secure the protection of the court in the context of domestic violence. Section 22 was enacted as a gender-neutral right but limited to a spouse. Critically, such intervention was, until 1996, limited exclusively to the protection of those who were parties to a marital union, identifying women who were married to their abusers as the sole victims entitled to such State intervention, as discussed below. The Family Law (Protection of Spouses and Children) Act 1981 extended the potential duration and scope of a barring

[18] 'Male Victims of Domestic Violence' (*The National Office for the Prevention of Domestic, Sexual and Gender-based Violence*, 2017) www.cosc.ie/en/COSC/Pages/WP09000005.

[19] Art 41.1.1 of the Constitution sets out the special position of the family and expressly identifies its elevated position and the superior nature of its status and associated rights: 'The State recognises the Family as the natural primary and fundamental unit group of society, and as a moral institution possessing inalienable and imprescriptible rights, antecedent and superior to all positive law.' Additionally, in light of this stated importance of the family, Art 41.2 provides: 'The State, therefore, guarantees to protect the Family in its constitution and authority, as the necessary basis of social order and as indispensable to the welfare of the Nation and the State.'

[20] A case in point is *N and N and another v G and G, the HSE and An Bórd Uchtála* [2006] 4 IR 374 where the marital family's right to State protection in respect of its constitution and authority, as expressly guaranteed by Art 41.2 superseded any conflicting rights that might be asserted by individual family members, in this case Baby Ann. A similar deference to the authority of the family unit is evident in the principal statute governing State capacity to intervene in a family unit where the life or wellbeing of a child is in danger; the Child Care Act 1991 operates on a presumption that a child is best placed with his/her family, resulting in an emphasis upon family support rather than family intervention. See also W Duncan, 'The Constitutional Protection of Parental Rights' in JM Eekelaar and P Sarcevic (eds), *Parenthood in Modern Society* (Dordrecht, Springer Netherlands, 1993).

[21] *Murray and Murray v Ireland* [1985] ILRM 542.

order to a period of up to 12 months,[22] while also introducing the protection order, an interim measure to better ensure the safety of an applicant in the period prior to the determination of a barring order application.[23] Subsequently, the Domestic Violence Act 1996 introduced the less restrictive safety order – a remedy which may be secured where there is insufficient evidence to justify the imposition of a barring order, yet where there is some danger to the safety or welfare of the applicant and/or any dependent children. This newly introduced safety order represented a crucial addition to the suite of remedies available to those in need of protection.

The legislative reluctance to include a statement or even guidelines relating to the evidentiary thresholds required to secure a barring order, safety order or protection order has always caused a significant level of uncertainty regarding the determination of applications for relief. The challenges posed for applicants are in turn compounded by the unavoidable exercise of judicial discretion in determining individual applications. The legislation requires the court to be satisfied that there exist reasonable grounds for believing that the safety or welfare of the applicant spouse and/or any child requires such a level of intervention to be ordered; without reference to the nature or extent of the danger to be proven.

A not unpredictable consequence of such vague and imprecise direction was the conservative approach adopted by the Supreme Court in *O'B v O'B*.[24] The plaintiff wife secured a High Court order from Costello J under section 22 of the 1976 Act, which directed the defendant to leave and not re-enter the family home, on the basis that he had behaved in an 'extremely reprehensible manner towards the plaintiff … [and] … that the marriage of the parties had broken down irretrievably'. The central ground of appeal was that neither the evidence nor the facts before the trial judge constituted 'proper or sufficient ground for the making of a barring order' under the 1976 Act. On appeal, the Supreme Court determined that the barring order was not justified in the circumstances. Chief Justice O'Higgins was of the view that while

> [t]he evidence of the plaintiff indicates that various incidents occurred – rudeness by the husband in front of the children, a lack of sensitivity in his manner to her and efforts by him at dominance in running the house … [there was] … no case of violence to be made against the husband.[25]

In considering the term 'welfare', O'Higgins CJ indicates his view 'that it was intended to provide for cases of neglect or fear or nervous injury brought about by the other spouse' thereby commendably suggesting an acceptance of the broader understanding of domestic violence, beyond the requirement of proof of physical injury. However, despite this acknowledgment by the Chief Justice of the distinct tests of safety or welfare, once the consequences of the barring order were considered by the court, namely removal of the respondent from his property, the threshold to be established became one of

> serious misconduct on the part of the offending spouse – something wilful and avoidable which causes, or is likely to cause, hurt or harm, not as a single occurrence but as something which

[22] Family Law (Protection of Spouses and Children) Act 1981, s 2(4).

[23] Where the court was of the opinion that there existed reasonable grounds for believing that the safety or welfare of the applicant spouse and/or any child required such intervention, it could order that the respondent spouse not use or threaten to use violence against, molest or put in fear the applicant spouse or the child, effective from the date of the application.

[24] *O'B v O'B* [1984] IR 182.

[25] ibid 190.

> is continuing or repetitive in its nature. Violence or threats of violence may clearly invoke the jurisdiction.[26]

Thus, it appears that the test for the granting of relief under both the 1976 Act and the 1981 Act shifted from a subjective test of danger to the safety or welfare of the applicant arising from neglect by the respondent, fear on the part of the applicant or nervous injury suffered by the applicant following the behaviour of the respondent, to an assessment of how wilful, how avoidable and indeed how frequent the misconduct was. No longer was the fact of a threat to the applicant sufficient, nor evidence as to the subjective impact of his behaviour on the applicant; rather the focus was on the behaviour of the respondent and whether it was deemed adequately dangerous to justify the penalty.

A particularly challenging aspect of the judgment delivered by O'Higgins CJ relates to the insistence that any threat arising to the applicant must be related to conduct on the part of the respondent, and not merely arising from his presence in the house. Thus, O'Higgins CJ stated that while the respondent remained the source of the threat to the applicant, and that

> it is clear that the plaintiff suffered severe nervous strain as a result of the defendant residing in the same house, it is equally clear that this did not stem from any particular conduct in his part, but rather because he was there.

Respectfully, if the fact of his presence represented a threat to the applicant, that in itself constitutes a form of conduct, or indeed behaviour that gives rise to the 'fear or nervous injury' both previously accepted by the Chief Justice as distinct aspects of the welfare of the applicant. In applying this view, O'Higgins CJ allowed the respondent husband's appeal, regarding his behaviour as at times rude and insensitive, but not amounting to serious misconduct.

On dissent, a quite different approach was adopted by Griffin J who, in the course of his judgment, documented much of the verbal and emotional abuse suffered by the applicant wife, concluding in favour of the applicant wife:

> I cannot agree that the conduct of the defendant husband was no more than what might be expected in the ordinary wear and tear of married life as I understand it … [and was] … bound to have an adverse effect on the physical and emotional health of the wife and of the children and the medical reports received in evidence at the hearing bore this out.[27]

Helpfully, and whilst noting the absence of physical violence in this case, Griffin J regarded welfare as ordinarily referring to 'health and well-being … both physical and emotional welfare' and refused to accept that the husband's behaviour 'was no more than what might be expected in the ordinary wear and tear of married life'.[28] In outlining the nature of the

[26] ibid 189.

[27] ibid 193–94, 'it is necessary to refer to some of the defendant's conduct which I would consider abnormal in married life by any standard …. He frequently told her that she was living off him, and should pay him rent and pay for her food; in the presence of the children he referred to her as a "lazy slut" and on occasions changed the words lazy to that of a different four-letter word. When the children attempted to bring cups and plates to the kitchen sink, as they had been trained to do, he directed them not to do so as this was their mother's job; he undermined any authority she had over the children by directing them not to do whatever she had just told them to do. When, on Sundays, they expressed a wish to go to visit their maternal grandparents with their mother, he physically pulled them away from the plaintiff and refused to allow them to go. He constantly indulged in things of the nature to which I have referred, being conduct which, in my opinion, no woman should be required to put up with in normal married life.'

[28] ibid 194.

behaviour in question, which included evidence of significant financial and verbal mistreatment and denigrating and degrading treatment of the applicant wife, Griffin J was in no doubt that the conduct in question 'was bound to have an adverse effect on the physical and emotional health of the plaintiff wife and of the children' as borne out by the medical reports presented to the court. Evidently, the impact of the respondent's conduct on the applicant wife and the children was the determining factor for Griffin J, demonstrating a more appropriate victim-centred view of the governing provision and the capacity for State intervention.

Unfortunately, the enactment of the Domestic Violence Act 1996, although progressive in other ways, did not provide any clarity or direction in respect of the evidentiary thresholds for securing protective relief. It remains the position that the court is required to grant the order sought where it is of the opinion that there are reasonable grounds for believing that the safety or welfare of the applicant and/or any dependent person requires that particular level of intervention. Providing direction to the judiciary in determining applications for relief in the context of domestic or relationship violence is undoubtedly challenging, especially given the subjective nature of the circumstances in every case. However, the current open-ended discretionary basis of adjudication relies almost entirely upon the views of the presiding judge, resulting in an inability to properly advise, insofar as might be possible, an already vulnerable applicant. This longstanding abdication of responsibility by the legislature places the arduous and complex task of determining sufficiency of evidence solely in the hands of the judiciary, operating in private sittings without statutory direction or accessible precedents.

Helpfully, the Domestic Violence Act 2018 includes an exhaustive list of factors or circumstances to which the court will be obliged to have regard in determining future applications for specified orders. 'Specified orders' refers to a safety order, barring order, interim barring order, emergency barring order or protection order, or an order varying or discharging any of these orders.[29] The guidelines did not feature in the Domestic Violence Bill 2017 as originally introduced before the Seanad but were added as a recommendation at Committee Stage. The lengthier, more comprehensive version, supplemented at the Report Stage[30] as included in the Act as passed by the Seanad, sets out the following as those factors or circumstances to which the court will now be obliged to have regard:

(a) any history of violence inflicted by the respondent on the applicant or a dependent person;
(b) any conviction of the respondent for an offence under the Criminal Justice (Theft and Fraud Offences) Act 2001 that involves loss to, or is to the prejudice of, the applicant or a dependent person;
(c) any conviction of the respondent for an offence that involves violence or the threat of violence to any person;
(d) whether any violence inflicted by the respondent on the applicant or a dependent person is increasing, or has increased, in severity or frequency over time;
(e) any exposure of any dependent person to violence inflicted by the respondent on the applicant or any other dependent person;
(f) any previous order under this Act or the Act of 1996 made against the respondent with regard to any person;
(g) any history of animal cruelty by the respondent;

[29] Domestic Violence Act 2018, s 5, as passed by Seanad Éireann, specified orders are defined by s 2 of the Act.
[30] 30 November 2017.

(h) any destruction or damage caused by the respondent to –
   (i) the personal property of the applicant, the respondent or a dependent person, or
   (ii) any place where the applicant or a dependent person resides;
(i) any action of the respondent, not being a criminal offence, which puts the applicant or a dependent person in fear for his or her own safety or welfare;
(j) any recent separation between the applicant and the respondent;
(k) substance abuse, including abuse of alcohol, by the respondent, the applicant or a dependent person;
(l) access to weapons by the respondent, the applicant or a dependent person;
(m) the applicant's perception of the risk to his or her own safety or welfare due to the behaviour of the respondent;
(n) the age and state of health (including pregnancy) of the applicant or any dependent person;
(o) any evidence of deterioration in the physical, psychological or emotional welfare of the applicant or a dependent person which is caused directly by fear of the behaviour of the respondent;
(p) whether the applicant is economically dependent on the respondent;
(q) any matter required to be considered by the court under, and in accordance with, *subsections (2)* and *(3)* of *section 29*;
(r) any other matter which appears to the court to be relevant to the safety or welfare of the applicant and any dependent person.[31]

While these factors will be instructive for the judiciary in determining applications for protective relief, dedicated training for all judges, most especially those presiding in the District Court remains essential to ensure that informed and considered decisions are reached. No one-size-fits-all rule will assist in this context, and judges will need a clear understanding of the law, the broader context of domestic violence, the power imbalance that arises in such relationships, and the particular challenges faced by those who bring applications before the courts. Certainly, the absence of public information, appropriate court facilities and adequate dedicated judicial training in respect of domestic violence applications was highlighted in the 2005 National Crime Council/ESRI report and the need for urgent attention and investment still remains.[32]

[31] With reference to existing guidelines in jurisdictions, including New Zealand and the State of British Columbia, Canada, see: Safe Ireland, *Briefing for Members of the Oireachtas Legislative Amendments Recommended to the Domestic Violence Bill 2017* (April 2017) 7, which outlined the rationale for advocating in favour of legislatively stated guidelines as follows: 'Judges deciding whether or not to grant a Domestic Violence Act order, and deciding which of these Orders to make, if any, would be assisted by these guidelines. They would also assist lawyers in providing useful advice to their clients. They could relate the facts of their client's case to the legislation, which would in turn assist their clients in giving their evidence to the court. Further, it would help to increase consistency of decision making from one District Court to another, and adherence to such guidelines would make it easier for the parties to appeal adverse decisions. It would also provide a measure of clarity and certainty about the application process and about the powers of the Court to applicants who are in need of protection, and finally, the law and its application might then develop, through a body of case law contributing to legal practice.' See Safe Ireland, *Briefing for Members of the Oireachtas Legislative Amendments Recommended to: Domestic Violence Bill 2017* (Safe Ireland 2017) www.safeireland.ie/wp-content/uploads/SAFE-Ireland-Domestic-Violence-Bill-2017-Recommendations-for-Legislative-Amendments-April-2017-.pdf.

[32] In relation to court procedures, the Report recommends that:

(1) Judges who sit in Family Law Courts should receive appropriate training in this area and should thereafter receive on-going training.
(2) The structures, resources and any necessary legislative changes should be put in place to ensure that, in appropriate cases, the Courts can make use of a wider range of sanctions, when dealing with the

Current Courts Service data is gender-neutral and provides an insight only into the nature and prevalence of applications and the determinations of the court. At the very least, the understanding of the current processes would be greatly assisted, for example, if the rate of non-attendance by applicants at the full hearing of an application could be recorded. In 2015, only 33 per cent of the 2,638 applications for barring orders were ultimately successful, increasing in 2016 to 50 per cent. What is unknown is whether these applications were refused on the basis of a failure to meet the evidentiary thresholds or whether in fact they were simply never pursued to full hearing.[33] The myriad of factors that influence the decision to pursue an application for a domestic violence order necessitates the capturing of the complexities involved, beyond the fact of application and the outcome of the case.

While little progress has been made in respect of developing dedicated Regional Family Law Courts for securing data relating to the gender, age group and available demographic details of parties to domestic violence proceedings, the judiciary are now being called on to account for the decisions reached in each case. Section 17 of the Domestic

perpetrators of domestic abuse. In particular, the Probation and Welfare Service should be adequately resourced to enable it to discharge its functions. Consideration should be given to the Service resuming the provision of reports in family law cases.

In relation to the Courts Service, the Council recommends that:

(1) The establishment of dedicated Regional Family Law Courts, using existing court facilities, be considered to protect the privacy of the parties.
(2) In its on-going court building and modernisation programme the Courts Service should take account of the possible increase in family law litigation thus leading to a requirement for additional accommodation for Family Law Courts with suitable ancillary services.
(3) Data on the gender, age group and available demographic details of applicants and respondents in family law cases be collected.
(4) Data on the gender, age group and available demographic details of both accused persons and injured parties in criminal law cases where domestic abuse is a contributory factor be collected.
(5) Data on applications for domestic violence orders i.e. Barring and/or Safety Orders which are withdrawn or struck out be recorded separately. The Courts Service should put in place a mechanism to monitor and respond to significant variations which may occur in the withdrawal or strike out rates at a regional level.

See D Watson and S Parsons, *Domestic Abuse of Women and Men in Ireland Report of the National Study of Domestic Abuse* (National Crime Council/ESRI, 2005) 17–18.

[33] Courts Service of Ireland, *Annual Report 2016* (Courts Service 2016) 52 www.courts.ie/Courts.ie/library3.nsf/(WebFiles)/300A3D2A10D824E88025816800370ED2/$FILE/Courts%20Service%20Annual%20Report%202016.pdf.

2016 District Court statistics:

Interim Barring Orders – 20% increase with 880 applications; 676 granted (77%)

Barring Orders – slight increase (20) with 2658 applications; 859 granted (50%)

Protection Orders – 5% increase with 5365 applications; 4627 granted (86%)

Safety Orders – 8% increase with 6069 applications; 3316 granted (55%)

Courts Service of Ireland, *Annual Report 2015* (Court's Service 2015) 46 www.courts.ie/Courts.ie/library3.nsf/(WebFiles)/B97E066344D48800802580830003407DF/$FILE/Courts%20Service%20Annual%20Report%202015.pdf.

2015 District Court statistics:

Interim Barring Orders – 731 applications; 563 granted (77%)

Barring Orders – 2638 applications; 859 granted (33%)

Protection Orders – 5108 applications; 4225 granted (83%)

Safety Orders – 5626 applications; 1917 granted (34%)

Violence Act 2018, once enacted, will require the presiding judge in every instance to give reasons for his/her decision:

(a) to grant or refuse the application;
(b) if applicable, to make the specified order subject to exceptions or conditions; and
(c) to vary the exceptions or conditions referred to in (b) above.

The inclusion of this mandatory requirement to rationalise the decision made will provide a mechanism to allow those party to proceedings, and indeed their legal counsel, to gain an understanding of the courts' interpretation of the governing provisions, and over time develop an understanding of the courts' interpretation of required evidentiary thresholds for each of the remedies available. Additionally, in requiring the judiciary to declare the reasoning for rulings delivered, the judges will be afforded the opportunity to deliver meaningful, considered and consistent judgments.

IV. The 'Deserving' Victim – Who is Eligible to Apply?

The judicial power created in 1976 to effect a barring order to protect a vulnerable spouse and dependent children represented one of the first legislative encroachments by the State in the private sphere of the family, deemed necessary in order to protect vulnerable family members. This State intervention in the context of domestic violence was recognised as entirely necessary and constitutionally sound.[34] Critically, however, such intervention was for many years limited exclusively to the protection of those who were parties to a marital union. While an especially welcome aspect of the 1981 Act was the introduction of the interim protection order, once again the capacity for the statutory provisions to protect victims of domestic violence was limited to spouses and their dependent children. Thus, the enactment of the Domestic Violence Act 1996 was ground-breaking insofar as it widened the categories of persons eligible to apply for protection. Crucially, in extending the right to apply to non-marital adult relationships, the Irish legislature finally acknowledged the myriad of domestic arrangements in modern Irish society, recognising the importance of providing protection for all victims of domestic abuse, irrespective of the status of the intimate relationship.

The statutory right to apply for relief was extended to include: the spouse of the respondent; a person who has lived with the respondent as husband or wife for six of the 12 months immediately prior to the application; a parent of the respondent where the respondent is aged 18 or over and is not dependent upon the parent; and a person aged 18 or over residing with the respondent in a non-contractual relationship.[35] In 2010, these categories were further extended to include civil partners, as defined by the Civil Partnership and Certain

[34] The Supreme Court noted that 'the legislation in respect of domestic violence has been passed by the Oireachtas for a vital social purpose: the protection of spouses and others against lawful assault and, on occasion terrorisation. There is sometimes necessity for such protection to be provided immediately in an acute situation.' *Eileen Goold v Mary Collins, a judge of the Dublin Metropolitan District Court, The DPP, Ireland, the Attorney General and John Joseph (otherwise Jackie) Gallagher* [2005] 1 ILRM 1 (Hardiman J).

[35] S 2(1)(a) defines the parameters of an 'an applicant' for a safety order, s 3(1) defines 'the applicant' for a barring order.

Rights and Obligations of Cohabitants Act 2010.[36] The less restrictive, but hugely important, safety order is available to a greater pool of persons who do not fulfil the more onerous evidentiary burden associated with a barring order, including the parent of a child whose other parent is the respondent, irrespective of their living arrangements.[37] However, the legislative efforts to broaden the availability and nature of accessible remedies was again hampered by perceptions of 'deserving' applicants, with the rights of non-property-owning applicants to secure protection being determined by legislatively fixed tests of eligibility. Under the 1996 Act, a cohabitant or a parent remained ineligible to apply for a barring order where the respondent held a greater legal or beneficial interest in the property than him/her.[38] This limitation on the rights of cohabitants and parents was justified by the superior constitutional right of an alleged abuser to own and enjoy his/her property and the duty to protect those rights in circumstances where a co-existing obligation to protect the marital family from the threat of violence does not arise. While it is difficult to ascertain definitive data relating to current property ownership in cohabiting relationships, what is certain is that the power imbalance arising in an abusive relationship is both supported and compounded by this approach to eligibility for a barring order, once again adopting the traditional Irish approach of the superior position of the property owner. This significant limitation on the right to seek the protection of the courts in the context of domestic violence was considered during the Parliamentary Select Committee on Legislation and Security, and it was noted by the then Minster for Equality and Law Reform, Deputy Mervyn Taylor, that to

> allow a respondent other than a spouse with an ownership interest to be barred on the application of a person with no such interest or with a lesser interest than the respondent, might not survive constitutional scrutiny … [as] … a barring order would constitute an infringement on that person's property rights which the State and its laws must respect under Article 40.3 of the Constitution. The position is different where parties are married. An infringement of a spouse's property rights is presumed to be justified on the basis that the rights of a family founded on marriage are protected by the Constitution and take precedence over property rights.[39]

[36] Pt 9 of the Civil Partnership and Certain Rights and Obligation of Cohabitants Act 2010 brings the civil partnership relationship within the remit of the Domestic Violence Act 1996 and equates the rights of the civil partner to that of a spouse.

[37] S 60(a) of the Civil Law (Miscellaneous Provisions) Act 2011, inserting sub-para (iv) in s 2(1)(a) of the Domestic Violence Act 1996. An application for a safety order can be made by an applicant who –

- (i) is the spouse of the respondent, or
- (ia) is the civil partner of the respondent, or a person who was a party to a civil partnership with the respondent that has been dissolved under the 2010 Act, or
- (ii) is not the spouse or civil partner within the meaning of the Act of 2010 of the respondent and is not related to the respondent within the prohibited degrees of relationship, but lived with the respondent in an intimate and committed relationship prior to the application for a safety order, or
- (iii) is a parent of the respondent and the respondent is a person of full age who is not, in relation the parent, a dependent person, or
- (iv) being of full age resides with the respondent in a relationship the basis of which is not primarily contractual or,
- (v) is a parent of a child whose other parent is the respondent.

Additionally, under s 6(2), the Child and Family Agency can apply for a barring order or a safety order on behalf of any of the above persons.

[38] Domestic Violence Act 1996, s 3(4)(a).

[39] Select Committee on Legislation and Security Debate (7 November 1995).

Thus, a married victim of abuse has long been regarded in law as deserving of protection, and such need being superior to those the claims of the property owner. Unfortunately, the rights of an unmarried cohabiting partner, irrespective of the duration or nature of the relationship is not so protected by the individual rights identified by Article 40.[40] In *DK v Judge Crowley, Ireland and the AG* Deputy Taylor noted however, that 'such persons will not be left unprotected' pointing to the (then) newly introduced safety order which was made available to cohabitants and others.[41] However, in placing limitations on the availability of some remedies to non-spouses, the legislature was again influenced by the nature and status of the adult relations in determining the extent to which the State could and should protect the persons seeking relief, and not by the nature or extent of the violence being perpetrated. This skewed approach demonstrates a dangerous deference to property owners, and in applying a strict combined ownership and temporal test, fails to even accord standing for the applicants to be heard. It was only following the signing of the Istanbul Convention that Ireland's lawmakers have been compelled to make emergency, short-term provision for unmarried non-property owning parties whose safety requires the removal of the alleged abuser from the home, as set out below.

A discriminatory mind-set regarding the woman as a dependent is evident in many aspects of Irish law (as noted throughout this volume), and has continuously influenced the manner in which Irish domestic violence laws and policies have developed. The longstanding (albeit now historical) punishing of an unmarried or separated woman who resides with a man in breach of the cohabitation rule, thereby defeating her entitlement to State income maintenance, had a hugely detrimental impact on women in Irish society. Although, from 1996, a cohabiting party could secure an order to protect herself from domestic or relationship violence, such a declaration of cohabitation would in itself trigger judgments by the State, resulting in detrimental financial consequences. Although suddenly deserving of protection from violence, she was now un-deserving of financial support. The cohabitation rule was based on the notion that women heads of one-parent families were presumed not to be capable of self-support;[42] it appears that the legislature's view was that once such a woman received the support of a man, the justification for State support ended and therefore the payments terminated. Cousins notes that the rule thus enforces women's dependence on men even in situations where they have no legal right to be supported.[43]

An especially heinous example of the presumed dominion of a husband over his wife of particular relevance to the issue of domestic violence was the absence of a crime of marital rape until January 1991, when the enactment of the Criminal Law Rape (Amendment) Act 1990 ('1990 Act') abolished any rule of law by virtue of which a husband could

[40] However, even if the rights of a married applicant are restricted where an interim barring order is secured, the ruling in *DK v Judge Crowley, Ireland and the AG* [2002] 2 IR 744 has limited the duration of such a protective order to a maximum of eight working days in order to properly vindicate the property and fair hearing rights of the accused.

[41] ibid.

[42] *Foley v Moulton* [1989] ILRM 169. The inevitable shortcomings of such a simplistic approach were evident in this flawed High Court ruling where the applicant's argument that the cohabitation rule ought to be interpreted in a purposive manner so as only to apply where actual financial support was being provided was rejected by the court. The fact that her cohabiting partner was in receipt of basic social welfare assistance and thus not in a position to provide her with any financial support, could not defeat the presumption that a woman associated with a man, sexually, socially *or* financially, was regarded in law as being dependent upon him.

[43] M Cousins, *The Irish Social Welfare System: Law and Social Policy* (Dublin, Round Hall Press, 1995) 89.

not be guilty of the rape of his wife. Prior to this development, a married woman was deemed not to be in a position to refuse consent to sexual intercourse with her husband, reflecting the common law position that rape could not occur within marriage, asserted in 1736 by Hale CJ: 'By their mutual matrimonial contract a wife hath given herself in kind unto the husband, which she cannot retract.'[44] However, since the introduction of the 1990 Act, there have only been three successful convictions for marital rape, most recently at the Central Criminal Court in October 2017.[45] Attempts were previously made to criminalise the act during the Dáil debate on the Criminal Law (Rape) Act 1981. It is reported that a briefing note prepared for the then Minister of State at the Department of Justice, Seán Doherty TD, had noted that marriage was a 'very complex relationship' and the introduction of an offence of marital rape 'could be very detrimental to the family' and might act as an obstacle to reconciliation attempts following a husband having sexual intercourse with his wife without consent. Once again, relentless efforts to maintain and protect the married family unit were used to justify the retention of this common law exemption.[46]

V. Domestic Violence Assault as a Criminal Offence: A Fundamental Flaw in the Irish Approach

The manner in which the Irish legal system, in both the civil and criminal contexts, processes incidents of domestic violence has continuously represented a failure to acknowledge the severity of the offences being committed and thus the harm being inflicted upon the (predominantly female) victims. In addition to the historic reluctance to intervene in the private sphere of the family unit, since intervention has been permitted, the legal measures and regulatory attitudes have not demonstrated sufficiently robust levels of intervention. A longstanding weakness has been that, while an act of assault, domestic or otherwise, is a crime under the Non-Fatal Offences Against the Person Act 1997,[47] in practice remedial measures lie predominantly within the sphere of civil proceedings, placing an inordinate pressure on victims to initiate the process of State intervention. Rather than ordinarily recognising domestic abuse as an act of criminal assault in the first instance, with the appropriate criminal proceedings being initiated following arrest and caution, too often it remains incumbent upon the victim to seek out civil remedies in the form of a barring order or safety order and to rely upon these reliefs to provide protection into the future.[48]

[44] *Historia Placitorum Coronæ, The History of the Pleas of the Crown* (1736).

[45] 'Man appeals against marital rape conviction' *The Irish Times* (Dublin, 31 October 2017) www.irishtimes.com/news/crime-and-law/courts/criminal-court/man-appeals-against-marital-rape-conviction-1.3275752.

[46] F Gartland, 'Marital Rape Law Rejected due to Family Concerns' *The Irish Times* (Dublin, 31 December 2011) www.irishtimes.com/news/marital-rape-law-rejected-due-to-family-concerns-1.17055.

[47] S 4(1) of the Non-Fatal Offences Against the Person Act 1997 provides that a person who intentionally or recklessly causes serious harm to another shall be guilty of an offence. A person guilty of an offence under this section shall be liable on conviction on indictment to a fine or to imprisonment for life or to both.

[48] The expectation that the victim of domestic abuse should pursue a civil order to secure protection serves to highlight the perception (and fact) that a criminal charge will typically only arise where the civil remedy has subsequently been breached by the abuser. Evidently criminal law proceedings in respect of the act of violence may be

Statistics reflecting the reluctance to charge offenders for criminal acts in the domestic context reflect the overwhelming perception of domestic violence offences as best resolved between the parties, unfairly pitting the victim against the abuser.[49] This normalisation of a civil-based response to an act of domestic violence suggests, deliberately or otherwise, that an act of violence in the domestic setting is regarded as a lessor form of assault than that committed outside that context.

The absence of comprehensive data in respect of incidents, reporting and conviction of domestic offences has also impeded informed law reform and policy making in Ireland. The 2014 *Crime Investigation* report from the Garda Inspectorate[50] highlights the practice of the incorrect recording of domestic violence offences, exacerbated by the absence of distinct Central Statistics Office statistics for acts of domestic violence, which are currently included with all other assaults.[51] The report highlighted that, as a consequence of this frequent failure to record cases of domestic violence correctly, such offences are much less likely to result in a criminal prosecution,[52] and/or that a large number of domestic incidents are moved to the non-crime category of 'Attention and Complaints'. This problem is further compounded by the absence of a formal risk assessment process at an incident of domestic violence, routinely conducted in many other jurisdictions, in order to identify those at the highest level of risk of abuse, with a view primarily to reduce the risk to those persons. The report highlighted the unavoidable consequence flowing from this failure, namely that the Gardaí all too often have to deal with the same victim repeatedly. Additionally, such repeat incidents of abuse have the very real potential to escalate to life-threatening violence.[53] This absence of a risk assessment with associated monitoring and interventions, coupled with the failure to record the fact of an offence in the absence of a victim statement, serve to fail the victim in every respect.

The need for a complete review of State practices surrounding the reporting and pursuit of incidents of domestic violence is long overdue. In their January 2017 submission

initiated under the more general laws governing assault, but statistics demonstrate that criminal prosecutions for domestic assaults are not very common.

[49] Garda Inspectorate, *Crime Investigation Report* (Garda Inspectorate, 2014) http://www.gsinsp.ie/en/GSINSP/Crime%20Investigation%20-%20Full%20Report.pdf/Files/Crime%20Investigation%20-%20Full%20Report.pdf.

[50] The Garda Inspectorate *Crime Investigation Report* (n 49) demonstrates that the rate of reported domestic violence incidents are difficult to determine as they are not classified distinctly because the Central Statistics Office crime statistics do not identify separate figures for acts of domestic violence, which are included with all other assaults. At pt 6 of the Report it is noted that in Ireland the *National Study of Domestic Abuse* (NSDA) found that 'a quarter of those severely affected by domestic abuse told the Gardaí'. Additionally such incidents are more likely not to be recorded officially on PULSE (Police Using Leading Systems Effectively – the computer system used by the Garda Síochána),). The 2014 Report (at 159) noted that 'in domestic violence cases, where a victim has injuries but is unwilling to make a statement of complaint, members sometimes do not record the incident on PULSE; or it is recorded on PULSE without details of any injuries to the victim and incorrectly categorised as a domestic dispute. In the latter case, this crime is categorised as a "domestic dispute – no offences disclosed". This matter is effectively closed and the assault is not recorded. This is a very unsafe practice for such a crime.' See *Crime Investigation Report* (n 49) 29.

[51] J Jones, 'Second Opinion: Strategies for domestic violence should focus on perpetrators' *The Irish Times*, (Dublin, 13 April 2015) www.irishtimes.com/life-and-style/health-family/second-opinion-strategies-for-domestic-violence-should-focus-on-perpetrators-1.2168913.

[52] Garda Inspectorate, *Crime Investigation Report* (n 49) Chart 6.16.

[53] ibid 42, noting the wide-ranging implications of the failure to record an assault or other crime.

to the United Nations Committee on the Elimination of Discrimination against Women (CEDAW),[54] the Dublin Rape Crisis Centre recommended, inter alia, that the State:

- Conduct a thorough, comprehensive analysis of the level of sexual violence in Ireland and the public attitudes to it, in order to provide a baseline and then regular updates.[55]
- Disaggregate the data collected through the Central Statistics Office, the Garda PULSE[56] system and the Courts Service, to better determine the categories of victims of sexual violence and the types of crimes reported, prosecuted and convicted.[57]
- Within the justice system: Resource Garda Protective Unit's country-wide. Audit all elements of the justice system, including police and courts, to ensure that the rights of victims of sexual offences are adequately protected at each and every stage of the criminal justice process.[58]

To be welcomed is the recently published *Policy of An Garda Síochána on Domestic Abuse Intervention*, which was published in consultation with the Office of the Director of Public Prosecutions and seeks to incorporate changes necessitated by the National Strategies on the Prevention of Domestic, Sexual and Gender-based violence and to comply with the State's obligations as a signatory to the Istanbul Convention.[59] The policy seeks to address the shortcomings relating to Garda responses to domestic violence, including a pro-arrest policy where the investigating Garda has reasonable cause to suspect that an offence has been committed and a power of arrest exists, even if no court order is in existence.[60] The policy document represents an impressively comprehensive understanding of the complexities of the abusive relationship and the cycle of abuse that typically occurs. To effectively manage the circumstances of an incident of abuse and to best protect the victim(s) in the circumstances, it identifies the three phases of domestic abuse – namely the tension-building phase, the violent/battering phase and the reconciliation/loving phase – acknowledging the manner in which abuse can escalate in terms of both frequency and severity. The policy is sensitive to the ongoing threat to the injured party, and the continuing risk that can often remain in the home, or elsewhere. Thus, it envisages robust monitoring of all incidents, the appropriate recording of such incidents on the Garda PULSE system and the ongoing investigation of incidents of abuse.[61] Crucially, as regards the decision to arrest the perpetrator of abuse, the policy states that 'it should not be the case that victim is asked if the abuser should be arrested. If a breach of an Order … occurs or an offence has been disclosed by the victim, a power of Arrest exists'.[62] The policy also identifies a proactive role for the Gardaí in relation to the provision of advice and

[54] Dublin Rape Crisis Centre, 'DRCC Submission to the Committee on the Elimination of all forms of Discrimination Against Women' (January 2017) www.drcc.ie/get-informed/policy-publications/jan-2017-cedaw/.

[55] ibid 2.

[56] PULSE (Police Using Leading Systems Effectively), introduced in November 1999, is a computer system used by An Garda Síochána.

[57] Dublin Rape Crisis Centre, 'DRCC Submission' (n 54) 2.

[58] ibid 7.

[59] An Garda Síochána, 'Policy of An Garda Síochána on Domestic Abuse Intervention: Incidents of Domestic Abuse and the Garda Response' (revised edition, 2017) www.garda.ie/en/Crime/Domestic-abuse/Domestic-Abuse-Intervention-Policy-2017.pdf.

[60] ibid para 3.9.

[61] ibid 4–7. Paragraph 3.18 provides that in cases of continuing risk of harm, the Member in Charge of the Garda Station must be informed of this by the responding Garda and the Member in Charge must ensure that details of the incident and such continuing risk are brought to the notice of the oncoming unit as well as the nominated Inspector with responsibility for domestic abuse intervention in the Division.

[62] ibid para 4.2.

support for victims of domestic abuse.[63] An emphasis is placed on maintaining a continued liaison with the complainant throughout the investigation and any prosecution by the same member of An Garda Síochána, with the Garda in question calling back to the complainant within one week of an incident.[64]

To accord respect to the victims of domestic abuse by treating such offences with an appropriate level of State intervention through the criminal justice system, it is recognised as vital that the key strategic partners, especially An Garda Síochána, implement a victim-centred policy and demonstrate effective investigative practices.[65] Thus, the response to the challenges surrounding the need to treat assaults in the domestic setting as criminal acts is currently being addressed in Ireland through enhanced Garda policies, rather than through the deliberate legislative identification of a criminal offence of domestic violence. The continuing inadequacies of failing to identify domestic violence assault as a criminal offence, thereby facilitating the capacity for mis-categorisation and devaluation of the domestic offences, were further highlighted in early March 2017 in the Concluding Observations of CEDAW on the combined sixth and seventh periodic reports of Ireland. Recommendation 27(c), which relates to Irish regulation of domestic violence, calls on the Irish government to 'Criminalise domestic violence and introduce a specific definition of domestic violence and other emerging forms of gender-based violence such as online stalking and harassment'.[66]

While domestic assault has not been categorised as a criminal offence in its own right, Irish law has now introduced an offence of coercion. Section 39 of the Domestic Violence Act 2018 provides that:

> (1) A person commits an offence where he or she knowingly and persistently engages in behaviour that –
>
> (a) is controlling or coercive,
> (b) has a serious effect on a relevant person, and
> (c) a reasonable person would consider likely to have a serious effect on a relevant person.

[63] Paragraph 11.5(a) provides that in all cases of domestic abuse, the investigating Garda shall provide the victim with a copy of the relevant domestic abuse information literature and make the victim aware of the relevant services, both statutory and voluntary.

[64] ibid para 11.5(c).

[65] ibid 44.

[66] In line with its general recommendation no 19 (1992) on violence against women, the Committee recommends that the State party:

> (a) Ensure that the National Office for the Prevention of Domestic, Sexual and Gender-based Violence and relevant institutions implement the 'gold standard' so that data on all forms of gender-based violence against women, including domestic violence, is systematically collected, analysed and that it is disaggregated by, inter alia, age, ethnicity and relationship with the perpetrator;
> (b) Intensify existing efforts to combat gender-based violence against women, including domestic violence, by ensuring that prosecutors and the police are properly trained to identify, investigate and prosecute cases of gender-based violence, including domestic violence, particularly targeting Traveller, Roma and migrant women and girls;
> (c) Criminalise domestic violence and introduce a specific definition of domestic violence and other emerging forms of gender-based violence such as online stalking and harassment;
> (d) Provide adequate financial resources to non-governmental organisations that provide services to victims of gender-based violence, including domestic violence; and
> (e) Expedite the ratification of the Council of Europe Convention on Preventing and Combating Violence against Women and Domestic Violence (the Istanbul Convention).

United Nations Committee on the Elimination of Discrimination Against Women, Concluding observations on the combined sixth and seventh periodic reports of Ireland (9 March 2017) UN Doc No. CEDAW/C/IRL/CO/6-7.

(2) For the purposes of [this offence], a person's behaviour will be regarded as having a serious effect on a relevant person if the behaviour causes the relevant person –

(a) to fear that violence will be used against him or her, or

(b) serious alarm or distress that has a substantial adverse impact on his or her usual day-to-day activities.

Difficulties will certainly arise with the evidentiary threshold required to prove that an offence has occurred, particularly given the typically vulnerable position of the person who is subject to the coercive treatment. However, the categorisation of the behaviour as criminal in nature does reflect a willingness on the part of the State to prosecute such actions, thereby recognising the severity of the behaviour and its impact.

In this context, and more broadly in respect of victims of domestic abuse where a breach of an order has occurred, the enactment of the Criminal Justice (Victims of Crime) Act 2017 which transposes into Irish law Directive 2012/29,[67] has required the Irish State to establish practices with minimum required standards in respect of the rights of victims of crime, in order to support and protect them in the course of the prosecution of the accused and after the sentencing, where relevant. The Act places an obligation on the Office of the Director of Public Prosecutions to ensure that there is improved engagement with victims, with a much greater obligation on the State to vindicate the right of the victim of a crime; on first contact,[68] regarding investigations and criminal proceedings,[69] decisions regarding prosecution of offences,[70] and the review of decisions in relation to prosecutions.[71]

Part 3 of the Act places an onus on the State to protect victims during investigations and criminal proceedings which includes best practice in relation to interviews, medical examination and assessments.[72] Victims of domestic abuse are likely to benefit from the power accorded to the courts under section 20 to exclude a person or the public from the court hearing where there is a need to protect the victim from 'secondary and repeat victimisation'.[73] Additionally, section 21 gives the court the power to give whatever directions it regards just and proper regarding any evidence adduced, or sought to be induced, and any question asked in cross-examination, where it relates to the private life of a victim and is unrelated to the offence at issue. The court can give such directions where it is satisfied that 'the nature or circumstances of the cases are such that there is a need to protect a victim of the offence from secondary and repeat victimisation, intimidation or retaliation'.[74]

These developments are of immense significance in the context of criminal prosecutions for domestic abuse, and will have a disproportionate benefit for women, who are predominantly the victims of such criminal acts. The enactment of the Criminal Justice (Victims of Crime) Act 2017 is a long overdue but welcome recognition of the very challenging role of a victim in criminal law proceedings, where they have historically been treated as simply

[67] Directive 2012/29/EU of the European Parliament and of the Council of 25 October 2012 establishing minimum standards on the rights, support and protection of victims of crime.

[68] Criminal Justice (Victims of Crime) Act 2017, s 7.

[69] ibid s 8.

[70] ibid s 9.

[71] ibid s 10.

[72] ibid ss 14–15.

[73] ibid s 20(1)(a).

[74] ibid s 21(a).

another witness for the prosecution with little acknowledgment within the legal process of their central role and often ongoing suffering at the hands of the accused.

VI. The Istanbul Convention – Impetus for Domestic Change

The Domestic Violence Act 2018, enacted on 8 May 2018, seeks to

> improve the protections available to victims of domestic violence, most critically for cohabitants and parents in crisis situations, by introducing a new emergency barring order which can last for up to 8 working days … [and] to make the court process easier for victims of domestic violence.[75]

The impetus for these reforms was heightened by Ireland finally becoming a signatory to the Istanbul Convention in November 2015.[76] As the first Council of Europe treaty to specifically target violence against women, the Convention sets out minimum standards on prevention, protection and prosecution, and mandates the development of integrated policies. In its preamble, the Convention recognises

> that violence against women is a manifestation of historically unequal power relations between women and men, which have led to domination over, and discrimination against, women by men and to the prevention of the full advancement of women … [and further recognises] … the structural nature of violence against women as gender-based violence, and that violence against women is one of the crucial social mechanisms by which women are forced into a subordinate position compared with men.[77]

The preamble also recognises that 'domestic violence affects women disproportionately, and that men may also be victims of domestic violence … [and] … that children are victims of domestic violence, including as witnesses of violence in the family' causing the Council to aspire to 'create a Europe free from violence against women and domestic violence'.[78]

The purposes of the Convention are identified in Article 1 as follows:

> (a) protect women against all forms of violence, and prevent, prosecute and eliminate violence against women and domestic violence;
> (b) contribute to the elimination of all forms of discrimination against women and promote substantive equality between women and men, including by empowering women;
> (c) design a comprehensive framework, policies and measures for the protection of and assistance to all victims of violence against women and domestic violence;
> (d) promote international co-operation with a view to eliminating violence against women and domestic violence;

[75] See Statement of Frances Fitzgerald, Minister for Justice and Equality upon publication of the Bill (3 February 2017) www.justice.ie/en/JELR/Pages/PR17000033. As regards better protecting victims of domestic violence within the court process, she pointed to the inclusion of measures whereby 'a victim will have the right to be accompanied to court by a family member, friend or support worker. A victim will be able to give evidence by live television link. There will be restrictions on attendance at both civil and criminal court proceedings and protections for the victim's anonymity.'

[76] Council of Europe, Council of Europe Convention on Preventing and Combating Violence against Women and Domestic Violence (12 April 2011) www.coe.int/en/web/conventions/full-list/-/conventions/treaty/210.

[77] ibid 5–6.

[78] ibid 6.

(e) provide support and assistance to organisations and law enforcement agencies to effectively co-operate in order to adopt an integrated approach to eliminating violence against women and domestic violence.

From the outset, Ireland purported to support in principle the aims of the Istanbul Convention, but was demonstrably reluctant given the perceived need, once again, to protect the competing property rights of persons accused of domestic offences. In particular, the State was required to satisfy itself that the ratification and implementation of the Convention requirements in respect of the availability of emergency barring orders under Article 52 would not interfere with the property rights of accused persons as protected by the Irish Constitution.[79] Article 52 of the Convention mandates signatory states to

> take the necessary legislative or other measures to ensure that the competent authorities are granted the power to order, in situations of immediate danger, a perpetrator of domestic violence to vacate the residence of the victim or person at risk for a sufficient period of time and to prohibit the perpetrator from entering the residence of or contacting the victim or person at risk.

This broadening of the availability of an emergency barring order based on the nature and immediacy of the threat, as opposed to the property status of the parties, is provided for in section 9 of the Domestic Violence Act 2018. This is a stand-alone order not made pending the hearing of a more substantive application, and if granted provides immediate effective protection for the applicant by removing the source of violence from his/her living environment. The impact of the order, although short-lived, is thus dramatic in effect. An emergency order can be sought by an applicant who –

(a) is not the spouse or civil partner of the respondent and is not related to the respondent within a prohibited degree of relationship but lived with the respondent in an intimate relationship prior to the application for the emergency barring order, or
(b) is a parent of the respondent and the respondent is a person of full age who is not, in relation to the parent, a dependent person.

The court can only make an emergency barring order in respect of a place where an applicant resides of a dependent person resides and where

(a) the respondent has a legal or beneficial interest in the place but the applicant has no such interest, or
(b) the applicant's legal or beneficial interest is, in the opinion of the court, less than that of the respondent.[80]

In facilitating accessibility to this relief, the Irish legislature has finally accepted the need to empower permit the courts to intervene as necessary, to ensure the safety of the an applicant irrespective of property ownership. Consequently, section 9(3) sets out a high evidentiary threshold for the applicant; in order to grant the short-term emergency barring order, the

[79] Ireland's reluctance to interfere with the property rights of alleged abusers was not as challenging an issue in most other signatory states, with 38 states signing the Convention in advance of Ireland. See further the criticisms of Amnesty International at that time: 'Ireland Must Sign and Ratify the Istanbul Convention to Fight Violence against Women and Girls' (Amnesty International, 1 August 2014) www.amnesty.ie/ireland-must-sign-ratify-istanbul-convention-fight-violence-women-girls/.

[80] Domestic Violence Act 2018, s 9(2). The interim barring order remains available under s 8 to those who are not married to the respondent but who have an equal or greater interest in the property at issue.

court must be satisfied that 'there are reasonable grounds for believing that there is an immediate risk of significant harm to the applicant or a dependent person if an order is not made immediately'. The application can be made on an ex parte basis,[81] or can be made unilaterally by the court in the context of an application by the applicant or the Child and Family Agency on his/her behalf for a direction under the Child Care Act 1991 and/or the Guardianship of Infants Act 1964, where the court determines that the evidentiary threshold has been met.[82]

The Domestic Violence Act 2018 includes many other welcome developments which serve to better acknowledge and respect the exceptionally harrowing and indeed vulnerable position of victims of domestic violence. In addition to the provision of factors to be taken into account by the court,[83] and the availability of an emergency barring order to all eligible victims in immediate need irrespective of their family status, as outlined above, the Act endeavours in numerous ways to redress the imbalance of power typically arising in cases of domestic abuse.

In order to combat the very real challenge of accessing protection when courts are not sitting, section 24 of the 2018 Act addresses the practical obstacles arising where a barring order is sought out of hours. It permits a member of the Garda not below the rank of sergeant, where he/she has been informed by a person seeking relief that he/she wishes to make an application for interim protection,[84] and at that time there is no District Court sitting in the relevant district court area, to request the Courts Service to arrange a special sitting of the District Court. Additionally, in the context of improved access to justice, new court procedures are introduced by the Act, including the provision for the applicant (but not the respondent) of the right to be accompanied in court by an individual (including a support worker) of the applicant's choice, in addition to the existing right to be accompanied by his/her legal representative.[85]

As regards the cross-examination of the victim and/or witnesses by the respondent, section 16 of the 2018 Act seeks to protect the victim where appropriate from further mistreatment, by requiring the court to prohibit such cross-examination of minors unless justice requires it while also permitting the court to prohibit such cross-examination of adult applicants/witnesses where justice requires it. The victim is further protected by the expressly mandated hearing of proceedings in private under section 34 of the Act where there has been a breach of an existing order. Evidence can also be given through a live television link (video or audio recorded) where appropriate.[86] Additionally, the Act expressly provides that the publication of any identifying information relating to any of the parties to the proceedings will constitute a criminal offence.[87]

Finally, in recognition of the especially egregious nature of domestic abuse, and the fact that such acts represent the exploitation of vulnerable persons in a relationship of trust and intimacy, the commission of an assault, rape or sexual assault against a spouse, civil partner

[81] ibid s 9(11).
[82] ibid s 9(3), with reference to orders sought under the Acts specified in s 15(2) of the 2018 Act.
[83] See Section II above.
[84] Such interim protection refers to an interim barring order, an emergency barring order or a protection order.
[85] ibid s 26. The court can refuse such permission where it would not be in the interests of justice for the individual concerned to accompany applicant but is required to explain the reason for so refusing.
[86] ibid s 25.
[87] ibid s 36.

or person with whom the respondent is or was in an intimate relationship, is now to be regarded as an aggravating factor in sentencing, requiring the court upon conviction to impose a sentence which is greater than that which would have been imposed if the parties had not been intimately connected.[88]

VII. Conclusion

Domestic violence is an especially heinous manifestation of abuse that occurs in innumerable ways but is premised upon a dynamic of control arising in the context of a current or historic close relationship between two people. The predominantly gendered nature of domestic and relationship abuse is well documented, as is the Irish State's failure to create a proactive framework of criminal accountability and universally available protection in order to safeguard those who suffer at the hands of perpetrators of abuse. These failures of laws, policies and processes have in turn failed the victims of this abuse, further weakening their already vulnerable position. For the most part, this has manifested as a failure to protect the affected women of Ireland. Several aspects of the 2018 Act, together with the 2017 Garda policy, do seek to address existing shortcomings, including access to urgent protective relief as well as the identification of key aspects of perpetrator behaviour that must influence the determination of applications for protective relief before the courts. Greater protection of the victim throughout the investigation and prosecution processes, together with heightened expectations regarding judicial reasoning and accountability, will hopefully provide a much-needed rebalancing of power in the pursuit of justice for the victims of domestic abuse.

[88] ibid s 40.

9

The Gendered Properties of Marriage Breakdown

DEIRDRE McGOWAN

I. Introduction

Historically, issues of gender, sex and property were central to the concept of marriage and how it was regulated by law. Until late in the nineteenth century, a wife's legal personality merged with that of her husband on marriage; everything she owned became his, and she could not subsequently own property or earn money on her own behalf.[1] Her only claim against him was for 'necessaries' and the test of what was necessary was a subjective one, dependent upon her husband's economic standing.[2] Laurence Stone has characterised historical marriage law as embodying a patriarchal set of values which made a married woman 'the nearest approximation in a free society to a slave'.[3]

In Ireland, during the nineteenth and early-twentieth centuries, marriages in rural areas were regularly contracted to facilitate (patrilineal) farm transmission.[4] And, as recently as 1973, Irish women were required to retire from public service employment upon marriage,[5] and married men in employment were habitually paid more than single men, reflecting an assumption that women adopted a domestic, dependent role following marriage and did not need to accumulate property during marriage.[6] Nineteenth and twentieth century reforms separated the legal personalities of spouses,[7] mandated equal pay

[1] See eg RS Roper, *A Treatise on the Law of Property arising from the Relation between Husband and Wife, Vol 2*, 2nd edn (London, Butterworth, 1820) for a detailed exposition of the effect of the doctrine of coverture and the support obligations of husbands at common law.

[2] As Blackstone explains, 'the husband is bound to provide his wife with necessaries by law, as much as himself; and if she contracts debts for them, he is obliged to pay them; but for anything besides necessaries he is not chargeable'. Sir William Blackstone, *Commentaries on the Laws of England*, 2nd edn (Oxford, Clarendon Press, 1799) 155.

[3] L Stone, *The Road To Divorce: England 1530–1987* (Oxford, Clarendon Press, 1990) 13.

[4] In a study of farm families in 1930s County Clare, Arensberg and Kimball describe a 'match' system which tied marriage to inheritance in a carefully choreographed economic transaction, C Arensberg and S Kimball, *Family and Community in Ireland*, 3rd edn (Clare Local Studies Project, Clasp Press, 2001).

[5] The public service marriage bar was removed by the Civil Service (Employment of Married Women) Act 1973.

[6] The Commission on the Status of Women, *Report to the Minister for Finance* (Dublin, Prl 2760, Stationery Office, 1972), contains a comprehensive account of the disadvantages suffered by women in employment, taxation and social welfare codes.

[7] For an account of campaigning leading to legislative change in Britain, see eg B Griffin, 'Class, Gender and Liberalism in Parliament 1868–1882, the Case of the Married Women's Property Acts' (2003) 46 *The Historical*

for equal work,[8] and constructed gender-neutral legal frameworks for the distribution of property following marital breakdown. Nonetheless, despite a gender-neutral appearance, and recent extension of marriage to same-sex couples,[9] the law governing property rights on the breakdown of marriage continues to struggle with gendered practices and assumptions.

This chapter begins with an outline of the substantive law governing property ownership during marriage, including an account of spousal maintenance obligations and the special position of family homes. The legal rules are then contextualised with an account of contemporary social practices and behaviours and how the adoption of gender-based roles in marriage affects property ownership. Next, the law governing property allocation on marital breakdown in the context of court applications for judicial separation and divorce is described. The legislative principles and how they are applied by the courts are set out, drawing particular attention to how the adoption of gendered roles in marriage affects property allocation upon breakdown. Reported marriage law decisions generally involve relatively well-off couples and are not representative of the vast bulk of marriages; alternatives to litigation are therefore discussed in order to illustrate the limitations of ancillary relief law in addressing the financial implications of marital breakdown. Finally, this chapter identifies some difficulties with the existing law from a gender perspective and the potential for, and limitations of, marriage law reform as a way to promote gender equality.

II. Substantive Law on Marriage and Property

A. During Marriage

As a basic proposition, all adults own their own property and income, and their right to do so is protected by Article 43 of the Irish Constitution. During an intact marriage, spouses each own their own property and income from earnings.[10] There is no general obligation to share, nor to exchange even basic information about property or income. However, any allowance made by one spouse to the other for the purpose of meeting household expenses and any property acquired from such allowance is the property of both, and spouses have a lifetime obligation to maintain each other.[11] Parents have an obligation to maintain their children, irrespective of marital status. Spouses do not have an explicit right to the use and enjoyment of one another's property, real or personal, but a right to occupy any home which

Journal 59. The Irish Married Women's Status Act 1957, s 5, effected the complete separation of the legal personality of husband and wife.

[8] The Anti-discrimination Pay Act 1974 became law on 31 December 1975 and required that men and women carrying out the same work be paid at the same rate.

[9] Marriage Act 2015. As noted in other contributions to this volume, same-sex civil partnership was available in Ireland between 2011 and 2015. The law governing distribution of property on dissolution of civil partnership is broadly similar to that which applies to judicial separation and divorce and is not specifically dealt with here. For an account of the law governing civil partnership, see eg F Ryan, 'The Rise and Fall of Civil Partnership' (2016) 19(3) *Irish Journal of Family Law* 50.

[10] The Married Women's Status Act 1957 removed all traces of the common law doctrine of coverture from Irish law.

[11] Family Law (Maintenance of Spouses and Children) Act 1976, ss 15 and 5.

they share is implicit in the Domestic Violence Act 1996, which allows one spouse to have the other barred from their shared home, even where the home is wholly owned by the excluded spouse.[12] Similarly, the Family Home Protection Act 1976 allows one spouse to veto the disposal of a home occupied by both irrespective of ownership rights, implying that a non-owning spouse occupies the family home as of right.[13] Where spouses own property together, normal property law rules apply and ownership rights are the same as they would be if the parties were strangers. So, where a dwelling is jointly owned, as joint tenants or tenants in common in equal or unequal shares, both spouses have a right to occupy the dwelling and one cannot exclude the other without an order of the court.[14] Further, the law presumes that financial transfers between spouses are irrevocable gifts, meaning that where the ownership of real property is registered in joint names – even where one spouse provides the entire purchase money – the law will generally infer ownership in equal shares.[15]

Marriage does not, in any legal sense, have a significant impact on property ownership. However, gendered differences in the actual ownership of property and income during marriage arise as a result of structural disadvantages endured by women and the choices made by individual families. In 2014, on average, women employees were paid 13.9 per cent less per hour than male employees and women, overall, are less likely to be in the labour force than men.[16] As noted by other contributors to this volume, in 2016, 51.5 per cent of women aged 15 years and over were in the labour force compared to 67.8 per cent of men. Ninety-eight per cent of those looking after a home or family in 2016 were women, and women who did work were more likely than men to have part-time hours. Three quarters of men in employment worked for 35 hours or more but only 52.3 per cent of women did. Married men worked longer hours in paid employment than married women; just 5 per cent of married men worked 20–29 hours per week compared with 22.2 per cent of married women. When a couple have children, women are more likely than men to leave the workforce or take up part-time work. In the 20-44 age group, the employment rates for men and women in couples are broadly similar, but once a child arrives employment rates for women are more than 25 points below those for men. These statistics indicate the persistence of gender differences in the assumption of caring responsibilities, leading to a corresponding gap in the earning of income. Women continue to give up paid employment, or significantly reduce the hours worked, when they marry and/or become parents, whereas men are more likely to continue working and increase their hours of work.

[12] Domestic Violence Act 1996, s 3.

[13] Family Home Protection Act 1976, s 3. A family home is defined in the Act as 'a dwelling in which a married couple ordinarily reside'.

[14] In *NK v HK* [2017] IECA 1, the Court of Appeal held that the court has no inherent jurisdiction to exclude one spouse from a family home owned by both of them and that any jurisdiction to do so arises only from the specific terms of the Domestic Violence Acts 1996–2001, the Family Law Act 1995 and the Family Law (Divorce) Act 1996.

[15] This is known as the presumption of advancement. The presumption is rebuttable where it can be shown that the transfer of beneficial ownership was not intended, *RF v MF* [1995] 2 ILRM 572. The presumption originally applied only to transfers from husband to wife but in view of the constitutional guarantee of equality is assumed to also apply to transfers from wife to husband, see H Delaney, *Equity and the Law of Trusts in Ireland*, 5th edn (Dublin, Roundhall, 2011) 172, as referenced with approval by Laffoy J in *Cawley v Lillis* [2011] IEHC 515.

[16] Central Statistics Office, *Women and Men in Ireland 2016* (18 October 2017) www.cso.ie/en/releasesandpublications/ep/p-wamii/womenandmeninireland2016/.

Participating in paid work facilitates the accumulation of wealth in the form of savings, pensions, real property and other investments. Married women who reduce their hours of work or give up work entirely lose this opportunity and at the same time become dependent on their husbands for day-to-day needs and to maintain their lifestyle. Although this is unlikely to cause difficulties in an intact marriage, this asymmetry inevitably creates problems when the relationship breaks down, particularly when the dependent spouse is the primary carer for minor children. While we are some distance from the position pertaining in the 1970s, when more than 75 per cent of married women did not work outside the home and family homes were generally owned by the husband,[17] addressing this type of dependency following marriage breakdown remains problematic. Evidence from other jurisdictions indicates that, following divorce, women caring for children suffer a significant decline in their finances while their ex-husbands do not.[18] The financial disadvantages suffered by women may initially be caused by the marriage breakdown, but they are exacerbated by general structural factors such as gender discrimination in finding employment and the difficulty of combining paid work with caring for young children. Time taken out of employment while caring for children during and after marriage impacts both career progression and pension contributions, and as noted above, women are, in any event, paid less than men and generally work for fewer hours.

B. Ancillary Relief on Judicial Separation and Divorce

Laws governing the distribution of property following marriage breakdown are, in part, intended to deal with the difficulties experienced by spouses who take on a dependent role during marriage. The vulnerable dependent housewife was central to debates surrounding divorce referenda in the 1980s and 1990s,[19] and a desire to protect her position is evident in the legal rules which facilitate the making of ancillary relief orders on judicial separation and divorce. An order for judicial separation suspends the cohabitation obligations of marriage, while a divorce dissolves marriage leaving the spouses free to remarry. On making either order, the court has power to adjust the property rights of the spouses to ensure that 'proper provision' is made for each of them and any dependent children.[20] In deciding to make financial orders, the court must have regard to a number of factors set out in legislation and may make orders only if it is in 'the interests of justice to do so'.[21] Crucially, financial orders can be made at the time of granting the judicial separation or divorce, or 'at any time

[17] T Callan and B Farrell, *Women's Participation in the Irish Labour Market* (Pl 8449, National Economic and Social Council, 1992) 18. Callan and Farrell identify a significant correlation between number and age of children and women's labour market status. They also note that labour market participation rates do not differentiate between full and part-time employment and that many married women with children engaged in part-time work, 29–36.

[18] H Fisher and H Low, 'Who Wins, Who Loses and Who Recovers from Divorce?' in J Miles and R Probert (eds), *Sharing Lives, Dividing Assets* (London, Bloomsbury, 2009) 254.

[19] For an account of historical development of Irish marriage law, see eg D McGowan, 'Governed by Marriage Law: An Irish Genealogy' (2016) 25(3) *Social and Legal Studies* 311–31.

[20] In the case of divorce 'proper provision' is one of the constitutional pre-requisites to a grant of divorce, see Constitution of Ireland, Article 41.3.2.

[21] Family Law (Divorce) Act 1996, s 20; Judicial Separation and Family Law Act 1995, s 16.

thereafter' and applications can be made to vary some orders if circumstances change after a divorce or judicial separation has been granted.[22] Further, orders made on judicial separation do not necessarily continue after divorce; the court is mandated to ensure 'proper provision' both when granting a judicial separation and again at the time of divorce.

As noted above, during marriage each spouse owns their own property and income. When a divorce or judicial separation is sought by one of them, the court may have recourse to all of the assets and income of both spouses whenever and however acquired in order to achieve proper provision. Property is thus held individually until relationship breakdown, at which point it becomes a pool available for distribution between the spouses in shares to be agreed by them or determined by the court. As Fennelly J explained in the Supreme Court:

> [A]ny property, whenever acquired, of either spouse and whenever and no matter how acquired, is in principle, available for the purpose of the provision. Thus, property acquired by inheritance, by chance, or by the exclusive labours of one spouse does not necessarily escape the net.[23]

Marriage breakdown therefore acts as a trigger for enforced sharing of property between spouses in order to achieve proper provision, but as the case law demonstrates there are no firm rules governing how it should be distributed. In *DT v CT* (Supreme Court), Keane CJ noted the wide discretion available to the trial judge in making orders for ancillary relief:

> [T]he circumstances of individual cases will vary so widely that, ultimately, where the parties are unable to agree, the trial judge must be regarded as having a relatively broad discretion in reaching what he or she considers a just resolution in the circumstances.[24]

The discretion, although wide, is not without bounds. Section 16 of the Family Law Act 1995 and section 20 of the Family Law (Divorce) 1996 Act require the trial judge to have regard to a number of factors, including the income of the spouses, their needs, the marital standard of living, the age of the parties, contributions made both economic and caring, loss of earning capacity caused by assumption of marital responsibilities, accommodation needs, and conduct if unjust to disregard. This mandatory nature of such consideration was emphasised by McGuinness J in *MK v JP (otherwise SK) and MB*:

> The provisions of the Act of 1996 leave a considerable area of discretion to the court in making proper financial provision for spouses in divorce cases. The discretion, however, is not to be exercised at large. The statute lays down mandatory guidelines. The court must have regard to all the factors set out in s 20, measuring their relevance and weight according to the facts of the individual case.[25]

As a matter of best practice, the court should give reasons explaining the manner in which they exercise their discretion in light of the statutory guidelines. However, this is not uniformly done and as indicated by the Court of Appeal in *QR v CT* the lack of a detailed analysis of the statutory factors in a written judgment will not be fatal to a decision.[26]

The only statutory factor upon which the courts have provided clear guidance is the 'conduct of the parties'. Judicial separation and divorce legislation provides that the conduct

[22] Family Law (Divorce) Act 1996, ss 13–16 and s. 22; Family Law Act 1995, ss 10–14 and s 18.
[23] *DT v CT* [2002] 3 IR 334, 416.
[24] ibid 365.
[25] *MK v JP (otherwise SK) and MB* [2001] 3 IR 371, 383–84.
[26] *QR v CT* [2016] IECA 421.

of spouses should be taken into account in making a decision on proper provision only where it would be 'unjust to disregard it',[27] and the courts have set a high threshold. In *DT v CT*, the Supreme Court held that only conduct that is 'obvious and gross' should result in the imposition of a financial penalty.[28] In *ML v SL*, Sheehan J refused to take a spouse's repeated infidelity into account;[29] similarly, in *DT v CT* the Supreme Court unanimously accepted that infidelity was a matter that ought not to be reflected in the courts' view as to what amounted to proper provision. Financial misconduct, particularly where it leads to the depletion of assets available for distribution may well be taken into account, although it is unlikely to have a substantial effect on how proper provision is achieved.[30]

Otherwise the courts have provided only limited guidance on the content of 'proper provision'. In the typical case, where the joint assets of the parties are not of any significant value, the courts consider the financial needs of the spouses and dependent children and how these needs, or indeed as is often the case, subsistence requirements, might be met from the available assets.[31] Needs in this sense are subjective. The court will look at the vouched outgoings of the parties and assess needs on that basis rather than by reference to any external measure or rule of thumb. In cases involving significant assets, the court will be guided by the standard of living enjoyed by both spouses before the breakdown of the marriage and financial orders will not be limited by needs, even when these are substantial. Justice Murray in *DT v CT* noted that:

> Proper provision for a spouse who falls into the category of a financially dependent spouse (where the other spouse is the source or owner of all or the bulk of income or assets of the marriage) should seek, so far as the circumstances of the case permit, to ensure that the spouse is not only in a position to meet her financial liabilities and obligations, continue with a standard of living commensurate with her standard of living during marriage but to enjoy what may reasonably be regarded as the fruits of the marriage so that she can live an independent life and have security in the control of her own affairs, with a personal dignity that such autonomy confers without necessarily being dependent on receiving periodic payments for the rest of her life from her former husband.[32]

This approach has led to significant variation in the types of provision which the courts consider proper, ranging from 'clean break' orders where assets are divided with neither party being ordered to pay spousal maintenance, to substantial periodic maintenance payments being ordered decades after a marriage has ended.[33]

The possibility for a 'clean break' under Irish law was first identified in *DT v CT*, an ample resources case involving a professional couple. The wife, a qualified medical doctor, had stepped back from her career to care for the couple's children and the husband developed a substantial solicitor's practice and property portfolio. While accepting that the bulk of the family's assets had been accumulated by the husband, the court noted that this would not

[27] Judicial Separation and Family Law Reform Act 1989, s 16(2)(i); Family Law (Divorce) Act 1996, s 20(2)(i).
[28] *DT v CT* [2002] 3 IR 334, Keane CJ, 370.
[29] *ML v SL* [2017] IEHC 438.
[30] *H v O'N* Unreported High Court, McMenamin J (23 June 2011).
[31] *DT v CT* [2002] 3 IR 334, Keane CJ, 365.
[32] ibid Murray J, 408.
[33] The term 'clean break' connotes an ending of inter-spousal responsibilities. Both parents have an irrevocable responsibility to support their children until they are 18 years or 23 years if in full time education.

have been possible without the wife's efforts in caring for the home and children. The wife sought a clean break through payment to her of a substantial lump sum, and Keane CJ in the Supreme Court noted that 'Irish law should be capable of accommodating those aspects of the "clean break" approach which are clearly beneficial'.[34] Although the possibility remained of a future application for maintenance, the court noted that the success of such an application was 'unlikely in the extreme'.[35]

Whether and how a clean break is to be achieved remains a matter for the individual judge and a wide variation is apparent in reported cases. In *MD v ND*, the Supreme Court granted a clean break on divorce with a 50/50 division of assets between spouses. The husband in that case was a farmer and the wife a public service professional.[36] The High Court in *LD v CD* achieved a clean break divorce for a two-income family based on a 60/40 split in the value of the family home in favour of the wife. The spouses had been living apart for seven years at the time of divorce and both had income from employment.[37] Similarly, in *LD v MA*, a professional couple with three children achieved a clean break judicial separation with assets being allocated between them but no ongoing spousal maintenance ordered.[38] An application for variation of the terms of a clean break divorce granted by the Circuit Court was refused by the High Court in *PCR v GR*. Justice White noted that 'if this court acceded to the application to vary, one would have to say that certainty of any sort in family law litigation would be impossible to achieve'.[39] There has been some attempt by the courts in recent years to achieve a type of deferred clean break by placing a time limit on maintenance payments to dependent spouses, providing a period of rehabilitation during which the dependency is to be brought to an end.[40] However, these are isolated cases and such orders remain subject to variation to meet changed circumstances.

Clean break orders, deferred or otherwise, are relatively rare in the superior courts. Ancillary orders providing ongoing support are more common in cases where one party (usually the husband) has substantial assets and income and the other has significantly less or none. In these cases, the courts can and do make orders for maintenance which are intended to continue the marital standard of living for the lifetime of the receiving spouse. In the recent divorce case of *CC v NC*, the Court of Appeal affirmed a maintenance order for a wife who had received, and dissipated, a substantial lump sum on judicial separation.[41] The parties in this case had separated in 2003 and divorced in 2011. The husband was very wealthy but the wife did not work after they married. Justice Hogan held that the wife was entitled to receive such maintenance as would enable her to maintain the standard of living enjoyed during marriage. Similarly, in *T v L*, ongoing maintenance was awarded to a wife 25 years after the breakdown of the marriage.[42]

[34] *DT v CT* [2002] 3 IR 334, 364.
[35] ibid Keane CJ, 372.
[36] *MD v ND* [2011] IESC 134.
[37] *LD v CD* [2012] IEHC 582, Circuit Court appeal.
[38] *LD v MA* [2012] IEHC 584, Circuit Court appeal. See also *CQ v IMcG* [2014] IEHC 699, Circuit Court appeal and *MC v AC* [2015] IEHC 492.
[39] *PCR v GR* [2013] IEHC 365, 9.
[40] See eg *KA v LTA* [2013] IEHC 634, *GR v NR* [2015] IEHC 856.
[41] *CC v NC* [2016] IECA 410.
[42] *T v L* [2015] IECA 362.

The Irish courts have not made any attempt to set out a comprehensive set of guiding principles regarding the distribution of property following marriage breakdown, preferring to retain a wide discretion that allows them to a respond to individual circumstances. In terms of accommodation for gender-based economic disparities, some attempt has been made to recognise the difficulties experienced by women who take on a dependent role. Justice Denham in the Supreme Court has specifically connected the requirement for proper provision with the text of Article 41.2 of the Constitution,[43] noting that value should be placed on the work of a spouse caring for dependents, the family and the home. She felt that in cases where there has been a long marriage in the primary childbearing years of a woman's life, significant weight ought to be attached to the role of the wife as carer.[44] Justice Murray in *DT v CT* endorsed this view, noting that

> in ensuring that proper provision is made for the spouses of a marriage before a decree of divorce, the courts should, in principle, attribute the same value to the contribution of a spouse who works primarily in the home as it does to that of a spouse who works primarily outside the home as the principal earner.[45]

Despite this rhetoric, dependent spouses are rarely awarded property adjustments amounting to 50 per cent of joint assets. A yardstick of one third as the lower threshold share for the dependent spouse was specifically rejected by the Supreme Court in *DT v CT*, with the court emphasising instead the need for flexibility to adapt to specific circumstances. No detailed statistical analysis of outcomes of marital property disputes is available, but the case law suggests that equal sharing of assets occurs only where the parties have similar incomes during marriage. Where one spouse has taken on a dependent role it is more usual that he or she receive considerably less than half of the joint assets.

C. Alternatives to Litigation

Decisions of the superior courts generally involve higher income families with the resources to fund litigation and assets available for distribution. These cases are therefore not representative of how marriage breakdown affects the property and income of the vast majority of separating and divorcing couples who either do not engage with the courts at all, or who bring their disputes before the District or Circuit Court. When a marriage breaks down, spouses can regulate their separation in a number of ways. They can simply walk away from the relationship and continue their lives independently. This is not uncommon. When both spouses are dependent on social support, in low paid employment, have no property or other assets, and are in agreement in relation to children, there may be no need to formalise a separation. Similarly, where individuals have a clear way to move on without engaging with the law, many will choose to avoid lawyers and the courts.

Where agreement is not possible, spouses can opt to use the summary jurisdiction of the District Court to obtain custody of and access to children, maintenance orders, and orders protecting them from domestic violence. Fahey and Lyons, in their study from the

[43] Constitution of Ireland, Art 41.2: 'In particular, the State recognises that by her life within the home, woman gives to the State a support without which the common good cannot be achieved.'

[44] *DT v CT* [2002] 3 IR 334, 381–82.

[45] ibid 307.

early 1990s, identified this group as the majority within the family court system.[46] Couples with assets, in need of more formal regulation of marital breakdown, can enter into a separation agreement. This is a legally binding document which typically sets out an agreement to live apart, details of custody, access and residence for children, and provisions regarding maintenance and property distribution. Individual couples are free to agree as they wish and there is no requirement to obtain legal advice, although it will likely be necessary if property division is agreed.[47]

When agreement is not possible, an application for judicial separation can be made, but if either spouse wishes to dissolve the marriage or to remarry, a divorce order will be necessary. The vast bulk of divorce decrees granted in Ireland are made in the Circuit Court and on a consent basis.[48] This means that the parties have agreed the terms of the divorce order in advance, their agreement is made an order of the court and their marriage is dissolved. Recent research indicates that consent orders are generally not reviewed in detail by the courts to ascertain whether proper provision exists and that they rarely include provision for spousal support.[49] No detailed analysis has been undertaken regarding the specific content of consent orders or the extent to which they reflect patterns established in the superior courts, although Roisin O'Shea in her observation of more than 1,800 cases in the Circuit Court concluded that litigants in these consent cases were 'invariably lay litigants, and there were little or no assets'.[50] In the absence of legal advice or assets it is likely that little or no engagement with the dicta of the superior courts has taken place.

III. Gender Considerations in Property Division

When considering the efficacy or otherwise of ancillary relief law in promoting gender equality, it is important to appreciate that a clear distinction exists between the law as applied to couples with the will and resources to litigate and those who must negotiate their

[46] T Fahey and M Lyons, *Marital Breakdown and Family Law in Ireland: A Sociological Study* (Cork, Oak Tree Press, 1995) 30–32. The volume of applications under these headings relative to the number of applications for judicial separation and divorce suggests that this remains the position. In 2016, there were 1353 applications for judicial separation and 4179 applications for divorce, the vast bulk of both in the Circuit Court. There were 15,227 applications to the District Court under domestic violence legislation and 8789 applications for maintenance. Courts Service, *Annual Report 2016* (Courts Service 2017) 40, 51. These statistics are simple counts and do not distinguish between first and subsequent applications by the same individual or between spousal and child maintenance. The statistics for maintenance and domestic violence also do not distinguish between married and non-married couples. Nonetheless, they indicate that applications for divorce and judicial separation represent only a small percentage of relationship disputes. And, of course, many couples part company without troubling the courts.

[47] It is not possible to agree an adjustment of pension rights; this can only be done by court order. A separation agreement may therefore be inadvisable where a pension forms part of the asset pool.

[48] In her observation of 1087 marriage law cases in the Circuit Court, Roisin O'Shea reported that 22% of litigants were unrepresented. O'Shea found a consent-order rate of 67% in Circuit family cases and noted that a substantial proportion of these involved lay litigants with little or no assets seeking divorce, see R O'Shea, *Judicial Separation and Divorce in the Circuit Court* (Unpublished PhD Thesis, Waterford Institute of Technology, 2014) 94. Lucy-Ann Buckley, in her study of solicitor case files completed between 1999 and 2003 and necessarily relating to represented clients, found a consent rate of 60%. L-A Buckley, 'Irish Matrimonial Property Division in Practice: A Case Study' (2007) (21) *International Journal of Law, Policy and the Family* 48, 63.

[49] O'Shea, *Judicial Separation and Divorce in the Circuit Court* (n 48) 46, 76.

[50] ibid 76.

way out of marriage, with or without legal assistance and court orders. For the better off, ancillary relief can operate to redress some of the disadvantages suffered by women who adopt a dependent role in marriage, but this often comes at the price of ongoing financial ties to a former spouse in the form of spousal support.[51] Where assets are available to provide a clean break, these are rarely divided equally by the courts; dependent spouses do not exit marriage on the same terms as wealth generators. For ordinary families, there are rarely adequate resources to provide compensation or maintenance to a dependent spouse and available evidence suggests that spousal maintenance is rarely sought by this group. Although proper provision is a constitutional and legal pre-requisite to the grant of a decree of divorce, it would appear that what constitutes proper provision is often simply what the parties agree.

The precedent set by ample resources cases in the superior courts, in which lump sums and large maintenance orders are made in favour of dependent spouses, is largely irrelevant to many families, but can be problematic for spouses in the middle-income bracket, who enjoy a comfortable life on one income while married, but must make significant compromises after the relationship has broken down. The compromises in such cases tend to be particularly felt by women.

The position is well illustrated by the High Court first instance divorce case *PH v FT*.[52] The parties were married in 1998 and obtained a divorce in 2006. The wife gave up employment early in the marriage to care for their twin daughters. Shortly after the relationship broke down, she attempted to move to another city to take up employment with the support of her extended family. The husband obtained an injunction preventing her doing so in order to facilitate his access to the children. This left her unable to work because she had no family to call upon to help with childcare and the terms of the divorce decree reflected this in awarding substantial maintenance to her. In an application by the husband for a variation of maintenance, Abbott J recognised the difficulties experienced by the wife and concluded that she could not work and therefore the husband should continue to pay maintenance. At no point in the judgment, however, does the court recognise the husband's responsibility for the care of the children beyond access and payment of maintenance. The husband had argued that the wife should attempt to earn and thus reduce his maintenance burden, but there is no indication that he offered, or the court expected, that he would facilitate her working through his own greater involvement in childcare. While this is just one case, it does highlight the limitations of ancillary relief orders in dealing with the gendered effects of dependency marriage. A court cannot order a parent to actively provide child care, but it can order the payment of money. It cannot order a spouse to work, but it can make financial orders that support a choice not to. Patterns of dependency established during marriage, particularly where the relationship was a long one, are not easy to displace when the spouses cease cohabitation.

IV. Potential for Reform

By focusing on the alleviation of post-relationship vulnerability, ancillary relief law can act to re-enforce and re-make marital dependency after marriage has ended. Further, the

[51] Maintenance payments cease on remarriage.
[52] *PH v FT* [2011] IEHC 233.

existence of rules which place responsibility for female post-relationship vulnerability on individual men can act to mask the role of public policy in maintaining gender inequality in other domains which affect women's ability to earn wages and accumulate assets. These types of difficulties have led radical feminists like Martha Fineman to call for the abolition of marriage law because of its role in reinforcing the culturally entrenched dependency of women, while others such as Carol Smart argue that relationship law should be remade so that it does not rely on concepts of marriage or coupledom.[53] Although these may be worthwhile aims, the difficulty of resolving issues arising from historic practices remain. Couples who married decades ago and are divorcing in the present need to regulate their futures, and cannot re-make the past. At the same time, the limitations of marriage law in accounting for structural inequalities must be acknowledged; the law should not raise unrealistic expectations of post-relationship security for spouses who take on a dependent role. It is only the very wealthy who can afford to completely compensate a home carer for the loss of a providing spouse.

No substantive proposals have been made by the Government to reform ancillary relief law although a proposal to reduce the wait time for divorce from four years to two has been accepted but a constitutional amendment will be necessary to implement it.[54] The four-year wait period was intended to create a period of adjustment for families and to avoid 'easy divorce' but there seems to be no specific rational for the choice of two years as an alternative. The wait period for a no fault judicial separation is one year and it would make more sense for the time periods to coincide, allowing divorce to operate as an alternative to judicial separation rather than as an additional step. Reducing the wait period to two years will allow earlier applications for financial orders for those who need them, but where need is urgent, an application for judicial separation will remain the only option within the two-year period, leaving in place the current two-step process whereby proper provision is assessed or agreed on judicial separation and again on divorce. It remains to be seen whether the Government will use the proposal as an opportunity to re-consider the law on ancillary relief. At the time of writing, no preparatory work in this regard has been undertaken and there seems little political appetite to address the issue.

Reform proposals from academic commentators have focused on uncertainty in ancillary relief law created by the lack of legislative guidance on the meaning and purpose of proper provision and the failure of the judiciary to develop a meaningful set of principles.[55] Louise Crowley argues that the Irish legislature has failed to address key questions such as the purpose of ancillary relief, the justification for ongoing financial ties following divorce, and the proper extent of spousal obligations after divorce.[56] Kathryn O'Sullivan points out that this lack of a principled approach impacts most on financially vulnerable spouses,[57] and that greater clarity could assist spouses in negotiating post-relationship lives.[58]

[53] M Fineman, *The Autonomy Myth* (New York, New Press, 2005) 133–34; C Smart, *The Ties that Bind; Law, Marriage and the Reproduction of Patriarchal Relations* (London, Routledge and Kegan Paul 1984) xi.

[54] The proposed 35th Amendment of the Constitution (Divorce) Bill 2016 contains a proposal to reduce the time which couples must live apart before making an application for divorce from four out of the previous five years to two out of the previous three years. The Bill completed Committee Stage in the Dáil on 6 April 2017.

[55] K O'Sullivan, 'Ancillary Relief and Private Ordering: The Vulnerability of Financially Weaker Spouses' (2016) 19(1) *Irish Journal of Family Law* 3; L Crowley, 'Irish Divorce Law in a Social Policy Vacuum – From the Unspoken to the Unknown' (2011) 33(3) *Journal of Social Welfare and Family Law* 227.

[56] Crowley, 'Irish Divorce Law in a Social Policy Vacuum' (n 55) 240.

[57] O'Sullivan, 'Ancillary Relief and Private Ordering' (n 55) 6.

[58] K O'Sullivan, 'Rethinking Ancillary Relief on Divorce in Ireland: The Challenges and Opportunities' (2016) 36(1) *Legal Studies* 111.

Evidence from the lower courts, however, suggests that many ordinary families are able to negotiate their way out of marriage and favour a clean break divorce without ongoing financial ties. When there are few assets beyond what is necessary to meet immediate needs, there is little room for dispute. In ample resources cases, the issues are often very complex and the imposition of fixed rules regarding assets splitting could lead to unfairness in individual cases.[59] Nonetheless, the superior courts could do more to promote equality in asset division for ample resources cases. Even in long dependency marriages, the courts rarely come close to a division of one third in favour of the home carer, despite repeated references to the equal value of caring and income-generating functions to the family in superior court decisions. The English House of Lords in *White v White* introduced a principle of equality into a discretionary ancillary relief scheme similar to that applicable in Ireland, although the courts have, unfortunately, subsequently rowed back from a position of strict equality.[60] A similar presumption of equal sharing could easily be incorporated into existing Irish law and would serve to highlight the significant benefit that a dependent spouse can confer on a wage earner and the substantial cost to an individual spouse in taking on that role.

V. Conclusion

Irish law governing marital property can be characterised as a type of deferred community of property system; each spouse owns his or her own property and income during marriage but enforced sharing applies once the relationship breaks down. There is no assumption that this sharing will be equal or create any defined shares for the spouses. No overriding principles or objectives apply to distribution of property and ancillary orders are potentially subject to variation during the lifetime of the spouses. While this uncertainty, and at times inconsistency, can be criticised, it does allow flexibility to deal with the significant diversity of relationship practices that arise. It is open to the courts to apply their discretion in a manner that promotes gender equality, but despite rhetoric supporting the equal value of family care work generally carried out by women, little has been done to recognise this value in a principled manner.

In any event, legal rules governing property distribution on marriage breakdown are of limited applicability to ordinary families without access to property and income adequate to support, let alone compensate, a home carer for the loss of a supporting spouse. Despite significant advances toward gender equity over the past 30 years, women continue to take on the bulk of caring responsibilities in marriage. When a long-term relationship breaks down, they are doubly disadvantaged; rarely compensated for care work by their spouses

[59] J Herring, *Family Law*, 7th edn (Harlow, Pearson, 2015) 285.

[60] *White v White* [2001] 1 AC 596. But, as Jonathan Herring notes, much of the subsequent case law in that jurisdiction effectively diminishes the significance of that principle through the development of additional principles of non-marital property, extraordinary contributions and pre-nuptial agreements. Post-*White* developments have led to the money-earner keeping more than half of the assets, to the detriment of the child carer and homemaker, see Herring, *Family Law* (n 59) 285.

and facing significant structural difficulties to self-sufficiency. Dependency arising after marriage is the direct result of dependency within marriage. Post-relationship poverty and diminution in living standards for separated and divorced women, particularly those having care of children, will not be alleviated with property law. Until a significant shift occurs in how economic roles are allocated within intimate relationships, women who take on a caring role will continue to be disproportionately disadvantaged by marital breakdown.

10

Hidden in Plain Sight? Gender in the Irish Financial Crisis

MARY DONNELLY

I. Introduction

On even minimal reflection, the gendered nature of the Irish financial crisis becomes obvious.[1] All of the key players in the Irish banking sector prior to the crisis were male[2] and men vastly outnumbered women on the boards of Irish banks.[3] The construction industry was male dominated and all of the major property developers were male.[4] The individuals with political and regulatory responsibility pre-crisis (the Financial Regulator; the Governor of the Central Bank; the Minister for Finance; and the Taoiseach) were all male. Notwithstanding changes of personnel as the crisis unfolded, these roles continued to be held by men throughout the crisis (and indeed still continue to be so held).[5] In July 2018, the board of the National Assets Management Agency (NAMA),[6] which has played a key role in dictating the ongoing response to the crisis, comprised seven men and two women.[7] The social and economic effects of the crisis are also experienced in a gendered way.[8]

[1] See M Murphy, 'Gendering the Narrative of the Irish Crisis' (2015) 30(2) *Irish Political Studies* 220.

[2] ibid 225.

[3] Writing in 2011, Blanaid Clarke noted that 20% of board members of the Irish banks then in existence (Allied Irish Bank; Anglo Irish Bank; Bank of Ireland; Irish Nationwide; EBS and Irish Life and Permanent) were women; however this percentage was not evenly distributed across the banks; when EBS was removed, the percentage dropped to 13% and Anglo Irish Bank and Irish Nationwide has no women board members: see B Clarke, 'Lessons Learned: The Corporate Governance for Credit Institutions and Insurance Undertakings' (2011) 33(1) *Dublin University Law Journal* 172.

[4] For accounts of the most high-profile developers, see F Connolly, *NAMA Land* (Dublin, Gill Books, 2017); F O'Toole, *Ship of Fools: How Stupidity and Corruption Sank the Celtic Tiger* (London, Faber, 2009).

[5] Eight members of the Central Bank Commission (which is responsible for ensuring that the statutory functions of the Central Bank are upheld) are men and three are women.

[6] NAMA was established by the National Assets Management Agency Act 2009 to facilitate the transfer of large non-performing loans in relation to development land from Irish banks. NAMA ultimately acquired loans with a face value of €74 billion, for which it paid €31.8 billion, thus becoming one of the most significant property companies globally.

[7] See www.nama.ie/about-us/board-and-committees/board-members/.

[8] See F Bettio et al, *The Impact of the Economic Crisis on the Situation of Women and Men and on Gender Equality Politics* (European Commission DG Justice, 2012); U Barry, *Economic Crisis and Gender Equality: Ireland and the EU* (Foundation for European Progressive Studies, 2014).

Both globally,[9] and in Ireland, there is evidence that austerity policies, homelessness and social inequality impact disproportionately on women.[10]

This chapter seeks to add to the gendered narratives of the financial crisis by exposing the role of gender in the case law in respect of 'sexually transmitted debt',[11] as this has played out in the Irish courts. The chapter has two goals; first, to illustrate the gendered nature of this corner of the financial crisis and, second, to illustrate some of the inherent difficulties in addressing gender-related issues in private law. The chapter begins by justifying its focus on, and explaining its understanding of, the concept of sexually transmitted debt. Looking first at the treatment of this issue outside of Ireland, it contrasts two dominant trends. These are the gender-neutral approach espoused by the House of Lords in *Royal Bank of Scotland plc v Etridge (No 2)*[12] and the gender-specific approach adopted by the High Court of Australia in *Garcia v National Australia Bank*.[13] The chapter then turns to the relevant corpus of Irish case law. It identifies broad patterns and selects cases for closer analysis both in terms of the gender narratives which emerge and the judicial approaches employed. Through this, the chapter makes visible the gendered nature of this aspect of the Irish financial crisis. This leads inexorably to the question of how the Irish courts *should* address the gendered nature of sexually transmitted debt. This is by no means an easy question to resolve. It will be shown that both gender-neutral and gender-specific responses are problematic, either because, in the first instance, they fail to represent reality or because, in the second, they serve to reinforce oppressive realities. The chapter concludes by locating the discussion within the broader context of feminist critiques of private law. Drawing on these, it advocates a structural analysis of private law in Ireland, grounded in the identification of the impact of factors, such as gender, which are otherwise hidden in plain sight.

II. Sexually Transmitted Debt: The Concept

The transmission of the consequences of indebtedness to those people with whom a debtor is in an intimate or close relationship is as old as the concept of debt itself.[14] Thus, the Mesopotamian Code of Hammurabi[15] provided for the pledging of all forms of 'property' of the

[9] See eg J Rubery and M Karamessini (eds), *Women and Austerity: The Economic Crisis and the Future for Gender Equality* (London, Routledge, 2013).

[10] See U Barry and P Conroy, *Ireland: Untold Story of the Crisis: Gender Equality and New Inequalities* (TASC Series 2012); U Barry and P Conroy, 'Ireland in Crisis 2008–2010: Gender, Equality and Austerity' in Rubery and Karamessini (eds) ibid.

[11] This memorable term seems to have originated in Australia: see N Howell, '"Sexually Transmitted Debt": A Feminist Analysis of Laws Regulating Guarantors and Co-Borrowers' (1995) 4 *The Australian Feminist Law Journal* 93, although it is now widely used.

[12] *Royal Bank of Scotland plc v Etridge (No 2)* [2001] 2 AC 773.

[13] *Garcia v National Australia Bank* [1998] HCA 48, (1998) 194 CLR 395.

[14] Credit and debt in one form or another have been part of human transactions for at least as long as written records, long preceding the invention of coinage: see D Graeber, *Debt: The First 5000 Years* (New York, Melville House Publishing, 2011) 39.

[15] This Code of law was decreed at sometime between 1752 and 1750 BCE.

debtor, including land, houses, utensils, children, slaves and wives.[16] In a contemporary context, the transmission of the consequences of debt is more indirect. Whenever indebtedness reaches a point where it interferes with a debtor's personal life, the consequences of this debt are likely to be transmitted to the debtor's spouse/partner (and indeed to his or her children).[17] While recognising this broader social phenomenon, however, this chapter is working with a more specific understanding of sexually transmitted debt, which is explained below.

A. Delimiting Sexually Transmitted Debt

This chapter adopts an updated version of the understanding of sexually transmitted debt as developed by scholars since the mid-1990s.[18] This views sexually transmitted debt as arising in a marital or intimate relationship, where one party incurs the debt and the other party assumes obligations in respect of the debt. This understanding has two aspects. First, it includes all situations where one spouse/intimate partner provides security (whether by providing a guarantee or security in rem, most typically over a share in a family home) for the business debt of the other. This includes a situation where the primary debt is assumed by a company and security is provided by the spouse/partner of a director or major shareholder. Second, it includes joint debts in a commercial context where both spouses/intimate partners assume formal liability for a joint loan or provide a guarantee of a loan to a company in which both are directors but one spouse is not actively involved in the operation of the business.

Sexually transmitted debt as analysed here can be distinguished from the broader category of emotionally transmitted debt, which encompasses situations where one (or more) person/s assume liability for the debt of another/s (very often through a contract of guarantee or indemnity) on the basis of their emotional connection with the debtor.[19] This may encompass a sexual/intimate connection but is not restricted to this and may also include family and parental bonds as well as friendship.[20] The narrower focus is adopted here so as

[16] See S Homer and R Sylla, *A History of Interest Rates*, 4th edn (Hoboken, Wylie Finance, 2005) 27. Wives were, however, afforded a higher degree of protection than other 'property' in that a wife's agreement was generally required (ibid).

[17] Although it would be difficult to identify a precise point at which this happens, some events such as the debtor's bankruptcy or application for relief under the Personal Insolvency Act 2012, could reasonably be assumed to have this effect. The statistics provided by the Insolvency Service of Ireland do not indicate the gender breakdown in respect of applications for bankruptcy (although it would be possible to do a manual breakdown based on the names provided); the disaggregated statistics in respect of applications for personal insolvency relief (from Q4 2013 to Q3 2017) show that 47.6% of applicants were female and 52.4% were male: see www.isi.gov.ie. However, without further information as to the causes of the debt (ie whether the debt in respect of which the relief was sought had, in its turn, been sexually transmitted), it is not possible to reach any definitive conclusions based on these data.

[18] See Howell, 'Sexually Transmitted Debt' (n 11); B Fehlberg, *Sexually Transmitted Debt: Surety Experience and English Law* (Oxford, Oxford University Press, 1997).

[19] See P Baron, 'The Exercise of Her Will: Women and Emotionally Transmitted Debt' (1995) 13 *Law in Context* 23.

[20] Classic examples from the case law include *Lloyds Bank Ltd v Bundy* [1975] QB 326; *Commercial Bank of Australia v Amadio* [1983] 151 CLR 447 and *Credit Lyonnais Bank Nederland NV v Burch* [1997] 1 FLR 11.

to allow a clearer exposition of the gendered elements of the relevant transactions, which can be obscured by the broader formulation.[21]

III. Developing a Judicial Response

The phenomenon of sexually transmitted debt, in the sense explored here, is relatively recent, having largely emerged with the shift to jointly owned family homes[22] which began in the 1980s.[23] Prior to this, the majority of women did not have the property interests to provide security,[24] and there is no suggestion from case law or elsewhere that husbands/male partners were being requested to provide security for their wives'/female partners' debts. Thus, the concept of sexually transmitted debt emerged as a gender-specific, male to female, phenomenon. The decision of the House of Lords in *National Westminster Bank v Morgan*[25] is generally regarded as having opened the floodgates to claims of this kind[26] (notwithstanding that Mrs Morgan was, in fact, unsuccessful in her claim). Thus began a complex line of case law which occupied the UK appellate courts (as well as the courts in many other jurisdictions) for the succeeding two decades. Broadly speaking, two trends can be identified: the UK gender-neutral approach and the gender-specific approach adopted in Australia. A brief overview of each helps to establish the context for the Irish discussion to follow.

A. The UK Gender-neutral Approach

The cases of sexually transmitted debt which emerged in the wake of *Morgan* all involved allegations by women of undue influence/misrepresentation by men and almost all involved married couples.[27] Nonetheless, when the issue again reached the House of Lords in *Barclays Bank v O'Brien*,[28] the House of Lords dismissed the 'special equity' theory which had been adopted by the Court of Appeal whereby wives (and possibly relationships falling into other categories) were entitled to special protection because of the particular vulnerability of their position.[29] Instead, Lord Browne Wilkinson relied on the equitable doctrine

[21] See J Scoular, 'The Revival of Equitable Doctrine in Scots Law: A Space for Gender Concerns?' in S Scott-Hunt and H Lim (eds), *Feminist Perspectives on Equity and Trusts* (London, Cavendish, 2001) 122.

[22] The right of married women to acquire and dispose of property in their own right had been established since the Married Women's Property Act 1882 (which extended to Ireland). However, property ownership continued to be largely male. There are various reasons for the shift to joint ownership of family homes including the new preference for this by lenders which emerged in the wake of the decision of the House of Lords in *Williams & Glyn's Bank v Boland* [1981] AC 487 in the UK and the Supreme Court decision in *Nestor v Murphy* [1979] IR 326 in Ireland.

[23] Although note occasional earlier examples, eg *Yerkey v Jones* (1939) 63 CLR 649, discussed at Section IV.B below, on 'The Australian Gender-specific Approach'.

[24] The Family Home Protection Act 1976 was a legislative attempt to deal with the consequences of the creation of security interests by husbands who were the sole owners of family homes.

[25] *National Westminster Bank v Morgan* [1985] 1 AC 686.

[26] R Auchmuty, 'The Rhetoric of Equality and the Problem of Heterosexuality' in L Mulcahy and S Wheeler, *Feminist Perspectives on Contract Law* (London, Glass House Press, 2005) 53.

[27] ibid 53–54.

[28] *Barclays Bank v O'Brien* [1994] AC 180.

[29] ibid 195.

of notice, finding that where a wife had acted as surety for her husband's debts, a lender was put on inquiry (regarding undue influence/misrepresentation) where the transaction was not, on its face, to the financial advantage of the wife and there was a substantial risk in transactions of that kind that, in procuring the wife's agreement, the husband had engaged in undue influence/misrepresentation.[30] Failure to take 'reasonable steps' to ensure that the wife's consent was properly obtained would fix the lender with constructive notice of the undue influence/misrepresentation.[31] Lord Browne Wilkinson was clear that the doctrine of notice operated in the same way in the context of cohabitation, 'whether heterosexual or homosexual', noting that 'Legal wives are not the only group which are now exposed to the emotional pressure of cohabitation'.[32] He also affirmed an earlier Court of Appeal decision[33] that other relationships (in the case in question, that between a son and his elderly parents) could also put a lender on inquiry.[34]

Although the House of Lords' revision of *O'Brien* in *Royal Bank of Scotland v Etridge (No 2)*[35] refined many aspects of the legal framework,[36] it remained committed to the gender-neutral approach. This was notwithstanding that broadly contemporaneous empirical investigation affirmed that sexually transmitted debt was a profoundly gendered phenomenon;[37] the vast majority of the extensive case law post *O'Brien* involved the exercise of undue influence by men (usually husbands) in respect of women (usually wives);[38] and all eight appellants in the conjoined appeals in *Etridge* were women.[39] Lord Nicholls found that a lender is put on inquiry regarding the possibility of third party undue influence where there is proof that a complainant had placed trust and confidence in the third party in relation to the management of the complainant's financial affairs 'coupled with a transaction which calls for explanation'.[40] Cohabitation was not a necessary prerequisite,[41] and Lord Nicholls was clear that 'the law does not regard sexual relationships as standing in some special category of their own so far as undue influence is concerned'.[42] Thus a lender should regard itself as 'put on inquiry' in every case where 'the relationship between the surety and the debtor is non-commercial'.[43] With no apparent intention of irony, however, Lord Nicholls (and the other members of the House of Lords) all used the term 'wife' as a shorthand to encompass all relevant sureties.

[30] ibid 196.
[31] ibid 196.
[32] ibid 198.
[33] *Avon Finance Company v Bridger* [1985] 2 All ER 281.
[34] [1994] AC 180, 198.
[35] [2002] 2 AC 773.
[36] Key doctrinal refinements included a movement away from constructive notice as the basis of the lender's obligations ([2002] 2 AC 773, 838 per Lord Scott) and clarification as to the nature of the 'reasonable steps' required (805–06 per Lord Nicholls).
[37] Fehlberg's empirical study of sureties impacted (primarily sourced from a bank pressure group) comprised 20 women and two men, see Fehlberg, *Sexually Transmitted Debt* (n 18) 92.
[38] See R Auchmuty, 'Men Behaving Badly: An Analysis of English Undue Influence Cases' (2002) 11(2) *Social and Legal Studies* 257.
[39] All cases concerned contracts of guarantee. Seven concerned an allegation of undue influence in respect of the appellant's husband (the eighth concerned a negligence action against a solicitor).
[40] [2002] 2 AC 773, 796.
[41] ibid 803.
[42] ibid 813.
[43] ibid 814.

B. The Australian Gender-specific Approach

The modern statement of the gender-specific position derives from the decision of the High Court of Australia in *Garcia v National Australia Bank Ltd*,[44] where a majority of the Court (to the surprise of many commentators[45]) endorsed the 'special equity' (or 'special wives equity') first propounded by that Court in the 1939 case of *Yerkey v Jones*.[46] Both *Yerkey* and *Garcia* concerned guarantees given by wives as security for loans to their husbands. The special equity was set out by Dixon J in *Yerkey* as follows:

> If a married woman's consent to become a surety for her husband's debt is procured by the husband and, without understanding its effect in essential respects, she executes an instrument of suretyship which the creditor accepts without dealing with her personally, she has a prima facie right to have it set aside.[47]

Explaining the 'basal reason' for the special equity, Dixon J stated that 'in substance, if not technically, the wife is a volunteer conferring an important advantage upon her husband who in virtue of his position has an opportunity of abusing the confidence she may be expected to place in him'.[48]

Reaffirming the special equity theory, some 60 years later, the High Court in *Garcia* decisively placed its decision within a gendered understanding of the nature of 1990s marriage in Australia.[49] Thus, the majority stated:

> That Australian society, and particularly the role of women in that society, has changed in the last six decades is undoubted. But some things are unchanged. There is still a significant number of women in Australian relationships which are, for many and varied reasons, marked by disparities of economic and other power between the parties.[50]

Nonetheless, the majority found that the wife's special equity as advanced in *Yerkey* had not derived from 'notions based on the subservience or inferior economic position of women'.[51] Instead it was based on the 'trust and confidence' between marriage partners. Thus, the majority stated that:

> The marriage relationship is such that one, often the woman, may well leave many, perhaps all, business judgments to the other spouse. In that kind of relationship, business decisions may be made with little consultation between the parties and with the most abbreviated explanation of their purport or effect.[52]

The majority acknowledged that the *Yerkey* principles could possibly be applied in other relationships 'more common now than was the case in 1939 – to long term and publically

[44] *Garcia v National Australia Bank* (1998) 194 CLR 395.

[45] See C Chew, 'Rethinking the Special Equity Rule for Wives: Post Garcia, Quo Vadis, Where to From Here?' (2007) 19(1) *Bond Law Review* 61, 65.

[46] *Yerkey v Jones* [1939] 63 CLR 649.

[47] ibid 683.

[48] ibid 684.

[49] See R Grossi, *Looking for Love in the Legal Discourse of Marriage* (Canberra, ANU Press, 2014) 72–73.

[50] [1998] 194 CLR 395, 403.

[51] ibid.

[52] ibid 404.

declared relationships short of marriage between members of the same or of opposite sex'.[53] However, it was not necessary in the case in question to offer a view on this or on the question of whether the principles would apply where a husband acted as surety for his wife.[54]

IV. Sexually Transmitted Debt in the Case Law of the Irish Crisis

Donovan and Murphy argue that the Irish crisis is best understood as four inter-related crises: a property market crisis; a banking crisis; a fiscal crisis; and, ultimately, a financial crisis which culminated in the EU/IMF programme.[55] The discussion here relates to the first of these crises and the dramatic fall in property values which began in 2007. While the other aspects of the crisis have had an impact on every person living in the State, this aspect of the crisis was felt primarily by those individuals who were exposed to the property market, usually through some form of property-related debt. It is not possible to provide an accurate picture of the extent, or indeed the impact, of sexually transmitted debt in this aspect of the crisis. Many situations of indebtedness were privately resolved (with the resolution generally including a confidentiality clause). For this reason, the discussion here focuses on what can be learned from the case law of the crisis. It begins by providing an overview of the relevant cases, from a gendered perspective. It then undertakes a more detailed analysis of the role of gender narratives in the case law. The focus on narratives reflects the proposition that legal judgments represent more than just a statement of the applicable legal position but also reflect the broader societal and normative contexts from which they come.[56]

A search of the crisis-related case law (from 2007 up until 31 December 2017) identified 12 cases[57] which fitted within the understanding of sexually transmitted debt used in this chapter.[58] To place this within a broader context, an additional four cases of emotionally

[53] ibid.

[54] ibid.

[55] D Donovan and A Murphy, *The Fall of the Celtic Tiger: Ireland and the Euro Debt Crisis* (Oxford, Oxford University Press, 2013) 7–8.

[56] See P Brooks and P Gewirtz (eds), *Law's Stories: Narrative and Rhetoric in the Law* (New Haven, Yale University Press, 1996).

[57] In reverse chronological order, the cases identified are as follows: *AIB plc v Rostaff Property Development Ltd* [2017] IEHC 533; *Bank of Ireland v Mellon* [2017] IEHC 501; *ACC Bank plc v Walsh* [2017] IECA 166; *Ulster Bank plc v De Kretser* [2016] IECA 371, [2015] IEHC 359; *Danske Bank A/S t/a Danske Bank v Miley* [2016] IEHC 105; *Allied Irish Bank v Yates* [2016] IEHC 60; *NAMA v Kessler* [2015] IEHC 6; *Bank of Scotland v Hickey* [2014] IEHC 207; *Friends First Finance v Lavelle* [2013] IEHC 201; *EBS Ltd v Campbell* [2013] IEHC 154; *Ulster Bank v Roche and Buttimer* [2012] IEHC 166; *IBRC v Quinn* [2011] IEHC 470. Cases which involved a first instance hearing and an appeal are treated as one case for the purposes of this calculation.

[58] Searches were conducted on www.courts.ie; www.bailii.org; www.staredecisishibernia.com using the search terms: 'husband/wife/debt'; 'partner/debt/defence'; 'undue influence' and 'non est factum' and these were cross-referred. Cases which involved defences based on emotional transmission of debt were excluded as were cases concerned solely with allegations of undue influence on the part of the lender (eg *Bank of Ireland v Cochrane* [2014] IEHC 605; *ACC Bank v Kelly and Anor* [2011] IEHC 7) and cases where the defendant did not attempt to assert that both parties were not involved in the business (eg *Allied Irish Bank v Fahey and Anor* [2016] IEHC 182; *O'Donnell v Bank of Ireland* [2014] IESC 77 and associated cases). *Whelan and Ors v AIB* [2014] IESC 3 was also excluded because of the peculiar and accidental nature of the transaction, which was never intended by any of the parties, including the lawyers, to transmit Philip Lynch's debt to his wife and children.

transmitted debt were identified within this period; three of these involved parents and children,[59] and one involved siblings.[60] None of these four cases were successful.

All cases involved a defence to enforcement proceedings and most involved an attempt to resist the lender's application for summary judgment. In the latter cases, there is a very low threshold for success in establishing a right to a plenary hearing and there is no need for the court to analyse defences raised in any detail beyond whether the defendants could raise 'an arguable defence'.[61] Ten of the cases employed a defence based on third party undue influence while four argued *non est factum* (with three cases arguing both). In five cases, the defendant's argument was successful. In three of the cases, this resulted in the defendant being afforded a right to a plenary hearing while in two, the defendant was entirely freed from liability.

Viewed from a gendered perspective, the striking feature is that in all the cases the primary debtor was male and the defendant was female. Although technically, this position is reversed in *Friends First Finance v Lavelle*,[62] as will be clear in the discussion below, this case in fact constituted one of the more egregious examples of male to female sexually transmitted debt. In nine of the cases, the parties were married. If one expands the category to encompass emotionally transmitted debt, it continues to be the case that the primary debtor was male; however, in two of the cases the defendant was also male (a father and a brother of the primary debtor). From this, it is clear that, insofar as can be ascertained from the cases, the pattern of the Irish financial crisis reflected that which had emerged in UK and Australian case law from more than two decades earlier. In light of this, it falls now to see what can be learned about the nature of sexually transmitted debt through a closer look at the case law.

V. Understanding the Nature of Sexually Transmitted Debt

In understanding how and why sexually transmitted debt happens, there are two possible narratives. The first, as advanced by Rosemary Auchmuty, is that sexually transmitted debt arises because of 'men behaving badly'.[63] Following a comprehensive study of English undue influence case law (up to 2002), Auchmuty concluded that 'morally reprehensible behaviour by men is so common as to seem normal and acceptable and, therefore, unworthy of comment'.[64] A second, rather more benign, representation is that of the High Court of Australia in *Garcia*, which characterised sexually transmitted debt as arising because of the relationship of trust and confidence between marriage partners.[65] Both narratives are represented in the Irish crisis case law (sometimes in the same case).

[59] *ACC Loan Management Ltd v Connolly* [2017] EWCA 119; *Bank of Ireland v Curran* [2016] EWCA 399; *ACC Bank plc v McEllin* [2013] IEHC 454.

[60] *ACC Loan Management Ltd v Sheehan* [2015] IEHC 818.

[61] The applicable standard is set out by Hardiman J in *Aer Rianta v Ryanair* [2001] IR 607, 627 in the following terms: 'is it very clear that the defendant has no case? Is there either no issue to be tried or only issues which are simple and easily determined? Do the defendant's affidavits fail to disclose even an arguable defence?'

[62] *Friends First Finance v Lavelle* [2013] IEHC 201.

[63] Auchmuty, 'Men Behaving Badly' (n 38).

[64] ibid 259.

[65] *Garcia v National Australia Bank* (1998) 194 CLR 395.

A. 'Men Behaving Badly'

In terms of 'men behaving badly', only in the leading undue influence case of *Ulster Bank Ireland Ltd v Roche and Buttimer*[66] is there evidence of overtly coercive behaviour by the male spouse/partner.[67] This case concerned enforcement proceedings in respect of a guarantee (limited in amount to €50,000) provided by Ms Buttimer of the borrowings of a motor trade company operated by Mr Roche, who was her 'partner in the personal sense of the term'.[68] Ms Buttimer was a hairdresser on a modest salary. She was not a shareholder in the company and Clarke J found that, although she was a director, she had no involvement with its operations.[69] Justice Clarke found that, at the time of the guarantee, Ms Buttimer was in 'the sort of dependent and abusive relationship with Mr Roche … that she would have done anything that he asked'.[70] Ms Buttimer's own evidence in this regard was verified by the evidence of a clinical psychologist whom she had been seeing at the time of the guarantee.

There are also instances of deliberate deception. In *Friends First Finance v Lavelle and Anor*,[71] a loan of €1.75 million had been advanced to Ms Lavelle in 2007, and guaranteed by her husband, the second defendant. However, to the knowledge of the lender, this arrangement was for 'tax planning reasons' only, and the real borrower was Mr Lavelle. The loan was invested by Mr Lavelle in a private investment fund operated by Quinlan Private Investments. Justice Charleton accepted the evidence of Ms Lavelle that the first time she knew that she had borrowed the money was in 2011 and that this had come as a shock to her. She accepted that she had signed the loan documents; however, she had done so when these were presented to her by her husband as part of a settlement in respect of a family trust, which had been set up for her and her children.[72] In respect of all subsequent communications from Quinlan Private Investments (which would have been marked with a large gold 'Q'), Charleton J found that, since Mr Lavelle worked from home, he had 'management of the post' and that he had used that control to prevent Ms Lavelle seeing the communications.[73] The appellant in *ACC Bank plc v Walsh and Anor*[74] also asserted acts of deception by her (now) estranged husband, although because this case concerned an application of the right to defend at plenary hearing, no finding of fact was made. The appellant denied having appended her signature to a joint loan contract (which bore the signatures of Mr and Ms Walsh), which had been used to top-up an earlier business loan to her husband in his sole name.[75]

[66] *Ulster Bank Ireland Ltd v Roche and Buttimer* [2012] IEHC 166.
[67] In *AIB plc v Rostaff Property Development Ltd and Ors* [2017] IEHC 533, the female defendant's affidavit alleged 'emotional pressure' by her former 'romantic partner' although further evidence in this regard was not provided.
[68] *Ulster Bank Ireland Ltd v Roche and Buttimer* [2012] IEHC 166 1.2.
[69] ibid 4.2.
[70] ibid 4.2.
[71] *Friends First Finance v Lavelle and Anor* [2013] IEHC 201.
[72] ibid 21.
[73] ibid 21.
[74] *ACC Bank plc v Walsh and Anor* [2017] IECA 166, [5].
[75] ibid 13.

If some of the male borrowers behaved badly, so too did the financial institutions, which in several instances can be seen to have colluded with the male borrowers in deceiving or excluding the female borrowers/guarantors. The most striking example is *Friends First Finance v Lavelle and Anor*, discussed above.[76] Here, the lender advanced a substantial loan to Ms Lavelle notwithstanding that, to its knowledge, the real borrower was Mr Lavelle.[77] Moreover, it delegated all normal procedures in terms of checking, witnessing and signing of documents in respect of the loan to Quinlan Private Investments (from whom an investment product funded by the loan was being purchased).[78] All communications in respect of the loan were directed to Mr Lavelle and no one made any attempt to meet Ms Lavelle. Instead, Mr Lavelle was asked to nominate the bank from which payments were to be made; to have the loan documentation signed; and to obtain a copy of his wife's passport and utility bill (for compliance with money laundering requirements). As described by Charleton J: 'Everyone seems to have forgotten that the plaintiff was making the loan and no one seems to show respect to the entitlement of Charlotte Lavelle as the supposed borrower to her statutory rights, never mind an entitlement to simply engaged [sic] in the process.'[79]

Other examples are less extreme but equally instructive; in both *Roche* and *Walsh*, all of the discussions of the loan were conducted between the lender and the male protagonists, to the exclusion of the female guarantor (in *Roche*) and the female joint borrower (in *Walsh*). In *Bank of Ireland v Mellon*,[80] the lender had at all times negotiated with the defendant's husband as regards management of his business loan portfolio, notwithstanding that the defendant had been requested to (and had) created a security interest in favour of the lender in respect of assets of which she was the joint owner.

B. Trust and Confidence

While the 'men behaving badly' narrative has been especially important in the successful cases, the 'trust and confidence' narrative has also been evident. *Friends First Finance v Lavelle and Anor* is again a useful representative example. As described by Charleton J, although Ms Lavelle had a reasonable level of English language training (she had moved from Germany in 2004), since her marriage, she had devoted herself to her family and 'trusted totally in the expertise, competence and honesty of her husband'.[81] In signing what she thought was a trust settlement document, she did not investigate further because 'As far as she was then concerned, her husband made money and he was able to spend it as he wished'.[82] Variations on this narrative are found in other cases. In *Bank of Ireland v Quinn*, Ms Quinn denied that she was a 'business lady' and stated that she had, in fact, been a homemaker for over 36 years and that her only role since her marriage at the age of 21 years had been 'rearing her family and taking care of her husband'.[83] In *Allied Irish Bank plc v Yates*,

[76] *Friends First Finance v Lavelle and Anor* [2013] IEHC 201.
[77] ibid 8.
[78] ibid 7.
[79] ibid 14.
[80] *Bank of Ireland v Mellon* [2017] IEHC 501.
[81] *Friends First Finance v Lavelle and Anor* [2013] IEHC 201, [20].
[82] ibid 21.
[83] *Bank of Ireland v Quinn* [2011] IEHC 470, [20].

Ms Yates stated on affidavit that, although she acted as director and secretary to Celtic Bookmakers Ltd (the company established by her husband and for which she had provided a secured guarantee): 'I never had any responsibility for financial matters. I had no qualifications or expertise in relation to financial matters and I have never professed to have such expertise.'[84] Although these narratives have to be viewed in the light of the overall goal of avoiding the imposition of liability, they do suggest that some aspects of the evaluation by the High Court of Australia in *Garcia* are still relevant in contemporary Ireland.

VI. Judicial Responses to Gender Narratives

In light of the preceding analysis, it falls then to consider how the Irish courts have responded to the gendered phenomenon that is sexually transmitted debt. For this, it becomes necessary to shift focus and structure the discussion around the 'neutral' question of doctrine.[85] In the Irish crisis case law, the questions of doctrine have been whether a (female) defendant can avoid liability (or have a chance to defend herself against liability in a plenary hearing) on the basis of either *non est factum* or third party undue influence.

A. *Non Est Factum*: The Relevance of Gender

It is well established that the common law defence of *non est factum* ('it is not my deed') is applied restrictively. This is on the basis that 'Much confusion and uncertainty would result in the field of contract and elsewhere if a man were permitted to try to disown his signature simply by asserting that he did not understand that which he had signed'.[86] The restrictive element of the defence tends to be most in evidence in the operation of the requirement that the defendant must not have acted negligently and must have taken all reasonable precautions to establish the nature of the document he or she signed.[87] Thus, in both *Quinn* and *Yates*, the courts were unimpressed by the defendants' arguments that they had not understood the nature of the loan/security documents signed and showed little sympathy for a (gender-based) 'trust and confidence' line of argument.[88] As summarised with some vigour by Kelly J in *Quinn*:

> Even the most cursory glances at the documents which bear her signature would alert any but the illiterate to the fact that this was some form of borrowing transaction. But it would appear that even such information was lost on Mrs Quinn because she apparently simply signed documents as part of a course of conduct without giving the matter a second thought.[89]

[84] *Allied Irish Bank plc v Yates* [2016] IEHC 60, 17.

[85] For a problematisation of doctrinal 'neutrality', see Auchmuty, 'Men Behaving Badly' (n 38) 266–67.

[86] *Muskham Finance Ltd v Howard* [1963] 1 QB 904, 913, cited with approval in *Allied Irish Bank plc v McKenna* [2014] IEHC 122, 27.

[87] See *Saunders v Anglia Building Society* [1971] AC 1004 as affirmed in *Tedcastle McCormack & Co Ltd v McCrystal*, Unreported, HC, Morris J, 15 March 1999. The other requirements are that there was a radical or fundamental difference between the document the person signed and what s/he thought s/he was signing and that the mistake was as to the general character of the document and not as to its legal character.

[88] The attempt to argue *non est factum* in *Ulster Bank plc v De Kretser* [2016] IECA 371, [2015] IEHC 359 also failed (having not been pressed by the defendant).

[89] *IBRC v Quinn* [2011] IEHC 470, 34. See also *Allied Irish Bank v Yates* [2016] IEHC 60, 33.

In contrast, the defence was argued successfully in *Friends First Finance v Lavelle and Anor.*[90] Justice Charleton found that Ms Lavelle had signed the loan documents presented to her without closer inquiry because 'she trusted [her husband] that he was doing this for her family as he was then in charge'.[91] He found that 'relying on a husband who states that documents have a character and effect in accord with a settled family strategy is not negligence because of the circumstances that surround the signature in the context of these documents'.[92] In reaching this conclusion, Charleton J gave no indication that Ms Lavelle's situation might fit within a broader gender or vulnerability context; instead, he placed great emphasis on the *sui generis* nature of the case, describing the situation as one which 'has rarely, if ever, been seen before'.[93] Thus, the judicial rhetoric is aimed at resolving what was undoubtedly a particularly egregious example of sexually transmitted debt, but also at limiting the precedential value of the decision. Thus, notwithstanding the successful defence by Ms Lavelle, the *non est factum* route cannot be said to have developed to any degree as the case law of the crisis unfolded.

B. Undue Influence: The Relevance of Gender

The conceptual development in the legal understanding of undue influence over the course of the crisis derives from the decision of Clarke J in *Ulster Bank v Roche and Buttimer.*[94] However, as will be seen, the role of gender remains unresolved and there is further conceptual work to be done.

As described above, *Roche* involved the only example of overtly coercive conduct by a principal debtor.[95] Surprisingly, given the volume of case law in other jurisdictions, the matter of third party undue influence had only come before the Irish courts on one occasion prior to *Roche*. The decision in *Ulster Bank v Fitzgerald and Williams*[96] was delivered just a few weeks after the decision of the House of Lords in *Royal Bank of Scotland v Etridge (No 2)*[97] and *Etridge* is not referred to in the judgment. Ms Williams had acted as guarantor in respect of the liabilities of a company in which her husband had an important stake. When the bank sought to enforce the guarantees, she argued that she had given the guarantees because of undue influence exercised by her husband and her concern that her marriage, which was already encountering difficulties, would be further harmed if she refused to give the guarantees.[98] Justice O'Donovan was prepared to accept that the defendant's husband may have 'exercised inordinate pressure on his wife' and that she 'believed that she had little option but to sign them'.[99] However, this was irrelevant because the lender did

[90] *Friends First Finance v Lavelle and Anor* [2013] IEHC 201.
[91] ibid 21.
[92] ibid.
[93] ibid 19.
[94] *Ulster Bank v Roche and Buttimer* [2012] IEHC 166.
[95] See discussion in Section V.A, 'Men Behaving Badly'.
[96] *Ulster Bank v Fitzgerald and Williams* [2001] IEHC 159.
[97] *Royal Bank of Scotland v Etridge (No 2)* [2002] 2 AC 773. See discussion in Section IV.B, 'The UK Gender-neutral Approach'.
[98] *Ulster Bank v Fitzgerald and Williams* [2001] IEHC 159, 7.
[99] ibid 8.

not have 'even an inkling' of the difficulties in the surety's marriage or that there was any reason why she might not be a 'free agent'.[100] He also found that Ms Williams had a stake in her husband's business, notwithstanding that she was neither a shareholder nor a director of the company, because she and her family relied on the income generated by the company for their day-to-day living.[101]

By any standards, *Fitzgerald* was extraordinarily generous to lenders, imposing obligations only where the lender had actual notice of an equitable wrong.[102] As was recognised by Clarke J in *Roche*, this gave 'insufficient protection to potentially vulnerable sureties'.[103] Justice Clarke established two important propositions. First, in any defence based on third party undue influence, it must first be established as a matter of fact that undue influence had in fact been exercised.[104] In this, *Roche* clearly differed from the special equity approach in *Yerkey* and *Garcia* which had established a wife's prima facie case to have a transaction set aside solely on the basis that the guarantee is procured by the husband without the wife understanding its effect in essential respects.[105] Second, the lender had a duty to inquire in the circumstances which arose in the case. As enumerated by Clarke J, these were: the lender was aware of the personal relationship between Ms Buttimer and Mr Roche; Ms Buttimer had no interest in the company whose debt she guaranteed, other than as a director; Ms Buttimer was in a less secure position than a spouse (or civil partner) who had 'certain potential legal rights in the assets or income of the other spouse or partner'.[106] These circumstances placed the situation at issue 'well on the side of whatever threshold might ultimately be fixed for determining the point at which a bank is placed on inquiry'.[107] Given that the lender had made no effort to take any steps to ensure that she was acting freely, Clarke J found that the lender's claim against Ms Buttimer must fail.[108]

Beyond this, Clarke J was circumspect. He acknowledged that the issue before him raised 'very difficult questions' and considered it unnecessary to explore the 'precise parameters of the circumstances in which a bank would be placed on inquiry'.[109] He did, however, indicate some scepticism about the scope of *Etridge*. He noted that the 'non-commercial relationship' test from *Etridge* would place a lender on inquiry where faced with a guarantee from business partners who were principals and equal shareholders in a business but who were also, to the lender's knowledge, same sex partners 'in the relationship sense of that term'.[110] Both partners in this context would require independent legal advice. He also noted the equal application of the *Etridge* principle between husband and wife, and wife and husband, and went on to state that 'Nothing in this judgment should be taken as, therefore,

[100] ibid.
[101] ibid 9.
[102] See J Mee, 'Undue Influence and Bank Guarantees' (2002) 27 *Irish Jurist* 292, 305.
[103] *Ulster Bank v Roche and Buttimer* [2012] IEHC 166, 5.14.
[104] ibid, 4.1.
[105] See *Yerkey v Jones* [1939] 63 CLR 649, 683, and *Garcia v National Australia Bank Ltd* (1998) 194 CLR 395, referenced above at Section IV.B, 'The Australian Gender-specific approach'. Neither of these cases is referred to in *Roche*.
[106] *Ulster Bank v Roche and Buttimer* [2012] IEHC 166, 5.14.
[107] ibid.
[108] ibid 6.1.
[109] ibid 5.12.
[110] ibid.

necessarily implying that the law in Ireland goes as far as the position in the United Kingdom as identified in *Etridge* in putting the bank on inquiry'.[111]

Subsequent case law has affirmed and refined some aspects of *Roche*. The requirement that undue influence must first be established as a matter of fact was accepted by a majority of the Court of Appeal in *Ulster Bank (Ireland) Ltd v De Kretser*.[112] Justice Hogan issued a dissenting judgment on this point, arguing that the female guarantor had put forward an arguable case that the lender was under an affirmative duty to insist that she obtain independent legal advice before she guaranteed the loan to her husband's company, regardless of whether or not undue influence had in fact occurred.[113] However, Hogan J subsequently accepted that the 'settled views' of the majority of the Court of Appeal were that undue influence must be established as a fact and, while still adhering to his earlier views regarding the lender's duties, he accepted that the requirement to establish undue influence represented the legal position 'as reflected by *stare decisis*'.[114]

The Court of Appeal has also indicated that the principle established in *Roche* in the context of a guarantee can, in some circumstances, apply also to a joint loan. In *ACC Bank plc v Walsh and Anor*, Peart J (on behalf of the Court of Appeal) found there to be

> arguably some equivalence between a spouse who is unduly influenced to join in a loan application being made by her husband and from which she is to derive no benefit, and one who is unduly influenced to provide a guarantee for her husband's primary loan and from which she is to derive no benefit.[115]

This case concerned an application for a plenary hearing, with the correspondingly low threshold for success, a point which was repeatedly emphasised by Peart J.[116] It is therefore not clear how much significance can be attached to this aspect of the Court's decision. Nonetheless, it may provide the basis for an expansion of the potential scope of lenders' duties in future cases.

In spite of these developments, the 'very difficult' issue of when a lender is put on inquiry (and the role of gender in this) remains unresolved. There is long established (albeit obiter) support for the gender-neutral approach (with reference to *Barclays Bank v O'Brien*[117]) in the decision of the Supreme Court in *Bank of Nova Scotia v Hogan*.[118] In fact, Murphy J (on behalf of the Court) was less inclined to view wives as vulnerable, describing this aspect of the decision in *O'Brien* as inappropriate 'as a matter of legal logic or … as an analysis of the rights or capabilities of women generally and married women in particular'.[119] More recently, Finlay Geoghegan J indicated some support for a gender-neutral approach when,

[111] ibid.

[112] *Ulster Bank (Ireland) Ltd v De Kretser* [2016] IECA 371, 31. As described by Birmingham J: 'It was for Ms Fox to adduce evidence that she had in fact acted under undue influence. That she has singularly failed to do.' Instead, all the evidence indicated that Ms Fox was an active partner in the business and an experienced business woman.

[113] ibid 32.

[114] *ACC Loan Management Ltd v Connolly and Anor* [2017] IECA 119, 27. The requirement that undue influence had to be established had also been affirmed by the Court of Appeal in *Bank of Ireland v Curran* [2016] IECA 399.

[115] *ACC Bank plc v Walsh and Anor* [2017] IECA 166, 39.

[116] See eg ibid 44.

[117] *Barclays Bank v O'Brien* [1994] AC 180.

[118] *Bank of Nova Scotia v Hogan* [1996] 3 IR 239.

[119] ibid 248.

in *ACC Loan Management Ltd v Connolly and Anor*,[120] she found it to be arguable that the approach in *Roche* 'should also apply to a relationship between a son and an elderly father with no commercial interest in the transaction'.[121] However, in the absence of any evidence of undue influence by the son in the case in question, the issue did not require resolution.[122] In the High Court decision in *AIB plc v Rostaff*,[123] Barrett J also appears to support a gender-neutral approach. While he acknowledged that the person taking on the debt was often a man and the person taking on liability was his wife or 'romantic partner', he considered that

> in our more enlightened times, when a variety of lawful adult relationships between partners who are, respectively for example, heterosexual, homosexual, bisexual *etc*, are properly recognised to exist, the issue of 'emotionally transmitted debt' is clearly one that can affect a more vulnerable and/or less business savvy partner in any such relationship.[124]

He also noted that 'there is, of course, no reason why in a male-female relationship, it would not today be the woman who is the primary earner and the man who is the more dependent partner'.[125] However, rather confusingly, Barrett J then went on to refer to the 'lessons of value' to be taken from the '*Yerkey-Garcia* line of case law which latterly seems more expressly to take account of concerned feminist legal commentary regarding the legal liability of vulnerable sureties'.[126] It may be the case that, in endorsing *Yerkey-Garcia*, Barrett J was concerned not with the issue of gender-specificity but rather with the special equity element of those cases which, as noted above, establishes a prima facie case to have a transaction set aside without a requirement to show evidence of third party undue influence.[127] If this is the case, however, it runs counter to the now solidly established principle that undue influence must be established as a matter of fact before a lender's duty to advise arises[128] and, short of a Supreme Court decision, this aspect of *Yerkey-Garcia* cannot form part of Irish law.

VII. Moving Forward: Gender-neutrality or Gender-specificity?

Given the recent expansion in Irish case law, it is likely that the courts will have to confront the role of gender in the context of sexually transmitted debt. This will be no easy task because both gender-neutral and gender-specific approaches are problematic.

[120] *ACC Loan Management Ltd v Connolly and Anor* [2017] EWCA 119.
[121] ibid 47.
[122] The Court of Appeal took a similar approach in another of the 'emotionally transmitted debt' cases: see *Bank of Ireland v Curran* [2016] IEHC 399, 32.
[123] *AIB plc v Rostaff* [2017] IEHC 533.
[124] ibid 6.
[125] ibid.
[126] ibid.
[127] See *Yerkey v Jones* [1939] 63 CLR 649, 683, and *Garcia v National Australia Bank Ltd* (1998) 194 CLR 395, referenced in Section IV.B above, 'The Australian Gender-specific approach'.
[128] See discussion in *Ulster Bank (Ireland) Ltd v De Kretser* [2016] IECA 371, 31, above in this section.

The difficulty with the gender-neutral approach is that it fails to recognise the gendered context in which this kind of debt is incurred. All of the evidence to date suggests that, in spite of our 'more enlightened times'[129] men do not take on sexually transmitted debt. This may, of course, change. However, as several feminist commentators have identified, it is not an accident that sexually transmitted debt is gendered. Rather, the preparedness of women to take on the debt of male intimate partners is profoundly grounded in gendered power dynamics and patriarchal societal norms.[130] Belinda Fehlberg identifies the 'economic reality of women's continuing partial economic dependence on men, particularly with the on-set of child-care responsibilities' and argues that because of this 'men are both likely to have greater control over financial arrangements, and to feel more entitled to mobilize the available resources for their personal use'.[131] While Fehlberg's data is dated (her book is published in 1997), it is worth noting (as other contributors to this volume have discussed[132]) that in the 2016 Census, 14.1 per cent of women in Ireland (as compared to 1.1 per cent of men) stated that they were looking after the home and/or family and that 98 per cent of all the people looking after the home/family were women.[133] Fehlberg also identifies the relevance of the social construction of gender to women's preparedness to take on a male partner's debt. Drawing on Carol Gilligan's work on gender differences in moral reasoning (which argues that women and girls place particular value on care and the preservation of relationships[134]), Fehlberg shows that this supports

> the proposition that a woman requested by her husband to execute a security would be likely to view her decision less in terms of law, economic considerations or property, than in terms of the negative impact that her refusal to act as surety would have on their relationship.[135]

On the other hand, the gender-specific approach is also problematic. Some of the reasons for this are outlined by Kirby J in his dissent in *Garcia v National Australia Bank*.[136] Justice Kirby identified five reasons why the High Court of Australia should not endorse the principle of a wife's special equity. First, the principle was a 'historical anachronism'; second, the principle reinforced discriminatory stereotypes which are 'offensive to the status of women' and should be rejected; third, given that marriage was not a suspect category in other respects, it was inconsistent that it should be in the surety context; fourth, the principle risked 'economically sterilising' the interest of married women in their homes, amounting to a 'judicial divestiture of a married woman's legal capacity to execute a guarantee'; fifth, the principle constituted unacceptable discrimination and the court should accept the

[129] [2017] IEHC 533, 6 (Barrett J).

[130] See eg Auchmuty, 'The Rhetoric of Equality and the Problem of Heterosexuality', 70. See also S Hepburn, 'The *Yerkey* Principle and Relationships of Trust and Confidence: *Garcia v National Australia Bank*' (1997) 4 *Deakin Law Review* 99, 101.

[131] Fehlberg, *Sexually Transmitted Debt* (n 18) 85.

[132] In this collection, see especially Deirdre McGowan on marriage breakdown and property (Chapter 9), Lucy-Ann Buckley's discussion of gender and employment law (Chapter 13), and Brian Tobin's discussion of parental rights (Chapter 6).

[133] CSO, *Census 2016 Results*, 15. www.cso.ie/en/census/. It is also worth noting the gender pay gap, which in 2017, was 14%.

[134] C Gilligan, *In a Different Voice: Psychological Theory and Women's Development* (Cambridge, Harvard University Press, 1982).

[135] Fehlberg, *Sexually Transmitted Debt* (n 18) 86.

[136] *Garcia v National Australia Bank* [1998] HCA 48; (1998) 194 CLR 395.

opportunity to 'refashion an equitable principle, so that it is not expressed, irrelevantly, in discriminatory terms'.[137]

In evaluating Kirby J's analysis, it should be remembered that the impugned special equity is not dependent on the establishment of undue influence as a fact and is therefore considerably more extensive than what is possible under current Irish law. Moreover, the evidence from the financial crisis raises doubts about his 'historical anachronism' argument in Ireland at any rate. Nonetheless, Kirby J's stereotyping; discrimination; and economic sterilisation arguments resonate in an Irish context. Indeed, in light of the limitations of the remedy available in Ireland, these arguments are stronger because under current Irish law, the costs of a gender-specific approach are not balanced by an expansive escape route for sureties. For this reason, it is suggested that the courts would (and should) apply the protections against undue influence without distinction on the grounds of gender, on the basis of the established facts of the case. However, in establishing these facts and understanding conduct, account should be taken of the feminist analysis which provides a structural explanation for actions which would otherwise be hidden within the discourse of private law. This could be significant, for example, in establishing a case for presumed undue influence. Although it is well established in Irish law that there is no autonomic presumption of undue influence between husband and wife,[138] the feminist analysis could be significant in making a case for a presumption of undue influence on the facts (which in turn would shift the burden of proof to the lender).

VIII. Conclusion

It is now more than three decades since feminist legal scholars began the task of identifying and theorising the gendered nature of private law.[139] While this work has extended far beyond simply 'asking the woman question', the identification of how law actually impacts on women has been core to the feminist legal endeavour.[140] By making women visible, feminist scholarship has drawn attention to the gendered dimensions of seemingly neutral legal concepts in private law.[141] The resultant analysis facilitates a better understanding of the role of private law and provides an essential context for its critique and ongoing development.[142]

[137] ibid 66.

[138] See eg *IBRC v Quinn* [2011] IEHC 770; *Danske Bank A/S t/a Danske Bank v Miley* [2016] IEHC 105, 26; *Ulster Bank plc v De Kretser* [2016] IECA 371, 15 (Hogan J).

[139] Classic early works include: C Dalton, 'An Essay in the Deconstruction of Contract Doctrine' (1985) 94 *Yale Law Journal* 997 and MJ Frug, 'Re-reading Contracts: A Feminist Analysis of a Contracts Casebook' (1985) 34 *American University Law Review* 1065.

[140] See K Bartlett, 'Feminist Legal Methods' (1990) 103 *Harvard Law Review* 829. For an early example of this approach in private law, see T Koenig and M Rustad, 'His and Her Tort Reform: Gender Injustice in Disguise' (1995) 70 *Washington Law Review* 1.

[141] See eg essays in L Mulcahy and S Wheeler (eds), *Feminist Perspectives on Contract Law* (London, Glass House Press, 2005); J Richardson and E Rackley, *Feminist Perspectives on Tort Law* (London, Routledge, 2012).

[142] In this, feminist scholarship makes an important contribution to developing 'social' theories of private law: see eg S Hedley, 'Looking Outward or Looking Inward? Obligations Scholarship in the Early 21st Century' in

Yet, despite this work, as Joanne Conaghan observes, it largely remains the case that 'In the jurisprudential imagination, law occupies a self-consciously artificial and gender devoid world'.[143] Private law is still perceived by many as concerning the resolution of individual disputes as if in a structural or societal vacuum.[144] In challenging this perspective, there is no substitute for grounded, contemporary, jurisdiction-specific investigation of how private law is actually impacting women (and men). This chapter has endeavoured to do this in one small, but significant, corner of private law. It has also shown that identifying the role of gender is more straightforward than finding appropriate ways to respond to this. Nonetheless, by making visible the hidden role of gender, we can at least establish an informed framework for legal discussion and provide a space for a more nuanced and careful application of the principles of private law.

A Robertson and H Tang, *The Goals of Private Law* (Oxford, Hart Publishing, 2009); S Hedley, 'Is Private Law Meaningless?' (2011) 64 *Current Legal Problems* 1.

[143] J Conaghan, *Law and Gender* (Oxford, Oxford University Press, 2013) 5.

[144] This derives in part at least from the prevalence of what Hedley describes as the 'radical internalist' approach to the law of obligations, Hedley, 'Looking Outward or Looking Inward?' (n 142) 194.

11

Gender Identity, Intersex and Law in Ireland

TANYA NÍ MHUIRTHILE

I. Introduction

The introduction of the Gender Recognition Act 2015 ('2015 Act') represented a seismic shift in the Irish legal landscape as regards the legal recognition of people whose preferred gender does not correspond with the sex noted upon the register of births. The 2015 Act is notable as it represents a loosening of the rigid division between the male and female gender. In essence, it maintains the need for a binary categorisation by gender of people but the boundary has become permeable and movement between the gender categories is now permissible.

Questions of identity go to the core of a person's dignity and thus are central to the inalienable rights we all enjoy as human beings.[1] This chapter will consider the circumstances leading to the introduction of the 2015 Act. It will examine how the legislative scheme evolved during its passage through the Oireachtas and analyse both the enacted legislation and the manner in which it is operationalised. Thus, it will consider whether the manner in which the right to recognition was realised in the 2015 Act fully respects the rights and dignity of those who may wish to avail of its provisions.

II. The *Foy* Cases

The requirement to formally declare a sex or gender for recognition by the law is a relatively recent development. It first appeared in the required particulars for Form A of the Act for the Registration of Births and Deaths in Ireland 1863. Prior to this date, there was a degree of flexibility evident in the law. Writing in the late 1600s, the then Lord Chief Justice, Sir Edward Coke, noted that 'Every heire is either a male, or female or an hermaphrodite, that is both male and female. And an hermaphrodite (which is also called Androgynous) – shall be heire, either as male or female, according to that kind of the sexe which doth prevaile.'[2]

[1] Making this precise point in his decision in *Sheffield & Horsham v UK*, Judge Van Dijk noted that it 'is at the basis of several of the rights laid down [in the European Convention on Human Rights]. Moreover, it is a vital element of the "inherent dignity" which, according to the Preamble to the Universal Declaration of Human Rights, constitutes the foundation of freedom, justice and peace in the world.' *Sheffield & Horsham v UK* [1999] 27 EHRR 163, 207.

[2] E Coke, *The First Part of the Institutes of the Law of England* (Robert H Smith, 1853) 225.

It was not until the case of *Foy v An tArd Chlaraitheoir (No 1)*[3] that the law in Ireland was required to define what precisely was meant by the terms male and female, or man and woman. The question arose in the context of a judicial review brought by a transgender (trans) woman, Dr Lydia Foy, who wished to amend the registration of her birth so that she could be recognised legally as a woman. Despite the fact that this was the first occasion upon which a court had to consider how to frame a legal test for recognition of gender, there is no discussion in the judgment of what that test might be.

Courts in other common law jurisdictions had developed two contrasting approaches. The first, a biological temporal test originated in the English case of *Corbett v Corbett.*[4] Here, the English court ruled that legal gender is determined by the congruence of the chromosomes, gonads and genitals at the moment of birth. This is determined as a question of law and, thus, once the congruence is present at birth, the legal gender is fixed.[5] The second approach, developed in *MT v JT*[6] considered gender to be a question of fact that is resolved at the moment when gender becomes legally relevant. Thus, once the anatomical sex of a person has been made to conform to their psychological gender, this harmonisation must be recognised by the law and the legal gender is the harmonised one.[7]

The Irish High Court in *Foy (No 1)* did not examine these alternative approaches. Rather it adopted the *Corbett* biological approach as the test in Ireland. It considered that the birth certificate was never intended to be an indicator of current legal status but rather functions as '"*a snap shot*" of matters on a particular day'.[8] The Court concluded that the entire system of birth registration would be undermined – rendered 'inoperable' – if it had to await the potential development of a trans identity, or not, prior to completion of the sex box on the register.[9]

Dr Foy's legal team advanced arguments drawing on both constitutional and European Convention on Human Rights (ECHR) entitlements, although neither were successful. The judgment of McKechnie J is compassionate and empathetic, but he concluded that applying the *Corbett* test did not enable the recognition of the preferred gender identity of the applicant. He noted that the question of how best to frame a scheme for gender recognition in Ireland was one best suited to the legislature and called upon the Oireachtas 'to urgently review the matter'.[10] Two days after the decision in *Foy (No 1)* the legal landscape shifted significantly with the decision of the European Court of Human Rights (ECtHR) in *Goodwin v UK.*[11]

The ECtHR had first considered the question of gender recognition in the case of *Van Oosterwijck v Belgium.*[12] The Court acknowledged that the right to recognition of preferred gender identity was an intrinsic, inseparable part of a person's status and person, and thus

[3] *Foy v An tArd Chlaraitheoir (No 1)* [2002] IEHC 116.
[4] *Corbett v Corbett (Otherwise Ashley)* [1970] 2 All ER 33.
[5] T Ní Mhuirthile, 'Legal Recognition of Preferred Gender Identity in Ireland: An Analysis of Proposed Legislation' in M Leane and E Kiely (eds), *Sexualities and Irish Society: A Reader* (Dublin, Orpen Press, 2014) 138.
[6] *MT v JT* [1976] 140 NJ Super 77.
[7] ibid 87.
[8] *Foy v An tArd Chlaraitheoir (No 1)* [2002] IEHC 116, [170].
[9] ibid [171].
[10] ibid [177].
[11] *Goodwin v United Kingdom* (2002) ECHR 588.
[12] *Van Oosterwijck v Belguim* (1980) 3 EHRR 557.

is a general principle of law.[13] However, in both this case and the ensuing line of cases until *Goodwin v UK*, the claim to recognition was unsuccessful: the lack of consensus among Member States enabling the margin of appreciation to operate to defeat such claims. Yet throughout the dissenting judgments, a growing minority of judges reasoned that the right to recognition, found in the Article 8 right to respect for private and family life, was an inherent part of the right to self-determination and respect for the innate dignity of the person.[14] This dissonance between the majority decisions and the increasing minority reasoning was resolved in *Goodwin*, where the Grand Chamber ruled unanimously that the persistent refusal of the respondent State to recognise the gender of the applicant was 'no longer sustainable'[15] and amounted to a violation of her Article 8 rights.

As a direct result of this decision, together with the incorporation of the ECHR into Ireland's domestic legal system through the passage of the European Convention of Human Rights Act 2003 ('ECHR Act 2003') and the changes made to the system of civil registration by the Civil Registration Act 2004, Dr Foy brought an appeal of the 2002 decision to the Supreme Court. As these three matters had not been considered by the High Court, the case was remitted back to the lower court for an initial judgment. Independently, Dr Foy sought, and was refused, a change of gender on her birth certificate on the basis that a mistake had been made in the recording of her birth and that this mistake should be corrected under sections 25, 63, 64 and 65 of the Civil Registration Act 2004. She then initiated judicial review proceedings of the refusal. Given the similarity within the cases, the remitted action and the new review were heard together. Unusually, the parties agreed that the conjoined cases would once again be adjudicated upon by McKechnie J, in light of his familiarity with the extensive expert testimony.[16] Dr Foy lost the remitted action as the three main grounds supporting it had not been law on the date of judgment. However, in the second case, her rights-based argument, centring on the *Goodwin* precedent, was successful.

Justice McKechnie found that the inability to recognise her gender of preference breached Dr Foy's Article 8 rights.[17] In those circumstances, the only legal remedy available to him was to issue a Declaration of Incompatibility under section 5 of the ECHR Act 2003. This McKechnie J did,[18] reiterating his call upon the Oireachtas to legislate in this area. He concluded by stating that:

> Everyone as a member of society has the right to human dignity, and with individual personalities, has the right to develop his being as he sees fit; subject only to the most minimal of State interference being essential for the convergence of the common good. Together with human freedom, a person, subject to the acquired rights of others, should be free to shape his personality in the way best suited to his person and to his life. All persons by virtue of their being are so entitled.[19]

Thus, the Court found that there is an obligation, based in human rights law and grounded upon the inherent respect and dignity that all people enjoy as members of the human race,

[13] ibid 577.

[14] T Ní Mhuirthile, 'Article 8 and the Realisation of the Right to Legal Gender Recognition' in S Egan, L Thornton and J Walsh (eds), *Ireland and the European Convention on Human Rights: 60 Years and Beyond* (Dublin, Bloomsbury, 2014) 201.

[15] *Goodwin v United Kingdom* (2002) ECHR 588, [90].

[16] *Foy v An tArd Chlaraitheoir & Ors (No 2)* [2007] IEHC 470.

[17] ibid [102].

[18] ibid [110].

[19] ibid [118].

on the State to recognise the preferred gender identity of people subject to the law. The precise manner in which this recognition was to be realised was left to the legislature to resolve.

III. Following *Foy*: The Route to Regulation of Recognition

The Declaration of Incompatibility issued by McKechnie J in *Foy (No 2)* was the first such Declaration to be made under the ECHR Act 2003. Hopes were high that this would prompt the introduction of a legislative scheme for recognition. Such had been the impact of an equivalent declaration of the UK's House of Lords in *Bellinger v Bellinger*,[20] which resulted in the introduction of the Gender Recognition Act 2004 in that jurisdiction. Things did not proceed quite so smoothly in Ireland.

Following the formal issuing of the Declaration of Incompatibility on Valentine's Day 2008, the State responded by appealing the decision to the Supreme Court, which paused the activation of the Declaration. Finally, in May 2010, the Government announced the establishment of a Gender Recognition Advisory Group (GRAG) which was charged with advising the Minister for Social Protection on how best to introduce legislation to enable recognition of preferred gender identity.[21] The following month in June 2010, the State announced it would withdraw the appeal.[22] The GRAG undertook an extensive public consultation and its report was published in July 2011.

The scheme recommended by the GRAG was, in essence, a carbon copy of the scheme in force in the UK under the Gender Recognition Act 2004 ('GRA 2004'). That legislation had been broadly welcomed when it was first introduced. The GRA 2004 was hailed for moving away from sex as the defining characteristic of legal status, and embracing gender as its champion.[23] Trans activists praised the introduction of a recognition scheme that relied on diagnosis of gender identity disorder rather than requiring that applicants be sterilised as a prerequisite to recognition.[24] Yet, since its introduction, a number of critiques of the 2004 GRA scheme had emerged and there were some specific jurisdictional issues that rendered its transplantation to the Irish context problematic.

Reflecting that of the GRA 2004, the GRAG proposed a scheme whereby an applicant of at least 18 years of age and whose birth was registered in Ireland, who had lived for at least two years in their preferred gender and had a clear and settled intention permanently to live in that gender, could make an application for that preferred gender to be recognised. In support of their application, applicants would have to supply evidence of diagnosis of gender identity disorder (GID), or evidence of having undergone gender reassignment surgery, or evidence of legal recognition of preferred gender identity by another

[20] *Bellinger v Bellinger* [2003] UKHL 21.

[21] Gender Recognition Advisory Group, *Report of the Gender Recognition Advisory Group* (Dublin, Stationery Office, 2011) 6.

[22] T Ní Mhuirthile, 'Legal Recognition of Preferred Gender Identity in Ireland: An Analysis of Proposed Legislation' in E Kiely, and M Leane (eds), *Sexualities in Irish Society: A Reader* (Dublin, Orpen Press, 2014) 144.

[23] S Cowan, '"Gender is No Substitute for Sex": A Comparative Human Rights Analysis of the Legal Regulation of Sexual Identity' (2005) 13 *Feminist Legal Studies* 67, 75.

[24] Press for Change, 'Transsexual Leaders Welcome Draft Bill to Allow Legal Change of Gender' (previously available online at www.pfc.org.uk/node/546).

jurisdiction. Furthermore, married or civilly partnered applicants would be excluded from the application process.[25]

There were three aspects of this proposed scheme that drew most criticism: the diagnostic criterion, the requirement to be single, and the age restriction. From the late 2000s, international human rights law had begun to stress that medical diagnosis should not serve a gate-keeping function in terms of access to legal rights.[26] Consequently the proposed scheme was criticised for pathologising access to legal rights. Furthermore, framing the medical certification in the context of a diagnosis of GID ensured that people with intersex variations,[27] who might well require access to legal gender recognition, were precluded from accessing those rights.[28]

The second criticism centred around a complication of constitutional compliance when importing the requirement that applicants be single from the 2004 UK GRA scheme. Effectively, this required married or civilly partnered applicants to dissolve their unions. It was argued that this would amount to an undue interference with the special constitutional position of the family based on marriage, as contained in Article 41.3.1° of the Constitution,[29] particularly in the context of a marriage that had survived the transition of gender. The third aspect of critique was the lack of provision for would-be applicants under the age of 18 years. Given that the majority of schools in Ireland remain single-sex, the impact that lack of recognition of preferred gender could have on access to education was a particular concern, especially in the context of children with intersex variations.[30]

It took some time following the publication of the GRAG report before Government-sponsored legislation emerged.[31] In the meantime, in the first half of 2013, two different Private Members Bills were presented on the floors of the Oireachtas on the matter. Aonghus Ó Snodaigh introduced the Gender Recognition Bill 2013 (Ó Snodaigh's Bill) in the Dáil on 22 May 2013 and Katherine Zappone introduced the Legal Recognition of Gender Bill 2013 (Zappone's Bill), in the Seanad on 27 June 2013. Inspiring both these legislative schemes was the recently enacted Argentinian Gender Identity Act 2012, which had introduced a simple administrative system of gender recognition that was based on self-declaration by

[25] Gender Recognition Advisory Group, *Report of the Gender Recognition Advisory Group* (Dublin, Stationery Office, 2011).

[26] Council of Europe Commissioner for Human Rights, *Discrimination on Grounds of Sexual Orientation and Gender Identity in Europe* (Strasbourg, Council of Europe Publishing, 2011); *Yogyakarta Principles on Sexual Orientation and Gender Identity* (2007) https://yogyakartaprinciples.org/.

[27] 'Intersex' is an umbrella term for a variety of conditions where a person's body combines both male and female biological traits, or where the body does not develop along typical male or female lines.

[28] Gender Identity Disorder is defined in the Diagnostic and Statistical Manual of Mental Disorders (Edition 4). One of the diagnostic criteria is that the patient cannot have a physical intersex condition and experience gender identity disorder. American Psychiatric Association, *Diagnostic and Statistical Manual of Mental Disorders*, 4th edn (Text Revision) (American Psychiatric Publishing, 2000).

[29] T Ní Mhuirthile, 'Legal Recognition of Preferred Gender Identity in Ireland: An Analysis of Proposed Legislation' in E Kiely, and M Leane (eds), *Sexualities in Irish Society: A Reader* (Dublin, Orpen Press, 2014) 150–52.

[30] See *S v An Bord Uchtála*, Unreported, High Court, Sheehan J, 9 December 2009. This case was a judicial review of the refusal of the Adoption Board to amend the gender marker of an intersex child on the Register of Intercountry Adoptions. The High Court granted the amendment in an ex tempore judgment. For analysis, see T Ní Mhuirthile, 'Building Bodies: A Legal History of Intersex in Ireland' in J Redmond et al (eds), *Sexual Politics in Ireland* (Newbridge, Irish Academic Press, 2014) 154.

[31] See T Ní Mhuirthile (ed), '5th Anniversary of Decision in *Foy v An tArd Chlaraitheoir (No 2)* [2007] IEHC 470' (Human Rights in Ireland, 9 October 2012) www.humanrights.ie/civil-liberties/5th-anniversary-of-decision-in-foy-v-an-tard-chlaraitheoir-no-2-2007-iehc-470/.

the applicant as to their gender.[32] Neither Private Members' Bill required applicants to be single, both included some form of recognition for minors: Ó Snodaigh's Bill enabled child applicants to apply to the District Court for recognition in section 6, while Zappone's Bill had a process, for 16–17 year olds, which enabled parents and guardians to make an application on behalf of their child in section 2(4), and enabled children between the ages of 16 and 18 to make an application on their own initiatives without the need for parental consent in section 2(5).[33]

Shortly after the publication of these Bills, in July 2013, the Minister for Social Protection published the General Scheme of the Gender Recognition Bill 2013 (the 2013 General Scheme). The legislation proposed in this General Scheme mirrored that outlined in the GRAG report. It was among the first pieces of legislation to undergo pre-legislative consideration by the Joint Oireachtas Committee on Education and Social Protection (the Joint Committee) in October 2013. As part of this process, the Joint Committee held two days of public hearings where it heard from trans people and parents of trans children, the civil servants leading the drafting process, medical professionals, academic lawyers, NGOs and civic society groups. The ensuing report on the 2013 General Scheme was published in January 2014.[34]

In this report, the Joint Committee engaged with the critiques of the scheme outlined above. On the diagnosis issue, the Joint Committee was cogniscent that requiring a diagnosis would amount to an official labelling of applicants as mentally disabled and recommended the wording be reconsidered to reduce the stigmatisation of applicants.[35] Regarding married applicants, the Joint Committee found 'that the fact that a person is in an existing marriage or a civil partnership should not prevent him or her from qualifying for a Gender Recognition Certificate, and urge[d] the Minister to revisit this issue'.[36] Finally, the Joint Committee recommended that the minimum age for applicants be reduced to 16 years for the grant of a Gender Recognition Certificate and that measures should be put in place to address the day-to-day concerns of the under-16s.[37]

Six months later, in June 2014, the Minister published a Revised General Scheme of Gender Recognition Bill 2014 (the 2014 Revised Scheme).[38] That the Department had reconsidered the proposed approach to recognition in light of the Joint Committee's report was evident. While the Revised Scheme maintained the requirement that applicants be single,[39] it did propose changes on the other two contentious issues: diagnosis and age.

[32] An English translation of Argentina's gender identity law, as approved by the Senate of Argentina on 8 May 2012, is available on the Transgender Europe website; Transgender Europe, 'English Translation of Argentina's Gender Identity Law as approved by the Senate of Argentina on May 8, 2012' www.tgeu.org/argentina-gender-identity-law/.

[33] For an analysis of the Zappone Bill, see T Ní Mhuirthile and F Ryan, 'Ní Mhuirthile and Ryan on the Legal Recognition of Gender Bill 2013' (Human Rights in Ireland, 3 July 2013) www.humanrights.ie/gender-sexuality-and-the-law/ni-mhuirthile-ryan-on-the-legal-recognition-of-gender-bill-2013/.

[34] Joint Oireachtas Committee on Education and Social Protection, *Report on the General Scheme of a Gender Recognition Bill 2013* (Houses of the Oireachtas, 2014).

[35] ibid 37.

[36] ibid.

[37] ibid.

[38] (Revised) General Scheme for Gender Recognition 2014 www.welfare.ie/en/downloads/Revised-General-Scheme-of-the-Gender-Recognition-Bill-2014.pdf.

[39] ibid Head 5.

Under the Revised Scheme, applicants would no longer need to supply evidence of diagnosis of GID; rather, they would submit supporting statements from two treating physicians. Head 7 of the Revised Scheme concerned applicants of less than 18 years of age. It proposed that those applicants aged 16 and 17 could apply to the Circuit Court for an exemption to the age criterion. Parents and guardians would be required to consent to the application. In addition, applicants would need to provide supporting statements from two medical professionals. There was no proposal contained in the Revised Scheme for children under 16 years of age. The Irish Human Rights and Equality Commission (the Commission) published a detailed analysis of the Revised Scheme.[40] While welcoming the revisions pertaining to trans young adults,[41] the Commission noted the limitation of the proposed legislation as regards persistent pathologisation, mandating marriage breakup, and the absence of provision for children under 16.

The Gender Recognition Bill 2014 ('2014 Bill') was finally published in December 2014 and introduced into the Seanad in January 2015. In the time between the publication of the Revised Scheme and the final text of the 2014 Bill, the scheme had undergone further mutation. In this iteration of the legislation, the medical evidentiary requirement had shifted once again, subtly but significantly. Now applicants would be required to present two supporting statements from medical practitioners 'following medical examination'. The insertions of these three words changed the emphasis of this evidence from a statement of support to what was termed on the floor of the House as 'diagnosis by any other name'.[42] The requirement for 'medical evaluation' was removed when the 2014 Bill came to Report Stage in the Seanad and the new text of section 10(1)(g) merely required medical certification.

On 25 May 2015, the Marriage Equality referendum was passed. Fortuitously, the 2014 Bill was still making its way through the Dáil, and the hope was that the requirement to be single would now be removed from the draft legislation. However, this hope was soon dashed and the Bill was enacted with the requirement for applicants to be single intact (as noted elsewhere in this volume, the result of the referendum was subject to legal challenge, see Chapter 5). Soon afterwards, however, section 24 of the Marriage Act 2015 amended the Gender Recognition Act 2015 to remove the requirement to be single. On a more positive note, the passage of the referendum did embolden the Government to omit a diagnosis requirement from the 2015 Act (although the referendum result did not specifically require this). Section 10 of the statute no longer requires any form of medical certification or support and, thus, the legislation adopts an approach to gender recognition based on a self-declaration model.

IV. Provisions of the Legislation

The Gender Recognition Act 2015 is revolutionary. It established a simple administrative system whereby applicants who are of at least 18 years of age can apply to the Minister

[40] Irish Human Rights and Equality Commission, *Observations on the Revised General Scheme of the Gender Recognition Bill 2014* (Irish Human Rights and Equality Commission, 2014).

[41] ibid 2–3.

[42] Sen David Norris, quoting Sara Philips, Chair of Transgender Equality Network Ireland, Seanad Debate, 3 February 2015, Vol 237, Col 7.

for Social Protection to have their preferred gender recognised for all legal purposes. The process is open to those whose births are registered in Ireland and who appear on either the register of births,[43] the adoption register,[44] foreign births register[45] or the register of intercountry adoptions.[46] People who are ordinarily resident in Ireland and whose births are either registered in accordance with the system of civil registration in their country of birth if there is one,[47] or whose birth is not so registered if there is no such system in their country of birth,[48] may also make an application under this process.

Section 10 of the 2015 Act sets out the evidentiary requirement which must be satisfied in support of such an application. Applicants must furnish the Minister with their name, PPS number and contact details;[49] the forename and surname by which they wish to be known;[50] proof of their identity;[51] proof of birth in accordance with the relevant system identified in section 9;[52] and non-nationals must provide proof that Ireland is their place of ordinary residence.[53] Finally, applicants must swear a statutory declaration that they have a settled and solemn intention of living permanently in the preferred gender;[54] understand the consequences of the application;[55] and make the application of their own free will.[56]

As discussed above, the 2015 Act makes provision for those aged 16 and 17 to make an application to the Circuit Court for an exemption on the lower age limit to enable them to apply to the Minister for recognition.[57] The application is not made directly by the person seeking recognition but rather by their 'next friend'.[58] In order to grant such an application, the Circuit Family Court must be satisfied that the child's parents or guardians consent to the application.[59] In addition an application must be accompanied by certification from the child's primary treating medical practitioner (understood in the legislation to be the endocrinologist or psychiatrist under whose care the applicant is being treated).[60] This certificate confirms that, in the professional medical opinion of the certifier, the young person is sufficiently mature to make an application for recognition;[61] understands the consequences of this decision;[62] makes the decision freely;[63] and has transitioned or is transitioning to the preferred gender.[64] A second endocrinologist or psychiatrist, who is not connected with

[43] Gender Recognition Act 2015, s 9(1)(a)(i).
[44] ibid s 9(1)(a)(ii).
[45] ibid s 9(1)(a)(iii).
[46] ibid s 9(1)(a)(iv).
[47] ibid s 9(1)(b)(i).
[48] ibid s 9(1)(b)(ii).
[49] ibid s 10(1)(a).
[50] ibid s 10(1)(b).
[51] ibid s 10(1)(c).
[52] ibid s 10(1)(d).
[53] ibid s 10(1)(e).
[54] ibid s 10(1)(f)(ii).
[55] ibid s 10(1)(f)(iii).
[56] ibid s 10(1)(f)(iv).
[57] ibid s 12.
[58] ibid s 12(2).
[59] ibid s 12(4)(a).
[60] ibid s 2.
[61] ibid s 12(4)(b)(i)(II)(A).
[62] ibid s 12(4)(b)(i)(II)(B).
[63] ibid s 12(4)(b)(i)(II)(C).
[64] ibid s 12(4)(b)(i)(II)(D).

the person seeking recognition, must also certify the same points.[65] The Court process is informal, in camera and an applicant will not be required to pay court costs.[66] The Court must make a determination based on the best interests of the child.[67] This includes making a determination to dispense with the consent of a parent or guardian in circumstances where that person cannot be identified or found, or where it would be unsafe for the child to seek them out.[68]

A Gender Recognition Certificate (GRC) attests the preferred name, gender and the date of birth of the individual who possesses it.[69] Henceforth this gender and name are those by which the bearer is legally known and they shall be treated as such for the remainder of their life.[70] In so doing it does not affect any action or responsibilities undertaken before recognition.[71] Thus, section 19 confirms that the fact that a person has been issued a GRC does not affect their status as mother or father of a child born prior to the date of issue of the certificate. Similarly, any entitlements arising under a will or other instrument are not negatively impacted upon.[72] Indeed, personal representatives and trustees are not permitted to make enquiries as to whether persons have been issued GRCs or whether such GRCs may have been revoked.[73] Where an expectation in relation to the disposal or devolution of property has been defeated as a result of a GRC being issued, the High Court may make any appropriate orders where it is satisfied that it is just to do so.[74] The only exception to this is in cases of gender-specific offences where that offence could only be committed or attempted by a person of the original gender.[75] The fact that the preferred gender has been recognised will not prevent the prosecution of such an offence. This echo of original gender persists in relation to both those who may commit or attempt such a gender-specific offence,[76] and those who may be the victim of a gender-specific offence.[77] For the elimination of doubt in this context, the 2015 Act confirms that a surgically constructed body part is the same as a body part that has not been surgically constructed.[78]

V. Critiques of the Act

The 2015 Act has been broadly welcomed by the community it was intended primarily to serve. Transgender Equality Network Ireland (TENI) heralded its introduction as 'an incredible day and a historic moment for the trans community in Ireland'.[79] Recalling

[65] ibid s 12(4)(b)(ii).
[66] ibid s 12(3).
[67] ibid s 12(6).
[68] ibid s 12(5).
[69] ibid s 13(1).
[70] ibid s 18(1).
[71] ibid s 18.
[72] ibid s 20.
[73] ibid s 21.
[74] ibid s 22.
[75] ibid s 23(1).
[76] ibid s 23(3)(a).
[77] ibid s 23(3)(b).
[78] ibid s 23(4).
[79] Press Release: 'Trans People Finally Exist in the Eyes of the State', Transgender Equality Network Ireland, 8 September 2015 www.teni.ie/news-post.aspx?contentid=1421.

the slow evolution of the legislation, Broden Giambrone, former CEO of TENI, noted that the introduction of the 2015 Act marked the end of Dr Lydia Foy's 22-year journey to be recognised. Calling the legislation compassionate, progressive and rights-affirming, Giambrone stated that adopting a self-declaration model was critical and 'marks an incredible shift in Irish society' towards protecting and honouring trans people.[80] However, Giambrone did not shy away from highlighting limitations within the legislative framework: 'There is still more work to be done to ensure that young, intersex and non-binary people will also be afforded rights.'[81]

Towards the end of the legislative process, the 2015 Act evolved quickly and dramatically. Between the publication of the final scheme in December 2014 and its enactment seven months later in July 2015, the process was de-pathologised entirely and medical gatekeepers were removed for adults. A limited process for the recognition of young people aged 16 and 17 years was introduced. The 2015 Act was passed with a requirement that applicants be single or divorced. However, as noted above, the passage of the Marriage Act 2015, 14 weeks later, removed this precondition from the legislative scheme.

Given the overhaul of the legislation in response to the Marriage Equality referendum, it seems particularly mean-spirited that the single requirement was maintained. Sharpe has suggested that homophobia is the unconscious subconscious of law.[82] While not an entirely relevant reflection on the 2015 Act as amended, enacting the 2015 Act with such single criterion to guard against potential same-sex (or seemingly same-sex) relationships suggests a latent legal heterophilia. That the scheme was not fully comprehensive was acknowledged during the legislative process. This is evidenced in the inclusion of a review of the Act as part of the scheme.[83] Introducing the review provision on the floor of the Seanad, Minister of State, Kevin Humphries TD (who had direct responsibility for the 2015 Act), stated that it was 'critical that the impact and effectiveness' of 'new and significant legislation such as this' be carefully assessed over time.[84]

In November 2017, the Minister for Employment Affairs and Social Protection, Regina Doherty TD, announced the establishment of a Group to review the 2015 Act.[85] The Group was charged with reporting back on the operation of the 2015 Act; arrangements for children aged 16 to 17 years; children aged under 16 years; non-binary people; and intersex people.[86] The Group invited submissions from the public on these points.[87] From a review of the submissions a number of points emerge.

[80] ibid.

[81] ibid.

[82] A Sharpe, *Transgender Jurisprudence: Dysphoric Bodies of Law* (London, Cavendish Publishing, 2002); A Sharpe, *Foucault's Monsters and the Challenge of Law* (Abingdon, Routledge, 2010).

[83] Gender Recognition Act 2015, s 7.

[84] Minister Kevin Humphries, Seanad Debate, 5 March 2015, Vol 870 No 3.

[85] Press Release: 'Minister Doherty Announces Moninne Griffith as Chair of Gender Recognition Act Review Group' (3 November 2017) www.welfare.ie/en/pressoffice/Pages/pa031117.aspx. [Note, the author of this chapter was appointed to this Group. At the time of writing, the Group has not yet reported to the Minister and thus the comments made are confined to those already in the public domain through the publication of the submissions that the Group received as part of the consultation process and are the opinion of the author who is not writing in the capacity as a member of the Group.]

[86] Press Release: 'Minister Doherty announces launch of Consultation Process under the Review of the Gender Recognition Act' (8 January 2018) www.welfare.ie/en/pressoffice/Pages/pr080118.aspx.

[87] All submissions received can be viewed online at www.welfare.ie/en/Pages/Review-of-the-Gender-Recognition-Act-2015.aspx.

VI. General Operation of the Act

Recent publicly available figures indicate that, since the introduction of the 2015 Act, 295 people have sought and been granted recognition,[88] nine of whom availed of the exemption process for 16 and 17 year olds.[89] In general, the feedback from those who engage with the system identifies it as a simple, efficient and quick service, the average processing time for GRCs in Client Identity Services is two to three days.[90] The Department of Social Protection notes that one of the most important aspects of process applications relations is quality data management, noting that 'Confidentiality is a vital component'.[91] Yet, it is difficulties with confidentiality that comprise the majority of the critiques contained in submissions regarding the operation of the 2015 Act generally. These issues with confidentiality have arisen in two ways: pre-recognition information being available to officials post-recognition and requiring proof of identification that inherently serves to out the applicant's trans status permanently.

In relation to the first point, Sub036 (Submission 036 to the Group) explains that, when visiting the local office of the Department to obtain a new Public Services Card following recognition, the administrator behind the desk had access to the original birth certificate of the submitter, thus their status as trans was revealed.[92] According to Minister Regina Doherty, in response to a parliamentary question on this very point: 'Only a small number of specifically trained officers [who] process these [GRC] applications … can access an individual's historical data after a Gender Recognition Certificate has been issued. System checks are in place to ensure that no other officers in the Department can access this data.'[93] Yet, the experience of the service user in Sub036 indicates that these system checks are not robust. Administrative 'echoes' of original sex undermines the confidentiality that was so important at the processing stage of the application and directly contradicts the policy of respecting privacy that purportedly underpins the entire gender recognition process.

The replacement birth certificate that a recognised person receives differs from original birth certificates in two ways. First, prior to 2002, the information on birth certificates was hand written and thus any certificate obtained of a birth registered prior to computerisation is a scan of the handwritten entry.[94] Therefore, when a replacement certificate is issued following a GRC, the information is typed rather than handwritten, which is unusual and

[88] Minister Regina Doherty, Written Answers to Parliamentary Question 578 to Minister for Employment Affairs and Social Protection (30 January 2018) www.oireachtas.ie/en/debates/question/2018-01-30/578/?highlight%5B0%5D=gender&highlight%5B1%5D=recognition.

[89] S Rogers, '230 "Gender Recognition Certificates" Issued Since 2015' *Irish Examiner* (Cork, 22 May 2017).

[90] Minister Leo Varadkar, Written Answers to Parliamentary Questions 269 and 270 to Minister for Social Protection (16 May 2017) www.oireachtas.ie/en/debates/question/2017-05-16/269/?highlight%5B0%5D=gender&highlight%5B1%5D=recognition&highlight%5B2%5D=gender&highlight%5B3%5D=recognition.

[91] Department of Social Protection, *Annual Report for 2016 of the Gender Recognition Act 2015* (2016) 2, www.welfare.ie/en/downloads/GRAAnnualReport2016.pdf.

[92] Sub036, Submission 001-088, 22 www.welfare.ie/en/downloads/Sub001-GRA2015.pdf.

[93] Minister Regina Doherty, Written Answers to Parliamentary Question 675 (10 October 2017) www.oireachtas.ie/en/debates/question/2017-10-10/675/?highlight%5B0%5D=gender&highlight%5B1%5D=gender&highlight%5B2%5D=recognition.

[94] The system was computerised in the early 2000s. Where a scan of the original entry was illegible, Part V of the Social Welfare (Miscellaneous Provisions) Act 2002 permitted that the relevant information be typed into the database.

may cause the holder of such a document to be asked questions that may lead towards a disclosure of their status as a recognised person. Second, all birth certificates issued carry a registration number. Replacement birth certificates issued do not have such a registration number. In their submission to the Group, FLAC reported anecdotal evidence of trans people experiencing difficulties resulting from this absence when interacting with the Gardaí, which resulted in disclosures of recognised status.[95]

Such inconsistencies in the appearance of documents create the type of encounter that the introduction of a process of gender recognition was intended to prevent. Furthermore, the existence of differences on the face of the two types of birth certificate is in violation of the privacy rights contained in Article 8 of the ECHR. Indeed, the text of the 2015 Act itself notes that the index linking the gender recognition register to the register of births is not open to public inspection and that 'no information from that index shall be given to any person except by order of a court'.[96] Where the reissued birth certificate draws attention to the potential that information may be on this index, it may itself be ipso facto in violation of the respect for privacy in the 2015 Act. The right to privacy is best respected by ensuring that the documents supplied on foot of a GRC do not inherently require the recipients to out themselves.

This undermining is further exacerbated by the practice in Client Identity Services in relation to a name change as part of the application for a GRC. As discussed above, section 10(1)(b) of the 2015 Act requires that applicants inform the Minister of 'the forename and surname by which he or she wishes to be known'. Applying the literal rule of legislative interpretation to this section suggests that the application for gender recognition would itself ground a name change. However, this is not how the section has been interpreted by the Department of Employment Affairs and Social Protection. According to its website, there are four methods by which a name change can be effected in Ireland: (1) by proof of two years' use and repute; (2) following marriage or civil partnership on production of marriage/civil partnership certificate; (3) reverting to pre-marriage/pre-civil partnership name on production of court documentation or correspondence from a solicitor showing that a divorce/dissolution has been initiated; and (4) following enrolment of a deed poll in the Central Office of the High Court.[97] Where an applicant does not satisfy the use and repute requirement, the current system in operation requires that such an applicant must enrol a deed poll with the Office of the High Court. The Deed Poll Register is a public document and is freely accessible online.[98] A system purporting to place a premium on privacy that requires publication of the very information the system is designed to conceal as a precondition to accessing that system is flawed, contradictory and incompatible with the legislative requirements found in the establishing legislation.[99] Thus, practice within

[95] Free Legal Advice Centres, 'Submission of FLAC to the Review Group on the Current Operation of the Gender Recognition Act 2015' Sub089, 20 https://www.welfare.ie/en/Pages/Review-of-the-Gender-Recognition-Act-2015.aspx accessed 10 May 2018. See also Sub0013 www.welfare.ie/en/Pages/Review-of-the-Gender-Recognition-Act-2015.aspx.

[96] Gender Recognition Act 2015, s 27, inserting s 30D in the Civil Registration Act 2004.

[97] Department of Employment Affairs and Social Protection, 'Public Services Identity: Changing Your Name' www.welfare.ie/en/Pages/Public-Service-Identity.aspx.

[98] Court Service Ireland, 'Deed Poll' www.courts.ie/Courts.ie/Library3.nsf/pagecurrent/075D7770C94358068025804B005C294B?opendocument&l=en#deed_poll_register.

[99] Gender Recognition Act 2015, s 27, inserting s 30D in the Civil Registration Act 2004.

the relevant section of the Department should be altered to interpret section 10(1)(b) as establishing a new, fifth, way to effect a name change in Ireland, ie on foot of an application for gender recognition.

VII. Young People

The 2015 Act introduced a limited form of recognition for those under 18 years. As discussed above, this is based on parental consent, supporting statements from two medical practitioners and with the consent of the court to make an application in these exceptional circumstances (as this is in the best interests of the child, who is aged either 16 or 17).[100] The onerous obligations imposed upon those young people who can access recognition, and the absence of any process for young children, even in circumstances where their parents consent, have been the main causes for criticism of the 2015 Act.[101]

Many of the personal submissions made to the Group note the impact that these restrictions have on the lives of young people. Sub005 (Submission 005 to the Group) discusses having come out as trans aged 14 years and being regularly mis-gendered in visceral terms as 'making my skin crawl with discomfort'.[102] A parent writing of behalf of their trans son noted that he feels like 'God made a mistake' by giving him the wrong body.[103]

That LGBTI+ children have the right to respect for their physical and psychological integrity, gender identity and emerging autonomy, was recently confirmed by the UN Committee on the Rights of the Child.[104] The age restriction of the current scheme and the fact that mature adolescents cannot initiate an application for recognition without their parents contravenes this obligation. Also implicated are the rights of children under Article 5 of the UN Convention on the Rights of the Child to exercise their rights under the direction and guidance of their parents in a manner consistent with their evolving capacities and for these parental responsibilities, rights and obligations to be respected by the State. These international obligations are confirmed by Article 42A of the Irish Constitution. In addition to violating the rights of children, the absence of provisions for young children also violates the rights of their parents under Articles 41 and 42 to make decisions on behalf of their children. The bar to interfere with such rights is set very high. Such interference is permissible only 'in exceptional circumstances where parents … fail in their duty towards their children'.[105] Sub023 and Sub042 (Submissions 023 and 042 to the Group) highlighted

[100] Gender Recognition Act, s 12.

[101] Department of Children and Youth Affairs, *LGBTI+ National Youth Strategy: Report of the Consultations with Young People in Ireland* (Department of Children and Youth Affairs, 2017) 34; Ombudsman for Children's Office, *Department of Employment Affairs and Social Protection: Review of the Gender Recognition Act 2015. Submission by the Ombudsman for Children's Office* (2018) www.welfare.ie/en/downloads/Sub053B-GRA2015.pdf; Children's Rights Alliance, *Submission on the Review of the Gender Recognition Act 2015* (2018) www.welfare.ie/en/downloads/Sub085-GRA2015.pdf.

[102] Sub005, www.welfare.ie/en/Pages/Review-of-the-Gender-Recognition-Act-2015.aspx.

[103] Sub0023, www.welfare.ie/en/Pages/Review-of-the-Gender-Recognition-Act-2015.aspx.

[104] UN Committee on the Rights of the Child, 'General Comment No.20 On the Implementation of the Rights of the Child During Adolescence' (6 December 2016) UN Doc No. CRC/C/GC/20, [33].

[105] Denham J (as she then was) *North Western Health Board v HW* [2001] IESC 90, [212].

the frustration parents feel in circumstances where they cannot achieve recognition of the preferred gender of their child.[106]

A further difficulty with the current scheme is the requirement to support an application for an exemption with certification of the child by two medical practitioners. The pool of potential practitioners who can provide such certification is small as it is confined to endocrinologists and psychiatrists.[107] Waiting lists for access to treating physicians are long and private care is costly. Therefore, some submissions noted that these factors operated as barriers to the exercise of the rights in the scheme.[108] The arguments noted earlier that access to legal rights should not be contingent upon engagement with medical practice are equally valid here in relation to children. This is strengthened by adoption, in 2015, of a 'Resolution on Discrimination Against Transgender People in Europe' by the Parliamentary Assembly of the Council of Europe, which states that recognition processes should be de-pathologised; based on self-determination; be quick, transparent and accessible and, as regards children, should place their best interests at the core.[109] In this context, the fact that issues relating to recognition of the preferred gender of children are central to the terms of reference of the Review Group is to be welcomed.

VIII. Non-Binary People

As discussed at the beginning of this chapter, at present Ireland operates a binary understanding of sex/gender. One must be declared as either male or female in order to become sui juris. In the absence of recognition within this paradigm, the law is not capable of interacting with an individual. The limitations of such an understanding of gender is evident in the decision of the Brisbane Family Court in the case of *In the Marriage of C and D (falsely called C)*.[110] Here, the Australian court recognised that the husband was a person with an intersex variation. Therefore, being neither male nor female, the Court held that the husband had no right to marry anyone at all. Consequently, his marriage was a nullity. Similarly, people who assert an identity outside the male/female dyad are excluded from participation in society on that basis.

The right to recognition outside the gender binary has long been an implied aspect of the right to gender recognition generally. This was explicitly articulated in the recently updated Yogyakarta Principles Plus 10. According to Principle 31 on *The Right to Legal Recognition*, where states continue to register sex and gender, multiple gender markers should be made available.[111]

[106] Sub0023, Sub042 www.welfare.ie/en/Pages/Review-of-the-Gender-Recognition-Act-2015.aspx.

[107] Gender Recognition Act 2-15, s 2.

[108] Sub013, Sub042, Sub044, Sub062, www.welfare.ie/en/Pages/Review-of-the-Gender-Recognition-Act-2015.aspx.

[109] Parliamentary Assembly of the Council of Europe, 'Resolution 2048(2015) Discrimination Against Transgender People in Europe' (22 April 2015).

[110] *In the Marriage of C and D (falsely called C)* (1979) 35 FLR 340.

[111] The Yogyakarta Principles Plus 10: Additional Principles and State Obligations on the Application of International Human Rights Law in Relation to Sexual Orientation, Gender Identity, Gender Expression and Sex Characteristics to complement the Yogyakarta Principles (2017) www.yogyakartaprinciples.org/principles-en/yp10/.

Many of the submissions received by the Review Group highlighted the detrimental impact that this lack of recognition has on the daily lives of non-binary people.[112] The introduction of a third gender marker is not novel. Many countries recognise non-binary people. Australia, Canada and Malta recognise third genders via a self-declaration administrative process.[113] Judicial determinations in both New South Wales and Germany have introduced non-binary recognition.[114] Thus, it is timely that the 2015 Act be amended to include recognition for non-binary people. This could be achieved by the introduction of a third gender marker. 'X' is a marker that has already achieved acceptance internationally and is recognised by the International Civil Aviation Authority. In addition, expanding the suite of honorifics to include a gender neutral 'Mx' would enable recognition of non-binary identities.[115]

IX. Intersex

Advocacy for intersex rights has two aims: recognition of the preferred gender identity of people with intersex variations and ending non-consensual medicalisation of their bodies. The 2015 Act responds to the first of these needs in a limited manner. By ensuring that the scheme for persons over 18 years of age is de-pathologised, this enables adults with intersex variations to be recognised in their preferred gender. However, children with intersex variations are left in legal limbo. The High Court decision of Sheehan J, in *S v An Bord Uchtála*, acknowledged the need of such children for documentation that reflects the gender in which they are being raised.[116] Yet the current scheme does not make provision for children under 16 years of age. Where a significant number of schools in Ireland are single-sex, this can create difficulties with access to education and other rights.[117] The social expectation that all people will be either male or female contributes to the pressure that parents experience to permit interventions on the bodies of their children with intersex variations.[118] The failure

[112] In particular see submissions Sub017, Sub046, Sub047, Sub049; and Sub088.

[113] Australian Government, *Australian Government Guidelines on the Recognition of Sex and Gender* (2013) www.ag.gov.au/Publications/Documents/AustralianGovernmentGuidelinesontheRecognitionofSexandGender/AustralianGovernmentGuidelinesontheRecognitionofSexandGender.pdf; Government of Canada, *Request for a travel document with 'X' in the sex field – Adult*, (2017) www.canada.ca/content/dam/ircc/migration/ircc/english/passport/forms/pdf/pptc633e.pdf; Y Pace, 'Malta Introduces 'X' on Passports, ID Cards and Work Permits' *Malta Today* (San Gwann, 5 September 2017) www.maltatoday.com.mt/news/national/80228/malta_introduces_x_marker_on_passports_id_cards_and_work_permits#.WvjdH6QvzIV.

[114] L Brown and A Brown, 'High Court recognises that "sex" in NSW may be other than male or female' (Human Rights Law Centre, 2 April 2014) www.hrlc.org.au/human-rights-case-summaries/high-court-recognises-that-sex-in-nsw-may-be-other-than-male-or-female; Decision of the German Federal Constitutional Court 1 BvR 2019/16, 10 October 2017 www.bundesverfassungsgericht.de/SharedDocs/Pressemitteilungen/EN/2017/bvg17-095.html.

[115] F Warfield and J Brady, 'Submission to Review of the Gender Recognition Act 2015' Sub051 www.welfare.ie/en/Pages/Review-of-the-Gender-Recognition-Act-2015.aspx, p 4.

[116] *S v An Bord Uchtála*, Unreported High Court, December 2009.

[117] M O'Connor, *Sé/Sí Gender in Irish Education* (Department of Education, 2007).

[118] G Davis, *Contesting Intersex: The Dubious Diagnosis* (New York, New York University Press, 2015); A Fausto-Sterling, *Sexing the Body: Gender Politics and the Construction of Sexuality* (New York, Basic Books, 2000); S Kessler, *Lessons from the Intersexed* (New Brunswick, Rutgers University Press, 1998); SE Preves, *Intersex and Identity: The Contested Self* (New Brunswick, Rutgers University Press, 2003); SE Sytsma (ed), *Ethics and Intersex* (Dordrecht, Springer, 2006).

of the 2015 Act to provide pathways to recognition for young children contributes to this pressure and fails to protect the bodily integrity rights of such children. This is something of which the Irish State should be cogniscent. Increasingly, the treaty bodies of the United Nations are calling upon the Irish State to clarify exactly how it protects medically irreversible and unnecessary sex assignment surgeries on vulnerable intersex children.[119]

In October 2017, the Parliamentary Assembly of the Council of Europe adopted a resolution requiring states to introduce gender recognition processes for people with intersex variations, including children, which are simple and based on self-determination.[120] The scheme created under the 2015 Act in no way meets international legal obligations in this regard.

X. Irish Citizens Whose Births are Registered in Northern Ireland

Under the Good Friday Agreement, all people born in Northern Ireland may choose to be identified as Irish or British citizens and may carry dual citizenship should they wish.[121] Thus, those born in Northern Ireland are entitled to all the rights of any other Irish citizen. However, due to the way that the 2015 Act is drafted, people born in Northern Ireland are excluded from making an application for a GRC.[122] Under section 9(1)(a), a person may make an application if their birth is registered in the register of births or the foreign births register or if their adoption is registered in the Adopted Children Register or the register of intercountry adoptions. Where a person was not born in the Irish State, but they are ordinarily resident in the State, they may also make an application for recognition under section 9(1)(b). People born in Northern Ireland will not have their births registered on the register of births in the Irish State. Section 27(2) of the Irish Nationality and Citizenship Act 1956, as amended,[123] identifies the births capable of being included in the foreign birth register as those occurring 'outside the island of Ireland'. People born in Northern Ireland, being already Irish citizens, do not require their births to be registered on the foreign births register to access citizenship and all its attendant rights. However, as the birth of a person born in Northern Ireland appears in neither the register of births nor the foreign births register, Irish citizens who were born, and continue to reside, in Northern Ireland are excluded from making applications for recognition under the 2015 Act. They satisfy neither the birth nor residence requirements for making an application.

[119] Committee on the Rights of the Child, 'Concluding observations on the combined third and fourth periodic reports of Ireland' (1 March 2016) UN Doc No. CRC/C/IRL/CO/3-4; Committee on the Elimination of All Forms of Discrimination Against Women, 'Concluding Observations on the Combined Sixth and Seventh Periodic Reports of Ireland' (9 March 2017) UN Doc No CEDAW/C/IRL/CO/6-7.

[120] Parliamentary Assembly of the Council of Europe, 'Resolution 2191 (2017) Promoting the Human Rights of and Eliminating Discrimination Against Intersex People' (12 October 2017).

[121] The Northern Ireland Peace Agreement: The Agreement Reached in the Multi-Party Negotiations (10 April 1998) Article 1, Para VI, www.taoiseach.gov.ie/attached_files/Pdf%20files/NIPeaceAgreement.pdf.

[122] See Sub018 www.welfare.ie/en/Pages/Review-of-the-Gender-Recognition-Act-2015.aspx.

[123] Irish Nationality and Citizenship Act 2001, s 7(b), amended s 27(2) so that the phrase 'birth outside Ireland' changed to 'birth outside the Island of Ireland' in order to ensure compliance with the Good Friday Agreement.

To ensure such citizens can access their right to gender recognition is a relatively simple matter. Inserting the words 'whose birth is registered in Northern Ireland, proof of which is a document issued in accordance with the system of birth registration in that jurisdiction' in section 9(1)(a) of the 2015 Act would ensure that people born in Northern Ireland, who do not live in the Republic, can access recognition.

Such recognition will necessarily have a limited effect. It will enable a recognised person to have a GRC and obtain a new Irish passport. It will not result in the issuing of a new birth certificate reflecting the preferred name and gender of the recognised person, as the Irish State has no competency to issue birth certificates for births not registered within the State. As the requirements under the 2004 Gender Recognition Act, which is in operation in Northern Ireland, are more invasive and restrictive than those in Ireland, it is unlikely that recognition within the Republic will result in recognition in Northern Ireland as the schemes are not equivalent.[124] Nonetheless, Northern Ireland born Irish citizens who reside north of the border may feel that recognition by the Irish State, however limited its practical use in Northern Ireland, is beneficial, and a citizenship right that they wish to exercise.

XI. Conclusion

The 2015 Act is transformative; it introduced a mechanism that enables trans and intersex people who meet the legislative requirements to be recognised in their gender of preference. The scheme, based on a self-declaration model, is among the best in the world. It respects the rights and dignity of trans and intersex adults. However, there is still room for improvement.

Systems surrounding the administration of the 2015 Act need to be tightened to ensure that the privacy of applicants is maintained. The pathway to recognition for 16 and 17 year olds should be de-pathologised to ensure that it meets the obligations of international human rights law. Pathways to recognise young children under the age of 16 should be introduced. Such an extension of the scheme would ensure that children with intersex variations can avail of recognition. The scheme excludes those who identify outside a binary gender paradigm and those born in Northern Ireland from its ambit. To be compliant with the human rights obligations, the scheme in the 2015 Act should be broadened so that all who would wish to access the rights therein can be recognised as their true selves. As McKechnie J concluded his judgment in *Foy (No 2)*, 'All persons by virtue of their being are so entitled'.[125]

[124] Gender Recognition Act 2004, s 2.
[125] *Foy v An tArd Chlaraitheoir & Ors (No 2)* [2007] IEHC 470, [118].

PART III

Law in a Changing Society

12

Gender and the Irish Constitution

Article 41.2, Symbolism and the Limitations of the Courts' Approach to Substantive Gender Inequality

ALAN DP BRADY

I. Introduction

Gender is not difficult to find in the 1937 Constitution. Some of the most significant cases in the Constitution's history have been directly or indirectly related to issues of gender and gender equality.[1] The most overt and deliberate statement regarding gender in the Constitution is contained in Article 41.2, which states:

> 1° In particular, the State recognises that by her life within the home, woman gives to the State a support without which the common good cannot be achieved.
>
> 2° The State shall, therefore, endeavour to ensure that mothers shall not be obliged by economic necessity to engage in labour to the neglect of their duties in the home.

Rereading the text of Article 41.2 continues to be a powerful experience. The language is arresting: the use of the generic 'woman' without any definite or indefinite article; 'her place' with its overtones of subservience. Article 41.2 is low-hanging fruit for feminist critique, but even still it is a quite stunning example of linguistic gender stereotyping and an appeal to a false universal notion of womanhood.

At the time of writing, it is anticipated that a referendum on changing Article 41.2 will be held in the near future. A removal of this gendered language will be an important symbol and is to be encouraged. However, a gender-neutral amendment of the text of Article 41.2 is unlikely to achieve much improvement in substantive gender equality in Ireland. Replacing

[1] *Attorney General v X* [1992] 1 IR 1; *A and B v Eastern Health Board* [1998] 1 IR 464; *de Burca v Attorney General* [1976] IR 38; *Murphy v Attorney General* [1986] IR 241; *CC v Ireland* [2006] 4 IR 1; *A v Governor of Arbour Hill* [2006] 4 IR 88. The term 'gender' is used here as it would have been understood by the Constitution's framers in a binary sense, which equates gender and biological sex. Questions of the meaningful recognition of the full diversity of gender identities, while an issue of pressing concern, is not explored herein, and is addressed in Chapter 11. See generally *Foy v An tArd-Chláraitheoir* [2012] 2 IR. The question of abortion and the 8th Amendment is addressed in Chapter 4.

a constitutional term which identifies women as having duties in the home with a gender-neutral recognition of care work cannot be expected to redress the gender imbalance in unpaid care work in Ireland. Nor should we expect any such new constitutional provision to be interpreted in a way which will improve the position of those (mostly women) who carry out such unpaid care work. The lessons of Article 41 and the superior courts' approach more broadly to questions of substantive inequality are such that there is every reason to expect that the status quo will be endorsed, if not entrenched, by any litigation arising from a new provision.

This chapter seeks to address the issue of care work, gender and the Constitution in three parts. First, the symbolism of Article 41.2 is addressed briefly, as are the reasons for supporting a removal of that symbol. Second, the jurisprudence on Article 41 as it relates to mothers in the home will be explored. Despite the limited case law on Article 41.2, it will be argued that the approach of the superior courts to Article 41 has been to endorse existing substantive inequalities in the name of preserving freedom between unequally situated parties. Third, drawing on that comparison, it will be argued that the Irish courts' deep resistance to positive obligations and socio-economic rights is both a perpetuating factor for gender inequality (regardless of the wording of Article 41.2) and also a reason to be sceptical about the potential for a gender-neutral recognition of care in the Constitution to achieve any meaningful change.

II. Constitutional Symbolism and Women in the Home

Constitutional lawyers have a tendency to focus on the overtly legal aspects of the Constitution, such as the technicalities of the separation of powers or the development of specific fundamental rights principles over decades of case law. As a result, it is possible to miss the relevance of symbols in the Constitution. The Constitution is a political, as well as a legal document. Symbols matter in the political life of a society.

The current wording of Article 41.2 attracted staunch resistance and critique from the outset.[2] At the time of the Constitution's introduction, the provisions regarding women were some of the most hotly debated. Hogan, in examining the debates at the time of the Constitution's introduction, has observed that

> [t]he Constitution's treatment of women was a matter of almost immediate controversy following publication and, indeed, remains so to this day. This was the single biggest policy issue which dominated much of the debate at the time both inside and outside the Dáil.[3]

A quarter of a century ago, Connelly criticised the stereotyping of women in the Constitution's text:

> Specific mention is made of the role of women in the home and as mothers (Article 40.3.3 and 41.2.1 & 2). Nowhere in the Constitution is the word father to be found; nor is the role of men in the domestic sphere specifically addressed. Furthermore, it is clear from the tenor of the relevant constitutional provisions that it is in their role as wives and mothers that women are especially valued.[4]

[2] See generally L Cahillane, 'Revisiting Article 41.2' (2017) 40(2) *Dublin University Law Journal* 107.
[3] G Hogan, *The Origins of the Irish Constitution, 1928–1941* (Dublin, Royal Irish Academy, 2012) 520.
[4] A Connelly, 'The Constitution' in A Connelly (ed), *Gender and the Law in Ireland* (Cork, Oak Tree Press, 1993) 5.

There is no attempt to universalise the experience or roles of men. Men are not mentioned and so, are by implication, presented both as neutral and as capable of individual diversity of experience and perspective. Doorley, writing two decades ago, mounted a scathing critique of the gendering contained in Article 41.2:

> The life given to important realities of home and family may not be the choice of some women. Where is their diversity valued in the universalizing thrust of the reference to 'woman'? Are these diverse women who choose not to marry, not to mother, either legitimated or valued under the normative simplicity in the concept 'woman'?[5]

This is the crux of the problem with the current wording. However much we might, as a society, generally accept that care work in the home is a positive and beneficial thing, the language used suggests both that this is exclusively women's work and that it is the only work that women should do.

The active use of the referendum under Article 47 has given the Irish electorate an ongoing relationship with their Constitution. No serious analysis of the public debates around the 31st Amendment on children and the 34th Amendment on marriage could dismiss the impact of symbols. Symbols are important to an understanding of the Constitution's purpose. The understanding of the Constitution's purpose, or more particularly, the understanding adopted by superior court judges, is itself of central relevance to how the constitutional jurisprudence develops, given the open texture of constitutional norms.[6] In this way, symbols can indirectly affect the substantive development of constitutional law.

Proposals for changes to Article 41.2 have tended to focus heavily on its symbolism and to recommend gender neutrality as a means of addressing the problem. For example, the UN Committee on the Elimination of Discrimination against Women ('the CEDAW Committee') criticised Ireland's retention of Article 41.2 in its current form as follows:

> The Committee is concerned at the persistence of traditional stereotypical views of the social roles and responsibilities of women and men in the family and in society at large which are reflected in article 41.2 of the Constitution and its male-oriented language
>
> …
>
> The Committee also suggests that the State party consider replacing male-oriented language with gender-sensitive language in the Constitution to convey the concept of gender equality more clearly.[7]

Gender-neutral recognition of the family and care work within it has formed the basis for a series of indigenous proposals for reform.[8] The 1996 Constitution Review Group report,[9] and both the 1997 and 2006 reports of the All-Party Oireachtas Committee on the

[5] D Doorley, 'Gendered Citizenship in the Irish Constitution' in T Murphy and P Twomey (eds), *Ireland's Evolving Constitution 1937–97: Collected Essays* (Oxford, Hart Publishing, 1998) 127.

[6] See generally R Dworkin, 'Hard Cases' (1975) 88 *Harvard Law Review* 1057, 1082–87. For a more critical account of the influence of judge's understandings of constitutional purpose, see P Schlag, 'Hiding the Ball' (1996) 71 *New York University Law Review* 1681.

[7] Committee on the Elimination of Discrimination against Women, Thirty Third Session, *Concluding Comments: Ireland* CEDAW/C/IRL/CO/4-5 at paras 24–25.

[8] L Cahillane, 'Revisiting Article 41.2' (n 2).

[9] *Report of the Constitution Review Group* (Dublin, Stationery Office, 1996) 311–12.

Constitution,[10] recommended such a change. The 2006 report, having referred to the decision of the Supreme Court in *DT v CT*,[11] went so far as to suggest that:

> The courts are disposed to interpret Article 41.2.1° as applying to either fathers or mothers caring in the home. The *need to change the Article to make it gender neutral is therefore not a legal necessity*.[12] (emphasis added)

This suggestion indicates a view that the *only* reason for changing the text was symbolic and that it would have no legal effect, since more recent superior court decisions were prepared to, tentatively, treat Article 41.2 as being gender-neutral in practice.

More recently, the Constitutional Convention recommended replacing Article 41.2 with a gender-neutral article mandating State support of carers.[13] In September 2017, the Government gave an indicative timetable for referendums it intends to hold throughout 2018 and 2019, which suggested a referendum on Article 41.2 could be expected in October 2018.[14]

The continued appetite for changing the language of Article 41.2, despite the All-Party Oireachtas Committee's view that it would be of no (or limited) legal effect, suggests that the symbol of women being confined to the home retains sufficient power to elicit substantial resistance. In an era when the majority of women with children work outside of the home, it is worth interrogating the reason for this resistance. If Article 41.2 was simply an anachronism with no resonance in contemporary life, then perhaps it would be of less concern. It seems plausible that the strength of the ongoing resistance to Article 41.2 is driven, not just by politico-legal symbolic concerns, but also by the socio-economic realities of life in Ireland for a great many women.

Gender inequality in Ireland, particularly in relation to unpaid care work, remains significant and is (as illustrated by other contributions to this volume, see Chapter 9) an incontrovertible fact. As of 2016, according to Central Statistics Office data,[15] the gender pay gap per hour worked is 13 per cent and the overall income pay gap is over 25 per cent. More than 90 per cent of lone parents are women and the ratio of women claiming carer's allowance to men is more than 3 to 1. However, fewer than 25 per cent of TDs (Teachta Dála, member of the Irish parliament or Oireachtas) and fewer than 20 per cent of Secretaries General in the Civil Service are women, and fewer than 35 per cent of those employed as managers, directors and senior officials are women, even though 60 per cent of women with children aged under four years are employed. National Women's Council of Ireland data from 2009 indicates that women bear a disproportionate share of informal, unpaid care commitments, particularly childcare: 86 per cent of supervision of children is done by women.[16]

[10] All-Party Oireachtas Committee on the Constitution, *First Progress Report* (Dublin, Stationery Office, 1997) 85; All-Party Oireachtas Committee on the Constitution, *Tenth Progress Report – The Family* (Dublin, Stationery Office, 2006) 126–28.

[11] *DT v CT* [2002] 3 IR 334.

[12] All-Party Oireachtas Committee on the Constitution, *Tenth Progress Report – The Family* (Dublin, Stationery Office, 2006) 120.

[13] *Second Report of the Convention on the Constitution* (Dublin, Stationery Office, May 2013).

[14] Press Release: *Government Sets Indicative Timetable for Referendums* 26 September 2017, available at www.merrionstreet.ie.

[15] *Women and Men in Ireland 2016* (Central Statistics Office, 2017) available at www.cso.ie.

[16] See generally *Who Cares? Challenging the Myths about Gender and Care in Ireland* (National Women's Council, 2009).

This chapter does not purport to be a comprehensive statistical analysis of the position of men and women in contemporary Irish society; however, even a cursory look at the statistics in this area shows a high degree of substantive inequality of economic and social power between men and women in Ireland. It seems likely that the symbol of Article 41.2 stings as much as it does because in Irish society women continue to wield much less power than men and continue to be expected to carry out the duties of homemaker, albeit often in an altered context which includes an overlapping group of lone parents and working mothers. If the desire to address substantive gender inequality forms any part of the reason for wanting to change the constitutional text, there is little reason to think that a change in the text will address this issue in any meaningful way. The remaining sections of this chapter argue for great pessimism on that front.

III. The Courts' Approach to Women in the Home: Resistance to Attempts to Address Substantive Inequality

It is generally accepted that Article 41.2 has been an under-litigated provision, relative to other parts of the Constitution's fundamental rights section, and has received relatively little judicial attention.[17] Cahillane argues that the 'only cases in which Article 41.2 has had any effect have been either in defeating equality claims or in cases of marital separation'.[18] In *Dennehy v Minister for Social Welfare*,[19] Barron J in the High Court used Article 41.2 as a justification for upholding a law that excluded men from deserted wives benefit under the social welfare system. He took the view that Article 41.2 recognised the special place of wives and mothers in Irish society and so the Oireachtas had not acted unreasonably in giving special financial support to wives who were also mothers.[20]

In *de Burca v Attorney General*,[21] the Supreme Court held that the default exclusion of women from the jury lists, with the option of applying to be included, was unconstitutional. Chief Justice O'Higgins dissented on this point on grounds that he linked expressly to Article 41.2 and took the view that it justified tempering or cushioning general obligations as they affected women having regard to the acceptance in Article 40.1 that laws can have regard to differences of capacity, physical and moral, and of social function.[22]

The most significant case to address substantive gender inequality in the context of Article 41.2 was *BL v ML*,[23] which involved an innovative attempt by the High Court to use the provision to protect wives engaged in care work in the home (ultimately overturned by the Supreme Court). The case concerned a family home on farm land that had been

[17] G Hogan and G White, *JM Kelly: The Irish Constitution*, 4th edn (Haywards Heath, Tottel, 2003) 1866–70; M Forde and D Leonard, *Constitutional Law of Ireland*, 3rd edn (Dublin, Bloomsbury Professional, 2013) 725–27, 729–30.

[18] L Cahillane, 'Revisiting Article 41.2' (n 2).

[19] *Dennehy v Minister for Social Welfare* (HC, 26 July 1984).

[20] See page 19 of the unreported judgment. This position was subsequently endorsed by Costello J in *Lowth v Minister for Social Welfare* [1998] 4 IR 321.

[21] *De Burca v Attorney General* [1976] IR 38.

[22] ibid 59.

[23] *BL v ML* [1992] 2 IR 77.

purchased in the husband's name only. Seventy-five per cent of the purchase price was funded by a gift from the husband's father and the remaining 25 per cent was a deferred payment discharged from farm income over the following years. Justice Barr accepted that, as a matter of the existing common law, it was not possible for the wife to obtain any share in the family home as she had not contributed money or money's worth to the upkeep of the household (which would have given her a beneficial interest by way of a resulting trust). However, the Court was prepared to find that Article 41.2 required an interpretation which treated work in the home as having monetary value. The judge held:

> In my view the judiciary has a positive obligation to interpret and develop the law in a way which is in harmony with the philosophy of Article 41 as to the status of woman in the home. It is also in harmony with that philosophy to regard marriage as an equal partnership in which a woman who elects to adopt the full-time role of wife and mother in the home may be obliged to make a sacrifice, both economic and emotional, in doing so. *In return for that voluntary sacrifice, which the Constitution recognises as being in the interest of the common good, she should receive some reasonable economic security within the marriage.* That concept can be achieved, at least in part, by recognising that as her role as full-time wife and mother precludes her from contributing, directly or indirectly, in money or money's worth from independent employment or avocation towards the acquisition by the husband of the family home and contents, her work as home-maker and in caring for the family should be taken into account in calculating her contribution towards that acquisition – *particularly as such work is of real monetary value.*[24] (emphasis added)

Justice Barr went on to recognise that the common law on resulting trusts would give a share in the family home to a wife who contributed to the family finances through paid work, and so indirectly subsidised the costs of the home. He accepted that the common law gave no credit to the woman who undertook work in the home and found that Article 41.2 mandated that such credit be given.[25] Justice Barr expressly limited the extent of his judgment as being subject to any arrangement or understanding between spouses,[26] and held that the wife did not have any interest in the husband's other assets, aside from the family home.[27] He excluded from his judgment marital homes which were acquired by a husband prior to the marriage. He also expressly referenced the likelihood of such matters being dealt with by legislation.[28]

Justice Barr's analysis is easily susceptible to the charge of accepting the false universalism contained in Article 41.2. As was set out above, the symbolic nature of Article 41.2 appeals to such false universals and is a significant issue with the wording of the provision. However, if, as is argued above, the underlying resistance to that symbolism is caused, at least in part, by the extent of substantive inequality in Ireland, Barr J's decision does at least use a flawed provision to achieve some substantive redress. His judgment, for all its use of the false universal, does give some level of financial protection to women who do not have an independent source of income arising from work outside of the home.

Women's lower socio-economic status in Irish society (which was even more acute in 1991 than it is now) was a social fact. The decision of Barr J raised the possibility of a married

[24] ibid 98–99.
[25] ibid 99–100.
[26] ibid 99.
[27] ibid 100.
[28] ibid 99.

woman developing *during and within* the marriage a financial interest in the marital home. This recognition of care work as work deserving of recognition as economically valuable placed the plaintiff's maintenance of the family home and her rearing of the couple's children on a par with her husband's farming and land speculation businesses. Justice Barr's judgment gave Article 41.2 some bite. It ate into the financial dominance of the husband's position by valuing the plaintiff's work in the only way that any work is ever truly valued in contemporary societies: by ascribing monetary value to it.

Justice Barr's judgment was, however, overturned by the Supreme Court. Chief Justice Finlay expressly accepted that joint ownership of the family home by both spouses was to be encouraged and that such joint ownership 'must directly contribute to the stability of the marriage, the institution of the family, and the common good'.[29] However, he queried whether the High Court was 'developing an existing law within the permissible limits of judicial interpretation, or whether in fact it would be legislating'.[30] He concluded that

> to identify this right in the circumstances set out in this case is not to develop any known principle of the common law, but is rather to identify a brand new right and to secure it to the plaintiff. Unless that is something clearly and unambiguously warranted by the Constitution or made necessary for the protection of either a specified or unspecified right under it, it must constitute legislation and be a usurpation by the courts of the function of the legislature.[31]

However, *in the next paragraph*, Finlay CJ accepts that the existing law on resulting trust was developed in the High Court in *C v C*[32] (just over a decade previously) and had only been approved by the Supreme Court in 1986.[33] In neither of those cases had Article 41.2 been part of the analysis of the Court. He concluded that, to uphold the High Court order, 'would be not to develop a doctrine, in my view, but to introduce a new one'.[34] Chief Justice Finlay's judgment involves *both* an acceptance that work in the home has monetary value by way of opportunity cost (as outside persons would have to be hired for money to do it otherwise) *and* an assertion that introducing this new doctrine is impermissible. This is despite the express constitutional basis for such a doctrine and the Supreme Court's acceptance that such a doctrine would contribute to the common good.

Chief Justice Finlay accepted that, in a marital breakdown case, it would be permissible to require a separated husband to pay alimony at a rate which did not require the separated mother to work outside of the home, if the husband was capable of making such provision, but could not countenance the transfer of any property right.[35] Justice O'Flaherty, in a short concurring judgment, observed that Article 41.2 is about mothers only and not about wives and so it cannot be 'called in aid to govern the division of property rights between spouses'.[36] He found that Article 41.2 did require the State to 'endeavour' to give economic aid to mothers in dire economic straits, but within the limits of the 'State's overall budgetary situation'.[37]

[29] ibid 107.
[30] ibid 107.
[31] ibid 107.
[32] *C v C* [1976] IR 254.
[33] *McC v McC* [1986] ILRM 1.
[34] *BL v ML* [1992] 2 IR 77, 108.
[35] ibid 109.
[36] ibid 112.
[37] ibid 112.

The effect of the Supreme Court judgment in *BL v ML* is that the duty of mothers in the home is reiterated, but any meaningful compensation for the unpaid care work done in the home by women is entirely dependent on either: (a) the means of the husband *after* marital breakdown; or (b) the assistance of the State, but subject to budgetary constraints in a way that that makes it entirely ineffective as a justiciable right. This is the worst of both worlds; the symbolism of Article 41.2 is endorsed in a manner which entrenches the existing economic disparities between men and women within the family; symbolic inequality gets judicial endorsement and substantive inequality gets judicial protection.

It is tempting to regard *BL v ML* as proving how diluted Article 41.2 ultimately became, and using it as a basis to write off Article 41.2 as a symbol only. However, this would be a mistake. When *BL v ML* is read in conjunction with *Re Article 26 and the Matrimonial Home Bill 1993*,[38] the extent of the effect of the Supreme Court's interpretation of Article 41 becomes clear.

In the Matrimonial Home Bill 1993, the Oireachtas had introduced the type of legislation suggested by the Supreme Court in *BL v ML* as being necessary to provide an interest in marital property. The Bill made provision for automatic joint ownership of the home of married couples. Section 4 of the Bill would have created a presumption that spouses owned the home where they lived as joint tenants, but with the option of the 'non-owning' spouse making a declaration that he or she had no financial interest in the home after receiving independent legal advice (section 7). In the absence of such a declaration, the 'owning' spouse could apply to court for a declaration taking the home out of the operation of the legislation (section 6).

This primary legislation, passed by both houses of the Oireachtas, constituted a very significant shift in the relative economic power of spouses in Ireland. Despite the repeated protestations in *BL v ML* that it was for the Oireachtas to decide if wives should have automatic rights to the family home, when the Oireachtas did exactly that, the Supreme Court found it repugnant to Article 41. It is worth noting that three of the five judges who sat in *BL v ML* decided the *Matrimonial Home Bill* case.

The Supreme Court accepted that encouraging joint ownership of marital property was an element of the common good and was conducive to the stability of marriage;[39] the Court expressly cited its own findings in *BL v ML* in this regard. The Supreme Court went on to find that the 'right of a married couple to make a joint decision as to the ownership of a matrimonial home is one of the rights possessed by the family' and protected by Article 41. No previous case law was cited for this proposition, suggesting that the worries expressed in *BL v ML* about finding new rights under Article 41 had dissipated somewhat in the intervening 26 months. The Supreme Court noted the automatic application of the legislation to any home occupied on or after 25 June 1993, regardless of whether the decision not to own jointly had been injurious or oppressive to the interests of one spouse. The Court then went on to speculate on the difficulties that would be faced by married couples who had decided against joint ownership years ago and were now forced to decide whether to opt out of the new system by way of declaration on independent legal advice. The Court observed that

> this means that the entire matter must again be reviewed between the spouses and that if a decision which has already existed in favour of ownership by one of them is to be continued, that the

[38] *Re Article 26 and the Matrimonial Home Bill 1993* [1994] 1 IR 305.
[39] ibid 325.

> non-owning spouse must register the declaration under section 7. In the event that such a joint decision has been made a considerable number of years ago, even though freely and fully agreed at that time, it may be that upon the passing of this Bill a non-owning spouse on grounds which could be reasonable or could be wholly unreasonable would not be willing to make the declaration under section 7.[40]

The Supreme Court then observed that, if a section 7 declaration were not forthcoming, a married couple 'who may well have been content though not enthusiastic about the arrangements which they had made and by which a substantial part of their married life had been governed' would be forced into litigation.[41] The Court criticised the Bill for automatically cancelling some decisions 'freely made by both spouses as part of the authority of the family',[42] and ultimately concluded that the Bill did not constitute a reasonably proportionate intervention by the State on the rights of the family and was a failure to protect the 'authority of the family' which it described as having 'extreme importance'.[43]

The logic of this two-page analysis from the Supreme Court is difficult to square with a vision of marriage that is best protected by assuming an equal partnership, despite the Court's express endorsement of the importance of equal partnership in the judgment. The assumption upon which the decision rests is that the spouses have freely and fairly decided for themselves that one spouse should own the marital home outright. Where this is the case, section 7 would have provided an easy remedy and so this is not, of itself, a reason to hold that the legislation was unconstitutional. The next step in the logic is where the sleight of hand occurs. The Supreme Court assumed that there would be cases where a free and fair decision was made by a couple in the past that one spouse should own the home; however, upon being forced to revisit the issue as of June 1993, that free and fair decision might be disrupted and reconsidered by the 'non-owning' spouse. That is the entire extent of the intrusion onto the family that was identified by the Court and yet it was sufficient to justify a finding of repugnancy to Article 41. If the problem posited by the Supreme Court had been expressed in openly gendered terms, the analysis is even harder to sustain: a man and a woman agree that the man should own the family home to the exclusion of the woman. In 1993, the Oireachtas requires the couple to revisit this decision and the woman says that she wants to own half of the family home. If the man wishes to prevent this, he has to go to court. Such is the level of intrusion contemplated by an 80 per cent male Supreme Court bench in this case. Yet, it formed the basis for a finding of unconstitutionality.

The analysis is comparable to that of the US Supreme Court in *Lochner v New York*.[44] In *Lochner*, the US Court found that an employer and an employee were free to enter into whatever contractual bargain they wished and it was constitutionally illegitimate for the legislature to intrude upon their privity of contract. An employee who agreed to work very long hours in poor conditions may wish to do so to make extra money. It was not for the legislature to second-guess the bargain made. The case led to almost three decades of decisions striking down legislation designed to protect workers, and *Lochner* impeded the ability of trade unions to obtain redistributive legislation.[45]

[40] ibid 326.
[41] ibid 326.
[42] ibid 326.
[43] ibid 326.
[44] *Lochner v New York* 198 US 45 (1905).
[45] M Tushnet, *The Constitution of the United States of America: A Contextual Analysis* (Oxford, Hart Publishing, 2009) 26–28.

Although *Lochner* is often associated with a critique of judicial activism, the difficulty of the logic of *Lochner* was the Supreme Court's decision to wilfully ignore substantive inequalities of bargaining power in the name of a near-absolute right to bargain freely. The same wilful ignorance is evident in the *Matrimonial Homes Bill* case. In both instances, entrenched disparities of power which protect certain members of society at the cost of others are not only treated as irrelevant; they are barely mentioned. To protect an existing power dynamic in this way, even by implication, is to endorse it and, just as *Lochner* endorsed the existing power interests of employers against employees, *Matrimonial Homes Bill* endorsed the existing power of husbands against wives.

Sunstein describes *Lochner* as a case about the courts applying a very specific standard of neutrality of their own making, which refers to a preservation of existing distributions of wealth and entitlements.[46] He argues that

> the common law categories were taken as a natural rather than social construct. The status of the common law as a part of nature undergirded the view that the common law should form the baseline from which to measure deviations from neutrality, or self-interested 'deals'.[47]

Understood in this way, Sunstein's critique applies just as forcefully to the Supreme Court's approach to Article 41 in the *Matrimonial Homes Bill*. This version of the Constitution, requiring neutrality as protection of the status quo, is far better as a means of explaining the approach of the Supreme Court than anything in the text of Article 41 itself. Despite the fact that the legislation was attempting to redress an acknowledged gender imbalance in marriages in Ireland, the decision-making around property in marriages is treated as pre-political; as unrelated to the politics of the society and so insulated from unwarranted State intrusion. This reading is particularly evident given that the Supreme Court *expressly accepted* that joint ownership of the marital home would be conductive to the stability of marriage and the protection of the family.

Sunstein acknowledges that gender equality law needs to challenge the status quo. He describes some of the developments in mid-twentieth century US gender discrimination law as breaking away from the *Lochner* approach and requiring the courts to challenge the status quo, rather than endorsing it in the name of neutrality. He argues:

> [T]he law of gender discrimination is an outgrowth of ideas that abandon the status quo as a neutral baseline and instead rely on a baseline of gender equality operating to some extent as a criticism of the existing order.[48]

A version of the approach suggested in *BL v ML* did eventually make its way into constitutional jurisprudence, but only as a result of the express terms of the 15th Amendment, which introduced divorce and only in relation to the distribution of property after the end of a marriage. After the 15th Amendment, Article 41.3.2°iii made it an express constitutional requirement for a divorce that 'proper provision' be made for the spouses. This constitutional imperative was read in light of Article 41.2. In *DT v CT*,[49] Murray J (as he then was),

[46] C Sunstein, 'Lochner's Legacy' (1987) 87 *Columbia Law Review* 873.
[47] ibid 879.
[48] ibid 899–900.
[49] *DT v CT* [2002] 3 IR 334.

drawing on the earlier case of *MK v JP*,[50] found that, having regard to Article 41.2, proper provision would require the contribution of a wife, who worked in the home, to be accounted for in deciding on the distribution of marital assets.

This decision goes some way to mitigating the effects of the Supreme Court decision in *BL v ML*, but it must be noted that it does nothing to improve the economic position of a woman during marriage. It only relates to proper provision being made in a divorce when the couple have four years of living apart. The resulting trust contemplated in the High Court in *BL v ML* and the operation of the Matrimonial Homes Bill would have provided greater economic power to women during the marriage itself.

It is also worth noting that prior to Ireland's membership of the EEC the Irish civil service was expressly excluded, by primary legislation,[51] from employing married women. No challenge to the constitutionality of the marriage ban was ever decided by the superior courts. In light of the foregoing jurisprudence, it is reasonable to assume that any such challenge would have had a very cold judicial reception. In this sense the effect of Article 41.2 may be as important for the cases that were not taken as for those that were.

IV. Limited Expectations for Gender-neutral Constitutional Recognition of Caring

The lessons of Article 41.2 to date give little reason to think that a gender-neutral text will be a forceful protection of care work. Smith writes of Article 41.2 that it

> ought, theoretically, at least, to bind the State towards creating the conditions necessary for the performance of care in such a way as to promote both the fundamental right to equality of treatment and the right to earn a livelihood. Not surprisingly, there has been little substantive worth attributed to the positive values implicit in Art.41.2.[52]

One of the most obvious limitations with proposals for a gender-neutral version of Article 41.2 is that the courts already purport to treat it as gender-neutral. In *Sinnott v Minister for Education*,[53] Denham J (as she then was) gave a general observation as to the meaning of Article 41.2 in the twenty-first century. She said:

> Article 41.2 does not assign women to a domestic role. Article 41.2 recognises the significant role played by wives and mothers in the home. This recognition and acknowledgement does not exclude women and mothers from other roles and activities. It is a recognition of the work performed by women in the home. The work is recognised because it has immense benefit for society. This recognition must be construed harmoniously with other Articles of the Constitution when a combination of Articles fall to be analysed.[54]

[50] *MK v JP* [2001] 3 IR 371.

[51] S 10 of the Civil Service Regulation Act 1956 required women to retire from the civil service upon marriage and s 16(2)(c) of the Civil Service Commissioners Act 1956 required that ordinarily only unmarried women and widows were permitted to apply for civil service positions. This legislation continued a rule that had been in place since the 1930s.

[52] O Smith, '"How Far from a "Right to Care"? Reconciling Care Work and Labour Market Work in Ireland' (2012) 47(1) *Irish Jurist* 143, 147.

[53] *Sinnott v Minister for Education* [2001] 2 IR 545.

[54] ibid 665.

Justice Denham also commented that 'The undefined and valuable role of the father was presumed and remained unenumerated by the drafters of the Constitution'.[55] The judge's analysis was contained in a part of her judgment in which she dissented from the rest of the Supreme Court; however, the gender-neutral approach was subsequently endorsed by the Court in *DT v CT*,[56] in which Murray J (as he then was) observed in relation to Article 41.2:

> I would observe, in passing, that the Constitution, as this court has stated on a number of occasions, is to be interpreted as a contemporary document. The duties and obligations of spouses are mutual and, without elaborating further since nothing turns on this point in this case, it seems to me, that it implicitly recognises similarly the value of a man's contribution in the home as a parent.[57]

Despite the gender-neutral approach of Denham J in *Sinnott*, the outcome of the case did nothing to improve the position of women engaged in unpaid informal care work. The case concerned two related actions; one brought on behalf of a 23-year-old autistic man who claimed his right to primary education had been violated and another brought by his mother who claimed that the State had failed to respect and vindicate her rights as the autistic man's mother. Justice Denham, dissenting from the rest of the Court, upheld the award of damages in favour of the mother. The majority of the Court accepted that she was separated from her husband and was a de facto single parent to nine children, including her autistic son, who was profoundly disabled. However, Keane CJ (with whom Murray, Hardiman and Fennelly JJ agreed) found that the mother's claim was 'wholly unsustainable'.

In the High Court, Barr J had found the mother's claim for damages to be sustained by the fact that the State's failure to meet its constitutional obligations to her son had imposed an 'inordinate burden'[58] on her which aggravated the problems of having such a disabled child. Justice Barr expressly cited Article 41.2 in his finding (albeit with limited analysis) and found that the mother had her own claim based on her constitutional rights.

Chief Justice Keane did not engage at all with these findings. He found that persons in the position of the mother 'naturally evoke our respect, admiration and compassion'[59] but held that, for her to be entitled to damages, would be to entitle every family member of a person with non-trivial injuries from a tort to damages from whiplash to quadriplegia. At no point did Keane CJ engage with the Article 41.2 issues, but his approach to the impact of injuries and disabilities on families indicates there will be no legal support found in the Constitution for those engaged in unpaid care work.

Justice Geoghegan, who also found against the mother, accepted that 'in an appropriate case'[60] a mother could claim breaches of Article 41.2, but found that in this case there had been no attack on the family justifying such a claim. By relegating any claim by the mother to being dependent on a claim of an attack on the family as a whole the bar for succeeding is raised to an unreachable degree and the mother is required to show that a whole group has been attacked, which further deprives the supposed protections of Article 41.2 of any force.

[55] ibid 664.
[56] *DT v CT* [2002] 3 IR 334.
[57] ibid 407.
[58] *Sinnott v Minister for Education* [2001] 2 IR 545, 589.
[59] *DT v CT* [2002] 3 IR 334, 641.
[60] ibid 725.

The approach of the majority in *Sinnott* indicates a great unwillingness on the part of the Supreme Court to place any positive obligation on the State for meeting the needs of those who cannot meet their needs themselves, even where there is explicit constitutional protection. This bodes ill for any constitutional recognition of unpaid care work. As such work is outside the labour market, it conflicts with any model that prioritises and requires all work to fit in a labour market model.[61] By treating the (highly legally constructed) labour market as the neutral or natural state of affairs, the law forces work that does not fit that model into a discretionary or charitable framework, denying equal dignity with other forms of work.

It is telling that Geoghegan's analysis of the son's case in *Sinnott* is rounded off[62] with a reference to Costello J's assessment of commutative versus distributive justice in *O'Reilly v Limerick Corporation*.[63] The dismissive approach taken by the majority to the mother's claim is entirely in keeping with that distinction. Suggestions that the Constitution might do something to assist any group with less means have tended to be rebuffed with dismissive arguments concerning the separation of powers or resource constraints. This is precisely the logic of *BL v ML*.

In *O'Reilly*, Costello J drew a distinction between distributive and commutative justice, which he saw as being distinguished by whether they dealt with relationships between individuals or relationships between individuals and those 'in authority in a political community' which holds goods in common for all. Justice Costello expressly accepted in *O'Reilly* that relationships between individuals could include relationships between individuals and servants of the State. As such, there is no impediment on that analysis to an award of damages against a range of State actors, which would impose a burden on common funds. Justice Costello saw claims based on relationships arising from mutual dealings as distinct from other, more general claims.

President Costello (as he became) subsequently took a different stance on this issue in respect of housing for members of the Travelling Community and accepted that his views on the matter had changed.[64] Despite this, the distinction between commutative and distributive justice has become the dominant approach and Costello J's dictum was repeatedly endorsed by the Supreme Court,[65] despite his own expressed misgivings. Although endorsed by the Supreme Court, Costello J's analysis does not bear much scrutiny. He expresses a concern for the distribution of the community's wealth, but expressly acknowledges that such wealth can be diminished by the bringing of an action against the State based on some mutual dealing. If tort law can form the basis for a payment from the community's wealth, it is difficult to understand why a statutory or constitutional duty cannot do the same. The obvious response to this is that socio-economic rights would involve the State in positive duties to expend resources. However, a wide range of civil and political rights engage such positive duties and the expenditure of resources.[66] The right to fair trial is not cheap to

[61] Smith, '"How Far from a "Right to Care"?' (n 52).
[62] *DT v CT* [2002] 3 IR 334, 641.
[63] *O'Reilly v Limerick Corporation* [1989] ILRM 181.
[64] *O'Brien v Wicklow UDC* (HC, 10 June 1994).
[65] *Sinnott v Minister for Education* [2001] 2 IR 545; *TD v Minister for Education* [2001] 4 IR 259.
[66] C Fabre, 'Constitutionalising Social Rights' (1998) 6 *Journal of Political Philosophy* 263.

protect, neither is the right to vote. Sunstein highlights the extent to which maintaining the status quo places positive obligations on governments to actively and affirmatively protect property rights and contract rights:

> There is, however, a peculiarity in the notion that the Constitution does not guarantee 'affirmative rights'. We have seen that the takings clause protects against repeals, partial or total, of the trespass laws. When a state abrogates the law of trespass, it is removing what might be seen as 'affirmative' protection; but its action does not become for that reason constitutionally acceptable. The protection of private contracts can be understood in similar terms. The contracts clause amounts to a right to state enforcement of contractual agreements; if the state fails to protect by refusing to enforce a contract, it is violating the clause.[67]

Even an assessment of the position of the defendant in *O'Reilly v Limerick Corporation* shows the extent to which existing non-socio-economic non-constitutional rights can intrude upon the community's common funds. Local authorities are required to discharge substantial portions of the community's wealth with some regularity. Local authorities can be sued in tort and regularly are. The right to litigate against a local authority carries with it the possibility of a very substantial costs order even if the underlying claim is not for damages.[68] The sums expended in such cases dwarf the costs of a serviced halting site. And so, the problem with socio-economic rights cannot really be said to be that they involve positive duties or cost money.

The extent to which a constitutional text can, of itself, redress substantive power imbalances is limited and to expect it to do so in the absence of political will is perhaps naïve. However, the Constitution is not neutral on the subject. Tribe has argued that constitutional space is shaped by the actions and omissions of the government and the courts as opposed to being a neutral area in which private individuals' actions affect only themselves free of State influence.[69] The social realities are legally constructed. Treating the effects of disparities of private power as outside of the realm of State responsibility is to ignore the State's construction of the circumstances that allow that private power to be abused. Tribe writes, in relation to judicial indifference to certain disparities of treatment of African Americans, that

> to announce that government bears no responsibility for these problems is to *legitimate* government's actions, and to relieve both governmental and nongovernmental actors of responsibility for solving these problems in institutionally appropriate ways.[70] (emphasis in original)

He suggests that:

> Discerning the social meaning of a challenged practice – of a legal space shaped by certain acts juxtaposed with certain omissions entails inquiry into how the practice affects the human geometry of the situation. Such inquiry in turn demands less an effort to uncover the hidden levers, gears or forces that translate governmental actions into objective effects, than an attempt to feel the contours of the world government has built – and to sense what those contours mean for those who might be trapped or excluded by them.[71]

[67] Sunstein, 'Lochner's Legacy' (n 46) 889.
[68] See eg *Walsh v Sligo County Council* [2013] 4 IR 417.
[69] L Tribe, 'The Curvature of Constitutional Space: What Lawyers Can Learn from Modern Physics' (1989) 103 *Harvard Law Review* 1.
[70] ibid 33–34.
[71] ibid 39.

There are indications in the jurisprudence cited above that the manner in which the constitutional space has been developed in Ireland by the senior judiciary has presented significant challenges for attempts to use the law to improve the substantive position of women in Ireland. In this sense, socio-economic rights are women's rights and they have been met with hostility from the bench. If substantive economic and political inequality between men and women in Ireland is an established fact (which, based on the statistics set out above, it seems it is), then for the Constitution to improve the position of those engaged in unpaid care work, who are overwhelmingly female, it is necessary for it to engage, at least to some extent, in addressing the substantive inequality.

The difficulty with socio-economic rights is perhaps more properly understood in the threat that they pose to the status quo. By their nature, they seek to challenge substantive economic and political inequality. By presenting opposition to them as neutrality and objectivity, the approach of cases such as *O'Reilly* and *Sinnott* manage to take a firm position in inequality while claiming to be doing nothing at all. MacKinnon has argued that gender power disparities are a particularly insidious example of power imbalance dressed up as an inevitable and objective status quo. She said of feminism that articulating women's experience

> defines our task not only because male dominance is perhaps the most pervasive and tenacious system of power in history, but because it is metaphysically nearly perfect. *Its point of view is the standard for point-of-viewlessness*, its particularity the meaning of universality. Its force is exercised as consent, its authority as participation, its supremacy as the paradigm of order, its control as the definition of legitimacy.[72] (emphasis added)

For the constitutional space to be defined as pursuing the goal of protecting neutrality, it must have a level-playing field to begin with (which it does not); otherwise the project becomes one of entrenching established interests. Where those established interests align so much more with protecting the power of men than they do with improving the position of women, the outcome of that constitutional space is inevitably the perpetuation of those imbalances. A gender-neutral ethic of care will not improve that.

Part of the ongoing difficulty with substantive inequality and the Irish Constitution is the deep unwillingness to countenance socio-economic constitutional rights *at all*, most famously in the judgment of Keane CJ in *TD v Minister for Education*.[73] Ó Cinneide has been critical of the lack of a 'social dimension' to the Irish constitutional order.[74] However, there is nothing inevitable in this – it has been driven by the approach taken by the courts. Article 45's 'directive principles of social policy' raises to the level of constitutional principle key markers of social justice. There have been some small indications over the years of a willingness in the High Court to develop the other fundamental rights provisions in light of Article 45,[75] but nothing as innovative as the jurisprudence of the Indian Supreme

[72] CA MacKinnon, *Towards a Feminist Theory of the State* (Cambridge MA, Harvard University Press, 1989) 116–17.

[73] *TD v Minister for Education* [2001] 4 IR 259, 282.

[74] C Ó'Cinneide, '"Zones of Constitutionalisation" and the Regulation of State Power: The Missing Social Dimension to the Irish Constitutional Order' (2014) 37(1) *Dublin University Law Journal* 173.

[75] See generally *Murtagh Properties v Cleary* [1972] IR 330; *McGee v Attorney General* [1974] IR 284 (HC).

Court has ever been attempted here,[76] despite the fact that the 'Directive Principles of State Policy' in Part IV of the Indian Constitution were openly modelled on Article 45 of the Irish Constitution.[77]

The Irish courts have not even given any great indication of a willingness to use such rights, even via Article 45, as a counterweight in constitutional adjudication to civil and political rights. The South African Constitutional Court has used the right to housing in section 26 of the South African Constitution as a means of justifying intrusions on the private property rights of landowners.[78] What little development of Article 45 there has been in the High Court has tended to be of this type, but it has been very limited. As was set out above in *BL v ML*, an attempt to consider Article 41.2 as eating into a husband's property rights was entirely dismissed.

Given this attitude to substantive inequality (both as it relates to gender and more broadly) in the Irish courts, there is very little reason to think that informal unpaid care work will be treated by the Irish courts as having direct monetary value. In the absence of such recognition, the lessons of the development of Irish constitutional jurisprudence and the shape of the constitutional space it has created give no reason to assume that a gender-neutral ethic of care will be meaningfully enforced or practically useful in anything other than a symbolic fashion.

V. Conclusion

If Article 41.2 was designed to keep women in the home raising children, it has been an utter failure. Most mothers in Ireland work outside of the home. If Article 41.2 was designed to ensure that work done by women in the home was valued it has also failed. The one attempt to give it teeth was overturned and, despite subsequent attempts to treat the provision as gender-neutral, the substantive inequality of men and women in Ireland continues. The extent to which constitutions can address substantive inequality may be inherently limited, but the way in which the constitutional space in Ireland has been developed by the superior courts has cut off any meaningful mechanism for putting socio-economic rights on the constitutional agenda. For as long as that remains the case, there is little or no reason to think that a gender-neutral recognition of care work would have anything other than a symbolic effect. As such, it is unlikely to be of any assistance in addressing substantive gender inequality.

[76] See generally *Mullin v Union Territory of Delhi* [1981] 1 SCC 608; *Olga Tellis v Bombay Corp* [1985] 3 SCC 545.

[77] See Hogan and Whyte, *JM Kelly: The Irish Constitution* (n 17) 2078–79.

[78] *Minister for Public Works v Kyalami Ridge Environmental Association* [2001] ZACC 19; *Port Elizabeth Municipality v Various Occupiers* [2004] ZACC 7.

13

'Doing Gender' and Irish Employment Law

LUCY-ANN BUCKLEY

I. Introduction

How does Irish employment law shape the context for 'doing gender', and why does it matter? These questions lie at the heart of this chapter. Irish equality law has made very significant advances in dealing with gender discrimination.[1] However, it is argued here that the binary conceptualisation of gender in Irish equality law is overly simplistic and reductionist. This leads to difficulties for non-binary groups and fails to address intersectional disadvantage. The chapter also highlights underlying normative assumptions in protective leave provisions that reinforce traditional gender roles, thus disadvantaging women and other gender groups who may wish or need to do gender differently.

The chapter begins with a brief explanation of 'doing gender', followed by a short outline of the historical background to the current legal context. It then examines the conceptualisation of gender in the Employment Equality Acts 1998–2015 (EEA), before discussing the legislative and judicial response to various instances of 'doing gender' in the workplace. This is followed by an analysis of the highly gendered protective leave structure. The chapter concludes by examining the effect of doing gender on labour market participation and considers how employment law contributes to this. Owing to constraints of space, the primary focus throughout is on gender rather than sexual orientation. However, the impact of particular gender norms on lesbian, gay, bisexual, transgender and intersex (LGBTI) groups is noted where appropriate (and discussed in other contributions to this volume, Chapters 5 and 11).

II. 'Doing Gender'

In their seminal article, 'Doing Gender', West and Zimmerman distinguish between sex, sex category, and gender.[2] 'Sex' traditionally refers to the individual's classification as male or female in light of biological characteristics. 'Sex category' refers to the individual's social

[1] For a full discussion of the current law on gender discrimination, see M Bolger, C Bruton and C Kimber, *Employment Equality Law*, 2nd edn (Dublin, Thomson Reuters, 2012).
[2] C West and DH Zimmerman, 'Doing Gender' (1987) 1 *Gender and Society* 125, 127.

designation as male or female in daily interactions, which is established by forms of signalling such as dress or mannerisms.[3] 'Gender', however, refers to an activity – specifically, the management of conduct in light of normative understandings of what is appropriate for the individual's sex category in situational contexts. 'Doing gender' therefore requires ongoing effort by the participants in interactions. It is essentially a form of work that helps individuals to become and to be perceived by themselves and others as being male or female.[4]

Normative understandings underpinning the activity of gender may include gender stereotypes (for instance, the assumption that men will be strong, and women will be nurturing) and the assumption of gender roles (for instance, men will be breadwinners and leaders, and women will be carers).[5] These norms are problematic for women, as they contribute to exclusion from and inequalities within the labour market. However, they are also problematic for men, as they are excluded from caring roles.[6] They may also be critiqued as heteronormative, that is, they rely on unspoken assumptions that reinforce heterosexual behavioural norms. Such norms have a structural impact, as they form the basis for social institutions. However, the assumptions themselves are so normalised as to remain invisible and uncontested.[7] Since heterosexuality is customarily premised on highly gendered social roles and stereotypes,[8] LGTBI individuals, in particular, may be disadvantaged by heteronormative employment structures.

The attribution of sex has also become contentious. Increasingly, science suggests that biological sex is constituted by more than procreative functions and encompasses broader genetic and physical criteria.[9] This suggests that sex might more correctly be regarded as a continuum,[10] and that assumptions of biological dichotomy are also socially constructed.[11] This has further implications for doing gender, since non-binary individuals may be forced to conform with (problematic) binary gender roles. Thus, Lembke notes, LGBTI individuals may be doubly disadvantaged by the assumption of dichotomous sexes and the inequality of binary gender roles.[12]

III. Historical Background to Gender in Irish Employment Law

Gender norms have been highly significant for the participation of Irish women in paid employment. The constitutional emphasis on the domestic contributions of women (discussed in Chapter 12) highlights dominant social expectations that are borne out by

[3] ibid.

[4] ibid 129.

[5] SAM Hennekam and JJ Ladge, 'When Lesbians Become Mothers: Identity Validation and the Role of Diversity Climate' (2017) 103 *Journal of Vocational Behaviour* 40.

[6] As noted by Brian Tobin in Chapter 6.

[7] D Bell, 'Heteronormativity' in N Thrift and B Kitchin (eds), *International Encyclopaedia of Human Geography* (Amsterdam, Elsevier, 2009) 115.

[8] Hennekam and Ladge, 'When Lesbians Become Mothers' (n 5) 40.

[9] U Lembke, 'Tackling Sex Discrimination to Achieve Gender Equality? Conceptions of Sex and Gender in EU Non-Discrimination Law and Policies' (2016) 2 *European Equality Law Review* 46, 47.

[10] ibid 47.

[11] ibid, citing J Butler, *Gender Trouble: Feminism and the Subversion of Identity* (London, Routledge, 1990).

[12] Lembke, 'Tackling Sex Discrimination to Achieve Gender Equality?' (n 9) 48.

data on labour market participation (discussed below).[13] Likewise, although the Constitution guarantees equality, it permits the State to have regard to 'differences of physical and moral capacity, and social function',[14] feeding directly into constitutionally sanctioned gender stereotypes. All citizens, both men and women, are recognised as having an equal right to an adequate means of livelihood, but this is qualified by the stipulation that the State shall ensure that citizens are not forced by economic necessity to 'enter vocations unsuited to their sex, age or strength'.[15] Indeed, the Constitution specifically provides that the State 'shall endeavour … to ensure that mothers are not obliged by economic necessity to engage in labour', to the neglect of their domestic duties.[16] Although case law overturned some gender inequalities on constitutional grounds,[17] it had little application in the employment context.

Constitutional and social norms discouraging women from working, particularly after marriage, were reinforced by structural barriers. Prior to 1974, married women were legally excluded from the Civil Service,[18] and the 'marriage bar' was also applied in practice by many private sector employers.[19] Although the bar was eventually abolished,[20] women who later returned to the labour market were left with reduced seniority and pension entitlements.[21] Other gender groups have also been historically disadvantaged. For instance, homosexual acts were not decriminalised until 1993; combined with a prevailing Catholic hegemony, the effect was to make sexual orientation invisible from an employment policy perspective (see Chapter 5).

The impetus for change came with Ireland's membership of the now European Union (EU), which has been foundational to the development of employment equality law in Ireland. Directives on equal pay[22] and equal treatment[23] were ground-breaking, as were subsequent directives on social security,[24] pregnancy,[25] parental leave,[26] race[27] and other grounds of discrimination.[28] These led to very significant national measures, such as the Anti-Discrimination (Pay) Act 1974 (prohibiting sex discrimination in relation to pay) and the Employment Equality Act 1977 (prohibiting discrimination in relation to access to employment and terms and conditions of employment). The 1977 Act prohibited discrimination based on marital status as well as sex; this has a clear gender relevance, particularly in the then context, only three years after the removal of the marriage bar. Both Acts were later repealed and replaced by the Employment Equality Act 1998, which added multiple

[13] Constitution of Ireland, Art 41.2.1.
[14] ibid Art 40.1.
[15] ibid Art 45.
[16] ibid Art 41.2.2. The repeal of constitutional references to women's domestic role will be considered in a forthcoming referendum.
[17] See eg *De Burca v Attorney General* [1976] IR 38.
[18] Civil Service Regulation Act 1956, s 10.
[19] I Lynch, 'Labour Law', in A Connelly (ed), *Gender and the Law in Ireland* (Dublin, Oak Tree Press, 1993) 52.
[20] Civil Service (Employment of Married Women) Act 1973, s 4.
[21] Government of Ireland, *National Pensions Framework* (Dublin, Stationery Office, 2010) [3.7].
[22] Directive 75/117, later consolidated in Directive 2006/54 ('Recast Directive').
[23] Directive 76/207, later consolidated in the Recast Directive.
[24] Directive 79/7.
[25] Directive 92/85.
[26] Directive 96/34.
[27] Directive 2000/43.
[28] Directive 2000/78 ('Framework Directive').

other protected grounds, including race, disability, age, religion and sexual orientation. The 1998 Act has since been significantly amended in line with EU requirements, and gender equality is now governed by the Employment Equality Acts 1998–2015 (EEA). Other key national measures deriving from EU law include the Maternity Protection Acts 1994–2004 and the Parental Leave Acts 1998–2006. The significance of these measures is considered below. However, it is worth noting at the outset that, while these measures represent huge advances in dealing with gender discrimination and the reconciliation of work and caring obligations, they have not fundamentally addressed social gender roles. On the contrary, they have sometimes reinforced particular ways of doing gender.

IV. The Concept of Gender in the Employment Equality Acts 1998–2015

The EEA prohibits discrimination on grounds of 'gender', rather than 'sex' (as under the previous legislation). This reflects evolving usages at EU level, analysed in detail by Lembke.[29] However, 'gender' is defined in binary terms; that is, the claimant and comparator must be a woman and a man, or vice-versa.[30] The EEA therefore does not offer explicit protection to transgender or non-binary persons, though the former are implicitly protected since the decision of the Court of Justice in *P v S and Cornwall County Council*.[31] In that case, the Court of Justice held that dismissing an employee who had undergone gender reassignment amounted to less favourable treatment on the ground of sex. Gender reassignment is now explicitly covered by the Recast Directive, which consolidated previous gender equality directives.[32]

The EEA offers more scope for gender protection than at first might appear, as it covers characteristics that are past, present, future or imputed.[33] This could include situations where less favourable treatment is based on previous or future gender (where a person has transitioned, or intends to do so), or on the perception of gender (where a claimant is treated less favourably depending on how their gender is perceived by others). However, this is not the approach that has been taken in practice.

Doing gender (or, indeed, transgender)[34] was at the heart of the leading Irish decision in *Hannon v First Direct Logistics Limited*.[35] In *Hannon*, the claimant, who was transgender, wished to dress and be identified as female within her workplace. Her employer asked her to alternate between her male and female identity on request (eg when meeting clients) and required her to work from home without a valid business justification for this. Ultimately the claimant was left with no option but to resign and claim constructive dismissal. The claimant had been diagnosed with gender identity disorder, and both parties accepted

[29] Lembke, 'Tackling Sex Discrimination to Achieve Gender Equality?' (n 9) 46.
[30] EEA, s 6(2)(a).
[31] *P v S and Cornwall County Council* [1996] IRLR 347.
[32] Directive 2006/54.
[33] EEA, s 6(1)(1).
[34] C Connell, 'Doing, Undoing or Redoing Gender? Learning from the Workplace Experiences of Transpeople' (2010) 24 *Gender and Society* 31.
[35] *Hannon v First Direct Logistics Limited* [2011] ELR 215.

that this was a disability within the meaning of the EEA. The Equality Officer held that the claimant had been denied reasonable accommodation in the employer's response to her transition. A key focus of the decision was on the claimant's medical need for uninterrupted 'real life experience' of living as a member of the other sex, including social interaction, which the employer had failed to accommodate. Although *Hannon* represented a good outcome from the claimant's perspective, it is deeply unfortunate that a need to do gender in a particular way should be characterised as a disability.

The claimant also succeeded in her claim of gender discrimination, but this too was problematic. The Equality Officer held that being asked to switch between male and female identities was both gender and disability discrimination, as was the request that the claimant should work from home. However, although the Equality Officer cited *P v S* as authority for the principle that the gender ground protects transgender persons from sex discrimination, it is not clear who Ms Hannon's comparator was for the purpose of her claim. This goes to the heart of the difficulty with the approach in *P v S*: the Court of Justice insisted on an opposite sex comparator, yet this is clearly difficult in transgender cases.[36] The solution adopted in *P v S* was essentially to compare the claimant with her own previous gender identity, and this appears to have been the reasoning in *Hannon* also, as the Equality Officer found that the claimant would not have been requested to work at home had she remained in her male identity. However, this cannot apply to another aspect of the finding, that allowing the claimant's co-workers to address her by her male name amounted to gender discrimination – clearly, had the claimant remained in her male identity, she would have been treated in the same fashion. Nor can one argue that a man would have been called by his chosen name while a woman would not, since other women working for the employer were not disadvantaged in this way. This suggests that the discrimination in this instance was more correctly based on a refusal to recognise the claimant's gender identity in the same way that the gender identity of a non-trans person would have been recognised. This is supported by an additional finding that the claimant had suffered gender discrimination through the refusal to give her a work email address in her new legal name. However, refusal to recognise gender identity in itself is not unlawful discrimination under the EEA, unless a comparator can be found. Again, it is not clear who this should be in a transgender context.

The issue has now partly been addressed by the Gender Recognition Act 2015 (GRA), which (as discussed in other chapters of this volume, particularly Chapter 11) permits an individual to apply for a gender recognition certificate in their 'preferred gender'. The term 'preferred gender' is left open, and simply means 'the gender a person applies to have specified or which is specified in a gender recognition certificate'.[37] This suggests that recognition of non-binary gender should be possible. However, the GRA then states that the effect of the certificate is that 'if the preferred gender is the male gender the person's sex becomes that of a man, and if it is the female gender the person's sex becomes that of a woman'.[38] This suggests that only binary gender categories may be recognised, significantly limiting the scope of the Act.

[36] M Bell, 'Shifting Conceptions of Sexual Discrimination at the Court of Justice: From *P v S* to *Grant v SWT*' (1999) 1 *European Law Journal* 63, 66.
[37] Gender Recognition Act 2015 (GRA), s 2.
[38] ibid s 18.

The GRA does not reference the EEA, but states that an individual's 'preferred gender' in a gender recognition certificate becomes their gender 'for all purposes'.[39] This would clearly include the purpose of claiming gender discrimination under the EEA. In *Hannon*, obtaining a gender recognition certificate (had one been available at the time) would have clarified that the claimant was female for comparative purposes. However, this would not have completely resolved matters. While Ms Hannon could have claimed she was less favourably treated than a man in terms of recognising her gender identity, the respondent could still have contended that this was not gender discrimination, as other women were not treated in this way. It is also worth noting the Equality Officer's comment that 'the respondent … presumed that there would be negative consequences because of the complainant's female identity'.[40] This suggests that the real issue from the employer's perspective was not whether the claimant was male or female, but rather that she had transitioned.[41] This might be captured by the Act's inclusion of discrimination based on a past characteristic (being male), or alternatively the employer may have imputed maleness to the claimant, notwithstanding that she was transitioning to female (and notwithstanding a gender recognition certificate, had one applied). However, the better approach would be to avoid difficulties of this kind altogether by reconfiguring the 'gender ground' (as currently defined) to include gender identity, gender expression and sex characteristics.[42]

Doing gender is inherent in pregnancy and childbirth, as employees who become mothers are performing a specifically female role.[43] However, pregnancy is not itself a protected characteristic in equality law, and pregnancy discrimination has primarily been conceptualised as gender discrimination. This has proved extremely challenging, as a pregnant woman originally had to show that she was less favourably treated than a similarly situated man – either one who was pregnant[44] or (in later judicial analysis) one who was sick.[45] Clearly, identifying a pregnant male comparator was impossible, while comparing a pregnant woman with a sick man was rightly criticised as inappropriate.[46] Pregnancy therefore highlights the limits of the comparator methodology. The difficulty was resolved at EU level by the decision in *Dekker*,[47] where the Court of Justice held that pregnancy discrimination constitutes direct gender discrimination, since only women can become pregnant.[48]

The EEA embeds *Dekker* by specifying that pregnancy discrimination amounts to gender discrimination.[49] However, it subsequently confuses matters by providing that the comparator for a pregnant woman in equal treatment claims (though not equal pay claims) may be either a man or a woman.[50] Pregnancy in the equal treatment context is thus essentially treated as a separate head of claim – a specific form of doing gender that

[39] ibid s 18.

[40] *Hannon v First Direct Logistics Limited* [2011] ELR 215 [4.9].

[41] This accords with Lembke, 'Tackling Sex Discrimination to Achieve Gender Equality?' (n 9) 51.

[42] This phrasing would include non-binary and transgender identity and expression; simply adding a 'gender reassignment' ground, such as that contained in s 7 of the Equality Act 2010 (UK), would accord with EU law, but would be less inclusive (eg of non-binary individuals).

[43] Hennekam and Ladge, 'When Lesbians Become Mothers' (n 5) 42.

[44] *Turley v Allders* [1980] ICR 66.

[45] *Hayes v Malleable Men's Working Club* [1985] ICR 703; *Long v Quinnsworth* EE 15/1991.

[46] Bolger, Bruton and Kimber, *Employment Equality Law* (n 1) 148.

[47] C-177/88 *Dekker* [1990] ECR I-3941.

[48] The reasoning in *Dekker* has been criticised: see eg S Honeyball, 'Pregnancy and Sex Discrimination' (2000) 29 *Industrial Law Journal* 43.

[49] EEA, s 6(2)(a).

[50] EEA, s 18(b).

is independently protected.[51] This makes it difficult to see why doing gender in the same way should be less protected in relation to pay. Furthermore, the EEA assumes that only women may become pregnant, yet pregnancy may also arise in the transgender and intersex context. This undermines the reasoning in *Dekker*, and makes it particularly important to permit comparison with women, since a (trans) man would be unable to compare himself with other men for equal pay purposes.[52] For these reasons, it would be preferable to recognise pregnancy as an independent protected characteristic.

The EEA's conception of gender is ultimately homogenous, and precludes any consideration of intersectional disadvantage. Intersectional theory was originally developed by Crenshaw to identify specific harms that affected black women, who were disadvantaged in ways that did not affect black men or white women.[53] Intersectional discrimination applies where a combination of characteristics (eg race/ethnicity, gender, disability, age, religion and sexual orientation) disadvantages a particular group. Thus, women with disabilities might be disadvantaged in ways that do not affect men with disabilities, or women without disabilities; older women may suffer disadvantages that do not affect older men or younger women. True intersectionality may be contrasted with 'additive' claims, where a claimant is disadvantaged on multiple separate grounds (eg a black woman suffers discrimination on grounds of both gender and of race, but discrimination is not limited to black women – black men and white women also suffer, though they are less impacted).[54]

Intersectional theory is important to this analysis because how gender is done varies with racial, cultural, religious and other norms. Members of sub-groups may therefore encounter barriers not faced by other gender groups. For example, a rule against wearing headscarves at work acts as a barrier to Muslim women, but not women in general or Muslim men. Specific stereotypes may also attach to particular gender groups, such as Traveller women, gay men, lesbians, Asian women, older women, black women, black men and women with disabilities. Individuals within these groups may be disadvantaged because of the stereotype, or for failing to comply with it.[55]

Unfortunately, while the EEA covers multiple protected grounds, these are individually applied. Section 6(1)(a) states that discrimination occurs where a person is treated less favourably 'on any of the grounds specified'; to date, this has been interpreted to permit claims under individual headings only. Although these may occur in tandem, each ground is pleaded and defended separately.[56] A few cases have appeared to conflate multiple

[51] This accords with Honeyball's analysis of pregnancy discrimination, in 'Pregnancy and Sex Discrimination' (n 48).

[52] The Gender Recognition Act 2015 does not prohibit the granting of a gender recognition certificate on grounds of pregnancy, although s 10 does require that the individual 'has a settled and solemn intention of living in the preferred gender for the rest of his or her life'. This raises an interesting question as to whether the Minister could revoke the certificate (under s 14) on the grounds that giving birth to a child does not demonstrate an intention to live as a man.

[53] K Crenshaw, 'Demarginalizing the Intersection of Race and Sex: A Black Feminist Critique of Antidiscrimination Doctrine, Feminist Theory and Antiracist Politics' (1989) *University of Chicago Legal Forum* 139.

[54] For a useful summary of intersectionality, see S Fredman, for the European network of legal experts in gender equality and non-discrimination, *Intersectional Discrimination in EU Gender Equality and Non-discrimination Law* (Brussels, European Commission, 2016) 27.

[55] For instance, in the English case *Bahl v Law Society* [2004] IRLR 799, the plaintiff alleged she had been disadvantaged because she was an assertive Asian woman.

[56] F Meenan, 'Expert Report – Ireland' in D Schiek and S Burri (eds), *Multiple Discrimination in EU Law: Opportunities for Legal Responses to Intersectional Gender Discrimination?* (Brussels, European Commission, 2009).

characteristics – for example in *Nyamhovsa v Boss World Productions*,[57] it was held that a 'white Irish male' would have been treated more favourably than the claimant. However, the detailed decision reveals an additive approach, where the claimant was considered disadvantaged by both race and gender stereotypes, rather than stereotypes about black women particularly.[58]

Essentially, therefore, the EEA's conception of gender does not recognise differences between gender groups, and the specific disadvantages that may affect them. This may leave some gender groups unprotected if they do gender differently to prevailing norms. It is unclear why intersectionality is not covered by the EEA: possibly, intersectional theory had simply not gained sufficient traction at the time the legislation was drafted (bearing in mind the 1998 Act was closely based on the Employment Equality Bill 1996, which was drafted when intersectional theory was still young).

Intersectional discrimination has been explored at the EU level,[59] though this has not yet resulted in any amendment to relevant directives. Individual jurisdictions have made some strides – most notably, the Canadian Human Rights Act provides that 'a discriminatory practice includes a practice based on one or more prohibited grounds of discrimination or on the effect of a combination of prohibited grounds'.[60] In the UK, the Equality Act 2010 permits claims of discrimination based on 'a combination of two relevant protected characteristics'.[61] However, the section does not cover indirect intersectional discrimination claims or claims based on more complex intersections. Ireland is obliged to address intersectional discrimination now that it has finally ratified the UN Convention on the Rights of Persons with Disabilities, which it signed in 2007. Article 6 of the Convention recognises the particular disadvantages faced by women with disabilities and requires states to address these disadvantages in the employment context and otherwise, and the importance of intersectional discrimination was further emphasised in the recent General Comment on Article 5 of the Convention.[62] Intersectional discrimination could be addressed by amending section 6 of the EEA to provide that discrimination occurs where a person is treated less favourably 'on any of the grounds specified, *or because of a combination of such grounds*'. This would extend the Act's general anti-discrimination provisions[63] to all intersectional groups, avoiding invidious distinctions. The sections of the Act dealing with discrimination on specific grounds would require greater consideration.[64]

V. The Response of Irish Equality Law to Socialised Gender Norms

How does Irish law respond to doing gender in the workplace? The protections offered by the EEA are extensive, covering access to employment, training and promotion,

[57] *Nyamhovsa v Boss World Productions* DEC-E2007-072.
[58] ibid [5.27].
[59] See eg Fredman, *Intersectional Discrimination* (n 54).
[60] Canadian Human Rights Act, RSC 1985, c. H-6, s 3(2).
[61] Equality Act 2010, s 14.
[62] General Comment on Article 5: Equality and Non-discrimination, adopted 9 March 2018.
[63] Pt II of the EEA.
[64] Pt III and Pt IV of the EEA.

discriminatory advertising, terms and conditions of employment, harassment and sexual harassment, remuneration and victimisation. Both direct and indirect discrimination are covered. For direct discrimination, the claimant must be less favourably treated on one of the protected grounds (such as gender or sexual orientation); the ground itself is therefore directly causative. For indirect discrimination, the claimant must demonstrate that a condition or requirement has a disadvantaging effect on a particular group to which the claimant belongs, and that the requirement is not objectively justified by a legitimate business aim.

Although direct discrimination claims are perhaps less common now,[65] they do arise, and frequently address gender assumptions. Sometimes these relate to gendered expectations, such as discriminatory interview questions that assume women will be primarily responsible for childcare: in *Chaney v UCD*,[66] questions about childcare arrangements essentially required the claimant to prove that she was available for work, whereas this would simply have been assumed of a man. Doing gender may also be an issue where women work in traditionally male areas and are accordingly identified as abnormal in some sense. In *Rodmell v University of Dublin, Trinity College*,[67] the claimant, who was the only female applicant for a position as a College electrician, alleged that she had been addressed as 'the lady electrician' by a member of the interview board. This was held to constitute unlawful gender discrimination. Effectively, the claimant was singled out by gender in a way that indicated she was stepping outside her gender role.

Doing gender may also be an issue in terms of the qualities and capacities attributed to employees. In *Boyle v Ely Property Group Ltd*,[68] the complainant was employed to manage student accommodation. She was dismissed because her employer wanted a manager who was capable of using physical force against the students, and considered that, as a woman, the complainant was not capable of doing this. This was unlawful discrimination. Doing gender may also arise in relation to appearances, though much will depend on the facts. In *Savage v Federal Security*,[69] the male complainant, who had waist-length hair, was asked at an interview if he would cut this; he refused, and was not offered a job as a security guard. At first sight, this suggests that the claimant was penalised for failing to comply with male gender norms, as long hair on a man might be regarded as inappropriate gender-signalling. However, the Equality Officer accepted that a similar request would have been made of a female applicant with long hair, as all hair had to be short enough to be concealed under a cap. Hence, the request was not discriminatory. Finally, gender may sometimes be a bona fide occupational requirement,[70] but this must be based on objective criteria. In *M v A Language School*,[71] the employer was not entitled to assume that only women were nurturing enough to fill the role of checking up on homesick foreign language students.

The response to inequalities arising from caring responsibilities is more problematic. As discussed below, maternity and adoptive leave are only available to mothers; however, absence from the workplace may lead to loss of seniority and reduced pay, and may prevent women from accessing pension schemes or other employment benefits. The Irish

[65] Bolger, Bruton and Kimber, *Employment Equality Law* (n 1) 138.
[66] *Chaney v UCD* EE15/1983.
[67] *Rodmell v University of Dublin, Trinity College* DEC-E2001-016.
[68] *Boyle v Ely Property Group Ltd.* DEC-E2009-013.
[69] *Savage v Federal Security* DEC-E2007-064.
[70] EEA, s 25.
[71] *M v A Language School* [2005] ELR 181.

courts have little latitude in responding to this, as the Court of Justice of the European Union has adopted various positions on this over time. In *Hill and Stapleton v Revenue Commissioners*,[72] the Court of Justice held that reclassifying (female) job-sharers so as to credit them with less experience, thus entitling them to lower pay, was discriminatory, as a job-sharer could acquire the same level of experience as a full-time worker. In *Gerster*,[73] the Court of Justice held that employers could not simply make a generalised claim that workers with longer service had more experience, as much would depend on individual circumstances. In *Cadman v HSE*,[74] however, the Court of Justice appeared to renege on this. Mrs Cadman was paid less than four male comparators for doing the same work, based on their greater length of service. She argued that linking pay to service indirectly discriminated against women, who were more likely to take time out of the workforce for caring reasons. The Court of Justice held that the service requirement was objectively justified as it permitted employers to reward experience, which enabled workers to perform better. However, the Court did not require the employer to show how the men's length of service made them more valuable or productive, and it was unclear whether the relevant business objective was rewarding loyalty or recognising better performance.[75] Subsequently, in the Irish case of *Brierton v Calor Teoranta*,[76] the Equality Tribunal held that *Cadman* required that a pay system should be sufficiently transparent to permit judicial scrutiny, and that an employer must be able to show why experience is required for the position in question, how it relates to other criteria such as merit and qualifications, and why it is rewarded proportionally. Bolger, Bruton and Kimber comment that this does not appear to be the correct interpretation of *Cadman*, and is probably best considered as an effort at mitigating that decision.[77]

Absence from work for caring reasons may also impact on promotion. In *Sheehy Skeffington v National University of Ireland Galway*,[78] applicants for promotion were asked to state whether they had taken protective leave. The objective was to permit the board of assessors to make allowance for such absences when assessing the candidates' career achievements. Although the question was neutral, it was only answered by women, four of whom indicated various caring leave periods. In the event, the women who answered the question were the lowest placed women in the competition, and the Equality Officer concluded that drawing attention to their caring responsibilities had disadvantaged the female applicants as against the male applicants. Thus, while the information was sought to permit the employer to compensate for gender disadvantage, 'the reality was that it had the opposite effect'.[79] This was unlawful discrimination.

[72] C-243/95 *Hill and Stapleton v Revenue Commissioners* [1998] ECR I-3739.

[73] Case C-1/5 *Gerster v Freistaat Bayern* [1997] ECR I-5253.

[74] Case C-17/05 *Cadman v HSE* [2006] ECR I-9583.

[75] G Beck, 'The State of EC Anti-Sex Discrimination Law and the Judgment in *Cadman*' (2007) 32 *European Law Review* 549.

[76] *Brierton v Calor Teoranta* DEC-E2010-034.

[77] Bolger, Bruton and Kimber, *Employment Equality Law* (n 1) 525.

[78] *Sheehy Skeffington v National University of Ireland Galway* DEC-E2014-078.

[79] S Quinlivan, 'Disrupting the Status Quo? Discrimination in Academic Promotions' (2017) 14(3) *Irish Employment Law Journal* 68, 70.

VI. Doing Gender and Protective Leave

For women, childcare has traditionally been an essential aspect of doing gender, in line with stereotypes about female nature. As noted previously, the narrative of women as carers is (currently) central to Irish constitutional law, and for many years women were actively prevented from stepping outside their designated gender role. Although women have gained greater access to the labour market, the legislative measures for balancing employment and caring responsibilities remain highly gendered.

Protective leave includes carers' leave and force majeure leave entitlements, but this chapter will focus on maternity, adoptive and parental leave. These are significantly informed by EU law: the Pregnant Workers Directive confers the right to 14 weeks' maternity leave,[80] and parental leave entitlements are conferred by the Parental Leave Directive.[81] EU law continues to develop; for example, in 2017, the EU Commission proposed a Directive on Work-Life Balance for Parents and Carers (not yet enacted).[82]

The current Irish law on maternity leave (the Maternity Protection Acts 1994–2004, as amended) considerably exceeds the minimum leave entitlement under the Pregnant Workers Directive, granting 26 weeks of 'paid' leave, two of which must be taken prior to the birth. An additional 16 weeks of 'unpaid' leave is available at the option of the worker, making a total of 42 weeks for those who wish or can afford to take unpaid leave. 'Paid' leave does not require the employer to pay the worker's salary during the leave period, but confers a social welfare entitlement. The Adoptive Leave Acts 1995–2005 confers a total of 40 weeks' leave on a similar basis (24 weeks of 'paid' leave following the adoption placement, and an additional 16 weeks of unpaid leave). In addition, 18 weeks' unpaid parental leave may be taken in respect of each qualifying child under the Parental Leave Acts 1998–2006. This is likely to be increased to 26 weeks in the near future.[83]

The Maternity Protection Acts apply to any pregnant employee, and may therefore apply in the transgender context, notwithstanding the use of feminised language throughout. There is no threshold service requirement. The rights granted extend beyond maternity leave, including for example the right to paid time off to attend pre-natal classes, paid time off for pre-natal and post natal care, and to time off or reduced hours for breastfeeding purposes. The legislation also provides that an employee who is absent on maternity leave or for other permitted purposes must be treated as if she had not been absent except in relation to pay. This prevents a break in continuity of service, which is essential for preserving the employee's statutory entitlements. The legislation specifies that 'protective leave' may not be treated as any other form of leave to which the employee may be entitled. Crucially, the Act provides that a purported termination of employment while the employee is absent on leave or for another permitted purpose will automatically be void, as will any purported suspension (with limited exceptions). Increased flexibility has been added over the years, with the facility to postpone or terminate the leave in certain circumstances. Finally, the legislation provides that an employee taking protective leave will be entitled to return to

[80] Dir 92/85/EEC.
[81] Dir 2010/18, replacing Dir 96/34/EC.
[82] For a summary of the proposal, see www.ec.europa.eu/social/main.jsp?catId=1311&langId=en.
[83] Parental Leave (Amendment) Bill 2017.

work, in the same job, for the same employer or an associated employer. The employee's terms and conditions of work must not be less favourable than if she had not been absent, and must incorporate any improvement to her employment conditions which would have applied had she not been absent. These protections and entitlements are largely mirrored in the adoptive leave context, with some omissions (eg there is no entitlement to time off for ante- or post-natal care, ante-natal classes or breastfeeding).

Notwithstanding the very significant advances made in maternity and adoptive leave, the legislation remains unnecessarily gendered. While protections relating to childbirth and breastfeeding are (largely) gender-specific, it does not follow that the entire maternity leave allocation should be restricted to the birth parent. Restricting the leave in this way perpetuates the assumption that childcare is primarily a female concern.[84] Even if the other parent (the father, for convenience, but see below) wishes to take on the role of primary carer, this is not permitted by the current legislation. Instead, the Act conceptualises fathers as having only a peripheral role, with limited rights to time off for ante-natal classes, and paid leave entitlements only if the mother dies. Gender performance is thus impacted in two ways – women are forced into the gendered role of primary carer, while men are forced into the equally gendered role of breadwinner.[85]

This characterisation may be partly due to the original presentation of the Pregnant Workers Directive as a health and safety measure, rather than an equality issue.[86] This fed into a highly gendered model of social care, which has been buttressed by limiting adoptive leave to adopting mothers only, unless there is a sole male adopter. There can be no health and safety justification for this; the adoptive leave model is therefore clearly premised on a normative understanding of gender roles.

Ironically, adoptive fathers were better off prior to the introduction of the Adoptive Leave Acts, as case law had held that where employers offered adoptive leave to female employees (which many did, even without a legal obligation), it was unlawful to deny it to men.[87] This position was altered by section 26(1) of the EEA, which specifies that it shall not be unlawful for an employer to confer benefits on women in connection with adoption. The Court of Justice has upheld this gendered approach, holding that an Italian law granting leave to adoptive mothers only was justified by the desire to match the conditions applying to the assimilation of a natural child within the family.[88] Accordingly, special provisions could be made for adoptive mothers without contravening the Equal Treatment Directive. More recently, however, the Court has placed greater emphasis on equal parenting. In *Roca Álvarez*,[89] the Court held that a Spanish provision granting leave to mothers for childcare purposes but not to fathers unless the child's mother was also employed, amounted to unlawful gender discrimination. The Court emphasised that both mothers and fathers might need to reduce their working time for childcare, and that keeping men in a subsidiary parenting role not only discriminated against men, but prevented the achievement of

[84] See also S Fredman, 'Reversing Roles: Bringing Men into the Frame' (2014) 10 *International Journal of Law in Context* 442.

[85] See Brian Tobin, Chapter 6, for an analysis of the impact of parental rights.

[86] Bolger, Bruton and Kimber, *Employment Equality Law* (n 1) 174.

[87] *O'Grady v Telecom Eireann* [1998] ELR 6.

[88] C-163/82 *Commission v Italy* [1983] ECR 3273.

[89] C-104/09 *Roca Álvarez v Sesa Start Espana ETT SA* [2010] ECR I-8661.

substantive equality for women. Applied logically, this suggests that the Irish provisions on both maternity and adoptive leave should be revisited, subject to the requirements of the Pregnant Workers Directive.

It is instructive to compare the Irish model with the Norwegian one. Norway provides a paid period of leave for the mother, a period for the father, and a period that may be taken by either parent, depending on their personal circumstances and preferences. The mother's and father's individual leave quotas are non-transferable, incentivising fathers to avail of their leave entitlements. Whereas initially the leave offered to fathers was relatively short (four weeks), it was gradually increased, and currently stands at 10 weeks, again encouraging fathers to avail of the leave. There were several underlying policy aims for this, most notably a desire to encourage mothers to return to the workforce sooner and to narrow the gender pay gap.[90] Although some scholars have suggested measures of this kind are ineffective or even counterproductive,[91] it appears that, when combined with greater availability of affordable childcare, the overall effect, in Norway at least, has been to encourage mothers to return to work more quickly, thereby reducing their long-term economic loss.[92] It also appears to have resulted in more favourable attitudes towards working mothers and to have created an expectation of paternal involvement in childcare.[93] As in the Irish model, therefore, both male and female gender roles are impacted, but in a more egalitarian way. It is interesting to note the suggestion of Ronsen and Kitterod that providing reserved leave for fathers (even if initially too short to lead to real role reversal) may have helped to stimulate public debate about parenting roles, and created the ground conditions (such as acclimating employers) for increased leave at a later stage.[94] None of this is to suggest that all mothers should engage in paid employment, or to devalue caring work. Rather, it shows the importance of offering genuine choice so that working parents are supported in their decisions regarding what best suits their family situation, instead of being compelled to perpetuate existing gender patterns for lack of any viable alternative, or because of social pressures. In the longer term, this may facilitate new ways of doing gender.

It was not until the Parental Leave Directive that a gender-neutral form of leave was required at the EU level.[95] The Directive was implemented in Irish law by the Parental Leave Acts 1998–2006. The 1998 Act was the first legislative recognition of parenting responsibilities other than those immediately connected with birth or adoption; it thus represents a departure from the idea that parenthood is purely a personal concern, irrelevant to the labour market. It was also the first legislation to accord equal rights to both parents. It therefore both spoke to issues of work-life balance and represented a clear step towards achieving parental equality and ending gender stereotyping.

[90] M Ronsen and RH Kitterod, 'Gender-Equalizing Family Policies and Mothers' Entry into Paid Work: Recent Evidence from Norway' (2015) 21 *Feminist Economics* 59.

[91] N Datta Gupta, N Smith and M Verner, 'The Impact of Nordic Countries' Family Friendly Policies on Employment, Wages, and Children' (2008) 6 *Review of Economics of the Household* 65; C Hakim, 'Is Gender Equality Legislation Becoming Counter-Productive?' (2008) 15 *Public Policy Research* 133.

[92] A similar leave model in Ireland might be less transformative, given the absence of equivalent levels of social supports such as affordable childcare. However, it is noteworthy that similar recommendations have recently been made in the UK context, for similar reasons (see House of Commons Women and Equalities Committee, *Fathers and the Workplace: First Report of Session 2017–19* (HC 358, 20 March 2018)).

[93] Ronsen and Kitterod, 'Gender-Equalizing Family Policies' (n 90).

[94] ibid.

[95] Directive 96/34/EC, replaced by Directive 2010/18.

Under the 1998–2006 Acts, an employee is entitled to an unpaid period of leave to care for a qualifying child. Crucially, the right attaches to each parent in respect of each child, and the leave entitlement is generally not transferable. Thus, a couple with two children is entitled to four periods of parental leave. The original parental leave scheme has benefited from amendments that significantly increased its duration and flexibility:[96] the leave period has increased from 14 to 18 weeks, and may be subdivided, subject to criteria. Some limitations apply, such as age limits for qualifying children. The leave normally cannot commence until the employee has a year's continuous service with the employer. An employer may postpone the commencement of the leave for up to six months for certain business reasons, subject to consultation with the worker. Finally, the leave can only be used for childcare, and may be terminated if it is abused.

The parental leave provisions represent a significant advance in reconciling work with caring responsibilities. However, although the leave entitlement is gender-neutral, it is also unpaid, unlike the Norwegian model where both parents have paid leave entitlements. In practice, it may be normatively difficult for men to take leave for childcare purposes; when this is considered in conjunction with the gender pay gap (discussed below), it is likely that parental leave will mostly be taken by women, as the cost to the family is lower.[97] This disadvantages women in the longer term in relation to their careers and pensions, and helps to maintain the gender pay gap.[98] Thus, structural gender disadvantage may be self-perpetuating. Recent indications of a move towards paid parental leave are therefore most welcome.[99]

More recently, Ireland took a small further step towards greater equality and recognising new ways of doing gender, by introducing a statutory entitlement to 'paid' paternity leave in 2016.[100] This is not an EU requirement, as the Court of Justice has held that it is lawful to limit paid leave to mothers only, both to protect women's health and safety during and immediately after pregnancy, and to protect the special relationship between mother and child in the immediate aftermath of the birth, which might be threatened by the simultaneous pursuit of employment.[101] However, as noted above in relation to *Roca Álvarez*, the Court now appears to have moved from this position, at least in relation to longer-term childcare.

Recognition of the role of fathers was only partially addressed by parental leave, since that is unpaid. The introduction of a statutory right to paid paternity leave was therefore significant, although the leave period is very brief (only two weeks). Unfortunately, take-up rates have been disappointing to date,[102] possibly due to normative expectations about how gender should be done. It is possible that (following the Norwegian example) a higher

[96] European Union (Parental Leave) Regulations 2013.

[97] See eg OECD, 'Parental Leave: Where are the Fathers?' (OECD Policy Brief, March 2016) www.oecd.org/policy-briefs/parental-leave-where-are-the-fathers.pdf.

[98] However, note the finding of Russell, Watson and Banks that unpaid parental leave was problematic for women also. H Russell, D Watson and J Banks, *Pregnancy at Work: A National Survey* (HSE Crisis Pregnancy Programme and the Equality Authority, 2011) xi, www.healthpromotion.ie/hp-files/docs/HCP01085.pdf.

[99] S Bardon, 'New Parents to Get Two Weeks' Paid Leave in this Year's Budget' *The Irish Times* (Dublin, 6 April 2018).

[100] Paternity Leave and Benefit Act 2016.

[101] C-184/83 *Hofmann v Barmer Ersatzkasse* [1994] ECR 3047.

[102] See eg C McQuinn, '"Costs to Blame" as Just Third of Dads take Paternity Leave' *Irish Independent* (9 August 2017).

rate of uptake will not be achieved unless the leave period is lengthened, though there are also recent indications that the leave may be made compulsory.[103] Additionally, since the 'payment' is a social welfare benefit rather than a full salary, there are financial implications to taking the leave at a time when the mother may also be on a reduced payment or on unpaid leave (paternity leave is only available for the first 26 weeks after the child's birth, thus overlapping with the extended maternity leave period).[104]

Maternity and adoptive leave may also be critiqued from an intersectional perspective. First, as noted above, 'paid' leave is a misnomer, as the 'payment' is limited to a social welfare entitlement. Employers are not required to pay the employee during the leave period (although in practice many do, and mothers may assign their statutory benefit to their employer in partial recompense).[105] For many women, therefore, maternity leave has an immediate economic cost, as their income is reduced even during the 'paid' leave period.[106] Extended maternity leave is entirely unpaid, and will be unaffordable for many women on lower salaries (including women from many intersectional groups).[107] In this sense, extended maternity and adoptive leave, along with parental leave, are highly privileged, and effectively facilitate those who are otherwise financially secure, rather than those who most need the leave. Thus, although the leave model encourages traditional methods of doing gender, it does little to make it affordable.

Second, the leave model is heteronormative.[108] As noted earlier, heterosexuality is customarily premised on highly gendered social roles and stereotypes, which have traditionally accorded men the 'breadwinner' role and women the 'homemaker' role. This is reflected in the assumption of Irish maternity and adoptive leave legislation that mothers will be the primary carers for children. This model has now been extended to same-sex parents, despite evidence that traditional heterosexual assumptions regarding role division may not apply in same-sex relationships.[109] The Children and Family Relationships Act 2015 amended the Maternity Protection Act 1994 to accord legal parentage of a child to the husband, civil partner or cohabitant of a woman who has conceived through donor-assisted human reproduction (subject to criteria),[110] thus according limited recognition (since not every child born to same-sex parents will be the result of donor-assisted human reproduction) to same-sex parents. However, the 2015 Act then simply extends the rights accorded to fathers under the maternity protection legislation to the 'father or other parent', as defined.[111] This assumes that same-sex relationships should follow the same leave pattern as heterosexual ones, essentially compelling one parent to adopt the heterosexual female

[103] Bardon, 'New Parents to Get Two Weeks' Paid Leave' (n 99).

[104] Paternity Leave and Benefit Act 2016, s 8.

[105] Russell, Watson and Banks found that 48% of women received top-up payments from their employers in addition to their State maternity benefit, but that this was more prevalent among women who were comparatively secure financially (eg not precariously employed). See Russell, Watson and Banks, *Pregnancy at Work* (n 98).

[106] Russell et al (ibid) found that 92% of women who had experienced pregnancy at work had taken paid maternity leave. However, the figure was lower for women who were self-employed, or who worked part-time or in temporary or casual jobs.

[107] Only 41% of women took extended leave in practice (ibid).

[108] On this point, I am indebted to Chapman's analysis of the Australian context: see A Chapman, 'Employment Entitlements to Carers Leave: Domesticating Diverse Subjectivities' (2009) 18(2) *Griffith Law Review* 453.

[109] ibid 454; R Leckey, 'Must Equal Mean Identical? Same Sex Couples and Marriage' (2014) 10 *International Journal of Law in Context* 5, 11.

[110] Children and Family Relationships Act 2015 (CFRA), s 5.

[111] CFRA, s 176.

role and the other to act as the putative male breadwinner (irrespective of gender). The 2015 Act also stipulates that, where an adopting couple are same-sex cohabitants or civil partners, they must elect which adopting parent will be classified as the 'adopting parent' for adoptive leave purposes;[112] the leave can thus be taken by one adopting parent only. Parental leave, which is also extended,[113] remains gender-neutral, but paternity leave follows the heteronormative model of maternity leave.[114]

Third, the maternity protection legislation may disadvantage women with disabilities, if they are unable to do gender in the 'normal' way. A notable instance of this occurred in *Z v A Government Department*,[115] where the complainant was born without a uterus and was unable to bear children. She succeeded in having a genetic child via a surrogacy arrangement in California, but was denied maternity leave in Ireland on the ground that she had not given birth. She was also unable to avail of adoptive leave, as she was not an adoptive mother (under Californian law, the commissioning parents are listed on the birth certificate). The claimant thus fell into a legislative limbo regarding the legal status of surrogate parents in Ireland and had no paid leave entitlement. She alleged both sex and disability discrimination. In a preliminary ruling, the Court of Justice rejected her claim on both counts. There was no sex discrimination as a commissioning father would have had no paid leave entitlements either, and there was no evidence that women were disadvantaged as compared with men. Although the claimant clearly had a disability within the meaning of the EEA, this did not prevent her from engaging in employment or advancing in her profession. She therefore did not have a disability, and had not suffered discrimination, within the meaning of the Framework Directive.

Z is an interesting case as it goes to the heart of a key gender question, what it means to be a mother. The Court of Justice's approach accords with the original health and safety basis of the Pregnant Workers Directive and also with its previous decision in *CD v ST*,[116] where it emphasised that the aim of the Pregnant Workers Directive was to protect women in the context of pregnancy and childbirth. It therefore applied only where the worker had been pregnant and had given birth: in *CD*, even breastfeeding her child was not sufficient to bring the commissioning mother within the scope of the Directive. This falls far short of social understandings of parenthood, and fails to grasp a key point relating to female labour market participation. The Court of Justice emphasised that the claimant was not prevented by her disability from engaging or progressing in employment, but in fact, given the gendered nature of caring norms, she was effectively denied the opportunity to reconcile family life and labour market participation on an equal basis with other mothers. She was compelled to use her sick leave allowance and to take unpaid parental leave (which is shorter than paid maternity or adoptive leave). She suffered severe stress as well as financial loss and loss of seniority, and felt she could not commission a second child to increase her family. *Z* is therefore an important example of intersectionality: Ms Z was disadvantaged

[112] CFRA, s 177.
[113] CFRA, s 178.
[114] Paternity Leave and Benefit Act 2016, s 5.
[115] Case C-363/12 *Z v A Government Department, The Board of Management of a Community School* [2014] IRLR 570.
[116] Case C-167/12 *CD v ST* EU:C:2014:169.

because, although a genetic parent and the primary carer to a baby, she was not a birth mother and could not do gender in the same way as a woman with a uterus. The denial of maternity leave resulted from Ms Z's particular disability, which could only affect women, and the harm she suffered must be understood in the broader context of gendered care roles and expectations. Ms Z was thus disadvantaged in a way that would not have affected either a non-disabled woman or a disabled man.

VII. The Effects of Doing Gender on Participation in the Labour Force

Although equality legislation has removed formal barriers to women's labour market participation, the pace of social change has been slow. Much of this is due to women's continuing role as primary family caregivers. In 1971, women accounted for 25.7 per cent of the labour force.[117] By 1997 (23 years after the abolition of the marriage bar) women's labour market participation rate stood at approximately 37 per cent.[118] Significantly, participation rates for married women increased from 14 per cent to over 52 per cent of the total female workforce over the same period.[119] However, this includes a significant element of part-time employment: in 1997, three quarters of workers engaged in part-time employment were women, and 65 per cent of women in regular part-time employment were married.[120] Only half of 25–29-year-old married women with children participated in the labour market, while over 90 per cent of married women without children and 87.6 per cent of single women in the same age group did so.[121] This fits with the finding of Fahey and Fitz Gerald that, by the early 1990s, the presence of children replaced marriage as the key factor affecting women's labour market participation.[122]

This finding is also supported by subsequent data. In 2001, 48.1 per cent of women participated in the labour force; this increased to 54.5 per cent in 2007 (the height of the economic boom), falling slightly to 52.8 per cent in 2012 and rising again to 53.6 per cent in 2016. At this point, women represented 44.1 per cent of the overall labour force. By contrast, 71.7 per cent of men participated in the labour force in 2001, rising to 73.6 per cent in 2007, falling to 67.8 per cent in 2012 and remaining more or less stable over the following years.[123]

Although the gap in male and female labour force participation rates narrowed significantly between 2001 and 2016 (decreasing from 23.6 per cent to 14.2 per cent), the continuing impact of family responsibilities becomes clear when women's labour force participation is

[117] F Ruane and J Sutherland, *Women in the Labour Force* (Dublin, Employment Equality Authority, 1999) 30.
[118] ibid.
[119] ibid.
[120] ibid 37.
[121] ibid 30.
[122] T Fahey and J Fitz Gerald, *Welfare Implications of Demographic Trends* (Dublin, Combat Poverty Agency, 1997) 67.
[123] Central Statistics Office, *Women and Men in Ireland 2016* (Dublin, CSO, 2016) www.cso.ie/en/releasesandpublications/ep/p-wamii/womenandmeninireland2016/.

analysed by age group. In 2016, just under half of the labour force[124] in the 15–19 age group was female, but this was the highest proportion of women across all age groups. The highest rate of labour force participation for women (77.8 per cent) occurred in the 25–34 age group, whereas the highest rate for men (91.8 per cent) was in the 35–44 age group.[125] Given that the average age for women giving birth to their first child has been rising in recent decades (30.5 years old in 2014,[126] up from 25.3 years in 1970),[127] it seems clear that women still drop out of the labour market in significant numbers following childbirth. This may have an enduring effect: in 2016, older women were much less likely to participate in the labour force than older men.[128] Furthermore, it must again be emphasised that participation in the labour market includes part-time work, and that this category of employment is heavily feminised.[129]

The employment rate for women also varied significantly depending on whether they had young children: 85.7 per cent of childless women were employed, compared with 60 per cent of women whose youngest child was aged between 4–5 years. The difference for men was far smaller, though an exact comparison is not possible from CSO (Central Statistics Office) data: 89.1 per cent of childless men were employed, compared with 83.9 per cent of men whose youngest child was aged 6 or over. Employment rates for lone parents are also indicative: only 58.5 per cent of male lone parents whose youngest child was aged 6 or over were employed, 26.5 per cent less than men in couples. Similarly, only 45.6 per cent of female lone parents whose youngest child was aged 3 or under were employed, 21.3 per cent less than women in couples. Significantly, more than 90 per cent of lone parents were women in 2016.[130] These figures demonstrate both the impact of childcare responsibilities, and the gendered nature of caregiving.

It is difficult to attribute the rise in women's labour market participation to a single cause. The ESRI (Economic and Social Research Institute) noted that women's labour market participation had increased significantly between 1997–2007, a period characterised by strong economic growth and labour market expansion, as well as the introduction of new employment rights (such as parental leave and the National Minimum Wage) and extensions to key existing rights, such as maternity leave.[131] One cannot single out any of these factors as causative. Nevertheless, it is noteworthy that the increased levels of female participation did not affect all female categories equally. Overall female activity rates (ie the proportion of the female population who were classified as employed or unemployed) increased from 57 per cent to 67 per cent, but the increase was much lower for women with children aged under 5, lone parents and young single women, than for other female groups.[132] The activity rate for young single women might be partly due to the pursuit of

[124] 49.2%.
[125] CSO, *Women and Men in Ireland 2016* (n 123).
[126] 32.7 years old if married, and 28 years old if unmarried.
[127] CSO, *Women and Men in Ireland 2016* (n 123).
[128] 39.5% of women aged 60–64, compared with 61.2% of men the same age.
[129] See the discussion of factors contributing to this: H Russell et al, *A Woman's Place: Female Participation in the Irish Labour Market* (Dublin, ESRI, 2009) 4.
[130] CSO, *Women and Men in Ireland 2016* (n 123).
[131] Russell et al, *A Woman's Place* (n 129) xi.
[132] ibid.

additional qualifications,[133] since the rates of increased activity were highest among women with low educational attainments.[134] However, the low rate of increase for the other groups (all characterised by high levels of caring responsibility), suggests the continued presence of structural barriers.

This view is supported by a comparison with other EU countries. The ESRI noted that Irish women's labour market participation rates are closest to those in countries whose welfare models encourage a 'male breadwinner' economic structure, such as Germany, France and Austria. However, it is much lower than countries whose welfare models assume a 'dual earner' arrangement, such as Denmark, Sweden and Finland.[135] Concluding that lower levels of labour force participation among mothers probably reflected both women's preferences and structural factors such as the availability of affordable childcare and flexible working arrangements,[136] the ESRI identified affordable childcare (especially for low earners) as a key policy initiative to support women's labour market participation.[137] Similar views were expressed by the OECD, which advocated income supplements to make childcare more affordable and encourage female labour force participation.[138] However, even where such measures are adopted, normative factors such as attitudes to women working are also highly influential, and may be slower to change.[139] Greater equality within the protective leave structure might assist with this.

Furthermore, even with equality legislation and maternity protection rights, pregnancy in the employment context continues to be problematic for many women. In a recent survey of 2,300 female employees who had experienced pregnancy at work, up to 30 per cent reported unfair treatment during pregnancy, including dismissal (reported by 5 per cent of women employed during pregnancy).[140] Other forms of unfavourable treatment included the loss of salary, bonuses or promotion (10 per cent), being given unsuitable work or workloads (12 per cent), unpleasant remarks by managers or co-workers (8 per cent), and being discouraged from attending pre-natal appointments during work time, despite a statutory right to do so (8 per cent). Additionally, 32 per cent of women experienced difficulties in connection with maternity leave, mostly regarding leave duration. More generally, 21 per cent of respondents felt that their training opportunities had decreased since they returned to work, while 24 per cent felt that their promotion opportunities had done so. It is clear that women continued to struggle with balancing work and home life: 33 per cent of mothers who had previously worked full-time reduced their hours after giving birth.[141] This may not have been entirely voluntary: 19 per cent of women had been refused parental leave, or had been granted leave in a different form to that requested.[142] Given the level of difficulty experienced, it is unsurprising that many women might choose to leave the workforce.

[133] The proportion of the female workforce with third level education rose from 29% to 43% over the period (ibid).
[134] ibid.
[135] ibid xii.
[136] ibid xiv.
[137] ibid xiii.
[138] OECD, *Economic Surveys: Ireland* (Paris, OECD, 2008).
[139] Russell et al, *A Woman's Place* (n 129) 5.
[140] Russell et al, *Pregnancy at Work* (n 98) xi.
[141] ibid.
[142] ibid.

Although women's labour market participation has increased, structural inequalities remain. A key indicator here is the gender pay gap (GPG), defined by Eurostat as the difference between male and female average hourly earnings as a percentage of male earnings (albeit not taking account of factors such as labour market experience, hours worked or educational differences). In 2014, Irish female employees were paid an average of 13.9 per cent less than male employees; this was lower than the average GPG in the EU, which stood at 16.3 per cent in 2015.[143] However, this average conceals some even more significant disparities. In the Industry sector, the Irish GPG was still as high as 22.6 per cent in 2014, although this was a considerable drop from over 40 per cent in the 1940s–1960s.[144] The 2014 figure represented a slight increase from the 2011 figure of 11.7 per cent, and in fact, the figures have fluctuated somewhat in recent years.[145] Precarious work has increased, and again disproportionately affects women.[146] Occupational segregation continues to be an issue: in 2016, the vast majority of workers in skilled trades (90.1 per cent) were male, as were 93.6 per cent of those employed in construction, while those employed in caring, leisure and other services were predominantly (83.5 per cent) female.[147] In 2009, the ESRI found that the level of vertical segregation within the marketplace had not significantly reduced, so that men were still twice as likely as women to occupy senior and middle management positions,[148] a finding confirmed by a recent study of the financial services sector.[149] Part-time work continues to be dominated by married women: 22.2 per cent of married women worked for 20–29 hours per week in 2016, compared with 5 per cent of married men.[150] Again, factors such as childcare and protective leave may be significant here. The ESRI notes that if women have shorter absences from paid employment (eg because they return to work sooner after having children), this may help to reduce the GPG,[151] though this is not the only relevant factor.

VIII. Conclusion

This chapter has highlighted some of the highly gendered normative assumptions underlying key aspects of Irish employment law, and has demonstrated how they shape the context in which employees do gender. This is most evident in the construction of maternity and adoptive leave, which effectively requires women and men to continue to do gender in traditional ways. This impacts women's labour market participation, which in turn contributes

[143] CSO, *Women and Men in Ireland 2016* (n 123).
[144] CSO, 'Historical Earnings 1938–2015', www.cso.ie/en/releasesandpublications/ep/p-hes/hes2015/ebg/.
[145] CSO, *Women and Men in Ireland 2013* (Dublin, Stationery Office, 2014) [3.4].
[146] ICTU, *'Insecure and Uncertain': Precarious Work in the Republic of Ireland and Northern Ireland* (Dublin, ICTU, 2017) https://static.rasset.ie/documents/news/2017/12/ictu-report.pdf.
[147] CSO, *Women and Men in Ireland 2016* (n 123).
[148] Russell et al, *A Woman's Place* (n 129) xiii.
[149] D McDonald, C Kelpie and A Weckler, 'Special Report: Almost 90 per cent of CEO Positions in Financial Services Held by Men' *Irish Independent* (11 January 2018).
[150] CSO, *Women and Men in Ireland 2016* (n 123). However, it should be noted that single men also worked longer hours than single women, 44% of single men working for 40 or more hours per week compared with 25.6% of single women.
[151] Russell et al, *A Woman's Place* (n 129) xii.

to the gender pay gap. This then makes it more viable for women than men to take unpaid leave such as parental leave, again reinforcing existing gender norms.

However, the chapter has also highlighted other aspects of the employment law architecture that impact on doing gender. These include the heteronormative aspects of protective leave, and the definition of gender itself, which struggles to accommodate non-binary persons and considerations of intersectionality. They also encompass the legal response to gender assumptions and to the economic costs of engaging in caring work. Sometimes these responses are adequate – most commonly when dealing with gender stereotypes – but it is evident that the law struggles to deal with structural disadvantage. This chapter concludes by arguing that Ireland needs to respond to these issues by broadening the scope of gender equality and restructuring protective leave (subject to EU legal constraints) to maximise inclusivity and move towards a more substantive version of equality.

14

Gender and Asylum Law

PATRICIA BRAZIL

I. Introduction

It has long been recognised that the Refugee Convention definition of a 'refugee' emphasises civil/political rights over socio-economic rights.[1] While the definition of a refugee is ostensibly gender-neutral, in practice difficulties can arise in securing recognition as a refugee for reasons relating to gender. It is well recognised in the research that substantive and procedural obstacles can arise in relation to advancing women's refugee claims.[2] In particular, the focus on civil/political rights can operate in such a way as to privilege male dominated 'public' activities over the activities of women, which may take place in the private sphere. This chapter will consider the theoretical framework which has developed regarding gender and asylum law, and will then assess the extent to which Irish law complies with international best practice concerning gender-based asylum claims.

II. Theoretical Framework Related to Gender and Asylum Law

The Convention Relating to the Status of Refugees 1951 ('the Convention'), signed in the aftermath of the Second World War, and the gross violations of rights associated therewith, established an individualised definition of a refugee as any person who

> owing to well-founded fear of being persecuted for reasons of race, religion, nationality, membership of a particular social group or political opinion, is outside the country of his nationality and is unable or, owing to such fear, is unwilling to avail himself of the protection of that country; or who,

[1] See eg N Kelly, 'Gender-Related Persecution: Assessing the Asylum Claims of Women' (1993) 26 *Cornell International Law Journal* 625; M Foster, *International Refugee Law and Socio-Economic Rights: Refuge from Deprivation* (Cambridge, Cambridge University Press, 2007); J Hathaway and M Foster, *The Law of Refugee Status*, 2nd edn (Cambridge, Cambridge University Press, 2014) 362–63.

[2] See eg J Bhabha, 'Embodied Rights: Gender Persecution, State Sovereignty, and Refugees' (1996) 32 *Public Culture* 3.

> not having a nationality and being outside the country of his former habitual residence as a result of such events, is unable or, owing to such fear, is unwilling to return to it.[3]

As Hathaway and Foster note, 'The Refugee Convention, unlike most constitutions and international human rights instruments, does not explicitly list sex or gender as a protected ground'.[4] However, it has long been recognised that gender-based claims can fall within the refugee definition in myriad different ways. In 1985, the Executive Committee of the United Nations Refugee Agency (UNHCR) issued its Conclusion No. 39 on 'Refugee Woman and International Protection', noting that 'refugee women and girls constitute the majority of the world refugee population and that many of them are exposed to special problems in the international protection field'.[5] The Conclusion went on to recognise that

> States, in the exercise of their sovereignty, are free to adopt the interpretation that women asylum-seekers who face harsh or inhuman treatment due to their having transgressed the social mores of the society in which they live may be considered as a 'particular social group' within the meaning of Article 1 A(2) of the 1951 United Nations Refugee Convention.[6]

The UNHCR Guidelines on Gender-related Persecution ('the Guidelines') recognise that gender can 'influence, or dictate, the type of persecution or harm suffered and the reasons for this treatment'.[7] The Guidelines also recognise that while 'gender-related claims may be brought by either women or men … due to particular types of persecution, they are more commonly brought by women'.[8] As Kelly notes:

> The majority of the world's refugees are female. Women as a group are often the first victims of political, economic and social repression. … This is in part because of laws and social mores which dictate gender-specific behavior and treatment. In addition, in societies facing economic, social and political upheaval, women are often left alone to care for children or elderly family members, and thus become the most exposed to violent attack during wars or ethnic crises. Women forced to flee their countries as refugees face continuing gender-related abuse including sexual harassment, rape, and torture by pirates, smugglers, border guards, camp administrators, and employers.[9]

Gender-based asylum claims can face particular difficulties in establishing persecution within the meaning of the refugee definition and also in linking that persecution to one of the Convention grounds ('the Convention nexus').

[3] Art 1A(2) of the 1951 Convention.

[4] Hathaway and Foster, *The Law of Refugee Status* (n 1) 436.

[5] UNHCR Excom, *Conclusion No. 39 – Refugee Woman and International Protection* (18 October 1985) at para (c).

[6] ibid at para (k). See also UNHCR, *Guidelines on International Protection (No. 1): Gender-Related Persecution Within the Context of Article 1A(2) of the 1951 Convention and/or its 1967 Protocol* (HCR/GIP/02/01, 7 May 2002) which state at para 30 that 'sex can properly be within the ambit of the social group category, with women being a clear example of a social subset defined by innate and immutable characteristics'.

[7] ibid para 6.

[8] ibid.

[9] Kelly, 'Gender-Related Persecution' (n 1) 625–26.

In relation to gender-based persecution, Bhabha notes that 'The refugee par excellence was someone heroically seeking to assert his (typically male) individuality against an oppressive state'.[10] As Kelly notes, the Convention has

> largely failed to recognize the political nature of seemingly private acts of and harm to women. For example, rape is often viewed as a private matter even when committed by a government official or in a political context.[11]

Some commentators have cautioned against overemphasising the public/private distinction and have called instead for an approach which focuses on the interconnectedness of the public and private spheres and the relationship of women to the State:

> The bifurcated version of society itself ignores the realm of women's lives outside domesticity, and creates a rhetorical and theoretical wall between domestic and social culture. It roots women's oppression in sexuality and private life, thereby disregarding oppression experienced in non-domestic circumstances, and the interconnections of the public and private spheres.[12]

Kelly notes the procedural obstacles that also contribute to advancing refugee claims in cases involving gender-based persecution, including treating women's claims as ultimately derivative of the claims of their male partners and poor practices in the assessment of credibility, including unrealistic expectations as to disclosure of sexual abuse and failure to consider cultural differences in demeanour.[13] Similar claims have also been made in the context of gender and sexuality, and are regularly highlighted in the experiences of LGBT asylum applicants in Ireland (as discussed in Chapter 5).[14] Crawley and Lester note in respect of the latter:

> Interviewers and decision-makers need to consider their impact on applicants, and also need to be wary of drawing conclusions about applicants' credibility based on culturally defined demeanour. The need for cultural sensitivity affects all asylum-seekers, but it can be particularly important for women, especially if they come from a culture where women's demeanour is expected to be different to that expected in Western culture. Thus, for women asylum-seekers, general cultural factors may be compounded by gender-specific cultural factors.[15]

Crawley and Lester note that failure to make eye contact while being interviewed may be regarded as suspicious in Western culture, but that 'in many authoritarian regimes and cultures, it is wrong, impolite, especially for a woman, to look superiors in the eye. The eyes must be cast down. This fact has been beaten into many a torture survivor.'[16] They cite in this regard the dictum of Lord Bingham in *R v Secretary of State ex parte*

[10] Bhabha, 'Embodied Rights' (n 2) 8.

[11] Kelly, 'Gender-Related Persecution' (n 1) 628.

[12] J Greatbatch, 'The Gender Difference: Feminist Critiques of Refugee Discourse' (1989) *International Journal of Refugee Law* 518, 526.

[13] Kelly, 'Gender-Related Persecution' (n 2) 629–30.

[14] See generally S Jansen and T Spijkerboer, *Fleeing Homophobia: Seeking Safety in Europe* (COC Nederland & VU University Amsterdam, 2011).

[15] H Crawley and T Lester, *Comparative Analysis of Gender-related Persecution in National Asylum Legislation and Practice in Europe* (UNHCR Evaluation and Policy Analysis Unit, 2004) at para 587.

[16] ibid para 588.

Dhirubhai Gordhanbhai Patel regarding the unreliability of drawing conclusions from demeanour: 'To rely on demeanour is in most cases to attach importance to deviations from a norm when in truth there is no norm.'[17]

In relation to the particular social group, Hathaway and Foster note that 'widespread state practice – across both common law and civil law states – now reflects the notion that women, sex or gender may constitute a particular social group for the purposes of refugee law'.[18] It is clear that gender is capable of being accommodated within the 'particular social group', either on the basis of gender as an innate or unalterable characteristic,[19] or a characteristic which is fundamental to identity, conscience or the exercise of human rights.[20] However, there is an 'ongoing reticence to recognise that women per se are capable of constituting a social group for refugee law purposes', reflected in the 'unfortunate tendency to formulate overly complicated and unnecessarily detailed social groups, rather than simply recognise that in most cases it is women *qua* woman that constitute the relevant social group'.[21] This approach gives rise to a risk that the group will be defined so narrowly that it will fail to qualify on the basis that it is defined only by the persecution feared,[22] leading to rejection of the claim. As Baroness Hale (as she then was) stated in *Fornah v Secretary of State for the Home Department*:

> This is a peculiarly cruel version of Catch 22: if not all the group are at risk, then the persecution cannot be caused by their membership of the group; if the group is reduced to those who are at risk, it is then defined by the persecution alone.[23]

Notwithstanding the difficulties identified above, the modern position in respect of gender-based asylum claims is best encapsulated by the following observation of Baroness Hale in *Fornah*:

> The world has woken up to the fact that women as a sex may be persecuted in ways which are different from the ways in which men are persecuted and that they may be persecuted because of the inferior status accorded to their gender in their home society.[24]

[17] *R v Secretary of State ex parte Dhirubhai Gordhanbhai Patel* [1986] Imm AR 515.

[18] Hathaway and Foster, *The Law of Refugee Status* (n 1) 437.

[19] *Matter of Acosta* 20 Immigration & Nationality Decisions 211 (BIA 1985).

[20] *Attorney General v Ward* (1993) 2 SCR 689. However, Aleinikoff acknowledges the difficulties that can arise in relation to the social perception approach, noting 'Exactly how, might it be asked, is an adjudicator to determine the "social perceptions" of other societies? Furthermore, whose perceptions count? Should an adjudicator examine the views of the alleged persecutors, a majority of the society, the views of the ruling elites? A major benefit of the protected characteristics approach is that it avoids some of these evidentiary problems': T Aleinikoff, 'Protected Characteristics and Social Perceptions: An Analysis of the Meaning of 'Membership of a Particular Social Group' in E Feller, V Turk and F Nicholson (eds), *Refugee Protection in International Law: UNHCR's Global Consultation on International Protection* (Cambridge, Cambridge University Press, 2003) 298.

[21] Hathaway and Foster, *The Law of Refugee Status* (n 1) at 439, cite as an extreme example of this phenomenon the decision of the Canadian Federal Court in *Litvinov v Canada* [1994] FCJ 1061 that the relevant group was 'women who have recently immigrated to Israel from the former Soviet Union and who, despite generous support by the host government, fail to integrate, are subsequently lured into prostitution, and are confronted with indifference by the front line supervisors responsible for their safety'. Hathaway and Foster regard the formulation of the particular social group in the seminal US decision of *Matter of Kasinga* (1996) 21 *Immigration and Nationality Decisions* 357 as 'only modestly less egregious', where the particular social group was defined as 'young women of the Tchamba-Kunsuntu Tribe who have not had FGM, as practised by that tribe, and who oppose the practice'.

[22] See further Hathaway and Foster, *The Law of Refugee Status* (n 1) 440.

[23] *Fornah v Secretary of State for the Home Department* [2006] UKHL 46, [2007] 1 AC 412, [2006] 3 WLR 733 at para 113.

[24] ibid para 86.

III. Legal Framework Related to Gender and Asylum Law in Ireland

Prior to 1996, the asylum system in Ireland operated on an ad hoc basis by way of administrative schemes.[25] The Refugee Act 1996 ('1996 Act') placed asylum law in Ireland on a legislative footing for the first time. Section 2 of the 1996 Act largely replicated the definition contained in Article 1A(2) of the Convention, providing that a 'refugee' means

> a person who, owing to a well founded fear of being persecuted for reasons of race, religion, nationality, membership of a particular social group or political opinion, is outside the country of his or her nationality and is unable or, owing to such fear, is unwilling to avail himself or herself of the protection of that country; or who, not having a nationality and being outside the country of his or her former habitual residence, is unable or, owing to such fear, is unwilling to return to it.

The innovation arose in section 1 of the 1996 Act – the interpretive section – which defined a 'particular social group' as including membership of a trade union, as well as membership of a group of persons whose 'defining characteristic is their belonging to the female or the male sex or having a particular sexual orientation'. Byrne notes that in this explicit enumeration of three groups constituting a particular social group, the 1996 Act 'pioneer[ed] a more expansive interpretation of the 1951 Convention'.[26] While it could be said that these grounds would in any event be included within the scope of the UNHCR general guidance on the particular social group,[27] the express recognition of these groups was undoubtedly a welcome statement of Ireland's recognition of the protection needs which may arise for members of these particular groups. However, Byrne made the important point that the application and extent of this enhanced interpretive provision depended to a large extent on the guidance given to asylum decision-makers, particularly in the context of gender-based claims, in order to heighten the skills and sensitivities of both interviewers and decision-makers to this class of claims.[28]

The next substantive amendment made to the definition of a refugee for the purposes of Irish law took place in 2006 with the transposition of the Qualification Directive[29] into Irish law by the European Communities (Eligibility for Protection) Regulations.[30] Acts of persecution were defined in regulation 9, transposing Article 9 of the Directive, as including:

> (a) acts of physical or mental violence, including acts of sexual violence;
> (b) legal, administrative, police, and/or judicial measures which are in themselves discriminatory or which are implemented in a discriminatory manner;

[25] The 'von Arnim' scheme operated between 1985 and 1997 and the 'Hope Hanlan' scheme operated between 1997 and 2000, named after the UNHCR representatives who negotiated the terms of the schemes with the Irish government. See generally S Farrell, 'Law and Practice Relating to the Interim Refugee Appeals Authority' (1997) 3(2) *Bar Review* 50 and W Farrell and C Gallagher, 'Refugee Law and Procedure' (2001) 6(7) *Bar Review* 431.

[26] R Byrne, 'At the Cross-roads: Refugee Protection in Ireland' in D O'Driscoll (ed), *Irish Human Rights Review 2000* (Dublin, Round Hall Sweet and Maxwell, 2000) 3–4.

[27] See eg UNHCR, *Handbook on Procedures and Criteria for Determining Refugee Status under the 1951 Convention and the 1967 Protocol relating to the Status of Refugees* (Reedited Geneva January, 1992) paras 77–79.

[28] Byrne, 'At the Cross-roads' (n 26) 5.

[29] Council Directive 2004/83/EC of 29 April 2004 on minimum standards for the qualification and status of third country nationals or stateless persons as refugees or as persons who otherwise need international protection and the content of the protection granted.

[30] SI No 518 of 2006.

(c) prosecution or punishment, which is disproportionate or discriminatory;
(d) denial of judicial redress resulting in a disproportionate or discriminatory punishment;
(e) prosecution or punishment for refusal to perform military service in a conflict where performing military service would include crimes or acts falling under the exclusion clauses as set out in section 2(c) of the 1996 Act;
(f) acts of a gender-specific or child-specific nature.

Regulation 10 dealt with the 'reasons for persecution', giving effect to Article 10 of the Directive, by providing that a protection decision-maker must take a number of factors into account when assessing the reasons for persecution, including:

> (d) a group shall be considered to form a particular social group where in particular –
> (i) members of that group share an innate characteristic, or a common background that cannot be changed, or share a characteristic or belief that is so fundamental to identity or conscience that a person should not be forced to renounce it, or
> (ii) that group has a distinct identity in the relevant country, because it is perceived as being different by the surrounding society;
>
> and, depending on the circumstances in the country of origin, a particular social group may include a group based on a common characteristic of sexual orientation. Sexual orientation shall not include acts considered to be criminal in the State: gender related aspects may be taken into account, without by themselves alone creating a presumption for the applicability of this Regulation; …

Hathaway and Foster describe the Qualification Directive's minimum standard in respect of gender-related aspects as 'regrettably more equivocal' than widespread state practice,[31] but given the express recognition in recital 8 of the power of Member States to 'introduce or maintain more favourable provisions',[32] it is clear that the more extensive recognition of the particular social group provided in section 1 of the 1996 Act continued to apply in Irish law.

The Refugee Act 1996 and the 2006 Protection Regulations were repealed and replaced by the International Protection Act 2015. Ireland opted not to take part in the Recast Qualification Directive,[33] and therefore remains subject to the provisions of the original Qualification Directive. Thus, acts of persecution are now provided for in section 7 of the 2015 Act, replicating the previous provisions of regulation 9 of the Protection Regulations. Similarly, the reasons for persecution now provided for in section 8 of the Act replicate the provisions of regulation 10 of the Protection Regulations. The only substantive change between the 2015 Act and the earlier domestic legal provisions arises in relation to the interpretive provision. The 2015 Act did not carry over the express recognition of gender, sexual orientation and trade union membership as particular social groups in section 1. This is a retrograde step, perhaps reflective of the generally restrictive provisions of the 2015 Act.[34]

[31] Hathaway and Foster, *The Law of Refugee Status* (n 1) 437.

[32] Recital (8) of the Qualification Directive.

[33] Directive 2011/95/EU of the European Parliament and of the Council of 13 December 2011 on standards for the qualification of third-country nationals or stateless persons as beneficiaries of international protection, for a uniform status for refugees or for persons eligible for subsidiary protection, and for the content of the protection granted (recast).

[34] See generally Irish Human Rights and Equality Commission, *Recommendations on the General Scheme of the International Protection Bill 2015* (June 2015).

IV. Jurisprudence of the Irish Courts on Gender and Asylum Law

A. Gender and the Convention Nexus

Despite the longstanding recognition in Irish law that gender can constitute a particular social group, in practice there are numerous examples of decision-makers failing to recognise gender-based claims. Thus, for example, in *AA v Refugee Appeals Tribunal*, the Refugee Appeals Tribunal rejected the gender-based element of a refugee claim on the following remarkable basis: 'As for the claim that she fears persecution on account of her gender I know of no precedent that has concluded that gender per se is a Convention ground.'[35]

In *AA*, the applicant was a Somali national who claimed asylum based on a fear of death, rape and other persecution by armed gangs on account of her membership of a minority clan and because of her past activities in campaigning against female genital mutilation (FGM). Although the High Court granted leave to seek judicial review of the Tribunal decision based largely on fair procedures issues relating to the use of country of origin information, perhaps even more remarkably leave was refused in respect of the Tribunal's finding on gender as a Convention ground, holding that 'the onus is on the applicant to show that women in Somalia are recognised as a particular social group for the purposes of s.2 of the Act of 1996 and … the applicant has failed to discharge this onus'.[36] Despite this problematic decision, which is clearly out of step with international best practice such as the UNHCR Guidelines,[37] subsequent cases have adopted a less restrictive approach to the interpretation of the particular social group in Irish law.[38]

It is not uncommon for gender-based claims in Ireland to be refused on the basis of a failure to establish a Convention nexus. In *CRDL v Refugee Appeals Tribunal*,[39] the applicant was a Bolivian woman who claimed asylum on the basis of a fear of persecution arising from her experience of harassment and threatening behaviour by a man in her country of origin. Her claim was rejected at first instance on the basis that

> while the applicant claims she was harassed by this man she stated she was not physically harmed or subjected to violence. Given that the applicant did not provide sufficient evidence to substantiate her claim of persecution or that she and her son would be at risk of physical harm if they returned to Bolivia.[40]

The applicant's claim was refused along with a finding pursuant to section 13(6) of the Refugee Act 1996 that she had showed either no basis, or a minimal basis, for the contention that she was a refugee, the effect of which was to deprive her of the right to an oral hearing

[35] *AA v Refugee Appeals Tribunal* [2010] IEHC 504.
[36] ibid para 28.
[37] UNHCR Guidelines (n 6).
[38] See eg *SJL v Refugee Appeals Tribunal* [2016] IECA 47 where the Court of Appeal accepted that a Chinese woman who feared persecution on the basis that she had breached the 'one child policy' in China could constitute a particular social group, rejecting the Tribunal's argument for a restrictive or narrow interpretation of this concept.
[39] *CRDL v Refugee Appeals Tribunal* [2015] IEHC 182.
[40] ibid para 16.

on appeal.[41] Amongst the reasons for this finding was the fact that the applicant 'appeared to be the victim of an opportunistic attack and she had not supplied sufficient evidence that she was targeted for any Convention reason'[42] and that the applicant's fear related to criminality and had no nexus to the Convention grounds. The applicant instituted judicial review proceedings seeking to challenge inter alia the failure of the first instance decision to consider gender as the Convention nexus. The High Court (Eagar J) rejected the applicant's contention that there was an error of jurisdiction in respect of the failure to consider the gender dimension, noting:

> The Applicant has indicated that she is being sexually harassed by an individual person who she does not know. Clearly this man has been involved in serious criminal conduct and the offences of harassment and sexual assault are widely regarded as serious offences. Nevertheless his criminal activities do not bring the applicant into membership of a particular social group or political opinion and the finding by the Refugee Applications Commissioner of obtaining a fear of returning to Bolivia due to criminality and showing that there is no nexus to [Convention] grounds is in my view a reasonable decision.[43]

The applicant in *CRDL* subsequently applied to Eagar J for a certificate of leave to appeal on the basis that the decision involved a point of law of exceptional public importance such that it was in the public interest that the appeal be taken. Eagar J declined the application, clarifying that although he accepted that gender did constitute a particular social group, the applicant could raise this issue as part of her appeal to the Refugee Appeals Tribunal.[44]

The recent decision of the High Court, in *SM v Refugee Appeals Tribunal*,[45] is to some extent more consistent with best practice guidelines on gender-based claims. The applicant was an Albanian national who was raped by her employer. At the time of the rape, she was three months pregnant by her husband. Three days later, the applicant reported the rape to the police. The police subsequently informed the applicant's employer and his wife of the rape complaint. As a result of the police having informed the employer of the rape allegation, the employer's wife left him taking their child. The police did not pursue any further investigation into the rape as, according to the applicant, her employer bribed the police. After she complained to the police, the applicant's employer began a daily campaign of harassment of her and regularly threatened to kill her for reporting the matter. The applicant reported the harassment and threats to the police but no action was taken. The applicant's in-laws, with whom she and her husband lived, became concerned at the extent of the harassment and intimated that their son would either have to divorce the applicant or that the couple would have to leave their home. The applicant and her husband then made a decision to leave Albania to get away from her assailant. In the course of their journey, the applicant became separated from her husband. She arrived in Ireland in November 2012 and applied for asylum. Her claim was refused at first instance on a number of grounds, including that the incident she complained of was an isolated criminal act; that her claim did not have a

[41] See generally R Byrne, 'Expediency in Refugee Determination Procedures' (2000) 35 *Irish Jurist* 149 and S McDonagh, 'Manifestly Unfounded Procedures and the Fear of Persecution' (2002) 7(5) *Bar Review* 284.

[42] At para 18 of the judgment.

[43] At para 29 of the judgment.

[44] *CRDL v Refugee Appeals Tribunal* [2015] IEHC 327.

[45] *SM v Refugee Appeals Tribunal* [2016] IEHC 638.

nexus to the Convention; and that state protection and internal relocation were available to the applicant.

The applicant appealed to the Refugee Appeals Tribunal, which accepted that she had been raped, and that she had suffered harassment at the hands of her assailant. Her claim to have been denied police protection was also accepted based on country of origin information referable to the issue of bribery of the police. On the issue of the Convention nexus, the Tribunal Member found as follows:

> The Tribunal finds that the appellant was not raped or persecuted by her former boss 'on account of' membership of a social group, or for any other Convention reason. Neither was his motivation in threatening her after she reported the rape to the police 'for reasons of' her social group. The question then is whether the state of Albania would be unable or unwilling to offer protection to the appellant for a Convention reason.
>
> The appellant submitted that she made a complaint to the local police in Albania but that no action was taken because the assailant bribed the local police. She stated that her assailant was not a man of note, but just the owner of the crèche in which she worked …
>
> The Tribunal finds that where the police were bribed by the man who raped the appellant and therefore failed to afford her protection, such failure of protection was not for a Convention reason. That is, the police did not refuse to assist the appellant for reasons of her membership of a particular social group or other Convention ground, but rather for money.[46]

The applicant subsequently challenged the decision by way of judicial review inter alia claiming that the Tribunal erred in law in finding that her claim did not have a Convention nexus. Justice Faherty noted that the crux of the challenge to the Tribunal decision on the 'nexus' ground centred on whether it could be said that the circumstances put forward by the applicant established a nexus to the Convention under the particular social group reason, and referred to the judgment of Bingham J in *K and Fornah v Secretary of State for the Home Department*[47] on the causal connection, where he stated:

> The text of article 1A(2) of the Convention makes plain that a person is entitled to claim recognition as a refugee only where the persecutory treatment of which the claimant has a well-founded fear is causally linked with the Convention ground on which the claimant relies. *The ground on which the claimant relies need not be the only or even the primary reason for the apprehended persecution. It is enough that the ground relied on is an effective reason.* The persecutory treatment need not be motivated by enmity, malignity or animus on the part of the persecutor, whose professed or apparent motives may or may not be the real reason for the persecution. What matters is the real reason. In deciding whether the causal link is established, a simple 'but for' test of causation is inappropriate: the Convention calls for a more sophisticated approach, appropriate to the context and taking account of all the facts and circumstances relevant to the particular case.[48] [Emphasis added]

Justice Faherty accepted that 'as a matter of first principle, there is no question but that women, generally, or women who are subjected to gender-based violence, may constitute a particular social group for the purposes of the Convention',[49] citing the seminal decision

[46] The reasoning of the Tribunal is set out in the judgment of Faherty J (ibid) at para 10.
[47] *K and Fornah v Secretary of State for the Home Department* [2007] 1 AC 412.
[48] ibid para 17.
[49] *SM v Refugee Appeals Tribunal* [2016] IEHC 638, para 54.

of the House of Lords in *Shah and Islam*.[50] Justice Faherty noted that the claim advanced before the Tribunal was not concerned with persecution of the applicant at the hands of the Albanian State, but rather at the hands of a non-state actor. Justice Faherty accepted that there was nothing in the subjective account given by the applicant of the rape and harassment, or in the objective evidence which was before the Tribunal, to persuade the court that the Tribunal Member was in error when she concluded that the assailant's motivation in raping the applicant and in threatening her thereafter was not Convention-related. It is arguable that this fails to accord with international best practice in respect of gender-based persecution.[51]

However, Faherty J noted that what was essentially in issue in the present case was whether the Albanian authorities' inability or unwillingness to provide protection to the applicant had its basis in a Convention reason. The Tribunal Member, albeit finding that the applicant would not be afforded state protection, was of the view that the failure of protection arose because of bribery (which she found was supported by country of origin information). In contending that the Tribunal Member erred in her determination that the absence of state protection was not Convention-related, the applicant's principal argument was that the decision-maker neglected to consider whether the country of origin information before the Tribunal had the necessary elements to illustrate that female victims of sexual violence in Albania are not afforded state protection by reason of their being women, thereby rendering them a particular social group for the purposes of the Convention. Counsel for the applicant relied on the content of country of origin information which was before the decision-maker, namely the US State Department '2013 Country Reports on Human Rights Practices – Albania'.[52]

The essence of the case put on behalf of the applicant was that there was objective material before the Tribunal sufficient to put the decision-maker on enquiry as to whether the failure of the police to afford her protection was because of discrimination on account of her gender. Justice Faherty noted that 'the question of whether there may be another reason (eg bribery) for the failure of State protection over and above any Convention-related reason would not … defeat a claim for protection under the Convention, if there was evidence that the Convention ground was "a relevant contributing factor"',[53] citing the UNHCR 2002 Guidelines and the decision in *Fornah v Secretary of State for the Home Department*.

Justice Faherty then summarised the country of origin information that was before the Tribunal Member, noting that it established that 'pervasive corruption in all branches of government and discrimination against women were "significant human rights problems" in Albania'.[54] Justice Faherty concluded as follows:

> [T]he country information which referred to discrimination against women and the lack of effective enforcement of laws prohibiting rape, together with the applicant's submissions in respect

[50] *Fornah and Islam v Secretary of State for the Home Department and R v Immigration Appeals Tribunal ex parte Shah* [1999] 2 AC 609.

[51] See eg UNHR, *Guidelines on International Protection: Gender-Related Persecution within the context of Article 1A(2) of the 1951 Convention and/or its 1967 Protocol relating to the Status of Refugee* (HCR/GIP/02/01, 7 May 2002), para 9 of which states: 'There is no doubt that rape and other forms of gender-related violence, such as dowry-related violence, female genital mutilation, domestic violence, and trafficking, are acts which inflict severe pain and suffering – both mental and physical – and which have been used as forms of persecution, whether perpetrated by State or private actors'.

[52] (27 February 2014).

[53] *SM v Refugee Appeals Tribunal* [2016] IEHC 638, para 66.

[54] ibid para 70.

> thereof should have been specifically considered by the Tribunal Member in the context of her assessment as to whether a nexus had been established, in the same way as she referenced the COI in aid of her finding that the absence of state protection arose because of bribery. Given the submissions that were made, it was not sufficient for the decision-maker, simply because the applicant had said that the police had been bribed, to accept that that was the reason for the failure of protection (even where the COI corroborated the applicant in this regard), in circumstances where the COI also had the potential to assist the decision-maker in deciding whether the absence of protection could be said to arise because of discriminatory practices surrounding the prosecution of or enforcement of laws against rape or sexual harassment respectively.[55]

The decision of Faherty J is significant for its findings on the appropriate test for causation in relation to establishing a Convention nexus, and for requiring a careful consideration by refugee decision-makers of the reasons for a lack of state protection and in particular whether the absence of such protection is for reasons of gender.

However, despite progress being made in such cases as *SM*, it is clear that challenges remain in advancing gender-based asylum claims in Ireland. Some decision-makers seem to be reluctant to accept violence against women as implicitly gender-based and structural, preferring instead to consider such claims on a case-by-case and individualised basis.[56] The decision of the High Court in *LAA (Bolivia) v Refugee Appeals Tribunal*[57] is one such example. The applicant was a Bolivian national who sought asylum on the basis of a fear of persecution at the hands of her husband who had subjected her to extensive domestic violence. Her claim was dismissed at first instance by the Refugee Applications Commissioner which found that this violence was motivated by her husband's alcoholism, not by the applicant's race, religion, nationality, membership of a particular social group or political opinion, and that her claim therefore had no Convention nexus.

On appeal, the Tribunal upheld the negative recommendation of the Commissioner. It is interesting to note that the decision of the Tribunal referred to country of origin information which had been submitted in support of the appeal, which stated:

> According to the Human Rights Reports on Bolivia, violence against women is a pervasive and under-reported problem. 70% of Bolivian women suffer some form of abuse. There is apparently a Police Family Protection Brigade but this lacks financial support and sufficient personnel to follow up and pursue unreported cases.[58]

Justice Stewart dismissed the applicant's challenge to the decision by way of judicial review, holding that

> when the decision is read as a whole, the tribunal member rejected the applicants' claim on the basis that, given the family's particular circumstances, state protection would be available to the family if they were to seek it. The tribunal member was particularly mindful of the difficult circumstance of the second named applicant and referred to the medical evidence before him. Nevertheless, he found that a consideration of those circumstances was not related to the claim of persecution and not within the jurisdiction of the tribunal.[59]

[55] ibid.

[56] Hathaway and Foster note that this approach generally only arises in relation to gender-based social groups and is often underpinned by a 'floodgates' concern: Hathaway and Foster, *The Law of Refugee Status* (n 1) 521.

[57] *LAA (Bolivia) v Refugee Appeals Tribunal* [2016] IEHC 12.

[58] ibid para 20.

[59] ibid para 17.

On the adequacy of state protection, Stewart J referred to the decision of Clarke J (as he then was) in *VI v Minister for Justice, Equality and Law Reform*[60] noting that state protection is not 'perfect protection'. Justice Stewart noted that the existence of formal legal measures is not in itself sufficient to demonstrate state protection, as enforcement of those laws is also required in order to demonstrate that the state is capable of providing protection. The court then stated at paragraph 20:

> According to the country of origin information before the decision-maker, domestic violence appeared to be endemic in Bolivia. The tribunal member then went on to assess whether the first named applicant's husband's connections were such that he could reasonably prevent her securing state protection. The tribunal found that his connections were not so influential so that state protection would not be forthcoming to the applicant. This amounts to an assessment of the adequacy of the state protection given the applicant's particular circumstances and therefore, I reject the applicants' contention that such an assessment was not performed. This assessment is within the jurisdiction of the tribunal and it is not open to this court on judicial review to supplant its own assessment for that of the decision-maker.

It is difficult to understand how a finding that state protection was available could be sustained in the face of country of origin information which established that domestic violence was 'pervasive' and that 70 per cent of Bolivian women suffer some form of abuse. In contrast to the decision of Faherty J in *SM*, Stewart J did not consider whether the adequacy of the state response was itself motivated by a Convention reason (ie gender). It is submitted that the decision of Faherty J in *SM* is more consistent with the international best practice guidelines, including the UNHCR 2002 Guidelines, and for that reason should be regarded as the more persuasive authority.

B. Gender-based Persecution

As noted above, Bhabha has suggested that 'the refugee par excellence was someone heroically seeking to assert his (typically male) individuality against an oppressive state'.[61] Furthermore, as Kelly notes, the Refugee Convention has 'largely failed to recognize the political nature of seemingly private acts of and harm to women'.[62] For example, rape is often viewed as a private matter even when committed by a government official or in a political context.

An example of this trend in the Irish context can be found in the case of *MM (Zimbabwe) v Refugee Appeals Tribunal*.[63] The applicant was a Zimbabwean national who claimed that she was a supporter of the Movement for Democratic Change (MDC) although she was not a member of the party. In, or around, April 2008, she attended a church meeting. ZANU-PF, the government party, wrongly believed that this was an MDC meeting and attacked it. The applicant and a number of other women were abducted and taken to a ZANU-PF camp where she was raped by four soldiers. She later contracted HIV which she attributed

[60] *VI v Minister for Justice, Equality and Law Reform* [2005] IEHC 150.
[61] Bhabha, 'Embodied Rights' (n 2) 8.
[62] Kelly, 'Gender-Related Persecution' (n 1) 628.
[63] *MM (Zimbabwe) v Refugee Appeals Tribunal* [2015] IEHC 325.

to this incident. She did not tell her husband about the rape and she could not support herself in Zimbabwe. She subsequently left Zimbabwe and after her arrival in the State in February 2008 she applied for asylum. The Refugee Applications Commissioner made a recommendation that the applicant's testimony fell short of what would be required in terms of credibility for her to be given the benefit of the doubt and therefore the applicant had failed to establish a well-founded fear of persecution in Zimbabwe based on a Convention ground. She appealed against this recommendation. Solicitors on behalf of the applicant submitted substantial grounds of appeal and in particular substantial country of origin information. The Tribunal subsequently affirmed the recommendation of the Refugee Applications Commissioner and the applicant instituted judicial review proceedings challenging the decision.

The two main grounds of challenge concerned a failure to make a clear finding on the applicant's credibility in the light of the country of origin information, and whether the Tribunal Member's conclusion that the applicant's fear was purely subjective was unlawful. In particular, the applicant challenged the Tribunal Member's finding that the attack on the applicant was only 'random' to the extent that not everyone in the meeting was abducted and she had not been specifically targeted, but it was not random in the sense of being conducted purely for the sexual gratification of the soldiers but was motivated by their beliefs that the persons at the meeting were opposition supporters.

Justice Eagar quashed the decision of the Tribunal that the applicant had not established a Convention nexus because the rape was a random act, holding:

> Rape by four or five soldiers is an extraordinarily brutal event and one which undoubtedly would scar the applicant for many years. The word 'random' suggests having no definite aim or purpose. The attack on the applicant in this case had a purpose. It had the purpose of harassment and intimidation of MDC supporters following elections on 29th March 2008.[64]

The court referred to country of origin information which had been submitted to the Tribunal to the effect that state security forces had punished and intimidated opposition party members and their suspected supporters, including the 'widespread use of rape squads by President Robert Mugabe's supporters to intimidate political opponents'.[65] Justice Eagar granted an order of certiorari quashing the Tribunal decision (at paragraph 54):

> Having regard to the description by the second named respondent of the appalling gang rape by members of ZANU-PF soldiers on the applicant as random acts of sexual desire rather than any politically motivated actions which is clearly documented in the country of origin information.

The decision in *MM (Zimbabwe)* is significant for its rejection of the attempt to characterise sexual violence as a purely private or criminal matter which is not within the scope of a Convention claim. It demonstrates the importance of sourcing and submitting relevant country of origin information on the circumstances in the country of origin and in particular the use of sexual violence as a means of persecution, albeit within a narrow context of state-sponsored sexual violence combined with imputed political opinion.

[64] ibid para 51.
[65] ibid para 53.

V. Conclusion

It is clear from a review of the literature and the jurisprudence, both international and domestic, that the Refugee Convention is capable of accommodating gender-based asylum claims. However, as Kelly states, this requires 'a reconceptualization of the presentation of women's cases, including an examination of the political nature of seemingly private acts and the ways in which many states fail to accord protection to their female populations'.[66] In addition to the substantive hurdles to securing recognition as a refugee in a gender-based claim, it is undoubtedly the case that many procedural obstacles can also arise. Recurring issues include the challenge of establishing credibility, in particular in some cases how to prove persecution which has occurred largely in the private sphere; the impact of trauma and the possibility of delayed disclosure; the absence of relevant country of origin information which is seen by some decision-makers as evidence of a lack of persecution; and a tendency for women's claims to be presented as derivative of male partners/head of household.[67] Despite some progress being apparent in some recent decisions of the High Court, such as *SM* and *MM (Zimbabwe)*, other decisions, such as *LAA (Bolivia)*, demonstrate the ongoing challenges that exist in advancing a gender-based asylum claim in Irish law.

[66] Kelly, 'Gender-Related Persecution' (n 1) 642.

[67] Kelly, 'Gender-Related Persecution' (n 1) 629. It is worth noting here that Crawley cautions against homogenised concept of the female refugee as a passive victim of male oppression: H Crawley, 'Gender, Persecution and the Concept of Politics in the Asylum Determination Process' (2000) 9 *Forced Migration Review* 17.

15

Redressing Gendered Mistreatment

Magdalene Laundries, Symphysiotomy and Mother and Baby Homes

JAMES GALLEN

I. Introduction

Historical abuse in Ireland is a product of the claimed noble intentions of institutions and professions, ill-designed and poorly resourced practices, and atrocious harms done to those individuals whom the institutions claimed to serve. After the establishment of the Irish Free State in 1922, the State maintained, adapted and added to the 'inherited networks of social control', including Magdalene institutions, County Homes, Mother and Baby Homes, Industrial and Reformatory Schools, psychiatric hospitals and prisons.[1] In addition, strong religious influence in politics and the medical profession shaped the nature of hospitals, which in turn influenced choices of medical procedure and the nature of care in the institutions.[2] Among these wide-ranging forms of historical abuse, this chapter will examine the cases of the Magdalene Laundries, the medical procedure of symphysiotomy, and Mother and Baby Homes. These institutions and practices particularly demonstrate the gendered dimension and nature of historical abuse and the modern-day efforts at addressing a legacy of human rights violations arising from these contexts.

Section II will examine the gendered nature of historical abuse in Ireland, with emphasis on these institutions and practices, and argue that these institutions formed part of a broader nation-building project in early-twentieth century Ireland, which had particular concern for the production of a narrow morality and role for women in Ireland as primarily mothers and the bearers of children. Section III will consider the nature and conditions under which these historical issues began to be investigated and redressed in modern Ireland. It will argue that, while these institutions and gendered harms have been addressed as part of a broader examination of Ireland's historical abuse, similarly to other

[1] E O'Sullivan and I O'Donnell, *Coercive Confinement in Post-Independence Ireland* (Manchester, Manchester University Press, 2012) 258.

[2] L Earner-Byrne, 'Moral Prescription: The Irish Medical Profession, the Roman Catholic Church and the Prohibition of Birth Control in Twentieth-Century Ireland' in C Cox and M Luddy (eds), *Cultures of Care in Irish Medical History, 1750–1970* (New York, Palgrave Macmillan 2010) 207–28.

consolidated democracies, there has been a gendered dimension in the manner in which harm against women and girls has been prioritised in the sequencing of investigation and redress. Sections IV, V and VI will evaluate the investigations and redress schemes to date regarding Magdalene Laundries, symphysiotomy and Mother and Baby Homes, and argue that a piecemeal approach that seeks to minimise the extent of the legal recognition of wrongdoing is consistent across these areas. Finally, the chapter will conclude by arguing that several shared structural challenges face those seeking to effectively redress the gendered nature of the harm and failures of redress strategies to date.

II. Elements of Irish Historical Abuse against Women

In Ireland, after the establishment of the Irish Free State in 1922, Church and State authorities engaged in a process of nation-building:

> [A]t the core of the relationship between Church and State was the ideological and spiritual construct of an imagined nation, that is, a nation of Irish Catholic virtues without the unnatural sexual vices that were seen by Free State ideologues, lay and clerical, as corrupting the rest of the world.[3]

This process of nation-building enabled the continued use of institutions that predated the Free State and accelerated the influence of the Catholic Church and Catholic morality. Máiréad Enright writes that 'in the post-colonial state, Catholicism became the defining characteristic of Irishness, understood in opposition to Englishness'.[4] Three manifestations of this nation-building process were Magdalene Laundries, Mother and Baby Homes, and the use of symphysiotomy (a surgical procedure).

The earliest Magdalene Laundries were established in the eighteenth century, throughout Europe, North America and Australia,[5] and operated in Ireland between 1795 and 1996. At an absolute minimum, approximately 14,607 women are known to have been detained in a Magdalene Laundry from the foundation of the Irish State in 1922 until the closure of the last Laundry in 1996, though victim-survivor groups suggest these figures are underestimated.[6] No new Magdalene Laundries were established after the foundation of the Irish State in 1922, but reliance on Church-run institutions was affirmed and fortified, continuing the 'civilising' mission of the Church begun under British rule of Ireland.[7]

[3] A Keating, 'Church, State, and Sexual Crime against Children in Ireland after 1922' (2004–2006) 5(7) *Radharc* 155, 157–58.

[4] M Enright, '"Involuntary Patriotism": Judgment, Women and the National Identity on the Island of Ireland' in M Enright, J McCandless and A O'Donoghue (eds), *Northern/Irish Feminist Judgments: Judges' Troubles and the Gendered Politics of Identity* (Oxford, Bloomsbury, 2017) 27–49, 31.

[5] 'Report of the Inter-Departmental Committee to Establish the Facts of State Involvement with the Magdalen Laundries' ('The McAleese Report') (Dublin, Department of Justice and Equality, 2013) ch 3, 69; J Franklin, 'Convent Slave Laundries? Magdalen Asylums in Australia' (2013) 34 *Journal of the Australian Catholic Historical Society* 70.

[6] Justice for Magdalenes, 'State Involvement in the Magdalene Laundries: JFM's Principal Submissions to the Inter-Departmental Committee to Establish the Facts of State Involvement with the Magdalene Laundries (February 2013) www.magdalenelaundries.com/State_Involvement_in_the_Magdalene_Laundries_public.pdf.

[7] T Inglis, *Moral Monopoly: The Rise and Fall of the Catholic Church in Modern Ireland* (Dublin, UCD Press, 1998) 140, 147–48.

Gender is a defining feature in the history of Magdalene Laundries and there are allegations of a variety of forms of gendered abuse.[8] The claimed purposes of the Laundries was to house and reform 'fallen women': those involved in prostitution, or (alleged to be) involved in extra-marital sexual activity, including unmarried mothers. James Smith suggests that the Magdalene system facilitated the creation of the post-colonial Irish State with a separate, Catholic identity, untainted by ideas of prostitution, single motherhood or sexual violence.[9]

Symphysiotomy is a surgical procedure designed to enlarge a woman's pelvis during childbirth by partially cutting the fibres which join the pubic bones at the front of the pelvis. While symphysiotomy was introduced in the late-eighteenth century, interest in the procedure revived in some Irish hospitals in the early-twentieth century until the 1960s and 1970s as an alternative to Caesarean section, which was viewed as dangerous and restricting the possibility of future pregnancies.[10] The State-commissioned Walsh Report concludes that approximately 1,500 symphysiotomies were carried out on women unknowingly and without consent between the late 1940s and early 1960s.[11] The revived use of symphysiotomy arose from a confluence of legal and religious gendered restrictions on women's bodily autonomy, with contraception illegal during this period, the Walsh Report concluded that 'the lack of options to control fertility was one of the key reasons for the return to symphysiotomy in mid-twentieth century Ireland'.[12] Although symphysiotomy may be useful in some situations, it carries a high risk of health problems for the mother and is now generally only recommended where there is no safe alternative.

In Ireland, unmarried mothers and their children were also considered as an explicitly gendered social problem from the 1920s,[13] and Mother and Baby Homes were established against this background. Maria Luddy articulates the perceived challenge posed by unmarried mothers and their children:

> Representing possible immorality, a drain on public finances and someone in need not only of rescue, but also of institutionalisation, the unmarried mother had become, by the foundation of the Irish Free State in 1922, a symbol of unacceptable sexual activity and a problem that had the potential to blight the reputation not only of the family but of the nation.[14]

O'Sullivan and Raftery also note that 'the language of criminality was deliberately invoked' in discussions of unmarried mothers 'highlighting the perception of such women as "criminal"'.[15] Diarmaid Ferriter describes the institutional solution to this perceived problem:

> The solution to the problem of illegitimate births was believed to lie in the establishment of antenatal homes for expectant unmarried mothers and institutions where the mother and children 'might be maintained together for at least the first year of the child's life' (the idea being that

[8] Justice for Magdalenes, 'Submission to the United Nations Committee Against Torture 46th Session' (May 2011) www.magdalenelaundries.com/jfm_comm_on_torture_210411.pdf.

[9] J Smith, *Ireland's Magdalen Laundries and the Nation's Architecture of Containment* (Indiana, University of Notre Dame Press, 2007).

[10] M O'Connor, *Bodily Harm: Symphysiotomy and Pubiotomy in Ireland, 1944–92* (Dublin, Evertype, 2001) 3; *Farrell v Ryan* [2015] IEHC 275 para 7.3.

[11] O Walsh, *Report on Symphysiotomy 1944–1984* (Dublin, Department of Health, 2012) 4.

[12] ibid 21.

[13] P Garrett, 'Unmarried Mothers in the Republic of Ireland' (2016) 16 *Journal of Social Work* 708.

[14] M Luddy, 'Unmarried Mothers in Ireland, 1880–1973' (2011) 20 *Women's History Review* 109, 110; M Luddy, 'Moral Rescue and Unmarried Mothers in Ireland in the 1920s' (2001) 30 *Women's Studies* 797.

[15] M Raftery and E O'Sullivan, *Suffer the Little Children: The Inside Story of Ireland's Industrial Schools* (Dublin, New Island, 1999) 73.

> the child could then be fostered). It was also believed that such homes were necessary 'where by appropriate training and example, self-respect is restored', preventing the women from staying in county homes at the expense of the ratepayers, or 'drifting into a life of degradation.' In the summer of 1922, proposals that unmarried mothers go to institutions other than workhouses (now referred to as county homes) were raised by the religious orders, the main concern being, it seems, that at that time such women were 'not segregated' from more 'hardened sinners'. The state's acceptance of such proposals laid the foundation for the infrastructure of religious order-run Mother and Baby Homes that operated from 1922 until the 1970s.[16]

Approximately 23,000 children were born into nine Mother and Baby Homes between 1922 and 1991.[17] Similar institutions, County Homes, operated until the 1960s and were funded and managed by the State, with some additional assistance from female religious congregations.[18] In 1966, there were 47 such homes.[19] Finally, there were around 300 private maternity homes in total registered under the 1934 Registration of Maternity Homes Act. Women in these homes were strongly encouraged to give up their children based on 'the firm conviction that unmarried mothers were fundamentally unfit to have custody of their own children'.[20] Mother and Baby Homes functioned as a 'form of internal exile' for many women.[21]

These institutions and practices contribute to a dominant interest of Church and State authorities with the management of perceived immorality and vice, especially for women, and the construction of a normative Irishwoman as a wife capable of bearing and rearing a large family of children in the context of marriage. The operation of these institutions and practices began to cease in the 1970s, although as noted the last Magdalene Laundry did not close until 1996. In this period, the tireless and lengthy work of activists changed Ireland, through the use of litigation and political activism, opening new if limited opportunities for women to control their bodies and choices beyond narrow nationalistic constructions of womanhood and vice, such as the eventual decriminalisation of contraception.[22] However, it is not until recent decades that Ireland has begun to investigate and redress its historical marginalisation, discrimination and harm against women.

III. From Crises to Process: The Dynamics of Investigating Historical Abuse

In recent decades, Ireland has begun to reckon with its past legacy of wrongdoing since the foundation of the State. Anne-Marie McAlinden identified three distinct periods of inquiries, some contemporary to events and some investigating historical abuses.[23]

[16] D Ferriter, *Occasions of Sin: Sex and Society in Modern Ireland* (London, Profile Books, 2009) 155.

[17] 'Report of the Inter-Departmental Group on Mother and Baby Homes' (Department of Children and Youth Affairs, 2014) 14 www.dcya.gov.ie/documents/publications/20140716InterdepartReportMothBabyHomes.pdf.

[18] ibid.

[19] Dáil Debate, 17 February 1966, Vol 266, No 12, 'Response to Parliamentary Question'.

[20] M Maguire, 'Foreign Adoptions and the Evolution of Irish Adoption Policy 1945–52' (2002) 36 *Journal of Social History* 387, 389.

[21] F O'Toole, 'Dark Elements of Our Past are Also Forces in our Present' *The Irish Times* (Dublin, 10 June 2014).

[22] Enright, 'Involuntary Patriotism' (n 4).

[23] AM McAlinden, 'An Inconvenient Truth: Barriers to Truth Recovery in the Aftermath of Institutional Child Abuse in Ireland' (2012) 33 *Legal Studies* 5.

From the 1930s to the 1970s, the focus was on the lack of basic care within institutional environments;[24] from the 1970s to the 1990s attention turned to abuse within the family and the failure of child protection services;[25] and from the late 1990s, four commissions of inquiry have examined child sexual abuse in diocesan and residential settings and the response of Church and State authorities,[26] with further investigations into State involvement in the Magdalene Laundries, the practice of symphysiotomy, and an ongoing Commission of Inquiry into the practices of Mother and Baby Homes and a representative sample of County Homes.

The starting point for investigating or redressing historical abuse in Ireland has tended to be denial of responsibility for wrongdoing from both State and private actors, including Church authorities.[27] The Irish Government's original position was that the State had no responsibility for, nor played any historical role in, the Magdalene Laundries.[28] In the context of Mother and Baby Homes, there were several attempts in the national media to deny the veracity of the historical records gathered by Catherine Corless regarding the extent and circumstances of deaths in the Mother and Baby Home in Tuam, Co Galway.[29] In the context of symphysiotomy, the Irish State has rejected the recommendations of the United Nations Human Rights Committee, concluding that obstetricians at the time were not perpetrators who should now be punished, and noted that Irish and international studies indicate that symphysiotomy is not a banned procedure but continues to have a place in obstetrics in certain limited circumstances.[30]

In Ireland, high-profile media reports, literature and memoirs, and legal cases of child sexual abuse across the Irish Church initially brought the broader issue of historical abuse into Irish public and political consciousness.[31] Subsequent inquiries into both residential institutions and diocesan child sexual abuse created the possibility to investigate Ireland's

[24] 'Report of the Commission of Inquiry into the Reformatory and Industrial School System, 1934' ('The Cussen Report') (Dublin, Department of Education, Stationery Office, 1936); 'Reformatory and Industrial Schools System Report' ('The Kennedy Report') (Dublin, Department of Health, Stationery Office, 1970).

[25] 'Report of the Kilkenny Incest Investigation' (Dublin, South Eastern Health Board, Stationery Office, 1993); 'Report of the Inquiry into the West of Ireland Farmer Case' (Manorhamilton, North Western Health Board, 1998).

[26] FD Murphy, H Buckley and L Joyce, 'Ferns Report' (Dublin, Department of Health and Children, Stationery Office, 2005); 'Report by Commission of Investigation into the Handling by Church and State Authorities of Allegations and Suspicions of Child Abuse Against Clerics of the Catholic Archdiocese of Dublin ('The Murphy Report') (Dublin, Department of Justice, Equality and Law Reform, Stationery Office, 2009); 'The Commission to Inquire into Child Abuse Report' ('The Ryan Report') (Dublin, Department of Children and Youth Affairs, Stationery Office, 2009); Commission of Investigation, 'Report into the Catholic Diocese of Cloyne' ('The Cloyne Report') (Dublin, Department of Justice and Law Reform, Stationery Office, 2011).

[27] S Cohen, 'State Crimes of Previous Regimes: Knowledge, Accountability and the Policing of the Past' (1995) 20 *Law and Social Inquiry* 7, 12–22.

[28] 'O'Keeffe Criticised for Referring to Magdalen Women as "Employees"' The Irish Times (Dublin, 19 September 2009); Irish Human Rights Commission, 'Assessment of the Human Rights Issues Arising in Relation to the "Magdalen Laundries"' (November 2010) para 8.

[29] 'Rush to Moralise over Tuam has Run Ahead of the Facts' *The Irish Times* (Dublin, 9 March 2017); 'John Waters Attacks Media "Hoax" over Tuam Scandal' *The Irish Times* (Dublin, 12 November 2017); Interview, 'Tuam and Ireland's Shame: Unedited Interview with Historian Diarmaid Ferriter' *YouTube* (27 June 2014) www.youtube.com/watch?v=fpMLB1icn0w.

[30] United Nations Human Rights Committee, 'Concluding Observations on the Fourth Periodic Report of Ireland Addendum: Information Received from Ireland on Follow-up to the Concluding Observations (CCPR /C/IRL/CO/4/Add.1, August 2014) para 23.

[31] 'How the Story of Abuse Emerged' *The Irish Times* (Dublin, 26 November 2009); M Flynn, *Nothing to Say: A Novel* (Dublin, Ward River Press, 1983); P Doyle, *The God Squad* (London, Corgi, 1988); *States of Fear* (RTÉ, April–May 1999); *Prime Time: Cardinal Secrets* (RTÉ, October 2002); Suing the Pope (BBC, March 2002).

historical abuse comprehensively. However, such early investigations had gendered consequences. While child sexual abuse in residential schools affected both men and women, several forms of institutional abuse and practice were specific to women and girls. As a result of investigations into historical institutional and child sexual abuse by religious actors especially, the dominant narrative largely concerned boys abused by priests and other religious figures in institutional settings and initially minimised the extent to which (a) familial sexual abuse of both boys and girls, and (b) historical non-sexual abuse of women, such as forced labour, detention or medical procedures, was addressed by State inquiries. Subsequent and separate efforts were required from victim-survivors and civil society to prompt the State to provide further forms of inquiry and redress for those who had survived Magdalene Laundries, Mother and Baby Homes, and the surgical procedure symphysiotomy – all of which primarily affected women and girls. These dynamics suggest that emergent social forces and the diffusion of norms regarding disclosure of abuse can create new forms of exclusion or minimisation of harm that must be consciously counteracted.

This fragmentation of investigating and redressing historical abuse is not cost-neutral from a victim-survivor perspective. It is now 19 years since the initial efforts of the State to investigate institutional child sex abuse were commenced through the Commission to Inquire into Child Abuse, representing a significant period of time for those who have been affected by institutions not initially investigated and redressed, or those who suffered harm through multiple forms of institutionalisation, such as in an Industrial School and a Mother and Baby Home. Relatedly, each subsequent inquiry and redress mechanism has also been cheaper than the last, suggesting an incentive for the State towards the minimisation of redress of historical abuse over time. The Commission of Investigation into Child Abuse cost approximately €86 million. The Residential Institutions Redress Board (RIRB) has cost the State in excess of €1 billion, while Church institutions have paid a minority of the bill for compensation to victims of abuse in residential schools, with recent figures suggesting a payment of a mere 13 per cent of the total bill.[32] In the context of symphysiotomy, part of the mandate given to Judge Yvonne Murphy for her 2014 report was to 'assess the merits and costs to the State of proceeding with an ex gratia scheme relative to allowing the court process to proceed'.[33] The current Commission of Investigation into Mother and Baby Homes is estimated to cost at least €21.5 million.[34] The Magdalene Restorative Justice scheme has cost approximately €25.7 million.[35] In 2011, the Public Accounts Committee reviewed the experience of Tribunals of Inquiry and endorsed the recommendation for the terms of reference of inquiries to be tightly drawn and that new lines of inquiry should be limited.[36] In light of significant resources and time which have been spent investigating and redressing historical abuse, the State's incentive for establishing a narrowly defined and restrictive approach is clear.

[32] Comptroller and Auditor General, 'Special Report 96 – Cost of Child Abuse Inquiry and Redress' (December 2016).

[33] Y Murphy, 'Independent Review of Issues relating to Symphysiotomy' (Dublin, Department of Health, 2014) 1.

[34] 'Terms of Reference', Commission of Investigation (Mother and Baby Homes and Certain Related Matters) Order, SI no 57 of 2015.

[35] Office of the Ombudsman, 'Opportunity Lost: An Investigation by the Ombudsman into the Administration of the Magdalene Restorative Justice Scheme' (Dublin, Office of the Ombudsman, November 2017) 66.

[36] Public Accounts Committee, 'Third Interim Report on the Procurement of Legal Services by Public Bodies' (Dublin, Dáil Éireann, January 2011) 25.

In this context, the efforts of victim-survivors and advocacy organisations to pursue investigations, accountability and redress for historical abuse must be understood as involving all available mechanisms including legal, political, cultural and moral means. Symphysiotomy gained national prominence in 2010 following a television documentary,[37] but advocacy efforts were greatly enhanced by successful national litigation. In 2012, in *Kearney v McQuillan*, the Irish High Court and Supreme Court agreed that symphysiotomy was not a generally approved obstetric practice in 1969 and awarded Olivia Kearney €325,000 for being subjected to a post-Caesarean section symphysiotomy.[38] An Inquiry into Mother and Baby Homes resulted from investigative journalism and dedicated historical research by local individuals, which led to worldwide media coverage of revelations of the discovery of a significant quantity of human remains of children and infants at the site of the Mother and Baby Home in Tuam, Co Galway.[39] In addition to these national-level approaches, it has been necessary to invoke international law and international human rights mechanisms to disrupt the attitude and process of the Irish State to historical abuse and to shame the State into more effectively addressing a legacy of historical abuse. Magdalene Laundries were originally excluded from State-led national inquiries into child sexual abuse commenced in the late-twentieth century. In 2011, the United Nations Committee against Torture criticised Ireland's failure to address the Magdalene Laundries, in which girls and women were detained arbitrarily and forced to engage in unpaid labour.[40] Similar efforts have been pursued in the symphysiotomy context,[41] while the issue of Mother and Baby Homes has also been referenced by several United Nations human rights treaty bodies.[42]

This role for international law and international human rights shows their use and potential for shaming and scrutinising Ireland's record on ensuring and enhancing the equality and empowerment of women in its laws and policies. The national investigations and redress mechanisms for each of these instances of historical abuse – Magdalene Laundries, symphysiotomy and Mother and Baby Homes – will now be considered.

IV. Magdalene Laundries

In 2011, prompted by a submission by the advocacy group, Justice for Magdalenes, the United Nations Committee against Torture expressed grave concern at Ireland's failure to protect girls and women who were involuntarily confined between 1922 and 1996 in the Laundries, by failing to regulate and inspect their operations, where it was alleged that

[37] *Symphysiotomy – A Brutal Practice* (RTÉ, 18 February 2010) https://www.rte.ie/news/player/2010/0218/2704182-brutal-procedure-the-symphysiotomy-scandal/.

[38] *Kearney v McQuillan* [2012] IESC 43.

[39] D Barry, 'The Lost Children of Tuam' *New York Times* (New York, 28 October 2017).

[40] United Nations Committee Against Torture, 'Concluding Observations' (CAT/C/IRL/CO/1, June 2011).

[41] United Nations Human Rights Committee, 'Concluding Observations on the Fourth Periodic Report of Ireland' (CCPR/C/IRL/CO/4, August 2014); United Nations Committee Against Torture, 'Concluding Observations' (CAT /C/IRL/CO/2, August 2017) paras 27–28; United Nations Committee on the Elimination of Discrimination against Women, 'Concluding Observations on the Combined Sixth and Seventh Periodic Reports of Ireland' (CEDAW/C/IRL/CO/6-7, March 2017) paras 14–15.

[42] United Nations Human Rights Committee, 'Concluding Observations on the Fourth Periodic Report of Ireland. Addendum: Information received from Ireland on Follow-up to the Concluding Observations' (CCPR /C/IRL/CO/4/Add.1, August 2014) paras 1–3.

physical and emotional abuses and other ill-treatment were committed, amounting to breaches of the Convention.[43] The Committee also recommended that Ireland institute investigations into all allegations of torture and other cruel, inhuman or degrading treatment or punishment; prosecute and punish the perpetrators, and ensure that all victims obtain redress and have an enforceable right to compensation, including the means for as full a rehabilitation as possible.[44]

In response, Ireland appointed an Inter-Departmental Committee (IDC) to establish the facts of State involvement with the Magdalene Laundries. The McAleese Report of the IDC included that approximately 14,607 women were detained in a Magdalene Laundry from the foundation of the Irish State in 1922 until the closure of the last Laundry in 1996, although victim-survivor groups suggest these figures are underestimated.[45] The Report concluded that of the cases in which routes of entry to Magdalene Laundries are known, only 26.5 per cent were referrals made or facilitated by the State.[46] Based on these findings, An Taoiseach (Prime Minister) Enda Kenny offered an apology in the Oireachtas to the women who resided in the Magdalene Laundries. The Taoiseach described the Magdalene Laundries as 'the nation's shame' and accepted the State's direct involvement:

> Therefore, I, as Taoiseach, on behalf of the State, the government and our citizens deeply regret and apologise unreservedly to all those women for the hurt that was done to them, and for any stigma they suffered, as a result of the time they spent in a Magdalene Laundry.[47]

This apology, while welcomed by some victims-survivors, eschewed framing the harm experienced as a question of legal rights and responsibilities. The McAleese Report presented the testimony of victim-survivors about their experiences in the Laundries as 'stories', rather than as evidence, and, claiming limitations arising due to its mandate, did not issue recommendations regarding accountability, responsibility or criminality.[48] The Report minimised the representation of harm in the Laundries, drawing favourable comparisons to harm experienced in Residential and Industrial Schools and in diocesan settings.[49] Máiréad Enright critiques the Report's findings, suggesting it

> consists of disjointed quotations from anonymised women, selected apparently at random. The women are allowed scant quotations in which to share their stories. This is in contrast to, for instance, the long passages of quotation from identified benign male authority figures later in the chapter.[50]

Two oral history projects counter the minimisation of harm and the lived experience of survivors in the presentation of the McAleese Report.[51]

[43] United Nations Committee Against Torture, 'Concluding Observations' (CAT/C/IRL/CO/1, June 2011) para 21.
[44] ibid.
[45] Justice for Magdalenes, 'JFM's Principal Submissions' (n 6).
[46] The McAleese Report (n 5), 'Introduction' para 2.
[47] 'In Full: Enda Kenny's State Apology to the Magdalene Women' (*The Journal*, 19 February 2013) www.thejournal.ie/full-text-enda-kenny-magdalene-apology-801132-Feb2013/.
[48] The McAleese Report (n 5), ch 19.
[49] ibid 'Introduction' 18.
[50] M Enright, 'Critiquing the McAleese Report' (Human Rights in Ireland, 8 February 2013) www.humanrights.ie/economic-rights/critiquing-the-mcaleese-report/.
[51] K O'Donnell, S Pembroke and C McGettrick, 'Magdalene Institutions: Recording an Oral and Archival History' (Government of Ireland Collaborative Research Project, Irish Research Council, Waterford Memories, 2013) www.waterfordmemories.com/recordings.

The Laundries can be considered to be a regime that operated in a discriminatory and gendered system of detention entirely for women and girls who shared economic dependence, poverty and social exclusion. The Laundries enabled Irish society, not merely State institutions, to enforce compliance with a restrictive and religious social morality – and to isolate or deny those who failed to comply with its strictures. In the view of the Irish Human Rights and Equality Commission, the McAleese Report indicates that the Laundries fulfilled a function that was otherwise the obligation of the State, as a significantly cheaper alternative to State care.[52] In addition, the conduct and findings of the McAleese Committee risk exacerbating the discriminatory and gendered forms of harm experienced by victim-survivors of the Laundries. Claire McGettrick of Justice for Magdalenes, describes the manner in which the Committee interviewed survivors of the Laundries:

> Initially, the committee didn't even want to speak to women in person, but we fought for that. The women gave their testimony verbally and then we were given very little notice of a second meeting where we were to look at the format of the initial testimony. Instead, the women were brought in one by one for a meeting with the commission where they asked repeated questions. Their overall impression was that they were being checked to ensure that their memories were correct. The women came out of those meetings very quiet and subdued. None of them, none of us, had been expecting for them to be questioned like that.[53]

Based on the McAleese Report, Mr Justice Quirke recommended an ex gratia scheme for the benefit of the women concerned, based on the length of their documented service in the Laundries, including access to the full range of State-provided health services. His Report concluded that the women were entitled to recognition, through monetary payment, that they worked 'within (and, arguably to an extent for), the State for a period of time'.[54] The Report concluded that the Magdalene women should be paid a minimum sum of €10,000 up to a maximum of €100,000, to reflect 'work undertaken'. Further recommendations included a memorial, payment equivalent to the State pension, and assistance to Magdalene women. In June 2013, the Irish Government accepted Judge Quirke's recommendation for an ex gratia lump sum payment scheme for women affected. The Redress for Women Resident in Certain Institutions Act 2015 also provided that the State shall make available health services to participants in the scheme without charge, including general medical practitioners, counselling services and physiotherapy.

The Quirke Scheme fundamentally fails to frame the question of State legal responsibility for the harm experienced, including acknowledgement for unpaid wages; nor does it address the broader question of the mistreatment of women while detained in the Laundries. In contrast to Reformatory and Industrial Schools, the relevant religious institutes have refused to contribute to the compensation fund for victim-survivors, an estimated 600 of whom were still alive in March 2014.[55] The Scheme also failed to include all relevant

[52] Irish Human Rights and Equality Commission, *Follow-Up Report on State Involvement with Magdalene Laundries* (Dublin, IHREC, June 2013) para 60.

[53] C McGettrick, 'Interviews Lacked Transparency' (Clerical Whispers, 7 February 2013) www.clericalwhispers.blogspot.ie/2013/02/interviews-lacked-transparency-say.html.

[54] 'Report of Mr Justice Quirke on the establishment of an ex gratia Scheme and related matters for the benefit of those women who were admitted to and worked in the Magdalen Laundries' (Dublin, Department of Justice and Equality, May 2013) paras 2.04–07, 2.11.

[55] 'Magdalene Compensation Snub is "Rejection of Laundry Women"' (Irish Post, 2 August 2013) http://irishpost.co.uk/magdalene-compensation-snub-is-rejection-of-laundry-women/.

institutions associated with Magdalene Laundries, in particular An Grianán Training Centre, High Park, which formed part of St Mary's Refuge in High Park, Drumcondra, Dublin.[56] Regarding this and similar facilities, the Office of the Ombudsman concluded that 'the actions of the Department in this regard constitute maladministration being actions based on erroneous or incomplete information and an undesirable administrative practice'.[57] In *MKL and DC v Minister for Justice and Equality*, two applicants sought and were granted judicial review of the decision to exclude their entry into the ex gratia scheme.[58] In his judgment, White J concluded that the Department of Justice and Equality did not apply fair procedures due to its failure to exchange with the applicants, for their consideration and comment, any documentation that it was considering when dealing with their eligibility.[59]

V. Symphysiotomy

After years of pressure from victim-survivors and advocacy organisations related to symphysiotomy since 2001, the Irish Government commissioned Professor Oonagh Walsh to report on symphysiotomy rates against maternal mortality rates from 1940 to present; critically appraise international reviews of symphysiotomy and associated rates in comparable countries and Ireland; review any guidelines and protocols that applied on symphysiotomy; and provide an accurate picture regarding its use in Ireland.[60] In her 2012 Report, Professor Walsh agreed with estimates that 1,500 women were subjected to symphysiotomy during childbirth between 1944 and 1984.[61] The Report concluded that 'Irish obstetrical practice was heavily influenced by and constrained within a widely accepted religious framework. This influence was not merely ideological but also shaped legislation in order to ensure conformity to certain religious principles.'[62] The Report also noted inappropriate use of symphysiotomy in a number of cases, where it was performed after delivery.[63] After the release of a draft report, Walsh engaged in consultations with relevant affected individuals and groups.[64] This process sought to address concerns arising from the draft report and to dispel misperceptions and falsehoods that arose from inaccurate media reporting regarding its contents. The consultation process also revealed the discomfort of some victim-survivors/those affected with the 'confrontational nature of the coverage' regarding the issue.[65] The final Report recommended the continuation and extension of processes of apology and redress for those affected by symphysiotomy.

While these political processes were ongoing, attempts to litigate for medical negligence arising out of the symphysiotomy procedure continued. In *Kearney v McQuillan*,

[56] Office of the Ombudsman (n 35), 'Opportunity Lost' 24–25.
[57] ibid 31.
[58] *MKL and DC v Minister for Justice and Equality* [2017] IEHC 389.
[59] ibid para 38.
[60] Walsh, *Report on Symphysiotomy* (n 11) 9.
[61] ibid 4.
[62] ibid 17.
[63] ibid 72– 73.
[64] ibid 74.
[65] ibid 83.

the plaintiff alleged that as a result of a symphysiotomy, conducted after the delivery of a child by Caesarean section, she suffered serious and permanent personal injuries.[66] In the substantive High Court judgment, Ryan J concluded this was not a case of a doctor deviating from a well-settled practice, but rather a case of a doctor who pursued a policy that a minority adhered to but which enjoyed a certain respectability because of the status of the people who shared the opinion. Even if the practice had enjoyed more general approbation, the Court concluded, it was attended by obvious inherent defects, being wholly unnecessary and having significant morbidity and, on any basis, the operation had required an essential justifying circumstance of pelvic disproportion which was absent.[67] As a result, the symphysiotomy operation was wholly unjustified. The decision was upheld by the Supreme Court although damages were reduced from €450,000 to €325,000.[68] However, litigation for symphysiotomy has not always been successful. In *Farrell v Ryan*, the High Court concluded that the plaintiff had failed to establish that there was 'no justification whatsoever in any circumstances for the performance of a symphysiotomy on the plaintiff at the time it was performed', in circumstances where symphysiotomy was performed as an alternative to Caesarean section.[69]

In November 2013, Minister for Health James Reilly appointed Judge Yvonne Murphy to review all relevant literature on symphysiotomy, assess the priorities of survivors, and assess whether an ex gratia scheme would be cheaper for the State than allowing litigation to proceed. In 2014, Judge Murphy issued her Report, detailing her meeting of 34 survivors, 16 family members, and insurers, lawyers and representatives of the Congregation of the Medical Missionaries of Mary, and approximately 300 letters provided in correspondence. The Report considered existing literature and discussions of symphysiotomy and noted that 154 High Court proceedings had been initiated regarding symphysiotomy. It also noted the preferences of victim-survivor representative organisation Survivors of Symphysiotomy to enable closure. These preferences were for a public apology that symphysiotomy and pubiotomy were wrong, amounted to medical negligence and were done without consent, and a payment of €250,000 to €450,000, according to an individualised assessment of the pain, suffering and disruption to normal life experienced.[70]

The Report cautioned that assessing the level of damage attributed to and caused by symphysiotomy in litigation would be a difficult assessment, largely involving expert evidence. The Report frames the desirability of the ex gratia scheme as a quid pro quo:

> [I]n considering of removing the burden of these issues [of proving liability, of the age and infirmity of the litigants] it reasonable to consider that the appropriate level of any sums awarded in the scheme be less than the sun that might be awarded to a successful litigant in a High Court.[71]

It also recommends a bar to litigation for those who enter a scheme to benefit the State 'in not having to litigate a large number of cases and bear the burden of costs associated with the

[66] *Kearney v McQuillan* [2006] IEHC 186.
[67] *Kearney v McQuillan* [2012] IEHC 127 para 53–54.
[68] *Kearney v McQuillan* [2012] IESC 43.
[69] *Farrell v Ryan* [2015] IEHC 275, para 11.6.
[70] Murphy, 'Issues relating to Symphysiotomy' (n 33). A pubiotomy involves cutting the pubic bone rather than the joint, as in the case of a symphysiotomy.
[71] ibid 48.

defence of those actions'.[72] Judge Murphy calculated that redress through the courts would cost €95 million, whereas redress through an ex gratia scheme would cost €34 million. As a result, the Report recommended a reduced scale of payment from €50,000 to €150,000 and declined to recommend an apology from Government. Both the Medical Missionaries of Mary and the Institute of Obstetricians and Gynaecologists have issued apologies, but the State has not apologised for its role.

In November 2014, the 'Surgical Symphysiotomy Ex Gratia Payment Scheme' was published, adopting Judge Murphy's recommendations regarding payments, and was to be administered 'as expeditiously as possible' by Judge Maureen Harding Clark. Several features of the Scheme differ widely from international best practice on addressing allegations of historical harm. First, the Scheme offered an incredibly short period of time for individuals to apply: 20 working days. This approach is in stark contrast to the application periods in other Irish ex gratia schemes, such those regarding Magdalene Laundries or the Residential Institutions Redress Board.[73] Second, payment of any award under the Scheme was conditional upon the applicant waiving their claim to litigate regarding symphysiotomy, without access to substantive appeal or oversight. Third, the redress Scheme is ex gratia in nature, which means 'by favour' and without admission of responsibility. This approach fails to adopt international law and best practice standards in the provision of reparation, which require the State to acknowledge its role in, or failure to prevent, the violation of individual rights.[74]

In 2016, the Report of Judge Maureen Harding Clark on this Scheme was published and indicated the Judge sought to pursue a 'compassionate and generous' approach. The Scheme awarded €29.8 million to 399 successful applicants. However, the Report did not merely detail the Scheme's administration, but evaluated again the Irish practice of symphysiotomy and the women concerned.

First, the Report differed from other Irish investigations into historical harm by failing to document the testimony of women subjected to the procedure. Second, the Report suggested that the Scheme was primarily premised on the expectation that symphysiotomy caused serious and life-long disability.[75] While over 35 per cent of successful applicants suffered significant disability, the emphasis on life-long disability neglected to adequately consider the harm and lack of patient consent involved in the use of symphysiotomy. The Report also emphasised that 'the vast majority of applicants became pregnant within a year of the symphysiotomy' and led healthy lives thereafter, calling into question the extent of the harm endured.[76] Recovery from harm by an individual over the course of their lifetime should in no way diminish the importance of the State acknowledging the initial wrongdoing.

[72] ibid 51– 53.

[73] 'Terms of the Surgical Symphysiotomy Ex Gratia Payment Scheme' (Dublin, Department of Health, 2014).

[74] Office of the High Commissioner for Human Rights, Basic Principles and Guidelines on the Right to a Remedy and Reparation for Victims of Gross Violations of International Human Rights Law and Serious Violations of International Humanitarian Law Adopted and proclaimed by General Assembly resolution 60/147 of 16 December 2005.

[75] Judge Maureen Harding Clark, 'Report on the Surgical Symphysiotomy Ex Gratia Payment Scheme' (Dublin, Department of Health, 2016) 5.

[76] ibid 33.

Third, the Report is inconsistent in its evaluation of medical expertise. On the one hand, the Report acknowledges the difficulty for its own medical team in establishing the existence of scars or other markers consistent with symphysiotomy, especially after several decades.[77] On the other hand, the Report is critical of evidence provided by applicants' doctors for not detailing an applicant's medical history through the years as a result of symphysiotomy, even though GPs would have limited awareness or exposure to this rare procedure.[78]

Fourth, the Report concluded that 185 claims (one out of three applicants) were ineligible. The Report was critical of 'intense' publicity and activism leading to the establishment of the Scheme. Remarkably, the Report speculated broadly as to the reasons why applicants made their claims. It concluded that 'suggestible women' were influenced by the possibility of financial payment into the 'self-serving adoption and embracing of the experiences described by others'.[79] It criticised the 'lurid accounts' of applicants, suggested their belief in conspiracy theories, and bemoaned the similarity of applicants' submissions – without having regard to the influence of the short application time period. Criticism of unsuccessful applicants and guesswork as to their reasons for applying are remarkable and highly inappropriate conclusions. Máiréad Enright argues:

> The report's approach undermines human rights campaigners, group organising, and social justice lawyering in one fell swoop, perhaps forgetting that without the work of these organisations the redress scheme – however flawed – would not have been set up at all, and many women would not have been able to access it.[80]

VI. Mother and Baby Homes

In 2014, the Irish Government established an Inter-Departmental Group, set up in response to revelations and public controversy regarding conditions in Mother and Baby Homes, centring on the high rate of deaths at the Mother and Baby Home in Tuam, Co Galway. Catherine Corless sourced details from public records of 796 child deaths in this home from 1925 to 1961.[81] The group was tasked with informing the Government on any decisions on the scope, format and terms of reference of a commission of investigation. In its Report, the group noted:

> Any consideration of the treatment of unmarried mothers over the period is likely to identify gender discrimination as being to the fore, while also acknowledging the role played by social class with different settings and patterns of treatment for those in different economic circumstances.[82]

As a result of this Inter-Departmental Group, in 2015, a Commission of Investigation was established regarding Mother and Baby Homes and a representative sample of

[77] ibid 45.
[78] ibid 55.
[79] ibid 97.
[80] M Enright, 'Notes on Judge Harding Clark's Report on the Symphysiotomy Payment Scheme' (Human Rights in Ireland, 24 November 2016).
[81] 'Report of the Inter-Departmental Group on Mother and Baby Homes July' (Dublin, Department of Children and Youth Affairs, 2014).
[82] ibid 8.

County Homes.[83] The Commission has a mandate to establish the circumstances and arrangements for the entry and exit of single women and children to and from these institutions, including practices of adoption of children; to establish the living conditions and care arrangements experienced by residents; and to examine mortality among mothers and children residing in these institutions, post-mortem practices, and compliance with relevant contemporary regulatory and ethical standards of systemic vaccine trials found by the Commission to have been conducted on children resident in one or more of these institutions.[84]

The Commission of Investigation has the power to hold public hearings, but at the time of writing has declined to do so. Instead its work is in private and operates via an Investigation Committee and a Confidential Committee. The Confidential Committee is intended to provide a forum for persons who were formerly resident in the homes listed, or who worked in these institutions, during the relevant period to provide accounts of their experience in these institutions in writing or orally, as informally as is possible in the circumstances.[85] In contrast, evidence given before the main Investigation Committee can be subject to cross-examination and refutation where it is the view of the Commission that such a process is required.[86] The Commission states it is 'obliged to furnish a summary of relevant evidence to those persons or bodies who may in turn seek an opportunity to cross examine you on the matters raised'.[87]

The most significant action of the Commission to date was its announcement regarding the Mother and Baby Home in Tuam, Co Galway. Technical examinations of the site began in 2015, with test excavations in 2016 and 2017, which revealed a long structure divided into 20 chambers. Significant quantities of human remains have been discovered in at least 17 of the 20 underground chambers which were examined. A small number of remains were recovered for the purpose of analysis and indicated individuals with age-at-death ranges from approximately 35 foetal weeks to 2–3 years dating from 1925 to 1961. The Commission has asked that the relevant State authorities, including the coroner, take responsibility for the appropriate treatment of the remains.[88] A decision on how to proceed with the remains at Tuam is expected in 2018 on foot of an expert technical group report and consultation with relevant stakeholders.

On 10 March 2017, the Minister for Children and Youth Affairs Katherine Zappone announced that she hoped to initiate a 'transitional justice' approach to meet the needs of survivors of Mother and Baby Homes, with a view to 'find out and record the truth, ensure accountability, make reparation, undertake institutional reform, and achieve reconciliation'.[89] At the time of writing, the transitional justice approach undertaken by the Department has resulted in national consultations with those affected by the issue of

[83] Commission of Investigation (Mother and Baby Homes and Certain Related Matters) Order 2015, SI no 57 of 2015.

[84] ibid s 1.

[85] ibid s 7(3).

[86] Commission of Investigation Act 2004, s 12.

[87] Clann Project, 'FAQs on Commission of Investigation' www.clannproject.org/faqs/faqs-on-the-commission-of-investigation/.

[88] 'Notice' (3 March 2017) www.mbhcoi.ie/MBH.nsf/page/Latest%20News-en.

[89] E Loughlin, 'Katherine Zappone: "We Will Find the Truth and Achieve Reconciliation"' *Irish Examiner* (Cork, 10 March 2017).

Mother and Baby Homes, monthly updates from the Department of Children and Youth Affairs as to developments on the issue, as well as the agreement from the Irish Government to invite the United Nations Special Rapporteur on the Promotion of Truth, Justice, Reparation and Guarantees of Non-recurrence, Pablo de Greiff, to engage in a country visit and examination of Ireland.

To date, the Commission of Investigation has issued three interim reports. In July 2016, following receipt of the Commission's 'First Interim Report', the Government agreed to the Commission's request to extend the timeframe for its Confidential Committee and social history reports.[90] In December 2017, on foot of receipt of the 'Third Interim Report', the Commission of Investigation and Department of Children confirmed the extension of the Commission's mandate for a further year with its final report due in February 2019.[91]

The 'Second Interim Report' addresses three substantive issues: the exclusion of some children's homes from the Residential Institutions Redress Board Scheme, the exclusion of some Mother and Baby Homes from the Commission's remit, and the false registration of births. The Report notes that children resident in Mother and Baby Homes without their mothers were in the same position as children who were resident in the Industrial Schools and orphanages which were covered by the RIRB and should logically be eligible to apply for redress in the same way and under the same conditions.[92] In April 2017, the Government rejected the extension of the RIRB to former residents of Mother and Baby Homes, in the absence of findings from the Commission regarding abuse and neglect.[93] It is possible such findings may form part of the final report of the Commission. It remains to be seen what findings the Commission will reach and what recommendations it makes. It hopes that increased engagement with civil society and victim-survivors will result in a more inclusive and legitimate process and outcome.

VII. Conclusion

Investigating and redressing historical abuse across Magdalene Laundries, symphysiotomy and Mother and Baby Homes share several challenges. None of the approaches adopted by the State prioritise a victim-survivor centred perspective, with limited public engagement with the views and preferences of those who experienced these institutions and practices. There was limited consultation in the design and practice of investigations. The adoption of an explicitly transitional justice approach to the Mother and Baby Home inquiry prompted subsequent consultations during the operation of the Commission, but could usefully be augmented by recognising the need for an overall coherent approach to historical abuse in Ireland from Government across all institutions and contexts.

[90] Mother and Baby Homes Commission of Investigation, 'First Interim Report' (July 2016) www.dcya.gov.ie/documents/mother_and_baby_homes/20160727MotherandBabyHomesInterimReportJuly2016.pdf; 'Second Interim Report' (September 2016) www.mbhcoi.ie/MBH.nsf/page/LPRN-ALCFND1238712-en/$File/MBHCOI%202nd%20Interim%20Report.pdf.

[91] Mother and Baby Homes Commission of Investigation, 'Third Interim Report' (September 2017) www.mbhcoi.ie/MBH.nsf/page/LPRN-ATSF5N1111226-en/$File/MBHThirdInterimReport.pdf.

[92] Mother and Baby Homes Commission of Investigation, 'Second Interim Report' (September 2016) para 4.4.

[93] 'Govt Rejects Immediate Redress for Mother and Baby Home Children' (RTÉ, 11 April 2017) www.rte.ie/news/ireland/2017/0411/866974-mother-and-baby-homes-report/.

The need for a coherent approach is acknowledged in international human rights treaty bodies. In 2017, the United Nations Committee for the Elimination of Discrimination against Women (CEDAW) concluded that the historical abuses in relation to the Magdalene Laundries, the Mother and Baby Homes, and the practice of symphysiotomy, gave rise to serious violations that have a continuing effect on the rights of victims-survivors of those violations.[94] The Committee urged Ireland to conduct prompt, independent and thorough investigations, in line with international human rights standards, into all allegations of abuse in Magdalene Laundries, children's institutions and Mother and Baby Homes, and allegations of symphysiotomy in order to prosecute and punish the perpetrators of those involved in violations of women's rights, and ensure that all victims-survivors of such abuse obtain an effective remedy, including appropriate compensation, official apologies, restitution, satisfaction and rehabilitative services.[95]

However, those seeking a more victim-survivor centred approach to investigating historical abuse face several challenges. First, the statute of limitations regime in Ireland is highly restrictive when compared to other common law jurisdictions, with the result that relevant individuals may not be able to pursue any litigation strategy.[96] The limitation regime in Ireland enables only a limited subset of victims and survivors of historical abuse to recover, where unconscionable conduct on the part of the defendant can be shown under the 1957 Statute of Limitations, where there was no reasonable prospect of discovering the injury arising from the historical abuse under the Statute of Limitations (Amendment) Act 1991, or where victims suffer a recognised psychiatric disability, which prevents them from initiating litigation where they suffer from sexual abuse, but not other forms of historical abuse, under the Statute of Limitations (Amendment) Act 2000.

Second, considerable risks of costs attach to those attempting to challenge Ireland's approach to historical abuse through the courts. Ireland does not have an effective mechanism for multi-party litigation, despite recommendations in 2005 from the Law Reform Commission to introduce a new procedure for multi-party action.[97] Multi-party action could enable a range of litigants, including victim-survivors, to overcome barriers with funding and standing that they may face taking actions individually.[98] Irish policy-makers may be relying on unquantified assertions that litigation floodgates would open. However, in the case of historical abuse, these arguments seem especially spurious. Existing reports and investigations identify, albeit imperfectly, the number of individuals concerned and even if interpreted liberally or with a foreseeable increase, would not cause disproportionate or catastrophic damage to the exchequer.

Third, what may be unique to Ireland is the limited nature and impact of the national conversation and debate that followed historical abuse inquiries.[99] Part of this may be

[94] United Nations Committee on the Elimination of Discrimination Against Women, 'Concluding Observations on the Combined Sixth and Seventh Periodic Reports of Ireland' (CEDAW/C/IRL/CO/6-7, March 2017) para 15.

[95] ibid.

[96] J Gallen, 'Historical Abuse and the Statute of Limitations' (2018) *Statute Law Review* (forthcoming).

[97] Law Reform Commission, 'Report on Multi-Party Litigation' (LRC-76-2005) (Dublin, Law Reform Commission, 2005).

[98] J Blennerhasset, *A Comparative Examination of Multi-Party Actions: The Case of Environmental Mass Harm* (Oxford, Hart, 2016) 256; Order 6, Rule 10, Circuit Court Rules 2001.

[99] Amnesty International, 'In Plain Sight: Responding to the Ferns, Ryan, Murphy and Cloyne Reports' (Dublin, Amnesty International Ireland, 2011) 20.

explained by the limited public and academic access to the archives of investigations into historical abuse. In Ireland, the records of investigation into the Magdalene Laundries have not been made public. Archives are vital to the successful operation and outcome of all transitional justice processes. They are crucial to the exercise of individual rights, such as the right to know the truth about the circumstances in which violations took place and, in the event of death or disappearance, about the victims' fate.[100] In 2015, the United Nations developed a set of general recommendations for truth commissions and archives as a standard for international best practice.[101] In particular, the recommendations state that archives should be made publicly accessible to the maximum extent possible, subject to assurance of confidentiality provided to victim-survivors and other witnesses. Public policy grounds for privacy should only be used when in full compliance with international human rights law.[102] The recommendations suggest the creation of general access rules

> such as what was previously public should remain public; victims, families, investigative and prosecutorial authorities, as well as legal defence teams, should have unhindered access to information on their specific case; there should be a presumption of public access to all State information with only limited exceptions; a procedure to make effective the right of access should be established; whatever access rules are determined for various categories of potential users (for example, victims, legal representatives, journalists, academics, and members of the general public) should apply to all members of the given category without discrimination.[103]

The risk is that in responding to historical abuse, Irish redress mechanisms treat victim-survivors paternalistically – as vulnerable objects to whom we, the non-vulnerable, are granting a remedy from our benevolence – only as far as suits us, and not as a matter of legal right or remedy. It remains to be seen whether the gendered mistreatment of women and girls will ever be effectively investigated and redressed.

[100] Updated Set of Principles for the Protection and Promotion of Human Rights through Action to Combat Impunity (E/CN.4/2005/102/Add.1, February 2005) principles 3–4.

[101] P De Greiff, 'Report of the Special Rapporteur on the Promotion of Truth, Justice, Reparation and Guarantees of Non-recurrence' (United Nations General Assembly, A/HRC/30/42, September 2015).

[102] ibid.

[103] ibid.

16

Gender and Politics

FIONA BUCKLEY AND YVONNE GALLIGAN

I. Introduction

Speaking at an Oireachtas committee in 2009 which examined women's participation in Irish politics, former minister Liz O'Donnell observed that 'many of the decisions taken at the highest levels in Ireland are made without women and therefore lack democratic credibility'.[1] In these few words, the issue and problem of women's political under-representation in Irish politics was crystallised. In the 90-year period between the Dáil's first sitting in January 1919 and Liz O'Donnell's comments, the proportion of women in Irish politics had never exceeded 14 per cent. Viewing it another way, the Dáil had always been at least 86 per cent men, a proportion that facilitated male dominance of political discourse, with just the minimum of female influence and perspective on policy-making. In an effort to redress this gender imbalance, legislative gender quotas were adopted as part of the Electoral (Amendment) (Political Funding) Act in 2012. This chapter will outline why legal gender quotas were adopted in Ireland. To do so, it reflects upon the status of women in Irish politics, paying particular attention to the role of political parties as gatekeepers. The decision to adopt legal gender quotas will be explored, as will the debates, challenges and controversies which greeted their implementation. Through an examination of the 2016 general election, the first at which legislative gender quotas applied, the impact of the quota on candidate selection processes and the election of women will be assessed. The chapter concludes that the gender quota law has had a positive impact on redressing the historical gender imbalance in Irish politics but a continual focus on women's political representation is required in order to ensure that gender parity is achieved.

II. Gender and Politics

In framing her chapter on gender and the legislative process in Alpha Connelly's *Gender and the Law in Ireland* in 1993,[2] Yvonne Galligan drew from EE Schattsneider's

[1] Sub-Committee on Women's Participation in Politics of the Joint Committee on Justice, Equality, Defence and Women's Rights, Houses of the Oireachtas 24 June 2009, reported in app D Transcripts of Public Hearings, 541, in Second Report of the Joint Committee on Justice, Equality, Defence and Women's Rights, *Women's Participation in Politics* ('Bacik Report') 2009.

[2] A Connelly (ed), *Gender and the Law in Ireland* (Cork, Oak Tree Press, 1993).

analogy of sport to describe politics and access, stating that 'whoever decides what the game is about also decides who can get into the game'.[3] This quote remains as relevant today, possibly even more so, as we reflect upon the reasons why legislative gender quotas were adopted in Ireland to facilitate women's entry into the political arena. Politics and political institutions in Ireland, as elsewhere, are shaped by gender power arrangements whereby gender is an attribute of power and in certain settings, notably politics, masculinity is dominant and privileged.[4] Because men established political institutions, masculinist frames of preference and 'domination' are embedded in, and associated with politics.[5] As political institutions remain 'sticky' to their masculinist foundations,[6] men, who are more aligned to masculinity than women (though not always congruently so), have gender power as a permeating resource to maintain their predominance.[7]

Masculinity is generally accepted to predominate in political institutions, shaping its institutional processes and practices.[8] Political institutions become 'gender captured' resulting from the numerical dominance of men in positions of power and as a result become 'gender biased' towards masculine preferences.[9] Drawing from March and Olsen,[10] Duerst-Lahti argues that institutions 'create formal and informal structures, rules, norms, and practices in response to the "preferences" of their founders and most influential incumbents throughout their histories'.[11] These rules, norms and practices shape the terms of recruitment and access into politics. But in European democracies such as Ireland, these terms privilege white, middle-class men. Anyone who differs from this norm are considered an 'other' and are contrasted against the 'native' male inhabitants. It is within this process of contrast that the masculinised basis and biases of political candidate recruitment are exposed. Within this male-gendered model of candidate recruitment, it is assumed that all have equal access to resources such as time, money, personal ambition and confidence. However, this is not the case. Gendered barriers such as care responsibilities, gender pay gaps and gender gaps in political ambition constrain women in their efforts to access political office. Coupled with this, masculinist frames of reference and preference in politics renders female candidacy

[3] EE Schattsneider, cited in Y Galligan, 'The Legislative Process' in Connelly (ed), *Gender and the Law in Ireland* (Cork, Oak Tree Press, 1993) 28.

[4] G Duerst-Lahti and RM Kelly (eds), *Gender Power, Leadership and Governance* (Ann Arbor, University of Michigan Press, 1995).

[5] G Duerst-Lahti, 'Institutional Gendering: Theoretical Insights into the Environment of Women Officeholders' in S Thomas and C Wilcox (eds), *Women and Elective Office: Past, Present, and Future*, 2nd edn (New York, Oxford University Press, 2005) 231–32.

[6] C Jillson and RK Wilson, *Congressional Dynamics: Structure, Coordination and Choice in the First American Congress, 1774–1789* (Stanford, Stanford University Press, 1994).

[7] Duerst-Lahti, 'Institutional Gendering' (n 5) 231.

[8] Duerst-Lahti and Kelly (eds), *Gender Power, Leadership and Governance* (n 4); J Lovenduski, 'Gendering Research in Political Science' (1998) 1 *Annual Review of Political Science* 333; M Kenny, 'Gender, Institutions and Power: A Critical Review' (2007) 27 *Politics* 91; ML Krook and F Mackay (eds), *Gender, Politics and Institutions: Towards a Feminist Institutionalism* (Basingstoke, Palgrave Macmillan, 2011).

[9] AM Goetz, 'Gender Justice, Citizenship and Entitlements: Core Concepts, Central Debates and New Directions for Research' in M Mukhopadhyay and N Singh (eds), *Gender Justice, Citizenship and Development* (Ottawa, International Development Research Centre, 2007); L Chappell and G Waylen 'Gender and the Hidden Life of Institutions' (2013) 91 *Public Administration* 599; G Waylen, 'Informal Institutions, Institutional Change, and Gender Equality' (2014) 67 *Political Research Quarterly* 212.

[10] JG March and JP Olsen, *Rediscovering Institutions: The Organizational Basis of Politics* (New York, Free Press, 1989).

[11] Duerst-Lahti, 'Institutional Gendering' (n 5) 231.

and office-holding as deviant from the norm, resulting in women being overlooked and side-lined. Political parties act as gatekeepers, using informal norms to sustain male power and institutionalise bias against the selection of women candidates.[12]

To combat this bias and to compensate for the gendered barriers that women face when accessing political office, gender quota measures have been adopted in 128 countries worldwide. Electoral quotas have been identified as an effective measure 'to increase the representation of historically excluded or under-represented groups',[13] and are considered a legitimate equal opportunity measure.[14] There are three main types of quotas: reserved seats, legislative quotas and voluntary or party quotas. Reserved seats are usually enshrined in a country's constitution and guarantee that a certain proportion or number of parliamentary seats are reserved for women. They are used primarily in African, Asian and the Middle Eastern countries. Legislative gender quotas 'are enshrined in the election law, political party law or other comparable law of a country'.[15] They usually apply to the nomination stage of candidate selection, ensuring that a certain proportion of candidates are women. These laws may also specify where on the ballot paper women are to be positioned (referred to as placement mandates) or that women are to be selected to run in winnable seats. Legislative quotas are used primarily in European and South American countries. Non-compliance with constitutional and legislative gender quotas may subject political parties to forfeits (such as a reduction in state funding) or penalties (such as financial fines or the barring of a party from contesting an election[16]). The third form of gender quota is the voluntary party quota. Gender quotas are voluntarily set by political parties to facilitate the nomination of a certain number or proportion of women candidates. Currently, of those countries employing gender quotas as a mechanism to ensure women's inclusion in politics, 41.5 per cent use voluntary party quotas, 40.8 per cent use legislative quotas and 17.7 per cent use reserved seats.[17] In Ireland, a legislative gender quota applies. The next two sections explain why this is the case. First, an overview of women's political representation in Irish politics is presented, before moving on to discuss why legislative gender quotas were adopted in 2012.

[12] V Randall and A Smyth, 'Bishops and Bailiwicks: Obstacles to Women's Political Participation in Ireland' (1987) 18 *The Economic and Social Review* 189; R Campbell, S Childs and J Lovenduski, 'Women's Equality Guarantees and the Conservative Party' (2006) 77 *The Political Quarterly* 18; E Bjarnegård, *Gender, Informal Institutions and Political Recruitment: Explaining Male Dominance in Parliamentary Representation* (Basingstoke, Palgrave Macmillan, 2013); M Kenny, *Gender and Political Recruitment: Theorizing Institutional Change* (Basingstoke, Palgrave Macmillan, 2013); T Verge and M De la Fuente, 'Playing With Different Cards: Party Politics, Gender Quotas and Women's Empowerment' (2014) 35 *International Political Science Review* 67.

[13] D Dahlerup, 'What are the Effects of Electoral Gender Quotas?' a paper presented at the World Congress of the *International Political Science Association* (Fukuoka, 2006) http://paperroom.ipsa.org/papers/paper_5301.pdf.

[14] ML Krook, *Quotas for Women in Politics: Gender and Candidate Selection Reform Worldwide* (New York, Oxford University Press, 2010) 37.

[15] S Larserud and R Taphorn, *Designing for Equality: Best-fit, Medium-fit and Non-favourable Combinations of Electoral Systems and Gender Quotas* (Stockholm, International Institute for Democracy and Electoral Assistance (IDEA), 2007) 8–9.

[16] Referred to as a list rejection, political parties who do not select the requisite proportion of women candidates by the close of nominations are usually given a period of grace in which time they must meet the quota threshold. If, after the period of grace, they still do not comply with the quota, the party's list of candidates is rejected, and essentially, the party is barred from contesting the election in the constituency/constituencies where their list of candidates is incompatible with the quota law.

[17] Data adapted from the *Quota Database* www.quotaproject.org/.

III. Women in Politics in Ireland: An Overview[18]

To the outside observer, resistance to women's participation in Irish political life does not come as a surprise, given Ireland's reputation for social conservatism. What is surprising, though, is that this resistance remained intact until recent times. What explains the durability of this resistance is the relatively stable value system that underpinned Irish political culture until the latter decades of the twentieth century. That value system is associated with what the sociologist RW Connell describes as the 'patriarchal dividend': the material, status and power advantages that men enjoy over women in developed capitalist countries and economies, and which, in turn, serve to exclude women from positions of power and influence.[19]

Political culture replicates, and often intensifies, the dominant social value system within which politics operates. In Ireland, personal identity was shaped by the twin forces of nationalism and Catholicism. Social politics was determined by these same forces, and societal values too expressed the preferences and priorities of these two hegemonies. Neither was particularly empowering of, or for, women. Yet, a political and social alliance between nationalism and Catholicism created the foundations of the independent Irish State and their shared values shaped Irish political culture.

Although the 1922 Irish Free State constitution advanced women's equality with men by providing equal citizenship (Article 3), full voting and other political rights – such as the right to stand for election (Articles 14 and 15) – the document was silent on the Easter Rising Proclamation's promise of equal opportunities.[20] Indeed, policy and law in the 1920s and 1930s eroded women's status as equal citizens, with women's jury service made discretionary, birth control outlawed, and women's employment opportunities restricted.[21] The promise and hope of advancement in women's opportunities that had occurred prior to independence was quickly eroded by nationalist governments in the new State in the face of opposition from elected and civil society feminists.[22] The re-inscription of the patriarchal dividend culminated in the majority public support for the 1937 Constitution which banned divorce (Article 41.3.2); confined women's citizenship to the home (Article 41.2.1); constitutionally restricted women's employment opportunities (Article 41.2.2); and enabled laws to take into account differences of capacity and social function (Article 40.1). The only dent women's activism could make in the patriarchal dividend was in securing recognition of women's right to equal citizenship with men (Articles 9 and 16).

Informing the rapid reassertion of male dominance in public, economic and social life was a world-view shaped by Catholicism. The relationship between Catholic religious belief,

[18] This section is drawn from an unpublished paper delivered at the 2013 Joint Sessions of the European Consortium for Political Research (ECPR) entitled '"Someday, girls, someday": Legislating for candidate gender quotas in Ireland' authored by F Buckley, Y Galligan and C McGing.

[19] RW Connell, 'Politics of Changing Men' (1996) 4 *Australian Humanities Review* www.australianhumanitiesreview.org/1996/12/01/politics-of-changing-men/.

[20] Constitution of the Irish Free State (Saorstat Eireann) Act 1922.

[21] C Beaumont, 'Women, Citizenship and Catholicism in the Irish Free State, 1922-1948' (1997) 6 *Women's History Review* 569–73.

[22] M O'Neill, *From Parnell to De Valera: A Biography of Jennie Wyse Power 1858–1941* (Dublin, Blackwater Press, 1991) 164–65.

nationalism and personal identity is an enduring feature of Irish culture and politics.[23] The role of the priest as political and community, as well as spiritual, leader was well established in the nineteenth century. By the time of the nationalist revolution, the identification of the Catholic clergy with the cause of Irish freedom was entrenched, leading to post-independence Ireland being described as a 'confessional state'.[24] Their shared vision of Ireland as a rural, traditional and Catholic nation, and the absence of an alternative social model, consolidated the influence of the Catholic hierarchy in the new nation. This position was further reinforced through the Catholic hierarchy's unchallenged control of the educational system, the notable loyalty of Catholics to the church, and the absence of countervailing pressures to challenge religious authoritarianism.[25] The new State accepted the role of the Church in other areas of social policy also – healthcare, social services, censorship, marriage, family life – and codified the 'special' position of the Catholic Church in the 1937 Constitution, though stopped short of making Catholicism the State religion (Article 44.1.2).[26] This interlacing of two powerful conservative forces left a gendered mark on the early years of the State that persisted throughout the twentieth century. Women's position in society was influenced by the ideal woman of Catholic social teaching – that of wife and mother – and through control of education, the Catholic clergy were in a position to instil moral principles of obedience, modesty and acceptance of Catholic moral prescriptions among girls and young women. Motherhood, in many instances enforced beyond the wishes of women, was reified. The scale and extent of this personal and societal internalisation of an unrealistic morality of purity was such that it remained unquestioned until the 1990s. Only then could a maturing secularisation uncover the scandals of clerical sexual abuse of children, the enslavement of unwed mothers and their children in enclosed convents, and a far from celibate priesthood.[27]

It is not surprising, then, to observe women's absence from public and political life in the decades after 1922. In the period between 1923 and 1975, just 18 women were elected to Dáil Éireann. All but three were related to a former male TD (Teachta Dála – a member of Dáil Éireann), revealing political parties' preference to limit female candidacy to those with familial links, or, as observed by Galligan and Buckley,[28] those networked into the political system through male relations, fathers or husbands who had died while serving in the Dáil (the so-called 'widows' and daughters' inheritance).

[23] JH Whyte, *Church and State in Modern Ireland 1923–1979* (Dublin, Gill and Macmillan, 1980); D Keogh, *The Vatican, the Bishops and Irish Politics 1919–1939* (Cambridge, Cambridge University Press, 1986); L O'Dowd, 'Church, State and Women: The Aftermath of Partition' in C Curtin, P Jackson and B O'Connor (eds), *Gender in Irish Society* (Galway, Galway University Press, 1987); JJ Lee, *Ireland 1912–1985: Politics and Society* (Cambridge, Cambridge University Press, 1990).

[24] K Andersen, 'Irish Secularization and Religious Identities: Evidence of an Emerging New Catholic Habitus' (2010) 57 *Social Compass* 17.

[25] J Coakley, 'Society and Political Culture' in J Coakley and M Gallagher (eds), *Politics in the Republic of Ireland*, 5th edn (London, Routledge/PSAI Press, 2010); Andersen, 'Irish Secularization and Religious Identities' (n 24) 17.

[26] This Art and Art 44.1.3 recognising other religious denominations – such as the Church of Ireland and Jewish congregations – were removed by referendum in 1973 (5th Amendment of the Constitution of Ireland).

[27] Such scandals included clerical sex abuse in the Diocese of Cloyne, burials at the Tuam Mother and Baby Home, and high-profile members of the Catholic Church clergy, including Bishop Eamon Casey, fathering children.

[28] Y Galligan and F Buckley, 'Women in Politics' in J Coakley and M Gallagher (eds), *Politics in the Republic of Ireland*, 6th edn (Abingdon, PSAI Press/Routledge, 2018).

However, indications of change emerged in 1977. In that election, six women were returned to Dáil Éireann, an outcome last achieved in 1921. It reflected a modernising Irish society, a pattern of change which began in the 1960s, as the economy transitioned from a reliance on agriculture to service provision, Vatican II reformed Catholic teaching, the spread of television brought alternative views and experiences into households, and a new generation of young, educated women sought to shape a lifestyle which was different to that of their mothers. Looking outwards after decades of introspection, the Irish economy moved from protectionism to being highly globalised, with the European Union playing a vital role in the social and economic modernisation of the country. With these developments came a rise in women's social and economic ambitions, and a general loosening, over time, of the bond between personal identity and Catholicism. Women began mobilising for change and during the 1970s, a plethora of new women's and feminist organisations emerged.[29] Among them was the Women's Political Association (WPA), formed in 1971, to campaign for women's election to parliament. The proportion of women elected to Dáil Éireann gradually began to rise, increasing from 4.1 per cent in 1977 to 8.4 per cent in 1987. In 1990, the election of left-wing feminist lawyer, Mary Robinson, as President of Ireland was a tangible indication that a modern, pluralist, Ireland was coming of age and Catholic-nationalist tropes of womanhood were being rejected.[30]

The mobilisation of women in support of Mary Robinson's presidential campaign did not go unnoticed by the political parties. Leveraging this 'women's vote', political parties, for the first time in their histories, took the issue of women's candidacy seriously. In the 1992 general election, the first held after the 1990 presidential election, there was a 71 per cent increase in female candidacy, up from 52 women candidates in 1989, to 89 in 1992. With more women on the ballot paper, the number of women elected increased by 54 per cent, up from 13 women TDs in 1989, to 20 in 1992. It seemed that Mary Robinson's election as President was the much-needed catalyst for change in Irish political party candidate selection processes. However, this change proved short-lived. In the five general elections between and including 1992 and 2011, women's candidacy was subject to reversals, and the number of women elected increased only marginally to 25 by 2011. Progress was static. Paradoxically, socio-economic patterns during this period pointed to a country experiencing socio-cultural change and modernisation, factors usually associated with increasing access to public life for women. In 1973, there were 287,800 women in paid employment, representing 27 per cent of the total number of people employed in Ireland. In the years that followed, the female employment rate (the number of women working as a proportion of the total number of women of working age available to work) increased steadily from 42 per cent in 1997 to 61 per cent in 2007, before reducing to 56 per cent in 2014 as a result of the economic recession.[31] In 1970, the fertility rate was 3.85. By 1990, it stood

[29] L Connolly, *The Irish Women's Movement: From Revolution to Devolution* (London and New York, Palgrave Macmillan, 2003); Y Galligan, *Women and Politics in Contemporary Ireland: From the Margins to the Mainstream* (London, Pinter, 1998).

[30] Y Galligan, 'Transforming the Irish Presidency: Activist Presidents and Gender Politics 1990–2011' (2012) 27 *Irish Political Studies*, 596.

[31] European Commission Representation in Ireland, 'The EU and Irish Women' 2018 www.ec.europa.eu/ireland/node/684_en; Central Statistics Office, 'Women and Men in Ireland 2013' 2014 www.cso.ie/en/releasesandpublications/ep/p-wamii/womenandmeninireland2013/employmentlist/employment/.

at 2.11 and decreased further to 2.05 by 2010.[32] Yet, women's participation in Irish politics remained obstinately low. The spotlight thus turned to political parties to assess the impact of their candidate recruitment and selection processes on women's political representation, in particular how these processes circumscribed women's candidacy in Irish elections.

IV. Candidate Selection for General Elections in Ireland

While the Electoral Acts and Constitution set out the eligibility criteria for candidature and membership of Dáil Éireann, the task of determining the rules and regulations of candidate selection, was, up to 2012, the sole preserve of political parties. This situation changed with the passage of the Electoral (Amendment) (Political Funding) Act 2012. Part 6 of the Act specifies that the amount of State funding that political parties receive under the Electoral Acts 'shall be reduced by 50 per cent, unless at least 30 per cent of the candidates whose candidatures were authenticated by the qualified party at the preceding general election were women and at least 30 per cent were men'.[33] The gender threshold will increase to 40 per cent from 2023 onwards. The provision is a recognition of the historic and contemporary gender imbalance in Irish politics, which has seen just 114 women elected to Dáil Éireann in comparison to approximately 1,181 men.[34]

Formally, the laws, rules and regulations surrounding candidate eligibility and selection do not negate against female candidacy, yet the informal dynamics and requirements of candidate recruitment do.

Under the provisions of Article 16.1.1 of the Constitution, the general criteria for membership of the Dáil is to be an Irish citizen, aged 21 years or over, who is not disqualified, by law or constitutional provision, of being a member of Dáil Éireann. Section 51(2) of the Electoral Act 1923 and section 41 of the Electoral Act 1992, as well as the Local Government (No 2) Act 2003 and Articles 12.6, 33.3 and 35.3 of the Constitution, set out the legal incapacities for membership of Dáil Éireann, which include membership of a local authority; membership of Seanad Éireann; officeholders such as the President, the Comptroller and Auditor General, the Attorney General and Judges; members of the Gardaí and Defence Forces; civil servants whose terms of employment prohibit membership of the Dáil; senior officials of the European Union; being a person of unsound mind; and being a person presently serving a prison term of longer than six months.[35]

To be formally nominated as a candidate for Dáil elections, a candidate must submit to the returning officer of the constituency in which they intend to contest, either a certificate of party affiliation or a statutory declaration of 30 assentors from that constituency supporting the candidature, or lodge a deposit of €500. The obligatory payment of a deposit by all candidates was found to be repugnant to the Constitution in the case of *Redmond v Minister*

[32] World Bank, *Fertility Rate: Ireland* (Public Data) www.google.ie/publicdata/explore?ds=d5bncppjof8f9_&met_y=sp_dyn_tfrt_in&hl=en&dl=en#!ctype=l&strail=false&bcs=d&nselm=h&met_y=sp_dyn_tfrt_in&scale_y=lin&ind_y=false&rdim=country&idim=country:IRL&ifdim=country&hl=en_US&dl=en&ind=false.

[33] Title of Pt 6 of the Act is *State Funding of Political Parties and Gender Balance*.

[34] Figures relate to elections from 1918 to 2016.

[35] J Kavanagh, 'Electoral Law in Ireland: Sustaining Electoral Integrity from Process, Procedures, and Precedent?' (2015) 30 *Irish Political Studies* 510, 517.

for the Environment[36] and since then the deposit is primarily paid by those who do not present a certificate of party affiliation or a list of 30 names.[37]

In relation to the candidate selection process, political parties are free to decide their own internal rules and regulations. The advent of gender quotas has not altered this freedom. Political parties have full discretion to decide how – or even if – they wish to apply the gender quota requirement. For the most part there is little variation across the political parties in terms of candidate selection processes. All registered party members, with membership of a certain duration and who have paid their membership fees, are entitled to vote in a candidate selection convention, operated under the one member one vote (OMOV) voting system. While the duration of party membership required to be eligible to vote in a selection convention can be as short as six months (as in the Labour party) or as long as two years (as in Fine Gael), there are no minimum requirements on length of party membership for candidacy. To be eligible to contest a selection convention all that is required is that the candidate must be a party member, a criterion which can be secured in a relatively short period of time if approval is granted by the party's local branch and national headquarters. This flexibility has facilitated the 'parachuting' in of candidates at short notice, usually high-profile local celebrities such as GAA (Gaelic Athletic Association) players.

Candidate selection operates within a framework which is best described as 'local selection, but with national approval'.[38] A central selection committee, based in party headquarters (HQ), manages the candidate selection process, issuing directives on the number of candidates to be selected, the geographical location of those candidates, and the gender profile of the candidacy team. Selection conventions are organised on a constituency basis and candidates are chosen locally by the party membership, but those selected 'must be ratified by the national executive, which reserves the right to deselect any candidate and add someone of its own liking to the party ticket'.[39] This interaction between the national and local organs of the party has resulted in many tensions and confrontations, leading to questions about the location and distribution of power within political parties with respect to candidate selection. 'This tension is often portrayed as the battle between the forces of democratisation and centralisation' and is a long running feature of party politics in Ireland.[40] Writing in 1994, Farrell observed that tensions emerge as party HQs, aiming to maximise their party vote and seat returns, issue strict orders on how many candidates to run, who to select, where those candidates are to be based, and which areas candidates are to canvas.[41] These orders are usually devised by party strategists on the basis of private polling conducted in constituencies to investigate the strength of the party vote. The strategisation and professionalism of the modern political party has seen a movement towards increased centralisation within all parties. This has exacerbated the tension between the centre and the periphery as Irish parties were always distinguishable for the considerable

[36] *Redmond v Minister for the Environment* [2001] 4 IR 61. Kavanagh, 'Electoral Law in Ireland' (n 35) 518.

[37] Where a candidate pays the deposit, they are entitled to a return of the deposit if their final total exceeds a quarter of the quota for the constituency in which they contested the election.

[38] L Weeks, 'Candidate Selection: Democratic Centralism or Managed Democracy?' in M Gallagher and M Marsh (eds), *How Ireland Voted 2007* (London, Palgrave Macmillan, 2008) 49.

[39] ibid.

[40] ibid 48.

[41] D Farrell, 'Ireland: Centralisation, Professionalisation and Competitive Pressures' in R Katz and P Mair (eds), *How Parties Organize* (London, Sage, 1994).

level of autonomy enjoyed by the party at the local level.[42] However, as Farrell observed, the movement away from decentralisation has been 'one of the more striking developments' in party organisation since the mid-1960s.[43]

As noted earlier, the formal rules of candidate selection do not discriminate against women, resulting in the framing of women's political under-representation 'as an unfortunate consequence of a gender-neutral, fair and effective system, which produces the best people for the job'.[44] But, as Culhane contends, 'these arguments, however, fail to take into account the "informal rules of the game" that bestow significant advantage to specific actors'.[45] As observed by Weeks, the formal rules tell only part of the story behind the process of candidate selection:

> By the night of the convention the crucial power struggles have often already taken place; the official selection 'is simply a formality which just puts the finishing touch on the work of the wire-pullers.' The interaction between the different wire-pullers within the parties denotes the existence of … informal rules of candidate selection … [but] because of their unwritten and private nature, it is difficult to outline what exactly these informal rules are.[46]

It is little wonder then that candidate selection is often described as the 'secret garden of politics'.[47]

There is a tacit understanding that incumbency and localism are key to the selection and election prospects of candidates in Irish elections. As parties seek to maximise their vote, incumbents are, by definition, experienced and quality candidates, who have proven their electability. Their re-selection is usually a mere formality as a result of the unfailing support of party loyalists, built up over many years. Given that the majority of incumbents are male, few women can take advantage of this informal requirement of candidate selection. In addition, localism privileges men.[48] Localism and personalism are reified in Irish politics because of the multi-seat and intra-party nature of the Irish electoral system, proportional representation by means of the single transferable vote (PR-STV). As Culhane points out, localism shapes ideas about what is considered an 'electable' and thereby a 'good' candidate.[49] Experience of local office, and being well-connected into the local community, are key to the recruitment and selection prospects of candidates. However as women's representation on local councils has never exceeded 21 per cent in Ireland, fewer women than men can harness this attribute.[50] Even though women occupy professions that network them into their local communities such as teachers, solicitors and accountants, and are involved in local campaigns and groups, Culhane's research finds that women have largely

[42] ibid 225.

[43] ibid.

[44] L Culhane, 'Local Heroes and "Cute Hoors": Informal Institutions, Male Over-representation and Candidate Selection in the Republic of Ireland' in G Waylen (ed), *Gender and Informal Institutions* (London, Rowman and Littlefield International, 2017) 48.

[45] ibid 48.

[46] Weeks, 'Candidate Selection' (n 38) 52.

[47] M Gallagher and M Marsh, *Candidate Selection in Comparative Perspective: The Secret Garden of Politics* (London, Sage, 1988).

[48] Culhane, 'Local Heroes and "Cute Hoors"' (n 44) 46.

[49] ibid.

[50] F Buckley et al, 'Is Local Office a Springboard for Women to Dáil Éireann?' (2015) 36 *Journal of Women, Politics Policy* 311.

been 'invisible' in the eyes of local selectors.[51] This is not due to a lack of presence she argues, but rather a privileging of a particular type of localism, that of the 'cute hoor' who wields *his* power through the 'wink and elbow language of masculinity' a trait perceived 'as incompatible with femininity'.[52] As a consequence, women have been largely overlooked and ignored, evidenced in the fact that despite women's membership of political parties hovering between 30 and 40 per cent, women's candidacy rates have rarely matched that of their membership rates.

Therefore, the informal norms of candidate recruitment and selection, are, in fact, gendered to favour male selection prospects. Compounding the problem of women's access into politics is the issue of time and funds. Time is a valuable resource for anyone wishing to carve out a career in politics, especially in Ireland, where personalism is so ingrained in the political culture. In addition, political candidacy requires personal financial investment. Yet 'gendered differences in pay and care commitments impact upon the availability of time and financial resources, meaning men are more likely than women to possess such capital to develop a political career'.[53] All things considered, access into politics is far from the gender-neutral image that is oftentimes portrayed, and it is certainly not a level playing pitch.

V. Why Legislative Gender Quotas?

It is no accident that the introduction of gender quotas coincided with a retreat away from all things associated with the 'cute hoor' way of doing politics in Ireland. The financial crisis of 2008 brought into focus and under scrutiny the interconnections between politics and banking, as well as the deeply ingrained personalism and cronyism that shaped those relationships. The decision of the Fianna Fáil/Green/Independent coalition Government to guarantee the loan books of the Irish banks in September 2008 proved controversial, in particular when it exacerbated the poor state of the public finances.[54] The financial crash resulted in the collapse of the construction sector, a decrease in property prices, unemployment, a return to emigration, mortgage arrears, homelessness and cutbacks in public services. The country eventually entered into a three-year financial bailout programme in November 2010 leading to a loss of financial sovereignty and a prolonged austerity programme.[55] The people were angry and, as Culhane surmises, the 'cute hoor' way of doing politics 'gained negative connotations' and became 'associated with political corruption, the Irish banking crisis and the unsavoury relationship between politicians and their political funding'.[56] In response, political parties engaged in a political reform discourse promising democratic renewal, change and a break from the past and the old way of doing politics. One of the

[51] Culhane, 'Local Heroes and "Cute Hoors"' (n 44) 56.

[52] ibid 58.

[53] M Brennan and F Buckley, 'The Irish Legislative Gender Quota: The First Election' (2017) 65 *Administration* 15, 19.

[54] T Reidy and F Buckley, 'Democratic Revolution? Evaluating the Political and Administrative Reform Landscape after the Economic Crisis' (2017) 65 *Administration* 1, 2.

[55] The bailout was funded by the International Monetary Fund, the European Central Bank and the European Commission.

[56] Culhane, 'Local Heroes and "Cute Hoors"' (n 44) 57.

first political reform measures announced by the Fine Gael/Labour coalition Government after they came into office in March 2011 were changes to the financing of political parties. The Electoral (Amendment) (Political Funding) Act was signed into law in July 2012 and addresses both State and private financing of political parties. As noted previously, the Act specifies that the amount of State funding that political parties receive under the Electoral Acts shall be reduced by 50 per cent, unless political parties select at least 30 per cent male candidates and 30 per cent female candidates.[57] The gender threshold will increase to 40 per cent from 2023 onwards. In terms of the private funding of politicians and political parties, the law provides for a reduction in the maximum donation that can be received, down from €2,539.47 to €1,000 for an individual and from €6,348.60 to €2,500 for a political party. An individual who gives a donation of more than €200 must register as a political donor with the Standards in Public Office Commission, and the maximum aggregate amount that an individual donor can give to multiple candidates has been reduced from €5,078.95 down to €1,500. Increased transparency and reductions in donation limits means political parties are heavily reliant on State funding. In addition to the funding that political parties receive under the Electoral Acts to cover party operating costs, they also receive what is known as a Parliamentary Activities Allowance,[58] the amount of which is determined by the number of TDs and Senators the party has. The money received is used to cover costs associated with parliamentary activities. In total, some 84 per cent of parties' income comes from the exchequer.[59]

The decision to adopt legislative gender quotas was the outcome of a collection of influences.[60] First, research from Ireland and elsewhere pointed to political parties as the gatekeepers to electoral politics, and to increase the supply of women, political parties needed to signal demand through the adoption of gender quotas. Second, voluntary gender quotas had been used by political parties in Ireland, but with no incentive to implement their self-imposed targets, political parties flouted such measures, curbing their transformative potential. As parties demonstrated their inability to deliver reform on their own, State intervention became necessary. Third, Ireland's poor record for women's political representation came in for severe criticism from the United Nations, and the Government was urged to introduce affirmative action to address the gender imbalance in Irish political life.[61] Fourth, the political reform discourse provided a platform to problematise the under-representation of women in Irish politics. As part of the reform agenda, two parliamentary committees – a Sub-Committee of the Joint Committee on Justice, Equality, Defence and Women's Rights and the Joint Committee on the Constitution – discussed women's participation in Irish politics. The former advocated the introduction of a legislative candidate selection quota.

[57] To be eligible for State funding, political parties must be listed on the Register of Political Parties, the Registrar of which is located in Leinster House, and obtain at least 2% of the first preference vote in the preceding general election.

[58] Formerly known as the Party Leader's Allowance.

[59] L Weeks, 'Parties and the Party System' in J Coakley and M Gallagher (eds), *Politics in the Republic of Ireland*, 6th edn (Abingdon, PSAI Press/Routledge, 2018) 130.

[60] F Buckley, 'Women and Politics in Ireland: The Road to Sex Quotas' (2013) 28 *Irish Political Studies* 341, 354.

[61] In 2005, the United Nations Committee on the Elimination of Discrimination Against Women (UN CEDAW), expressed concern about what they described as the 'significant under-representation of women in elected political structures, particularly in the Oireachtas' and they recommended the adoption of 'sustained measures to increase the representation of women in elected bodies'. See UN CEDAW's *Concluding Comments: Ireland* (2005) 8.

The latter recommended that the public funding of parties be 'regulated so that a proportion of the funding allocated to a party would be determined by the number of women candidates it nominates for election'.[62] These recommendations shaped the quota provision contained in the legislation.[63] Fifth, feminist activism, both inside and outside parliament, brought salience to the issue of women's political under-representation and ensured the issue remained on the political agenda. Feminist politicians such as Senator Ivana Bacik and organisations such as 'The 5050 Group', the National Women's Council of Ireland, Labour Women, and Women for Election coalesced to agitate for legislative change, demonstrating the importance of alliances in advocacy campaigns. Finally, the presence of ministers in Cabinet who were strongly in support of gender balancing mechanisms for election candidacy was key to their adoption, illustrating the impact of critical actors on policy-making. Together, all of these factors contributed to the adoption of legislative gender quotas.

VI. Critiques and Challenges

The implementation of legislative gender quotas in Ireland was not without debate. As the candidate selection conventions for the 2016 general election took place, discourses and resistance emerged, raising questions about merit, fairness, democracy and male displacement. Some of this commentary betrayed the latent, sometimes blatant, sexism inherent in politics whereby women's candidate selection is subject to query, question and scrutiny at levels rarely experienced by men, a consequence of the gender power arrangements in politics whereby masculine assumptions underpin the norms that become 'normal' in politics, appropriating men as the archetype politician.[64]

As the gender quota was implemented, male candidacy and merit was rarely questioned. The opposite was the case for women, with women frequently accused of being selected, not on the basis of merit, but on the basis of their biological sex. Taking experience of political office as a measure of merit, Buckley et al demonstrate that, in the 2016 general election, some 52 per cent of female candidates had experience of political office in comparison to 61 per cent of male candidates (see Table 16.1).[65] The data shows that not all men (39 per cent) and women (48 per cent) had experience of serving in elected office prior to contesting a general election, but yet, it was only women's experience and lack thereof that was queried and questioned.

[62] Joint Committee on the Constitution, *Fourth Report: Review of the Electoral System for the Election of Members to Dáil Éireann* (Dublin, Government Publications, 2010) 18 www.oireachtas.ie/documents/committees30thdail/j-constitution/report_2008/20100722.pdf.

[63] Buckley, 'Women and Politics in Ireland' (n 6) 353.

[64] Duerst-Lahti and Kelly (eds), *Gender Power, Leadership and Governance* (n 4); Duerst-Lahti, 'Institutional Gendering' (n 5); M Hawkesworth, 'Engendering Political Science: An Immodest Proposal' (2005) 1 *Politics and Gender* 141.

[65] F Buckley, Y Galligan and C McGing, 'Women and the Election: Assessing the Impact of Gender Quotas' in M Gallagher and M Marsh (eds), *How Ireland Voted: The Election that Nobody Won* (Basingstoke, Palgrave Macmillan, 2017) 192.

Table 16.1 Proportion of Female and Male Candidates with Previous Office-holding Experience, 2016 General Election

Party	Female Candidates %	Male Candidates %
All candidates	52	61
Fianna Fáil	73	86
Fine Gael	74	97
Labour	92	100
Sinn Féin	72	88

Source: Figures adapted from F Buckley, Y Galligan and C McGing, 'Women and the Election: Assessing the Impact of Gender Quotas' in M Gallagher and M Marsh (eds), *How Ireland Voted: The Election that Nobody Won* (Basingstoke, Palgrave Macmillan, 2017).

As noted previously, party HQs regularly issue directives to their constituency conventions to guide the candidate selection process. For the 2016 general election, a total of 12 gender directives were issued across Fine Gael (five), Fianna Fáil (six) and Sinn Féin (one). In nine of these conventions, party members were instructed to select a gender balanced candidate slate – one man and one woman. In three of these cases, a woman-only directive was issued, instructing party members to select one female candidate. In some cases, the official announcement of the directive was left as late as the night of the convention to confirm, leading to much controversy at the selection convention. Accusations of unfairness and undemocratic practices were levelled at party HQs as party members were left disgruntled that they could not vote for their preferred candidate and questions were raised about the legitimacy of candidates selected in such a manner, especially if the contest was unopposed.

The timing of the announcement of directives must be reviewed. Regardless of the nature of the directive (gender, geography or numerical), to delay its announcement until close to the actual convention leads to a lot of annoyance and disappointment, particularly among those who invested time and energy into selection campaigns. In cases where the directive instructed the nomination of one woman candidate, the selection of that woman was often met with much resistance and resentment, as was the case in Fianna Fáil's selection convention in Longford. There, the selection of Connie Geraghty-Quinn resulted in a backlash and the constituency party signalling their intent to select an 'unofficial' candidate to run against her. They didn't, but many party members refused to canvas for Connie Geraghty-Quinn. In the end, Geraghty-Quinn came very close to winning a Dáil seat, but her experience of party politics was a bruising one, whereby she was subjected to sexist taunts about her ability to stand and her legitimate right to contest the general election. Much of this could have been avoided through better management of the selection process by Fianna Fáil HQ, but the reaction to Geraghty-Quinn's selection revealed a sense of male entitlement to political power within the constituency party. This becomes even more evident when the selection process of the other candidate selected by Fianna Fáil to contest the Longford-Westmeath constituency is considered. That candidate was the male incumbent TD, Robert Troy, who was selected unopposed. If upholding the fairness and the democratic nature of the selection process was tantamount to the Fianna Fáil party in the Longford-Westmeath constituency, why was there no negative reaction to the automatic selection of Robert Troy or questions regarding his legitimacy to stand? It points to the privileging of the informal norm of incumbency in the selection processes for Irish elections. However, given that there are more male TDs than female TDs, more men than women can take advantage of this informal norm in candidate selection conventions.

A constitutional challenge to the Electoral (Amendment) (Political Funding) Act was taken by Brian Mohan, a Fianna Fáil party member in the Dublin Central constituency. On the night of the selection convention in that constituency, Fianna Fáil HQ issued a directive instructing that one candidate be selected and that that candidate be a woman. Brian Mohan challenged the Act, primarily on the grounds that:

> Section 17 (4B) of the Electoral Act 1997, inserted by Section 42 of the Electoral (Amendment) (Political Funding) Act 2012 contravenes Article 40 of Bunreacht na hÉireann in regard to freedom of expression, of assembly, of association, and of equality. He also contends that the said sections contravene Article 16 of Bunreacht na hÉireann which guarantees the right of every citizen having reached a specified age and eligibility criteria to stand in Dáil Éireann elections and to vote in those elections for candidates without distinction of sex.[66]

Justice Keane adjudged that Brian Mohan did not have locus standi to mount the challenge and 'failed to demonstrate that any of his interests [were] adversely affected' by the operation of section 17 (4B).[67] This decision was upheld by the Court of Appeal in February 2018. In July 2018, the Supreme Court agreed to hear an appeal concerning the interpretation of the rule regarding legal entitlement to bring a challenge to the Electoral (Amendment) (Political Funding) Act.

VII. Impact of Legislative Gender Quotas

As illustrated in Table 16.2, the introduction of legislative gender quotas saw a 90 per cent increase in the number of women candidates contesting the 2016 general election when compared to 2011. A total of 163 women ran for election, the highest number of women to ever contest a general election in Ireland.

Table 16.2 Women Candidates in the 2011 and 2016 General Elections

2011			**2016**			**Difference 2011–2016**
Party	*Total number of candidates*	*Women candidates N (%)*	*Party*	*Total number of candidates*	*Women candidates N (%)*	*Percentage difference*
Fianna Fáil	75	11 (14.7%)	Fianna Fáil	71	22 (31.0%)	↑100%
Fine Gael	104	16 (15.4%)	Fine Gael	88	27 (30.7%)	↑69%
Labour	68	18 (26.5%)	Labour	36	13 (36.1%)	↓28%

(continued)

[66] Plaintiff's Outline Legal Submissions, December 2015.
[67] *Mohan v Ireland and the Attorney General* [2016] IEHC 35 (Keane J).

Table 16.2 *(Continued)*

2011			**2016**			**Difference 2011–2016**
Party	*Total number of candidates*	*Women candidates N (%)*	*Party*	*Total number of candidates*	*Women candidates N (%)*	*Percentage difference*
Sinn Féin	41	8 (19.5%)	Sinn Féin	50	18 (36.0%)	↑125%
Greens	43	8 (18.6%)	Greens	40	14 (35.0%)	↑75%
United Left Alliance	20	5 (25.0%)	AAA-PBP	31	13 (42.0%)	↑160%
–	–	–	Renua	26	8 (30.8%)	–
–	–	–	Social Democrats	14	6 (42.9%)	–
Independents	197	19 (9.6%)	Independents	165	33 (20.0%)	↑74%
Others	17	1 (5.9%)	Others	30	9 (30.0%)	↑800%
Total	**566**	**86 (15.2%)**	**Total**	**551**	**163 (29.6%)**	**↑90%**

Source: F Buckley, Y Galligan and C McGing, 'Women and the Election: Assessing the Impact of Gender Quotas' in M Gallagher and M Marsh (eds), *How Ireland Voted: The Election that Nobody Won* (Basingstoke, Palgrave Macmillan, 2017) 188.

Across the four main parties of Fianna Fáil, Fine Gael, Sinn Féin and Labour, there was a total of 80 women candidates. Of these, the majority were selected through the traditional mechanisms of the selection convention without gender directive (61.25 per cent) or added-on when the conventions were complete (23.75 per cent). Just 15 per cent were selected through a gender directive (see Table 16.3). As the majority of women contesting the election came through without a gender directive, it confirms what the research had long suggested, that to increase the supply of women, political parties need to signal demand through the adoption of gender quotas. Women are available to contest elections, and the quota law ensured that political parties could no longer ignore them. Thus, the legislative gender quota has effected a cultural change as well as a shift in the mind-set of party strategists. In tandem with this, the quota, the discourses surrounding it, and the general discussion about the under-representation of women in politics, has provided women with a platform to 'speak up and speak out' about their experiences of sexism in politics.[68] The quota debate may have also contributed to the 74 per cent increase in the number of women running as Independents in 2016 when compared to the 2011 general election. While the legislative gender quota applies only to political parties, its introduction may have had a diffusion or spillover effect, signalling to all women, party and non, that the political system is a more accessible and welcoming space for them.

[68] F Buckley, Y Galligan and C McGing, 'Women and the Election' (n 65).

Table 16.3 Routes to Candidate Selection

	Number of women selected	Selection Convention	Added-on	Gender Directive
Fine Gael	27	13	9	5
Fianna Fáil	22	8	8	6
Sinn Féin	18	15	2	1
Labour	13	13	–	–
Total	80	49 (61.25%)	19 (23.75%)	12 (15%)

Source: Authors' own calculations.

VIII. Monitoring Progress

The 2016 general election saw the election of 35 women TDs, a 40 per cent increase in the number of women elected when compared to 2011. Women account for 22 per cent of the members of Dáil Éireann following that election. As highlighted by Buckley et al, in just one five-year electoral cycle, women's political representation in the Dáil rose by seven percentage points, an increase which previously took five electoral cycles and 22 years to achieve.[69] This can be directly related to the greater availability of women candidates on the ballot paper as a result of the legislative gender quota.

Yet, there can be no room for complacency. In October 2018, Ireland still languished in 82nd position in the Inter-Parliamentary Union's (IPU) league table for women's political representation.[70] Political party gender recruitment practices and candidate selection strategies must be continually monitored to ensure that the effectiveness of gender quotas is maintained and not undermined. At the 2016 general election, there is evidence to suggest that Fine Gael engaged in a 'sacrificial lamb' strategy, using the mechanism of the 'add-on' to include women on the ticket who were more likely to contest non-competitive races.[71] In some countries where legislative gender quotas apply, laws encourage the selection of women to contest winnable seats, to prevent a 'sacrificial lamb' approach to candidate selection. All political parties in Ireland should pledge to uphold the spirit of the law, embracing it as an opportunity to increase women's candidacy and election, rather than engaging in strategies to undermine it.

The financial provisions associated with the gender quota law incentivise parties to comply. If they do not, they forfeit half of the State funding they receive under the Electoral Acts. In comparison to the financial compliance mechanisms used in other countries, the Irish financial provision may seem harsh as it is applied to parties in a uniform manner, whether they miss the quota threshold by one percentage point or 10 percentage points.[72] While political parties stand to lose significant sums of money if they ignore the quota law, ranging from €109,373 as in the case of Renua, to €878,508 as in the case of Fine Gael

[69] ibid 201.

[70] Out of 187 ranked positions.

[71] F Buckley et al, 'Gender and Political Reform in Ireland: An Analysis of Three Elections' paper presented at the Annual Meeting of the *American Political Science Association*, San Francisco, California, September 2017.

[72] The most severe form of compliance mechanism is the list rejection.

(based on 2016 data),[73] it must be noted that this is not the only source of State funding that political parties receive. Under the Parliamentary Activities Allowance, political parties with representatives in Dáil Éireann and Seanad Éireann receive State funding which ranges from €13,541, as in the case of the Socialist Party, to €2,247,031 as in the case of Fianna Fáil (again, based on 2016 data).[74] Indeed, in 2016, Fianna Fáil received a total of €3,773,819 (€1,526,788 from the Electoral Acts and €2,247,031 from the Parliamentary Activities Allowance) from the State. If it did not apply the quota in 2016, it would have lost €763,394, just 20.22 per cent of its total State funding allocation. So, what may sound like a significant financial penalty on one's first reading of the gender quota law, it is not that severe or acute in practice. In theory, a wealthy party could ignore the gender quota law, as was the case in France when legislative quotas were first introduced in 2000. There, the larger and wealthier political parties were willing to pay the fine rather than select women. Laws in France were tightened up in the years that followed to combat this behaviour, but the French case-study is a salutary lesson for Ireland. Irish political parties must be monitored to ensure they do not engage in similar behaviour to that of their French counterparts.

Where legal gender quotas are applied elsewhere, they are usually in place at multiple levels of the political system. In Ireland, gender quotas apply only at the national level. As discussed in this chapter, localism and local government experience is crucial for the selection and election prospects of candidates in Dáil elections. The extension of legislative gender quotas to local elections would facilitate the election of higher numbers of women at that level, which in turn would increase the supply of high quality women candidates with local profile, name recognition and elected office experience to contest Dáil elections.

IX. Conclusion

The discourse and debate surrounding gender quotas and the under-representation of women in Irish politics has generated a discussion about the requisite and desired qualities of political candidates. This is welcomed and indicates a maturing Irish democracy. At the time of writing, political parties are engaging in candidate selection conventions for the second election under the 30 per cent gender quota rules. At this early stage of the process, there has been little or no gender related controversy, indicating a normalisation of the gender quota in party mind-sets and party selection processes. Yet, as demonstrated in 2016, we know that resistance exists and there is evidence to suggest that some political parties engaged in strategies to undermine the effectiveness of the quota law. It indicates that without the presence of the law, political parties may revert to their old ways and stymie women's access into political office. Therefore, it is essential that the Electoral (Amendment) (Political Funding) Act 2012 is maintained and its implementation is continually monitored, as without it, progress could be subject to reversals.

[73] Figures adapted from Standards in Public Office, *Exchequer Funding of Political Parties in 2016* (Dublin, Government Publications, 2017) 7 www.sipo.ie/en/Reports/State-Financing/Expenditure-of-State-Funding/2016-Exchequer-Funding-received-by-Political-Parties/Exchequer-Funding-Report-2016.pdf.

[74] Figures adapted from Standards in Public Office, *Appendix* www.sipo.ie/en/Reports/State-Financing/Funding-received-under-Parliamentary-Activities-Allowance/2016-Expenditure-of-the-Parliamentary-Activities-Allowance/Appendix.html.

17

Women in Law

MARY O'TOOLE[1]

I. Introduction

For almost 100 years, women in Ireland and England have been lawfully entitled to enter the legal profession. The Sex Disqualification (Removal) Act 1919 became law in Ireland and England in April 1920 and removed the legal bar to women being appointed to public office. Prior to the enactment of the 1919 Act, the Solicitor's Act 1843 governed entry to the profession. It provided that any 'person' with the required qualification was entitled to train as a solicitor. On the face of it, surely, that provision encompassed males and females. The judges, all male, did not agree. In proceedings brought in 1913 against the Law Society in England, it was held that a woman was not a 'person' within the meaning of the 1843 Act, because of the long established common law principle that no woman could hold public office. Thus, the need for the 1919 Act. It effectively removed the barriers for entry of women into both branches of the legal profession. It also provided for the removal of official barriers in the Statutes of Charters of British and Irish Universities regarding the admission of women as students.

We've come a long way since 1920. Women today form a large part of both the Solicitors and the Barristers profession. Indeed, by the end of 2014 there were 4,623 female practising solicitors in Ireland compared with 4,609 male practising solicitors. It is believed that this was the first time a female majority has existed in any legal profession anywhere in the world.[2] The figures from the Bar Council in 2016 show total Law Library membership at 2,234, with 772 female members. Thus, 39 per cent of the Bar were women, with 61 per cent men. The most recent Bar Council figures (January 2018) show little change in that picture, with a slight decrease in female membership to 38 per cent.

It is probably fair to say that the influx of women into the legal profession did not start until the 1970s and 1980s in Ireland. It was only during the 1990s that significant numbers of women began entering the profession. Law Society figures show that in 1970 there were 71 women solicitors, compared to 1,278 men. By 1990 that number had increased to 946 women, compared to 2,593 men. At the end of 2014, as we have seen, women in fact represented the majority in the profession.

[1] With thanks to Natalie McDonnell BL for her invaluable contribution to this chapter. Thanks are also due to Aedamair Gallagher Policy and Research Assistant at the Bar of Ireland and to Grainne Larkin BL for their generous assistance.

[2] T Kelly, 'Profession's Perfect Parity' (2015) Jan/Feb *Law Society Gazette* 20.

So, have we cracked it? Can we say that there is no gender inequality in the legal profession in Ireland? Well, it seems that the answer to that question is 'no'. There are few studies or surveys of women lawyers in Ireland, but those that do exist all show a consistent and discouraging similarity over the last number of decades. They all cite the same core problems experienced by women in the legal profession, with remarkably little progress in tackling those problems. Thus, it is fair to say that we have progressed to the point of equal access of women and men to the legal professions; however what happens after entry into the professions remains of concern. Retaining women in the profession is still a problem.

I was called to the Bar in 1980. At that time sexism was a normal everyday experience for many women, in all areas of life in Ireland. At the Bar, it was no different. I can recall being told that, in common with all female counsel, I had little prospect of succeeding as an advocate as a woman's voice was just 'too light' for court. I heard of discussions at partners' meetings at big Dublin solicitors' firms on the subject of whether to brief women counsel – at all. One colleague told me of an incident when she was pregnant, when a male solicitor requested that she return the brief he had sent her. It became apparent to her that the reason for this request was that the solicitor was of the view that women went 'funny in the head' during pregnancy. Being a pregnant practising barrister was considered quite unnatural in some quarters. Women barristers wearing trousers to work was controversial. But that was the 1980s – times have changed, and those kinds of attitudes have completely died out. Or so one likes to think. Nowadays such attitudes and prejudices seem almost comical. Yet if this chapter demonstrates anything, it is that sexism and gender discrimination have not died out and are still experienced by women practitioners to the present day, perhaps in a somewhat different form.

II. The Situation in 1993

In 1993, *Gender and the Law in Ireland* considered issues pertaining to women in the law.[3] In a chapter devoted to the legal profession, written by Alpha Connelly and Betty Hilliard, the authors sought to question a range of women about their own experiences of practice and their perceptions of the experiences of women generally in both branches of the legal profession in Ireland.[4] The authors spoke with women who were starting out on a career as well as those long established, including women working in full-time and part-time positions, and in different types of practice and work. This exercise did not purport to be a systemic study of women in the legal profession at that time. It primarily consisted of the interviews with selected women practitioners. The problems identified by those women, however, bear considerable resemblance to the problems that women lawyers experience today.

The authors noted the significant change in the proportion of women entering the legal profession during the two decades up to 1993 and concluded that the experience of women in the profession is markedly different from that of men in a number of ways. The authors

[3] A Connelly (ed), *Gender and the Law in Ireland* (Dublin, Oak Tree Press, 1993).

[4] A Connelly and B Hilliard, 'The Legal Profession' in A Connelly (ed), *Gender and the Law in Ireland* (Dublin, Oak Tree Press, 1993).

found that in early 1992, approximately half of those entering the solicitor's branch of the profession were female. In the barrister's branch of the profession, approximately one-quarter of the members of the Law Library were female.[5] More women chose to become solicitors than barristers. This, the authors discovered, was because a career as a solicitor was considered a more practical option than a career at the Bar, especially for those women who did not have strong family or other connections in the legal world.

Interestingly, the women interviewed suggested that different qualities were required to become a successful barrister as opposed to a solicitor. The interviewees identified the traits required to be a solicitor as more likely to reside in a woman. Whereas the traits required to be a barrister were more likely to reside in a man. The interviewees also saw the Bar as male-dominated and reflecting values that they saw as typical of the male, rather than the female: maximisation of income, competitiveness and detachment. That view is not reflected in the later surveys or studies. However, the interviewees also identified the necessity for barristers to have family, political and/or social networks in order to succeed at the Bar. They were of the view that those networks, centred around 'structured leisure activities and informal socialising', were much less accessible to women for a variety of reasons.[6] This view is reflected in the 2003 study, where golf is identified as being particularly gender exclusive by those women who experienced networking exclusion as a form of discrimination[7] (some 31 per cent of women surveyed). Given the prevalence of male-only membership of golf clubs in the 1980s and 1990s this is perhaps not a surprising finding. In the 2016 survey conducted by the Bar Council, there were no complaints about leisure activities and informal socialising that excluded women. However, being able to engage in social activities remains important for one's career, it seems. Women practitioners with children reported in 2016 that because of childcare constraints they had difficulty attending early morning or late evening events, including social events and CPD (continuing professional development) events, and expressed concern about maintaining 'visibility' as a professional and being 'out of the loop'.[8]

The women lawyers interviewed in 1993 were noted to be interested in having a balance between career and personal life. The authors noted that among the respondents 'there seemed to be relatively low levels of ambition'.[9] This was not because they did not aspire to success in their chosen careers. Rather, their ideas of doing well meant more than seniority and financial success. Personal satisfaction and balancing career advancement with other aspects of life were instead seen as a priority.[10] A major factor of such balancing was identified as parenthood. There was an acceptance by those interviewed that women bore the brunt of the responsibility for childcare even when they were working full-time in professional employment. The authors noted considerable stress and resentment arising from this situation. The women voiced the reality that their partners did not share in the childcare burden, which fell entirely to them. This is echoed, perhaps in slightly different terms, in the later surveys. In 1993 there was also evidence of interruption of women's career path as

[5] ibid 235–37.

[6] ibid 233.

[7] I Bacik, C Costello and E Drew, *Gender InJustice: Feminising the Legal Professions* (Dublin, Trinity College Law School, 2003) 296.

[8] A Gallagher, 'Women's Issues?' (2016) 21 *The Bar Review Volume* 50, 51.

[9] Connelly and Hilliard, 'The Legal Profession' (n 4) 233.

[10] ibid 233.

a result of their parenting roles. The study also found evidence that women lawyers tended to cluster into areas of work, particularly into lower paid areas, and there was a preponderance of women among part-time lawyers. Unsurprisingly perhaps, there were few women at senior levels in the profession.

The authors of the 1993 study commented that there appeared to be very little organised effort to secure the changes needed to ease the difficulties experienced by women lawyers.[11] In general, the response to the difficulties was to deal with the situation as they found it, rather than seeking to change it. The authors believed that an explanation for this may have been that women lawyers internalised the norms and expectations of the work world in which they found themselves. In becoming incorporated into that world, they no longer perceived how little it catered to their interests, and hence failed to confront those aspects of it which exacerbate their difficulties, especially the difficulties of combining careers with parenthood. Whatever the reason, and they are no doubt many and complex, this 'work world' failed to cater for women's interests, particularly in relation to parenthood, if the later studies are anything to go by.

The 1993 interviewees also reported sexist attitudes and behaviours, which had been encountered from all sources – colleagues, clients and judges. A significant dimension of this sexism appeared to be that different standards were applied to men and women. There was a strong and widespread perception among those interviewed that to succeed, whether as a solicitor or a barrister, a woman had to be considerably better at the job than a man.

It is important to bear in mind that this was not a systemic survey of the female practitioners in 1993, nor did it purport to be. It is, however, anecdotal evidence of the difficulties experienced by women in the professions at that time. The key issues identified by those women were:

(a) interruption to women's careers as a result of parenthood;
(b) exclusion from networking;
(c) exist attitudes and behaviours.

These factors were still relevant in 2003, as we will see, and even in 2016 problems such as sexism and combining a career with parenthood persisted.

III. The Situation in 2003

In 2003 the first, and to date the only, systemic study of women in law in Ireland was carried out. This extensive study of law and gender was undertaken by Bacik, Costello and Drew and resulted in the publication of *Gender InJustice: Feminising the Legal Profession*.[12] The study is very comprehensive and looks at both branches of the legal profession in Ireland, providing extensive information about women in the Irish legal profession from the 1920s onwards, including statistics and analysis, and comparing these to the statistics available in other jurisdictions. The study examines international literature on 'women in law' as well as reports and surveys from the professional bodies of other jurisdictions on the subject.

[11] ibid 234.
[12] Bacik et al, *Gender InJustice* (n 7).

One of the aims of the study was to document the momentous changes that had taken place in the legal profession in Ireland up to that point, in a clearly quantifiable way. The study also sought to document Irish women lawyers' experiences, particularly those of early pioneers and to acknowledge their contribution.

In 2002, Bar Council figures showed that 34 per cent of the Bar was female, up from 25 per cent in 1992.[13] The proportion of women senior counsel to men was low. In 2003, there were 23 women out of 247 senior counsel, 9 per cent of the total number.[14] The study noted that 5 per cent of women barristers were senior counsel in 2003, compared with 22 per cent of male barristers. Figures for 1993 are not available but the number of women who were senior counsel at that stage would have amounted to no more than a handful.

The 2003 study found that women often entered the profession with equal if not more academic 'capital' than men.[15] However, having entered the profession, men tended to do better, and more quickly than women. This sentiment is mirrored in the 2016 Bar of Ireland survey, where respondents said that male colleagues' careers took off more quickly than their female counterparts.

The 2003 study looked at many aspects of life in the profession for women. Notable however, was the fact that by 2003, a decade after the 1993 commentary, combining parenthood with a successful legal career was still enormously difficult. The study found that 'There is a strong prevailing view among women lawyers that, unlike their male counterparts, it is not possible for women to "have it all" (a successful legal career and a family)'.[16] The fact of having children and maintaining a career continued to be a major issue for women lawyers. While many respondents suggested creative ways to improve work/life balance, many others saw it as an inevitable struggle. The study identified the fact that fewer than one in 10 women with children (9 per cent) relied on a partner in the home for childcare, compared to 65 per cent of men.[17] Disproportionately more men than women had a partner/spouse working full-time in the home, 39 per cent of men, compared with only 4 per cent of women.[18] The study also found that although statutory maternity leave was available to the respondents, half had never taken any leave, other than their holidays.[19] A high proportion of women are only entitled to statutory benefit when they take maternity leave, rather than having access to maternity leave with full pay (in accordance with best practice). Women lawyers tend to experience serious difficulties even in seeking to take statutory maternity leave, with many suggesting that taking such leave was seen as a form of weakness. Some returned to work only days after giving birth. Of those that took leave, one-fifth of women considered that taking leave had affected them a lot in the workplace, and a further 19 per cent reported that it had affected them a little. Men did not tend to take any form of family-related leave, in many cases because it would not have been seen as acceptable for them to do so. Although nearly half of women who had taken leave had cover assigned (even a locum appointed or a colleague filling in for them), only 31 per cent of men had this experience. Women lawyers felt that the adoption of a part-time or reduced

[13] ibid 72.
[14] ibid 76.
[15] ibid 141.
[16] ibid 328.
[17] ibid 244.
[18] ibid 242.
[19] ibid 245-47.

hours scheme would be advantageous to them in the workplace, and that it was easier to juggle home and work responsibilities by working a four-day week than by working reduced hours every day. These results suggested that, in practice, things had not changed much since 1993. There is little point in having statutory maternity leave when the ethos of the workplace is such as to make it impossible for women, and indeed men, to take up that leave, for fear of the consequences to their career of so doing.

The 2016 Bar of Ireland survey echoes similar problems concerning maternity leave for women barristers. Respondents reported pressure to return to work very shortly after giving birth, and to do otherwise risked being perceived as not sufficiently committed to their practice.[20] It would be very interesting to have an up-to-date survey of women solicitors, to see how much progress or otherwise has been made in the area of maternity leave since the 2003 survey, and whether the experience of women solicitors is any better than the reported experience of self-employed barristers in 2016.

The 2003 study also looked at gendered legal specialisation and pay gaps between women and men in terms of income and pension entitlements. Within legal practice, the most 'gendered' areas of work are: personal injury, criminal, family and corporate/commercial law, with women particularly more likely to be involved in family law than men (47 per cent of women practice family law compared with 35 per cent of men). For male lawyers the most time-consuming area of legal work is personal injury/negligence while for women it is property (including conveyancing/probate).[21]

The 2003 study found a significant gender gap in income levels of men and women, with 42 per cent of men earning over €100,000 per annum compared with 19 per cent of women. Conversely, 27 per cent of men have incomes of €35,000 per annum or less compared with 35 per cent of women.[22] The study found that this gender gap remains even when the figures are controlled for age, and in fact the disparity actually increases; a male lawyer who was aged 50 years or over has a 60 per cent probability of earning in excess of €100,000 per annum while this is the case for only 20 per cent of women lawyers aged 50 years or over.[23] Further, significantly more men (82 per cent) have a pension arrangement compared with only 66 per cent of women.[24] The 2003 study is the only study examining the question of pay equality. It appears that this pay gap was an international phenomenon in 2003 and indeed appears to continue in jurisdictions such as the United States, as discussed later in this chapter. It seems unlikely therefore that things are different in Ireland although there is no later study which examines this issue.

There was widespread concern among women in 2003 about the lack of transparency and potential for gender bias in the briefing practices of some of the larger institutional clients, like insurance companies.[25] A survey of briefing practices shows that public sector organisations like the Office of the Director of Public Prosecutions are making efforts to address this perception, but that private companies are less aware of the problem. Again, this is a problem which persists and is cited in the 2016 Bar of Ireland survey. In that

[20] Gallagher, 'Women's Issues?' (n 8) 51.
[21] Bacik et al, *Gender InJustice* (n 7) 328.
[22] ibid 265.
[23] ibid 266.
[24] ibid 267–68.
[25] ibid 268–73.

survey, it is the briefing policies of the State and public sector bodies that are the subject of complaint; the low number of women briefed in criminal prosecution work is particularly evident.

In addition, the 2003 study looked at the different perceptions of men and women as to whether discrimination continues in the legal profession. It found that a significantly higher proportion of women than men have experienced gender discrimination in their legal career; at least a fifth to a quarter of women respondents had experienced at least one form of discrimination. They found that fewer than 10 per cent of all men surveyed had any experience of discrimination. The study finds that the most common forms of discrimination experienced by women are 'inappropriate comments' (36 per cent of all women surveyed) and 'network exclusion' (31 per cent of all women surveyed).[26] This certainly resonates with the experience of women lawyers in 1993 regarding both forms of discrimination. In 2016 'inappropriate comments' as a form of sexism in the workplace persisted.[27]

Out of a total of 506 women respondents, 21 per cent had experienced discrimination from a colleague, and 29 per cent from a superior.[28] This again resonates with the experience of women lawyers in 1993 and 2016. Discrimination in 2003 appears especially common in practice on circuit, compared with practice in Dublin. Many women described being subjected to multiple forms of discrimination and use the phrase 'old boys club' or 'old boys network' to describe their experience of sexist workplace cultures. Over one-third of women respondents (36 per cent) had experienced the use of inappropriate comments in the workplace. Some had been called 'good girl' by colleagues or superiors or had been otherwise belittled through language. Nearly one in five women respondents (19 per cent) had been assigned 'inappropriate tasks' such as making tea or doing other 'domestic' jobs for colleagues. More than one in 10 women (14 per cent) had experienced sexual harassment or bullying in the workplace. Types of harassment or bullying reported range from actual sexual assault, to being physically molested or experience of attempted molestation, to sexually loaded comments.[29] Sexual harassment in the workplace was also a problem for the respondents to the 2016 survey. The 2003 study also documented several instances of discrimination against women lawyers in court, including the use of sexist or inappropriate language by judges. The study found, in common with the situation in 1993, that 'structured leisure activities', golf outings, in particular, are seen as being particularly gender exclusive by those women who experience networking exclusion as a form of discrimination: 79 per cent of women and 64 per cent of men believe that an interest in sport is helpful in furthering a legal career, and golf was identified as being the most helpful sport.[30]

Proportionately more women (60 per cent) than men (31 per cent) said that gender makes a difference in their career/professional job.[31] Over half (56 per cent) of women compared with a quarter of men, felt that, based on their knowledge or experience in their legal career, discrimination against women was either normal, common or very common.

[26] ibid 276.
[27] Gallagher, 'Women's Issues?' (n 8) 52.
[28] Bacik et al, *Gender InJustice* (n 7) 278.
[29] See ibid 281–86 for fuller discussion.
[30] ibid 296–97.
[31] ibid 281.

The issue of parenthood for women was again a significant factor. The adverse effect of family responsibilities and parenthood on women's career progress was particularly noted. It seems nothing much had changed since 1993 on that front. Respondents, both male and female, overwhelmingly cited family commitments/children or pregnancy as the most significant obstacles in women's career advancement.[32] At least by 2003 this issue was recognised by both sexes.

Three out of every 10 women have experienced discrimination in their level of income or earnings and 28 per cent have experienced discrimination in 'not getting certain work'.[33] This problem persists to the present day, at least for women barristers, according to the 2016 Bar of Ireland survey set out below. Some respondents, mainly men, felt that discrimination had occurred in the past, but was unlikely to happen now. They tended to be hostile to the view that obstacles might exist for women's career progression.[34] The authors of the 2003 survey thought that this was a very common view and makes it difficult to acknowledge and tackle the very real obstacles confronting women in progressing their careers. It is likely that this is still the prevailing attitude.

Gender is the most common ground of discrimination, with fewer respondents reporting any experience of discrimination on other grounds. Since the Bacik, Costello and Drew study in 2003, there has not been any other extensive study of the experience of women practitioners in both branches of the legal professional in Ireland. The only recent survey was that carried out by the Bar of Ireland, published in February 2016, entitled 'Women at the Bar'.

IV. The Situation in 2016

'Women at the Bar' was a survey of the female members of the Bar. The survey looked at female barristers' views and experiences of life at the Bar. The survey also questioned why the rate of attrition for female barristers is somewhat higher than those of their male counterparts, and why the proportion of women being called to the Inner Bar is significantly lower. The results of the survey were published in 2016.[35]

By 2016, 39 per cent of Law Library membership was female, a surprisingly small increase over the 13-year period since 2003. Of 329 senior counsel, only 16 per cent were female.[36] This figure represents an improvement on the figure of 9 per cent in 2003 but falls significantly short of the sort of numbers one might expect. Depressingly, but perhaps unsurprisingly, the top issues for female counsel found by the survey were:

(a) access to work;
(b) childcare, family responsibilities, and maternity leave;
(c) working environment and culture;
(d) stability and structure.

[32] ibid, see generally ch 7.
[33] ibid 276.
[34] ibid 295.
[35] Gallagher, 'Women's Issues?' (n 8).
[36] ibid 50.

A. Access to Work[37]

Some respondents felt that the Bar was not meritocratic. Nepotism and political alignments have resulted in areas of practice that are effectively 'closed shops'. While this presents a barrier for male and female practitioners alike, female respondents frequently cited gender bias and a preference for male counsel as a major obstacle in pursuing particular areas of practice. Respondents noted that the careers of male colleagues have taken off more quickly than those of their female counterparts. Some respondents felt that there were areas of law that were 'less available' to females. Commercial law, criminal law and chancery, for example, are regarded as typically male-dominated areas of practice with solicitors and clients tending to give preference to male counsel.

What is notable about the 2016 responses is their similarity to earlier surveys. For example, comments by female members of the Bar who responded to the 2016 survey included: 'commercial briefs tend to flow from male solicitors to male barristers'; 'criminal defence work is very difficult to get into if you are a woman'; 'I was once told by a female solicitor that you would not brief a woman, as clients are more impressed by male counsel'; and 'male clients do not want female counsel, as it would seem weak to be defended by a woman'. These statements are remarkably similar to the responses in 1993 and 2003, and suggest that, perhaps to a surprising extent, gender bias is widespread in society.

The 2016 survey provided a breakdown of female Law Library members according to type of work. It showed low percentages of women working in commercial law (21 per cent), criminal prosecution (5 per cent), criminal defence (32 per cent) and chancery (30 per cent), relative to the higher percentages of women working in general practice (68 per cent), personal injuries (65 per cent), and non-personal injury common law/non-jury or general common law (48 per cent). However, it is difficult to attribute these figures to gender discrimination alone. Other factors such as poor earnings, particularly in the field of legal aid, difficulty securing a master in an area of interest, and limited access to State panels were also cited as obstacles and these arguably affect both male and female practitioners. Many respondents said they experienced no pressure or expectation to work in a particular field of law. However, some did express a feeling of being 'pigeon-holed' into certain areas of practice because they were female. One respondent said that she got family law work simply because she was female, even though she did not seek it out or want it. Family law is often associated with being 'women's work' and this perception may well be reflected in the relatively large percentage of female practitioners practising in this area (42 per cent, though down from 47 per cent in 2003). It should be noted that these percentages represented those who responded to the survey and are therefore an indication only of practice areas of the overall female membership.

The survey highlighted the notably low percentage of women engaged in criminal prosecutions (5 per cent). Women are well represented on prosecutions panels, representing approximately 6 per cent of the female membership of the Law Library. By way of comparison, approximately 7 per cent of the male members of the Law Library are on the criminal prosecution panel. Yet the number of women receiving prosecution work is very low.

[37] ibid 50–51.

B. Childcare, Family Responsibilities and Maternity Leave[38]

As cited by respondents, balancing childcare and family responsibilities with a career at the Bar is one of the most challenging issues facing female counsel. Some respondents felt that being self-employed, and the freedom and flexibility it can provide in terms of hours of work, is ideal when you have children, but a significant proportion stated otherwise. Many respondents felt that the profession is not conducive to family life, as its demands and unpredictability make it very difficult to plan childcare and take parental leave where necessary. Constrained by inflexible crèche hours, many women find it more difficult to attend early morning consultations, late court sittings, or evening social and CPD events, leading to a perception that they are 'less available, less reliable, less dedicated and less successful'. Difficulties in maintaining 'visibility' have led some women to feel they are 'out of the loop' and less able to compete.

Pregnancy and maternity leave continue to pose significant challenges for women at the Bar. Respondents complained that workflow slows down at about five or six months into the pregnancy. Other respondents complained that taking maternity leave meant that they were 'written off' by many solicitors. Another said that she kept her pregnancy under cover for as long as she could because she did not want solicitors sending work elsewhere. Another respondent said following the birth of her baby she felt that she had to get back to work as soon as possible and was drafting pleadings six days after giving birth and on her feet in court after four weeks. These examples give a depressing insight into how little things have changed in the decades since the 1980s. While solicitors may not now believe that pregnancy 'softens the brain', it is still the case that pregnancy means a significant falling off in work for many women. This may be because solicitors do not want to brief a counsel with work when that counsel is likely to be taking leave in the near future. This is directly related to another aspect of the difficulty of being a sole practitioner and one remarked upon by the respondents who complained that there is very little practical support for women. Any cases that are handed over while on maternity leave are not handed back and no fees accrue while on leave. This also has the effect of putting huge pressure on the woman concerned to commence working again as soon as the baby is born. A long period of absence can result in having to 'start again', with many women experiencing a substantial drop in income and a stalling in the developing of their practice. One respondent said her practice nearly fell away after she had her first child even though she only took eight weeks off. Another respondent said that she returned to a decimated diary and almost no new cases, and it had an enduring adverse effect on her career.

C. Working Environment and Culture[39]

Some 37 per cent of respondents said that they had encountered individuals who had exerted a negative influence on their career, recalling instances at the hands of their masters, colleagues, solicitors and members of the judiciary. Such encounters are undoubtedly

[38] ibid 51.
[39] ibid 51–52.

experienced by both male and female practitioners. However, some 62 per cent of respondents had experienced direct and/or indirect discrimination during their career, and this problem is specific to women practitioners. Although they were not asked to specify or elaborate the types of discrimination encountered, an overwhelming number of respondents' comments refer to either personal experience of, or awareness of, casual sexism and sexual harassment. Many respondents felt that there was a culture of silence and an underbelly of acceptance of inappropriate comments and behaviour, exacerbated by the absence of an explicit internal policy or complaints mechanism which could penalise, discourage and eradicate such practices. Normal employment law policies that address such issues as dignity at work and harassment do not have the same application within a profession made up of sole traders.

This survey tells us that sexism is alive and well and having a deleterious effect on women practitioners. That this was so in 2016, among some of the most highly educated members of our society, is as awful as it is depressing. Doubtless, the phenomenon of the '#MeToo' movement may help to change such behaviour and create an environment in which such unacceptable behaviour can be exposed and discussed. However, the 'culture of silence' complained of has a particularly pernicious effect, especially when encountered in a relatively small and hierarchical professional environment such as the Bar.

One respondent noted that the Code of Conduct prohibits discrimination on any of the nine grounds listed in the Employment Equality Act 1998 but does not refer to harassment. The Code of Conduct was subsequently amended by a General Meeting of the Bar in 2016.[40] However, implementation of the change awaits coordination with the new Legal Services regime.[41]

D. Stability and Structure[42]

Inconsistency in terms of work and income make it very difficult to sustain a practice. This undoubtedly is true for both male and female practitioners. However, respondents felt that women in particular were uncomfortable with the high levels of risk and uncertainty associated with the profession, causing them to leave the Bar in search of more protected, structured and reliable sources of income. Women also wanted work that could accommodate a better work-life balance, and which provided access to benefits such as paid maternity leave and a guaranteed job on return. Further, childcare is prohibitively expensive and the precarious nature of earning at the Bar makes it very difficult to justify the cost of full-time childcare.

In the first quarter of 2015/16, 54 per cent of those leaving the Bar were women. The 2016 survey found that the top seven challenges causing women to leave were:

(a) lack of job stability, structure, and financial security;
(b) family responsibility;

[40] Code of Conduct for the Bar of Ireland, available at www.lawlibrary.ie/Documents/Code-of-Conduct-for-the-Bar-of-Ireland-adopted-25.aspx.

[41] Following the Legal Services Regulation Act 2015, a new framework for regulating the barristers' and solicitors' professions has been established in Ireland. Many aspects of this are yet to be commenced.

[42] Gallagher, 'Women's Issues?' (n 8) 52.

(c) inadequate support during and after maternity leave;
(d) insufficient volume of work;
(e) male-dominated profession;
(f) gender bias;
(g) childcare costs.

Many respondents cited the fact that criminal defence work was very difficult to get into for women, and others noted that commercial briefs tended to flow from male solicitors to male barristers. Others felt that they were not given the same opportunities because of the perception among colleagues and solicitors that female counsel were not in the profession 'for the long term'. Others cited childcare costs and noted that they were paying somebody a few hundred euros a week to mind their children, so that they could go out to work, very often for free. These comments hark back to the experiences of women in 1993 and suggest that little has changed since then.

It is interesting that the survey cites the desire of women practitioners to have a more secure and structured work environment. This seems to run contrary to the notion of a self-employed barrister, and for some will beg the question as to why women come into the Bar at all, if job security is what they require. This is a highly simplistic view of matters, however. Further, it seems to be the complaint of women who have suffered disruption to their careers because of parenthood. Establishing a career at the Bar is a difficult process, whether one is male or female. The complaint that women make is that they suffer additional barriers to establishing and progressing a career over and above those of their male counterparts. For any barrister, regardless of gender, establishing a practice sufficient to provide a reasonable income will take at least five to seven years, unless one is well connected and talented. It is usually necessary to have some other source of income in order to survive until one's practice is established, however long that takes. It is hardly surprising that women practitioners, having struggled to establish a reasonable living only to find that motherhood puts them back to square one, will wish for a more secure and structured form of employment. That self-employed women find themselves in such a predicament is a reflection of the disproportionately adverse effects of parenthood on a woman's career, and the lack of progress we have made in accommodating women's interests in the workplace, as noted in 1993.

E. Taking Silk

At 16 per cent, the proportion of female barristers 'taking silk' is significantly low.[43] It is encouraging that respondents who have applied for silk find that there are no aspects of the application process that are particularly challenging as a female applicant. The fact that female silks are in the minority however is not encouraging for junior practitioners and may act as a deterrent. Despite this, 64 per cent of respondents felt positive about their future at the Bar.[44] Respondents gave various reasons for this positivity, citing the type of work, that it was a job with great integrity, that the Bar was held in high esteem owing to

[43] ibid 50. 'Taking silk' refers to the procedure by which junior counsel can become senior counsel. Junior counsel can apply for admission to the Inner Bar after a period of years spent in practice.
[44] ibid 52.

its independence, and that colleagues generally strived to ensure that standards were high. Respondents also noted that the self-employed status of the Bar facilitated the autonomy, freedom, and flexibility of being one's own boss, and that there was a huge level of independence in respect of the structure and content of work. Respondents also felt that the varied nature of the work was interesting; that the work was challenging and stimulating, and they felt they could really make a difference. Further, 77 per cent of respondents identified their master as having a positive bearing on their career, with 60 per cent praising the friendship and mentorship of colleagues.

However, 41 per cent of respondents stated that they felt less confident than their male colleagues, leading some respondents to believe that women were 'underselling' themselves as a consequence.[45] The respondents felt that women could be more critical and self-doubting, which held them back from putting themselves out there and creating the opportunities needed to succeed.

A number of respondents proposed education and CPD initiatives in the development of 'soft skills' such as networking and an increased focus on the business side of practice. Supporting women to develop greater levels of self-confidence can help to address the frustration of being overqualified and under-utilised. That a significant proportion felt that they were less confident than their male counterparts is an issue which would require a separate paper to explore. It seems to suggest deeply embedded cultural and social attitudes which have been internalised by many women to the extent that even academic and professional success cannot eradicate them, or at least not entirely.[46]

Some 15 per cent of respondents expressed an interest in having on-site childcare facilities at the Bar, particularly one that was open during the legal year and did not charge during the vacation, as well as a facility that would work with the vagaries of a barrister's schedule.[47] Respondents also expressed a strong desire to see greater support and protection for women on maternity leave and wanted the Bar Council to introduce some formal way of assisting women during maternity leave so that their work remained their own. It was recommended that the Bar Council take greater steps to 'normalise the idea of maternity leave for more than a few weeks'. Having a formal support mechanism in place whereby mothers are supported and encouraged to take adequate maternity leave can avoid situations where women are returning to work before they are physically or mentally ready. A tiered approach to the payment of subscription fees upon return from maternity leave is also heavily advocated by respondents. Suggestions were also made to relax the rules in relation to practising while on maternity leave.

In May 2013, the Bar of Ireland amended the rules on maternity leave, permitting and recognising that all members are entitled to leave defined as maternity, paternity and adoptive leave for up to nine months prior to and one year after the birth of their child or adoption of a child. The period is not to exceed 12 months in total and a member should be deemed to be in practice at the Bar during any period of parental leave and must retain the necessary professional indemnity insurance. Members continue to enjoy the right to vote in any election or general meeting or poll and the designation of any period of leave

[45] ibid 52.
[46] ibid 52.
[47] ibid 52.

as parental leave shall be a function of their own Library Committee on the application of a member.[48]

It appears from the 2016 survey, that there is a high attrition rate in relation to membership of the Law Library, but there are greater numbers of women leaving than men. In relation to taking silk, it was suggested that there should be promotion and encouragement of an increase in the number of female applicants to the Inner Bar. It is necessary to raise awareness of the need for more female silks, to provide guidance on what are deemed desirable qualities in prospective applicants, and to facilitate mentorship by female silks.

The results of the study would suggest that 13 years after the 2003 study, women continue to experience huge difficulties in balancing parenthood and full-time employment at the Bar and women's careers remain disproportionately affected by parenthood. Women also continue to experience 'gendered areas of work and lack of transparency in briefing policies'. Thirteen years later, there was still concern among female practitioners about the lack of transparency in the briefing policies of large organisations, the State being cited in the 2016 survey. The survey demonstrated that despite the number of women practitioners listed on the prosecution panel, almost twice as many men as women are prosecutors, and that there is a much smaller fraction of women defence lawyers.

Although the 2016 Bar of Ireland survey did not encompass the area of pay disparity, anecdotally the sense is that women are paid less than men in the professions. International studies would seem to substantiate this view. The American Bar Association, in March 2016, suggested that full-time female lawyers earn 77 per cent of male lawyers' pay.[49]

V. Women Judges

The first woman judge ever appointed in Ireland was Eileen Kennedy who was appointed as a District Justice in 1963. In *Gender Injustice*, the authors tell us:

> Her courtroom was 'crowded for days with people coming to witness the novelty of it all' and she created a legal precedent in another way too; she was the 'the first female to sit in a court with her head uncovered!' Kotsonouris recall that, as a solicitor's apprentice herself at the time, she remembers 'the *frisson* of excitement at such daring!'[50]

However, it was to be a long time before another woman judge was appointed to our courts. In 1980, Mella Carroll SC was appointed a judge of the High Court. She was called to the Bar in 1957 and took silk in 1976, only the second woman to do so, and the first woman to practice as a senior counsel. She was also the first, and to date only, female Chair of the Bar Council. Susan Denham SC was the second woman to be appointed a judge of the High Court, and this did not happen until 1991. In January 1993, she was appointed as a judge of the Supreme Court, and in 2011 she was appointed Chief Justice. Catherine McGuinness SC was called to the Bar in 1977, and was appointed a Circuit Court judge in 1993, a High

[48] See Bar of Ireland Parental Leave Policy, available at www.lawlibrary.ie/secure/parental-support-hub/parental-leave-policy.aspx.

[49] D Cassens Weiss, 'Full-time female lawyers earn 77 percent of male lawyer pay' (ABA Journal, 17 March 2016) www.abajournal.com/news/article/pay_gap_is_greatest_in_legal_occupations/.

[50] Bacik et al, *Gender Injustice* (n 7) 59.

Court judge in 1996, and was appointed to the Supreme Court in 2000. She was the first person to progress as a judge through all three court levels.[51]

In 1993, Ireland had one female Supreme Court judge, one female High Court judge and one female Circuit Court judge. By 2003, of the 8 Supreme Court judges, 2 were female: Susan Denham and Catherine McGuinness. Of the 28 High Court judges, 3 were female (10.71 per cent). In the Circuit Court, of the 31 judges, 9 were female (29.03 per cent). In the District Court comprised of 53 judges, 11 were female (20.75 per cent). There was a notably higher proportion of female District Justices sitting in the Dublin Metropolitan District Area. Out of 15 ordinary District Justices sitting in this district area, 7 were women (47 per cent of the total). However, conversely, women judges at District Court level were relatively rare outside Dublin: only 4 out of 37, or 11 per cent of the total.[52]

As the authors of the 2003 survey pointed out, the number of women judges as a percentage of the total number of judges was low, considering the proportion of women in the professions generally. Compared to other common law jurisdictions however, the number of female judges was relatively high, with Ireland coming second only to Canada as having the highest proportion of female judges in the common law world.

By 2016, there were approximately 36 judges of the High Court, of whom 11 were female (30.55 per cent). Of the 37 members of the Circuit Court, 15 were female (40.54 per cent). Of the 63 members of the District Court, 23 were female (36.50 per cent). The Court of Appeal, which was established in 2014, had 9 judges, 2 of whom were female (22.22 per cent). These figures are, on the whole, very encouraging and are certainly moving in the right direction. In addition, in recent years many of the highest law offices in the State have been occupied by women. In 2011, the first female Chief Justice, Susan Denham SC was appointed.[53] The first female Attorney General, Maire Whelan SC, was appointed in 2011. She was appointed to the Court of Appeal in 2017. The first female Chief State Solicitor, Eileen Creedon, was appointed in 2012 and became a High Court judge in 2017. The first female Director of Public Prosecutions, Claire Loftus, was appointed in 2011. This is also very encouraging, and points to the availability of senior female practitioners to fill these diverse roles.

VI. Representation of Women on Professional Governing Bodies[54]

Representation of women on the governing bodies of the legal profession is somewhat uneven. The solicitors' profession has the highest number of women on its governing body, the Council of the Law Society of Ireland. Membership of the Law Society's Council for 2017/18 comprised 31 elected members, 11 of whom were female (approximately 35 per cent) approximately. There were also 4 provincial delegates and 13 nominated

[51] ibid 59.
[52] ibid 63–64.
[53] Chief Justice Denham retired in 2018.
[54] The author thanks the relevant governing bodies for their co-operation and provision of the figures used herein.

members from the Law Society of Northern Ireland, the Dublin Solicitors Bar Association and the Southern Law Association. Of these, 7 were female. Thus, the overall representation of women on the Council of the Law Society was 37.5 per cent, which is a very respectable figure.

Figures for the Bar Council, the governing body for barristers, are not as high. The Bar Council consists of 20 elected members, and 4 co-optees. Of the elected members, 10 are from the ranks of senior counsel and 10 from the ranks of junior counsel. In 2017/18, of the 10 senior counsel elected, one was a woman, and of the 10 junior counsel, 4 were women. There are also 4 co-optees, 2 of whom were women. Overall, female representation on the Council was approximately 25 per cent. The disparity between the number of female senior counsel and junior counsel may be explained by the relatively small numbers of female seniors. The Honourable Society of the King's Inns are the body responsible for the running of the King's Inns, and thus the education of barristers. The Society is run by the Benchers, a group which consists of all of the superior court judges who become Honorary Benchers once appointed as a judge.[55] In addition, practising barristers may be elected Benchers by the existing cohort of Benchers. Such elected Benchers are referred to as 'Bar Benchers'. Election as a Bar Bencher is a mark of the respect and esteem in which the barrister elected is held by his or her colleagues and is considered a great honour by practitioners. By the beginning of 2018, of the 131 Benchers of the Honourable Society of King's Inns, 23 were women (18 per cent). When account is taken of the number of female Honorary Benchers, it is apparent that the number of female Bar Benchers is very small indeed.

VII. Retaining Women in the Legal Profession

The surveys show that the problem is not attracting and recruiting women into the professions. The problem is keeping them there. This apparently is not a phenomenon exclusive to Ireland. In a presentation to the World Bar Conference in April 2016, Grainne Larkin BL spoke of the gender experience in other jurisdictions.[56] In New Zealand, in 2016, for example, she cited figures showing that the majority of female membership of the Bar fell into the category of under 20 years in practice. In multi-lawyer firms, 24 per cent of partners were female, compared with 76 per cent male. The relatively low numbers of women advancing to partnerships and Queens Counsel status in New Zealand is acknowledged in that jurisdiction. Again, the position is that while almost half of all lawyers in New Zealand law firms are women, only 21 per cent of them are partners.

A similar phenomenon has been encountered in England and Wales. In July 2015 the Bar Council of England and Wales published two reports on gender diversity. Again, the reports showed that there was an equal balance of men and women being called to the Bar but consistently a larger number of women left the profession at a young age. The reports identified that the greatest challenge was the retention of women. Again, female barristers

[55] Superior court judges are judges from the High Court up to the Supreme Court.

[56] G Larkin, 'Diversity Focusing on Gender', Presentation at the World Bar Conference, 16 April 2016, available at wbc.advocates.org.uk/grainnelarkin.pdf.

cited the problem of balancing a career and caring responsibilities. In addition, many felt that they were being pushed into traditional 'women's practice areas'.

It is the same story in Australia, where steps are being taken to encourage women to remain at the Bar. In 2013, women comprised 20.43 per cent of all barristers in Australia. The percentage of female senior counsel was 11 per cent, although as Larkin pointed out in her paper, it is important to note that of the 50 barristers appointed as senior counsel between 2014 and 2016, 19 were women, so perhaps this bodes well for the future. In Australia, the retention statistics for men and women are comparable.

A number of Bar Associations in Australia have taken active steps to encourage and support gender equality and diversity. The South Australian Bar implemented gender quotas for representation of the Law Society. The Victoria Bar has been a leader among the Australian Bar Associations in this area. The Bar of New South Wales has looked at gender equality since 1995 when it first established the gender issues committee, now known as the Equal Opportunity Committee. The New South Wales Bar Association has addressed equality and diversity issues by means of specialist committees and sections, with the Association putting specific measures in place to assist.

From her review of other jurisdictions, Larkin has concluded:

> The figures statistically at the Bar of Ireland, Bar of England and Wales, NZBA, the bar associations of Australia show that women are under-represented as Silks with statistics showing that women comprise between 11% to 16% of the total number of Silks. The number of women taking Silk will only improve if we can improve the retention of woman in the profession as a whole. Recent heightened awareness of this issue is a global phenomenon, as is evidenced by the research undertaken by individual Bar Councils, who in turn have set up specialist committees and working groups to implement and effect change.[57]

Larkin identified the initiatives and policies that are common to all Bar Councils and Associations to support gender equality as:

(a) equitable briefing policies;
(b) formal mentoring programmes;
(c) professional conduct rules addressing bullying and harassment;
(d) forum for discussion on gender;
(e) supporting barristers with family responsibilities by establishing a successful childcare scheme.[58]

Since the 2016 survey, the Bar of Ireland has sought to implement measures to assist its female membership.[59] It has put in place a working group to review the findings of the survey, and work is underway to make recommendations to the Bar of Ireland for consideration under three main headings:

(a) creating awareness;
(b) education and training;
(c) policy and research.

[57] ibid 12.
[58] ibid 12.
[59] 'The Bar of Ireland Considering a Range of Measures to Support Women at the Bar' (21 April 2016) available at www.lawlibrary.ie/News/The-Bar-of-Ireland-considering-a-range-of-measures.aspx.

Particular attention is being paid to the suggestions and solutions put forward by the respondents to the survey, and discussion is taking place around the feasibility of some of the initiatives proposed. On the issue of respondents feeling less confident than their male colleagues and the concern that women are 'under selling' themselves as a consequence, respondents proposed education and CPD initiatives on the development of 'soft skills' such as networking, and increasing the focus on the business side of practice.

However, where respondents had expressed an interest in having on-site childcare facilities, the working group concluded, in consultation with various experts, that unfortunately an on-site childcare facility was not a viable option. The working group is currently engaged with a number of childcare agencies which may be able to provide a suitable alternative, by way of temporary and flexible childcare, to establish the best available options that are most suited to the profession.

Further, the working group has considered a mechanism to provide a staggered approach to Law Library subscription fees following a period of maternity leave, and that proposal is currently being researched. The primary aim was to support and facilitate women who would like to return to work to the Bar on a phased basis in the first six months following the birth of their child and recognising that their supply of work in the pipeline is likely to have significantly reduced during their period of maternity leave. This measure, together with flexible childcare, could provide an effective support system for women returning to the Bar after having had a child. The working group is also engaging in research in relation to briefing policies specific to women in other jurisdictions around the world for consideration in this jurisdiction. In addition, as a result of the survey a pilot mentoring scheme was launched in January 2016 providing mentoring training for more senior members of the Bar, with a view to assisting the younger female membership. An expansion of this scheme to assist female members considering taking silk is to be considered.

One of the concerns that arose from the survey was in relation to experiences of inappropriate behaviour directed at female barristers. A proposal to amend the Code of Conduct with a provision that explicitly states that barristers must not engage in conduct that may constitute victimisation, harassment or sexual harassment of another barrister, and providing for an adequate complaints procedure that can address any instances of inappropriate behaviour of this nature, was successful, and the Code of Conduct was amended in 2016. As set out above, this amendment has not yet been implemented because of the necessity of coordinating with the new Legal Services regime.

VIII. Conclusion

Women practitioners have much to celebrate, we have come very far, and achieved a great deal. We will only have attained the goal of equality, however, when it is no longer relevant to write about or discuss issues of gender discrimination in the legal professions. We are some way off that goal as things stand. Longstanding barriers to progress persist, as the studies since 1993 highlight. Although the level of entry of women into the legal profession in Ireland is on par with male entrants, participation and progression within the legal professions remains problematical for women for additional reasons attributable to their gender.

Recent research conducted by the Bar of Ireland confirms that issues such as sexual harassment, preferential treatment of male counsel in briefing policies and structural difficulties relating to self-employment combine to create difficult working conditions and augment the other barriers to remaining in the profession and progressing within it.

These problems no doubt reflect wider societal and cultural attitudes to women. It may well be argued that the kind of cultural and structural change in society necessary to eliminate, for example, the disproportionate disadvantage to a woman's career as a result of parenthood, is the type of change that takes a very long time indeed. It is, however, difficult to attribute the persistence of sexual harassment and preferential treatment of males in briefing policies to anything other than good old-fashioned misogyny. Changing a culture that tolerates sexual harassment, changing how women professionals are viewed and treated on a day-to-day basis is something within the power of every thinking person in the workplace. There is no excuse for the persistence of these kinds of attitudes, particularly among the most educated, not to say privileged, members of our society, such as are found in the legal professions. Such attitudes inevitably tend to undermine the status of and respect due to women practitioners and constitute another unnecessary barrier for women lawyers.

On the positive side, we have witnessed in recent years seismic shifts in social attitudes in Irish society. Everything from marriage equality to the repeal of the 8th amendment. This hopefully augurs well for the position of women in general and women lawyers in particular. It is to be hoped that the initiatives taken by the Bar Council following the 2016 survey of the female membership will assist in this progress. The creation of a non-sexist workplace requires challenging the culture that tolerates such practices. To do this successfully requires persistence, humour and above all the ability to have conversations that raise awareness and properly communicate the corrosive nature of the problem.

One of the points made by Bacik et al in 2003 is that it does not appear to be the case that the increase in the number of women practitioners will inevitably lead to change and gender equality being achieved across the board within the professions.

> While it is undoubtedly true that much has changed for women in the legal professions, particularly within the last decade, the assumption that change occurs inevitably is not borne out by the empirical data. If the assumption was accurate, then change should have occurred for women more quickly, given that women and men have been entering law schools in equal numbers for nearly twenty years. Nor does this view of inevitable change take into account the real concerns of, and difficulties faced by, many women who responded to this survey with their personal accounts of discrimination experienced in their careers. In particular both men and women lawyers agree that more needs to be done to provide greater work/life balance within the workplace. It is thus clear that some positive actions must be taken in order to address these concerns and difficulties, improve the work/life balance of lawyers generally, and provide further improvements in the position of women in the law.[60]

These observations appear to largely hold true today. Of course, as there is no up-to-date survey which includes women solicitors, we are left to wonder whether the results of the Bar survey would be replicated in a survey of that profession. It is likely that in broad terms the results of the Bar survey would be replicated, as female solicitors are likely to experience, broadly, the same type of workplace practices and difficulties as female barristers.

[60] Bacik et al, *Gender InJustice* (n 7), 316.

Bacik et al also concluded that one of the greatest difficulties in dealing with the barriers facing women lawyers is the prevailing assumption that no such barriers exist, and that there are no longer any, or any serious, disadvantages suffered by women lawyers. This observation is even more relevant today. The value of surveys such as the 2016 Bar survey is to highlight the real difficulties faced by women lawyers, simply by virtue of their gender.

It is very important not to overlook the enormous progress that has been achieved by women lawyers since the 1920s. It is also fair to say that even since 2003 there has been progress. We have far greater numbers of women judges, and women office holders at every level in the legal system. We must therefore take confidence and pride in our achievements thus far. While we are still grappling with the issue of sexist comments and attitudes in the workplace, and the disproportionate impact of parenthood on a woman's career, these problems reflect the attitude and culture of the society we live in, and not just the culture of the legal profession. We have a considerable distance to go to deal with those problems, and they have proved persistent. We should not, however, despair. Enormous change has been wrought in the last number of decades, and still more change can be achieved. We must keep on keeping on.

18

Conclusions and Analysis

LYNSEY BLACK AND PETER DUNNE

I. Introduction

This edited volume has explored the relationship between law and gender in modern Ireland. Addressing 17 distinct, yet inter-related, areas of the Irish legal system, and drawing upon a wealth of academic and practitioner expertise, this book assesses – 25 years after the last major scholarly intervention – gender-based reform and the lived-experience of law in twenty-first century Ireland.

In some ways, this book serves as a cause for celebration – acknowledging important rights advancements in fields including reproductive justice, LGBT protections and the sexual exploitation of women. Yet, as the various contributors have illustrated, modern Irish law continues, at core junctures, to operate through deeply-engrained gendered inequalities, restricting access to and enjoyment of key entitlements. From stereotype-framed employment rules to gender-insensitive family protections, and from the legal erasure of vulnerable demographics (transgender children, unmarried survivors of domestic violence, etc) to the invisibility of women in public spaces, the Irish legal system remains, in key respects, characterised by the failure to acknowledge and presently redress historic gender imbalances.

In this concluding chapter, the editors offer conclusions on the foregoing discussions and debates. The chapter is not an extensive overview of the various contributions, nor do the editors propose recommendations for the transformation of Ireland's legal framework. Rather, identifying common themes and recurring questions across the 17 chapters, the editors engage in a holistic analysis of the current (and evolving) relationship between law and gender in modern Ireland.

II. Activism and Cultural Change

A clear thread, running throughout the volume, is the impact of activism-led movements in achieving social change. In recent years, there has been sustained, organised and impassioned activism, leading to tangible legal reforms in Ireland. Such movements are perhaps best illustrated by the work of advocates in the 2015 Yes Equality campaign for same-gender marriage (discussed by Fergus Ryan) and the 2018 Together for Yes campaign to remove the '8th Amendment' (discussed by Máiréad Enright). Both of these movements – fuelled and sustained by (years of) grassroots activism – speak to the power of people and community-led advocacy in creating substantive reform in Irish law.

The various contributions to this volume document the achievements of activism-based campaigns. Their successes signal a changed (and changing) Ireland, different in many respects from the country that existed 25 years ago. Activist campaigning has been central to the changes, which have taken place over recent decades. These movements have emerged from shifts in public discourse and have also helped to drive it. While reform cannot occur in an environment of absolute hostility, activism has allowed small opportunities to be translated into societal momentum. Feeding into the successes of activism, the role of investigative journalism, in facilitating the voices of victim-survivors, as well as the resources and efforts of non-government organisations (NGOs) and academics, have come together in various coalitions for progressive reform, joining research with passion.

James Gallen's analysis of the redress schemes, established in response to historical mistreatment, highlights a masterclass in activism. Gallen cites the efforts of the groups, which brought historical gendered abuse into the political foreground. Organisations such as Justice for Magdalenes and Survivors of Symphysiotomy have compiled victim-survivor testimony, often carrying out their own research where no such efforts were forthcoming from successive Irish governments. In his chapter, Gallen emphasises how the State was, and remains, resistant to many of the arguments made, and has been wary of expansive interpretations at every turn. For example, the Report of the Inter-Departmental Committee to Establish the Facts of State Involvement with the Magdalen Laundries (the 'McAleese Report') pitted institutional Catholic Church accounts against victim-survivor memories, creating a deeply unsatisfactory document. Similarly, victim-survivor testimony was downgraded in the report of Maureen Harding Clark J in the case of symphysiotomy.

Activism not only creates the optimal conditions for action; sometimes it is the only means of achieving State recognition of mistreatment. Crucially, State recognition builds slowly from public awareness, and public disquiet. In cases, such as those examined by Gallen, it is clear that activism was a necessary alchemy, and continues to be so in the face of official obstruction. Activist groups have been crucial in amplifying the voices of women where reluctant government approaches have consistently minimised their voices. Activism has, therefore, been particularly necessary to ensure that the gendered harms of Ireland's past, and present, are recognised.

Ivana Bacik's chapter on prostitution and sex work reminds us, however, that activism does not proceed from a monolithic ideological position. Bacik highlights the role of activism in driving debate and law reform on the legislation governing prostitution. She cites the importance of 'Turn Off the Red Light' (TORL), a campaigning coalition comprised of various organisations in support of the 'Nordic model' (discussed in detail in Section VI below). These campaigning groups found favour with government actors, who recognised the need for reform. Similarly, NGOs, such as Ruhama and the Immigrant Council of Ireland, offered a campaigning platform, as noted in Monica O'Connor and Nusha Yonkova's chapter on trafficking for sexual exploitation. On the other hand, however, organisations, including the Sex Workers Alliance Ireland, prefer an alternative approach, focusing on harm reduction and labour rights. The often-divisive nature of the debate on this issue was brought into clear focus when the International Council Meeting of Amnesty International, meeting in Dublin in August 2015, voted to decriminalise sex work and prostitution, as well as voting for the decriminalisation of the purchase of sex. Amnesty's current policy is therefore in conflict with the Irish Government approach, and with the Criminal Law (Sexual Offences) Act 2017.

Division among activist communities can also be seen in Fergus Ryan's contribution on sexual orientation rights – particularly during the debates surrounding passage of the Civil Partnership and Certain Rights and Obligations of Cohabitants Act 2010 ('2010 Act'). As Ryan notes, while many – perhaps more established and institutionally situated – advocates favoured the incremental rights development, which civil partnership would guarantee (particularly for those same-gender couples who, for various reasons, were in need of immediate protection), other community members, particularly among younger populations, rejected civil partnership as legally enshrined second-class citizenship. In many ways, the divisions over the 2010 Act were more complex than the competing positions adopted in the sex work and prostitution debate. While, in the latter discussions, as Bacik explains, the various activist groups advocated different substantive outcomes (most obviously, in the legal consequences for individuals who purchase sex), both sides of the civil partnership debate were ultimately looking to achieve the same thing: marriage equality. However, while some organisations and individuals preferred a more cautious, developmental strategy, other lesbian, gay and bisexual (LGB) persons believed that accepting anything less than immediate marital rights would be an impossible compromise.

Ryan's discussion of intra-community disagreement among LGB activists may be contrasted with the (at least publicly) more united front presented by trans activists during legislative campaigns for legal gender recognition, as described by Tanya Ní Mhuirthile. Despite the multiplicity of experiences of gender which are visible within Ireland's trans community, those advocating for, and advising on, the Gender Recognition Act 2015 presented a clear, consistent message in terms of the appropriate (and necessary contours) of legislative reform. In many ways, this uniform approach both assisted parliamentarians in understanding the requirement to formally acknowledge preferred gender, and removed possible ambiguity as to what gender identity rights would be acceptable. Although debates on the 2015 Act may have lacked the diversity of opinions identified by Bacik and Ryan in the spheres of sex work and civil partnership, there were key strategic advantages where all stakeholders for the 2015 Act – political, civil society and grassroots community – pursued a common, agreed goal.

Activism can also crystallise at moments of cultural and generational shift, not least the receding moral authority of the Catholic Church from the mid-1990s onwards. A notable example of changing culture can be seen in the 'The 5050 Group', which campaigned on women's political representation. This movement led ultimately to the Electoral (Amendment) (Political Funding) Act 2012, which introduced a gender quota system into Irish national politics. Fiona Buckley and Yvonne Galligan document a moment of change in Ireland in the wake of the 2008 financial crisis. In this climate, the 'cute hoor' mechanisms of Irish politics became unpalatable to many and gender quotas enjoyed support in an atmosphere of demands for increased transparency.

The role of individuals as lightning-bearers should not be ignored. Both Ryan, and Buckley and Galligan, reference the symbolic importance of the election of Mary Robinson as President of Ireland in 1990. Her gender and her noted credentials as an advocate for progressive causes, offered a visible marker of a sea change in Irish society. Similarly, and in more tragic circumstances, Savita Halappanavar – a young woman who, in 2012, died after being initially denied abortion-related medical services in an Irish hospital – became (and remains) a potent symbol for the need to acknowledge and expand reproductive rights.

The past two decades have shown the critical part which activist-litigation (particularly strategic litigation) can play in facilitating, and building upon, social change. This is nowhere more evident than in the case of *Zappone and Gilligan v Revenue Commissioners*, which brought the issue of same-gender marriage into many Irish homes for the first time. Public litigation can raise the profile of marginalised groups through compelling personal stories. James Gallen explains how litigation was a particularly effective tool for breaking ground in bringing the harms of symphysiotomy to greater public notice. Similarly, as Tanya Ní Mhuirthile acknowledges, it was Dr Lydia Foy's two decades of litigation against the Irish State (often in the face of overwhelming media hostility) which raised Irish public consciousness on trans-related issues, and created the framework (and the legal obligation) for the Gender Recognition Act 2015.

In some situations, litigation (even if it does not provide a desired remedy) can expose legal and social inequalities of which the wider public are either unaware or towards which they have shown historical ambivalence. In her contribution on 'sexually transmitted debt', May Donnelly investigates recent case law from the 2008 financial crisis. The judgments examined often involve women who, in guaranteeing (sometimes without proper knowledge) their male partners' businesses and property speculation, are placed in positions of extreme financial vulnerability. While, in many cases, the Irish courts were unwilling to accept the women's defences to actions brought by financial institutions, the judgments are nevertheless an important mechanism through which to highlight troubling commercial and family-based practices, which, even in 2018, continue to disproportionately burden women.

Social media sites, such as Twitter and Facebook, have been central to activist discourse on gender in Ireland. Online media services – both commercial and personal – have played, and continue to play, a key role in encouraging and shaping legal reform in this jurisdiction (as illustrated by disagreements over access to, and use of, social media advertising during the 2018 referendum to remove the '8th Amendment'). In particular, social media developments offer an important platform for ordinary citizens – many of whom who have been historically shut out from political and legal discourse – to share their personal narratives, and to shape ongoing reform debates. The democractising potential of online resources has been clear visible in recent legislative and constitutional debates, as Máiréad Enright (repealing the 8th Amendment), Fergus Ryan (same-gender marriage) and Tanya Ní Mhuirthile (gender identity) make clear. Of course, however, social media is not an absolute social good. For women, in particular, online spaces can represent a dangerous, even oppressive, environment. However, overall, as the various chapters reveal, social media has played a crucial (mostly positive) role in facilitate progressive social change, and has created a space in which individuals – irrespective of position or status – can share and control their own stories.

III. Consent and Agency

It is impossible to consider the themes which have emerged from a review of gender and the law in modern Ireland, and not situate 'consent and agency' front and centre.

As a lens through which to view the legal frameworks on gender, these are essential concepts – encompassing ideas of autonomy, of personhood, and of citizenship on equal terms – that are inextricably linked to this endeavour.

In Susan Leahy's chapter, these issues are addressed explicitly. In her consideration of sexual offence law in Ireland, Leahy focuses on consent. This has two effects: it illuminates one area of the law on sexual offences, and it acts as a cipher for the knotty questions of women's position in Irish society. As Leahy outlines, consent was not positively defined in Ireland until 2017. The new legislation has introduced ideas of communicative sexuality and mutuality into the Irish law for the first time. However, the definition of consent continues to orient around the idea of force. This can be used to exemplify some broader issues around consent and agency, such as the impact of context and circumstances on decision-making, which require us to ask whether consent has been freely given. Leahy also criticises the failure to reform the 'honest belief' defence, which again can be used as an example of wider issues. Consent and agency are essential in identifying the point at which male perspectives assume dominance over the female perspective. Not only are there limits to the extent to which female consent can be tolerated, but these are explicitly provided for in law.

While Leahy examines the nature of consent in its substantive form as a matter in sexual offence trials, other contributors consider more abstract meanings of consent and agency. Ivana Bacik delves into the idea of consent and agency fundamental to the debate on the nature of prostitution/sex work. Under a radical feminist perspective, prostitution is exploitative and evidence of oppressive gender hierarchies. In this conception, women's agency to consent is restricted by their economic and social circumstances. However, under the competing sex work perspective, such choices are emblematic of agency. Bacik's argument in favour of the former emphasises the need to recognise the role of structure over a neo-liberal prioritisation of individual choice.

Monica O'Connor and Nusha Yonkova offer comparable analyses of consent and agency in their discussion of trafficking for sexual exploitation. Again, the authors note that the lived-experience of trafficked women cautions against viewing their actions within the terminology of choice. The reality of trafficking for prostitution is that 'consumers' – mostly men – ignore signs of coercion, and may react negatively to indicators that women are not participating voluntarily. This invokes the spectre, and indeed the reality, of further violence. Within these scenarios, there is a further layer of meaning, in which women feign consent and agency to avoid physical repercussions.

In a consideration of consent then, should there be a dual-pronged approach to analysis. In the first instance, can we say there is express consent? Second, however, even in cases of explicit consent, is the consent voluntarily given? This approach goes further in ensuring that agency is acknowledged. In particular, in the chapters from Bacik, and O'Connor and Yonkova, the need to look beyond the visible indicators of consent is necessary. In the context of sexual exploitation in a globalised world, issues of power differentials, and of class position, ethnicity, race and nationality complicate any simplistic definition of consent.

One of the areas in Irish law where consent has historically been denied is consent regarding bodily autonomy during pregnancy. The inability of Irish women to make decisions about their bodies during pregnancy had long constituted a serious human rights failing, creating the context of unwanted pregnancy and forced birth, as well as the need for women to leave the jurisdiction to avail of healthcare abroad. While 'care' and 'compassion' may have been the most obvious and frequently used terminology in the referendum to repeal the 8th Amendment, that public vote was – at its core – a symbolic recognition of women's right to make autonomous, agentic decisions about their own bodies and futures. In the wake of the May 2018 referendum, that focus on choice and agency has now been (largely) enshrined in subsequently adopted legislation, which permits individuals to access terminations without restriction before the twelfth week of pregnancy.

The case study of abortion is illustrative of a wider historical failure in Irish law and society to prioritise women's agency. As James Gallen notes in relation to consent for medical procedures, there have tended to be more highly valued imperatives, namely, the preservation of women as child-bearers. Symphysiotomy, which was widely used in Ireland in the 1960s and 1970s, was preferred as an alternative to Caesarean sections, which were considered a risk to potential future pregnancies. The procedure was often carried out against the standards of best practice and contrary to the interests of the patient, and many women experienced harmful effects. Gallen also demonstrates the futility of consent in circumstances which offered no good alternative. Within an Ireland in which the stigma towards illegitimacy was overwhelming, and which offered no State support which could have made such a life bearable, the decisions made by some women to avail of institutional support cannot be considered, uncritically, as voluntary.

In contemporary settings too, there are often problematic issues relating to agency and consent in the domestic sphere, as demonstrated in Mary O'Toole recounting of female experiences at the Irish Bar, Mary Donnelly's analysis of sexually transmitted debt, Deirdre McGowan's examination of marriage breakdown, and Alan DP Brady's discussion of constitutional frameworks on the family. Women's relative lack of financial autonomy in such settings results from the gendered legal regimes, as well as cultural and social norms. Lucy-Ann Buckley's examination of the protective leave framework throws further doubt on the issue of women's agency, and 'choice', in a legal structure which pushes women into child-caring roles through heavily gendered leave entitlements. These factors create a dilemma; it is often a mistake to assume agency, as women's role in marriage and the family has been heavily constrained, however there are many voices critical of such an approach who decry what they see as the victimhood of feminist arguments. However, why is there an assumption that women are free actors in such cases when a review of structural determinants would suggest otherwise? We are compelled, then, to critically interrogate what we mean by consent and agency.

Such critical analysis is particularly relevant for ongoing debates relating to the regulation of surrogacy practices in Ireland. As Andrea Mulligan notes in her contribution, an especially pertinent critique of surrogacy industries is their potential exploitation of vulnerable – financially and socially – women. In many surrogacy cases, the individuals who are commissioning the arrangement enjoy disproportionately higher levels of privilege than the women who gestate their children. Against that background, there is a fear that disadvantaged women may be unduly influenced by their financial circumstances to compromise their bodily autonomy – thus bringing into question the validity of the consent which these women offer for the surrogacy arrangement. In response, Irish policy-makers have sought to institute a number of safeguards into the proposed surrogacy legislation, which are intended to curb the potential for exploitative arrangements. Perhaps most importantly, any Irish surrogacy framework will operate – like the current law in the United Kingdom – on an exclusively non-commercial basis. Those seeking to create a surrogacy agreement with a gestational mother in Ireland will be legally barred from purchasing those services through a financial transaction. By removing financial incentives from any proposed surrogacy regime, Irish policy-makers hope to avoid (or at least minimise) situations where commissioning actors are effectively 'buying' the consent of women who subsequently gestate their children.

IV. Recognising Gender

One of the difficulties in finding justice at the intersection of gender and the law, evident throughout this volume, is the problem of ostensibly gender-neutral laws, which perpetuate gender injustice. Throughout the contributions, examples of laws which failed to recognise a 'gender reality' often imposed a 'gender harm'. In such instances, these failures to reflect lived-experience perpetuated and compounded the discrimination experienced. By failing to acknowledge the gendered characteristic of social phenomena, we cannot innovate policies which respond to the lived-experience of individuals. Issues such as trafficking for sexual exploitation, prostitution and sex work, sexual offences and domestic violence have strikingly gendered profiles, and the victims are overwhelmingly women and girls. However, the fact that gendered power differentials are often left unexamined can reveal powerful vested interests. As Alan DP Brady argues in his discussion of *Re Article 26 and the Matrimonial Homes Bill 1993*, gender neutrality can protect the status quo. Although the status quo in this case was expressly more favourable to men, this state of affairs was viewed as 'natural', and beyond the scope of legislative interference.

In her chapter, Ivana Bacik presents prostitution and sex work as an example of a fundamentally unequal gender regime, and argues that any legal framework imposed must reflect the reality of that situation. Similarly, in Monica O'Connor and Nusha Yonkova's analysis of trafficking for sexual exploitation, the authors again point to the research which demonstrates that, overwhelmingly, it is women who sell sex, and men who buy sex. O'Connor and Yonkova are emphatic in their recommendation that laws governing trafficking should not be gender-neutral and are highly critical of the current legislative schema which fails to recognise the reality of trafficking. The authors suggest that this failure stems from the controversy over prostitution and sex work, which the EU is unwilling to face. Therefore, there are clearly barriers to reflecting sex work as gendered exploitation, and therefore to embedding gender in the law itself. Meanwhile, the existing European and Irish legal provisions cannot contemplate, and do not speak to, the intractable links between gender, migration, trafficking for sexual exploitation, and prostitution and sex work. In her discussion of gender within Ireland's asylum framework, Patricia Brazil similarly observes that, while women and young girls experience unique vulnerabilities and dangers when they travel across borders to flee persecution, Irish law (and its application) has, on the whole, been incapable (or unwilling) to address the gendered dynamics of asylum.

Fiona Buckley and Yvonne Galligan turn the spotlight on one recent legislative innovation in Ireland which seeks to explicitly reintroduce the reality of gender into the law. Discussing the Electoral (Amendment) (Political Funding) Act 2012, which introduced gender quotas, the authors itemise the gender disadvantages which can accumulate in gender-blind regimes. Although prior to 2012, there were no direct barriers to women's involvement in politics, between 1918 and 2016, only 114 women were elected to Dáil Eireann, compared to 1,181 men. Despite the presence of obvious obstacles then, women were not participating in the public life of the country to anywhere near the same extent as men.

Additionally, the authors outline the political culture in which women found it harder to make inroads. The informality of processes created barriers to women's participation, a phenomenon which Mary O'Toole also cites as obstructing the progress of women within the Irish legal profession, particularly within the Law Library. Compounding this the problem of Ireland's political culture, Buckley and Galligan further highlight how Ireland's multi-seat constituencies also privileged localism. While routes to candidacy for men often included local council membership, women's representation on local councils never exceeded 21 per cent. These features were exacerbated by the power of incumbency. Incumbents tended to have much higher chances of success, a system which perpetuated the gender representation skew. Further, candidates must draw from a deep well of resources, time and money, which can be difficult for women who are more likely to have caring responsibilities.

When women do put themselves forward, Buckley and Galligan note that they often face criticism and challenges relating to their qualifications. The authors suggest that this exposes the acceptance of 'Man' as the archetypal politician, an entitlement flowing from gender, which women must fight to achieve. The political landscape demonstrated how gender neutrality in the law created the misleading assumption that women's lack of representation was just an unfortunately gendered outcome of a meritocracy. Instead, gender blindness was privileging male experience, and ignoring the structural barriers to women's participation in public life. Again, this phenomenon is also evident in women's experiences of the Irish legal profession, with Mary O'Toole observing that, in order to access even baseline opportunities, female practitioners must achieve noticeably higher standards than comparably situated male colleagues. There is also an unwillingness among male legal professionals to even acknowledge that such differentiation exists, reproducing the troubling myth that formally equal professional frameworks are sufficient to create substantively equal opportunities for women. On a positive note, however, Buckley and Galligan point out that, in the general election of 2016, the first since the legislation was passed, there was a 90 per cent increase in the number of women candidates contesting the general election, which led to a 40 per cent increase in the number of women TDs.

The fact of gender injustice is evident in the need for anti-discrimination provisions, as outlined by Lucy-Ann Buckley in her chapter on employment. There must be a balance between gender neutrality and gendered roles carved out by law; an equitable formulation which recognises, and does not perpetuate, injustice. Buckley discusses maternity, parental and adoptive leave provisions which reinforce women's childcare functions. For example, in 2016 Ireland introduced legislative provision for two weeks 'paid' paternity leave, which is in itself misleading. The two weeks is not in the form of salary, but rather comes in the shape of a social welfare payment, which undermines its appeal. Meanwhile, parental leave provisions are gender-neutral. However, because of the gender pay gap most women earn less than most men. Parental leave is therefore more likely to be taken by women. Therefore, this structural gender disadvantage may be self-perpetuating. Again, it is clear that sometimes gender-neutral legal provisions do little to recognise and reflect the reality of a situation.

Crucially, the Irish Constitution is far from gender-neutral. If the Constitution is not gender-neutral, it appears counter-productive to create legislative provisions which are blind to gender. Alan DP Brady considers what the result would be of removing gender-specific provisions from the Constitution. In relation to Article 41.2 and the role of women as mothers in the home, a gender-neutral amendment would do little to redress the imbalance of unpaid care work in Ireland. While the Constitutional Convention recommended the insertion of a gender-neutral provision which valorised State support of carers, it is difficult to see what changes such an amendment would bring in reality. As Brady notes, women's explicit mention in the Constitution brought no tangible benefits for women in the form of State assistance or protection from hardship. Such provisions acted instead as potent symbols of the kind of society Ireland imagined itself to be.

Strikingly, in many cases, an overt (and necessary) gendered analysis is lacking. As Mary Donnelly writes, 'on even minimal reflection, the gendered nature of the Irish financial crisis becomes obvious'. The actors and institutions were male-dominated, and the repercussions have also been felt in keenly gendered ways. Donnelly's exploration of 'sexually transmitted debt' exposes the issues with either a gender-neutral or a gender-specific response, and brings an awareness that each is problematic in its own way – representing the danger of either not acknowledging a reality, or else reinforcing existing discrimination. Donnelly concludes by instead advocating a structural analysis of private law in Ireland which can take account for gendered lives.

One barrier to gender-specific provisions is the case of 'exceptions' and the inability of gender-specific provisions to accommodate all scenarios. As Louise Crowley notes of domestic violence, the evidence stacks up to suggest that women experience domestic violence at higher rates than men, and that the form of abuse is qualitatively different, involving more sexual abuse and greater physical harm. However, many men also experience domestic violence. The question which arises is how can we account for these cases if the law is framed around the gender of the 'majority'? Similarly, laws on pregnancy which are premised on the idea that only women can become pregnant ignore the experiences of transgender men. Arguments in this vein have provoked ire from some feminists, as diminishing women's experience. Equally, one of the questions that arises out of this volume is the extent to which there should be a relationship between gender and the law. Is it false universalism, or reflective of lived-experiences? If it is social fact, does enshrining gender in law ossify this? Law should reflect reality and attempt to ameliorate discrimination. Many contributors herein have shown how law can both facilitate gender discrimination, but also how law can be made to act as an impediment to inequality. These questions have led some to suggest that gender should not be part of the law. In her contribution, Tanya Ní Mhuirthile observes how, in recent years, Ireland has been brought to a greater awareness of gender through the Gender Recognition Act 2015. Yet, even here, one should acknowledge that many transgender individuals – some of whom may have waited for official acknowledgement of their preferred gender for numerous years (if not decades) – would not support movements away from the intersections of law and gender.

V. Gender and Nation-Building

On independence in 1922, all women and men aged over 21 years were granted the vote. However, women's role in the new Irish Free State almost immediately came under attack from conservative forces. Constraints were imposed on women's civic participation, in the form of the Juries Acts 1924 and 1927 and in legislation from the 1930s that restricted married women's employment opportunities in the civil service. Women had been extended equal franchise, but women's citizenship rights became contested.

Key to these efforts to circumscribe women's role in the newly independent State was a template of womanhood that revolved around the idea of woman as 'mother'. As the contributions throughout this volume emphasise, women's participation in Irish life has, until very recently, been restricted to a private, domestic space. As Alan DP Brady observes, even the Irish Constitution has defined 'woman' through her 'life within the home'. The corollary was, of course, that women's voices were minimised and marginalised (with the legal identities of certain women, including lesbians and transgender women, being completely erased). These historical truths have inevitably shaped the law's conception of womanhood, as policy-makers attempted to fashion a legal mould to fit the preferred archetype.

As a powerful example, women's political representation after 1922, as addressed by Fiona Buckley and Yvonne Galligan, fell far short of the hopes pre-independence. The inevitable result was that political discourse, the speech which shaped national aspirations and values, was male discourse. At no time in the decades after 1922 did women's political representation exceed 14 per cent. The causes and consequences of this fact are felt throughout the book: in the institutional responses to non-conforming women, the failure to legislate adequately for sexual and domestic violence, women's lack of access to reproductive healthcare, and women's remarkably low participation in the workforce. As James Gallen concludes, many of the policies and laws implemented in the post-independence period were fundamental to, and shaped by, a wider project and desire for nation-building. It is also important to acknowledge that, when laws and policies were passed and implemented, their compliance and application has been, as Mary O'Toole recalls, overwhelmingly been ensured by an older, middle-class, heterosexual and male judiciary.

Lucy-Ann Buckley's exploration of gender and employment demonstrates how the gender norms prevalent from independence shaped women's participation in the workforce, ensuring that, for decades, women undertook unpaid care work in the home. Constitutional provisions which enshrined, and continue to enshrine, such labour as a common good both reflected and reinforced contemporary thinking. Deirdre McGowan, in her chapter on the gendered nature of marriage breakdown and division of assets, notes that wage inequality was built into the male remuneration schemes as married men were paid more than single men, with the presumption that they would provide for a family, including a wife who was not in paid employment. As Brian Tobin observes in his exploration of parental rights, these social, legal and constitutional structures also have had gendered consequences for men – creating a State-sponsored regime which denies (and financially punishes) Irish men's desire to engage in caring or home-centred work.

Women's lack of paid employment inevitably contributes to their low stake in the family home, a theme which Mary Donnelly explores. Donnelly analyses recent case law on 'sexually transmitted debt' – a relatively recent phenomenon in Ireland as, prior to the 1980s and the advent of jointly-owned homes, most women did not have the property interests necessary to provide security for loans.

Deirdre McGowan also delves into women's unequal property interests, as she teases out the question of marital breakdown. McGowan cites the special position of the family home, again understood as a public good, whereby, although the property is owned by one spouse, the non-owning spouse has veto over disposal. McGowan suggests that, on the face of it, marriage has little significant impact on property ownership; however, the structural, gendered context of society ensures that this is not the case in reality – in 2016, 98 per cent of those looking after a home or family were women. In very real terms, it is clear that if more men are working, and working longer hours, earning higher wages, men will accumulate more wealth. When a marriage breaks down, this leaves women especially vulnerable to financial hardship. Although law attempts to compensate for this weaker position at the point of marriage breakdown, once the legal process has ended there is little in the way of compensation for a woman who has devoted her adult life to unpaid care work in the home. 'Proper provision' rarely matches the contributions of women to a marriage in the form of long-term caring. Furthermore, as Deirdre McGowan, Alan DP Brady and Louise Crowley have all illustrated, Irish superior courts (particularly the Supreme Court) are reluctant to expand women's (married and unmarried) property entitlements in circumstances where there is a clash with existing (usually property) rights.

The paramount importance of woman as maternal pervades the various chapters. As Lucy-Ann Buckley notes, maternity, parental, and adoptive leave provisions all reify a heterosexual model of parenting in which women are carers and nurturers and men are providers. As noted, Brian Tobin's analysis of gender and parental rights presents the starkly gendered patterns of parenting in Ireland. While an unmarried mother has immediate guardianship rights over her child at birth, unmarried fathers in Ireland remain in a more tenuous, contingent position. The gendered legal framework on parental rights reinforces Catholic Ireland's celebration of womanhood as motherhood and reinforces the secondary role of the father. Historically, the impact of such differences was clear in the shame experienced by unmarried mothers and in the network of institutional sites which responded to 'illegitimate' pregnancy. One of the intended consequences of the reification of women as mothers, within a socially conservative and Catholic nation, was the demonisation of women who became pregnant outside of marriage. The confinement of unmarried pregnant women in Magdalene Laundries and Mother and Baby Homes constitutes an incredibly gender-specific social abuse. James Gallen's exposition of gendered historical abuse underlines the primacy of fertility too, in the preference for symphysiotomy over Caesarean sections in order to preserve female fertility.

Throughout this book, the Catholic Church emerges as an imposing character. Catholic social teaching informed the views of many in government, and members of the Catholic hierarchy offered policy contributions where they could, on matters integral to the creation of a Catholic society. Such input disproportionately impacted on the lives of women and girls, as morality, sexuality and maternity became focal points for concern. In his discussion of sexual orientation rights, Fergus Ryan notes how the infamous section 37 of the Employment Equality Act 1998 stifled any expression of gay, lesbian and bisexual identities in education and healthcare institutions, where such identities were perceived as incompatible with an existing religious ethos (effectively excluding the vast majority of gay teachers from coming out at work, given the monopoly which the Catholic Church continues to exercise in the provision of education across Ireland). Ryan also observes the powerful impact of religious considerations when David Norris' challenge to Irish sodomy laws was heard before the Supreme Court in the early 1980s.

Within newly independent Ireland, the family, based on marriage, became the social unit par excellence, in which a mother and a father would raise and care for children. The familial ideal is enshrined in the Irish Constitution. This 'ideal' had many pernicious consequences, including the prioritisation of heterosexual relationships, as well as the protections afforded to 'marriage' above and beyond the protections afforded to individual women.

Louise Crowley's analysis of State responses to domestic violence illustrates this point powerfully. As Crowley notes, there has been 'historical reluctance to intervene' in domestic violence, a reluctance associated with rights of privacy and property. This resulted in, inter alia, a failure to criminalise marital rape until 1990. Prior to this, a married woman was not in a legal position to refuse consent to sexual activity with her husband. Previous attempts to criminalise marital rape were met with resistance due to the prized position of marriage, and fears that wives' allegations of rape could jeopardise *potential future* reconciliation. Alan DP Brady's analysis of the Matrimonial Home Bill likewise illustrates the deferential status given to the family, and the impetus to protect the status quo within marital relations. As Fergus Ryan's discussion of the events leading up to the Marriage Act 2015 reminds us, while there are, and can be, many formulations of family in Ireland, only marriage attracts the protection of Article 41 of the Constitution.

Given the priority which the Irish State has historically placed upon family, and the preservation of marriage, it was somewhat counter-intuitive that, in its original form (passed before the marriage equality referendum had been ratified by the courts), the Gender Recognition Act 2015 obliged married applicants to divorce prior to obtaining a Gender Recognition Certificate. The justification for such pre-condition was the avoidance of unconstitutional same-gender marital unions. Yet, the requirement appears inconsistent with State preferences for maintaining (seemingly at all costs) validly existing marriages. It should also be observed that, while the Government's proposed regulation of surrogacy is a promising step towards acknowledging the diversity of family formations that exist in Ireland, such regulation must, as Andrea Mulligan observes, be introduced in a manner which respects and promotes the rights and dignity of all women who may play a part in the surrogacy process.

VI. International Law

It is clear, from many contributions to this volume, that the relationship between law and gender in this jurisdiction has been highly influenced – in important ways – by international, regional and comparative sources. This influence is undoubtedly most obvious in those aspects of Ireland's legal system which, in recent decades, have been amended (or added) to comply with the State's external obligations. In her chapter on transgender and intersex rights, Tanya Ní Mhuirthile explains how the introduction of the Gender Recognition Act 2015 was a direct consequence of Ireland's membership of the Council of Europe. While, in *Foy v Registrar General (No 1)*, McKechnie J (High Court) observed that the applicant, Dr Lydia Foy, had no constitutional or common law right to legal gender recognition, the same judge concluded, in *Foy (No 2)*, that Dr Foy could rely upon Article 8 of the European Convention on Human Rights (ECHR) to obtain an amended birth certificate.

A similar result prevailed in *Norris v Ireland*, described by Fergus Ryan in his contribution on sexual orientation. Although, in the earlier domestic litigation, *Norris v Attorney General*, a majority of the Irish Supreme Court affirmed the constitutionality of anti-sodomy statutes, the European Court of Human Rights, applying *Dudgeon v United Kingdom*, found that such rules disproportionately interfered with private life under Article 8 ECHR. In her contribution on surrogacy reform, Andrea Mulligan warns that, considering recent Strasbourg case law (*Mennesson v France*), Irish law-makers may be compelled to recognise the legal relationship between a child born through cross-border surrogacy and its biological father, even where the surrogacy arrangement was commercial in nature.

Outside of litigation, international and regional standards have served as the impetus for important legislative and executive reform. In her exploration of amendments to Irish domestic violence laws (Domestic Violence Act 2018), Louise Crowley notes the crucial impact of the Council of Europe Convention on Preventing and Combating Violence against Women and Domestic Violence (the 'Istanbul Convention'). It is the Istanbul Convention which, in situations of emergency posing immediate threats of violence, has finally convinced Irish law-makers – who (as discussed) have historically prioritised the constitutional rights of property owners – to embrace a more protection-centred model, foregrounding (in admittedly limited circumstances) safety for victim-survivors. Similarly, in her contribution, Lucy-Ann Buckley observes the transformative influence of the European Union on Irish employment law and practice. Recalling the introduction of successive directives dealing with, inter alia, equal pay, equal treatment, social security, pregnancy and parental leave, Buckley explains how these EU measures have compelled the State to enact meaningful safeguards for female employees both accessing and operating within Irish workplaces.

International oversight, even when it cannot require immediate legislative reform, has often acted as a significant check on the exercise of State power, particularly executive power. In his chapter on historical mistreatment and movements for redress, James Gallen acknowledges the key role of United Nations supervisory bodies, including the Committee against Torture and the Committee on the Elimination of Discrimination against Women (CEDAW Committee). These bodies have: (a) critiqued past abuse, such as the Magdalene Laundries and Mother and Baby Homes; and (b) encouraged Ireland to promptly investigate, prosecute and remedy (including through financial compensation) proven rights violations.

UN-level criticism has also been levelled at Article 41.2 of the Constitution. Alan DP Brady observes, in his contribution on gender in Bunreacht na hEireann, that, although this provision has not had any substantive impact on public law jurisprudence (and certainly has not enhanced the constitutional status of women), it has been condemned by the CEDAW Committee as symbolically reinforcing stereotypical attitudes. Fiona Buckley and Yvonne Galligan note that the same committee has complained about the absence of female representation within Irish political life, and suggest that the committee's strong rebuke was a contributing motivation for the Electoral (Amendment) (Political Funding) Act 2012.

The international and comparative dimensions of law and gender are not limited to Ireland's compliance with binding and soft-law obligations. As the various contributions in this volume attest, the Irish State has – increasingly in recent decades – become aware of its position as a legal actor within a global community. As successive Irish governments and parliaments have grappled with complex issues of social, economic and cultural concern, there has been a growing willingness among Irish policy-makers to explore reform models in other jurisdictions, and to consider the applicability of those models within an Irish context.

This new-found openness to comparative analysis is a logical and welcome development. As is clear from the preceding chapters, many (if not all) of the gendered questions which legislators have confronted, and continue to confront, are not unique to Ireland. Concerns, such as abortion, employment discrimination and sexually transmitted debt, also arise in other countries. They have required policy-makers in those jurisdictions to consider the same competing factors which press against Irish authorities, and to apply practical solutions which balance public acceptability and fundamental guarantees. For Irish law-makers, who (owing to the country's small population) often address social and cultural questions after they have already emerged in larger states, there is merit in reflecting upon the analysis of those who have already acted. In addition, as Monica O'Connor and Nusha Yonkova observe in their discussion of human trafficking, some legal problems present no clearly delineated boundaries in their national and international dimensions. To adequately and effectively address the root causes of those problems, even within a single jurisdiction, domestic authorities must be open to transnational perspectives.

Across the various contributions, there is considerable evidence of Irish law-makers drawing from (if not directly mirroring) measures which have already been adopted in other jurisdictions. In describing the recent overhaul of Ireland's prostitution and sex work rules, Ivana Bacik notes that the Oireachtas has implemented the so-called 'Nordic Model' – an approach to regulation applied across Northern European countries, and first developed by policy-makers in Sweden (Lucy-Ann Buckley suggests that Ireland should also look to Nordic jurisdictions, particularly Norway, in order to reform its parental leave entitlements). As noted, the Nordic Model involves the decriminalisation of the sale of sex work, as a means of protecting vulnerable individuals. However, it prohibits the purchase of such services on the basis that supressing purchase will supress demand, and will reduce exploitative supply chains. While outlawing purchasing rights has drawn heavy criticism from sex work advocates, Bacik suggests that Irish politicians were likely influenced by the prior introduction of similar structures by the Northern Ireland Assembly in 2015.

This phenomenon of 'policy-transfer' or 'neighbour effect' is also evident in other areas of Irish law. In his reflections upon movements towards sexual orientation rights in Ireland, Fergus Ryan acknowledges how various reforms in the United Kingdom, including the Civil Partnership Act 2004 and the Marriage (Same-Sex Couples) Act 2013, inspired and legitimised similar measures in this country. Indeed, during the marriage equality referendum, although there was public consciousness that Ireland would be unique in affirming same-gender unions through public vote, there was equally an appreciation that, by 2015, a majority of peer-nations had already permitted 'gay marriage'. The United Kingdom (in particular, the Human Fertilisation and Embryology Act 2008) also appears to have strongly influenced proposed interventions in the sphere of surrogacy. Like the 2008 Act, the Irish Government's General Scheme of the Assisted Reproduction Bill 2017 creates a uniquely non-commercial surrogacy framework, recognises gestation as the prima facie defining characteristic of legal motherhood, and prioritises the consent of birth mothers.

Understanding Ireland's position within a global community not only encourages legislators to take inspiration from other jurisdictions, it also increases consciousness that those jurisdictions may place a critical eye upon Irish laws. An interesting feature of Alan DP Brady's discussion of Article 41.2 of the Irish Constitution is the fact that, although this provision has not (as noted) significantly impacted domestic law, there remains considerable will for its removal or amendment. In many ways, this appetite for reform reveals a concern as much about how Article 41.2 portrays modern Ireland as it does any substantive need to address existing harm.

In the same way, although there has been, for many decades, vocal opposition against restricting access to safe and legal abortions, there was (at least during the 2018 referendum) a palpable awareness of how the 8th Amendment – with its disregard for women's autonomy, and its exporting of crisis pregnancies – presents Irish society to the world. Indeed, in his contribution on historical mistreatment, James Gallen suggests that the fact that institution-based scandals, such as the Magdalene Laundries, became global news stories increased pressure on State actors to investigate and redress allegations of abuse. This is somewhat ironic because, as Gallen recalls, in the early and mid-twentieth century, the existence of such institutions had been justified as protecting the Irish State from the international shame associated with 'fallen women'.

It is, however, important to acknowledge that, in some situations, Irish law has gone beyond, and continues to go beyond, what is strictly required by international law. First, in the sphere of sexual orientation rights, Ireland created employment non-discrimination protections before these rights were guaranteed by EU legislation. In fact, although the Irish State only decriminalised sodomy in 1993, the Irish Government was soon thereafter a key actor in having sexual orientation safeguards included in the Treaty of Amsterdam. Under current national law (the Equal Status Act 2000), gay, lesbian and bisexual persons enjoy equality guarantees in accessing goods, services, accommodations and education. They benefit from these rights even though the EU legislator has been unable to agree similar protections at the supranational level. The Irish State has also provided for same-gender marriage protections, even though the European Court of Human Rights has (on a number of occasions) confirmed that no such entitlement currently exists under the ECHR.

Second, in her contribution, Lucy-Ann Buckley notes that, while the European Economic Community served as the catalyst for greater pregnancy rights in Ireland, domestic guarantees in the field of maternity leave now considerably outstrip the minimum entitlements which Member States of the European Union must respect. Finally, in the area of transgender and intersex rights, *Goodwin v United Kingdom* ensures that all Contracting Parties to the Council of Europe are obliged to offer some process – administrative or legal – through which persons can be formally acknowledged in their preferred gender. However, Irish law significantly exceeds the minimum ECHR requirements by allowing adult applicants to obtain a Gender Recognition Certificate through a model of self-determination.

VII. Intersectionality

Throughout this book, there is consistent evidence of the intersectional ways in which individuals have experienced, and continue to experience, gendered inequalities in Ireland.

Considering the demographics of women who suffered institutional and State-sponsored abuse during the twentieth century, James Gallen observes the disproportionately high number of economically and socially marginalised persons who were coerced into Magdalene Laundries and Mother and Baby Homes. While historic mistreatment is a cultural phenomenon, which impacted upon all sections of Irish society, it was primarily a mechanism through which to control the bodies and identities of poorer, disenfranchised women. This is also true of the State's restrictive abortion laws, particularly following passage of the 12th Amendment to the Irish Constitution. While, post-1992, individuals with sufficient resources were able to procure abortions outside Ireland (typically in the UK and the Netherlands), the near-total prohibition on terminations placed uneven burdens upon financially constrained persons, who lacked sufficient funds to travel outside the jurisdiction. It also disadvantaged migrant women, particularly individuals navigating Ireland's asylum procedures, who may have had neither the right nor the necessary travel documentation to lawfully exit (and re-enter) the Irish State.

Thinking about intersectionality helps to identify: (a) those areas of law where multiple hardships and discriminations are not yet sufficiently acknowledged, and (b) necessary law reforms to appropriately account for lived-realities.

In her discussion of 'proper provision' on the breakdown of marriage, Deirdre McGowan highlights the deficiency of existing judge-made rules, which regulate general family law but which are typically developed in only 'big money' cases (ie litigation where there are substantial assets for division between the spouses). For McGowan, 'big money' disputes are an unfortunate background against which to develop broader principles, because they reflect the experiences of one, privileged category of litigant, and are ill-placed to accommodate the intersecting issues of class, opportunity and resources, which are often central to disputes regarding asset division. Similarly, as Mary Donnelly observes in her contribution on 'sexually transmitted debt', it is typically the most affluent individuals who have the means to challenge actions for repossession. While it is clear that the effects of the financial crisis were not limited only to those with sufficient means, Donnelly's analysis suggests that it is economically privileged individuals who have greater capacities to defend against financial institutions.

In her exploration of Irish employment law, Lucy-Ann Buckley observes that, although the Employment Equality Acts 1998–2015 foresee the existence of discrimination on multiple grounds, they recognise only additive rather than intersectional claims. A person may bring an action alleging discrimination on the basis of gender and race, but she cannot advance a claim as a woman of colour. The result, therefore, is that, while Irish law acknowledges that female employees may experience inequality on grounds in addition to their gender, it cannot understand how those grounds intersect with gender to distinguish different women's experiences of discrimination. Similarly, in their chapter, Monica O'Connor and Nusha Yonkova suggest that, without emphasising poorer women and women who lack access to substantive rights, Irish and European efforts to counteract human trafficking can have only limited effect. Indeed, the same is arguably true in the sphere of surrogacy law. In recognising past and existing abuses of vulnerable (often Global South) women who act as surrogates for wealthy commissioning parents, the General Scheme of the Assisted Reproduction Bill 2017 proposes a model which reduces potential commercial exploitation and foregrounds the consent of gestational mothers.

Being aware of intersectionality also requires a critical perspective on recent reforms which have been achieved on questions of law and gender. While the Gender Recognition Act 2015 was a landmark moment for transgender rights in Ireland, it places highly restrictive pre-conditions on young persons who wish to be formally acknowledged (and fully excludes persons under 16 years). Incorporating medical assessment and parental consent requirements, the 2015 Act disadvantages those (many) transgender minors who live at the intersections of healthcare and social inequality. The statute creates an access structure through which only well-resourced, supported transgender adolescents will obtain a Gender Recognition Certificate. Similarly, one must also consider the ultimate beneficiaries of the Marriage Act 2015. While, in the abstract, the recognition of same-gender marital unions undoubtedly enhances the equality of LGB persons in Ireland, Fergus Ryan rightly questions whose lives are substantively improved by access to marital protections. Within a wider LGBT community which suffers higher levels of mental ill-health, higher unemployment rates and higher instances of violence, does a narrow focus on marriage rights (while symbolically important) hide the other, intersectional vulnerabilities which LGBT persons in this jurisdiction face?

VIII. Limitations of the Law

A striking commonality among the various chapters is the extent to which they expose certain weaknesses of the law in creating social change. While, in recent years, Irish society (and Irish law in particular) has undergone significant transformations, one must not overstate the capacity of *legal* reforms to eradicate discrimination or erase historical abuse. Enhanced bodily rights, stronger employment and family law protections, and the official recognition of diverse experiences of gender and sexuality are all welcome features of a modern, outward-looking Ireland. Yet, as the various contributors to this volume explain, simply amending legal frameworks, even where those amendments improve lived-experiences, can have only limited impact without accompanying efforts to address the social, economic and cultural factors which drive gender-based inequality.

In her chapter on sexual offences, Susan Leahy provides a detailed account of recent legislative interventions, most notably the Criminal Law (Sexual Offences) Act 2017, which aims to establish, inter alia, more robust response structures regarding the crime of rape, particularly in relation to consent. However, while there was (and remains) an undoubted need to recalibrate the applicable rules and standards where an allegation of rape is made, Leahy observes that true reform – whereby women both: (a) suffer lower rates of sexual violence; and (b) experience a more accessible legal system if such violence takes place – necessitates a fundamental shift in the way society understands female sexuality. Although one can applaud movements towards communicative sexuality and mutuality, these reforms are unlikely to create substantive change without society-led challenges to rape myths, proper education (especially for young men) regarding consent, and a commitment among legal professionals (both judges and practitioners) to respect the dignity of victim-survivors.

In her contribution, Deirdre McGowan also identifies constraints of legal interventions. Referring to the High Court case of *PH v FT* – where Abbot J refused to reduce the maintenance payments owed by a male litigant to his former wife – McGowan notes that, while the legal solution proposed responded to the immediate precarity in which the female individual found herself, the judgment did nothing to create empowerment or redress historic imbalances. The High Court acknowledged that proper provision required continuing payments to maintain the former wife, who was primary carer for the parties' children. Yet, as McGowan observes, Abbot J was unable to deal with the underlying social factors, which created the wife's financial vulnerability. In particular, the judge placed no obligation upon the male litigant to engage in further child care responsibilities so that his former wife might be able to re-enter the labour market.

Similar limitations of the law are evident in numerous other chapters throughout the volume. Alan DP Brady explores the gendered nature of the Irish Constitution, and considers to what extent Bunreacht na hEireann can be (and has been) used to enhance gendered experiences of constitutional rights. Noting (as discussed above) a manifest reluctance among Ireland's superior courts to extend constitutional protections to female litigants, Brady suggests that symbolically including women within constitutional frameworks has only limited effect if, in practice, women suffer disproportionate economic and social marginalisation. Patricia Brazil observes a similar phenomenon whereby, even during the period when Ireland's asylum laws made specific reference to gender and sexual orientation, decision-makers (and the superior courts on appeal) were either unwilling or unable to, in many cases, adequately identify and respond to the vulnerability of women, young girls and LGB asylum applicants.

In their contribution, Monica O'Connor and Nusha Yonkova outline recent European and Irish efforts to combat and criminalise human trafficking. Although O'Connor and Yonkova recognise the symbolic (and in many ways practical) importance of legal reforms to address the cross-border sale of humans, they argue that, without broader cultural shifts against the sexual commodification of human bodies, such reforms will not displace European and Irish human trafficking networks. Finally, in her reflections on 'doing gender' in Ireland's employment law sphere, Lucy-Ann Buckley observes that, despite the recent introduction of long-advocated-for paid paternity leave entitlements, society-entrenched gender norms may still be discouraging men from exercising these rights.

A particularly notable limitation of legal solutions – evident throughout the volume – is the creation of binary 'good-bad' categorisations. This is, perhaps, nowhere more obvious than in movements for reproductive choice. While, since the introduction of the 8th Amendment in 1983, advocates for choice, and politician-allies, have been strategising for reform, their efforts have – at various junctures over the past 35 years – been hampered by the restrictive nature of potential legal frameworks.

In particular, advocates have struggled with the knowledge that, in foregrounding or agreeing to politically-palatable proposals, such as abortion rights in cases of rape, incest and fatal foetal abnormalities, they would be distinguishing the acceptability of different women's choices. This, in turn, would mark certain women as insufficiently worthy of bodily autonomy. The lingering shadow of the 'bad' abortion impeded, for many years, a cohesive civil society voice on abortion rights, and divided women's rights organisations on questions of reproductive justice. Indeed, it is unsurprising that, only when civil society and political actors showed a willingness to frame reproductive rights through the lens of experience and choice rather than levels of worth, meaningful progress – culminating in the repeal of the 8th Amendment in 2018 – was achieved.

The capacity (even propensity) of law to box individuals into 'good/bad' classifications can also be seen in other contributions. As noted above, in her reflections upon domestic violence, Louise Crowley observes how Irish law has historically disadvantaged persons – most often women – who experience abuse in circumstances where they are neither married to the perpetrator nor have a property interest in the shared home. Until the Domestic Violence Act 1996, unmarried women could not apply to remove a violent partner from a property which the parties shared, but in which the woman had no interest. Although, under the current applicable rules, non-spouses and partners enjoy increased access to barring orders, they still benefit from fewer remedies than their married counterparts.

These distinctions create a worrying perception about how the Irish State differentiates the value of victim-survivors. It appears to imply that, should women make a personal choice to forgo marriage or be unable to substantively contribute to the acquisition of property, they forfeit their right to State protection.

A similar perception regarding the forfeiture of rights arises in Susan Leahy's chapter on sexual offences. Through her exploration of Ireland's rape laws, Leahy identifies a criminal law system which tolerates (and even facilitates) broad assumptions that women's clothes, their consumption of alcohol, and their sexual history reduces their legitimate expectation to be free from violence.

In his contribution, Fergus Ryan also refers to assumptions; although these are not assumptions that, in certain circumstances, LGBT persons surrender their rights. Rather, Ryan discusses emerging social (and even intra-LGBT) assumptions that, having gained access to civil-marriage entitlements, all non-heterosexual couples will now exercise those rights. For Ryan, such an assumption may potentially disadvantage the many same-gender partners who consciously choose to organise their lives – both separate and intertwined – outside formal structures. The fear is that, having embraced 'good' LGBT individuals within marital frameworks, the law will now censure (and will encourage society to censure) those 'bad' couples who remain outside marriage norms.

While these limitations of legal intervention clearly arise from law's restricted capacity to challenge cultural norms, they also reinforce the gendered processes (discussed above) through which Ireland's legal framework is produced. In their contribution, Fiona Buckley and Yvonne Galligan consider the extent to which male-identified individuals have historically dominated, and continue to dominate, Irish law-making institutions. Although, in recent years, and specifically through the operation of the Electoral (Amendment) (Political Funding) Act 2012, more women have ascended to legislative and governance positions, creating law remains an overwhelmingly male enterprise in this country. It is unsurprising that where: (a) the negative effects of legal norms are disproportionately experienced by women; but (b) efforts to address those effects are typically proposed and introduced by men (and, as Mary O'Toole notes, legally overseen by a largely male judiciary), law-based solutions to gendered inequality will have only a limited (sometimes counter productive) impact. Until the voices of women are appropriately incorporated into legislative and judicial practices, the results of those practices will have an inevitable detachment from the reality of women's lives.

IX. Conclusion

The relationship between law and gender in Ireland has evolved rapidly over the past three decades. Increased bodily autonomy, the formal acknowledgement of diverse familial arrangements and a reconceptualisation of how individuals can and should 'do' gender, has expanded social and political consciousness, and created a pathway for significant and meaningful legislative reform. In many cases, amendments to Irish law and policy have been grassroots-led, with political and public actors responding to overwhelming shifts in Irish public attitudes. The recent referenda campaigns to enshrine same-gender marriage rights, and to remove constitutional prohibitions on abortion, are just two (high profile) examples of wider, public-empowered movements to create gender-based reform.

Yet, as the above discussion and the substantive contributions to this edited volume attest, gender inequality and gender stereotyping remain a significant (if not always explicitly visible) characteristic of the Irish legal system – both in terms of the rules and policies that are applied, and the processes by which law is made, experienced and enforced. At numerous junctions, and within numerous legal spheres, women and those who transgress social gender norms are either: (a) unable to access legal structures which vindicate their basic rights; or (b) positively disadvantaged (sometimes under the guise of protection) by existing legal frameworks. The contributions to this edited volume, while celebrating the momentous advancements of the past 25 years, advocate a more nuanced, reflective and sensitive relationship between gender and law in the modern Irish State. While, as noted, law cannot be the sole answer to Ireland's problems of economic, political and social gender disparity, recalibrating existing legal structures to acknowledge and address gendered-realities can be an important – both practically and symbolically – first step.

INDEX

www.ingramcontent.com/pod-product-compliance
Ingram Content Group UK Ltd.
Pitfield, Milton Keynes, MK11 3LW, UK
UKHW051931150926
475560UK00005B/345

9 781509 917211